THE FOREIGN POLICY OF CANNING

1822–1827

Canning speaking in the House of Commons
12th. Dec. 1826
from the portrait by Sir Thomas Lawrence P.R.A.
in the National Portrait Gallery

THE FOREIGN POLICY OF CANNING
1822 - 1827

England, the Neo-Holy Alliance, and
the New World

HAROLD TEMPERLEY

with a New Introduction by
HERBERT BUTTERFIELD

ARCHON BOOKS
1966

Published by Frank Cass & Co. Ltd.,
10 Woburn Walk, London W.C.1
by arrangement with G. Bell & Sons Ltd.

Published in the United States in 1966
by Archon Books,
The Shoe String Press, Inc.,
Hamden, Connecticut.

First Edition   1925
Second Edition   1966

Printed in Great Britain

NEW INTRODUCTION

by

HERBERT BUTTERFIELD

HAROLD TEMPERLEY
AND GEORGE CANNING

1. THE LIFE OF CANNING

I⊤ is now over a quarter of a century since Harold Temperley died at the age of sixty. A new generation will hardly be able to realise the powerful position he once held amongst historians in Great Britain, on the Continent and in the United States. In so far as this was due to his published work and not to the play of a forceful personality, he owed it to something more than his remarkable technical accomplishment as a diplomatic historian. What impressed his colleagues was the character that he managed to give to his historical writing, the spirited way in which his mind seemed to work, and the extraordinary richness of the experience out of which his judgments sprang. For a long time, the chief basis of his fame was his study of the later Canning—the book that is reprinted here.

His working life is marked by a fairly clear division in 1924–25, when he completed and published the present volume. There had been a preliminary period when, as a post-graduate student, he had devoted himself to English constitutional history. He had moved in this direction because, in 1901, the prescribed subject for the Members' English Essay Prize in Cambridge had been: "The Office of Prime Minister under the Hanoverian Dynasty". He had won the prize in that year, when D. A. Winstanley, who was to devote so much of his life to this field, was amongst the group of people receiving "honourable mention". For a time, after this, he himself had continued writing in the same field; but the significant beginning of his career came in 1905, when he published his *Life of Canning* and made the first of his many visits to Serbia. During the next twenty years, he was extremely prodigal in his activities and published books on a variety of subjects, but he was known to the world chiefly as an expert on Canning and an authority on the Western Balkans. Then, from 1925 (while the present work was appearing) down to nearly the end of his life, his principal concern was with the *British Documents on the Origins of the War,* which he had been commissioned to edit, along with Dr. G. P. Gooch. In a sense the two halves of his career over-lapped, for he had been deeply involved in the First World War and had edited a little later the *History of the Peace Conference of Paris.* He had already been seriously engaged, therefore, with contemporary history.

What the future will never be able to recapture is the extra-ordinary exuberance of his personality—the tremendous exhilaration with which his mind seemed to work—an exhilara-tion which he was able to communicate to his pupils and others. There was an admirable uninhibitedness in all this—he gained more than he lost from the fact that he was never held in by the fear of looking silly before other people. As an historian, he pushed his mind forward into his material, somewhat as a thinker who is courting adventure. He was the reverse of that dry kind of scholar who contributes nothing out of his personality because he is governed chiefly by the fear of making mistakes. In his very earliest writings, the thing that is disconcerting is his exuberance in both thought and style. One of the first of his productions—an essay on the Hungarian novelist, Jokai, in the *Contemporary Review* for 1904—is surprisingly florid and betrays the fact that he had ambitions of a more literary kind. His conversation showed the heartiness with which he would take an academic point or treat the paradoxes of life—the energies apparently leaping out of his ebullient nature—his voice cracking before it exploded into a roar of laughter. He was lucky because he had been endowed with a plentiful supply of the forces that only required to be tamed—the horse itself was lively enough, so there was some point in applying the curb. Once he had brought things under control he could produce writing which showed ample signs of the resulting tension, giving the impression of powerful forces held in check.

This control, however, had not been quite achieved when, at the age of twenty-six, he produced his first book—the *Life*

of Canning—in 1905. His actual prose had been pruned a little
by this time; but the thought, whether by way of commentary
or of generalisation, seemed to come in incessant waves, surging
on without any check. The volume, therefore, gives one the
impression of juvenile audacity and bounce. He had clearly
been a rapid worker, for, in 1904, he had still been engaged on
a dissertation about "Cabinet Government". Why he chose the
new subject is not clear. He was certainly impressed because
Lord Acton, "when passing in review all the great ministries of
England had pronounced that 'no Foreign Secretary has
equalled Canning' ".[1] He himself wrote that Canning "was of
all our English party leaders the most philosophic, the one with
the soundest grasp of principle". And he added: "Lord Acton
ranked Burke alone above him, and Burke could never have
formed a party".[2] He used the diplomatic despatches of
Canning at the Public Record Office, some of his letters at the
British Museum, and the papers and correspondence of Sir
Robert Wilson, as well as a formidable body of printed material.
These, he said, "for the first time enable an estimate to be made
of Canning's work and character". His information, he wrote,

> might be corrected in detail from foreign archives and from
> private and as yet unpublished letters, but the evidence is
> comparatively complete and at least sufficient to remove
> some of the vast accretion of tradition and calumny, which
> has accumulated around the names of Castlereagh and
> Canning.[3]

He was aware of the imperfection of his materials, therefore,
and at a later date he considerably tightened his view of what
a work of scholarship required. For the time being, however,
he was satisfied that "Canning has waited long enough for a
biographer and to delay any longer in the hope that fresh
materials will be found is as though Columbus were to put off
crossing the Atlantic until steam was invented".[4]

The result was a racy book, written with tremendous zest,
a book which, in slashing strokes, made it clear why Canning
had become Temperley's hero. "A great part of his life-work

[1] *Life of Canning*, 268.
[2] Ibid. 108.
[3] Ibid. 13.
[4] Ibid. 11.

was the dissolution of the so-called Holy Alliance", he wrote. "The first object of Canning's policy in its widest and most European aspect was to dissolve the Holy Alliance".[5] At a much later date, Professor Halévy was surprised to find him so enthusiastic about this point. "You leave the reader under the impression", he wrote, "that Canning disliked the Holy Alliance on the very grounds which made it, according to your views, a counterpart of the League of Nations".[6] More important still to him, perhaps, was Canning's insistence on allowing countries to determine their form of government and even have a revolution, if they liked, without interference from foreign powers. Temperley was unwearied in the assertion of "the principle that every nation had the right to manage its own affairs". He wrote: "It is now a recognized principle of international law—and it had before Canning's time been asserted by Kant and Vattel—that no one nation has the least right to interfere with the government of another except in the case of anarchy".[7] Once again, it is not clear that his principle would be entirely accepted today—entirely accepted by the twentieth-century enemies of "international revolution". The book shows in general a hearty approval of the spirit of nationality, and Temperley writes with patriotic fervour when he defends the British attack on Copenhagen during Canning's first career as a Foreign Minister in 1807. "The doctrine of nationality", he says, ". . . was first advanced and asserted by Canning".[8] This statesman, in his view, was superior to Pitt in that he disapproved of the policy of creating coalitions against France by the granting of subsidies to continental states. From 1809, he preferred to grant financial aid only to those nations which had decided to resist the power of Napoleon on their own account. "He thus early recognized and foretold that the chief hope of Napoleon's overthrow lay in the awakening of the spirit of nationalism against his universal supremacy".[9] Also he "was one of the first to perceive the advantages of a vigorous prosecution of war in Spain, and with Wellesley was

---

[5] Ibid. 9; 270; cf. p. 280.
[6] Halévy to Temperley, 4 July 1922.
[7] *Life of Canning*, 9, 270.
[8] Ibid. 280.
[9] Ibid. 83–4.

the first to dream that Napoleon was not invincible".[10] He "insisted on the appointment of Wellesley to the supreme command in Portugal in face of opposition both in public and in the Cabinet".[11] In addition to all this, he was "the first important statesman to proclaim and avow the existence of the Cabinet". He "both assisted and perceived the development of the power of the Prime Minister", and in 1809 "laid it down as a principle, from which he would not depart, that the Prime Minister should be a member of the House of Commons".[12] He was opposed to parliamentary reform, but he believed in the "mighty power of Public Opinion, embodied in a Free Press". Indeed, "to the people . . . he would grant anything save more direct representation".

> He did much to extend and create a popular interest in affairs by the liberal publication of state papers, and by his popular progresses and circuits. He was the first minister of importance who habitually delivered addresses to his constituents. He was the first Foreign Secretary who elaborately explained and expounded his policy beyond the four walls of St. Stephen's.[13]

2. TEMPERLEY AND WEBSTER

A REMARKABLE feature of this early biography is the way in which Castlereagh is set up against Canning, and the hostile manner in which the former is treated. Temperley tells us that Fyffe, in his *History of Modern Europe*, "was the first Englishman to appreciate the connection between Castlereagh and Canning".[14] The juxtaposition of the two men was to become a matter of importance, and it is relevant to see the way in which Castlereagh was treated by Temperley in 1905:

> His domestic record is almost the worst of any notable English statesman . . . He hated publicity in international affairs . . . over-ruled the popular wishes, but neglected

[10] Ibid. 84.
[11] Ibid. 88.
[12] Ibid. 98–9.
[13] Ibid. 102–03.
[14] Ibid. 14.

our true interests at [the Congress of] Vienna and so
lowered our prestige in subsequent years that England
stood but fourth in a great Confederation . . . He seems
to have concealed more from parliament than a constitutional minister should. How is it . . . that a man of his
resolution should have pursued in diplomacy a course so
tortuous and inconsistent? . . . Poorly supplied with
knowledge and ideas and narrow in prejudice he was
unable to grasp or formulate great schemes of policy, or to
gauge the force of great movements at a time of unexampled
turbulence and revolution. The hopeless confusion of
ideas, prevalent in his speeches and in some of his despatches, seems to have extended in a less degree to his
views on la haute Politique, so that he looked to others for
advice. He groped clumsily in the dark, and was forced
to beg oil from others, to kindle the lamp of his understanding . . . Canning had the intuitive perceptions, the
humour and the imagination of a great statesman, in
addition to a courage and strength of will at least as great
as that of Castlereagh.[15]

These are the views of a hearty young man who sees Castlereagh as a foil to Canning and makes a dramatic issue of the
contrast between the two, at a time when the modern expositor
of Castlereagh has not yet arisen. They represent only the
beginning of the story; for, if Temperley was to carry out a
great amount of further research in the next two decades, it was
significant also that, in about 1910, the later Sir Charles
Webster began his parallel work on the diplomacy of Castlereagh. And now the confrontation became more dramatic. If
statesman was set up against statesman, the encounter was
duplicated in the interactions between historian and historian.
To the outside world for a considerable period the very names
of Temperley and Webster seemed to have become interlocked.
Both men had originally been students of history at King's
College, Cambridge, though Webster had been the junior by a
few years. Both of them could appear as booming giants,
cumbersome and dangerous to crockery, bulging with warmth
and good feeling, yet capable of overbearingness—terrible lions

[15] Ibid. 147–50.

if you trod on their tails. Sometimes they seemed inseparable, glorious in their collaborations, charming in their avowals of indebtedness to one another—boosting one another at International Congresses, each for ever making reference to his "distinguished friend". One critic of their books was reminded later of Stubbs buttering Freeman and Freeman buttering Stubbs.[16] Both gave so freely of their personalities that they took the International Congress by storm when, after the First World War, it renewed its activities at Brussels in 1923. But both, in spite of their intellects, were like innocents in the world in one sense—somehow primitive or crude in what one might call their emotional structure, and capable of appearing in postures, or producing situations, which made them twice as human as anybody else but revealed in them also a certain quality that was almost Dickensian. During the struggle with Germany, Temperley had served at the War Office while Webster had been at the Foreign Office. This—like their historical work—tended to tighten their friendship but also to increase the possibility of a collision between them. In the Combination Room at Peterhouse we would hold our breath on occasion if one of them began a story with the words, "When I was at the Foreign Office . . ."; for we knew very well that the other would intervene to crown it with an anecdote beginning, "When I was at the War Office . . .". Neither would be content to have less than the whole room as his audience; and we knew in advance that the competition would be carried further—the thing would escalade—and ultimately there would be a head-on clash. It would be distressing to the observers, but, at the end of it all, these fabulous creatures seemed to the audience only more endearing than ever. Furthermore, in spite of their Olympian airs and their attachment to academic ideals, both men managed to make themselves almost the professional defenders of their respective heroes. The question would arise whether, on one occasion or another, Castlereagh or Canning had been in the right— whether Temperley in the early biography had been unfair in his account of the various conflicts between the two statesmen. Occasionally the controversy would take place in print, but it would involve the element of collaboration as well as the

[16] W. F. Reddaway, in the *Cambridge Review*, 10 June 1925.

element of conflict, and the cause of truth undoubtedly benefited from the debate. By the time their major works appeared, the balance had been struck—all passion spent—and the books seemed chiefly to complement one another. Amongst the acknowledgments at the beginning of the present treatise Temperley mentions his debt to Webster and says of him that "his work on Castlereagh has been planned in collaboration with mine". Webster, in his corresponding Preface, writes of Temperley: "Without his encouragement this book would probably never have been attempted". Temperley also tells how Webster and Alison Phillips "have happily done much to settle the tedious and unworthy dispute about the respective merits of Castlereagh and Canning". He says that, in the past, "Castlereagh has had certainly less, Canning perhaps more, than his meed of praise". He has now come to the view that "both men, though in different ways, rendered immortal services to their country".

On one significant point Temperley had by this time seriously qualified the extravagance of his original views. He had written in 1905 that Canning, after 1818, had been "the main cause of Castlereagh's change of front" in the face of the Holy Alliance. He had gone further than this, and had said that Canning's policy in the years 1807–09 had foreshadowed that of his later ministry; "his debt to Castlereagh was small, therefore". He had changed his mind very much about this in 1923, and by 1925, he properly attributed to Castlereagh the merit for the famous state paper of 5 May 1820—"the first statement of general principles to which English diplomacy had ever committed itself". This represented the "change of front" to which he had attached importance in his earlier book; but now he merely says that Canning always declared it to be "the foundation of his own foreign policy."[17]

The parallel labours of Temperley and Webster would seem to have had their place in the development of the study of

---

[17] *Life of Canning*, 27; *Foreign Policy of Canning*, 14. Cf. Webster, *The Foreign Policy of Castlereagh, 1815–22*, 246: [referring to Temperley's revised views in *Cambridge History of British Foreign Policy II* (1923) 622]: "The final judgment is the same as that held by Mr. Temperley, who was the first historian to realise the importance of this paper, that 'the main responsibility rests with Castlereagh' but that the tone of the paper was influenced by Canning and others in the Cabinet, and made rather more explicit and incisive than it would otherwise have been".

diplomatic history in England. The subject had progressed more slowly in this country than on the Continent, and G. W. Prothero's Presidential Address to the Royal Historical Society in 1904 had called particular attention to "the neglect" with which nineteenth-century history in general was still treated here. Quoting Hubert Hall, he said that the British Foreign Office papers were then "open to 1781, and by special permission to 1850".[18] By this time some good work had been done on the French Revolutionary and Napoleonic era, however; but even in these fields our diplomatic documents had been used (and even published sometimes) by Continental scholars first of all. Oscar Browning had printed in 1885 the despatches of Earl Gower, who had been the British ambassador in Paris from 1790 to 1792. He had then noted that:

> the documents from which this history can be alone composed are allowed to sleep in the obscurity of the Record Office, or to moulder in the lumber rooms of country houses . . . An example which we may wisely imitate is set us by foreign nations [France, Austria, Prussia and Russia] . . . Indeed . . . we can learn the extent of our own resources better from French and German than from English writers.[19]

When Holland Rose produced his *Life of Napoleon I* in 1901, he pointed out the way in which historians in France, Austria, Russia and Prussia had used the archives of their own country for that period, and he said: "It is surely discreditable to our research that . . . few English works have appeared that are based on the official records of the period".[20] If Holland Rose carried the researches into British documents down to 1815, our historiography for the period after the fall of Napoleon remained in a primitive state until Temperley emerged. In 1897 W. Alison Phillips had produced for the Cambridge Historical Series a book on one of the episodes in which the later Canning was involved—*The Greek War of Independence*—but this was merely a compilation from a number of German writers. In

---

[18] *Transactions of the Royal Historical Society* New Series XVIII (1904), 12, 26. Cf. ibid. XX (1906), P. Ashley, "The study of nineteenth-century history" especially 133–35, 139–40.

[19] *The Despatches of Earl Gower,* Preface xi.

[20] Preface viii.

1903 he had produced, from a few printed sources only, a diminutive life of *Canning*.

Speaking at Richmond, Virginia, in 1924, Webster declared that "before 1914 the scientific study of nineteenth-century British foreign policy was almost confined to a group of Cambridge historians".[21] These included not only Holland Rose, Temperley and Webster himself but also a small number of research-students. Webster was concentrating on the work of Castlereagh in the age of Napoleon; and it was W. Alison Phillips—an Oxford man—who between 1907 and 1913 (and then again, after the war) studied the Congresses that followed the fall of Napoleon, using this time the Foreign Office documents. It is possible that, once the First World War was over, the *Cambridge History of British Foreign Policy, 1783–1919,* though it has so many defects, especially in its later volumes, played a useful part in the development of diplomatic history, so far as England was concerned. Since it appeared in 1922 and the subsequent years, it was bound to be very unsatisfactory for much of the nineteenth century; but such a survey of the field can be excellent as a fresh starting-point—sometimes a stimulus to further work, so that it brings the study to a new stage. Along with Holland Rose, for the Napoleonic period, and W. Alison Phillips, for the age of the international Congresses, Webster and Temperley made important contributions to the earlier part of the work, and by this time their studies reached a new stage. American scholars had begun to appear in the same field, and their work on the Monroe Doctrine was relevant to the student of Canning. By 1919, the Peace Conference of Paris had produced a distinct revival of interest in the Congress of Vienna, and was helping to bring about a new assessment of its work. From this date, diplomatic history had a kind of heyday in England, and one of the important services of Temperley and Webster was the part they played in the training of future scholars. Diplomatic history became a favourite subject for the writers of Ph.D. dissertations, justified on educational grounds because of the precision-work that it required and the convenient and orderly way in which diplomatic documents are preserved. As the years passed, the work of research gradually moved forward to later and later periods of

[21] *American Historical Review* XXX (1925), 728.

the nineteenth century. In his paper on "The study of diplomatic history" in 1924, Webster took his bearings for that year:

> It may perhaps be said that for the period 1815–1830 the Foreign Office records in the Record Office have been practically all read and an attempt made to survey them as a whole and most of the correspondence of the foreign ambassadors and ministers is known in one shape or another; for the period 1830–1848 some important work has been done, but in more piecemeal fashion and with little reference to unpublished foreign sources; for the period 1848–1860 the British records have been used more for the elucidation of the foreign policy of other countries than for that of Great Britain.[22]

In 1924 Austen Chamberlain announced that the records, which in 1914 had been available with certain restrictions to 1860, were to be open to scholars for the period down to 1878. The research into nineteenth-century diplomacy went on moving forward after this—moving to later periods—until there was pressure on the means of subsistence, as the study was brought near to the new closure period at the Record Office. By the middle of the 1930's there was a tremendous concentration—the simultaneous appearance of a host of books—on the Eastern Question, 1875–78.[23] Then in the later 1930's, partly owing to the influence of Marxist ideas on non-Marxists—an influence very remarkable at that date—it became the fashion to decry diplomatic history, especially the sort that is written straight from diplomatic documents. For a long time after this, the number of research-students in the field declined. Temperley, who died in 1939, had been the leading teacher of the subject for over thirty years.

3. TEMPERLEY AND RESEARCH

THERE were signal episodes in even the earlier life of Canning to which Temperley would continually return. One of these was the question: who, in July 1807, brought from Tilsit the

---

[22] Ibid. 736.

[23] Works listed in my article, "Tendencies in Historical Study in England", *Irish Historical Studies* IV (1945), 211n.

news of the plans adopted by Napoleon and the Czar—the news which induced Canning to authorise the famous attack on Copenhagen? Another was the question of the responsi-.bility for the dispute which led to the duel between Canning and Castlereagh in 1809. Like Acton, Temperley had a love for the sensational episode—the picturesque moment that carried the element of melodrama—and he vividly envisaged it, perpetually turning his mind to the problem involved, especially if there was something of mystery attached to it, crucial evidence that had not yet come to light. Like Acton, he managed to have a certain *flair* for such things, without always possessing, in the last resort, the delicacy of judgment required for making the right guess (as Ranke was capable of doing) in spite of the defects in the evidence. In 1905 it was his view that "there was a man on the raft at Tilsit", who was able to overhear the discussions between Napoleon and the Czar Alexander I; but he also held that some elevated person had made further dis-closures, and "this was probably Talleyrand". The topic became a matter of controversy, and on both these points his views were subjected to serious criticism as the debate pro-ceeded. He claimed later that his Talleyrand hypothesis was supported by what he had learned about the tradition handed down in an important family in France—a family which, how-ever, refused to allow itself to be named.[24] But, like Acton, he was liable to attach too great importance to the backstairs knowledge that reached him occasionally by this kind of privileged route. For twenty years he kept his eyes open for further evidence, and instructed his pupils to be on the look-out for anything that might serve as a clue. In 1922 he reasserted his belief that Talleyrand was involved in the story and he insisted that the news which reached Canning must have come "in a discreditable way". In 1923 he wrote to the Napoleonic historian, Driault, that he had found some further evidence in the private papers of Leveson-Gower, and was inclined to think that his original conclusions were "not far wrong". A private letter from Canning himself had also made it clear that he had received information direct from Tilsit—information leaving that region at the crucial moment. A British fleet was already

---

[24] Letter to *The Times*, written 30 June 1922.

assembled for some kind of demonstration against Denmark; and now it was directed to a more drastic purpose.

By the early 1920's his views on the subject of historical research had greatly developed. He had become more conscious of the mental operations involved, more precise and concrete in his maxims, and at the same time more exacting in his demands. He came to the view that it is impossible to study properly even the diplomacy of one's own country from merely the papers of one's own Foreign Office. As a teacher, he followed the important principle that no student can be properly trained as a diplomatic historian if he uses the archives of only a single country. "Unfortunately", he wrote in his manuscript notes on this subject, "there are few historians who [write?] on diplomacy in this country who delve in the records of two or more countries to illuminate the policy of one". In a list that he drew up, he mentioned only Webster and himself in Great Britain as using records "outside as well as inside their own country", though there was Lord in the United States and Weil in France, as well as Stern and Wertheimer in Germany. Temperley and Webster owe their importance in the development of our diplomatic history to the fact that they extended their work to a number of foreign archives. "You *never* will write a true account of a diplomatic problem from English archives alone", Temperley wrote. Indeed he felt that if the archives of only a single foreign country were consulted too, the whole standard of research was raised to a higher level. "Vienna is the great place", he says. "Paris not so good. Petrograd is better." But he mentions also Berlin and Brussels. In 1930 and 1931 certain books appeared which made him wonder whether there might not be a danger of carrying his principle too far. Students, rushing from capital to capital, might traverse too hurriedly vast areas of archival material, giving themselves too little opportunity to collate all their varied sources at every inch of the story. He himself tended to have his mind concentrated on certain problems, and went to his sources with some sense of what he needed from them. He will perhaps be regarded as having struck a happy balance.

He had seized upon another important point, however—one to which Acton had already drawn attention in his manuscript notes. The opening of the archives in the nineteenth century had made it clear that the first necessity for the diplomatic historian is a completely free play with the official sources—the papers of the Foreign Offices themselves. It transpired, however, that the papers of a given Foreign Office do not necessarily provide us with the hidden springs of policy, the ultimate reason why one course rather than another has been adopted. This may be a cabinet matter, or it may be threshed out between a Foreign Secretary and a Prime Minister; and at any rate it may not be communicated in full in the instruction to the ambassador abroad who has to carry out the policy. For this reason—particularly perhaps at certain periods—though the official papers are the first requirement of all, the ultimate source, and the repository of the crucial secrets, may be private letters. The resort to private archives became an important factor in the work of Temperley and Webster in the early 1920's.

In his manuscripts on this subject Temperley takes over from Acton the dictum: "The partial use of manuscripts was as misleading as the partial use of books". He quotes also, as the "final conclusion" of Ranke, the view "that it is not science to extract modern history from anything less than the entire body of written evidence". In the course of criticising Lytton Strachey, he writes:

> There is an immense difference between a knowledge of fifty per cent of the material available and a knowledge of ninety per cent of it. For the last part of knowledge matters a good deal more than the first part of it. Even a man of supreme insight may be wrong in the first case, a very ordinary man may be right in the second.

Independent of all this, he comes to distrust more radically than before the thing which he calls the literary, as distinct from the historical, imagination. He goes on to criticise Macaulay. He says that Macaulay was "a pioneer of research, who had delved into diplomatic and naval archives and read hundreds of pamphlets. For his age he was a prodigy of learning and the most professional of historians. But—in the end—his literary bias found him out and misled his historical judgment". In another manuscript he writes:

> The artistic use of the imagination for the discovery of truth has never been displayed more effectively than by

Maitland, but I question sometimes whether the imaginative brilliance did not occasionally impair his critical acumen. Speaking with all reverence, I doubt if his results, though infinitely important, are final. And I think there is a sense in which [I wonder if] the stern art of labour is not triumphant over everything. The advance of history depends on the certainty of information acquired and there are fields where all doubt has been laid to rest by the labours of a hundred patient workers. Do not think I wish the artistic imagination to be driven from history, but the imagination must be yoked with patient industry before the land be ploughed and the seed returns an hundredfold.

In his Inaugural Lecture in 1930, he developed some of these ideas further. A great historian to him is the one whose work gives a hint of "vast hidden wells and crypts of knowledge". He tells us more precisely what he means by that historical imagination, "without which no true history can exist".

This kind of imagination, different from the purely literary one, was possessed in an eminent degree by Ranke, by Gierke, by Stubbs, and in this generation by Bury and by Tout. The power of discovering and establishing the truth, of piecing together and forming a coherent theory out of apparently unrelated scraps of evidence, is one of the greatest an historian can possess. It is a faculty demanding insight of the highest kind, it is a kind of constructive detective work.[25]

He now produced a further precept for the research-student.

It is very dangerous for him to begin his research with printed selections or summaries of documents printed in books. Here is a pitfall, and of the largest size. I am informed, some universities have already awarded degrees for research based only on the printed sources of the Origins of the War, such as the *Grosse Politik* and the British series of documents, which are now being supplemented by similar publications from other countries. Now, on whatever scale such documents are published, they must always be a selection, and usually a very small selection, from a great mass of unpublished material. I speak from

[25] *Research and Modern History* (1930), 9.

experience when I say that such selections contain a great deal of meaning to the selectors, and even a certain amount of meaning to highly-trained historians. But they can hardly convey any meaning at all to the apprentice in research. What he wants to do is to learn the detail and routine of a foreign office or a policy or a cartulary or a set of accounts. When he has done that his imagination may be able to fill in the gaps which occur in selected material. It will not do so without that training. To set him to work in the first instance on printed selections is to destroy in him the aptitude for research.[26]

Coming from one of the editors of the *British Documents on the Origins of the War*, this advice is significant, and it was intended to apply to this series as well as other selections of documents. It is not clear, however, that, in this respect, his standards have always been maintained, or the real point of his remarks always understood.

4. THE FOREIGN POLICY OF CANNING

IF Temperley sometimes said that he had spent twenty years on his study of the later Canning, he readily admitted that he had packed a great many other things into those years. His papers suggest that he was a rapid worker and concentrated a great deal of the research into a comparatively short period—first of all the period during which he was preparing his chapter for volume II of *The Cambridge History of British Foreign Policy*, a volume that appeared in 1923. On 21 June 1923 he wrote to Professor Halévy:

I have just recently refurbished my knowledge about [Canning] in view of the chapter I have written on him in the Cambridge History of Foreign Policy, Vol. II. I propose in a year or two from now to write what I think will be my final judgment on his foreign policy.

It is in 1923 and 1924 that his researches seem to become most intensive, and his surviving letters show him most preoccupied with the task. The chapter written for the Cambridge co-operative history has some references to documents in the

[26] Ibid. 11–12.

Vienna archives, but some of these were supplied by Professor Webster and some he may have read in London. By 1923, if not by 1922, documents from Vienna were being sent to the British Foreign Office for his use. He procured also a certain number of volumes for me—despatches relating to an earlier period altogether; and I read these under Stephen Gaselee's eye at the Foreign Office. It would seem to have been in about 1923–24 that he did his main work in foreign archives; and it was certainly in this period that he made his great attempt to gain access to papers still remaining in private hands. For years he was in constant correspondence with Sir Ernest Satow to whom he appealed for information concerning international law and practice. He would write on occasion to Sir Stephen Gaselee, the Librarian of the Foreign Office, for further enlightenment on the methods of diplomacy. On 24 January 1924, he sent to Lord Curzon one of his chapters, probably chapter XII of the present book, since he submits it as describing the "first occasion on which business methods appeared at the Foreign Office".

Perhaps the most exciting episode in his quest for private papers was the securing of a copy of the Diary of Princess Lieven,[27] fragments of which had been reproduced by Professor Theodor Schiemann in 1902 and by the Grand Duke Nicholas Mikhailovitch in 1910. Temperley tells us elsewhere:

> In 1923 a transcript of the Diary proper (1825–1830), . . . taken by a person who had had access to it, came into my hands. This disclosed some important secrets of Russian diplomacy. I published some extracts from it in the *English Historical Review,* January 1924, and in my book on *Canning's Foreign Policy* (1925). Since that time the transcript has been compared with the original, by permission of the Russian Bolshevik Government, and transcripts of

[27] There exists the copy of a letter from Temperley to the later Sir Harold Nicolson, 22 September 1923 which begins: "I have read with great interest the whole diary of Princess Lieven, and will bring it back on Tuesday". It ends: "I confess I do not know any private papers of this kind which in so short a space enclose so much that is of novel interest". Lord Carnock (Sir Harold Nicolson's father, and former ambassador at St. Petersburg) wrote to Temperley, 27 Jan. 1924 that he had lent his transcripts of portions of Princess Lieven's Diary to Mackenzie Wallace, who had evidently taken some extracts. He added that he wished he had copied the whole.

certain other important political sketches also made. The authenticity of them all is now firmly established.[28] Stephen Gaselee, and the British Embassy in Moscow, helped to smooth the way for this. Montgomery Hyde points out that the Lieven papers "being of a more intimate nature than her letters, and never apparently intended for publication" were more interesting than anything relating to the Princess which had hitherto appeared".[29] Less fortunate was Temperley's attempt to secure access to the papers in the possession of Lord Lascelles, though in June 1922 Arthur Balfour had provided him with a recommendation. At first Lord Lascelles was under the impression that he had nothing of interest connected with George Canning. Later he provided what Temperley describes as "valuable information as to the papers of Canning in his possession", and invited the historian to see a portrait of the statesman that he possessed. On p. 29 of the present work, a footnote states: "I am informed by Lord Lascelles that he possesses letters which indicate this conclusion". In 1938, however, Dorothy Marshall published *The Rise of George Canning,* a much fuller account of the man's youth than Temperley had been able to give in 1905; and her work was "very largely based upon private papers hitherto unpublished and now in the possession of the Right Hon. the Earl of Harewood". When it was too late, Temperley made contact with a correspondent, whose reply, on 15 July 1925, pointed to a more radical kind of misfortune. This man wrote:

> A friend of mine, who was the executor of Miss Canning (the last surviving daughter of Lord Stratford de Redcliffe) told me some time ago he had boxes of papers, mainly letters that had been written by and to the Cannings and did not know what to do with them and did not want to send them to the Public Record Office before somebody went through them.

The letter describes this collection of papers as having been entirely destroyed.

Webster's study of the later Castlereagh (1815–22) appeared in 1925 before his larger work on the earlier period (1812–15),

[28] H. Temperley: *The Unpublished Diary and Political Sketches of Princess Lieven* (London, 1925) 12.

[29] H. Montgomery Hyde, *Princess Lieven,* 10.

and a few months before the present study of the later Canning by Temperley. The works came from the same publisher and were similar in form. The partnership in Holy Alliance studies seemed complete. The appearance of the two books was timely: a certain amount of disillusionment with the Peace Conference of 1919 had created a disposition to see that the Congress of Vienna might have had more virtue than men had once believed. The question of the reconstruction of Europe after a great war had provoked a greater interest in the period of Congresses that came after the downfall of Napoleon. The world had reached the centenary of the events that were being narrated—the year 1923 had revived an interest in the Monroe Doctrine, for example. It was recognised that these two treatises represented something new in diplomatic history so far as this country was concerned—something, moreover, which would not easily be attained again. By now, the names of Castlereagh and Canning had been in the air for a long time, and it was felt that Temperley's work was most new or most striking in respect of Britain's relations with the American countries— a point of some significance to readers in the middle of the 1920's. There was also a special interest in the chapter concerning the Foreign Office and the handling of "Canning the Man". Some critics, in spite of their admiration, felt that the use of foreign archives had not quite counterbalanced the impressions made on the authors by the British Foreign Office papers—that in both books the real hero was British foreign policy, defended authoritatively and almost officially—always too unquestionably right, and with the Continental diplomacy serving somewhat as a foil. Perhaps there is an imaginable international history in which, when everything is shaken down, the lines of the general picture will come to fall differently in the long run. Indeed, Metternich himself has never had quite his Temperley or his Webster, partly because he is so colossal; and even Srbik found that it was too much to extend his work to the manuscript sources. Temperley, in the Inaugural Lecture of 1930, says very rightly that "international history in the true sense has hardly even begun".[30] Some of the critics felt also that each author, while recognising faults in his subject and avoiding the grosser forms of partiality, had under-

[30] *Research and Modern History,* 20.

stood his hero's point of view almost too well, or had identified himself with it too closely; so that there was perhaps a little too much hero-worship still. It would seem that, of the two authors, Webster may have worked the more widely in foreign archives, visiting them as early as 1913 and extending his researches to St. Petersburg. It was Temperley, however, who received from the critics very considerable praise for a certain imaginativeness in his writing—a prose sometimes colourful, an exposition sometimes brilliant, and repeated examples of deftness—so that the reader is not left with just the dry lines of diplomatic history.

Both authors had to a certain degree the feeling that finality can be achieved by the historian and that the methods they had adopted had enabled them to attain something of the sort. It is this view which is bound to be tested as time proceeds; but one can predict that the two books will not be easily or quickly superseded, in spite of the correction to which they may be liable here and there. They will prove vulnerable in time, perhaps, chiefly in respect of the outer framework of the story and their setting of the European scene—chiefly in respect of their treatment of the policies of foreign powers. Possibly it would only be the coming of "international history" that might produce anything like a radical change in the staging of the whole story.

PREFACE TO THE FIRST EDITION

THE history of a foreign policy is not the same thing as the biography of a Foreign Minister. The former aims at showing what a foreign policy was, the latter at what a Foreign Minister was. The latter is pure biography, while this book aims at placing the individual in his proper relation to other diplomatic personalities and to events. The plan of the book will illustrate the nature of this attempt.

The first chapter shows the diplomatic forces at war in Europe, just before Canning's accession to power ; the second shows the political ideas of the man himself. The third describes the Congress of Verona ; the fourth shows how the Neo-Holy Alliance surrendered the initiative in the Spanish question to France. The fifth chapter deals with the extraordinarily important events in the New World, which resulted in the Polignac Memorandum and the Monroe Doctrine. Yet, even during 1824, Canning's power is not sufficient to control the stream of events. At one time he diverts it, at another he is swept away by it. But in 1825 there is, at last, an English policy which can be separated from that of Europe, and the personality of Canning begins to dominate both. In that year he overthrows a Ministry in Portugal, negotiates the Independence of Brazil, recognises the Spanish Colonies as independent, and gives the final blow to the Congress System. In 1826 he prevents any possible revival by substituting a new combination for it, and by acting separately with Russia over Greece. He defeats the concealed designs of Metternich and the open enmity of Spain by sending British troops to Portugal. The signature of the Treaty over Greece in July 1827 puts the finishing touch to his policy, and marks the culmination of his fame.

But it was only by degrees that Europe was leavened with

the leaven of Canning's policy. The old bands of diplomacy were tough and were not broken in a moment. And, thus, the narrative begins by exhibiting a crowd of men and forces, and ends by showing an individual who was able to control them. It would be more personal, and certainly more artistic, to exhibit Canning in full control of the team as soon as he took his seat on the box. But this method would trample history beneath the feet of biography.

The main sources of this book are the unpublished papers in the official archives of London, Paris, and Vienna. My study has extended over twenty years, and every despatch of Canning himself at the British Record Office has been read. To these sources must be added the private and unpublished papers of statesmen of the time, which have been generously shown me by their present possessors. Among these are the invaluable *Granville Papers*, for access to which I have to thank the Dowager Countess Granville and the present Earl Granville. Some unpublished parts of the *Bathurst Papers* have kindly been shown me by Earl Bathurst, and, similarly, unpublished parts of the *Bagot Papers* have been shown to me by Mrs Cropper. Viscount Lascelles has given me valuable information as to the papers of Canning in his possession. I have to thank a friend, who prefers anonymity, for enabling me to get a transcript of some Russian papers, and to use the famous *Diary* of Madame Lieven. This work, hitherto supposed to be as lost as some books of Livy, is unlike them in having been genuinely recovered. These, and a number of printed materials, are enough to show the tendencies of Russian policy.

Not the least valuable among the private papers of the period are three collections deposited in the Record Office. Some parts of the *Woodbine Parish* and of the *Stratford Canning Papers* have been published, but the latter has a rich remainder. *The Papers of Lord Howard de Walden*, Canning's Under-Secretary, are of even greater value, for they give much of that miscellaneous, yet unavowed, material on which foreign policy is based. A similar work of interest for a short period—*Notes on Spain*, 1824–5—has been supplied me by the kindness of Mr S. Gaselee, the Librarian of the Foreign Office.

The acknowledgments which I should make to brother

historians are so numerous that I have placed them on pp. xxiii, xxiv. I can only mention here my friend Professor Webster, a colleague in peace and war, whose recent book on Castlereagh will become a classic work on our diplomacy, and for whose criticism at every stage I am profoundly grateful.

My first publication on Canning was in 1905, and, after twenty years, opinions alter, new materials and new judgments of historians are to hand. Practical experience of war and diplomacy during the years 1914–21 has taught much that no historian could acquire by mere diligence. In so far as I may venture to express any views, they would be to the effect that increased knowledge of the practice of diplomacy makes one recognise the great difficulties which always beset the practical man, and the much greater difficulties which confront any historian who has to pass judgment upon him. I have not thought it right to disguise my opinions at times, because the statement of a view is more likely to put the reader on his guard against bias or prejudice than the expression of that opinion through the more colourless medium of quotation or inference. But experience tends to diminish that certainty and confidence which a historian sometimes has when he judges from documents, without regard to their human setting. The despatches of a statesman can be searched with infinite care, but they seldom form a decisive clue to his motives.

On the other hand, there seems no doubt that personality is the true key to diplomatic success, and that quality Canning certainly possessed. And, if something of youthful enthusiasm is diminished by experience, there is nothing to suggest that Canning was not one of the greatest of our Foreign Ministers, or that any historian is likely to dethrone him from that eminence. It is easy to see his defects and to point to some questions on which his judgment was at fault. But there is no British (or perhaps any other) statesman of whom the same cannot be said. And it is certain that no greater intellect than his has been placed at the service of British diplomacy.

My friends—Professor Webster and Professor Alison-Phillips—have happily done much to settle the tedious and unworthy dispute about the respective merits of Castlereagh and Canning. During the most crucial years of the nineteenth century these two men guided the destinies of England. If the one possessed constructive qualities, serene steadfastness, and cosmopolitan detachment, the other had infinite resource, intellectual imagination, and a hitherto unexampled power of national and popular appeal. Both men, though in different ways, rendered immortal services to their country.

It is time to dissipate that cloud of controversy which has long floated dustily over the place where they sleep together in peace. It should be enough to remember that the two bodies lie at the foot of the grave of Pitt, whom both men acknowledged as their model and their master.

1925   HAROLD TEMPERLEY.

NOTE ON THE SYSTEM OF REFERENCES

I. Unpublished Manuscripts, Official.

1. *F.O.* These refer to the Foreign Office papers in the British Public Record Office. In some cases I quote from the Foreign Office copy ; in others from the Archives of Embassy copy.
   Thus—*F.O. Portugal,* 63/269, represents the Foreign Office copy of some despatches of 1822.
   F.O. Portugal, 179/23, is the duplicate Archives copy. In not a few cases the latter is the more valuable, as containing the original despatch of the Foreign Secretary.

2. *A.O.* Audit Office papers.

3. *B.M.* Add. MSS. British Museum Additional Manuscripts, followed by the number of the manuscript and the reference to the folio. *B*(ritish) *M*(useum) *Add*(itional) *MSS.*, 31,237, *f*(olio) 258.

4. *V.S.A. Wiener Staats Archiv.* I adopt the British form of Vienna for the abbreviation. The despatch *to* the specific country is given thus—*V*(iener) *S*(taats) *A*(rchiv), Weisungen nach Frankreich. Metternich to Vincent, 26th November 1823. That *from* a country thus—*V.S.A.*, Berichte aus England. Neumann to Metternich, 30th November 1823.

5. *A.A.E. Archives Affaires Etrangères,* Paris. The reference is to *Angleterre* (despatches to and from London), unless otherwise stated. The number of the volume follows these letters. Thus— *A*(rchives) *A*(ffaires) *E*(trangères) (Angleterre tome), 618. The reference of the writer follows—" Polignac to Chateaubriand, 12th March 1824."

II. Unpublished Manuscripts, Private.

1. (*Bag. MSS.*). These refer to a few papers not published by Colonel Bagot in his *George Canning and his Friends.*

2. (*Bath. MSS.*). *Bathurst MSS.* (A selection of the Bathurst Papers has been published in the Historical Manuscripts Commission, 1923.) This abbreviation refers to unpublished ones.

3. (*Gr. MSS.*). *Granville MSS.* Many of these have been published by Stapleton ; this reference is to the unpublished ones.

4. (*H. de W. MSS.*). *Howard de Walden MSS.* The secret papers of Canning, mostly intercepted letters of Continental diplomats. They are in *F.O.* 360/1–5.

5. (*Lie. MSS.*). *Madame Lieven's Diary* and papers transcribed from the St Petersburg Archives. Some of Madame Lieven's letters are in the Granville MSS.

6. (*Strat. MSS.*). These are the private papers of Stratford Canning in *F.O.* 352/8–17.

III. SHORT LIST OF PRINTED AUTHORITIES.

1. Stap., *P.L.* A. G. Stapleton, *Political Life* (1831), 3 vols.

2. Stap., *G.C. & T.* A. G. Stapleton, *George Canning and his Times* (1859).

3. Stap., *Corr.* E. J. Stapleton, *Political Correspondence* (1888), 2 vols.

4. Bagot, *G.C. & F.* *George Canning and his Friends* (1909).

5. *Speeches.* *George Canning*, ed. G. Therry (1836), 6 vols.

6. *W.N.D.* Wellington, *Despatches, Correspondence, and Memoranda,* i.–iv. (1867–71).

7. *B.F.S.P.* *British and Foreign State Papers*, x.–xiv. (1823–28).

8. *A.H.R.* *American Historical Review.*

9. *E.H.R.* *English Historical Review.*

10. *Hans. Deb.* *Hansard Parliamentary Debates.*

11. *Hans. Deb.*, N.S. *Hansard Parliamentary Debates*, New Series.

CONTENTS

CHAPTER VI

CALLING THE NEW WORLD INTO EXISTENCE (1824)

CHAPTER VII

THE LATER AMERICAN POLICY

PART IV

PORTUGAL AND BRAZIL (1823–5)

CHAPTER VIII

THE RECOVERY OF BRITISH INFLUENCE IN PORTUGAL

PART V

CANNING AND ENGLAND

CHAPTER X

CANNING, THE MAN

CHAPTER XI

CONQUERING THE KING

CHAPTER XII

THE DAY'S WORK AT THE FOREIGN OFFICE

CHAPTER XIII
The Press and Public Opinion

PART VI
THE AWAKENING OF GREECE AND THE DIPLOMATIC REVOLUTION

CHAPTER XIV
The Neo-Holy Alliance and the Greek Insurrection
(1821–4)

CHAPTER XV

The Greek Protocol of 4th April 1826; the Diplomatic Revolution

PART VII

THE RESULTS OF THE DIPLOMATIC REVOLUTION

CHAPTER XVI

The British Triumph in Portugal (1826)

CHAPTER XVII
THE FREEDOM OF GREECE

PART VIII
THE TRIUMPH AND LEGACY OF CANNING

CHAPTER XVIII
THE HUNDRED DAYS OF CANNING

CONTENTS

LIST OF ILLUSTRATIONS

ACKNOWLEDGEMENTS

THE thanks due to owners for granting me access to private papers of the periods have already been acknowledged in the Preface. Here I wish to express the thanks due to historians on both sides of the Atlantic. My thanks are due to Sir Ernest Satow, who not only read the proofs but gave me the benefit of his unrivalled practical and historical knowledge of diplomacy on the many points on which I consulted him. To Professor Webster my debt is even deeper, for his work on Castlereagh has been planned in collaboration with mine, and I have, for many years, had the benefit of his great historical and diplomatic knowledge. He has added to his kindness by reading the proofs, and, despite a few differences, I am happy to say that we are nowhere fundamentally in disagreement on the many problems of the period. I have to thank also Miss L. M. Penson of the London University for reading the proofs and for helpful suggestions. Mr C. N. Crawley, Fellow of Trinity Hall, has been very useful in correcting and adding to my knowledge on the Greek question. To Professor W. Alison-Phillips I owe much. Mr Reddaway, Fellow of King's College, Cambridge, was good enough to lend me his aid on the Monroe Doctrine. To Professor Elie Halévy, who knows so well the internal history of England in this period, I owe much, both for his books and for his counsel.

Many historians of the American Continent have helped me. Professor W. S. Robertson of Illinois University read the proofs of the Spanish-American chapters and gave me the benefit of his unrivalled knowledge on this question. I must thank Don Agustin Edwards, formerly Chilean Minister to this country, for a similar service. The chapters on Portugal and Brazil owe much to my friend M. Oliveira de Lima, whose knowledge of diplomacy both in history and at first hand has made his studies on this subject, and his advice to me, of the greatest importance and value.

On the vexed question of the Monroe Doctrine I owe much to Professor A. B. Hart of Harvard University and to Professor E. D. Adams of Leland Stanford University. Two other authorities have aided me. Mr H. Dexter Perkins, whom I examined for the Ph.D. at Harvard University, has returned the compliment by instructing me. And to S. E. Morison, Professor of American History at Oxford, I owe thanks for a criticism of my views and a clear exposition of his own. Professor J. M. Callahan of West Virginia University has helped me on some points by correspondence. I need scarcely add that none of those who have aided me should be held responsible for any inaccuracies that may be contained in this book.

I am indebted to my friends Mr G. N. Clark and Dr. J. F. Jameson, Editors respectively of the *English Historical*, and *American Historical Reviews*, to reproduce certain passages used in articles written for them.

My last, but not least, thanks are due to the Custodians of Archives. I have already mentioned in the Preface Mr Gaselee for his help as the Librarian of the Foreign Office, and should like to add also my recognition of that of Mr J. W. Headlam Morley. To M. Rigaud of the *Archives des Affaires Etrangères* at Paris, to Dr Redlich and to Dr Gross at Vienna I owe a deep debt of thanks. To the British Public Record Office I owe even more, especially to the Secretary, Mr A. E. Stamp, to Mr Hilary Jenkinson and to Mr Headlam. The Embassy Archives (as distinct from the Foreign Office copies) of the despatches of the period are deposited at Cambridge, and it is due to this fact that I have been able to read everything that Canning has written. To Mr Wright, under whose charge these records are at Cambridge, I am most grateful for unfailing courtesy and attention. It is difficult for any historian adequately to express his thanks to the keepers of archives, in view of the trouble he so persistently gives them.

PART I

THE NEO-HOLY ALLIANCE AND THE NEW MAN

CHAPTER I
REVOLUTION AND THE NEO-HOLY ALLIANCE (1820–22)

CHAPTER II
THE ADVENT OF THE NEW MAN: HIS POLITICAL SYSTEM

CHAPTER I

REVOLUTION AND THE NEO-HOLY ALLIANCE
(1820–22)[1]

I. THE PRELUDE (1818–20)

" Peuples, formez une Sainte Alliance ! "—BÉRANGER.

AT the beginning of 1820 Europe was still governed by
Alexander, by Metternich, and by Castlereagh. They were
a trio not unworthy of fame, for they had overthrown
Napoleon. Alexander's armies had given him his first great
defeat in 1812 ; Metternich's diplomacy had brought Austria
against him in 1813 ; Castlereagh had rallied the wavering
Coalition and ensured his downfall in 1814. In a sense these
triumphs were unfortunate for their fame, for they could
never again face so great an adversary or achieve such great
renown. Yet at the Congresses of Vienna and of Aix-la-
Chapelle all three played distinguished parts, and their union
and friendship still remained to ensure the peace of the world
in 1820. Yet for all three failure and shame were waiting.
Castlereagh and Alexander were to die miserably, separated
from their Allies, and with a sense of failure resting over their
labours and dimming their fame. Metternich was to live on
to an extreme old age, to experience defeat at the hands of
Canning, and to fly, thirty years later, to England, leaving
behind him nothing but the wreck of his life-work and of his
renown. In 1820 the result of the labours of all three men
still promised fair. Yet within a few months the prospects
of a long European peace vanished. Castlereagh took a course
that was to separate England from Europe ; Alexander and

---

[1] I give only a few references in this chapter to the authorities or events.
The whole has been handled more ably and fully than I could manage by
my friend, Professor Webster, in chapters i., vi., and vii. of *The Foreign Policy
of Castlereagh* (1925).

3

Metternich one that was to expose them to the hatred of all Liberals in the Old World and to the destruction of their system in the New. Events and ideas were to prove stronger than armies or despots, and the waves of revolution were already undermining the fabric of 1815.

On the basis of the European system all three were agreed ; they differed only as to the superstructure. The system of alliances built up from the Treaty of Chaumont, as modified by the Treaty of 20th November 1815, was the chief bond. This committed the Four Allies for twenty years to the defence of the territorial provisions of the Treaty of Vienna, and also to concerted action against any attempt to restore the Napoleonic dynasty to France. To this obligation of the Quadruple Alliance, to this steel structure of European peace, all three subscribed. Article VI. of the Treaty of 20th November 1815 provided for the periodical reunion of ministers and sovereigns, and this clause, due to Castlereagh, ensured collective discussion on European events, and kept up the idea of a possible extension of obligations. The three men looked at the Treaties in a different way. Metternich said Englishmen viewed a treaty ' like a civil contract,' and that Russians regarded not its precise stipulations but took the spirit for their guide. Castlereagh, though not at all anxious to break with the Alliance, did not consider that England was bound by that obligation to do more than join in attacking France, if she violated the territorial settlement or restored Napoleon. In the case of revolution or disturbance in France they were bound indeed to meet and discuss together, but Castlereagh denied that he had promised to do more than that. Alexander, however, held that this bond could be extended to cover a general and active interference or suppression of revolution in any State wishing to attempt such experiments. Metternich was too much of an opportunist to stop as short as Castlereagh or to go as far as Alexander. It might be convenient at one time to extend the Quadruple Alliance to include the suppression of revolution, and very inconvenient to do so at another time. Metternich had no desire to see Cossacks restoring order in Germany, but he might want to see Austrians restoring it in Italy. What Metternich most wanted was a display of moral solidarity among rulers in order that revolutionaries might be intimidated. But he was statesman enough to see that if he pushed Castlereagh too far in the direction of Alexander, the Quadruple Alliance would fall in pieces. Hence he tried to balance between the hard legal practicality of the one and the vague cosmopolitan mysticism of the other. His formula of 'moral solidarity' was constructed to prevent the material intervention of Alexander and the possible defection of Castlereagh.

Alexander had a certain case for extending the obligations of the Alliance. His scheme, known as the 'Holy Alliance,' had been signed in 1815 by every monarch in Europe except one. And even the Prince Regent of England, who could not publicly concur with a document not countersigned by any minister, wrote privately approving of it. It was intended by the Kings to be a union of sovereigns alone, on the basis of Christian charity and love. Perhaps because they were not consulted, their Ministers were less reverent. A 'piece of sublime mysticism and nonsense,' said the down-right Castlereagh, invented by a monarch whose mind was 'not entirely sound.' Metternich cynically declared that Madame de Krüdener and Alexander had summoned Christ to take part in their mystical conferences and had gone so far as to set a chair for Him at the table. Certainly neither Metternich nor Castlereagh attached any importance to it in 1815. They did not regard it as an official act, nor consider that it formed any part of the Peace Treaties as such.

But Alexander's view that the spirit was more important than the letter of treaties was pressed at Aix-la-Chapelle in 1818. He came forward with new and very extensive proposals for extending the reign of peace and love by guaranteeing sovereigns against revolution. Castlereagh told the Russian Ministers to leave out 'the parts where the Apocalypse showed itself.' Alexander then suggested a guarantee, not only of territory but also of institutions, by an international army, and claimed that the other Powers had already subscribed to these doctrines by signing the 'Holy Alliance.' The British Minister said that, as the British Constitution forbade her monarch to sign such a compact without a ministerial counter-signature, England could not be bound by any obligation which the 'Holy Alliance' contained. Moreover, as he

stated in a memorandum to the Conference, the idea of an
Alliance solidaire or of general guarantee was not contemplated in the Treaties, nor was it one which England could
accept.   Such acceptance might give " an almost irresistible
claim [to Russia] to march through the territories of all
the confederate States to the most distant points of Europe
to fulfil her guarantee."   England could make, and had made,
" no engagements beyond the immediate objects which were
made matter of regulation in the Treaties themselves."
Metternich's task of evasion was more difficult.   He held
the view that the ' Holy Alliance ' was not a registered Act
and therefore not binding.   It was the ' Quadruple Alliance,'
he said, that was ' our political religion,' and the ' Holy
Alliance ' was merely ' a moral part ' of it.   There was a good
deal of difference, he thought, between religious and moral
ideas.[1]   Finally, the three agreed on a vague formula which,
while declaring the object of the union of the Powers to be
peace on the basis of the Treaties, referred also to the intention
of the Powers to maintain the intimate union, strengthened
by the ties of Christian brotherhood, contracted by the
sovereigns.   This meant little to Metternich and Castlereagh,
but very much to Alexander.

A more practical step was the addition of France, now
regenerated and forgiven, to the European Concert by creating
a new Alliance known as the Quintuple.   The Quadruple
Alliance provided for action against France in the case of an
attempt by her to violate the territorial limits of Vienna or
to restore Napoleon.   To that France herself could not be
a party.   But under Article VI. of the Treaty of 20th November
1815 she could be, and was, admitted to the periodic congresses
or unions, and this admission served to restore her self-respect
and to enable her to resume her place in the European family.
It did not, however, destroy or affect the obligations of the
Quadruple Alliance.

The differences of opinion had, however, revealed considerable dangers.   Castlereagh was by no means satisfied with the

---

[1] Metternich does not explain what the difference was.   I infer that
dogmas were binding, and that morality was not.   The Treaty of Vienna,
at any rate, has clauses which have diplomatic meanings, but the ' Holy
Alliance ' speaks of charity, brotherhood, and Christian love, terms not
definable in diplomatic dictionaries.

formula which had saved the face of Alexander ; the British Cabinet even doubted whether the periodic reunions of the Powers should be continued ; and the British Parliament was becoming steadily more hostile to the ' entangling Alliance ' with the military despots of the Continent. It was strange to hear Alexander speaking of a reign of universal peace and love, while maintaining a Russian army of a million men,[1] and describing it as a ' European force.' Diplomacy may despise dreamers, but it cannot afford to despise formidably armed ones. Grave as were the doubts of Metternich, and graver as were those of Castlereagh, they hoped that their judicious use of a formula would prevent Alexander's injudicious use of an army.

The result of Aix-la-Chapelle was that the ' cracks ' were ' papered over ' for the time. In 1819 Metternich set himself to erect his masterpiece by the organisation of the new Confederation of Germany. By this system, embodied in the Carlsbad Resolutions and confirmed in a Congress at Vienna, Metternich secured Austria's predominance, and in effect her control, over all Germany. The Emperor, the Five Kings, the Grand Dukes, and the Free Cities were bound by a Federal Bond in chains at the feet of Metternich. Constitutions, where they existed, were discouraged or ' scotched ' ; measures of police supervision and press censorship penetrated throughout Germany, to control, to intimidate, or to suppress the utterances of professors, the outpourings of journalists, the organisation of students' unions or of gymnastic associations —everything which could criticise, or modify, or attack the existing order of Legitimate Monarchs. The right of interference in the internal affairs of German States, thus conceded to Metternich, enabled him to stifle opposition to his views. The finishing touch to the structure was put in 1820, just as revolution broke out in the Mediterranean lands. It is but fair to Metternich to say that his machinery stood the strain, and that in Germany alone was profound tranquillity maintained during 1820. From this work Castlereagh stood aside, though he did not dissent, and Alexander ventured only on a half-hearted remonstrance. In 1819 no real divergence of view had yet appeared over Germany or over Italy. In both

---

[1] Wellington thought half that number would have been sufficient.

of these countries Metternich maintained a rigid police and censorial control over the puny potentates who ruled the divided territories of what are now great nations.

The year 1818 had seen the military evacuation of France. She was no longer an object of terror, and this fact weakened the common bond which had united the Allies for six years in keeping watch over her. Henceforth France was to be kept strictly within the territorial limits assigned to her by treaty. Her violation of these frontiers was still to be resisted by the whole force of the Quadruple Alliance. But such violation was not, in fact, feared, and hence the different interests of the Four Allies tended to diverge. Alexander wished to continue that system of spasmodic interference in France by setting up and pulling down ministries and working on parties, which his ambassador Pozzo di Borgo had pursued with some success from 1815 to 1818. Castlereagh and Metternich preferred to leave her alone. So also with Spain. One man, complained Metternich in 1820, governed Spain, and by the methods of the Middle Ages and the Inquisition. It was Tatischev, the Russian Ambassador at Madrid. Metternich foresaw trouble, and wished Alexander would stop managing ' other people's business ' in Spain and in France. He was alarmed about both countries.[1] The monarchy in France seemed to him more than alien to the country, the loyalty of the army was doubtful, the ministries were fleeting, the bureaucracy was still full of old revolutionaries. Spain was a chaos of absurdities and corruption, but he did not think foreign interference had done, or would do, any good. About Alexander's theories he cared little, so long as they led to no practical action. What seemed to him important was the continuance of a period of static peace, which Alexander's meddling might disturb. The moral force of the Alliance, overshadowing France, was the best bulwark of peace and the chief means of discouraging revolution.

Castlereagh's position was not quite the same. ' The most European and least insular ' of British statesmen had devised, and obtained great results from, the system of government by conference. He had found that half a dozen men sitting

[1] *V.S.A.*, Weisungen nach Russland, Bd. 12. Metternich to Lebzeltern, Mar. 4/20.

round a table could regulate the destinies of Europe and draw up an instrument which gave peace to the world. Not only that, but his scheme of periodical reunions had tended to preserve and to improve that peace, and he was reluctant to abandon so useful an instrument. His difficulties became greater as the need for unity and concerted action declined. The vague and mystic theories of Alexander were more serious to him, for Metternich thought them faults which did not materially affect the development of a repressive regime. Castlereagh, though an Irishman, had a truly English distrust of all theories. He had been driven almost frantic by his own domestic problems, by the disturbances and bloodshed at Peterloo in 1819, by the conspiracy of Thistlewood, and by the riots over Queen Caroline. He may perhaps have believed that these were connected with international revolutionaries on the Continent, and he corresponded with the sympathetic Metternich about the vigorous life of the ' monster Radicalism ' in England. But he had no idea of suppressing it by bringing Alexander's Cossacks to put down riots in Hyde Park, by instituting a European police, or by accepting a theory of general international intervention. Theories were dangerous things to handle at conferences, for rumours of them got into the Press and incited the mob leaders without to denunciation of the Alliance and its ways. He had had much trouble in explaining the ' Holy Alliance ' to Parliament in 1816, and he knew that he could not defend any new-fangled theory of Divine Right, based on the Apocalypse, before the hostile orators in the Commons. It was his nature to work quietly and unobtrusively for the good of England and of Europe ; publicity disturbed and alarmed his honourable, but sub-terranean, labours. Hence, after 1818 he went in constant dread of being called upon to explain his connection with despotic rulers, whose arguments and theories he could oppose in private but did not want to repudiate in public. Metternich could be trusted to keep his mouth shut and to avoid inconvenient appeals to the public. Alexander could not ; and hence Castlereagh watched him with a growing sense of alarm and mistrust.

2. The Revolution in Spain (1820)

" Ainsi fut couronnée la tyrannie par la couardise, le manque de foi par le parjure."—CHATEAUBRIAND.

Thus, though Europe seemed at peace in 1820, it was an uneasy and eventful slumber. Crude attempts at revolution and cruder attempts at repression were soon to provoke those new forces which were to rule the modern world. Four revolutions broke out in Europe in 1820, a fifth was heralded in Greece. In North America revolution was already stable and triumphant; half of the South was already liberated, and the other half was gathering itself for the final effort to tear the crowns of New Spain and New Granada from the head of the despot at Madrid. It was indeed the effort to reconquer his dominions in America which proved fatal to Ferdinand in Spain. For it was the attempt to fit out an expedition for the New World which caused a military revolt among a handful of starved, ill-paid, and discontented soldiers at Cadiz. It was thus New Spain which provoked a revolt in the Mother Country. The Spanish revolt was created by a vain and foolish officer called Riego, ' a greater but a more insane hero than Don Quixote.' The flame could not be stamped out by the government of a blind, obstinate, and stupid despot, who had, said Spaniards, ' the heart of a tiger and the head of a mule '; whose rule Metternich himself condemned as unspeakably inefficient and corrupt. Riego's vanity was fanned by his success, and his demands increased with his followers. He proclaimed himself the hero of democratic freedom, and demanded that Ferdinand should accept the Spanish Constitution of 1812. That was an experiment in the wildest democracy. It was a constitution without an aristocracy, without a second chamber, without ministers sitting in the lower house, without stability, and without any reasonable hope of it. The Spanish people, thus endowed with complete powers, were brutishly ignorant and superstitious, as much a tool in the hands of ambitious soldiers and of flamboyant politicians as they had been in those of Ferdinand. Whoever ruled in Spain, it was not to be the people. None the less Ferdinand's obstinacy, which had so long resisted even Napoleon, had to bow to lesser men. He was alone, he was deserted by his grandees and his priests. Riego and his myrmidons were at the door, the armies of Alexander were far away. He solemnly accepted the crazy constitution, admitted loud-voiced politicians to his Cabinet, and did solemn penance for his absolutist sins. He appeared on the balcony of his palace and bowed his stubborn neck to the crowd below, while a mother held up to him a child whose father he had executed. This typical scene produced the most profound impression throughout Europe. His brother despots beheld a king accepting an ultra-democratic constitution and felt shamed and humiliated in his person.

All men with real information knew that Ferdinand had not accepted either the constitution or his humiliation with sincerity. His personal qualities excited the greatest contempt; his preference for low company and bad advisers, his insane obstinacy and inefficiency were known to all diplomats. But they all knew that he was a convinced absolutist, and that he only yielded for the moment to the storm. Hence his submission was not the end, but the beginning, of revolution. To avert further consequences, the Czar of Russia decided to summon the monarchs to unite together and display their concerted purpose to the world.

Alexander was a strange, brilliant, and unhappy figure. No man had had more triumphs, no one was more many-sided, few had finer intelligence, none a more sympathetic imagination. Napoleon said he had great qualities but lacked something. Wellington said what he lacked was moderation. It was true. In youth a disciple of La Harpe, of democracy and nationality, he had outstripped all statesmen of Europe in liberality. Napoleon had attacked him in Moscow; Alexander had replied by deposing him and by dictating peace in Paris, by giving constitutions to France and to a regenerated Poland, and by forcing the 'Holy Alliance' upon the monarchs of Europe. His inconsistencies were always abundant. While talking of general peace and of grand general objects, he vigorously pushed the particular ends of Russia. While maintaining a huge army, he yet talked seriously of disarmament and of international armies and fleets. And his inconsistencies had now become apparent. By 1818 he found that France resented the advice of her liberator, that Poland unmistakably showed her distrust of him, that the Ministers, if not the monarchs, of Europe laughed at his ' Holy Alliance.' Then came denunciations of it by German students and by English journalists, the murder of Kotzebue, the murder of the Duc de Berri, the assassination plot of Thistlewood and the riots over Queen Caroline in London, rumours of a rising in Greece, the revolt of the army in Spain. These blows smote like a hammer in relentless succession on the sensitive and excitable Czar. Was there not a universal international conspiracy against monarchs, above all against him—the most splendid of monarchs? Surely these individual murders, popular out-cries, sporadic riots, military mutinies, all had a common root. He was wrong, but he did not know that he was. The ruler, whose face expressed benevolence and love, whose instincts were kindly, whose faith was sincere, was about to become the most relentless of despots, more ' ultra than the ultraists.' For the absence of moderation and balance turned his philan-thropic instincts to hatred. His vanity and his fears whispered to one another and aided the conversion. His ambassador Tatischev had governed Spain and been overthrown even be-fore Ferdinand, and, for all his benevolence, Alexander seldom neglected the interests of Russia.[1] The Spanish Revolution had triumphed because soldiers had forsworn their obedience at Madrid. If soldiers could revolt, no monarch was safe, and it was the duty of every sovereign to suppress military mutiny wherever found. He could bring the most numerous of armies to aid the Spanish King, and thus benefit not only Spain but all Europe. Would not the flames lighted in Spain extend across the Continent unless they were immediately extinguished? It was his task to save Europe from de-mocracy, just as he had once saved it from Napoleon. But Europe must not be saved by him alone. He would only head the international army and preside over the international union of sovereigns. A united front must be shown by all kings so that all revolutionaries might tremble.

---

[1] Tatischev left Spain Oct. 1819 and never returned, v. Webster, 226.

3. CASTLEREAGH'S STATE PAPER OF 5TH MAY 1820

" It was not with the desire of claiming to himself any merit that belonged to them [his colleagues] *. . . he now felt himself called upon to repeat . . . that he* [Canning] *had found in the records of his office a state paper, laying down the principle of non-interference, with all the qualification properly belonging to it."*—CANNING in the Commons, 14th April 1823.

Hence on the 3rd March, as soon as he heard of the revolt, Alexander suggested that the Allies should at once confidentially discuss their measures or attitude (1) in case the King should suppress the revolt ; (2) in case he should spontaneously ask for support from his Allies ; (3) in case the insurrection should be protracted. At the end of March he suggested the reference of the whole Spanish question to the Ambassadors' Conference at Paris. On the 30th April he went further still, for he had been approached by the new Constitutional Minister of Spain at St Petersburg, and he sent out a circular to his Allies indicating the tone of his reply, and asking for their support. He said that " The Revolution of the peninsula draws on it the eyes of two Worlds. The interests which it is going to decide are the interests of the Universe." He claimed that the Allied Sovereigns had given Spain to understand at Aix-la-Chapelle that, neither in New World nor Old could constitutions prosper unless " granted by the benevolence of the sovereign as a voluntary concession." In virtue of the engagements of Aix-la-Chapelle the Czar condemned " with the strongest, and most solemn, reprobation the revolutionary means put to work to give new institutions to Spain." " The Spanish Government to-day ought to make an expiation to the peoples of the two hemispheres." There could be " no relations of amity or trust with Spain until it improves its constitution." He added, ominously for Castlereagh, " The Emperor does not doubt that his Allies will approve [his sentiments]."

This eloquent and melodramatic appeal smote idly on the cold marble of Castlereagh's mind. Sober, serene, and practical, he despised the alarms, as much as he distrusted the threats, of Alexander. Crusades were as out of date as high words were dangerous. Russia's influence was already great. In recent years she had menaced Persia, the Adriatic, the American Continent, and the British maritime power and practice. It was time to call a halt both to the practical and theoretical progress of this Colossus of the North, and to tell him plainly what the view of England was. With this idea in his mind Castlereagh produced his famous state paper of 5th May 1820, the first statement of general principles to which English diplomacy had ever committed itself, and which was, as Canning afterwards declared, the foundation of his own foreign policy.

Castlereagh began by objecting to a reunion of sovereigns for the purpose of deliberation on Spain as being unlikely to achieve the end in view. The Spanish Revolution was remote, and " fearful as is the example of an army in revolt . . . there is no ground for apprehension that Europe is likely to be speedily endangered by Spanish arms." Intervention by any Power was always a very delicate question. England would, for instance, interfere to prevent Belgium from being annexed to France, but she certainly would not interfere in the German Confederation even if ' the flame of military Revolt ' extended itself there. In any case military intervention carried with it of necessity military occupation, and "no rational states-man would found his prospects of security on such a calcu-lation."

Castlereagh admitted " the general danger which menaces more or less the stability of all existing government, from the Principles which are afloat and from the circumstances that so many States of Europe are now employed in the difficult task of casting anew their governments upon the Representative Principle." But to control or regulate such experiments ' by foreign counsel or by foreign force ' would be ' as dangerous to avow as it would be impossible to execute.' All that England would consent to, as thought likely to be effectual in Spain, would be the tendering of good offices or advice by the Four, or Five, Great Powers after the freest interchange of views amongst themselves. But there should be no reunion of sovereigns or public or formal deliberation. That was likely to provoke the susceptibilities of Spain, which in Wellington's view was " of all the European people that which will least brook interference from abroad."

In the special case of Spain it was not then advisable for any Power to intervene by military force, though Castlereagh had already admitted that cases demanding intervention might arise. But they were, in his view, cases to be determined on their merits and by the action or interests of individual Powers. England intended to combat the view that " whenever any great Political Event shall occur, as in Spain, it is to be regarded almost as a matter of course that it belongs to the Allies to charge themselves collectively with the Responsibility of exercising some Jurisdiction regarding possible or eventual Danger." For such responsibility eventually implied force, and to a generalised system of intervention, implying or supported by force, England was unalterably opposed. The Alliance to which she belonged was framed to protect the territorial settlement of Vienna. " It never, however, was intended for the Government of the World, or for the superintendence of the Internal Affairs of other States."

Castlereagh then proceeded to define the obligations of the Quadruple Alliance, the specific territorial guarantees, the provision against the return of Napoleon, and he admitted that it " designated the Revolutionary Power which had convulsed France and desolated Europe as the object of its constant solicitude, but it was the Revolutionary Power more particularly in its military character against which it intended to take precautions, *rather* [1] than against the Democratic principles, then as now, but too generally spread throughout Europe." Castlereagh seems to have felt himself on thin ice here. His language lacks precision, and gave some handle both to the wider interpretation as to intervention adopted by Metternich, and to the extremer views of Alexander. He therefore proceeded to use arguments of expediency and to contrast the power of a despot (Alexander) in such cases with the limitations imposed by public opinion on King George. " H.I.M.'s mind is settled on these points, his action is free and his means are in his own hands." But the King of Spain was unpopular in England. King George, even if he embarked in a war on the advice of his Ministers, would not be permitted by the ' Voice of the country ' to continue it. England would not recognise that her safety was menaced, unless Spanish revolutionaries attacked Portugal. As she had resolved not

---

[1] Italics my own. *Vide* generally Webster, pp. 226–46.

to interfere forcibly to restore order in the Spanish American
Colonies, she was equally bound to eschew the use of force
in Old Spain. Castlereagh admitted that there was treason and
disaffection in certain manufacturing districts in England,
and said that interference abroad would only excite it further.[1]
" The fact is that we do not and cannot feel alike upon all
subjects." It was better to recognise this fact, for representative governments must keep within the ' common-sense
limits ' of the Alliance or they will create an " impression that
they have made a surrender of [their] first principles " if they
acted contrary to the sense of their people, in order to preserve
unified action with despotic governments. The minimum
was all that could be offered, and this precluded the sanctioning of armed external interference in Spain, or (and more
important) anywhere else, save in a case defined by treaty
or in one specially affecting England's interests.

He concluded by saying, " We shall be found in our place
when actual danger menaces the system of Europe, but this
country cannot and will not act upon abstract and speculative
Principles of Precaution. The Alliance which exists had no
such purpose in view in its original formation. It was never
so explained to Parliament, and it would be a breach of faith
to Parliament now to extend it." He added, a little ironically,
that this view had already been fully stated in a memorandum
presented at Aix-la-Chapelle, to which he now referred his
Allies.

The tone of this communication was not always urbane,
and Alexander, whose ' common sense ' was called in question
and whose proposals were declined, was naturally irate. From
this time forward dates the antagonism of England and
Alexander, the closer connection between the latter and
Metternich, and the consequent remodelling of Alliances on
the narrower basis of the closer union of Prussia, Austria,
and Russia, the three eastern despotic and military monarchies,
against revolution. The bond cannot accurately be called
the ' Holy Alliance,' but might not unfairly be described as
the *Neo-Holy* Alliance. It was a new and real union based

---

[1] He seems also to have mutiny of troops in his mind. In June 1820
Wellington addressed a letter to Liverpool in which he referred to ' acts
of mutiny and disorder ' in the Guards. *W.N.D.*, i. 127.

on the memory of an old and vague understanding. It was a union of three sovereigns, all despots, and it displaced that union of three men—Alexander, Metternich, and Castlereagh—which had governed Europe since 1815.

Castlereagh and Alexander had denounced one another from opposing pulpits; Metternich hoped to bridge the chasm. Of Castlereagh's protest Metternich took little notice, hoping that it might soon be forgotten. But Alexander's project, which threatened or implied action, must be met at once, so he took a line which, he thought, might reconcile both parties. He opposed ' an international army,' because England and France would not join it. It was a project which ought to be examined, but was not likely to end in good practical results.[1] Though he did not say so, he did not in fact want a Russian army to pass through Germany, even for the desirable object of overthrowing a constitution in Spain. The only Power which could attack Spain was France, but he thought that the French Army could not be trusted. If it was loyal, it ought to remain to protect Louis XVIII.; if it was not, it would overthrow him, either on being ordered to Spain, or on its return from that country. He did not think that armed foreign intervention would produce benefits in Spain. If the worst came to the worst he might support the Spanish Royalists with money and arms, but in any case at their suggestion and on their initiative. The application of moral force, the demonstration of the unity of the Allies, was his sovereign and only remedy for the evil. Revolutionary ideas would exhaust themselves, and at the critical moment the Allies could step in and give authoritative advice to ' mend or end ' the constitution. He did not even want a conference or a union of sovereigns, for the public might be unfavourably impressed by such a demonstration of solidarity. If the monarchs united in such a demonstration it would show that they were afraid of the revolutionaries. So argued Metternich, shrewdly and wisely enough, in circulars to the Powers during June and July 1820.

[1] *V.S.A.*, Russland Weisungen, Bd. 1. Metternich to Lebzeltern, May 7/20.

4. The Revolutions in Naples and Piedmont

" La constitution de Cadiz avoit été imposé à Naples : Naples en fut pour son caprice ; il lui fallut retourner à son soleil et à ses fleurs."—
CHATEAUBRIAND.

But in July a new complication occurred. A revolution broke out in Naples, and Piedmont was disturbed. Ferdinand of Naples yielded openly to the storm and elaborately swore to the ultra-democratic Constitution of 1812, imported like a hot-cake from Madrid. Metternich changed his tone at once. He had been against both action and conferences before ; now he was for both. Ferdinand of Naples was as bigoted, though not as stupid, as his brother Bourbon and namesake at Madrid. The revolutions at Naples and Turin not only showed that the ' moral contagion ' was spreading, but they directly touched the interests of Austria. Metternich resolved to act, and to act at once, by sending armed forces to overawe Piedmont, and to put down revolution in Naples in the name of the kings and of European order. Austria was to be the instrument of the Alliance, which was not to be allowed directly to interfere. The spread of revolution caused Metternich to think that there really was something to be said for a reunion of sovereigns after all. For a reunion of sovereigns would bless the intervention of Austria, and exhibit their moral solidarity to the world. But Austria was to act for herself under the blessing of the Conference.

In the course of one month Metternich had executed a complete change of position and principle. On the 4th March he had argued strongly against any more conferences. It was much better for Alexander to express his individual opinion separately, " than to see him present at conferences our ideas clothed in forms that are not ours." [1] On the 7th he wrote, " The very nature of my thesis excludes all idea of foreign inter- ference for France *as for other countries*.[2] No one can govern for a government, and there are cases where the appearance of support does more than feebleness itself." Yet this judicious observer was about to overthrow two constitutions in Italy with armed force, and to support one tottering

[1] *V.S.A.*, Weisungen nach Russland, Bd. 12. Metternich to Lebzeltern, Mar. 4, 7/20.
[2] Italics my own.

government by a military occupation for eight years. Even at the end of May he still refused to believe that Spain could be 'restored to calm by intervention and foreign aid.' He wished only a strong moral condemnation by the Powers of the culpable methods (*i.e.* military revolt) by which the constitution had been obtained. Even in mid June[1] he wrote, " The Powers can do nothing at once, much in the future by closing the ranks." Then came the news of the revolution at Naples, and of another Ferdinand and another Bourbon prostrate before Carbonari and military conspirators. This one not only swore to obey the Constitution of 1812, but did so in defiance of a previous treaty pledge to Metternich. With incomparable ease the latter changed his point of view. This news placed Austria ' in the first line' ; ' we mean action here ' ; and the Austrian Army at once began to concentrate in Lombardy. A conference, formerly a dangerous luxury, suddenly became a prime necessity. For, while Alexander's material influence must be kept out of Spain, his moral pressure must be brought to bear upon Naples. Events had at last finished the Czar's conversion on " the day when this [innovating] spirit sought and found its means of action in the ranks of that force which sustains and menaces, to an equal degree, an empire founded on the sole power of the monarch."[2] Metternich was not blind to the immense ascendancy he might secure over Russia and its Czar, now at length a repentant liberal and an unrepentant despot. So, on the 1st September, Metternich at last accepted Alexander's renewed invitation to a reunion of sovereigns. But he intended now to lead, and not to follow. Austria was to be strengthened, not to be hindered, by Alexander. This is clearly shown by Metternich's utterance : " Whatever Alexander's answer, we shall take our own course in Naples."[3] All this seems clear enough. Castlereagh, in one of the few unreserved utterances of his life, allowed himself once to write privately of the ' complete double-dealing ' of Prince Metternich. The best commentary on that text is his kaleidoscopic change between March and August 1820.

[1] *V.S.A.*, Weisungen nach Russland, Bd. 12. Metternich to Lebzeltern, May 24, June 16/20.
[2] *V.S.A.*, Weisungen nach England, Bd. 213. Metternich to Esterházy, Aug. 12/20. Metternich means the revolt of the Spanish Army.
[3] *Ibid.*, Aug. 26/20.

The real difficulty lay in the attitude of the two parliamentary States, England and France (more particularly England), and in the difference between Castlereagh and Alexander on the principle of intervention. But here a new revolution, for once, became pleasing to Metternich. In September Portugal had raised a rebellious head. The authority of the absent king was overthrown, and an ultra-democratic constitution was once again proclaimed. Metternich hoped to appeal to Castlereagh on this count. England was bound closely by treaty to Portugal, and Metternich was quite willing to leave this whole question to her. Castlereagh, in return for a free hand in Portugal, might grant Metternich one in Italy. For he was bound by pledges there, and the ' faith of treaties ' appealed to one who looked on them in the light of ' a civil contract.' On the other hand, even Castlereagh could no longer hold that Spain was an isolated problem. For the ' dreaded moral contagion ' had flown from Madrid to Naples, had swept back from Turin to Lisbon, and was spreading in Epirus and in the Morea. A conference was obviously justified in considering what was now a general problem. On the first of September Metternich therefore accepted Alexander's offer of a conference. But England still demurred. Metternich reported Castlereagh's brother (Lord Charles Stewart, the Ambassador at Vienna) as ' frightened into the proposed reunion at Troppau.' ' I am not,' said Metternich.[1] For he was not blind to the incomparable opportunity which it offered of binding Alexander to his chariot.

The Austrian chancellor had consented to Alexander's projected congress, and it remained to devise a method for including England and France. He devised an ingenious scheme to overcome the resistance of Castlereagh and the reluctance of France. The three Eastern despots with their ministers would meet in a rather informal congress, the two Western or parliamentary States need not send their sovereigns but only ministers plenipotentiary. Even if they acted merely as observers, as Castlereagh instructed the British representative to do, their presence would prevent any breach in moral

[1] V.S.A., Weisungen nach England, Bd. 213. Metternich to Esterházy, Sept. 21/20.

solidarity. On these lines the congress met at Troppau in October. Alexander, as soon as he appeared on the 24th October, hastened to assure Metternich that he regretted all that he had said and done during the years 1814–18, but that his purpose was now ' unshakable.' Alexander's aim was of course to draw closer the bonds of union on the basis of the old ' Holy Alliance,' an instrument he could interpret at his will and to his advantage. That instrument was derided by Metternich to every one except the Czar, and was not one he was prepared to accept or, in any way, to work. But he also foresaw that the old form of the Quadruple Alliance was no longer possible. Metternich stated to Vincent on the 7th April that he had originally favoured the Quadruple Alliance (as indeed had Castlereagh), and both had resisted the Russian attempt to transform it in 1818. He now used these memorable words : " It is no longer in the form of the Quadruple Alliance that we can seek the remedies. There is happening to-day what I have never ceased to predict in the years which prepared the actual catastrophe. They have broken a mould which might have become of even greater utility in moments of disaster ; we must remake it to-day and the elements are no longer the same. Russia is going to make a demand on us, but it is impossible to count on the assent of England. Of all faults in politics those which bear the bitterest fruits are *changes of system*." [1] He saw the danger of a breach with England as with Russia. He would not have the ' Holy Alliance ' as Alexander conceived it, but he thought that he might go some way to meet him by fashioning a new system, which we have called the Neo-Holy Alliance, out of the old ' Quadruple Bond.'

It might be thought that Metternich now had Alexander in control. But, as Canning said later of the Czar, ' be assured that no man living has him in control.' Metternich had mounted the horse and held the reins, but the steed was

---

[1] *V.S.A.*, Weisungen nach Frankreich, Bd. 343. Metternich to Vincent particulière, Apr. 7/20. Vincent was ' to keep this idea wholly to himself.' What Metternich meant was that the Quadruple Alliance was an intelligible bond because embodied in diplomatic formulæ. The ' Holy Alliance ' was mere nonsense, and its adoption in any form might commit the Powers to Alexander, who claimed the right of interpreting his nonsense to his own advantage. So a modification of the ' Holy Alliance ' was a ' change of system,' but the Quadruple Bond might be extended.

mettlesome and might run away with him. Even though Alexander had changed, he still wished to lead. Metternich afterwards complained of the divided Russian Cabinet and of ' their dangerous and incorrect phrases,' which they preferred to simple reasonings. Certainly there have been few phrases which have produced more consequences or awakened more indignation than those connected with Troppau. For Alexander's time had come. Metternich, once in a conference, was not able to resist the New Holy Alliance, as he resisted and evaded the old one in 1815. The outcome of Troppau was a proclamation of high-flying doctrine, followed by an outburst of popular hatred against monarchs, exactly as Metternich had foreseen. Metternich was the new Mazeppa, borne away by the wild horse Alexander, and the wolves of liberalism ran howling and snapping at their heels.

5. The Troppau Circular (8th December 1820); Castlereagh's Reply (19th January 1821)

Apparently much against Metternich's wish, the three Eastern Powers signed a circular at Troppau (8th December 1820) which may be taken as the manifesto of their political faith.   Here is the real formation of the Neo-Holy Alliance of the three great eastern military monarchs of Russia, Austria, and Prussia, based on a new doctrine and on a new faith of reaction, and backed by hundreds of thousands of bayonets. Its professions were remarkable.

The circular began by alluding to the revolutions in Spain and Naples and to the ' catastrophe ' of Portugal.   Revolution had ' raised its head ' and the Powers must use " the same means happily employed in that memorable struggle which delivered Europe from a yoke it had borne for twenty years," in order to " put a bridle on a new power, not less tyrannical, not less detestable, in its power of insurrection and of crime. These were the motives and aims of the reunion of Troppau."

Insurrections such as these were a " flagrant violation of the pact guaranteeing to all European governments their territorial integrity."   It was necessary to act at once against the constitutional regime in Naples. No insurrectionary government could be recognised by the three sovereigns.

" They demand only the right of maintaining peace, of delivering Europe from the scourge of revolution, of diverting or checking according to their means, the evils resulting from the violation of all the principles of order and morality." England and France were invited to concur in this circular.

The doctrine thus proclaimed was that revolution or insurrection, even if purely an affair of internal change, could never be recognised by the three military despots of East Europe. Their moral force would always be exerted against such governments. They did not pledge themselves to suppress every insurrectionary government by material means, but they did intend to suppress that in Naples. Here, then, is the origin of the Neo-Holy Alliance. It is fully developed, and claims an unlimited right of interference in the internal affairs of other states, if they chose to change their govern- ments or try new experiments in political science. In principle the European ' Areopagus,' the European ' police system,' the right of the Monarchical Trades Union to protect brother kings against their subjects, is fully proclaimed. It is limited only by power and by expediency.

There is ample evidence that Metternich objected to the circular.   Three years afterwards he wrote to his most trusted subordinate : " Remember the famous Circular of December 1820, meant to spread wide (*répandre*) the view of the results of the Congress of Troppau, and how much I fought against it, and which first provoked a formal protest on the part of the British Government." [1] Had he not been run away with by Alexander, he would never have committed. himself publicly to such dangerous sentiments. Castlereagh knew this well enough, but was, none the less, furiously angry. England's government was founded on revolution, and she could not consent to doctrines which denied her origin. Moreover, Castlereagh held that he had not been adequately consulted, and that his state paper of 5th May 1820 had been contemptuously set aside. He well knew the storm which awaited him, both in Parliament and the Press, when the circular became public, and he prepared, therefore, to make it

---

[1] *V.S.A.*, Weisungen nach Russland, Bd. 8. Metternich to Lebzeltern, Jan. 15/25. Secrète ad. no. 2. He says later that Capodistrias, for his own purposes, widened the split between Russia and England.

publicly known that England dissented from the Neo-Holy Alliance doctrines, and denied that they were implied in the obligations of 1815.   On the 19th January 1821 he published his famous circular of dissent, a document which repeated in vigorous terms the principles of the state paper of 5th May 1820.

The three Allies were already at Laibach sitting in congress on the question of Naples, with France and England as onlookers.   Alexander did not let the Congress break up without issuing more foolish circulars of the ' high-flying ' ultra type.   Meanwhile the Austrian Army was let loose on Naples, and had overturned the constitution and entered the capital (24th March).   Castlereagh approved of the suppression of the Naples movement because he thought (as did Canning) that Austria had a right by treaty to suppress disturbance in Italy.   But he was in the highest degree roused by the circulars, as were the British public.   In the Commons he declared (21st June 1821) that he agreed with the criticisms of these circulars. " He would not recognise the principle that one State was entitled to interfere with another because changes might be effected in its Government in a way which the former State disapproved.   For certain States to erect themselves into a tribunal to judge of the internal affairs of others was to arrogate to themselves a power which could only be assumed in defiance of the law of nations and the principles of common sense."   None the less he did not think it necessary to make a fresh protest.

6. The Last of Castlereagh (12th August 1822)

" Let him pass, he hates him
That would upon the rack of this tough world
Stretch him out longer."—" King Lear."

Here are outlined sharply the two principles: that of intervention held by the Neo-Holy Alliance; that of non-intervention held by England.   The principles of despotism and of parliamentary government were thus actually in conflict.   For the Neo-Holy Alliance regarded the engagements of Vienna as giving them the right to intervene in the internal affairs of States, while Castlereagh denied any such interpreta-tion, and thought it impossible for any parliamentary government to recognise it. The issue was fairly joined. The struggle between these two principles went on during the next half-dozen years, and was more active under Canning than under Castlereagh.

Towards the end of 1821 Castlereagh met Metternich at Hanover and endeavoured to arrive at an agreement over the question of Turkey. So he was unfortunately again drawn into the Congress System in this special case. The danger of Russia going to war with her was so great that Castlereagh and Metternich endeavoured to act together, despite their differences in principle. They ultimately agreed that the summoning of a congress alone was likely to prevent Alexander from going to war. Such was the origin of the Congress of Verona, and Castlereagh's last act was to draft instructions for it, or rather for himself, as he proposed attending in person. The situation was so serious in the middle of 1822 that it may be doubted whether even Castlereagh's diplomatic arts could have produced a successful outcome at Verona; even if agreement had been reached, it is still more doubtful if he could have reconciled Parliament and public to the spectacle of further harmony between himself and the Neo-Holy Alliance. But the experiment, as he conceived it, was not destined to be tried.

During the summer of 1822 Castlereagh's mind and body were both failing. For a time his cold, serene face forbade anyone to guess at the agitation and distractions which were consuming his life. Though weary, he seemed to the world as imperturbable and as unassailable as ever. On the 30th May he appeared at a dress ball at the Opera, splendid and handsome ' in a fine coat covered with diamonds.' But on the 3rd June he told Lord Tavistock that " he was sick of the concern, and that if he could well get out of it would never get into it again." Parliament ended, and he hoped to secure rest in July. Early in August his manner became strange; he talked of spies and of men who threatened his life and—what he cared more for—his honour. He kept still to his work, the last document he signed being dated the 9th August. Before this date his friends had become thoroughly alarmed not only for his health, but for his mind; his attendants removed his pistols and his razors, but forgot one small knife.

The omission was fatal. On the 13th, witnesses reported to the jury that they had found him on the 12th stretched on the floor of his dressing-room, covered with blood, his carotid artery severed, his eyes staring glassily upward, and the small knife in his stiff right hand.

The hatred of his enemies pursued him even when dead, and a body of ruffians shouted with triumph as his mortal remains sank from view in Westminster Abbey. It was a sad close to the career of a great public servant, who had laboured till the last moment of his strength as unselfishly as any man in English history, and whose services to his country were such as no public adulation could ever have rewarded. But there was one ready to fill his place. As the helm of state fell from the dying hands of Pitt only to be grasped by his old rival Fox, who carried on his policy with a vigour and a mastery arousing universal admiration, so Canning was now to receive the rudder from Castlereagh and to pilot the ship of state along the dangerous course which lay before it.

CHAPTER II

THE ADVENT OF THE NEW MAN: HIS POLITICAL SYSTEM

1. Coming into Office (August–September 1822)

" Canning is a genius, almost a universal one . . . and no man of talent can long pursue the path of his late predecessor, Lord C[astlereagh]. If ever man saved his country, Canning CAN but WILL he? I, for one, hope so."—BYRON.

HE who was now to succeed to the heritage of Castlereagh had preceded him in the office of Foreign Minister. During 1807–9 he had held power and shown great resolution at the most perilous moment of England's fate. His measures in Denmark and in Portugal had withdrawn from Napoleon's grasp as many ships of the line as Nelson destroyed at Trafalgar; and his policy in committing England irrevocably to the defence of Spain ultimately cost that great conqueror half a million of men. This record was a very remarkable one, though it did not excel that of Castlereagh in consolidating the Alliance in 1814, nor equal his great constructive work in rebuilding Europe in 1815. The unfortunate incidents which led to the retirement of Castlereagh and Canning from the Cabinet and to their duel in 1809 had caused great excitement and had left a lasting impression. Canning received a wound in the duel, and bore ever afterwards (though somewhat unjustly) both moral and material scars. His political career had been fatally injured, while Castlereagh went on to achieve a power such as few men have ever enjoyed. At the moment when Castlereagh was giving the law to Europe, Canning played the humble part of Ambassador to Lisbon (1814–1816). In 1816 he entered the Cabinet once more as President of the (India) Board of Control, thus definitely renouncing independence and accepting defeat. There he had distinguished

27

himself by attacking the Radicals with a vigour and bitterness which even exceeded their own, and became, for a time, the best-hated man in a thoroughly unpopular ministry. Then came George IV.'s accession and his attempt to divorce Queen Caroline. From this campaign Canning, who had been her personal friend, stood aside, and finally resigned when the King's efforts forced the ministers towards penal measures. Canning took care to say on his resignation that it was on this point alone that he differed from the ministers. It was one over which the public was more concerned for the moment than over foreign policy, and they considered it much in his favour. For the London mob espoused the cause of the ' injured Queen ' with frantic enthusiasm, and Brougham had fanned their hatred of the King to white-heat during the trial before the Peers. Neither Castlereagh nor Wellington could appear in public without being insulted, the indignation with the King was even greater, and the throne itself in some danger. Canning by his resignation had regained some of his lost popularity, but for that very reason his re-entry into the ministry was not welcomed by most of his colleagues, and was bitterly opposed by the King. It was not pleasant to them to hear Brougham praising ' the noble and manly conduct of Mr Canning.'

In August 1822 the situation was that Canning had already accepted the Governor-Generalship of India, and that the ship was actually waiting in the Thames to convey him to his gilded and imperial exile. On hearing of the death of Castlereagh he played his game with admirable coolness and skill. A fortnight passed and there was no overture yet from the Government, and he had made no overture to them. His old friend Granville wrote warning him of the danger ' that the K[ing] and his faction ' might offer him less than the whole heritage of Castlereagh [*i.e.* less than the lead in the Commons and the Foreign Secretaryship] and advising him in such case to refuse altogether. Canning answered him on the 25th August from Liverpool : " I must use this abominable slippery paper and a pen no bigger than a pin . . . all the implements I can get at my friend Ewart's country house, where I am spending the day." . . . " I am *inclined* to agree in the [your] former opinion, and agree entirely upon the latter " [*i.e.* to insist on the whole heritage] . . . " upon the *former* I have some doubts . . . upon the latter none. . . . Gladstone and Ewart are distinctly of my opinion on this last point." He thought that Eldon would wish to deny him, and that Liverpool would be unable to obtain for him, this irreducible minimum.

" My expectation is still that I shall go. My unqualified wish and unalterable opinion, were I alone in the world, would be that way. There is nothing in domestic politicks to tempt me, and as to foreign politicks what is there remaining but the husk without the kernel ? Ten years have taken away all that was desirable, and ten such years have taken away almost the desire itself.

" For the sake of others, however, I will, in a certain case [the whole heritage] submit to the sacrifice (for it is one), and it is a great happiness to know that except in that case the sacrifice would not be acceptable or allowed.

" How can people write upon such paper as this ? It is walking in a ploughed field—and further, here is the company assembled for dinner,—so Good-bye.

" Ever affectionately yours,

" G. C." [1]

Other letters of the period exist, but they are less intimate in character and were written after his acceptance of office. Here we seem to have the man's authentic thought. It seems probable that he really wished to go, though his wife and daughter wished him to stay. If he stayed at home he would have but a modest income, would be hampered and vexed by the dislike of the King, and by the jealousy and suspicion of most of his colleagues. In India he would acquire a princely fortune for himself to repair that of his wife's, which he had almost spent.[2] He would govern millions with a power that he well knew would be almost uncontrolled, surrounded by the glamour and mystery of the East.

A week more passed and still there was no sign. On the

---

[1] Square brackets not in original. *Gr. MSS.* Canning to Granville, Aug. 25/22. The Gladstone is Sir John Gladstone, the father of the great Gladstone, who took both his Christian names from ' my friend Ewart.'

[2] I am informed by Lord Lascelles that he possesses letters which indicate this conclusion.

30th August he delivered his farewell speech to his constituents at Liverpool, loftily declaring that he had made no change in his arrangements but would consider any offer that the government made him, if they did make it, upon its merits. After this the ministers knew that he would only return with ‘ the whole heritage ’ of Castlereagh. The ministers were divided, but after nearly five weeks’ delay Wellington decided that the offer was necessary, won over the Cabinet, and, with more difficulty, the sullen King. On the 9th September Canning received a letter from Lord Liverpool, on the 11th he was offered ‘ the whole heritage.’ On the 15th he accepted it. On the 16th September he wrote to a friend at 6.15 p.m. from the Foreign Office : “ I cannot refrain from letting you see by the evidence of a *date* that the proposal *was* that which, as you know, I could alone have accepted ; that I *have* accepted it ; and that in consequence *here* I am.” [1]

The very reason that had caused the offer made Canning’s position one of difficulty. He was not asked to join because he was wanted by most of his colleagues, but because his talents were considered indispensable to save them from Parliamentary shipwreck. It was a bargain of interest on either side, and such bargains do not usually produce bonds of affection. Distressing incidents at once occurred. Castlereagh’s widow actually protested to Wellington against Canning’s appointment ; his half-brother resigned his post at Vienna and told Wellington that in a few years Canning ‘ would force himself to the head of His Majesty’s Councils ’ ; [2] Lord Clanwilliam threw up his Under-Secretaryship at the Foreign Office, and Canning had to offer it to three persons, before a fourth would accept it.

Finally he selected Lord Francis Conyngham ; ‘ Canningham,’ as some wits called him. For a moment this was a good stroke, as his mother, the Marchioness of Conyngham, was the King’s avowed mistress. George was delighted ; in January he sent Canning his portrait, and was seen walking at Brighton, by the end of the month, with his arm round the minister’s neck.[3]

[1] *Gr. MSS.* I think this shows that he was not actually at work in the Foreign Office till the 16th. *Vide* p. 53.
[2] Londonderry’s own admission, May 2/27. *Hans. Deb.*, N.S., xvii. 485–6.
[3] *Creevey Papers*, ii. 59.

But the affection of George was as fleeting as it was embarrassing, and did Canning little good with his colleagues.

Canning's opponents in the Cabinet included six peers, Eldon, Wellington, Bathurst, Westmoreland, Sidmouth (Addington), and Maryborough. Not only were they the friends of Castlereagh, but they were ultra-Tories in principle. Of the others, three—Liverpool, the Prime Minister, Lord Melville, and Robinson—were his friends and more liberal in policy; while four—Peel, Harrowby, Vansittart, and Wynn—were the doubtful factors. Canning was disliked by some of his colleagues for other reasons than for his political views. Sidmouth (the quondam ' Doctor ') was a very Saint Sebastian, stuck full of the arrows of his wit. Canning's tongue and pen alike had dropped vitriol on ' Brother Bragge ' (a relative both of Bathurst and of Sidmouth, who were both in the Cabinet) and on ' pound-foolish ' Vansittart, whose attempts to regulate the exchange he had likened to those of the Inquisition to make the sun move round the earth. Other jests had circulated in private. Wynn had a particularly shrill voice, and when he stood for Speaker Canning said he would address him, if elected, as ' Mr Squeaker.' Wynn's relative, the Duke of Buckingham, had been ridiculed as the Ph(at) D(uke) ; Westmoreland, Privy Seal, with a weakness for secret sources of inspiration, was called ' le sot (sceau) privé.' There were other difficulties too. Though Canning was of good birth on one side, he felt himself a new man or, as others said, ' a plebeian.' In after years Grey opposed him because, he said, " He regarded the son of an actress as being *de facto* incapacitated from being premier of England." To such manifestations of aristocratic prejudice he had already returned a public and haughty reply. He would never admit, he said, that any great aristocratic confederacy had the power of distributing the favours of the Crown. ' I will look,' he quoted from Burke, ' these proud combinations in the face.' On his election at Liverpool on the 12th June 1826 he replied to the Whig accusation that he was ' an adventurer ': " To this charge, as I understand it, I am willing to plead guilty. A representative of the people, I am one of the people ; and I present myself to those who choose me only with the claims of character (be they what they may)

unaccredited by patrician patronage or party recommendation.
. . . I would not exchange that situation, to whatever taunts
it may expose me, for all the advantages which might be
derived from an ancestry of a hundred generations." It was
on this connection with the people, first as member for Liverpool, then as one who made speeches outside Parliament,
that his safety, his fame, and his power must depend. It was
not by explanation to his colleagues but to Parliament and to
the public that he must win his way. He had everything to
gain by being straightforward and making his private actions
square with his public ones. That might be the way to overawe his opponents in the Cabinet; it was not the way to
conciliate them.

There were other reasons for suspicion besides his desire
for popularity. Canning had been brought up in a Whig
family as the friend of Fox and Sheridan. As a schoolboy
at Eton he had denounced Pitt; it was even said that he had
been ' a great Jacobin.' Then he abandoned the Whigs for
Pitt, and produced that immortal satire, *The Anti-Jacobin.*
A hail of sarcasms had followed him, which he had returned
with interest. Even in 1822 these bitter memories still lived.
Lansdowne remembered the gibe that he was ' the Roscius
of the State, new-breathed and harnessed for debate '; Erskine
that he was ' Chancellor Ego '; Lamb and Southey recalled
untrue attacks on their private characters. Grey had long
been his enemy; Brougham and Creevey had both been routed
by him at the elections at Liverpool. Lambton (Lord Durham)
had been compared to a ' dolt ' or an ' idiot '; Burdett and
Cobbett had been mercilessly satirised. Mr Creevey had been
crushed beneath mountains of ridicule when he brought
forward a motion on the Board of Control, and bore an undying
hatred to Canning ever afterwards. ' His lash,' said Wilberforce, ' would have fetched the hide off a rhinoceros.' Erskine
said that Castlereagh never made a speech without making a
friend, or Canning one without making an enemy. And
ridicule is in Parliament a dangerous and two-edged weapon.
His sallies made even men of wit and humour lose their judgments, as well as their tempers. Brougham said that, even
when he was discussing measures for ameliorating the Poor Law
or for transportation of convicts, Canning turned everything

into ridicule ; Cobbett said he made ' a jest of the groans ' of the poor ; Lamb called him ' the zany of debate.' ' When he is jocular,' wrote Sydney Smith, ' he is strong ; when he is serious he is like Samson in a wig ! ' Byron said, ' though bred a statesman, he was born a wit.' In those days many thought the functions incompatible. Was he serious at all ? He had abandoned Fox, but, curiously enough, he had not abandoned liberal ideas. Was he a Whig or a Tory ? It was hard to say, for he seemed to fit into no party category, indeed into no known category. Was he not merely a trifler or an adventurer, playing with ideas or policies for pleasure or for interest ? There were many who openly attacked his character, as the intriguer, the new man, the tactician. Ward (afterwards to be one of his greatest admirers) had said that Castlereagh and Canning showed the difference between character and talents. Lord John Russell suggested that Canning had ' to bury himself in India ' in order to redeem his character ; or, as Mr Creevey gaily put it, his fate was ' banishment to India for want of honesty.' On his taking office, the *Times* called him ' a hired advocate,' and Leigh Hunt said ' he had neither faith nor principles.' Even his cousin, Stratford Canning, only contended that he was ' in the main an honest man.'

It was unfortunate that a man, suspected of incurable levity, and worse, should succeed one dowered with portentous gravity. Castlereagh had led the Commons though almost the worst speaker in it ; Canning was now to lead them though indisputably the best. Castlereagh, though an Irishman, had typical British qualities. As powerful and as unassuming as Marlborough, obviously an aristocrat and a gentleman, mild and calm, he was the ideal of the ponderous fox-hunters of the Back-benchers, of the stately peers, and of the timid citizens who feared revolution. He never joked with intention, and his very failures as a speaker awakened in them a sympathetic chord. His alienation from the despots of the Continent was not wholly understood ; most Tories thought that, in such matters, one must go slow, and anyhow that one could trust Lord Castlereagh. By the Whigs and by the mass of the people he was certainly detested, but such detestation was the measure of his greatness to many of the Tories. The peculiarly middle position held by Canning suggested to Tories that he would abandon, and to Whigs that he would maintain, the principles of his predecessor. For he was so unlike him— he was egoistic where Castlereagh was modest, volatile where he was solid, communicative where he was restrained, irritable where he was calm, dominating where he was persuasive.

Enough has been said to show the baffling character of the new leader. Contemporaries admitted great qualities in Castlereagh, but denied him genius. Few denied it to Canning, most indeed thought it the chief source of his defects. ' Now we have got rid of these confounded men of genius ' chuckled one old Tory lord on Canning's fall in 1809. To John Bull genius is always strange and often alarming. The fear and hatred which pursued Disraeli pursued his equally mysterious forerunner. Yet the real Canning differed as much from the legendary Canning, as he differed from his predecessor.

Castlereagh had many personal friends and moved in the highest society, charming all with his bland and gentle manners. But in the last resort Castlereagh was not an open, perhaps not a warm-hearted, man ; he was repressed, reserved, and impenetrable. Canning, with even more affectionate friends, had once been ' a diner-out of the highest lustre,' a man whose social brilliance equalled that of George Selwyn or Tickell. But he had long ago forsaken high society. His absence from fashionable levées was noticed at once both by diplomats and by society, who contrasted him with the sociable Castlereagh. To those whom he met he was frank, open, and communicative, but he did not meet many. But the attitude was characteristic of the man. It was not merely that he was almost an invalid with the gout, and that he preferred his own circle and his own hearth to state dinners and to society dances. He did not think he would learn what England thought from the King, from great lords, from great ladies, from great diplomats, or from great dinners. When he wanted to learn that he dropped into the lobby of the Commons to hear the chatter of Back-benchers, he received deputations from merchants, he read the papers, he ' talked with men who walked the streets,' or took the even bolder step of making public speeches outside Parliament.

2. CANNING AS THE PHILOSOPHIC TORY

Canning had a political creed of his own, and one which has strangely perplexed many students of it. But as it is the key to his foreign policy it must be examined. At first sight it is a bundle of inconsistencies. He resisted the Repeal of the Test Acts for Dissenters in England, he championed Catholic Emancipation for Ireland. He opposed Parliamentary Reform and supported the suspension of Habeas Corpus; he advocated Freedom of Trade and the eventual Abolition of Slavery. " His Whiggism is for Peers and his Toryism for peasants," wrote Lytton; " with the same zeal he advocates the Catholic question and the Manchester Massacre." If we can explain these paradoxes we shall have no difficulty in understanding why the Anti-Jacobin and the enemy of Napoleon was to destroy the Neo-Holy Alliance in Europe, and to recognise republics in South America. In truth the creed was, in many respects, not very different from that of Castlereagh, whom none ever charged with lack of sincerity. Castlereagh opposed Parliamentary Reform, but he also wanted the repeal of the Navigation Acts, Catholic Emancipation, and, towards the end of his life, a relaxation of the duties on corn. In 1822 the two men showed some difference of opinion in two friendly little contests. Canning introduced a Bill for giving full privileges to Roman Catholic Peers; Castlereagh, though in favour of the general principle, opposed the particular measure as premature. Castlereagh was defeated and Canning carried his Bill by a majority of twelve. On the Corn Importation Bill Canning proposed an amendment, which Castlereagh opposed. Canning divided the House, only to find himself in a great minority. Such differences were not great, but they are enough to show a shade of distinction between the ideas of the two men.

' Burke,' wrote Canning in 1823, is ' still the manual of my politics,' and Burke's influence enables us to understand them. That great man had taught Canning that history was the key to politics, that society was a vital organism, a compact between the dead and the living. It was the greatest institution for promoting human liberty that had ever existed, a ' living mystic tree ' rooted in the past and stretching arms towards the future. You might lop, or prune, or graft, but you must never assail the trunk. Canning hoped never to see the day when England became a " democracy inlaid (for ornament's sake) with an aristocracy and topped (for suffer-ance) with a crown." The King, the Lords, the Commons, and the masses each had their powers and their rights but also their limits. None should be too powerful or too supreme. The Crown, and not the Commons, should have the right of patronage ; the Peers should have the right of rejecting Bills ; the Commons should have the right of resisting popular pressure if that seemed necessary or desirable. A Member of Parliament must resist his constituents if his conscience so dictated. While he sat for Liverpool, Canning sometimes voted in Parliament in accordance with the expressed wish of his constituents. Sometimes he laid their petitions on the table and said that he did not agree with them.[1] Similarly he thought Parliament ought sometimes to lead, and some-times to oppose, popular opinion. Check and balance, ad-justment and compromise, were the essence of the British Constitution.

It is strange that a mind so keen-sighted as that of Canning should have held to so rigid a doctrine as regards fundamentals, a doctrine that must ultimately have turned the Constitution into a museum and Englishmen into Chinamen. For he sustained the paradox that the England of 1820, which was predominantly industrial, should be content with the electoral system of 1688, which was based on ' the divine right of the [agricultural] freeholders.' The system had even then been full of anomaly and evil ; it was now fuller of both by the accretions of a long century of parliamentary corruption. But Canning had started public life in the midst of the French Revolution, which had set out by destroying all privileges and precedents in the name of a perfect and simple system. In his eyes ' all simple governments are bad,' whether simple monarchy, simple aristocracy, or simple democracy. For such things were ' struck out at a heat,' and offered no barrier, no resistance to sudden change, no homage to time nor to

---

[1] *E.g. Hans. Deb.*, xl. 909–10. Canning presented a petition from Liverpool *against* the Foreign Enlistment Bill, and spoke and voted *for* it (June 3/19). This is in the true tradition of Burke.

history. He had seen a French king lose his throne ' by too obsequious subservience to temporary popularity '; he had seen an English one retain his by resisting parliamentary reform, by gagging the Press, and by imprisoning the agitators. As he saw it, the great danger in 1822, as in 1792, was from irresponsible agitators driving on a blind majority to abolish old institutions, in obedience to reckless passions and in deference to abstract principles.

A people, said Canning, was no longer a people when they became a mob ; a people was no longer free when it could no longer be restrained. Even the very word ' people ' did not mean to him what it means to most of us to-day. What was the meaning of the word ' people ' ? he asked on 22nd December 1819. " The people as synonymous to (sic) a nation, meant a great community, congregated under a head, united in the same system of civil polity for mutual aid and mutual protection, respecting and maintaining various orders and ranks, and not only allowing the fair and just gradations of society, but absolutely built upon them. That was a ' people.' But in a mass of persons, first stript of the government, then stript of the aristocracy, then stript of the clergy, then stript of the magistracy, then stript of its landed proprietors, then stript of its lawyers, then stript of its learning, then stript of everything which ornamented and dignified human nature— in such a mass he could no more recognise the people than he could recognise in the tub [1] [bird ?] of Diogenes the man of Plato. A mere populace, deprived of everything essential to what by common consent was called a nation, could not, without the grossest perversion of terms, be called a nation. But when the term ' people ' was applied to a portion of the community arrayed against the interests of the nation ; not only distinct from, but hostile to the nation ; when the term was applied to such as these, it tended directly to encourage insurrection and rebellion." [2]

Thus he held the doctrine that a nation really had a ' general will ' not always represented in the majority but always represented in institutions, interests, and classes.

---

[1] This is in Hansard, but it is obvious that ' bird ' is meant, for that was the whimsical term by which Diogenes described man.

[2] Dec. 22/19. *Hans. Deb.*, xli. 1500.

Under the constitution the King, the Peers, the Commons, and the masses were blended into one harmonious whole. Parliamentary reform, as he held, would adulterate the blend and upset the balance. He did not wish Parliament to be corrupt. Where corruption was proved, as at Grampound, he would agree to disfranchisement, but that was the exception which proved the rule. Parliament must remain diverse not uniform in its franchise, with a system based on history and not upon theory. It seemed excellent that Old Sarum should have only three electors, Liverpool as few as four thousand, while Westminster had a franchise that was practically democratic. In such diversity lay safety. Though " he would have been glad to see a larger infusion of the popular spirit in the representative system of Scotland " (which numbered only a few thousand electors for a whole nation), " he would not regret it. . . . He saw nothing in the representative system which required redress ; and even if he could have discovered anything which required amendment, he saw no means of effecting such amendment without introducing into the system far greater evils." [1]

The arguments thus marshalled met with the plain man's retort. " Mr Canning was an eloquent man but even *he* could not say that a rotting tree stump was the *people*." A member might be and was returned by a borough which had been for some centuries under the sea. How were the people represented in this process ? Canning would have answered that such anomalies were actually useful, for they prevented uniformity of representation, and destroyed the possibility of ' simple democracy ' and the will of a ' vague irresponsible multitude.' It was a paradox, indeed, though a highly intellectual paradox. In just the same strain he argued that electors of one district should not listen to the orators of another, but that Middlesex should hear speakers only from London, and that Orator Hunt should not visit Manchester. This argument for the historic and the particular and the local seems overstrained. Yet it is the same argument, enlarged and sublimated, which explains his passionate national patriotism. For it was England in its very historic defects that he thought so perfect.

[1] Apr. 13/26. *Hans. Deb.*, N.S., xv. 182-3.

So far Canning's creed seemed purely Tory. It was conservative, like that of Burke, in the framework; that is, as to
reform of Parliament. It was liberal in the particulars; that
is, in all sorts of legislative reform. "They who resist indiscriminately all improvements as innovations," said he,
"may find themselves compelled at last to submit to innovations although they are not improvements" (24th February
1826). He once said that the two problems most near his
heart were those of Catholic Emancipation and of foreign
policy, and during the coming years he threatened to resign
over both. He regarded them from the standpoint of a
robust and vigorous nationalist, and desired a liberal policy
in both. The Protestant ascendancy had imposed upon
Ireland "an accursed system, an accumulated mass of cold
and chilling enactments which had congealed and benumbed
a nation" (29th January 1817). Here was the point; it was
a system to which the majority of a nation were opposed. It
had been devised for purposes now obsolete and unhistoric.
Above all, it tended to make Catholics look beyond England
and Ireland for aid from a foreign Power. True English
policy should look precisely the other way. He would say:
"Efface the line of separation which divides the inhabitants
of the British islands into two classes, and strengthen the
line of demarcation which separates British from foreign
influence."[1] Hence he argued for Catholic Emancipation in
the interests of British patriotism—as the completion of
"the circle of gold which was to bind together the whole
community."

But, while a strong advocate of religious freedom in the
interests of nationality, he was a limited champion of it in
other respects. He wanted the Church of England to retain
control of education. He did not want to repeal the Test
Acts in favour of Dissenters in England, for they were not
in the majority and must not therefore be placed on an
equality with Churchmen. "The business of the British
Constitution is to redress practical grievances, not to run after
theoretical perfection." As the Annual Indemnity Acts
removed such grievances he saw no reason to repeal the
Test Acts. A similar combination of apparently inconsistent

[1] Feb. 28/25. *Hans. Deb.*, N.S., xii. 794.

views explains his policy in regard to the Press and public opinion in India while President of the Board of Control. On the 20th June 1822 he opposed the forcible abolition of the *suttee*, the practice of burning Hindu widows, for that was a custom deeply rooted in the religious and racial life of Hinduism. Our ties to India were so slender that such forcible reforms might snap them. And India was " a state of society which had no resemblance in the whole world." He declined to curtail the freedom of the Indian Press at the request of the East India Company,[1] though at this very same moment he was supporting Castlereagh in a curtailment of the freedom of the Press in England (1819–20). He was perfectly consistent, for he held that the Indian Press was not then exciting people to seditious acts, and that the British Press was. There was ' inflammability ' in England, there was none in India. This incident is a good example of how he acted in a liberal, or in a reactionary, sense according as circumstances altered cases. It is doubtful if any of his colleagues would have acted in the same way, or have understood the reasons of his action.

With his preference for the ' middle way ' Canning naturally regarded the middle class, ' which interposes between the two extremes ' of democracy and aristocracy, as the most stable element of the country. They were the " most valuable part of the population, in which the staple interest, as well as the staple good sense, of the community reside " (15th March 1820). But, for the very reason that his principles forbade him to give them more parliamentary representation, he was impelled to promote their interests in every other kind of remedial legislation. One such object was administrative reform in all directions, though his loyalty to his colleagues sometimes compelled him to defend such things as state lotteries or large pensions to Royal Dukes.[2] But where his own department was concerned, as at the Board of Control or the Foreign Office, he was an ardent promoter of economy, and his influence inspired and supported Robinson and Huskisson in their revision of expenditure in other depart-

---

[1] *Vide* his explanation, May 25/24. *Hans. Deb.*, N.S., xi. 879–80.
[2] He was, however, in favour of supporting the splendour of the Monarchy and (May 2/20) opposed any diminution of the Civil List.

ments. He had had an unusual and varied official experience. Besides having been Foreign Secretary he had been Ambassador in Portugal, Treasurer of the Navy, President of the Board of Control. Both as an official and as member for Liverpool, he had thus learnt at first-hand the needs of a business community, and been familiarised with commercial and naval problems. The interests of the Indian Empire— ' that great, anomalous, and astonishing part of our Empire ' —were more familiar to him than to any contemporary statesman. He realised fully the basis of our imperial power. " The sea, which separates all nations from one another, unites them to Great Britain." He recognised Singapore as " the *unum necessarium* for making the British Empire in India complete," by securing the strategic command of the Straits of Malacca and the control of the spice trade. He refused to give up the north-west coast of British Columbia because that would surrender the future prospect of trade with China, a fact that the great Dominion perhaps does not recognise to-day. Castlereagh had recognised the commercial flags of the South American States in 1822, and Canning the Greeks as belligerents in 1823, and they thus safeguarded their country's commerce long before other nations recognised the same necessity. His promotion of the Repeal of the Navigation Acts was intended to increase the trade between England, Europe, and America, and to develop commerce along its natural channels in accordance with the ideas propounded by Adam Smith and practised by Pitt. The interests of the Colonies were not forgotten, for while the Navigation Laws were relaxed, the coasting trade was reserved to British (including colonial) ships, and large differential duties secured to the Colonies what was, in effect, an imperial preference on corn and other articles of their produce. As regards more purely English interests the mercantile community was equally favoured. Under the direction of his friend Huskisson the obsolete tariff was revised, and, most important of all, the Silk Duties repealed. Finally the Corn Duty was to be greatly reduced in the interests of the masses. " We are on the brink," said he in his last days, " of a great struggle between property and population; . . . such a struggle is only to be averted by the mildest and most liberal legislation.

Mark my words, that struggle will some day come, when probably I may be removed from the scene." Twenty years later, Peel, his old colleague in the Cabinet, averted that struggle by conceding Free Trade.

These ideas, set forth with glitter of rhetoric and brilliance of illustration, were dazzling enough for a time. But they could not conceal the fact that Canning and Huskisson, with their remedial measures for the middle class, were but fortunate accidents. They were neither of them products of the oligarchic regime. The middle class were not a real part of the existing system of government, and relied purely on such far-sighted men to help them to their ends. They were not permanently going to be content with a system which placed Liverpool and Manchester on an inferiority to Old Sarum, nor were Nonconformists going to endure for ever that theoretical injustice for which practical freedom in no way atones. Nor was the policy of the 'Six Acts,' with all its limitations on personal freedom, going to be made agreeable to the masses by measures facilitating the import of corn. The fact is that the political theory of Canning resembled the body of that prince in the 'Arabian Nights,' on whom a magician had worked his will. The upper part of his body was living human flesh; the lower half had been turned to stone. One side of the theory was static and impenetrable to new ideas, the other was an expanding, elastic, and vital force. In Canning's internal policy lurked the germs of decay and death; in his foreign policy there was life and promise for the future.

3. CANNING'S IDEAS ON FOREIGN POLICY

All Canning's ideas, whether for home or for foreign policy, sprang from his intense belief in the virtues of a vigorous nationality, based not on theory but on history. He started from the standpoint of his own country. For England was the " model of rational liberty, the protectress of national independence, powerful in foreign exertions beyond the natural proportions of her physical force—whose ' pigmy body,' animated and o'er-informed by the spirit of her free constitution, was strong enough to deliver Europe from the grasp of the oppressor."[1] That oppressor had been Napoleon. There were two new oppressors now—the spirit of Revolution or ' simple democracy,' and the spirit of ' simple Despotism.' Canning was equally opposed to both. Nations could not, he thought, be governed by universal rules, whether imposed by despots at Aix-la-Chapelle, by Jacobins at Paris, or by Carbonari in Italy. England was in ' the temperate zone of freedom,' not in the Arctic zone of despotism or the torrid zone of democracy. Her liberty, ordered and graduated and balanced, could serve as a model to despots and to democrats, and restrain the excesses of unbridled freedom and of unbridled power. In this sense English policy could contribute to the happiness of other nations, for a free England meant the possibility of a free world on either side of the Atlantic.

Canning had thus expressed his views in public in 1817. He began to fight in the Cabinet for the ' English ' policy as against the ' European ' one of Castlereagh as early as the time of the Congress of Aix-la-Chapelle. His views are described in a letter written by Lord Bathurst to Castlereagh on the 20th October 1818, and based on the assumption that Castlereagh had been inclined to approve ' the decision ' by the Four Allies " of meeting at fixed periods, . . . to be announced in a circular letter to the other [smaller] Powers, with such declarations as may satisfy them." Bathurst intimated that the Cabinet, while not objecting to the system, did object ' to the expediency of declaring it in a circular letter.' They thought, too, that the subject for which any reunion was summoned ought to be specific (as *e.g.* France) and not general. Any arrangement as to a meeting for general purposes might produce ' much inconvenient discussion in Parliament.' He went on to say that one member of the Cabinet went further than this.

" The objections which Canning feels on this subject are not confined to the inexpediency of announcing a decision at fixed periods, but to the system itself. He does not consider the Ninth Article[2] as having been generally understood to

---

[1] Jan. 29/17. *Hans. Deb.*, xxxv. 131.
[2] This seems to be an error. The Sixth Article of the Second Treaty of Paris seems to be referred to. It runs as follows:—" To facilitate and to secure the execution of the present Treaty, and to consolidate the connections which at the present moment so closely unite the Four

apply to any meetings, except for the purpose of watching
the internal state of France, as far as it may endanger the
public tranquillity. He thinks that system of periodical
meetings of the four great Powers, with a view to the general
concerns of Europe, new, and of very questionable policy ;
that it will necessarily involve us deeply in all the politics
of the Continent, whereas our true policy has always been
not to interfere except in great emergencies, and then with a
commanding force. He thinks that all other [*i.e.* smaller]
States must protest against such an attempt to place them
under subjection ; that the meetings may become a scene of
cabal and intrigue ; and that the people of this country may
be taught to look with great jealousy for their liberties, if our
Court is engaged . . . with great despotic monarchs, deliberating
upon what degree of revolutionary spirit may endanger the
public security, and therefore require the interference of the
Alliance. This last, however, he only stated as a popular
argument.

" I do not subscribe to Canning's arguments, nor did any
of the Cabinet who attended.[1] But, if this is felt by him, it
is not unreasonable that it may be felt by many other persons,
as well as by our decided opponents. . . . Why take the bull
by the horns ? . . . All that you need do now is to fix the
next meeting ; and you will observe that even Canning does
not make any objection to such a decision." [2]

It does not appear that Castlereagh had gone as far as the
Cabinet feared. His management of the Allies was skilful,
but, as he complained, he could not hope for ' a pure vocabulary '
when Russia was using the language of exaltation. He did not
think Canning was right in wishing to exclude public mention
of the 'Holy Alliance' when the Prince Regent had sent a letter

Sovereigns for the happiness of the world, the High Contracting Parties
have agreed to renew their meetings at fixed periods, either under the
immediate auspices of the Sovereigns themselves, or by their respective
Ministers, for the purpose of consulting upon their common needs, interests,
and for the consideration of the measures which at each of those periods
shall be considered most salutary for the repose and prosperity of Nations,
and for the maintenance of the Peace of Europe." Hertslet, *Map of
Europe by Treaty* (1875), i. 375.

[1] They were—Liverpool, Vansittart, Sidmouth, Melville, Canning, and
Bathurst.

[2] Correspondence, ed. C. W. Vane—*Despatches and other Papers of
Viscount Castlereagh, Marquess of Londonderry* (London, 1853), 3rd ser.,
iv. (xii.) 56–7. Bathurst to Castlereagh, Oct. 20/18.

to Alexander approving of it, and he did not therefore entirely
adopt his suggestions.

Canning's view was not, indeed, entirely accurate as a
comment on the text of the Treaty, but it is of priceless value
as a key to his policy in the future. All the characteristic
views he expressed later are here ; the strict limitation of the
Quadruple Alliance to the duty of watching over France ;
the scorn of the 'Holy Alliance'; the fear that the Quadruple
Alliance would extend its functions so as to intimidate small
States, and would cause ministries to be suspected by the
British people of betraying British liberties at the behest of
foreign despots ; the belief that England must only occasionally
interfere on the Continent, but ' then with a commanding
force.'

Castlereagh and the other members of the Cabinet moved
definitely in the direction of a more ' English ' policy as the
Neo-Holy Alliance developed in 1820. The famous state
paper of the 5th May 1820, in which Castlereagh at last told
the Neo-Holies what he thought of them, was indeed his own.
But Canning had anticipated his fears and now supported his
expression of them. Stratford Canning notes the following
in his Diary—on the 28th May 1820, about a week after this
state paper was finished : " I congratulated him [George
Canning] on the line which I knew had been taken [by England]
with the Allied Courts on the subject of the late revolutionary
events in Spain, and as I *had reason to believe from a former
conversation with him in obedience to his suggestions.* ' Yes,' he
said, ' we shall have no more congresses, thank God ! They
were all very well for such matters as the disputes between
Baden and Bavaria, but he had always been convinced that
they would prove useless for the settlement of any such dis-
location as that of Spain. The Emperor of Russia still had a
fancy for them, and was wanting the Allied Powers to agree
beforehand upon some plan of action in case of the King of
France's death, or some new explosion in the country.' " [1]

Canning can have had little further direct influence on
foreign policy, for he left the country in August 1820 and

---

[1] S. L. Poole, *Life of Stratford Canning,* [1888], i. 291. Italics my own.
Castlereagh declined Alexander's proposals *re* the King of France's death
with some indignation.

resigned from the Cabinet in December. Castlereagh wrote him a graceful letter saying they agreed on all questions of foreign policy, an opinion which Canning endorsed.

That Canning was quite satisfied with the state paper of 5th May 1820, and with its publication in a slightly different form early in 1821, is certain. But the violent popular resentment provoked in England by the despotic principles proclaimed at the Congresses of Troppau and Laibach, and by the Austrian armed attack on the Constitution of Naples, led him to a most important utterance indicating his views. This was made on the 20th March 1821.[1] Being out of office, he spoke with a freedom which no minister could imitate. But he declared that the right policy of England towards both Naples and the Neo-Holies was ' neutrality in word and deed.' No man in the Commons " was disposed to view with less distrust an extension of the principles of freedom and good government throughout the Continent of Europe than he was." . . . " He saw the principles of liberty were in operation, and he should be one of the last individuals who would attempt to restrain them " . . . Unless, however, England was really prepared to support the Constitution of Naples against the Neo-Holies by force, ' all mention of support was a fraud.' It was absurd to go to war because " we were so angry with the foolish and pedantic state papers of the [Neo-Holy] Allies. . . ." The principles that the democrats of the world wanted enforced were not those of the British Constitution, and, in any case, " the idea of establishing it [the British Constitution] in other countries by the force of the sword was too chimerical to be entertained.

" Whatever might be the result of the present portentous struggle, it was not in our power to lead the parties to the point we wished, either by persuasion, remonstrance, or force . . . let us not, in the foolish spirit of romance, suppose that we alone could regenerate Europe. Let us not forget that we were rather likely to mar the experiment by our interference ; let us recollect that the interference of strangers was always sure to become, either sooner or later, an object of jealousy. Show him the duty that called for the interference of Great Britain, and then, how great soever the sacrifice, he

---

[1] *Hans Deb.*, N.S., iv. 1365–76, of Mar. 20/21.

should say that duty must be performed : but obligation in this case he saw none.   Here the spirit of monarchy [despotism] was at war to crush every principle of freedom, said the one party ; and there, said the other, the spirit of democracy was labouring to destroy all monarchies.   We ourselves had in our Constitution enough of democracy to temper monarchy, and enough of monarchy to restrain the caprices of democracy. Where was, then, the necessity for our incurring those risks, which other countries, not possessed of a tempered Constitution like our own, might laudably encounter ? "

One reason, and that the strongest, why England did not interfere in Naples was because Castlereagh had, in 1815, secretly approved the Austrian Treaty with Naples.   This Treaty bound the King of Naples not to accept a constitution without Austria's consent.   This obligation Canning did not, and, as an ex-minister, could not, disclose.[1]   But it may be doubted whether he would have thought the protection of Naples worth a war in any case.   Here neither the honour nor interest of England was sufficiently concerned.

The real importance of this speech, however, is that he now publicly stated, and in the clearest form, the true basis of his principles, viz., the isolation of England, her interference only at a great moment and with a force sufficient to support it, her general policy of a rigid non-intervention in the internal affairs of other nations, her disapproval either of despotic or of democratic excesses.

After this speech Canning said little as to foreign policy, and we can only guess at his thoughts.   In June 1821 Liverpool, who had the best means of knowing, reported him as still at one with the Cabinet as regards internal and external policy. But towards the end of 1821 he seems to have feared that the ' English ' policy of 5th May 1820 was not being pursued. It seems probable that he disliked the *rapprochement* between Castlereagh and Metternich at Hanover in November 1821. For there is some evidence at least that his views on the Greek question differed from those of Castlereagh, and that he thought

---

[1] Two years later, referring to this speech, Canning told Esterházy that he had avoided condemning the Austrian interference in Naples.   He did not mean to say that interference was never, but that it was not always, justifiable.   *V.S.A.*, Berichte aus England, Bd. 220.   Esterházy to Metternich, July 27/23.

that a further congress would not solve the difficulty.[1] For he thought that the British public would only cast further obloquy on British Ministers for attending secret conclaves with foreign despots. But his differences with the Castlereagh policy were rather of shade and of emphasis than in fundamentals, and of method and exception rather than of principle. Castlereagh desired just as much as he to extend British influence and to check foreign aggression, but Castlereagh was bound by his past and by his friendships, while Canning was not. Castlereagh despised popularity, Canning did not think it wise to do so. Therein lies the true difference between the two men.

In Canning's view it was essential that future foreign policy should be both intelligible and popular. Herein it was that he differed from Castlereagh, from Wellington, from Metternich, from Alexander, and from all those men whose iron resolution had overthrown Napoleon. Those men did not see that what is successful in war is not always successful in peace time. For in war one must be ruthless and firm, not popular or diplomatic. Canning knew that such methods were out of date in a period of peace. England's foreign policy could not be successful unless it was generally supported by the nation. " They had now [31st May 1827] all the advantages of a free press, and he valued a free press as highly as any man," and he took care not to forget its influence. His methods and machinery were alike new, and amounted to revolution.

But it must not be thought that this revolution was effected with ease. As will have been seen, there was much in his policy that was too intellectual and too refined for the people, or even for Parliament or for his colleagues, to understand. Like Gladstone, he combined the gift of popular appeal with ' the microscopic subtlety of a thirteenth-century schoolman,'

---

[1] Planta, the permanent Under-Secretary, expressed views on Greece strikingly different from those of Castlereagh in 1821, and he was then in very close touch with Canning, v. an article by Mr C. N. Crawley in *Cambridge Historical Journal*, No. 2, pp. 209–13. It is perhaps legitimate to infer that Canning objected to the summoning of the Congress of Verona, which Castlereagh certainly did not. Stap., *P.L.*, ii. 36, says he objected strongly to the Congresses of Troppau and Laibach, and adds: " Had he been in office three months before the meeting at Verona no English Minister would probably have assisted at it." Stapleton is not always accurate, but I am inclined to think that there is something in this.

and it was the latter quality which was conspicuous in 1822. Like Gladstone, too, and not altogether undeservedly, he had a reputation for impulsiveness and recklessness. With the King and most of his colleagues against him, with a sullen diplomatic staff, with a doubtful parliamentary following, and a suspicious parliamentary opposition, he might well hesitate to take office. One quality, however, he had. In after days, Gladstone, who thought him ' too clever ' for the House of Commons, pronounced that he possessed ' great parliamentary courage.' And it was not in Parliament alone that courage was needed. In Europe and in America revolution raised its menacing head. Monarchy armed its hand for resistance at Vienna, at Berlin, at St Petersburg, at Paris. England, said Canning in 1821, was treading " a plank which lay across a roaring stream. Attempts might be made to bear us down on one side or the other." In 1822 the waters were still rising on every side, and Canning had now to tread the plank alone.

PART II

FRANCE, THE NEO-HOLY ALLIANCE, AND BRITISH NON-INTERVENTION

CHAPTER III
FRANCE AND THE CONGRESS OF VERONA

CHAPTER IV
THE FRENCH INVASION AND THE FALL OF CONSTITUTIONALISM IN SPAIN

CHAPTER III

FRANCE AND THE CONGRESS OF VERONA

1. The Instructions of Castlereagh

A GRAVE diplomatic crisis faced Canning at the very moment at which he assumed office. He seems not to have been aware of it, for on the 23rd August 1822 he said at Liverpool, " I see no near prospect of a call upon this country for any foreign exertion." He apparently imagined that more imminent difficulties and dangers lay at home. But then he had been eighteen months out of office, and to be out of office is not only to be without power, but to be without that knowledge which is more important than power. Further—and apparently by design—the instructions of Wellington had finally been signed and given to him by Bathurst (the Acting Foreign Secretary) on the 14th September. Thus Canning had neither part nor lot in the drafting of the instructions nor in the appointment of Wellington as plenipotentiary to Verona.[1]

Castlereagh's instructions are of interest as forming his political testament. He ranked the questions to be discussed in order of their significance as follows : First, the Turkish question ; next, that of Spanish America and of European Spain ; last, the affairs of Italy.[2]

As regards Turkey, he expected Russia to be dissatisfied with Turkish proposals of settlement and considered that

---

[1] Canning said afterwards that he had been little over forty-eight hours in office when Wellington left for Verona. The Duke left on the 17th, and the official communication of Canning's taking office was issued to diplomats under date of the 16th. He was not in the Foreign Office on the 14th and probably not on the 15th. *Vide* p. 30. At any rate, the 16th is the first day on which he signed documents.

[2] *W.N.D.*, i. 284–8. (I omit the slight reference he made to three more purely British questions : (*a*) The Slave Trade (see Webster, p. 466); (*b*) The Austrian debt (see Webster, pp. 401-2); (*c*) The Russian Ukase on North-West America, *v. infra*.)

' the progress made by the Greeks towards the formation of a government ' might possibly necessitate their recognition by England as belligerents. If this became necessary, however, it was to be done " with caution and without ostentation, lest it should render the Turks wholly inaccessible to our remonstrances." English mediation between Turks and Greeks was not to go " beyond the limits of good offices. Engagements in the nature of a guarantee are to be considered altogether inadmissible."

Castlereagh went at length into the question of Spanish America. He regarded it ' rather as a matter of time than of principle.' He distinguished between three classes of colonies, according as they were then struggling, or negotiating, with Spain, or had ended the struggle by expelling the Spaniards. In the third case he plainly regarded recognition as probably near. The case of American Spain he regarded as ' of a more serious nature than that of European Spain.' The basis of policy towards the latter comprised " solicitude for the safety of the royal family, observance of our engagements with Portugal, and a rigid abstinence from any interference in the internal affairs of that country."

The affairs of Italy he regarded as of very secondary importance for England.

It did not take Canning very long to find out that these instructions by no means conformed with the facts as they existed in September.[1] The very seat of the Congress was transferred from Vienna to Verona. In reality, leaving Italy aside, the scale of importance in which Castlereagh graded the three main topics proved exactly the opposite of the truth. The least important proved to be the Turkish question ; that of Spanish America was not the main one ; far the most important proved to be that of European Spain. Instead of Turkey being the chief subject on the carpet and Russia the chief power to be conciliated, Spain provided the chief topic of discussion and France proved the power most difficult to manage. As it happened, the Congress of Verona turned

---

[1] In justice to Castlereagh it should be pointed out that this Spanish part of the instructions must have been written before he heard of the outbreak in Spain in July. As his instructions were drafted for his own information he probably did not trouble to alter them. For he would thus obtain a freer hand (v. Webster, pp. 476-8).

mainly on the attitude and relations of England and of France. The policy of the latter was determined, or rather swayed, mainly by the strife of parties within France herself, and this fact necessitates a brief sketch of the principles, personalities, and ideas which controlled the restored Bourbon Monarchy.

2. THE FRENCH MINISTRY AND THEIR IDEAS

" *Si les lâchetés de Louis XV., si le partage de la Pologne retombèrent sur la tête de Louis XVI. et l'abattirent, que ne pouvait-on craindre pour Louis XVIII. ou pour Charles X. après l'humiliation des traités de Vienne.*"— CHATEAUBRIAND.

Of the little group of French statesmen who had conducted the policy of the Restoration, the high-minded Richelieu was gone. The King remained, older, goutier, and wittier than ever. One thing, though a Bourbon, he knew indeed by heart the works of Horace. Much else escaped his memory or his energy, though little his natural good sense. Not without dignity, convinced of his right Divine, he yet tempered it with a certain homely shrewdness and insight. And so long as he lived, his cynical good sense imposed some check upon the unfortunate tendencies of the ultra-Royalists.

Of the other Bourbon princes, the Heir—Monsieur (afterwards Charles X.)—was the quondam Comte d'Artois of the exquisite satin breeches, into which he had been lifted by four valets, in order that they might be without wrinkle. He was pronounced by a lady to be ' pale, old, adorable.' Yet he was still vain and weak, and his influence, though great, was neither prudent nor wise. Of the younger generation, his son, the Duc d'Angoulême, was the best and the most promising. He had rectitude, judgment, and good sense. Though awkward in manner and apt to stand too much upon his dignity, he had played an honourable and useful part in striving to avert Royalist excesses in France after 1815, and was again about to win that same distinction in Spain.

The curse of Divine Right fell heavily across the path of the Bourbon princes. Their personal will was exerted in matters which the ministers could not always resist, and which destroyed any theory of the collective responsibility of the Cabinet. Angoulême disgraced the Duc de Belluno, the quondam Marshal Victor, to the dismay of the ministers. Monsieur, his father, disgraced Chateaubriand and subsequently refused to readmit him to the Ministry—one of the worst blunders of his unhappy reign. For a king cannot be constitutional unless he subdues his personal predilections, and, in rejecting Chateaubriand, the Bourbons flung away the strongest prop of the throne. The hand of Monsieur is visible in other dark and dangerous intrigues, in which his crony Polignac played a part, till both vanished together with the White Flag and Divine Right in 1830. Louis XVIII., though the wisest, was also the most indolent of the Bourbons. Sometimes he went to sleep at the Council, at others he told stories to make Chateaubriand laugh. The *communiqués* daily announced that the King was closeted with Villèle, but omitted to add that three-quarters of his conversation was about the latest scandal or the last new novel. His private conversation was not always discreet, and his relations with Madame du Caylas outraged propriety.[1] But Louis sometimes rose to an occasion, as for instance on Christmas Day 1822. Again, in the last days of his life, he appeared at the *levée* with a smiling face and stood unmoved while suffering the most excruciating tortures. When Talleyrand cast the banner of France into his grave, he bade farewell not only to the last Bourbon of the elder line who died on the throne, but also to the last who deserved to do so.

The doctrine of Divine Right led to unauthorised and irregular interference in many matters of importance, sometimes by the King, oftener by Monsieur, or by Angoulême. The Foreign Secretary was never sure that his situation was secure, and the diplomats had to choose between obeying and evading the formal orders that they received, and were often reduced to the latter course by a whisper from a great personage, or by a private letter from the President of the Council. The result was chaos. For it was equally perilous to obey or to disobey your instructions. Diplomats like Hyde de

---

[1] Vincent, with a discreet grin, relates that on one occasion Madame du Caylas sank on her knees before Louis XVIII. and kissed his hands. The King, in endeavouring to raise her, fell on the floor, and his great bulk forced him to remain there. Alarmed by the noise, a lackey rushed into the room and found the King and his mistress rolling on the floor. He decorously assisted them to rise. Even a Bourbon could hardly retain his dignity on such an occasion.

Neuville in Portugal, or de Moustier in Spain, or Polignac in England pursued a personal policy regardless of their official instructions.[1] The more timid French diplomats, like those at St Petersburg or at Vienna, thought that a purely passive attitude was the safest. In no case were such policies to the advantage of France.

During this period, however, a French policy existed and was fitfully pursued. The chief aim was to emancipate France from the humiliating control of foreigners, and to assert her independent action and influence. It took the form at first of holding out to other nations the advantages of adopting the French Constitution of 1814, a constitution *octroyée* by the sovereign and permitting a limited exercise of personal prerogative. In 1820–1 this aim was pursued with regard to Naples and Piedmont, with the idea of withdrawing them from Austrian influence and bringing them within the orbit of French policy. It was also attempted with modifications in Spain in 1823, where it eventually broke down before the opposition of Metternich and Alexander, and in Portugal where Canning administered the *coup de grâce* in 1825. The still more ambitious dream of planting Bourbon princelets in Spanish America was also shattered by Canning.

If France dreamed of independence, she could not love the Neo-Holy Alliance. France, as Chateaubriand said, had painful memories of Conferences and Protocols, which had been the instruments of her humiliation in 1814 and 1815. French suspicions were aroused by the claims of the Neo-Holy Alliance to reform by armed force the internal institutions of Naples or Spain. For such processes might be applied to France. To avoid such a catastrophe, it was essential that France should take the lead in any enterprise in which she was interested. It was impossible to put her in a position in which the Left Wing of her Parliament could say that she was being dragged at the tail of the Alliance, and was obeying the influence of foreign countries.[2] But France could not break with the Neo-Holy Alliance, for she would then be thrown on

---

[1] Cp. *F.O. France*, 146/63. "Whether M. Reinhard (French Minister to German Diet), like Hyde de Neuville, and (as I sometimes suspect) M. de Polignac takes steps without instructions in the subsequent faith of being approved, I do not know." Canning to Sir C. Stuart, Aug. 3/24.

[2] *A.A.E.*, tome 616. Chateaubriand to Marcellus, Jan. 30/24.

her own resources and brought face to face with England, her old and hereditary foe. Hence the scheme was to induce the Neo-Holies to bring their pressure to bear upon England, but, at the same time, to preserve to France the sole initiative in Spain. These seem to have been the basic ideas of French policy, as conceived by Villèle, the most important man in France. But they were not universally held. Montmorency, for example, anxious to support the altar and the throne, had a standpoint in sympathy with the Neo-Holy Alliance; Chateaubriand balanced between these two extremes. And France therefore halted at times between a purely French policy and one of deference to other Powers.

Villèle, who at last attained the height of his ambition as President of the Council in September 1822, was for some half-dozen years to be the most powerful man in France. But for a time his power, though real, was not complete. It depended on many circumstances: on his cajolery of the King through Madame du Caylas, on his influence with Monsieur and Angoulême, on his corruption of ministers and of deputies, and on his control of the Press.[1] Some of these influences made themselves felt but gradually, yet Villèle ultimately prevailed over all obstacles. His position was singular, for he led a fanatical party though he himself loved neither fanaticism nor clericalism nor reaction. Adroit as a parliamentary manager and tactician, he was primarily an administrator and financier, and in both capacities rendered immense services to France. Metternich said he was 'a man of wit, of decided will and courage,' but that he lacked the highest attribute of a statesman—'the critical spirit.'[2] This judgment was true. With excellent sense, he had no great imagination or insight. His knowledge of foreign policy was limited, and his public references to it not always marked by diplomatic *savoir faire*. As to his character, foreigners were less complimentary. Apponyi said he was 'shifty.' Canning was even

---

[1] *F.O. France*, 146/57. Sir C. Stuart to G. Canning, Jan. 22/24, No. 46, states that he corrupted even the Opposition Press. Pozzo said that Royalist journals, and perhaps Madame du Caylas, were in his pay, v. Martens, xv. 32–41. I have not thought it necessary to describe Damas' policy. He was merely the instrument of Villèle from 1824–7.

[2] *V.S.A.*, Weisungen nach Frankreich, Bd. 377. Metternich to Apponyi, Jan. 29/27, and Berichte aus Frankreich, Apponyi to Metternich, Jan. 1/27.

more severe. " I fear—I very much fear—that Villèle himself is radically tricky, and that he would rather come by the same end through a roundabout and intricate path, than through a straightforward one." [1]   Eleven months later Granville confirmed this by saying, ' It would be vain to expect sincerity or plain dealing ' from Villèle, and shortly afterwards Canning again referred to his ' restless and crooked policy.' [2]

Villèle ruled partly by parliamentary means, partly by the intrigues of the closet and the backstairs. He therefore could hardly avoid questionable methods. Yet his duplicity can be proved; for, on being reproached by Austria for joining England and Russia in the Treaty of 6th July 1827, he explained at great length that such a union was monstrous. He had done so merely in order to weaken and divide the two Powers with whom he had signed the Treaty, and he hated both. [3]   No one could surely avow himself a more complete Machiavellian!   And though the alternative, that he was not speaking the truth, may be held, it is one that can only save his intelligence at the expense of his candour.

Yet some of Villèle's faults were actually beneficial to France. He was, said Canning, " pre-eminently among Ministers tenacious of office (even to a degree to which the glutinous adhesiveness of Westmoreland [in England] is no more than a parallel)." A man who could ' glutinously ' stick to office for half a dozen years was eminently a benefit to France, which had seen ministers tumbling down like cocoa-nuts since 1815. Other Frenchmen had little confidence in him, but they knew that they could not deceive him; and all feared his resolute will, his infinite tactical resources, his silent and secret power of manœuvre. Montmorency and Chateaubriand, to be successively his Foreign Ministers, were each to oppose him. But in each case, as Metternich said, ' the earthen pot got broken.' Though neither a good nor a great minister, he was eminently a useful one, for he represented the sole centre of stability and union in France. He was, said Canning, ' the only man able to steer the boat.'

The chief difficulty about the control of French foreign

[1] Stap., *G. C. & T.*   Private letter to Granville, Nov. 15/24, p. 404.
[2] *F.O. Spain*, 185/101.   Canning to F. Lamb, Dec. 30/25, No. 33.
[3] *V.S.A.*, Berichte aus Frankreich, Bd. 378.   Apponyi to Metternich, June 5/27, No. 25, Litt. A.

policy during the years 1822–7 was that it never lay entirely
in a single hand. Divine Right rendered that impossible, so
that even Villèle was not all-powerful. Moreover, he himself
had no diplomatic training nor expert knowledge, and of the
three Foreign Ministers of the period only the literary man,
Chateaubriand, had had any diplomatic experience whatsoever before assuming office. Of Montmorency little need be
said. Once a revolutionist, he was now a devout, if somewhat
pompous, clerical aristocrat, little fitted by his breeding or
decorum to understand the intrigues or to endure the
acerbities of French politics. Chateaubriand, his successor,
was a man of different mould. Unsurpassed as a writer in
his own age, renowned for the beauty of his style and the
superabundance of his imagination, he aspired to become as
great a statesman as he had once been a writer. As a propagandist he was unrivalled. He was the restorer of Christian
modes of thought in literature, the assailant of Napoleon, the
glorifier of the Bourbon constitutional dynasty. He flung
around the uninspiring Bourbons the purple of his eloquence,
he brought water from the Jordan to baptise a son of France,
he ‘ bore, among lilies, the pilgrim’s cross.’ From a pam-
phleteer he rose to be a diplomat and ambassador to England
(1820–1), then to be Plenipotentiary to Verona, and finally
(28th December 1822) to be Foreign Minister. In spite of his
extremely brilliant gifts he was not to justify his claims.
Metternich shook his head sadly at the news. “ More a man
of letters than one of affairs, qualities too often found in
opposition to one another.” And later, “ with measureless
ambition and vanity, he possessed none of the elements which
form a statesman.” [1] Chateaubriand professed the loftiest
sentiments of chivalry towards colleagues and of morality
towards all. He had the highest regard, he said, for Montmorency and Villèle. But at Verona he intrigued against the
one, and tried, though vainly, to deceive the other. Vincent
thought he worked little, had endless distractions, showed
‘ little mean and rancorous passions,’ and was a ‘ tergiversator.’ [2]

[1] *V.S.A.*, Weisungen nach Frankreich. Metternich to Vincent, Jan.
18/23. *V.S.A.*, Weisungen nach Russland, Bd. 6. Reservée. Metternich
to Lebzeltern, July 14/24.

[2] *V.S.A.*, Berichte aus Frankreich, Bd. 356. Vincent to Metternich,
Jan. 12, Feb. 27, and March 7/24.

Canning, who knew him well personally, had a correspondence with him marked by exquisite literary grace on both sides. But Canning thought little more of him as a diplomat than Frederic did of Voltaire. He had no belief in him, and told Stuart to tell him that, though he was always asking for confidential communication, "he can hardly reckon on a confidence so purely unilateral" as he expected.[1] Stuart complained that, after making an offer, Chateaubriand twice verbally disclaimed it.[2] It is but too clear that Chateaubriand was no match for trained diplomats at their own game. Ready to intrigue, he was too hasty and excitable to deceive men who knew every turn of diplomatic fence. In fact, he was always acting a part and trying to make himself out more important than he was. He was a 'brilliant impostor,' said one critic; but at any rate his brilliancy imposed neither on Canning, on Metternich, nor on Villèle. On one man, however, he did impose, and completely, and that was on Alexander the Czar: one whose imagination, sentiment, sympathy, and vanity were akin to his own. That fact brings us into contact with one of the most formidable influences on French policy.

The Russian Ambassador in France, Count Pozzo di Borgo, was certainly one of the most remarkable and influential men of the period. A Corsican by birth, an adventurer by trade, and ultimately a diplomat by profession, he possessed remarkable knowledge and subtlety, together with graces of person and, when he chose, an exquisite and insinuating courtesy. He had espoused the English side in opposition to the French in Corsican politics, had been always at feud with Napoleon, and claimed (with some justification) to have contributed greatly to his overthrow. At first an adventurer under the English flag, he had gradually drifted to Vienna, where he impressed Metternich and Gentz, and finally to Alexander, who made him first a Russian general and then his Ambassador to Paris in 1814, where he remained for twenty years. Alexander distrusted but, none the less, greatly valued him, and used him as an instrument in his ambitious schemes for meddling perpetually in French politics. Pozzo himself was possessed of inordinate vanity and ambition, which often led him to

---

[1] *F.O. France*, 146/62. Canning to Stuart, Feb. 20/24, No. 14.
[2] *Ibid.*, 146/58. Stuart to Canning, June 8/24, No. 290.

pursue a personal policy.   His enemies said he pursued nothing else, and it seems likely that he at one time received money from the French Government, and certain that at another he used his official position to speculate in a Spanish loan to his own great discredit.   Yet, though certainly corrupt, he was not an ignoble character.   In his temperament Sancho Panza was blended with Don Quixote, and he was as capable of high ideals as of low motives or of extreme views.   His chief defect was an inordinate love of and skill in intrigue.   He had a perfect genius for influencing back-bench politicians and journalists and for setting one member of a Cabinet against another.   He was a bitter enemy of England, whose Ministers unsparingly returned his animosity.   Wellington and Canning agreed at least in their hatred of Pozzo, and even the serene Castlereagh became violent when his name was mentioned. Metternich was his personal enemy, and so was Villèle.   Yet, in spite of everything, he exercised extraordinary influence. In the period 1814–18 his power was at its greatest, and the dismissals and appointments of several French Ministers were directly due to him.   After that his influence waned slightly, but it is probable that Chateaubriand owed his high place to the favourable impression he had made upon Pozzo and Alexander.   Villèle, however, did not intend to be ruled either by Pozzo or by his nominee, and the main interest of French politics, during 1823 and the first half of 1824, consists in Villèle's determination to get rid of Chateaubriand and Pozzo's attempt to sustain him.

The French Government was weak, and conscious of its weakness, and hence there were many methods of influencing it.   The French Foreign Office had purified the ranks of the higher officials, but the revolutionary elements remained influential among the clerks at the Quai d'Orsai.   Leakage of important official secrets was frequent, sometimes for reasons of corruption, sometimes by design, sometimes by mere blunder.   The Government was under pressure now from the ultra-Royalist Right, now from the revolutionary Left, and again from the Liberals of the Legislature.   Of these it is here necessary to mention only one, the wisest and most renowned man in France, perhaps even in Europe.   Talley- rand had rendered great services to the Directory, to the

Empire, to the restored Bourbon Monarchy, and was to render as great services in the future to the Orleanist Monarchy. By this time he was soured and disappointed, and lacked a little of his old versatility and skill. The cynical old ex-bishop could win no sympathy from the Clericals, the ex-revolutionist could find no favour with the advocates of Divine Right. But his enormous experience and sagacity made him universally respected, for it was felt that he stood for moderation and for that central line of policy which represented the true interests of France. It was not the least of the difficulties of Villèle that Talleyrand opposed himself to a policy of adventure in Spain.[1]

3. Canning's 'Come what may' Instruction to Wellington (27th September 1822)

The French Plenipotentiaries at Verona were Montmorency, Chateaubriand, and de Ferronays. The last was a cipher; the first two were almost openly at variance with one another. Villèle saw Wellington as he was passing through Paris, and gave him quite a new idea of French policy. Owing to the disturbances in Spain, a large French force had already been massed on the southern frontier, professedly to maintain a 'cordon sanitaire,' in order to prevent yellow fever from passing into France. The scales soon fell from the eyes of all observers. It was a moral, not a material, contagion that was feared. In October the 'cordon sanitaire' was ominously renamed Corps d'Observation, and its object was avowed to be the establishment of a quarantine, not against yellow fever, but against revolutionary principles.

On the 20th September Villèle explained the situation to Wellington, who appears to have been previously ignorant that 100,000 Frenchmen were within striking distance of the Spanish frontier. Villèle was almost disconcertingly frank. King Louis could not allow his brother Bourbon to be deposed or murdered, and the Spanish Revolution was of the kind likely to lead to foreign war. The French plan was to advance quickly on Madrid to defend the King, and to make arrange-

---

[1] The Government took a somewhat mean revenge on him in the middle of 1823 by refusing to suppress the memoirs of Savary, which implicated him in the execution of the Duc d'Enghien.

ments for reforming the Spanish Constitution on the French model. Villèle admitted objections to this plan and was not explicitly committed to it. But he said bluntly, "his whole policy in relation to Spain was founded upon French interests, and that it was entirely unconnected with anything the Congress might determine. He should ask no assistance from any other Power; nay, more, he could not receive it, and should oppose it if endeavoured to be forced upon him, if the assistance to be given was to be a body of troops to be passed through France." The Congress would be valuable as giving moral, but not as giving material, support to France. Pressed by Wellington as to what view he took of the assembly of an 'Army of the Alliance' in Germany, he said he thought the affair would be over before it could assemble, and that the point was one 'to which he, as Minister of France, was not under the necessity of paying much attention.' [1]

Canning replied to Wellington on the 27th September. He perceived at once that Villèle's policy offered an opportunity for separating France from the Neo-Holy Alliance. It was their collective intervention he especially desired to thwart. A collective *démarche* had just been made by the Neo-Holy Alliance. A protest had been delivered to Canning by the Austrian and Prussian *chargé d'affaires*, who brought a despatch from the Russian *chargé* and apologised for his absence. They remonstrated against the journey of Sir William À Court, the new British Minister, who was now on his way to Spain; they asked Canning to stop him before he arrived there. The French *chargé d'affaires* arrived designedly at a later time, with a similar remonstrance and request. Canning treated the matter 'as lightly as possible,' and said that it was impossible to stop À Court, for he had already reached Bordeaux on the 13th September. But, putting the facts together, and observing the distinction between French policy and that of the Neo-Holy Alliance, he decided to give the Duke a memorable instruction. He did not want, he said, if it could be avoided, to introduce disunion or a partial separation into the Congress, but would take this step in case menaces or the notion of an armed interference in Spain proceeded from the Alliance. " If, as I confess I see reason to apprehend, in the

[1] *W.N.D.*, i. 288–94. Wellington to Canning, Sept. 21/22.

late communications both from Paris and Vienna, there is entertained by the Allies a determined project of interference by
force, or by menace, in the present struggle in Spain, so convinced are His Majesty's Government of the uselessness and
danger of any such interference—so objectionable does it
appear to them in principle, and so utterly impracticable in
execution—that, if the necessity should arise, or (I would
rather say) if the opportunity should offer, I am to instruct
your Grace at once frankly and peremptorily to declare, that
to any such interference, *come what may*, His Majesty will not
be a party." [1]   In these few words Canning decisively traced
England's line of action and pronounced the ultimate failure
of the Congress.

4. Montmorency's Questions (20th October 1822); and the Answers of the Neo-Holy Alliance

Wellington, on proceeding to Vienna, found that the Congress
was to be transferred to Verona. On the 4th October he
found Metternich still anxious ' to leave the Spaniards to
themselves ' and desirous of not incurring any risks in the
matter. Alexander was still burning to lead his international
army to Madrid, and painfully surprised to learn that Villèle
did not wish to give it passage. On the 18th the Duke
reported, on his arrival at Verona, " all notion of what is called
an European army, or any offensive operation against Spain,"
as ' at an end.' Yet the diplomatic disputes at Verona were
soon to become as fierce as those between the Montagues and
Capulets of old. On the 20th, Montmorency laid three famous
queries before the Congress. They were as follows :—

1. " In case France should find herself under the necessity
of recalling her Minister from Madrid, and of breaking off all
diplomatic relations with Spain, will the High Courts be disposed to adopt the like measures and recall their respective
Ministers ? "

2. " Should war break out between France and Spain,
under what form and by what acts would the High Powers
afford to France that moral support which would give to Her

---

[1] *W.N.D.*, i. 304. Canning to Wellington, Sept. 27/23. Italics my own.

measures the weight and authority of the Alliance, and inspire a salutary dread in the Revolutionists of all countries ? "

3. " What, in short, is the intention of the High Powers, as to the extent and the form of the effective assistance (' *secours matériel* ') which they would be disposed to give to France, in case active interference should, at her demand, become necessary ? "

To these formidable queries the answers of the Four Allies were different. Alexander at once welcomed the French overture with enthusiasm, said he would march 150,000 men across Germany and post them in Piedmont either to fall upon the Jacobins in France if the French Army were absent in Spain, or to reinforce that army if it required assistance.[1] He offered also at once to conclude a treaty to that effect. But Pozzo, in making this communication to Montmorency, discovered that France not only objected to the assembling of Russian forces in Piedmont, but would actually object to the formation of any army for that ultimate purpose. " A Russian army in Europe was equally objectionable to Prussia and to Austria." ' All Europe would rise in arms,' said Metternich, though he shrewdly thought it was much better for France than for Austria to sustain the objections.[2] By discouraging the scheme he hoped to avert it altogether. If Metternich was lukewarm, Wellington was icy cold. The only difference was that Metternich believed in a concerted moral action, with veiled menaces, against Spain, and the Duke believed that remonstrances, if made, should be individual, not collective. Wellington had been instructed, if necessary, to break the unity of the Congress ; Metternich had decided at all hazards to preserve it.

Matters came to a head on the 30th October, when the answers of the Powers were delivered to Montmorency. In all three cases Alexander promised his sincere support to France. In the first case Metternich and Prussia both promised to sever diplomatic relations with Spain ; in the second case both promised moral, but not material, support to France on the outbreak of war with Spain ; in the third

---

[1] *W.N.D.*, i. 457–60. Wellington to Canning, Oct. 29/22.
[2] *W.N.D.*, i. 476. Memo by Londonderry (Lord Charles Stewart), Oct. 29/22.

case both Powers 'hedged.' They would only agree to give France armed aid if matters were decided with full consent and concert of all Powers concerned as to the ' extent, quality, and direction of this aid.' [1] This was a polite method of shelving the third question.

5. 30TH OCTOBER—WELLINGTON'S BOMBSHELL

It was Wellington who delivered the bombshell. His memorandum (30th October) declared that " such an inter- ference appeared to be an unnecessary assumption of responsibility." He declined to commit himself or his government in any of the three hypothetical cases advanced, and suggested that disturbance in Spain was more likely to be produced than allayed by a general rupture of diplomatic relations. Finally, while admitting the right of France to maintain a *corps d'observation* on the frontier, in view of the civil war in Spain, he expressed a strong disbelief in the theory that the Spanish Revolution threatened other nations with its ' moral contagion.'

Here was a rent in a somewhat tattered garment, a rent which gaped and widened. On the 30th and 31st, Metternich drafted diplomatic formulæ, and Montmorency quoted news- papers and police reports, in order to move the Duke from his position. But Wellington remained inflexible, saying that he must know " the exact ground of complaint and the exact cause of war " before he could lend any support to the other members of the Alliance.

There was clearly nothing to be done with Wellington, and from this time forward the other Powers concerted their policy in secret deliberations without him, summoning him only to formal conferences. On hearing of these discussions, Canning approved the attitude of the Duke, but clearly foresaw that France at least might be driven into war.[2] One result only came from Wellington's attitude : that the action of France was ultimately separated from that of the Neo-Holy Alliance. On the 12th November Wellington saw Montmorency's draft

---

[1] *W.N.D.*, i. 497–8. The Austrians promised to give aid if the matter were decided in full Congress ; Prussia was a little more vague.

[2] *W.N.D.*, i. 518. Wellington to Sir C. Stuart, Nov. 12/22.

of his Spanish despatch, told him he thought it 'highly objectionable,' and moderated some of its language. Finally, the three Powers signed a *procès-verbal* on the 15th November, which they explained was 'neither a treaty nor a protocol,' but which defined the *casus fœderis* which would cause them to give aid to France. These were: attacks on France by Spain ; the deposition, trial, or death of the Spanish King or members of the Royal Family ; or provocative diffusion of propaganda in France by persons in the employment of Spain. Unforeseen cases were to be referred to the Conference of the Allied Ministers at Paris. On the 20th November Wellington formally declined being a party to any such proceedings, drily stating that the British Minister at Madrid would confine himself " to allay the ferment which these communications must occasion." Finally, Montmorency departed to lay these documents before his government, having broken with England, but having preserved a precarious and artificial unity with the Neo-Holy Alliance. After a last warning to Alexander on the 29th, Wellington himself left Verona on the 30th November. He was ' *mécontent de nous tous*,' said Metternich, and declared that ' we ' were entirely in the wrong.

6. France pursues a Separate Policy ; The de la Garde Despatch (25th December 1822)

The Duke reached Paris on the 9th December, where he found that the Neo-Holy Allies had not yet instructed their Ministers to leave Madrid, and that Villèle was still relatively apathetic. The President of the Council had informed him that he had requested the Neo-Holy Allies to suspend their letters of recall. Personally, Villèle believed (though Metternich did not) that the withdrawal of diplomatic representatives from Madrid meant war, at any rate for France. Wellington was instructed by Canning on the 13th December to offer British mediation between France and Spain *before* the decisive step of recalling the various diplomatic representatives from Madrid was taken by the Neo-Holies. Wellington presented a formal note offering British mediation on the 17th. Neither Montmorency nor Villèle gave him much encouragement. On the 19th and 20th both said they must await the arrival of Chateaubriand from the Congress with the latest information. Wellington then left Paris, believing, for reasons known only to himself, that peace was assured.

In fact, so far as the Neo-Holy Allies were concerned, the die had already been cast. For on the 14th December the three Powers had signed a circular despatch, announcing their intention of withdrawing their representatives from Madrid. But the moment for this decisive step was not yet determined. Metternich thought that he had already triumphed and had averted everything but a ' moral demonstration.' The Allies, he said, must take this step, for otherwise the Congress would have done nothing. On the 27th November he wrote to Vincent at Paris that Montmorency left Verona ' *d'accord uniquement avec moi.*' A letter from Montmorency himself on the 5th December confirmed this view, which he answered on the 14th, expressing his delight that Louis XVIII. had approved of the plan and policy of the Neo-Holies.[1] Shortly afterwards he was informed that Montmorency had been made a Duke for his services at Verona. Metternich was undeceived when Chateaubriand arrived at Paris (20th December) with the despatches and the latest news from Verona.[2] What followed is as important as it is obscure. Montmorency, as Wellington had already perceived, was acting in a sense more purely European than French, and had agreed at Verona to withdraw the French Ambassador simultaneously with those of the Neo-Holy Allies. He still adhered to this view. But Villèle was determined, at all hazards, not to follow at the tail of the Alliance, and to move France along her own line of policy. On Christmas Day, the season of ' peace to all men of good will,' the French Cabinet came to a grave decision in the presence of the King.

This decision was embodied in a despatch, dated the 25th December, and addressed to de la Garde, the French Ambassador at Madrid. The despatch began by referring to the Revolution in Spain of May 1820, saying: " France, despite the dangers threatened by this revolution, has devoted

---

[1] *V.S.A.*, Kongress-Akten, Verona, Bd. 43. Metternich to Vincent, Dec. 2 ; Montmorency to Metternich, Dec. 5 ; Metternich to Montmorency, Dec. 14/22.

[2] It is of some significance that all the French journals of the 17th December were pacific, except *L'Etoile*, the organ of Montmorency.

all her care to strengthening the bonds which unite the two kings, and to maintaining the existing relations between the two peoples." But the fact that the Constitution had not been established by Ferdinand on reassuming the crown (1814), and that the Revolution of 1820 was ' the product of a military insurrection,' had encouraged revolt and disturbance in Spain. The mutiny of the Royal Guard, and the existence of civil war on the boundaries adjoining France, had compelled her to assemble forces on her frontier.

France had explained to the Congress why she had been compelled to arm, and the eventual use she was to make of her armaments. " The Continental Powers have taken the resolution to unite to aid her (if ever there was need) to maintain her dignity and tranquillity."

France is, " for the moment, well content with a resolution at once so friendly and honourable to her," but the three Courts of Austria, Russia, and Prussia have decided to suspend diplomatic relations with Spain.[1] France had not, however, taken this course. But she associated herself with the Allied wishes that " the noble Spanish nation will find a remedy for its ills, ills of a nature to disturb the governments of Europe, and to impose on them *des précautions toujours pénibles.*"

De la Garde was, however, instructed to give the following explanations, on behalf of France, to the Spanish Government :—

" You will take special care to make it known, that the peoples of the Peninsula, restored to tranquillity, will find loyal and sincere friends in their neighbours. In consequence you will assure the Cabinet of Madrid that help of every kind (*les secours de tous genres*) of which France can dispose in favour of Spain, will always be offered to assure her good fortune and to increase her prosperity ; but you will declare to her at the same time that France will in no way relax the precautionary measures (*des mesures préservatrices*) which she has taken, so long as Spain continues to be torn by factions. His Majesty's Government will not even hesitate to recall you from Madrid, and to find her security in more efficacious dispositions, if her essential interests continue to be compromised, and if she loses the hope of an improvement, which

---

[1] Apparently on the 23rd December.

may be expected from the sentiments which have so long united Spaniards and Frenchmen in the love of their kings and of a wise liberty."

These instructions were to be presented at Madrid simultaneously with the communications from Russia, Austria, and Prussia.

The best explanation of this despatch is, in fact, the simplest. If the Neo-Holy Allies withdrew their diplomatic representatives and France retained hers, the latter had an advantage. France had a means of depriving England of the chance of playing mediator between France and Spain, as she would for the moment be on better terms with the latter than were the Neo-Holies.[1] And this explanation is borne out by the fact that next day (26th December) the British offer of mediation was formally declined by France.[2] Yet the actual contents of the despatch were rendered more unpleasant to the Spaniards, because it was published on the 27th in the *Moniteur*, by what Chateaubriand called " *une mesure un peu insolite en Diplomatie, mais qui, chez la nation française, devait réussir.*"[3] However it might succeed in France, it was not likely to do so in Spain, whose ministers actually first learnt of this threatening despatch from the newspapers. Whether they were revolutionaries or ultras, Spaniards retained all their old pride and dignity, and both were wounded by so undiplomatic a disregard of their feelings.

This despatch was, as Wellington said, ' too emphatic,' but none the less somewhat mysterious. It went beyond the Neo-Holy despatches in one direction, and not so far in another. For, though it did not sever diplomatic relations, yet, as Canning wrote, it was " still vicious in principle, as at once demanding of Spain something to be done in the arrangement of Her internal concerns and denouncing (in however comparatively distant and obscure a manner) War as the consequence of refusal."[4] The despatch did imply the independent action of France, and for that reason

---

[1] Duvergier de Hauranne, *Histoire Parlementaire*, 1865, vii. 210, 217–25.

[2] Montmorency addressed this reply, though Villèle signed the de la Garde despatch.

[3] *A.A.E.*, 616. Chateaubriand to Marcellus, Jan. 1/23.

[4] Canning to Sir William À Court, Dec. 29/22 (published Apr. 14/23), *B.F.S.P.*, x. 29–30.

Montmorency resigned. The uncertainty in the minds of French Ministers is reflected in the despatch itself. But the actual decision to send it appears to have been taken by the King and Villèle in opposition to the rest of the Cabinet, and thus in the true spirit of Divine Right. Louis closed the debate with an epigram : " I cannot recall my minister from Madrid until I send a hundred thousand men over the Pyrenees."

Chateaubriand was not present at the Cabinet and the despatch was signed by Villèle, as acting Foreign Minister. But on the 28th December, after some not very sincere professions of reluctance, Chateaubriand obeyed the command of the King and became Foreign Minister. With ill-concealed delight he allowed himself to be dragged up to the summit of his ambition, avowing himself (incorrectly) the faithful follower of Villèle. His appointment did not render war certain, but it made it more probable. For he now became leader of the war party and was recognised as such by public opinion. And behind him was Pozzo and Russia. Metternich had written on 2nd December that Pozzo was greatly inciting the French Government to war, but thought that Montmorency would prevent him from being successful.[1] He was wrong, for Chateaubriand brought back the latest views of Alexander, which were too important to be disregarded. Villèle, in fact, in an undiplomatic utterance, revealed the truth. On the 25th February 1824 he confessed in Parliament ' qu'il falloit attaquer le midi pour échapper au Nord.' The only way to prevent a Russian army coming into France was to send a French one into Spain. With the violence of Spanish Liberals, with the secret appeals of their King, with the weakness of French Ministers, with the fear of Alexander, with the ambitions of Chateaubriand and Pozzo, the chances of preserving peace were very small at the end of 1822.

---

[1] *V.S.A.*, Weisungen nach Frankreich, Bd. 350. Metternich to Vincent, Dec. 2/23. Secrette, Berichte aus Frankreich, Bd. 351. Vincent to Metternich, Mar. 22/23, says, ' he [Pozzo] was always for armed intervention.'

7. The Results of Verona

" In short, I scarce could count a minute
Ere the ice dome, and all within it,
Kings, Fiddlers, Emperors, all were gone."
                                         TOM MOORE.

But, for the moment, the question of Spain was actually less important than the moral effect produced, first by British and then by French action, upon the Congressional System. Other decisions, and by no means unimportant decisions, were taken at Verona as to the Slave Trade, South America, Greece, and Italy. Over these questions a semblance of unity was preserved. Over the Spanish question England had broken away altogether ; France, though reluctantly concurring at the Congress, revoked her assent immediately afterwards. To Metternich this breach was very fatal to the Congress System. Its essence was that Europe should present an entirely united front to cow the revolutionaries in all parts of Europe, and the scene had been carefully staged at Verona for the purpose. There were present two emperors, three kings, three reigning grand dukes, one cardinal representing the Pope, one viceroy, three foreign secretaries, twenty ambassadors, and twelve ministers. Cajoleries had not been spared to the hesitating envoys of France and of England. Metternich succeeded in winning over Montmorency ; Alexander flattered Chateaubriand and spoke to him ' as friend to friend ' with a picturesque eloquence akin to his own. He invited Wellington to dine with him alone, as if he were a brother sovereign. Metternich induced Napoleon's widow, Marie Louise—already with child by her paramour—to play cards with the conqueror of her husband. Madame Lieven amused the lighter moments of the Duke. All the dignitaries appeared in state at the old Roman amphitheatre, where the first players of Europe amused ' those other actors, the kings.' It was truly the last muster, the last splendid pageant of those forces which had ruled the world since 1815. But the harmony of the scene remained purely theatrical, and neither words nor flatteries could prevent the divergent interests from being revealed to the world. By the end of 1822 it was clear that they would no longer march in unison. Chateaubriand, in eloquent retrospect, pronounced that Verona would recall to men not Metternich but Shakespeare, not the speeches of the Congress but the love tale of Romeo and Juliet. All that was left were " sentiments that are extinguished, chimeras outworn, although once nursed, like those of the dwellers of Herculaneum, at the bosom of Hope." On the 14th April 1823, Canning, in less rhetorical phrases, quoted the de la Garde despatch of the 25th December to prove that England's attitude had broken up the Congress by confining within due bounds the ' predominating Areopagitic spirit ' which was threatening to govern the world. " The success of a [' *wholly European* '] policy . . . would have been completely secured, if England had thought she could concur in them." Perhaps the French separatist action would, in any case, have wrecked the ' European ' policy. But its combination with Canning's instruction to Wellington of 27th September made failure certain. The gaps in the fabric could not be concealed from the world, and it was doubtful whether any new congress could succeed. The sense of failure rested heavy upon this one, and, ever after this, Metternich and Alexander feared that the summoning of a congress might only expose their divisions to the world. Congresses had hitherto been a meeting of almost supernatural beings, whose secret and solemn decisions carried with them a sense of awe and mystery. It was at Verona that the ' archangels ' were ' damaged.' Wellington's attitude had been negative and one of protest; Villèle's attitude was positive and one of independence. On Christmas Day the European aspect of the Spanish question gave way to a more purely French one. And as soon as it became purely a matter for France, England, her old enemy, became awake to the gravity of the situation. A war between France and Spain, a war by one Bourbon to restore another, suggested a revival of the *Pacte de Famille*,[1] and might be followed by attempts to reconquer Spanish America for Ferdinand. Here England's most vital interests were touched, and thus France came face to face with her.

---

[1] The ' Family Compact ' was based on three separate Treaties between France and Spain of 1733, 1743, and 1761. Their essence was combination against England by the Bourbon kinsmen of Paris and Madrid. A clause of the Anglo-Spanish Treaty of 1814 forbade any such union in future. This clause, though secret, was published by Canning during the crisis of 1823.

CHAPTER IV

THE FRENCH INVASION AND THE FALL OF CONSTITUTIONALISM IN SPAIN

1. THE LAST BRITISH EFFORT FOR PEACE (JANUARY TO FEBRUARY 1823)

" France said to Spain—' Your revolution disquiets me ' ; and Spain replied to France—' Your army of observation disquiets me.' There were but two remedies to this state of things : war or concession."—CANNING in the Commons, 30th April 1824.

WELLINGTON returned from Verona in the belief that peace would be maintained. He overrated his influence alike over Metternich, over Alexander, and over French politicians. Between 1815 and 1818 he had not only directed the military policy of the Allies in France, but he had, in fact, settled nearly all the financial difficulties, and had often overruled all the Allied Ambassadors together over purely diplomatic questions. The experience was unfortunate, for Wellington had previously been modest enough when dealing with politicians. He now got the idea that he could direct diplomacy as well as he could direct war. He still thought at Verona that his wishes and his utterances would be as weighty as they had once been at Paris. He was mistaken, but he did not recognise his mistake. He thought that his attitude at Verona had prevented common action by the Allies in Spain, and that his utterances at Paris would prevent separate action by France. He therefore pressed Villèle and Montmorency hard, and offered the mediation of England for the settlement of French difficulties with Spain (17th December). The reception was not favourable, and the Duke left Paris on the 20th. A formal refusal of mediation by the French Government, together with an acceptance of the good offices of England in the Spanish question, followed the Duke to London on the 26th. His view was, however, still optimistic as to the preservation of peace, an impression which Canning did not share. And at this point begins the coolness between the two men, which afterwards terminated in such bitter strife.

France, though she had rejected the mediation of England, had not refused to avail herself of her ' good offices.' To soothe the vanity of Spain, Wellington, in his capacity as a Spanish grandee, was asked to send Lord Fitzroy Somerset to assist Sir William A Court at Madrid, by pressing on the Spanish Government his suggestions for conciliating France. Canning said that these were, in effect, the suggestions of the British Government. " But we do not, like France, demand anything of this sort as the price of our forbearance to break with Spain." [1] Though couched in vague terms, their general meaning was clear. Everyone, including most Spaniards, admitted the defects of the Constitution of 1812. There was no second Chamber ; ministers could not sit in the Cortes, and the members of one Cortes were not to sit in the next one. The remedy was to strengthen the King's prerogative and to provide elements of stability by making a second Chamber. Any chance of success these negotiations might have had was ruined by the fact that letters of recall were demanded on the 9th January 1823 by the representative of Prussia at Madrid, and on the 10th by those of Austria and Russia, and all ' in most violent and offensive language.' By the middle of the month the Neo-Allied representatives had left, though the Frenchman still remained. This was most unfortunate, for it interfered with a measure promoted by Canning in order to conciliate Spain. England had recently taken a very strong line by sending out a naval squadron to the West Indies, with instructions to protect British shipping by force against pirates in Spanish America. On the 10th December 1822 Canning announced this step to all diplomats ; but on the 7th January 1823 he suspended all such instructions, offered to negotiate a commercial convention with Spain, and suspended all operations against them. This wise and moderate overture did not reach Spain until the Neo-Holy representatives had left.[2] By that time, however, it was too late. On the 10th

---

[1] *W.N.D.*, ii. 9, to Fitzroy Somerset, Jan. 6/23.

[2] It reached Madrid on the 22nd, and the last of the Neo-Holies left on Jan. 16/23. *F.O. Spain*, 185/91. Canning to À Court, Jan. 7/23, No. 2. A commercial convention was signed on Mar. 12. . The policy as to this

January, smarting with resentment at the Neo-Holy Alliance, the Spanish Government instructed their Ambassador at Paris to refuse all concessions to France. On the 13th, repenting of their haste, they solicited the ' good offices ' of England in their dispute with France. But the Spanish despatch of the 10th had done its work at Paris, and on the 18th Chateaubriand instructed de la Garde to demand his passports, adding, on the 20th, that the Spanish instruction of the 13th made no difference in this respect.

Though the clouds were gathering darkly round Madrid, Canning did not abandon all hope. Besides official despatches he wrote five intimate personal letters to Chateaubriand before the 28th January, of which the burden was ' peace, peace, peace.' Chateaubriand replied gracefully, telling de la Garde in private to ' put no trust in the English.' Villèle was meanwhile assuring Canning, ' as a secret,' that he was really pacific and would fall in with British intentions.[1] Canning was not the dupe of either confidence, and the events of the 28th January showed that he was right. On that day the King of France delivered his speech from the throne on the opening of Parliament.

2. THE FRENCH KING'S SPEECH (28TH JANUARY) AND THE BRITISH PROTEST

" The infatuation . . . at Madrid," said Louis XVIII., " left little hope of maintaining peace." The French Minister had been recalled.

" A hundred thousand French are ready to march " under a son of France to the aid of a brother Bourbon. So far the speech was directed against Spain, though it contained a suggestion of the renewal of the ' Family Compact.' But one passage caused the greatest sensation in England. For it reasserted, in their most offensive form, those doctrines of Legitimacy of which England had already had enough in the circulars of Troppau and Laibach. " Let Ferdinand be free to give to his people the institutions they cannot hold but

convention may be defined both as an attempt to settle disputes of the past, and as a move towards closer relations for the future.

[1] *F.O. Spain*, 185/91. Canning to À Court, Jan. 10/23, enclosing Sir C. Stuart to Canning of Jan. 2/23. Canning commented with much suspicion on Villèle and his ' secret.'

from him." As these words were uttered, Pozzo di Borgo sprang up and threw his hat in the air with exultation. So, at least, reported the newspapers.

This speech, the most famous ever made to a Parliament by a King of France, in reality gave Canning his opportunity. Hitherto he had been humble enough in his solicitations both to France and to Spain. His tone at once altered. For France had proclaimed, in the strongest terms, a doctrine implying interference in the internal affairs of independent States, in which no English Minister could acquiesce. If there was to be a war, not of armies, but of opinions, then British public opinion was to count. Canning immediately began to assert the standpoint of his own people in the Cabinet of nations. From the moment that he publicly challenged this doctrine he became, in the eyes of the majority of his countrymen, the first man in England. This position he held until the last years of his life, when he abandoned it only to become the first man in Europe. The formidable power which he was to wield was the power of awakening public feeling—at first in his own country and afterwards elsewhere—to challenge the unblest doctrines of force, and to assert in the face of the world the principles of freedom. What Castlereagh had done in notes and circulars he was now to do in Parliament and on platforms, and his utterances were to reach to the farthest bounds of Europe and to carry light over the ocean to the New World.

That his action was justified seems to be shown by the effect of the French King's speech even on persons of Legitimist sympathy. Shrewd old Talleyrand, the former high-priest of Legitimacy, deprecated the sentiments. In London Lieven the Russian, and Esterházy the Austrian, Ambassador thought such sentiments had better have been omitted. Three ultra-Tory members of the Cabinet—Westmoreland, Harrowby, and Wellington—thought them too strong. Canning and Liverpool were more vehement, and they represented the almost universal condemnation of the public and the Press. The *Star* spoke of ' great indignation,' the *Times* of a ' burst of absolute horror ' upon the Stock Exchange, and eight other journals upraised their voices in condemnation.[1] It was defended only,

[1] *New Times, Morning Chronicle, Morning Herald, Morning Post, Morning Advertiser, British Press, British Public Ledger, Examiner.*

and not very convincingly, by the *Courier* (which owed much to French information and probably something to French gold), and by the fractious and irresponsible Cobbett.

The Stock Exchange or the newspapers might feel contempt for the proclamation of high-flying absolutist doctrines by a foreign sovereign to-day, but they would scarcely show ' horror ' or passionate ' indignation.' The situation was different in 1823. For the result of 1815 was that unlimited monarchy had regained its sway over two-thirds of Europe, and that it had become aggressive against the constitutional movement everywhere during 1820 and 1821. The few and feeble constitutions of Germany were being gradually stifled ; in Naples and Piedmont they had been put down with an iron absolutistic hand ; that of Spain was now threatened. Most Englishmen thought, not perhaps correctly, that it was the people and the Parliament who had won liberty and a constitution for England, and that the ' glorious revolution of 1688 ' was the palladium of their present freedom and the source of their present dynasty. Canning wrote at once to France on the 3rd February that England could recommend Spain to modify her constitution, but not on the principle proclaimed by the King of France—" a principle which strikes at the roots of the British Constitution." France might enjoy freedom and happiness under " institutions emanating from the will of the sovereign, and described as *octroyées* from the throne. But it [England] could not countenance a pretension on the part of France to make her example a rule for other nations, and still less could it admit a peculiar right in France to force that example specifically upon Spain, in virtue of the consanguinity of the reigning dynasties of the two kingdoms." This latter reason would, on the contrary, suggest recollections and considerations which must obviously make it impossible for Great Britain to be the advocate of pretensions founded upon it.[1] Here, in a few words, lay the objections of England : popular indignation at the threat of spreading by arms a doctrine opposed to English ideas of liberty ; diplomatic objection to the assistance to a Bourbon,

[1] Chateaubriand endeavoured to explain away the construction as to the constitution by saying he meant a reform of the constitution agreed between the King and the Cortes. Sir C. Stuart to Canning, Feb. 10/23. *B.F.S.P.*, x. 56–7.

when Spain had solemnly pledged herself to England by treaty not to revive the *Pacte de Famille.*

Brougham sounded the tocsin on the 4th February in the Commons by denouncing the conduct of the Neo-Holy Alliance towards Spain as ' abominably iniquitous,' as ' displaying the malignity of demons,' as ' prodigiously beyond endurance,' as ' worse than Bonaparte ' ; and the French King's speech as dictated by his parasites, and as ' worse than the principles of the [Neo-]Holy Alliance.'

Canning's endeavour was now to work on French fears by pointing to the display of feeling in England. The young and astute French *chargé d'affaires* at London, Marcellus, had to face formidable interviews with both Liverpool and Canning on the 30th January, the day after they knew of the speech. On the 4th February, Canning told him it was *malheureux* and ' disarms us completely.' On the 7th, Liverpool told him ' all England condemns the speech,' and added the graver intelligence that " he [Liverpool] has had to omit the word neutrality [as between France and Spain] in the English King's speech." Canning told Marcellus, after Liverpool had left, that to insert it would have been to invite the attack of the Opposition. On the 11th, Canning made a public speech at Harwich ' of a menacing character.' What he said was : " If unhappily a state of hostilities should be eventually unavoidable, the country was fully prepared to meet the emergency. If it were assumed that exhaustion had succeeded to our gigantic efforts in the late war, that was certainly a most erroneous conclusion." On the 1st he had written a private letter direct to Monsieur (the Comte d'Artois), stating that " the effect [produced by the speech] in this country " was " such as I have witnessed, I think, but twice in my life—the tumultuous expression of feeling in the City of London which hailed the renewal of war with Bonaparte in 1803," and again the sympathy called out in defence of Spain in 1808.[1] To this grave warning the Prince gave an evasive answer.

Chateaubriand was greatly impressed by the omission of the word neutrality, and summoned the Austrian, Russian, and Prussian representatives to a conference on the 17th

---

[1] Stap., *Corr.*, i. 73–4. Canning to Monsieur, Feb. 1/23.

February. They " all agreed that the three Courts should have explanations with England, in case she thought seriously of breaking her neutrality and of taking the side of Spain." They unanimously thought that their Courts would have no diffi- culty in declaring to England that, " if she attacked [France], the Continental Powers would be obliged to make common cause with us." [1] But they added that they would at first make friendly communications, not a formal declaration.

Canning did not, in fact, mean war. In a Cabinet memorandum of this period he said that we could not fight in Europe; we had no troops ready, and naval support would not materially aid Spain.[2] Besides, if the Allies supported France, Prussia and Russia might threaten Hanover and Portugal. In two cases only he proposed to fight: if France tried to aid Spain to recover Spanish America, or if she attacked Portugal. But these contingencies for the moment were remote. Nor did Canning even threaten war though he provided for it by announcing (19th· February) an increase of the navy from 21,000 to 25,000 men. As he wrote proudly to A Court on 9th February, " a menace not intended to be executed is an engine which Great Britain could never condescend to employ." Meanwhile he did everything he could to strengthen Spain and to make the task of invasion difficult for France. With this view the embargo on the export of arms to Spain and Spanish America was lifted on the 21st February. On the 16th February the Duc di San Lorenzo, the Spanish Ambassador who had been dismissed from Paris, arrived in England. He was received at the pier- head at Dover with cheers for Spanish liberty, and dragged in triumph by the London mob to the Spanish Legation, which happened unfortunately to be opposite the house of Marcellus. So much for what the public thought. Canning showed what he thought on the 2nd March, when he appeared in public at the Opera with the Duke. He stopped on the staircase, with the Duchess of San Lorenzo on his arm, to express to Marcellus his regret for the tone of a speech made by

[1] *A.A.E.*, 616. Chateaubriand to Marcellus, Feb. 17/23. *V.S.A.*, Berichte aus Frankreich, Bd. 351. Vincent to Metternich, Feb. 17/23.
[2] Stap., *Corr.*, i. 85–8. It is dated February, but must have been before Feb. 10, for a memo of Wellington's of that date (*W.N.D.*, ii. 31–3) is plainly a reply to it.

Chateaubriand on the 25th February.   Canning clearly meant to suggest to France that he wished well to Spain, and that French action towards her might so exasperate England's public opinion as to drive her unwilling government into war.

Canning always maintained that war hung on a hair in 1823, that Villèle did not wish it, and that, " had the British Government been rightly understood " in France, " the invasion of Spain would never have taken place.   In this faith I shall die." [1]   But British policy was not ' rightly understood,' and the chief reason was that misunderstanding was deliberately promoted in the critical weeks of February and March, notably by King George, but also by some of Canning's colleagues in the Cabinet.   George IV. was the worst offender.   On the 14th February he expressed interest in the French cause, and said " he sees with joy the rights of Legitimate Royalty " sustained ;   on the 3rd March he told Esterházy he disapproved of the British export of arms to Spain, whom he would not support in her obstinacy, said he wished Castlereagh was alive, and regretted Wellington's action at Verona.   On the 25th he said that his government must come out of its ' shameful uncertainty.'   On the 11th February ' several ministers ' told Marcellus that a French army ought to go at once to Madrid, as England would remain neutral if they got there quickly.   They suggested that Marcellus should let his government know this.   On the 14th, Marcellus met Lords Westmoreland and Harrowby coming out from the Cabinet.   "Are your troops already in Spain ? " asked the one.   "Who stops you ? " queried the other.   Wellington was a little more diplomatic.   On the 3rd January he told Marcellus, " you will go to Madrid without delay and without danger. But what could you do there ? "   Peel and the Duke of York let it be known they would oppose war with France.   With the King and two colleagues openly approving the French invasion ;   with Wellington advising a rapid march on Madrid as a good military measure ;   with another colleague and a Royal Duke opposing war with France, it is not surprising

---

[1] Stap., *G.C. & T.*, 528.   To Liverpool, Oct. 16/26.   So thought Sir R. Wilson, a man well-informed as to the facts though not impeccable in judgment.   Vide *B.M. Add. MSS.*, 30, 132, 466–7, 471.

that Canning and Liverpool failed to make themselves ' rightly understood ' at Paris.[1]

3. CANNING'S DESPATCH OF THE 31ST MARCH 1823

" The hinge between war and peace is indeed a dangerous juncture to Ministers."—BURKE.

By the middle of March, Canning's attempt to influence the constitutional party in Spain, and his appeal to the moderate party in France, had definitely failed. On the 13th he heard that the Spanish Government refused to make any modifica- tions in the constitution. On the 15th the Duc d'Angoulême left Paris to command the French Army on the frontier. On the 21st, Canning therefore accepted the inevitable and informed Marcellus that England would observe neutrality in the impending contest. On the 23rd he told him that he was going to publish the various documents on the question, a decision which horrified Chateaubriand, Wellington, and Metternich, and provoked protest in each case.

Just before he did this he summed up his views in a despatch of 31st March, which was published *only five days after* it was communicated to the French Government.[2]

The importance of this despatch was enhanced by the fact that it was sent " for the purpose of being communicated to the French Minister." In diplomacy this is an unusual step to take. It was, indeed, practically an ultimatum, or a declaration that war with England would follow if France broke any of the three pledges which she was regarded as having given—

(*a*) not to establish a permanent military occupation of Spain ;

(*b*) not to appropriate any part of the Spanish Colonies ;

(*c*) not to violate the territorial integrity of Portugal.

Chateaubriand and Villèle heard it on the 9th April, and

---

[1] *A.A.E.*, 616. Marcellus to Chateaubriand, Jan. 3, 7, Feb. 11, 14, Mar. 25/23. *V.S.A.*, Berichte aus Frankreich, Bd. 351. Vincent to Metter- nich, Mar. 3/23. *V.S.A.*, Berichte aus England. Esterházy to Metternich, Mar. 3/23.

[2] I infer that Canning instructed Stuart, by private letter, not to present this despatch until the French crossed into Spain. Otherwise Stuart must have withheld the despatch on his own responsibility from Apr. 3 to 9, which is highly improbable. The despatch is in *B.F.S.P.*, x. 64-70.

made no direct reply to what was, in effect, a challenge. They could hardly do so, partly for reasons of dignity, partly because the renewal of their disclaimers at the moment would have been to admit that their previous assurances had been worth-less. As regards (a) and (b), their previous pledges had been of a general character—" as recognising the sacred obligations of treaties," as not wishing to revive the *Pacte de Famille* or to harbour aggressive designs. In respect to (c), Portugal, their pledges had been specific in February and were renewed in August.[1] For the moment, Canning seems to have assumed that silence implied that they harboured no designs on Spain and Spanish America.

After recounting the failure of British attempts to mediate or to interpose their good offices between France and con-stitutional Spain, Canning indicated that he now regarded war as practically certain. He concluded with the following grave warning, which must be given in full, as almost every word has to be carefully weighed.

" It remains only to describe the Conduct which it is His Majesty's desire and intention to observe, in a conflict between two Nations, to each of whom His Majesty is bound by the ties of Amity and Alliance.

" The repeated disavowal, by His Most Christian Majesty's Government, of all views of ambition and aggrandisement, forbids the suspicion of any design on the part of France, to establish a permanent military occupation of Spain ; or to force His Catholick Majesty into any measures, derogatory to the independence of his Crown, or to his existing relations with other Powers.

" The repeated assurances which His Majesty has received, of the determination of France to respect the dominions of His Most Faithful Majesty, relieve His Majesty from any apprehension of being called upon to fulfil the obligations of that intimate defensive Connection, which has so long sub-sisted between the Crowns of Great Britain and Portugal.

" With respect to the Provinces in America, which have thrown off their allegiance to the Crown of Spain, time and

---

[1] *F.O. Spain*, 185/91. Canning to À Court, Aug. 20/23, mentions " a most positive assurance from Polignac *re* Portugal."

the course of events appear to have substantially decided their separation from the Mother Country ; although the formal recognition of those Provinces, as Independent States, by His Majesty, may be hastened or retarded by various external circumstances, as well as by the more or less satisfactory progress, in each State, towards a regular and settled form of Government. Spain has long been apprised of His Majesty's opinions upon this subject. Disclaiming in the most solemn manner any intention of appropriating to Himself the smallest portion of the late Spanish possessions in America, His Majesty is satisfied that no attempt will be made by France, to bring under her dominion any of those possessions, either by conquest, or by cession, from Spain.

" This frank explanation upon the points on which perhaps alone the possibility of any collision of France with Great Britain can be apprehended in a War between France and Spain, your Excellency will represent to M. de Chateaubriand, as dictated by an earnest desire to be enabled to preserve, in that War, a strict and undeviating Neutrality : a Neutrality not liable to alteration towards either Party, so long as the Honour and just Interests of Great Britain are equally respected by both."

This despatch contains, in itself, a compendium of Canning's whole future policy as regards Spain, Portugal, France, and Spanish America. It hints at the possibility of war if Portugal is attacked, and at the recognition of the Spanish Colonies if France continues to occupy Spain. It stops short of war, indeed, but it makes clear that the breach between France and England is a wide one, and may become wider still. It may be a ' perfect neutrality ' that is here proclaimed, but it is one that, in three defined cases, may end in armed intervention. Strong words here are plainly meant as the prelude to strong action.[1] Its effect was enhanced because it was directed to be read in full to Chateaubriand, a step which is a strong one for any minister to take. It is interesting, however,

[1] A supplementary despatch draws attention to the abrogation of the *Pacte de Famille* in the separate article of the Anglo-Spanish Treaty of July 5/14—the article being afterwards published by Canning. À Court, on Jan. 27, had stated to Canning that a despatch of Chateaubriand to Madrid spoke of restoring the ancient intimate connection between France and Spain.

to note that Metternich, when he read it, intimated approval
and stated that, if France contemplated any of the three
measures, "Austria would join Great Britain in her efforts
to counteract them."[1]   It was seldom that Metternich
approved of Canning's policy, and still more seldom that he
offered to support it.   Other evidence permits us to doubt
if he now really did either.

4. THE FRENCH INVASION AND CANNING'S REPLY
IN PARLIAMENT

" And I did pluck allegiance from men's hearts,
Loud shouts and salutations from their mouths,
Even in the presence of the crownèd King."
"HENRY IV."

On the 6th April the French forces crossed the Bidassoa,
and war began.   On the 14th, Canning came to the Bar of the
House of Commons with his papers in his hand—papers which,
together with his speech, revealed the whole course of the
negotiations.   His speech did little more than repeat the
arguments of his state papers.   But it made a great sensation
that a minister should say the same thing in public as in private,
and that the 31st March despatch should be published only five
days after it had been communicated.   Canning's dissection
of Chateaubriand's contention that his policy was '*toute
Européenne et toute française*,'[2] was merciless in its logic, for
it revealed that not only was it exclusively French, but that
French action had dissolved the European Areopagus.   He
denounced the doctrine of the French King's speech, saying
that "no member of the House thought of it with more disgust
and abhorrence than he did," and that "not a day nor an hour
was lost in protesting against it."   He alluded to himself
jestingly 'as a Liberal, yea, a Radical Minister,' but recommended the Opposition not to call European sovereigns
'wretches' and 'barbarians,' not to think of war as a light
thing, as it might be in the mouth of "an irresponsible writer
—with the safety of a country on his lips and none of the
responsibility on his shoulders."   Then, varying an expression

[1] *F.O. Austria*, 120/56. Wellesley to Canning, May 5/23.
[2] Marcellus, at any rate, did not believe in it. He wrote privately to
Chateaubriand that he used the phrase, '*pour contenter les fantasques*';
Marcellus, *Politique de la Restauration*, [1853], p. 76.

in one of his despatches, he said : " The country which menaces war ought always to be ready to carry these menaces into execution." He made no such menace, but said England had decided for a neutrality, and for an honest neutrality. " Indifference we can never feel towards the affairs of Spain : and I earnestly hope and trust that she may come *triumphantly* out of the struggle." [1]

It was the last phrase of this speech which astounded the diplomats of Europe. Brougham welcomed the new minister as uttering sentiments " which did him the highest honour, which will surprise and delight the country, and which will crown him with the ardent applause of the country : most heartily do I and all my friends pray for the success of the Spanish people in this war. . . . The Spaniards are to be punished because they wish to be free. I hope in God, however, they will succeed against their enemies. . . . Should the war end (as I sincerely hope it may) in the discomfiture of the Bourbons . . . they will perish amidst the delight of every man in Europe." When Canning spoke again on the 30th in a more moderate tone, saying " so long as it is honourable to remain pacific it is rash to become belligerent," Brougham went even further in his praise of Canning for denouncing the ' atrocious aggression of France.'

These tributes and these exaggerations were an embarrassment to Canning, for they seemed to suggest a connection between his diplomacy and the extravagance of Brougham.

The Ministry secured a great triumph, for on the 30th April, by a majority of 372 to 20, the Commons approved the policy of neutrality. " I wish," wrote Canning to his friend Bagot, " you could have seen the *ultrageous* faces—ultra in either extreme—the first time I met them after the 30th April." Canning saw the ' ultrageous face ' of Marcellus at the Opera on the 4th May. The latter reported Canning as saying : [2] " The Ministry owes to him [Canning] its preservation and its triumph by means of the system he had adopted for three months [*i.e.* since the news of the French King's speech on the 30th January], and into which he has brought Lord Liverpool. He has decided the crisis in favour of the Ministry and has

---

[1] Italics my own.
[2] *A.A.E.*, 616. Marcellus to Chateaubriand, May 4/23.

since then brought round to his opinions the most dissentient colleagues as Peel, Harrowby, etc." All his colleagues, however, did not approve, nor did the King. On the 7th May, George IV. told Esterházy, the Austrian Ambassador, that he was very angry with Canning's speech, that Wellington agreed with him, and that he had written a letter to Canning reproving him. At the next levée Canning appeared and said : " I have to express to your Majesty all my thanks for the letter you have done me the favour to address me." George owned he was a little startled at the thanks, but recommended him in future to keep strictly to the matter in hand. Esterházy seized the opportunity to present to the King a letter (of course without Canning's knowledge) from the Emperor Francis, congratulating George on ' his noble sentiments.' Lieven, the Russian Ambassador, now entered the room. George repeated his previous sentiments, and instructed both to tell their masters that " his own [' ultrageous '] sentiments remained unchangeable." [1] Wellington, in more prudent language, announced his regret for Canning's speeches, and said he thought that he had improved. The Duke expressed his delight that the French Army had shown good discipline and *moral*. Other ministers— even, it was claimed, a majority—were less prudent and wished success to the French arms.[2]

But whatever his colleagues or foreign statesmen might think or say, a new man, wielding a new power, had arisen to trouble the placid waters of conventional diplomacy. Metternich said he did not know why Canning had spoken as he did unless he wished to win the votes of revolutionaries. Canning appeared to desire to " acquire a sort of popularity that I continually regard as a pretension that is misplaced in a statesman " (an illuminating phrase !). When Wellington's brother, Sir Henry Wellesley, reported a similar utterance from Vienna, Canning answered him directly " that no set of ministers could expect to remain at the head of affairs if they did not take care that their language in Parliament accorded, in some degree at least, with the feelings of the people," and that any other attitude " might very possibly have led to a change of government," and he said Metternich himself always spoke of " a

[1] *V.S.A.*, Berichte aus England. Esterházy to Metternich, May 7/23.
[2] *V.S.A.*, Berichte aus England, Mar. 17/23. Esterházy to Metternich.

change of [British] Ministers as the greatest misfortune which could befall Europe." The strength of the position of ministers depended not only on the language which they used but on "the firm belief of the nation that that language was sincere . . . it was the confidence in our *real* feeling of all that we expressed that satisfied the country." In future, at any rate, there was to be no difference between the language in the Cabinet and the language in Parliament.[1] Canning's letter got to Metternich, who remained unconvinced. He knew of the resentment of the King, of Wellington and others of the Cabinet, and Sir Henry Wellesley had already told him that Canning did not mean what he said. He concluded, therefore, that Canning was merely using words to frighten France, which Castlereagh, ' his noble predecessor,' would never have done. It was distressing, indeed, that Liverpool had used language in the Lords as strong as that of Canning in the Commons, but the King and the majority of the Cabinet were men who possessed the sensible (*saine*) view. The attempt therefore must be made to set the ' *ministres bien pensants* ' against Canning. With this object Metternich addressed various despatches, which were to be read confidentially to Wellington and the King, but to be withheld from Canning. Private letters also passed between the Duke and the Austrian Chancellor. Here began a discreditable intrigue against the Foreign Minister, which was after eighteen months to founder on the rock of his popularity.

It would have been better if Metternich had followed the advice of Marcellus, who judged the situation with remarkable insight. Even in April he wrote to Chateaubriand that neither the opposition of King nor Cabinet could overthrow Canning. " Do not hope for it. . . . When the ship which was to transport Canning far from the political scene waited on the shore, I saw him vanquish the King, the Ministers, and the aristocracy and seat himself at the helm of State." In his last despatches before leaving England in July, Marcellus said that Canning was ' dangerous ' . . . " *Il nous faut la chute, ou son changement.*" He must be turned out, or his views must be altered. " He will not fall. His chief enemy in the

---

[1] Stap., *G.C. & T.*, 372–3, 378–9. Canning to Sir H. Wellesley, Aug. 27, Sept. 16/23. He was told to communicate the substance of this to Metternich.

Cabinet, the Chancellor [Eldon], egoistical, leader of a vanishing influence, had been unable to exile him to the throne of the Indies. Mr Peel, young, firm, and patient, advances slowly but fearlessly towards the position of Prime Minister. I know that Mr Canning does not enjoy enough reputation to aspire to that position. The Duke of Wellington, *guerrier peu redoutable sur le champs de l'intrigue*, has had to yield to the popularity and the talents of Mr Canning. Lords Harrowby and Westmoreland are weak opponents. Supported on Lord Liverpool, whose mind he has entirely captivated, Canning will not fall." His views therefore must be changed. He must be made a good European. How was this to be done? " Flatter him, assemble a congress, make him familiar with friendly discussions, he is without honour and a born plebeian, let Europe load him with gifts and favours, as so many ties attaching him to her." [1]

To do Metternich justice, he would have preferred intrigue or cajolery to remonstrance. So far he agreed with Marcellus. He differed from him in thinking that Canning could be turned out. But his hand, as so often, was forced by Russia. Bagot, our Ambassador at St Petersburg, had already told Canning that remonstrance was coming, and suggested in a private letter that he could either " lay the official complaint on the table at the Cabinet *or place it in the little room adjoining*." As a Russian remonstrance over Canning's speeches was on its way, the Austrian, Esterházy, was told to support it. At the end of July he drew particular attention to the wishes expressed by Canning for the triumph of Spain. Canning replied that, as Spain was attacked, he wished to preserve her independence. " If, in a similar position, I express such wishes it will not be for those whom we regard as the aggressors." As Minister of England he was bound to do this, for external interference was not always justifiable, as it had been at Naples. If Spain had been left alone, " the anarchy, to which this unfortunate country was a prey, would have infallibly provoked a crisis, which would have re-established order in a more stable manner than would be the case with foreign influence. This necessarily left behind it the germ of future troubles." He

---

[1] *A.A.E.*, 617. Marcellus to Chateaubriand, Apr. 19, July 11, 18. Polignac, who knew England well, endorsed these ideas on July 22.

added that he did not think the (Neo-Holy) Alliance support
of France was calculated to serve their principles.[1]

5. THE FRENCH OUTWIT METTERNICH (MARCH–MAY 1823)

Canning's last suggestion was a truth which the Allies had
already been finding out to their cost. On the 29th March,
when war between France and England seemed possible,
Alexander had offered to support the former by arms, and
massed an army in West Russia for the purpose. On the 4th
April, Metternich offered to concentrate Austrian forces in
Italy to aid France if necessary.[2] But Villèle and Chateaubriand had already received Canning's assurance of neutrality,
and they therefore found these offers not only unwelcome but
embarrassing. The Neo-Holy Allies now proceeded to demand
that Ambassadors' Conferences should be held at Paris to
express the moral solidarity of the Alliance (apart from
England), or, in less urbane language, in order to enable the
Neo-Holy Alliance to control French action in Spain. To
this Villèle was thoroughly opposed. But, despite himself,
he had to consent to a series of reunions, beginning on the
22nd April, which sought to tie up the action of France, and
to prevent her from acting independently of the Neo-Holy
Alliance.

With characteristic astuteness Villèle succeeded in out-
witting his Allies. His policy was, as already indicated, to
revise the Spanish Constitution in the French sense and to
prevent the concentration of any Allied armies near France.
The Neo-Holy Allies, at least, wished to abolish the Spanish
Constitution, and two wished to bring in a Russian force.
But events went too fast for them. Angoulême and his troops
moved forward in what proved to be a military promenade.
The Revolutionists might be supreme at Madrid or at Cadiz,
but in the provinces the priests and their parishioners were all
for absolutism. Napoleon, when he came as the Apostle of

---

[1] V.S.A., Berichte aus England, Bd. 220. Esterházy to Metternich,
July 27/23; Lieven was instructed to remonstrate both with Liverpool
and Canning on June 26, and reported on Aug. 7 that they denied all
offence. Martens, xv. 308. His report can hardly be correct.

[2] For Alexander's despatch, v. Chateaubriand, Œuvres (1912), xii.
236–8, and Martens, xv. 17–8; for Metternich's, v. V.S.A., Weisungen nach
Paris, Apr. 4/23, to Vincent.

Enlightenment, had been received everywhere with black looks or with bullets. Angoulême, surrounded by priests and with ' the spirit of St Louis hovering over his banners,' entered town after town welcomed by maidens with flowers and by men with beribboned guitars, surrounded by crowds shouting " Death to the Constitution! Death to Jews and Jacobins! " While he was being entertained by the civic authorities with dinners and with bull-fights, a few fusillades took place in the distance, in the ' wings ' as it were, which only served to enhance the unreal and theatrical character of the proceedings.[1] On the 24th May he entered Madrid ' according to programme,' and without any serious fighting. The next day he issued a proclamation appointing a regency, consisting of Spanish notables, who were of course in reality the nominees of France.   He had gained less than he thought, for even these nominees, like all Spaniards of the period, proved very intractable to any foreign influence.

None the less Villèle had ingeniously defeated Metternich. The latter's view of the situation was that no modifications ought to be made in the constitution at all, for to tinker with the Constitution of 1812 was to touch an unhallowed instrument of democracy.   In order to prevent any such design, he had put forward the clever scheme of making Ferdinand of Naples Regent until Ferdinand of Spain was set at liberty. He thought France would find this proposal hard to resist, since Ferdinand of Naples was a Bourbon.   Moreover, as Naples was occupied by Austrian troops and Ferdinand was under Metternich's eye at Vienna, he could be trusted to destroy the Constitution of 1812 in Spain, as he had already destroyed it at Naples.   But Angoulême's Madrid proclamation of a Spanish Regency blew the Naples Regency scheme into thin air.   Metternich was much annoyed.   He succeeded in getting the Naples Regency discussed at three successive reunions at Paris, but he could not get Villèle to accept the project.

[1] The only area where there was serious resistance was in Catalonia, where General Mina held out.   But this did not affect the advance on Madrid.

6. The French Advance and the Fall of Cadiz
(30th September 1823)

" The profession of kindness with that sword in his hand, and that de-mand of surrender, is one of the most provoking acts of his hostility."—Burke.

As the French advanced, the Spanish Constitutionalists prudently retired to Seville. There on the 11th June, after scenes of much violence, they decided to withdraw to Cadiz, and requested the King to accompany them. Ferdinand answered that ' they might as well put a pistol to his head,' and suggested that yellow fever made Cadiz unsuitable as a residence. The ministers answered by declaring him incapable of ruling and by appointing a Spanish Constitutionalist Regency. This was the third Spanish Regency now in existence. In 1822 there had been formed an ultra-Loyalist Regency at Urgel, which France had refused to recognise. Angoulême had just formed a new Spanish Regency at Madrid. Each refused to recognise the other. Now there was a third one at Cadiz. There were thus three kings, or regencies, of Brentford.[1] Canning, in responding to a note from the Spanish (Angoulême) Regency, informed them that he had already received communications from two Regencies (the Urgel and the Spanish Constitutionalist). He could not recognise any regency, but out of politeness had acknowledged their letter, which he had not done in the two other cases. He published the correspondence at once. The comfort was cold ; there is a good deal of difference between acknowledging a letter and acknowledging a government.

7. Canning's Instructions to À Court
(June–December 1823)

Sir William À Court, acting under instructions which had anticipated the possibility of Ferdinand being put under restraint, followed the King to Seville. But he declined to accompany him to Cadiz, as he was ' in manifest duress ' and thus no longer in effect king. Canning approved this action at the end of June, but instructed him that, if the King

[1] Four, if we count Metternich's scheme for a Naples Regency, which never materialised.

were personally in danger, he should proceed to Gibraltar,
which he ultimately did.[1] Canning had no intention of co-
operating either with the Neo-Holy Alliance or with France.
On the 19th August, Villèle suggested that there would be
a separation between France and the Neo-Holies over the
question of Spain, and that he desired 'the intervention and
support of Great Britain.' Canning coldly replied: "After our
counsels offered to and rejected by both belligerents, until it
is demanded by both we shall abstain from all uncalled-for
interference unless our direct interests, faith, or honour are
affected."[2] There was a clear hint here that France had not
given definite pledges as to terminating her military occupation of Spain or as to waiving all claim to restore the Spanish
King to his dominions in America. It was obvious that
on the fall of Cadiz, which could hardly be long deferred,
these grave questions would come up for decision, and on that
decision would depend the future British attitude to France.
If there had not been war about the French invasion of Spain,
there might be war over a prolonged occupation, and there was
certain to be war if a French force landed in Spanish America.

When the Constitutionalists were being bombarded by
French guns at Cadiz they naturally bethought themselves of
English aid. They petitioned Sir William À Court for British
mediation between them and King Ferdinand and Angoulême.
À Court made overtures to Angoulême, who declined the offer.
The Spaniards also asked À Court to guarantee their constitution, a request which he promptly refused. In approving
that decision Canning seized the opportunity not only to state
the British doctrine of guarantee, but incidentally to show
what dangers lay in the disregard of this doctrine by the
Neo-Holy Alliance and by France.[3] The despatch is equally
admirable whether we regard the masterly logic of the
argument, which has made it a classic, or the immediate

---

[1] Canning subsequently (Sept. 15) instructed À Court not to shut
himself up in a blockaded place. This question of blockaded diplomats
has since attracted much attention, especially during the siege of Paris in
1870-1. Sir E. Satow, *Diplomatic Practice* (1922), i. 350-1, quotes this
despatch in full and adds the encomium: "Could the question be more
clearly stated if 'Paris' were substituted for Cadiz?" It earned the
later approval of Bismarck over the question of the Paris blockade in 1870.
[2] *F.O. France*, 146/56. Canning to Sir C. Stuart, Aug. 19/23, No. 67.
[3] The text of this most important despatch is in App. II. (a).

warning which it conveyed to France and to the Neo-Holy Allies.

The sequel was to show that Canning was right.   He had, as yet, won victories only of logic and reason, and these prevail but slowly over the passions of men.   But Angoulême had won a victory of fact.   For on the 30th September Cadiz surrendered, and next day the French entered the town and released Ferdinand from his imprisonment.   They little knew what was to come.   Canning had taken his decision.   He would have neither part nor lot in settling or arranging the restoration of the rule of Ferdinand.   England's counsels had been disregarded both by Ferdinand and by France.   So England would stand aside and throw all the responsibility upon them.

" Vous l'avez voulu, Georges Dandin," Canning said, with reference to Angoulême, when war began.   And he thought that the result of his wishes would be satisfactory to nobody. Now he watched from afar, with silent contempt, the generous but ineffectual efforts of Angoulême to protect the hapless victims of Ferdinand.   Canning defined his policy before the end of the year in no uncertain terms.   " The time may come when His Catholic Majesty himself, grown weary of the agitations and the animosities with which he is surrounded, and of the perpetual transfer of the offices of state from one incompetent minister to another, may select some individual, worthy of his confidence, and capable of giving stability to his counsels.   With an administration so formed it will be the duty of the British Minister to cultivate the most intimate and confidential relations, and to employ the influence of his Government for the only purpose to which it can be properly applied—the recommendation of a moderate and healing policy, and of such measures as may conduce to the happiness of Spain.   But while the present uncertainty and fluctuations of counsel prevail, you cannot too studiously avoid the appearance of advising or controlling, or of being the setter up or puller down of successive ministries." [1]   It will be noticed that he says nothing as to the fall of Constitutionalism. He had encouraged the Constitutionalists as long as he could, because they were opposing France.   But when Ferdinand

[1] *F.O. Spain*, 72/268, to À Court, Dec. 29/23.

was restored, it was not England's business to advise him to retain the constitution.

8. France, the Neo-Holy Alliance, and the Spanish Terror (October 1823–1825)

> " The best of the sight is, all allow,
> . . . At the very scaffold's foot, I trow."
> BROWNING.

It might have been thought that Angoulême, who had restored Ferdinand to his throne, would have had some claim upon his gratitude. But Ferdinand acted up to his well-earned reputation, showing ' the head of a mule ' towards his ally, and the ' heart of a tiger ' towards his subjects. Angoulême had not only pressed an amnesty upon him, but his letters of the 4th and 7th September had given some hints as to granting representative institutions on the French model. Ferdinand took no notice of either suggestion.[1] Under pressure from his subjects he had signed a general amnesty on the 30th September ; he revoked it the next day as soon as he was free. He appointed his confessor as universal minister ; he announced his intention publicly of offering to God ' holocausts of piety.' He incited irregular bands to plunder and to murder the ordinary Constitution-alists ; he employed more regular agents to imprison, to hang, and to shoot the more eminent. Angoulême saw that his dignity would be compromised by remaining, and departed before the end of October, leaving a strong French garrison behind him. Just as he left, Pozzo di Borgo arrived from Paris, hoping to influence Ferdinand on the side of mercy. His efforts were equally fruitless. The massacres and executions of lesser victims went on unchecked, and on the 7th November it was the turn of the arch-Constitutionalist, Riego.

This defeated champion of Constitutionalism had already experienced all the vicissitudes of fortune. He had once before been a fugitive with a few followers ; he had twice been arrested and twice restored to his admirers in Madrid. He

---

[1] It must have added to Angoulême's humiliation that at the Conference of Ambassadors at Paris the Neo-Holy representatives forced Chateaubriand to repudiate all idea of a Spanish Constitution (Sept. 18), v. my article, *A.H.R.*, Oct. 1924, pp. 21–2.

had not often shown prudence, not always even courage, but he received the news of his sentence with stoical firmness, and went to die like a valiant man of Spain. He passed on his last journey before the same crowd, which, two years before, had deafened him with their *vivas* and received him more royally than a king. A priest, bearing a cross, preceded a clay-cart dragged by an ass. In it sat the pale victim, stripped of his uniform, clad in a white shirt, bonneted with a green cap, crowned in mockery with oak leaves. The body hung on a gallows fifty feet high, and, as it was cut down, a wretch dashed his fist in the dead man's face. Even the crowd, hitherto silent, murmured then. The body was divided into five parts, and sent to be publicly exposed in the five towns where he had been best known.[1] Six days later Ferdinand made his public entry into Madrid and was received with raptures of applause. 'The holocausts of piety' were only beginning.

To do him justice, Pozzo di Borgo was horrified at these atrocities. He protested violently, he overturned one or two ministers, but despaired of further success and hastily returned to Paris. He then started an extraordinary experiment, endeavouring to coerce Spain by, an Allied Conference of Ambassadors at Paris, of which he was the head, and by a similar subordinate organisation at Madrid.[2] This attempt was quite in accordance with the Neo-Holy Alliance doctrine of general or forcible intervention in the internal affairs of disturbed States. It went on even until 1826. But it was resisted covertly by France and openly by Spain.

Ferdinand was no more inclined to bow his stiff neck to the Neo-Holy Alliance than to France. He was induced with great difficulty to summon a Congress on Spanish-American affairs, and his method of doing so practically ensured its failure. He rejected with contempt, first the French scheme of planting Bourbon princes in Spanish America, and next any idea of granting any of them independence, and to these views he steadily adhered. During the whole of 1824 he received much good advice from the Conferences of

---

[1] Riego's wife and children found refuge in England, where a subscription was raised for them.

[2] For details, *v.* my article in *A.H.R.*, Oct. 1924, *passim.*

Ambassadors at Paris and at Madrid.   They counselled him to
govern well, to pay his debts, to organise his government,
to stop shooting his subjects, and to grant an amnesty.   He
refused every demand except the last.   And when his amnesty
appeared (20th May 1824) it was found to contain so many
exceptions that his ferocious courts-martial were able to
proceed almost unchecked in their savagery for another
twelve months.   The Allied Ambassadors at Paris made a
great effort in July 1824 and succeeded in appointing Zea,
a moderate, as the Prime Minister of Ferdinand.   But he was
surrounded by so many ultras and reactionaries, he found the
state of inefficiency so appalling and his master so obstinate,
that he effected little.   The comments of the Allies were
biting.   Villèle said ' there was no sense in the men of Spain,'
and Metternich agreed with him ; Pozzo di Borgo said Spain
was subject to ' a royal anarchy,' and denounced the ' ignorance
and imbecility of his ministers.'   Ferdinand returned the
compliments of his Allies with interest, and in October 1825
dismissed their nominee Zea.   He followed up this measure
by a proclamation which intimated that this step had been
taken because Zea had been agreeable to the Allies, and that,
henceforth, Spain would submit to no interference in her
internal affairs.   The British Minister said of it : " There is
one unmixed good.   It is a Spanish measure decided upon and
carried into effect without the advice or convenience of any
Foreign   Power   whatever." [1]   Though   the   French   troops
continued in Spain till 1827, it was, in fact, the end of
effective interference either by France or by the Neo-Holy
Alliance.

This event of 1825 is a far cry from those of 1823.   Yet the
connection is evident.   France had attempted to control
Spain by garrisoning her country, and by obtaining a position
from which to give authoritative advice.   She had been
hindered partly by the interference of the Neo-Holy Alliance,
partly by the inconceivable inefficiency of her government,
and most of all by the immovable obstinacy of Ferdinand.

---

[1] *F.O. Spain*, 185/102.   Lamb to Canning, Oct. 29/25.

9. CANNING'S ATTITUDE TO SPANISH AMERICA
(OCTOBER 1823)

In the autumn of 1823, however, these effects could not be foreseen. Ferdinand, at any rate, was deeply angered with England, which had sent him only good advice—a commodity he never appreciated—and had tried to prevent France from coming to his aid. There was, in Canning's view, the obvious danger that the Family Compact might induce France and Spain to unite to oppose English interests and influence in Europe. That result he had failed to prevent, and England's prestige had suffered accordingly. In his despatch of 31st March, Canning had intimated that he was not only concerned with Spain in Europe. If he had failed to prevent a French invasion of Old Spain, that was no reason why he should permit their interference in the Spain that was over the water. If the barrier of the Pyrenees could not be defended by a British army, the gates of the Atlantic could be held by a British fleet. If France could humble Spain on the land, England could humble France on the sea. So on the 3rd October, even before he knew that Cadiz had fallen, Canning summoned Polignac to a conference and asked him his intentions with regard to Spanish America.

PART III

NEW WORLDS FOR OLD

CHAPTER V
THE POLIGNAC CONFERENCE AND THE
MONROE DOCTRINE

CHAPTER VI
CALLING THE NEW WORLD INTO EXISTENCE

CHAPTER VII
THE LATER AMERICAN POLICY

CHAPTER V

THE POLIGNAC CONFERENCE AND THE MONROE DOCTRINE

I. THE POSITION IN SPANISH AMERICA IN 1823

" Every day convinces me more and more, that in the present state of the World, in the present state of the [Spanish] Peninsula, and in the present state of the country, the American questions are out of all proportion more important to us than the European, and that, if we do not seize and turn them to our advantage in time, we shall rue the loss of an opportunity never, never to be recovered."—CANNING to Wellington, 8th November 1822.

CANNING, with that imaginative insight which was so peculiarly his, had recognised the vast possibilities of Latin America in his first Ministry of half a generation back. He had induced the Portuguese Regent to retire from his native country to Brazil ; he had proclaimed Talavera as a victory for us because it had opened to us the commerce and the harbours of Spanish America. He had known that Castlereagh had forced all Powers to disavow aggressive designs on these Colonies at Aix-la-Chapelle in 1818. He feared now that these designs were reviving. The French project of planting Bourbon princes on the thrones of Mexico, Colombia, Peru, and Chile had long been known to everybody. And Castlereagh, in 1820, had addressed vigorous protests to France when he found she had secretly negotiated with Spain and with the Argentine Republic to establish the Bourbon Prince of Lucca as the ruler of Buenos Aires. It does not seem probable that, in this instance at least, force was actually contemplated by France. Canning saw that the question might be different in 1823, when she had already invaded the Old Spain, and he had evidence which, he thought, justified suspicion of French designs on the New. In any case, Canning had to win diplomatic prestige over Spanish America as a set-off to his diplomatic defeat in Europe.

The question of Spanish America had three aspects in 1823.

First there was the attitude of Russia, whose Czar was extending a long arm over the Pacific.   There was next the policy
to be pursued towards Spain herself, whose nerveless grasp
was relaxing on her old-time possessions, and who seemed to
be falling under the influence and arms of France.   There was
third the question of French designs in the West Indies and
Latin America.   The second or purely Spanish aspect was dealt
with by Canning alone from a purely British point of view.
In the matter of Russia and France, Canning attempted (and
unsuccessfully) to co-operate with the United States in a joint
policy.   Canning solved the French problem by the Polignac
Memorandum, Adams the Russian one by the Monroe
Doctrine.

2. THE RUSSIAN ASPECT

" *The indignant Tsar, when just about*
To issue a sublime ukase—
' *Whereas, all light must be kept out,*'
Dissolved to nothing in its blaze."

TOM MOORE.

Russia was at this time, through her possessions in Alaska,
an American Power, and Alexander was the foremost champion
of monarchy against revolution and of the Neo-Holy Alliance
against liberty.   That being so—the issue of a ukase dealing
with North-West America on the 28th September 1821 was
more alarming than it would have been in the case of a
sovereign of less power and less exalted pretensions.   It
followed, significantly enough, on the high-flying proclamations of Troppau and Laibach.   It forbade all except Russian
subjects to fish, trade, or navigate within a hundred Italian
miles of the west of the Behring Sea to the 51st degree of
latitude on the west of North America, and from the Behring
coast of Siberia to the 45th degree of latitude (*i.e.* to the cape
south of Urup Isle).   This ukase affected the rights of trade,
discovery, and occupation   both   of English and United
States subjects.[1]

Castlereagh received this ukase with displeasure, and made
a provisional protest in London at once, which he transmitted
to Petersburg at the beginning of 1822,[2] stating that England

[1] In *A.H.R.*, Oct. 1912, 309–45; Jan. 1913, 537–62, is much Russian
correspondence on this ukase, but there seems no clear explanation of it,
v. infra, pp. 491–3, and Webster, 452–3.
[2] *F.O. Russia*, 181/48. Castlereagh to Bagot, Jan. 19/22.

would not admit either the exclusive sovereignty or the
exclusive navigation of Russia in these waters or areas.
Lord Stowell—the greatest of international lawyers—condemned Russia's pretensions as ' very insupportable.'   Little
was done to clear the matter up at Verona, and, though both
the United States and England had shown signs of concerted
resistance, nothing had actually been settled by the autumn
of 1823.   Canning viewed the matter with some humour,
declaring that Alexander had proclaimed " as a *mare clausum*
an ocean four thousand miles across," and treating the whole
matter as ridiculous.   He had heard rumours of Alexander's
intermeddling farther south in the West Indies as well, but he
did not credit them.[1]   He was right.   Alexander was at this
time fully occupied with European Spain and with Turkey,
and, though he favoured armed intervention in Spanish America
in principle, he did nothing to put it into practice or to urge
it on his Allies in 1823.   Russia, Canning held, could be disregarded in this connection.   He said she could not act alone.
It was only in conjunction with France that she could threaten
Spanish America.

The view of the United States was not quite the same.
To them the proclamations of a despot were naturally an
object of suspicion.   And, when pressed by Adams, Tuyll, the
Russian Minister at Washington, replied by proclaiming the
most extravagant doctrines of absolutism.   The republican
blood of Adams was deeply stirred.   This Russian action,
though it hardly affected Canning at all, was to have a serious
influence upon the government of Washington.   For the
proclamation of absolutist principles by Russia necessitated
a rejoinder on the virtues of republicanism by Adams.   Russia,
however, had no influence on the Polignac Memorandum,
though she exercised a good deal upon the formation of the
Monroe Doctrine.   We may therefore leave this matter till
later in the chapter.

[1] *F.O. France,* 146/56. Canning to Stuart, July 23/23, secret and separate.
He had heard that Alexander was trying to induce President Boyer of
Haiti to cede the Isles des Vaches, but does not think it necessarily true.
Russian agents were also reported in Colombia. *Vide* notes to this
chapter, pp. 491–3.

3. THE ATTITUDE OF SPAIN

" Crowned above queens, a withered beldame now
Brooding on ancient fame."

KIPLING.

In 1822 the Spanish-American question demanded a speedy solution. Castlereagh had not only recognised the Spanish Colonial flags in June 1822, but in other ways had brought things so far that a British recognition of the independence of Colombia at last seemed imminent. The Colombians had captured Quito and a large number of Royalists in May, and Brazil revolted from Portugal in September. The island of Cuba presented another difficulty, for it was infested with pirates who preyed on British shipping. Spain refused all compensation to British mercantile owners, and proved totally unable to repress the piratical depredations. During the Congress of Verona, therefore, Canning took a decisive step. He considered the choice lay between recognition of some of the Spanish Colonies and " some vindication against Spain herself of the injuries we have suffered either from her hostility or from her helplessness." The third course—" continued acquiescence in such injuries without vindication and without redress "—could not be considered nor defended in Parliament.[1] Meanwhile fresh reports of piratical attacks arrived during the whole of November. So he decided to apply ' a local remedy ' by effectively policing the West Indies with a British squadron.

On the 1st December, Canning sent a despatch to Paris informing Villèle that a new British naval armament had been sent to the West Indies, and that they had orders, if the consent of the Spanish Governor was refused, to land in Cuba and attack the pirates in their hiding-places. They were also to demand redress from Spain for the various injuries. Canning ended by a solemn and, under the circumstances, very necessary disclaimer by England that, though she meant to land in Cuba, she had no aggressive designs.[2]

[1] *W.N.D.*, i. 468. Canning to Wellington, Oct. 29.
[2] *F.O. France*, 146/50, No. 14. Canning to Sir C. Stuart, Dec. 1/22. The instruction to the naval armament is of Nov. 23/22. Canning to Bathurst, *Hist. MSS. Commn.*, Bathurst papers, [1923], pp. 534–7. Canning's Cabinet Memo., Nov. 15/22, is in Stap., *Corr.*, i. 48–63.

This vigorous action brought Spain to her senses. Her Constitutional Government first offered to give England commercial advantages in Spanish America in return for support against France. Canning rejected this offer, but on the 7th January 1823 he suspended the operations against the pirates, as the Spaniards were in difficulties with France and now offered full compensation to England. Canning accepted the offer and negotiated a convention for the settlement of outstanding difficulties. He had drawn up a list of consuls for the chief towns in Spanish America in December 1822, and he now likewise suspended this measure with the view of giving the Constitutional Ministers in Spain as much moral support as possible, and as, in addition, they were negotiating with Buenos Aires on the basis of her independence. Further, any immediate recognition would destroy the chance of the restoration of monarchy in any Spanish colony. It was not till October 1823 that he took any further measures which could in any way affect Spain, and that was after the French had liberated Ferdinand, who had overthrown the Spanish Constitution and might be threatening Spanish America. On the 10th October he took two important steps. He actually accredited consuls to the chief towns of Spanish America ; and he despatched Special Commissions of Inquiry to Colombia and to Mexico to report on the question of their recognition by Great Britain.[1] The step of accrediting consuls was intended to be a purely commercial measure, without political significance, but the despatch of Commissions of Inquiry indicated that England was seeking for information in order to decide on the question of recognition. These steps showed that British policy towards Spain and her Colonies was considered by Canning to be a question which she was not going to submit to a congress, with its possibilities of intervention or of menace. It did not seem impossible that Russia might combine her efforts with France to trouble the lands, as well as the waters, of the New World. The United States feared the Czar, England the French Bourbon, so the elements of unity were at hand.

[1] The instructions to Mexico were drawn in July, but Canning apparently heard of the fall of Cadiz on Oct. 10, and then altered them.

4. French Designs on Spanish America (1822–3)

" That plan, which Monsieur made himself,
Soon downed all others to the shelf,
And was received by acclamation
As truly worthy the Grande Nation."
                                                    Tom Moore.

Canning had inserted in his despatch of the 1st December
1822 to Stuart the following, very solemn, disavowal of aggressive designs on the part of Great Britain. " His Majesty
would deem it both dishonourable and unjust to take
advantage of the present difficulties of Spain to appropriate to
Himself any part of Spanish America, and the King would
feel, that He did wrong to any Government, to which He did
not give full credit for being actuated by similar principles."
This communication was plainly meant to reassure France,
and doubtless intended to produce a similar disclaimer from
her. Villèle received this communication on the 9th of
December and pronounced it as ' very important.' On the
10th he had an interview with Wellington (then on his way
back from Verona), and expressed much annoyance about
British action in Cuba, saying : " France could not submit to
an extension of our [commercial] advantages and our territory
[in Spanish America]." Wellington had already disclaimed
territorial designs on our part, and he now denied that we
claimed ' any exclusive commercial advantage.' Villèle
had already made the ominous statement : " If the Spanish
Government wished to send an Infant to Mexico or Peru,
or to any port of Spanish America, attended by troops, with
a view to make an endeavour to renew the connection between
those Colonies and Spain, the expedition now fitting in the
ports of France should be at the orders of the Spanish Government to convey the Infant and the troops wherever they
pleased." [1] On the 14th December the *Journal des Débats*,
an organ in touch with Villèle, emphasised the project of
planting Bourbon princes in Mexico and Peru, and added
that French naval support had been promised. The French
despatch to Spain of the 26th December 1822 promised ' aid

---

[1] *W.N.D.*, i. 639. Wellington to Canning, Dec. 10; Canning to
Wellington, Dec. 13/22, p. 650. *Vide* my article, *E.H.R.*, Jan. 1925.

of all kinds ' to Spain, and, on the 11th March 1823, Chateaubriand explained to the Austrian Ambassador that this meant
French naval support and money to Spain " pour conserver
une partie des Colonies qui n'étaient pas entièrement detachées
de la métropole." [1] It is pretty clear that Monsieur, Polignac,
and the extreme Ultras went further than this.

Naval support given and money lent to Spanish expeditions
against the revolted Colonies seem to imply the use of some
force or menace by France. Villèle elaborated the scheme
still further to Angoulême in July, plotting out the principalities, and suggesting ' a few troops ' as well as ships.[2] The
prudent prince replied by the suggestion that it was better to
wait till the Spanish King was at liberty before proceeding
with the design. This was wise, because both King and
Infantas were at that moment imprisoned in Cadiz. It was
subsequently found out that each Infanta objected to the other
obtaining a throne in America, " the King [Ferdinand] extending, as I am assured, the same amiable feeling to both His
Brothers." [3] Villèle pursued the subject with Angoulême,
stating (18th July 1823) that all France would support the
use of the French Marine for this purpose in Peru, in Chile,
and in Mexico, but that the matter could wait till the more
pressing problems of Old Spain were settled. Obviously
nothing could be settled until Cadiz fell, and it did not fall
soon enough. For on the 1st October Canning summoned
Polignac to give him explanations as to French intentions
in Spanish America. Cadiz actually fell on the 30th September, but the news did not reach England until the 10th
October, one day after the explanations had been satisfactorily concluded.

Canning had now made up his mind " that France meditates
and has all along meditated a direct interference in Spanish
America." [4] In his instructions to the Commissioners of
Colombia and Mexico he stated that, though England was not
unfavourable to the establishment of monarchy or the Spanish

---

[1] V.S.A., Berichte aus Frankreich, Bd. 351. Mar. 11/23, No. 85A.
Vincent to Metternich. Probably Mexico at least, as well as Cuba, is
indicated.
[2] Villèle, Mémoires, [1904], iv. 200–1, to Angoulême, July 5/23.
[3] F.O. Spain, 185/102. Lamb to Canning, June 9/25.
[4] W.N.D., ii. 137, to Wellington, Sept. 24/23.

Infantas in the New World, the Commissioners were not to suggest the idea, though they were to encourage it if proposed to them. They were, however, to insist that any " negotiation for a Spanish Prince is to be carried on with Spain alone, and that no foreign [*i.e.* French] force should be employed to conduct the Spanish Prince to Mexico." It was added that the French designs on America were ' notorious to all the world.' [1]

5. CANNING'S INTERVIEW WITH RUSH
(AUGUST–SEPTEMBER)

" *In August* 1823 *Mr Rush* ' said that, IF WE WOULD PLACE OURSELVES ON THE SAME LINE *with the* UNITED STATES *by acknowledging the* S[outh] A[*merican*] *States, he would say, swear, sign, anything* SUB SPIRITU.' "— CANNING to Bagot, 9th January 1824.

Before the Polignac Conference opened, Canning had had several highly important interviews with Rush, the American Minister in London. The first was on the 16th August, on a matter unconnected with Spanish America. It was only incidentally that this question was discussed, and it was introduced, not by Canning, but by Rush. It seems difficult, however, to suppose that Canning had not already contemplated some such step, for within four days he submitted privately to him a most important proposal.

His letter, dated the 20th August, was as follows :—

" Is not the moment come when our governments might understand each other as to the Spanish-American Colonies ? And if we can arrive at such an understanding, would it not be expedient for ourselves and beneficial for all the world that the principles of it should be clearly settled and plainly avowed ?

" 1. For ourselves we have no disguise. We conceive the recovery of the Colonies by Spain to be hopeless.

" 2. We conceive the question of the recognition of them as independent states to be one of time and circumstances.

---

[1] To Hervey (Mexico), Oct. 10/23, enclosed in *F.O. Spain*, 185/95. Canning to À Court, Jan. 31/24 ; and *F.O. Colombia*, 135/1, to Hamilton, Oct. 10/23.

" 3. We are, however, by no means disposed to throw any impediment in the way of an arrangement between them and the mother country by amicable negotiation.

" 4. We aim not at the possession of any portion of them ourselves.

" 5. We could not see any portion of them transferred to any other Power with indifference.

" If these opinions and feelings are, as I firmly believe them to be, common to your government with ours, why should we hesitate mutually to confide them to each other, and to declare them in the face of the world ?

" If there be any European Power which cherishes other projects which look to a forcible enterprise for reducing the Colonies to subjugation on the behalf or in the name of Spain, or which meditates the acquisition of any part of them to itself by cession or by conquest, such a declaration on the part of your government and ours would be at once the most effectual and the least offensive mode of intimating our joint disapprobation of such projects.   It would at the same time put an end to all the jealousies of Spain with respect to her remaining Colonies, and to the agitation which prevails in those Colonies, an agitation which it would be but humane to allay, being determined (as we are) not to profit by encouraging it.

" Do you conceive that under the power which you have recently received you are authorised to enter into negotiation and to sign any convention upon this subject ?   Do you conceive, if that be not within your competence, you could exchange with me ministerial notes upon it ?

" Nothing could be more gratifying to me than to join with you in such a work, and I am persuaded there has seldom in the history of the world occurred an opportunity when so small an effort of two friendly governments might produce so unequivocal a good and prevent such extensive calamities."

This most important communication was one in which United States policy largely concurred with the British. On the 23rd August, Canning wrote again to Rush that he had " received notice that, so soon as the French military object in Spain was achieved (and he thought it would be very soon) a proposal will be made for a Congress—upon the affairs of Spanish America." At a dinner at Liverpool on the 25th August, Canning proposed the health of the American Minister, Mr Hughes, a friend and a man witty both with pen and tongue, who was on his way to Sweden. Canning paid the usual compliments to the Minister, and alluded to the two countries as united in their true interests " by a common language, a common spirit of commercial enterprise, and a common regard for well-regulated liberty." Dissensions had been forgotten, " the force of blood again prevails, and the daughter and the mother stand together against the world." [1] There can be no mistaking the importance of this utterance in the mouth of a diplomat speaking outside the walls of Parliament. He did not then know that the daughter and the mother, though they both were soon to stand against the world, were to stand against it in separation.

Rush was at first greatly impressed by Canning's earnestness, and he offered on the 28th, though without instructions, to make an explicit declaration " in the name of my Goverment, that it will not remain inactive under an attack upon the independence of these States by the Holy Alliance." [2] But he attached one condition to this declaration : that Canning should recognise the independence of the Spanish Colonies beforehand. Canning was not prepared for this, and his reply of 31st August betrayed coldness and disappointment. He always maintained that he had been ' sounding ' Rush, and the exploratory process did not seem satisfactory. Rush even thought that the overture had definitely ended.

But in September Canning raised the matter again and demanded an instant decision ; Rush, who could not receive instructions in time, offered on the 26th September to sign a joint declaration on his own authority, provided that England would recognise the independence of the Spanish-American Republics. All Canning could offer was a promise of ' future acknowledgment.' For the step itself Canning

[1] *Speeches*, vi. 413–4. Canning was pleased to find that Adams repeated to Addington "the phrase ' the mother and the daughter ' as one quite familiar to their vocabulary." Bagot, *G.C. & F.*, ii. 216.

[2] Rush to Adams, Aug. 28/23, quoted in *A.H.R.*, vii. 683.

was not prepared. He certainly could not have got the consent of either Cabinet or King in 1823, and he himself seems to have doubted of its wisdom at the moment.[1] Hence the negotiation failed, for Rush refused to sign. On the 10th October he reported suspiciously that Mr Canning had suddenly dropped the whole subject, and wondered why he had come ' to so full and sudden a pause with me.'

If we now consider the terms of Canning's letter to Rush of the 20th August we find that, as regards points 1 and 3, the United States agreed entirely with Canning : as regards points 4 and 5 Adams was at one with him in principle, though he did not wish absolutely to pledge the United States not to annex any part of the Spanish America, or, at least, not to incorporate such part as a member of the union. Such a pledge was ' substantial ' and might be ' inconvenient.' Even here, however, the difficulties were not insuperable. The real crux of the question lay in point 2. The United States had already recognised these Colonies, while Great Britain had not. And the two policies differed in this respect. Adams believed in ' the independence of nations ' (a sort of anticipation of the doctrine of self-determination). He believed also in the republican form of government and in the establishment and recognition of republics on the American Continent. Thus he was suspicious of Canning, and doubted if he believed in either ideal. " It is France," wrote Rush on the 10th October, " that must not be aggrandised, not South America that must be set free." And the suspicions thus entertained by Rush combined with Canning's demands for an immediate declaration to cause the failure of the negotiation.

---

[1] It can be proved that he deferred all thought of recognition at the end of 1822 and during nine months of 1823, because he wished to help the Spanish Constitutionalists (Stap., *Corr.*, i. 51. Memo., Nov. 15/22). It seems that in the autumn of 1823 he deferred recognition again (a) because he thought a monarchy might arise in Mexico and perhaps elsewhere, (b) because he had not given up hope of negotiating Spain into granting recognition.

6. The Polignac Conference and Memorandum
(3rd–9th October 1823)

" Sextus Pompeius
Hath given the dare to Cæsar, and commands
The Empire of the Sea."
" Antony and Cleopatra."

The reason Canning dropped the matter was a simple one. It was impossible now to prevent the European Powers from proposing a congress by the expedient of an Anglo-American declaration. So he decided to act by himself and to eliminate France from South America. If France was eliminated, Russia, he held, could not act alone. He foresaw at the beginning of October that Cadiz would fall, that Ferdinand would rise, and that France would triumph in Spain. So he summoned Polignac on the 3rd October to a conference which lasted over several days, and asked him his intentions as to Spanish America. The step was a strong one, but had been foreshadowed by his despatch of the 31st March (*v.* pp. 83–6).

What passed at these several conferences we do not know in detail, though the general result is clear. It appears that Polignac pressed the proposal of a Spanish-American Congress, and that Canning retaliated by hinting strong suspicions of French designs on Spanish America. The record of the Polignac Conference was drawn up by Canning. He sent it to Polignac, asked him to sign it, and proposed to circulate it to the diplomats of Europe. Polignac was astonished and dismayed. He made several alterations and many attempts to get out of it, but all of them in vain.

Canning held him to his bond, and Polignac was unable to deny his own words. The Polignac Memorandum was not circulated definitely to the European Cabinets until November. But its substance was certainly known to Austria and to Russia, as well as to France, by the third week of October. It was not circulated to Rush until the 13th December, though Canning communicated it to him by word of mouth on the 24th November. The importance of the Polignac Memorandum was therefore European, and it seems certain that it did not reach Washington in time to affect the President's message which proclaimed the Monroe Doctrine.

The principles laid down in the Polignac Memorandum (of which parts remained unpublished) were as follows :—

CANNING

1. Canning declared that England conceived " any attempt to bring Spanish America under its ancient submission to Spain, must be utterly hopeless." England would, however, facilitate negotiation if " founded upon a basis which appeared to them to be practicable. . . . But that the junction of any Foreign Power, in an enterprise of Spain against the Colonies, would be viewed by them as constituting an entirely new question, and one upon which they must take such decision as the Interests of Great Britain might require."

2. The British Government disclaimed any desire for exclusive territorial advantages and " any intention of forming any political connection with them (the Spanish Colonies), beyond that of Amity and Commercial Intercourse." England sought no exclusive preference with the Spanish Colonies, but wished to be on the most favoured nation basis ' equally with others' but ' after' the Mother Country, which was entitled to ' preference.' England considered the commercial and coast laws of Spain with regard to her Colonies as ' tacitly repealed.' Any attempt to renew the obsolete interdiction . . . " might be best cut short by a speedy and unqualified Recognition of the independence of the Spanish American States."

POLIGNAC

1. Polignac " declared that his Government believed it to be utterly hopeless to reduce Spanish America to the state of its former relation to Spain."

2. Polignac disclaimed " any intention or desire," on the part of France, " to appropriate to Herself any part of the Spanish Possessions in America, or to obtain for Herself any exclusive advantages."

He agreed with Canning's view as to commercial preference to the Mother Country, and equal commercial privileges for other nations.

3. Canning said that England regarded recognition as not dependent upon Spain, but upon time and circumstances.

But "it (England) would consider any Foreign (*i.e.* French) interference, by force or by menace, in the dispute between Spain and the Colonies, as a motive for recognising the latter, without delay."

(*N.B.*—Canning subsequently explained that the passage was worded thus to inform the European Powers that such instant recognition would not result from the mere assembling of a congress, "in which England might refuse to join, without any reference to the nature of the propositions entertained by it." *F.O. France*, 146/56. Canning to Stuart, 9th November 1823.)

Polignac said that "She (France) abjured, in any case, any design of acting against the Colonies by force of arms." ["Mr Canning having alluded to certain reports in the newspapers, of some attack, or intended attack, by a French Naval Force against the Independents in Colombia, the Prince de Polignac said that, so far from intending any hostile act, the French Government had recalled the only line of battleship in those seas, . . . which is on its return to France."]

4. Great Britain was not prepared to go into "a joint deliberation upon the subject of Spanish America upon an equal footing with other Powers, whose minds were less formed upon that question and whose interests were less implicated in the decision of it."

4. Polignac said France had no opinion as to an arrangement with the Colonies till the Spanish King was at liberty, when she would discuss the matter with her Allies, including England. "In observing upon what Mr Canning had said, with respect to the peculiar state of Great Britain, in reference to such a Conference [Concert][1] the Prince de Polignac declared that he saw no difficulty which should prevent England from taking part in the Conference [Congress][1] however she might now announce the difference in the view which she took of the question, from that taken by the

---

[1] These words were thus altered because Canning admitted that England might enter a conference (*i.e.* of subordinate ministers), but refused to accept the idea of a congress (*i.e.* of leading statesmen).

Allies. The refusal of England to co-operate in the work of reconciliation might afford reason to think, either that She did not really wish for that reconciliation, or that She had some ulterior object in contemplation; two suppositions equally injurious to the honour and good faith of the British Cabinet." . . .

Polignac then suggested that the revolted Colonies were ' distracted by Civil Wars,' had no government, and that recognition would be ' nothing less than a real sanction of anarchy.'

"Mr Canning, without entering into discussion on [these] abstract principles, contented himself with saying that—however desirable the establishment of a Monarchical form of Government, in any of those Provinces might be, [he saw great difficulties in the way of it, nor could his Government take upon itself to recommend it "].

The Prince de Polignac added, "that in the interest of humanity and especially in that of the Spanish Colonies, it would be worthy of the European Governments to concert together the means of calming, in those distant and scarcely civilised regions, passions blinded by party spirit; and . . . to bring back to a principle of Union in Government, whether Monarchical or Aristocratical, People among whom dangerous and absurd theories were now keeping up agitation and disunion."

["Mr Canning further remarked that he could not understand how an *European* Congress could discuss Spanish-American Affairs without calling to their Counsels a Power so eminently interested, as the United States of *America*, while Austria, Russia, and Prussia, Powers so much less concerned in the subject, were in consultation upon it."]

["The Prince de Polignac professed himself unprovided with any opinion of His Government upon what respected the United States of America, but did not *for himself* see any insuperable difficulty to such an association."[1]]

---

[1] The passages in square brackets are the suppressed parts of the Memorandum. The published version is in *B.F.S.P.*, xi. 49–53. The suppressed passages were printed, for the first time, by me in *Cambridge History of British Foreign Policy*, [1923], ·ii. 633–7. The only

The restoration of the suppressed passages of the Polignac Memorandum throw an entirely new light upon its meaning and purport. The main principles are three. First, England would recognise the Spanish Colonies if any attempt was made to restrict her existing trade with them. Secondly, France was definitely warned off from any interference ' by force or by menace,' and, under stress, definitely abjured any such attempt. Thirdly (and here is the revelation), Canning declined, on the ground of British interests, to enter upon joint deliberation on ' an equal footing ' with other European Powers, and said, in effect, that he would not do so unless the United States were invited to become a member.

7. Effects on Europe of the Polignac Memorandum

To take the question of France first, Canning's attitude produced immediate effects. Chateaubriand and Villèle hastened to reassure him that they had no hostile intentions, that their fleet was being laid up, and that the idea of erecting French or Spanish Bourbon princelets on the thrones of Spanish America had been definitely abandoned. Chateaubriand also promised not to interfere between Spain and Revolutionaries in Cuba. These protests were not wholly sincere. They revived the Bourbon prince project again and again till so late as 1825 ; they sent out troops secretly to the West Indies, and French naval squadrons to Brazil and Peru in 1824 and to Hayti in 1825, under circumstances which awakened suspicion. But the disavowal of armed projects, forced from them by the Polignac Memorandum, was not a pledge on which they could openly go back. On the 12th March 1824, Rush told Polignac that the publication of the Polignac Memorandum would reassure his country as to the designs of France.[1] About the same time Metternich wrote sadly that the Polignac Memorandum had rendered Canning ' master of the terrain,' that he had isolated France from the Neo-Holy Alliance, and that " his manœuvre was cleverer

important part omitted in the extracts given above is a long argument between Canning and Polignac as to whether Wellington at Verona had proposed to treat the Spanish-American question by the congress method. For an important interpretation of the Polignac Memorandum by Canning himself, v. Appendix III (b).

[1] A.A.E., 618. Polignac to Chateaubriand, Mar. 12/24.

than that of the French Ministers." He thought the negotiations connected with the Polignac Memorandum would, one day, 'form interesting materials for history.'[1] At the Ambassadors' Conference at Paris on the 21st March 1824, it was proposed by the other Powers that France should interfere by armed force in Spanish America, and Chateaubriand had to remind them that he could not do so because of his promise to Canning in the Polignac Memorandum.[2]

It appears therefore certain that the pledge thus given was of importance, and that, if it had not been obtained in October 1823, France would have been freer in her future action and more inclined to obey the counsels of her Allies.

Canning did not publish the Polignac Memorandum until March 1824, but it was known to European diplomats in October 1823. He emphasized the lesson by one of those public utterances which he was fond of making when he wished to impress the European diplomats with the power of English public opinion. Speaking at Plymouth on the 28th October 1823, he uttered words as remarkable for their literary beauty as significant for their political import. Though England had preserved the peace when France invaded Spain, she might not be able to do so when her special interests were more gravely compromised. " But . . . let it not be said that we cultivate peace, either because we fear, or because we are unprepared for, war. . . . Our present repose is no more a proof of inability to act, than the state of inertness and inactivity in which I have seen those mighty masses that float in the waters above your town, is a proof they are devoid of strength, and incapable of being fitted out for action. You well know how soon one of those stupendous masses, now reposing on their shadows in perfect stillness—how soon, upon any call of patriotism, or of necessity, it would assume the likeness of an animated thing, instinct with life and motion —how soon it would ruffle, as it were, its swelling plumage— how quickly it would collect all its beauty and its bravery, collect its scattered elements of strength, and awaken its dormant thunder. Such as is one of these magnificent

[1] *V.S.A.*, Weisungen nach Frankreich. Metternich to Vincent, Mar. 18/24.
[2] My article in *A.H.R.*, Oct. 1924, pp. 22-3, and later, p. 35, n. 17.

machines when springing from inaction into a display of its might—such is England herself : while apparently passive and motionless, she silently concentrates the power to be put forth on an adequate occasion."

The British public were profoundly impressed, though to them these words had but a general application. But the diplomats of Europe knew well that the ' adequate occasion ' for the use of England's sea power would be a French attack on Spanish America. What is surprising is that the public warning, which was thus given, did not prevent either the Neo-Holy Allies or France from raising the question again.

So much for the menace of French designs on Spanish America. The pressing question was now that of the congress, and Canning's suggestion, that the United States should be invited, excited great consternation. Chateaubriand strongly opposed it, putting forward the logical argument that the United States, having already recognised the Spanish Colonies, could not well be invited to a congress to discuss their future status. Neumann, the Austrian *chargé d'affaires* in London, wrote (7th November) : " It is impossible to express the astonishment of the diplomats." Metternich, adopting the airs and phrases of Alexander, declared that the United States were opposed " to the fundamental principles, forms of government, manners, doctrines, and civil and political regime of Europe." [1] The interest of the Neo-Holy Alliance in Spanish America was more elevated and less material than that of the United States. He hoped Canning was not serious, as Austria thought that the United States would never be able to take part in a European Congress.

In one sense, Metternich was right. Canning's proposed invitation to the United States was a mere expedient,[2] for

[1] *V.S.A.*, Weisungen nach Frankreich. Metternich to Vincent, Nov. 26/23.

[2] *W.N.D.*, ii. 137, where, in a letter to Wellington, he says the invitation to the U.S.A. is the " one way of avoiding it [the congress] altogether, or neutralising its efforts," and *F.O. France*, 146/57, where he tells Sir C. Stuart (Jan. 9/24) " If the United States had been invited, I have good reason to think they would have declined the invitation." Canning was right (*v. F.O. America*, 5/177). Addington to Canning (No. 25 of Dec. 1/23) reports Adams as saying that the United States would not join, unless the invitation ' were extended to the Spanish American Republics,' a condition to which none of the Allies would have consented.

he thought she would refuse to attend, but he hoped that the mere suggestion would stop discussions as to the Congress being held. Canning warned the Neo-Holy representatives, at an interview on the 24th November, that the presence of the United States would not be wholly desirable, but he also said that England's interest in the Spanish Colonies " were of a nature so delicate, so diversified and different from those of other Powers that they could *not* be submitted to any general deliberation." [1] But he intimated that he might invite France to try a joint mediation with England.[2] France dared not act apart from her Allies, so this suggestion failed of effect. But the Neo-Holies and France together were still urging the question of bringing England into the Congress, when they received a formidable message from over the water. On the 12th December Monroe's message was reported in an obscure form, on the 26th and 27th it went broadcast through all Europe.

8. THE FORMULATION OF THE MONROE DOCTRINE
(OCTOBER–DECEMBER 1823)

" He chose alone, yet turned the balance too,
So much the weight of one brave man can do !"
DRYDEN.

Stapleton goes so far as to say that what " passed between Mr Canning and Mr Rush mainly encouraged, if it did not originate to the Government of the United States, the idea of taking so firm and decisive a tone." [3] But this opinion does not take into account the personality and the character of the great State Secretary at Washington. Adams was a man of the greatest ability, a shrewd New Englander, forceful, resolute, prudent, well versed in law and in diplomacy, strong and hard as a rock. When Minister at Washington, Stratford Canning had struck fire from this flint ; his cousin was to do so more than once. Adams received the first news of these over-tures from Rush on the 9th October. President Monroe was so impressed with them that he sent copies to his two famous predecessors, Madison and Jefferson. Both were inclined to

[1] *V.S.A.*, Berichte aus England. Bd. 220. Neumann to Metternich, Nov. 30/23.
[2] *V.S.A.*, Berichte aus England. Bd. 220. Neumann to Metternich, Nov. 30, reporting Polignac's account of an interview with Planta.
[3] Stap., *P.L.*, ii. 39.

accept Canning's offer, and Monroe seemed favourable also. But the decision was not to lie with the two ex-Presidents, or with the existing one, but with Adams.

In one sense even Adams was greatly impressed with Canning's overture. It was the first proposal for a joint policy ever made on the British side since America had won her independence. It was therefore highly flattering to the United States to learn that Canning's " belief was founded upon the large share of the maritime power of the world which Great Britain and the United States shared between them, and the consequent influence which the knowledge that they held a common opinion upon a ' question ' on which such large maritime interests, present and future, could not fail to produce upon the rest of the world." [1] This tribute from the greatest naval Power in the world was one which any rising State would value.

Addington, the British Minister at Washington, commented on Adams' manner as " open and cordial, and exempt from harshness or haughtiness. In truth, ever since the receipt of Mr Rush's correspondence [on 9th October], he has been singularly cheerful and complaisant, and assumed a frankness and unreservedness in deportment and conversation altogether unusual to him." [2] And again, " Mr Adams was evidently much pleased with the manner in which the proposition had been made, as well as the opening thus afforded for his country to play so prominent a part in the affairs of the world." [3]

On the 1st December Addington recorded that he had met Adams at a dinner and been informed that he had received further despatches from Rush (detailing the interview with Canning of 16th September). This contained Canning's well-turned appeal for a common policy in response to Rush's refusal. " The United States . . . were the first Power established on the Continent, *and now confessedly the leading Power*. . . . Could Europe expect this indifference? " [4]

---

[1] *A.H.R.*, vii. 681. Canning's words on Aug. 16.

[2] *F.O. America*, 5/177. Addington to Canning, Nov. 20/23, No. 20. Private and confidential.

[3] *F.O. America*, 5/177. Addington to Canning, Dec. 1/23, No. 25. This conversation took place ' shortly after the President's return to the Capital.' This was on Nov. 5, and Addington says that Adams had only received the first of Rush's communications, which arrived on Oct. 9.

[4] Reddaway, *Monroe Doctrine*, [1898], 50–1. Italics my own.

Adams seemed "extremely gratified, and evidently contemplated his country as already placed by it on a much
higher elevation than that on which she had hitherto stood." [1]
Here we have the key-note to the policy of Adams. He
knew England attached great importance to the attitude of
the United States, he knew also that England would fight
France if she assailed Spanish America. " My reliance upon
the co-operation of Great Britain," he said later, " rested not
upon her principles, but her interest." [2] It was, therefore, safe
for the United States to act alone, and to proclaim a separate
policy. In this way he would "make up an American policy,
and adhere inflexibly to that " and, at the same time, he would
prevent the United States from circulating as a satellite in the
orbit of Great Britain.

The views of Adams were bold and original, and they were
not favoured by Monroe. For Adams differed from him and
from many other Americans in that he disbelieved in the
danger from the ' Holy Alliance.' If there was such, England
was more committed to repelling it than the United States.
Adams had been much annoyed by the Russian Minister,
Tuyll, who had extravagantly proclaimed absolutist doctrines
to him. Accordingly, at the Cabinet of the 7th November he
explained that the Russian communications " afforded a very
suitable and convenient opportunity for us to take our stand
against the ' Holy Alliance,' and at the same time to decline
the overture of Great Britain. It would be more candid as
well as more dignified, to avow our principles explicitly to
Russia and to France than to come in as a cock-boat in the
wake of the British man-of-war." [3] That is the spirit which
ultimately prevailed in the Monroe Message. He had to fight
hard in the Cabinet to win his case, and, during the struggle,
one further point (and of the greatest importance) emerged.
Wirt, the Attorney-General, a man of supreme common sense,
asked him if it was wise to threaten without meaning to strike.
Did he mean to fight, or not ? Adams was obliged to ' hedge.'

[1] *F.O. America*, 5/177. Addington to Canning, Dec. 1/23. The
reference is not to the conversation shortly after Nov. 5, but to one at the
end of November after Adams had received Rush's second budget, dated
Sept. 16.
[2] Adams' *Memoirs*, [Phila. 1875], Nov. 24/23, vi. 203.
[3] Adams' *Memoirs*, vi. 178. A polite refusal was sent to Canning on
Nov. 30, *v. A.H.R.*, viii. 46–8.

He had to admit that the Executive could not pledge the country to war without consent of Congress. He denied the immediate possibility of war, and said that England was more committed than the United States.[1] So it is really true that he was proclaiming the Monroe Doctrine beneath the shelter of the British Fleet. He was not prepared to fight, but he did not believe that the ' Holy Alliance ' was either. As the ' Holy Alliance ' had lectured him, he proposed ' to return the compliment.' And he did so in a way which will never be forgotten.

9. The Monroe Message and Doctrine

" *The explicit and manly tone especially, with which the President has treated the subject of European interference in . . . this hemisphere . . . has evidently found in every bosom a chord which vibrates in strict unison with the sentiments so conveyed. They have been echoed from one end of the Union to the other.*"—ADDINGTON to Canning, 5th January 1824, on the President's Message, 3rd December 1823.

The Monroe Doctrine concerns us mainly in its relation to Canning's policy, but a summary of its principles must here be given.[2]

President Monroe announced in his message that :—

1. The United States desired " the liberty and happiness of their fellow-men on that side of the Atlantic. In the wars of the European Powers in matters relating to themselves we have never taken any part, nor does it comport with our policy to do so. . . . Our policy in regard to Europe, which was adopted at an early stage of the wars which have so long agitated that quarter of the globe, nevertheless remains the same, which is, not to interfere in the internal concerns of any of its Powers ; to consider the government *de facto* as the legitimate government for us ; to cultivate friendly relations with it, and to preserve those relations by a frank, firm, and manly policy, meeting in all instances the just claims of every Power, submitting to injuries from none.

2. " The political system of the Allied Powers is essentially different in this respect from that of America. This difference proceeds from that which exists in their respective Govern-

---

[1] Adams' *Memoirs*, vi. 203.

[2] I have altered the order of some of the sentences as delivered, placing together the passages expressing each of the three principles.

ments, and to the defense of our own, which has been achieved by the loss of so much blood and treasure, and matured by the wisdom of their most enlightened citizens, and under which we have enjoyed unexampled felicity, this whole nation is devoted. We owe it, therefore, to candor and to the amicable relations existing between the United States and those Powers to declare that we should consider any attempt on their part to extend their system to any portion of this hemisphere as dangerous to our peace and safety. With the existing colonies or dependencies of any European Power we have not interfered and shall not interfere. But with the Governments who have declared their independence and maintained it, and whose independence we have, on great consideration and on just principles, acknowledged, we could not view any interposition for the purpose of oppressing them, or controlling in any other manner their destiny, by any European Power in any other light than as the manifestation of an unfriendly disposition toward the United States. . . . It is impossible that the Allied Powers should extend their political system to any portion of either continent without endangering our peace and happiness ; nor can anyone believe that our southern brethren, if left to themselves, would adopt it of their own accord. It is equally impossible, therefore, that we should behold such interposition in any form with indifference."

3. After referring to the Russian Ukase of 1821 the Message stated, " In the discussions to which this interest has given rise, and in the arrangements by which they may terminate, the occasion has been judged proper for asserting a principle in which the rights and interests of the United States are involved, that the American Continents, by the free and independent condition, which they have assumed and main-tained, are henceforth not to be considered as subjects for future colonisation by any European Powers . . . with the existing colonies or dependencies of any European Power we have not interfered and shall not interfere."

10. Canning's View of the Monroe Doctrine

" I have very little doubt that the President was encouraged to make his declaration about the South American States by his knowledge of our sentiments."—Canning to Bagot, 22nd January 1824.

Of these three principles, the first definitely follows Washington's warning against complications, and Jefferson's against ' entangling alliances,' with Europe.[1] It laid down (and most significantly in view of Canning's offer of co-operation) the policy of separation from Europe, the policy of two hemispheres closed to one another. The second point is the reverse of this medal. The United States (and by implication other purely American Powers) will not intervene actively in Europe, but they assert that Europe must not intervene in the New World. There was to be a perfect equality of America with Europe, a complete separation of one from the other, on the basis of mutual non-intervention. In the third principle Adams asserted, with special reference to Russia, that the American Continent, except in so far as existing European Colonies were concerned, was to be considered as ' staked out ' for the independent American Republics. Underlying and informing all these principles is a fourth. The aspiration to republican freedom and equality is the natural birthright of men, and the countries of America, whether in the United States, in the Spanish Republics, or even Cuba, are entitled to live their own life, and to develop their own individuality without interference from Europe. "Whenever a body of men in occupation of a determinable territory desired to rule themselves they had an inherent right to carry their desire into effect." [2] This is the doctrine of self-determination in embryo.

These utterances were highly important a generation later, as they formed the American ideal, and gave a name and a programme to the foreign policy of the United States. But their value at the time lay not in their novelty nor in their boldness, but in the power of the United States to assert them in practice. European intervention, Adams said, would

---

[1] Washington implies but does not use the phrase ' entangling alliances ' in his address of 1796. Jefferson does in his of 1801.

[2] Reddaway, *Monroe Doctrine*, 78. These are not the actual words of Adams.

be "the manifestation of an unfriendly disposition to the United States." We would not behold "such interposition, in any form, with indifference." We "submit to injuries from none." "When our rights are invaded or seriously menaced . . . we resent injuries or make preparations for defence." In ordinary diplomatic parlance these statements mean that Adams was ready to fight in such instances. We know, however, that he was not.[1] It is in this direction that his skill and address are most conspicuous. He knew that England would fight, he thought that the Neo-Holy Alliance would not. Hence the United States could safely blow a blast on the republican trumpet, while sheltered behind the shield of England. In fact Canning had failed to perceive that there could be no co-operation unless he recognised the Spanish Colonies. Thus he was hasty in his overture, and Adams, like a skilful diplomat, made use of this opportunity to turn Canning's strength against himself. For a few weeks the ruse was successful, but the diplomatic bluff was called soon enough. For in the last resort, the Monroe Doctrine in 1823 was a policy, an ideal, or, in Adams' own phrase, ' a lecture.' And in diplomacy lectures have importance for the future, but do not permanently affect the present.

Canning was, in one sense, seriously annoyed at this utterance. He did not like the United States proclaiming itself the head of a sort of Pan-American League, from which both England and Europe were to be excluded. He had heard rumours that Guatemala was ready to join the Union and that Adams was ready to receive her.[2] He did not like, either, the assertion that all undiscovered or unoccupied America was staked out for its republics, for this might have a serious bearing on the dispute between England and the United States in the Oregon Territory. He took an early opportunity of putting a question to Rush. "Suppose," said he (2nd January 1824), "any new British expedition were to end in the discovery of land proximate to either part of the American Continent, North or South, would the United States object to Great Britain planting a colony there?" This question

---

[1] Except, of course, where the special interests of the United States were concerned, as in Cuba (v. infra, pp. 166, 171–2).

[2] F.O., 352/8. Strat. MSS., Stratford to George Canning, May 6/23.

Rush found unanswerable. Canning followed this up. " If we were to be repelled from the shores of America, it would not matter to us whether that repulsion were effected by the Ukase of Russia excluding us from the sea ; or by the new doctrine of the President prohibiting us from the land. But we cannot yield obedience to either." Rush had no instructions nor official knowledge of the Message. He found it hard to proclaim natural law in the face of this common-sense logic.[1] Canning plainly thought that the utterances both of Alexander and Adams were of a piece. They were the politics of the bazaar or of the auction-room.

Canning was never very much impressed by, or regardful of, abstract principles as such, and still less by a doctrine he thought ' apparently extravagant ' and ' not very intelligibly stated.' It was with the practical issues that he was mainly concerned. He thought that the Message implied that the United States condemned, or perhaps was even prepared to resist, the interference of Spain herself in Spanish America. If so, that would be a serious matter. It would, he wrote, " constitute as important a difference between his (Adams') view of the subject and ours as perhaps it is possible to conceive." He perhaps misinterpreted a report of a conversation of Adams himself.[2] At any rate, Adams himself disclaimed any such purpose to the Colombian Government on the 6th August 1824.[3] So that this misunderstanding was of no practical importance.

One other difference lay in the fact that the United States had recognised the Spanish Colonies as independent, whereas England had not. Apart from these points, however, Canning saw that the immediate effect of the Message was all

[1] Reddaway, 96–7, v. Canning to Bagot, Jan. 9/24, G.C. & F., ii. 208–9. " Where one Power proclaims a *mare clausum* . . . four thousand miles across, the other may have thought it a fair set-off to prohibit colonisation over the whole coasts of that continent, with a view to which the *mare clausum* was attempted to be established." It appears that the Monroe Message was never formally communicated to diplomats in Europe. It was, therefore, a domestic communication.

[2] F.O. America, 5/177. Addington to Canning, Dec. 1/23, No. 25. " The United States allowed a full right on the part of these islands [Cuba, Porto Rico] to act for themselves in submitting to Spain despotic or in resisting her . . . but the Government would never admit a right on the part of any third Power to interfere in subjugating them for Spain, or on the part of Spain to cede them to another Power."

[3] W. S. Robertson, *Hispanic-American Relations*, [1923], 50.

in his favour, and he used it, as was his wont, for his own practical ends. His first impression was recorded in a letter to Granville just after he had received it.

" One cannot help wishing that Pozzo di Borgo (the Russian Ambassador at Paris) had been at work preparing a plan of operations against S[panish] A[merica] for the approbation of Alexander and Metternich when first my Memorand : [the Polignac] and then this document [Monroe's Message] fell upon their table.

" You see what prevented direct co-operation [*i.e.* the joint declaration] was the step in advance which the U[nited] S[tates] had taken by recognition [of the Spanish Colonies]. But the effect is the same, though the form is varied by our respective positions." [1] And on the last day of the year he wrote to À Court at Madrid : " Pozzo may bustle and Ferdinand may swear. . . . The Spanish-American question is essentially settled. There will be no Congress upon it, and things will take their own course on that Continent, which cannot be otherwise than favourable to us." He goes on to say that he favours monarchy in Mexico and Brazil, as that " would cure the evils of universal democracy and prevent the drawing of the line of demarcation which I most dread—America *versus* Europe.

" The United States, naturally enough, aim at this division and cherish the democracy which leads to it. But I do not much apprehend their influence." He then describes the failure of his ' sounding ' of Rush. " In the meantime they have aided us materially. The Congress was broken in all its limbs before, but the President's Speech gives it the *coup de grâce.* . . . I send you some copies of the [Polignac] Memorandum, which you may use as your discretion suggests ; it must not be published [it was, in March 1824] ; but short of that it cannot be too generally known. Its date is most important, both in reference to the state of things which then existed, and in reference to the American Speech which it so long preceded." [2]

[1] Canning to Granville, Dec. 28/23. *Gr. MSS.* The Monroe Message came to England in a garbled form on Dec. 12—was known by Canning on the 24th, and was in one newspaper on the 26th and in all on the 27th.
[2] Stap., *G.C. & T.*, 394-5. *Cp.* his more guarded utterance in the Commons, Feb. 3/24. *Hans. Deb.*, N.S., x. 74. I have not space here

Canning, therefore, definitely claimed that he had safe-guarded Latin America, allowing that Monroe had later assisted him. We may add to this another and more characteristic utterance : " The effect of the ultra-liberalism of our Yankee co-operators, or the ultra-despotism of Aix-la-Chapelle Allies, gives me just the balance that I wanted." [1]

to go into the reception of the Monroe Doctrine on the Continent.   Until next January the European diplomats suspected the Message to be the product of an understanding with England, and this was of advantage to Canning.   Subsequently they were disillusioned, and Lieven informed Canning, that " The message of the President of the United States had pro-duced no more effect in Europe than in the [Spanish] Colonies, that it did not appear that the latter had since drawn closer to the Washington Govern-ment, so much did they regard England as the preponderant Power in this business, that the Continental Powers would not easily be intimi-dated by menaces like those of Mr Monroe, which had remained without result."   Vide V.S.A., Berichte aus England, Bd. 224.   Neumann to Metternich.   Vide also other documents quoted by me, E.H.R., Oct. 1924, pp. 590–3.

[1] Canning to Bagot, Jan. 22/24.   Bagot, G.C. & F., ii. 217–8.

CHAPTER VI

CALLING THE NEW WORLD INTO EXISTENCE

1. INTRODUCTORY

In the history of the Spanish-American Colonies the year 1824 is the crucial one. At the beginning of that year it was still conceivable that a congress might regulate the affairs of the New World, that monarchies might arise there, or that England might negotiate the peaceful separation of some of them from Spain. On the last day of the last month these possibilities had vanished because Canning took steps to recognise three New Republics.

With Canning the paramount consideration was, as always, to secure the unimpeded intercourse of British trade with the Spanish-American Colonies. His way of looking at the whole matter, as he constantly told the Allied Ambassadors, was commercial rather than diplomatic. After the Polignac Memorandum he had little to fear from the Neo-Holy Alliance direct, and his refusal to join their congress put the finishing touch to their impotence. Indirectly, however, they were more formidable because they could, and did, encourage Spain to refuse recognition. Spain, as Canning contended, had given for some years a ' tacit sanction ' to British trade with Spanish America, but there was always a chance that her refusal to sanction it further might embarrass the merchants. When in February 1824 she showed some signs of grace, and issued a decree throwing open the Spanish-American trade to the ships of European nations, Canning tried to clinch matters by a separate and direct negotiation with the Mother Country herself, in a last hope of obtaining her recognition of her revolted daughters (April). This method, successfully pursued by him in the case of Brazil, would have been the best way of securing the British trade, of conciliating Europe, and of stabilising the Spanish-American Colonies.   When that hope vanished, recognition became dependent on ' various external circumstances ' which might accelerate or retard it.   The first was ' force or menace ' from Europe, the second was the attitude of the United States. The third was that Canning was not unwilling to delay recog-nition, if any of the Spanish-American States showed the intention of re-establishing constitutional monarchy, for, without actively instigating, he wished passively to encourage that tendency.   By the middle of 1824 the possibility of monarchies in Spanish America had disappeared and recog-nition became urgent for a monarchy like England.   For, if she delayed too long over recognition, the young States might fall into the Republican arms of the United States which had already recognised them.   The last consideration, and, as it turned out, the deciding one at the crisis, was France. For Canning was not going to permit France indefinitely to occupy Spain, and at the same time to assert Spain's un-diminished sovereignty over America.   If Spain remained obstinate in her refusal to recognise her Colonies, and France obstinate in her refusal to evacuate Spanish soil, Canning did not see why he should consider the scruples or prejudices of either.   If France had obtained political ascendancy by force of arms in Old Spain, England could obtain commercial ascendancy by diplomatic means in Spanish America.   Hence, at the end of 1824, Canning refused any longer delay and recognised the Spanish-American State in defiance of the Neo-Holy Alliance, as an endeavour to compete with the United States in their favour, as a means of securing their trade, and, finally, as a protest against the French occupation of Old Spain.   The moment of recognition was, in fact, decided by this last consideration.

In all this policy Canning lays himself open, like so many diplomats, to the charge of opportunism.   But it was an opportunism within the limits of what he conceived to be fair.   Provided that our trade with Spanish America remained unimpaired, he did not wish to accelerate the separation. His actual recognition was, in fact, retarded for a time by his preference for monarchy, by his attempt to obtain Spain's

consent, and by his desire to see the Republics settle their own
affairs. After the middle of 1824 he seems to have conceived
that, while fully justified on the facts in giving recognition,
at any rate, to Buenos Aires, he was justified also in waiting
to give it at the time he conceived most favourable to England's
interests. That moment arrived when France refused to
evacuate at the end of 1824, but he certainly made no attempt
to recognise the Colonies before he considered that the facts
justified his action. In that sense he spoke truly when he
wrote that the separation from Spain was ' neither our wish
nor our work.'

2. The Refusal of Canning to join the Congress on Spanish-American Affairs (30th January 1824)

" At such a point
When half to half the World opposed."
                    " Antony and Cleopatra."

After the Polignac Conference, France, having once more
publicly renounced the idea of armed intervention in Spanish
America, could only fall back on the Neo-Holy Alliance,
whose Congress System might put moral pressure on England.
If England were invited to a congress on Spanish America,
she would be in a minority of one to four and might be compelled to accept the decisions of the others. One thing, however, France seems to have forgotten, and that was that
England might refuse the invitation to the congress.

The idea of summoning a congress on Spanish America
had been mooted at Verona. It was clearly indicated in
August 1823, and Louis XVIII. had suggested it again in
October and hinted that Wellington would be preferable to
Canning as England's representative.[1] As already related,
Polignac's suggestions on the subject in October were met
by Canning's demand that the United States should be invited, as one of the Powers most concerned ; a demand which
equally terrified Austria and France. Two secret conferences,
attended by Neo-Holy Ambassadors and by the French
Foreign Minister, were held at Paris on the 13th and 20th

---

[1] On Oct. 11. *V.S.A.*, Berichte aus Frankreich, Bd. 353. Vincent to
Metternich, Oct. 14/23.

October, at which it was decided ' to ask for a congress on
the Spanish Colonies.' In order to commit England, Sir
Charles Stuart was asked to attend a conference of Ambassadors, but refused to do so, an action highly approved
by Canning.[1] On the 31st October Polignac suggested to
Chateaubriand that Canning might refuse to attend a congress
sitting as a tribunal in judgment on other nations, but he
would find it hard to refuse if Spain invited her Allies to give
her their advice in a congress. Chateaubriand replied that
a congress had painful memories for France, but that a
conference of Ambassadors of the Great Powers (which he
meant should meet at Paris) would be just as good.[2]

Unmistakable signs now appeared that England was unlikely to enter a congress. They were clearly indicated in
the Polignac Conference. Wellington told the Austrian
chargé d'affaires that she would not ; on the 24th November,
Canning made the same statement separately to all the
diplomats of the Great Powers. But Chateaubriand pressed
on the project of which, wrote he, ' the advantages were
evident ' (6th December). On the 8th he reported Spain as
having drawn up her invitation requesting Allied intervention
in the colonial question, but in a form which he considered
bad, as it suggested that armed aid was intended.[3] This
mistake had to be corrected, and others soon appeared.
Knowing England's strong feelings on the commercial question,
Chateaubriand conceived the ingenious idea that Spain should
issue a decree granting freedom of trade with her Colonies
to all nations. This step would make it difficult for England
to refuse a congress, and would, he thought, encourage the pro-
Spanish parties in America to overthrow the Revolutionists.
Ferdinand's obstinacy again upset everything. Early in
December he issued a decree asserting his full rights over the
Colonies, a most unfortunate preliminary to a congress. He
did issue the invitations to the congress at the end of the
month, but it was not until February 1824 (when too late

---

[1] *F.O. France*, 146/56. Canning to Stuart, Oct. 28/23.
[2] *A.A.E.*, 617. Polignac, Oct. 31 ; Chateaubriand, Nov. 17/23.
[3] Even as ultimately drawn up, certain phrases in the invitation might
imply armed aid, a point to which Sir James Mackintosh drew attention.
Vide *Hans. Deb.*, N.S., xi., 1371, June 15/24. He said it meant ' interference by menace.' Canning in his despatch of Jan. 30 said force was
' not distinctly disclaimed.'

to have any effect) that he issued the decree concerning freedom of commerce.

None the less on the 26th December he had formally issued an invitation to ' his dear and faithful Allies ' to assist him at a congress on Spanish-American affairs. As he had no accredited minister in London he could only issue the invitation indirectly to England through her representative at Madrid.[1] High hopes were entertained that England would consent. On the 15th January France was reported as having accepted the congress, and Canning as being ' much disconcerted.' On the 21st Canning told Neumann, the Austrian *chargé d'affaires*, that there should be free communication of ideas, but that England would attend no congress on Spanish America, least of all at Paris. The day before he told Polignac that " conferences are useless or dangerous ; useless if we are in agreement, dangerous if we are not," and that he had already written a despatch to Spain to that effect. Chateaubriand, in great alarm, sat down and composed, on the 26th January, a magnificent piece of eloquence, denouncing the South American Colonies as the homes of militarism and anarchy, and demanding a congress in the name of Monarchy and Right. It was too late. Canning never answered it, for on the 30th January[2] he had sent off his despatch to Spain refusing the congress. On the 2nd February he assembled the diplomats and informed them of the fact. On the 7th February he told the disconsolate Polignac that " the British Government had already taken its decision and that nothing could change it." Had the Allies believed him, they would have been spared much needless humiliation.

Chateaubriand professed to receive this refusal ' without surprise or regret,' though his face showed ' evident proofs of mortification.' He lost his head completely and offered to waive all the arguments in his letter of the 26th January, ' if it were thought they were calculated to estrange the policy of France ' from that of England. Polignac thought ' the

---

[1] The same conduct was pursued in regard to Prussia, and for the same reason. Canning's insinuation, in his reply of Jan. 30, that England was not invited is not quite fair.

[2] Canning's despatch, Jan. 30, is in *B.F.S.P.*, xi. 58–63. Chateaubriand's of Jan. 26 in Stap., *Corr.*, i. 138–44. Canning prepared a series of notes on Chateaubriand for his diplomats to use as material. This unpublished document is printed in App. III. (*a*).

game was up,' and Villèle truly said that now ' independence '
must precede the holding of a congress and might be acknowledged by England more rapidly than France would admit.
On the 7th February Neumann said ' a great question has
just been decided,' ' the separation of England from Europe.'
But the masters of the Neo-Holy Alliance were not disposed
to admit defeat, even if France was.   Metternich protested
violently to Wellington.   England was the only " Power
which took the United States into its calculation," the principles of England and Europe had diverged ; Canning's international law was bad, and he had sacrificed everything ' to
the factions.'   But Wellington, though not in favour of
recognition or of republicans, did not think a congress on
South America would do good.   He wrote to Metternich to
this effect on the 24th February, and on the 4th May he used
stronger expressions, saying that the majority of Englishmen
would " not expose their interests to the imputation and even
to the risk of being bought and sold in conferences at Paris
and Madrid."

In March Canning resorted to his favourite weapon of
publicity, and laid before Parliament the Polignac Memorandum, and the despatch of the 30th January 1824, in which
he declined to enter the congress.   He hoped by these means
to cut ' the thread of this twisted policy ' :   Wellington protested because, once papers were before Parliament, their
subject-matter was no longer in the control of diplomats.
But Parliament and public rejoiced greatly at the British
policy thus laid bare to their view.   Even yet, however, the
Allies persisted in believing that Canning might consent to
a congress.   They thought, said Canning, we were ' throwing
a little dust in the eyes of Parliament ' and implored us
' to cease our funning.'

The Neo-Holy Alliance suspected that France would
give way to England.   On the 21st February their three
Ambassadors at Paris met, without summoning a French
representative, criticised England's refusal strongly, and
decided to put pressure on France.   On the 21st March a
new conference met, and Chateaubriand, who was present,
was forced by the Neo-Holy Alliance to disclaim any idea of
recognising Spanish-American independence without their

leave. He retaliated on them, when they pressed him to aid in recovering Spanish America by force, by saying that France had promised in the now published Polignac Memorandum to abjure any such idea.[1] These dissensions, however, prevented neither France nor the Neo-Holy Allies from renewing the assault on Canning. In March Russia asked him to reconsider his decision. In April Chateaubriand was still regretting his absence, and Metternich was sending a message to say how happy he would be to see England in the conference. In May Polignac renewed the invitation, but Canning showed himself, perhaps excusably, ' very irritated,' especially at the proposal to hold the congress or conference at Frankfurt, instead of Paris. Finally, when, on the 4th July, Neumann, at the instigation of Metternich, reopened the subject, Canning spoke with disconcerting plainness. This utterance did not end the conferences on Spanish-American affairs (for the Allies continued them until the next year), but it did convince them that England would have neither part nor lot in them, so long as Canning was Foreign Minister. The refusal, originally made on the 30th January 1824, was now confirmed. It convinced Metternich and Pozzo that the decision was " to separate the interests of Europe from those of America." In Canning's view his decision had reunited them, and made England the bridge between the two hemispheres.

3. Canning's Negotiations and Last Effort with Spain (1822 to May 1824)

In January 1824 Canning had again offered to mediate between Spain and her Colonies, and in April he made a last desperate effort to obtain a settlement of the question by Spain. Her sovereignty he considered as ' purely passive,' for her active forces held out only in three of the Colonies. The castle of San Juan d'Ulloa, which dominates the port of Vera Cruz in Mexico, the island of Chiloe off Chile, were still held by Spanish garrisons; in Peru, Royalists still faced the Revolutionists in the open and with superior forces, backed

---

[1] Chateaubriand and Villèle had not only endorsed the Polignac Memorandum, but had followed it up by a whole sheaf of further pledges on the subject, v. F.O. France, 146/54. Stuart to Canning, Nov. 3, 7, 13, 18, 24, Dec. 4, 8/23; and my article, E.H.R., Jan. 1925, pp. 42-3.

by a powerful fleet.   Canning thought that it was still possible
to obtain a peaceful separation.   He was also favourable
to the suggestion of establishing monarchies in some of
these countries.   In 1822 Iturbide had been proclaimed
' constitutional Emperor ' of Mexico, and Canning had sent
out a secret agent (Dr Mackie), who was personally known to
the Emperor, to report on the situation.   Mackie arrived to
find the ' Emperor ' dethroned and an exile, and then engaged
in negotiations with the republic, which were promptly discovered.   Canning decided that Iturbide's adventure had
" disgusted the Mexicans with the form of elective monarchy,"
but thought that the hereditary or constitutional form of
monarchy might find favour in that country.   His instructions
to Mr Hervey, his Commissioner of Inquiry to Mexico, of
the 10th October 1823, make his views clear.   England wanted
an agreement between Spain and Mexico, but on condition
that Spain " was not, in any shape, subjected or subservient
to France ;   nor employing the intervention of French arms
to restore its [Spanish] supremacy in the Colonies."   Polignac's
disavowal (9th October 1823) of French projects of force or
menace, enabled Canning to add a more secret instruction
on the 10th October.   If the Mexicans wanted a Spanish
prince ' on the basis of Mexican independence,' Hervey was
to co-operate with them and support the project, which would
be approved by the British Government.   But he was not
to take the initiative in this suggestion, " not to attempt to
prescribe to the Mexican authorities this, or any particular
course of action." [1]   They were to make their own choice un-
hampered, " and no foreign [*i.e.* French] force should be
employed to conduct the Spanish prince to Mexico."   He said,
elsewhere, that monarchy in Mexico would form a barrier to
the ' pushing policy ' (*politique envahissante*) of the United States.

Canning had intimated to Villèle, in answer to an inquiry,
that " we attach great importance to its [monarchy's] continuance in Brazil."   On the 24th November 1823 he had

[1] *F.O. Mexico*, 50/3.   Instructions to Hervey, Oct. 10/23, No. 1 and No.
5, secret.   Canning states that he had not touched on the monarchy
project in July 1823 (when instructions No. 1 were first drawn) because
the then condition of Spain " afforded no immediate probability that a
Spanish prince would be available otherwise than through the contrivance,
and with the aid, and under the superintendence of France."

received all the representatives of the Neo-Holy Alliance
separately, and informed them, that he thought that ' Republican principles had taken too deep root ' in Buenos Aires
and Venezuela (Colombia), but that they might yet hope
' to strengthen monarchic and aristocratic principles ' in
Mexico, Peru, and Chile.[1] He was also avowedly in favour
of monarchy in Brazil. It might be argued that thus to prefer
monarchy was to pursue a legitimist or unneutral policy.
That was not Canning's view. He thought that constitutional
monarchy was the true *via media* between democracy and
despotism. He did not object to some republics in Spanish
America, for democracies there would be a useful counter-
balance to despotisms in Europe. But he thought the
republican mixture rather too strong in the new world, and
would have preferred to add a mild monarchic flavour. He
wished therefore to delay the recognition of republics, until
it was clear that the cause of constitutional kings was lost.
But he did nothing actively to promote the monarchical
principle.[2]

In the early part of 1824, while he was still awaiting the
reports of his Mexican and Colombian Commissioners, Canning
tried a last separate negotiation with Spain. Having declined
a congress on Spanish America in January, he secretly offered
on the 2nd April ' by a formal engagement ' (averse as England
was from giving guarantees) to guarantee the Isle of Cuba to
Spain by our maritime power, provided Spain would agree to
a peaceful separation with her Colonies. On the 3rd May
Spain definitely refused this offer, " which, if not clogged with
such conditions, would have been thankfully accepted." [3]

[1] *V.S.A.*, Berichte aus England. Neumann to Metternich, Feb. 7/24.
Cf. Canning to À Court, Dec. 31/23 (p. 129). My friend, Mr Dawson, has
shown me a letter from Leopold (King of Belgium) to the effect that a
number of Mexicans discussed with Canning the plan of setting Leopold
(afterwards of Belgium) on their throne. Leopold adds that he declined
because " it would have been ' unbearable ' for Victoria (aged 7 in 1827 !)
to have sent me so far away." So I doubt its value.

[2] It was suggested by French and Austrian diplomats that Canning's
commissioners in Mexico had secret instructions to advocate monarchy.
This is correct, if it means they were to encourage it, when proposed to
them by Mexicans. It is incorrect if it means they were to suggest it in
the first instance.

[3] *F.O. Spain*, 185/95, Apr. 2, No. 14, secret. Received Apr. 14. Canning
to À Court; 185/96, May 5. À Court to Canning. Canning added that
our principle of non-interference would have prevented us from intervening in the internal disputes of Cuba, and that defence ' by maritime

A few days before, to wit on the 30th April, Ofalia, the new Spanish Foreign Minister, had sent a note, deploring Canning's refusal of a congress on the 30th January and re-newing the invitation. Canning scented in it the hand of the Neo-Holy Alliance, and it was, in fact, approved by the Ambassadors' Conference of Paris. "Whence comes the Spanish Answer?" wrote Canning. "Ask where's the North?"

"The voice is the voice of Ofalia but the hand is the hand of Pozzo :—Pozzo's hand, however, not so rough as the natural hand of Esau, but a kid glove on—the hairy side turned *inwards*. Nothing can be more smooth than the style of the Spanish Note—There is not a word to find fault with : but the matter is (as Ofalia thought it) ruinous to Spain—being intended to be only detrimental to England. Well, we cannot help. *Liberavimus animas nostras*. And there's an end." [1]

In a more official style he instructed À Court that he should send no reply and that the " result of it is simply that His Majesty reserves to himself the right of taking, at His own time, such steps as His Majesty may think proper, in respect to the several States of Spanish America, without further reference to the Court of Madrid." [2]

4. Canning Rejects the Congress Policy in the New World (July 1824)

" Let's not confound the time
With Conference harsh."
"Antony and Cleopatra."

This was Canning's last effort with Spain; henceforth he was concerned with Spanish America direct. In April 1824 he had received the report of Hervey, the chief of his Com-missioners to Mexico. He was amazed that they had reported so soon ; and he did not think that they had laid enough

power' did not extend to landing of troops. This secret transaction was revealed by the indiscretion, *or worse*, of Wellington to Neumann, who reported it to Metternich. *V.S.A.*, Berichte aus England, Bd. 222, May 30/24 ; and also by À Court (Apr. 28) to the Prussian Minister in Lisbon. *V.S.A.*, Berichte aus Frankreich. Vincent to Metternich, May 8/24, No. 22 B.

[1] May 29/24, to Bagot, private. Bagot, *G.C. & F.*, ii. 239-40. The Spanish answer of Apr. 30/24 is printed in *B.F.S.P.*, xii. 958-62.

[2] *F.O. Spain*, 185/95. Canning to À Court, May 17/24 (recd. May 31), No. 18.

stress on the monarchical elements in the country. He, however, concurred in the judgment, but still delayed because he hoped that Mexico might obtain recognition from Spain.[1] He further explained to the Austrian representative on the 7th July, that he had delayed the recognition of Colombia and Buenos Aires because they were Republican.[2] He did not want to have his hand forced by recognising republics until he was sure that Spain would not do so. But even in March he had said, " We cannot delay much longer." His enemies did their best to delay matters for him, and the dark intrigue to discredit him with the King and to overthrow him in the Cabinet, which had been started in 1823, was now revived by Metternich and Lieven in the hope of affecting the Spanish-American question. On the 30th May Wellington indiscreetly (or perhaps deliberately) revealed the British offer to guarantee Cuba to Neumann. Another member of the ' healthy party ' (la saine partie) in the Cabinet (probably Westmoreland) proposed on the same day that Metternich should make a proposal on the subject to the British Government " which would give [us] weapons against Mr Canning whom they would like to overthrow," . . . " but there was no time to be lost." George IV. approved this project and sent a secret message to Metternich. Thus the enemies of Canning in the Cabinet, with the royal aid, were actually intriguing with a foreign Power to overthrow him.

The Austrian Chancellor replied to this intrigue by a proposition to Canning via Neumann, which was received on the 4th July, and which was intended to supply ' the weapons ' in question. Canning, whose suspicions had been aroused, replied with disconcerting emphasis. It was impossible, he said, to let these Colonies fall under the moral domination of the United States. The British Government itself had been the result of a revolution, so that they could not regard revolutionary States as did the Neo-Holy Alliance. " The Powers believed that they could constitute themselves into a tribunal to exert influence on all sorts of matters,—this error had existed since the Congress of Vienna " ; but in fact the

---

[1] F.O. Spain, 185/95, to À Court, Apr. 23/24, enclosing despatch of same date to Hervey.

[2] V.S.A., Berichte aus England, Bd. 223. Neumann to Metternich, July 4/24, No. 25 Litt. B.

control had been directed against France and confined to special cases, and it was now desired to extend it generally. "The history of the most recent times was divided into three periods—that of Naples, Verona, and to-day. In the first England had separated herself from the Alliance; this separation had been shown by the answer the English Cabinet had had to make to the Circular of Laibach. At Verona England had protested against everything then done, and had taken an attitude of neutrality between France and Spain. The war had happily been of short duration, so that British neutrality had not been compromised. The period since Verona had seen the raising of a question wholly maritime and commercial. Consequently "it was the concern of England (*du domaine d'Angleterre*). . . . The influence of the [Continental] Powers ceased with the bounds of Europe."[1] All Metternich could do was to direct that Wellington and the King should be secretly informed that everything in Canning's words was '*blamable et faux*,' that no minister of a king ought to distinguish between recognition *de facto* and *de jure*, and that this attitude would more than ever injure England's position in regard to the first Courts of Europe.

5. THE BRITISH MERCHANTS AND THE BUENOS AIRES DECISION (23RD JULY)

But the venom of Metternich and the opposition of Canning's colleagues was countered by another force. For he was now to reap the fruits of his assiduous cultivation of the commercial classes and of parliamentary opinion. Ever since 1823 petitions of merchants had been flowing in on him with prayers to safeguard their interests in Latin America, and now at this critical moment, on the 15th June, Sir James Mackintosh presented a petition from the London merchants for recognition of the independence of Spanish-American States which had established independent governments. The petition bore on it some of the great names of the city—Baring, Montefiore, Ricardo, and Benjamin Shaw, who "as Chairman of Lloyd's coffee-house represents the most numerous and

[1] *V.S.A.*, Berichte aus England, Bd. 223, July 4/24. Neumann to Metternich. Weisungen nach England, Bd. 224. Metternich to Esterházy, July 18 (two despatches).

diverse interests of traffic." There was also an important petition from Liverpool, Canning's old constituency. Mackintosh, in an eloquent speech, praised Canning's despatches as " containing a body of liberal maxims of policy and just principles of public law " and as " models and masterpieces of diplomatic composition." But he complained of the government's undue tenderness towards European Spain. He also pointed out, with a good deal of acumen, that Castlereagh's provision in the Act of 1822, recognising the commercial flags of Spanish America, in effect committed us much further, and that Canning's appointment of Consuls in 1823, " is as much an act of recognition as the appointment of higher ministers." Then, taking Canning's despatch of the 31st March 1823, he showed that the question of recognition was there regarded as one only of time and expediency. And he further argued that the Polignac Memorandum of the 9th October 1823, and Canning's rejection of a congress in the despatch of the 30th January 1824, had in fact removed all European obstacles to recognition, and therefore all objections whatsoever.

Canning was very willing to be pressed upon the line which Mackintosh had so ably argued, but as yet he could not answer for his colleagues. So he contented himself with stating that he could not accept the view that all the South American Republics should be recognised in the mass; he maintained that each case should be considered on its merits. He likewise drew a distinction between two kinds of recognition, which he termed *de jure* and *de facto*. " If the Colonies say to the mother country, ' We assert our independence,' and the mother country answers, ' I admit it,' that is recognition in one sense (*de jure*)." " If the Colonies say to another State, ' We are independent,' and that other State replies, ' I allow that you are so,' that is recognition in another sense of the term (*de facto*)." It was better for the Colonies themselves to get *de jure* recognition if that was possible, and it was not wise to give *de facto* recognition " if the mere effect of that acknowledgment shall be to mix parties again in internal squabbles, if not in open hostility." He concluded by informing the House that Spain had (30th April) repeated her invitation to a congress, which the British Government had again refused.

This was a plain public intimation that Spain would no longer be consulted by England with regard to Spanish America, and that, if she did not recognise the new States soon, England would.[1]

The Parliamentary and public interest aroused on the question enabled Canning, against the keen opposition of Wellington, to induce the Cabinet to take the first step towards recognition. On the 23rd July the Cabinet forwarded a minute to the King, in which they reviewed the whole question of Spanish America. On Chile there was little information, that on Mexico was unsatisfactory; in Peru there was still a struggle, into which Colombia had been drawn. Action as to all these could be delayed for a time. But as to Buenos Aires, ' no such disqualification,' such as absence of information or unsettled conditions, could be pleaded. Some decisive step was demanded by the need for protecting commercial interests and by the " danger that might accrue to Europe and to civilised society if so large a portion of the world should continue much longer without any recognised political relations " with the Old World ; and exclusively connected with the *one* State (*i.e.* the United States), to which they are already indebted for recognition. Therefore they recommended that a full power be sent to the British Consul-General at Buenos Aires to negotiate a commercial treaty. The British ratification of such a treaty " would amount to diplomatic recognition of the State with which it had been concluded."[2]

This decision has never had the importance in history which should be attributed to it. The chief reason was that the relations of Buenos Aires with other parts of the Argentine Republic were still unsettled, and Canning did not mean to act until they were arranged. Another reason was that the decision was concealed from foreign diplomats at the time, and was only known when the steps to recognise two other States became public. The King gave a broad hint to Neumann on the 29th July, stating that, while he had refused to appoint a minister or to recognise the independence of these provinces, commercial arrangements must be made with them.[3] Metter-

[1] *Hans. Deb.*, N.S., xi. 1344-1406.
[2] Stap., *G.C. & T.*, 397-400. Cabinet Minute, July 23/24.
[3] *V.S.A.*, Berichte aus England, Bd. 223. Conversation du Roi avec M. de Neumann, July 29/24.

nich responded (17th October) that ' such a policy meant nothing for us but defeat,' and that the King was to be told that ' Canning cannot last.' Wellington was furiously angry, vainly tried to delay the despatch of the full power to Buenos Aires, sought to depreciate the power of British business interests and of popular opinion, and finally in October engaged in an unseemly personal quarrel with Canning.[1]

6. THE STRUGGLE WITH THE CABINET AND THE KING OVER RECOGNITION (DECEMBER 1824)

" *Novus Sæclorum nascitur ordo.*"—Quoted by CANNING to Granville, 17th December 1824.

But Canning had now his opponents both in the Cabinet and in Europe on an incline, and he slowly pressed them down it. The Report from the Commissioners in Colombia, which was in favour of recognition, reached him on the 23rd October. At about the same time he received highly favourable reports from Buenos Aires. At the end of November Liverpool circulated a Memorandum to the Cabinet, in which the hand of Canning is evident. It advised the recognition of Colombia and Mexico.[2] Could you leave " one-fourth of the habitable globe . . . in a state of *outlawry* ? " In the end these States could force recognition by imposing high duties on non-recognising Powers. Austria, Russia, Prussia indeed refused to recognise them on principles of Legitimacy, but " that principle is eternal, . . . will it not be as good twenty years hence as to-day ? " " The *pierre de touche* is the recognition of Great Britain." Further delay would mean advantages to the commercial, and consequently to the military marine, of the United States. " Sooner or later we shall probably have to contend with the combined maritime power of France and the United States. The disposition of the new States is at present highly favourable to England. If we take advantage of that disposition we may establish through our influence with them a fair counterpoise to that combined maritime power. Let us not, then, throw the present golden

[1] See my article in *E.H.R.*, Apr. 1923, pp. 218–20.
[2] That of Buenos Aires was, of course, already decided in principle. For instructions to Commissioners *v.* Notes to this Chapter, pp. 500–1.

opportunity away, which once lost may never be recovered." [1] On the 7th December the Cabinet resolved (all except one) [2] " that the question should be decided without reference to the opinions of Continental Allied Powers." All agreed that Spain need not be further consulted, and that the actual recognition should be given on the merits of each individual State. The main question was still unsettled.

The first Memorandum had not convinced everybody, and Canning now resorted to an ingenious manœuvre. He drew attention to the position of France and her influence in the matter, and pressed home, by a modern instance, a danger he had already illustrated from history. The first Memorandum pointed out that in 1711 England had proposed to assign European Spain to a French Bourbon, but had decided to cut off the West Indies (*i.e.* Spanish America) from his rule. The failure to adhere to this decision in 1713 had had the result that " during the greater part of the last century Spain followed France in her external policy," throwing Spanish America into the scale. This danger from the ' Family Compact ' Canning now proceeded to show was an actual one. On the 3rd December he demanded of Granville at Paris as to whether France would promise, or not, to evacuate her military force from Old Spain in a definite time. Both Villèle and Damas gave courteous but evasive replies, which information reached England on the 9th December.[3] Liverpool then drew up a second Memorandum, and Canning seized his opportunity and circulated a third Memorandum about the 14th December. " The great practical question for us seems to be how, in the event of an actual incorporation of the resources of Spain with those of France, such an accession to the power of France can best be counteracted. I have no hesitation in saying that this must be by a separation of the resources of Spanish America from those of Spain." He argued strongly for the recognition of Mexico, because of British capital sunk in mining and

---

[1] *W.N.D.*, ii. 354–8, and *v.* Notes to Chapter VI., pp. 550–4.

[2] The third Memorandum refers to Bathurst as suggesting consultation with the Allies (p. 551). On July 11 it was stated that Wellington never would separate from them over this question, *v. Bathurst Papers*, p. 571. Wellington's attitude in December may be summed up as ' Don't do it now,' but he did not then suggest consulting the Allies, *v.* Notes to Chapter VI., p. 551.

[3] *F.O. France*, 146/64. Canning to Granville, Dec. 10/24.

territorial concerns, and because of its contiguity to the United States, to whose 'ambition and ascendancy' "an amicable connection with Mexico would oppose a powerful barrier." The case of Colombia he admitted to be more difficult. He and Liverpool had "made up their minds to be satisfied with Mexico," but at the last moment, by the aid of Granville's despatch and the second and third Memoranda, they 'carried Colombia too.' [1] They had to fight hard, for Wellington, who had already offered to resign, now again threatened to do so. On the 14th December Liverpool and Canning laid a Minute before the Cabinet recommending recognition of Buenos Aires, Mexico, and Colombia, and stating they would resign if it was not accepted. Faced with this threat, the 'Die Hards'—Wellington, Bathurst, Westmore-land (the *sot privé*), and Eldon—gave way on the 15th. The battle was won, and the Minute went to the King on the same day.

There was a great resistance on the part of His Majesty. "He consents," wrote Canning, "but he does not concur." George tried first to get the Cabinet to consult the Allies before any step was taken, and then demanded individual opinions from his ministers *seriatim* as to whether the great principles of 1814, 1815, and 1818 'are, or are not, to be abandoned.' The Cabinet declined to give individual opinions, and pointed out to George that he had dissented from the Allies in 1821. Wellington, though sore at his defeat, now showed his good sense. He told Esterházy that he was very sorry that he had brought Canning into the Cabinet in 1822, but that he could not be dismissed. And he told the King that, if he did not consent, there might be an exposure in Parliament and a *coup d'état*. This threat thoroughly frightened the King, who gave way (30th January). In reality, Canning had not waited for His Majesty and had taken the final plunge on the last day of December.

[1] For the authorship of these Memoranda, see Notes to this chapter and Appendix III. (*c*) for text of the third.

7. Canning's Despatch (31st December 1824) announcing his Intention to Recognise Three Spanish-American States.

Canning's despatch, announcing his intentions to Spain, is of such grave importance that it was read to Count d'Ofalia, and must be reproduced here at length.[1]

" I send this Messenger to you for the express purpose of conveying to you His Majesty's Commands with respect to a communication which you are to make to the Government of His Catholic Majesty.

" It is not to be expected that any delicacy of form or gentleness of expression can reconcile the Court of Spain to the Substance of that communication ; but it is one for which His Catholic Majesty's Ministers must have been long prepared, as well by the progress of Events, as by the language and conduct of the British Government.

" The Declarations of His Majesty's Government to His Parliament,—to His Allies, and to Spain Herself, have left no ambiguity as to His Majesty's Intentions on the Subject of this communication, whenever the period for carrying them into effect should arrive: and M. de Zea therefore cannot be surprised to hear, that the Time is now come at which, conformably with those Declarations, His Majesty's Confidential Servants feel themselves called upon to advise His Majesty to take a new step towards certain of the Spanish-American Provinces, which have separated themselves from Spain.[2]

" It has been uniformly declared by the British Government that as to the Time at which any such new step should be taken, His Majesty's Government would be guided, 1st, ' By the Reports which the British Government might receive of the situation of Affairs in the several American Provinces ' ; 2ndly, By considerations regarding the essential Interests of

[1] *F.O. Spain*, 185/96, No. 7. Canning to Bosanquet, Dec. 31/24. Received Jan. 9/25. This is the original despatch. A circular, somewhat differently worded, was addressed to the other diplomatic centres.

[2] The circular of Dec. 31/24 to Courts other than Spain stated, somewhat optimistically, that " His Majesty had been graciously pleased to comply with the advice of his Confidential Servants."

His Majesty's Subjects, and by the Relations of the Old World with the New.

" From the period at which this Declaration was last made (in my letter to Sir William À Court, of the 30th January last, which was communicated to the Condé d'Ofalia, then His Catholic Majesty's Minister for Foreign Affairs) to the present, the States of Mexico and Columbia (*sic*) have been gradually advancing in the consolidation of their Internal Institutions, and in the capacity to maintain whatever Relations they may contract with Foreign Powers.

" The Commerce and Navigation of His Majesty's Subjects in that part of the World, have increased in a corresponding proportion.

" Spain has, during the same interval, refused to listen to offers of Mediation on the part of Great Britain, which were accompanied by conditions eminently favourable to Her Interest.[1]

" In looking at the present situation of Mexico and Columbia (*sic*) and comparing it with that of Spain, every impartial judgment will be convinced of the utter hopelessness of the success of any attempt to bring those Provinces again under subjection to the Mother Country ;—nor can it be deemed that a much longer continuance of so large a portion of the Globe without any recognised existence, or any definite connexion with the Governments of Europe whose subjects are in daily intercourse with them, must be productive of the greatest embarrassments to such Governments, and greatly injurious to the Interests of their Subjects, as well as to the General Commercial Interests of the World.

" The condition to which Mexico and Columbia (*sic*) have now advanced, has been for some time past the condition of Buenos Ayres (*sic*).

" Accordingly, eventual Instructions have been sent to the same effect with those which are now in the course of transmission to Mexico and Columbia (*sic*).

" In Peru, a struggle is still maintained in behalf of the Mother Country. With regard to Peru, therefore, a just consideration for the rights of Spain, and for the chance, whatever it may be, of the practical assertion of them,

[1] Referring, of course, to the offer to guarantee Cuba, *v*. pp. 139, 169.

forbids any interference on the part of His Majesty's Government.

" With respect to Chili (*sic*), we have not sufficient information to enable us to form any opinion as to the fitness or expediency of any further measure of approximation to that Province, at the present moment.

" With Mexico and Columbia (*sic*), as well as with Buenos Ayres (*sic*), His Majesty, in His paternal care for the Commerce and Navigation of His Dominions, has been pleased to decide that measures should be taken forthwith for negotiating Commercial Treaties. The effect of such Treaties, when severally ratified by His Majesty, will be a Diplomatick Recognition of the ' *De facto* ' Governments of those three countries.

" In adherence to the Declarations uniformly made in His Majesty's name, His Majesty has forbidden the introduction into those Treaties of any Stipulations which should be adverse to the Commerce of other Nations.

" Should Spain hereafter be willing to avail herself of His Majesty's Good Offices for the Establishment of a friendly understanding with countries, which she can no longer hope to reduce under Her Control, His Majesty will most willingly lend his best assistance to promote such an arrangement on Terms honourable and advantageous to Spain.

" I purposely abstain from mixing any other matter with that of this Despatch, or even from sending to you Instructions by the same opportunity on any other questions pending between the two Governments.[1]

" His Majesty would not on any account that the steps taken towards the Countries of America should appear to be influenced in any degree, by any other motives than those which really produce them, still less by any feelings at all unfriendly to Spain.

" Much rather would the British Government have been (as it has over and over again offered Itself to be) the Channel of reconciliatory communication, and the Instrument of

---

[1] In point of fact another despatch did accompany this one. For, after writing it, Canning received an overture from Spain as to a commercial treaty. He wrote a despatch, No. 8 of Dec. 31, welcoming this overture, but separating it from " That great question . . . with respect to which our conduct is governed by considerations beyond all human control."

amicable arrangement between Spain and Her late Colonies :
—but the determination of Spain having rendered those offers
unavailing, and time and the course of events having effectually precluded any useful renewal of them, His Majesty has
been compelled, at length, to take for Himself that course,
which the Interests of His own Subjects, and those of the
general Commerce of the World prescribed.

" You will read this Despatch to His Catholick Majesty's
Minister."

Much deference is here shown to the opinions of Spain,
though there is no suggestion that it was necessary to regard
those of other European Powers, and, still less, of the congress.
The second argument of the despatch mentions " considerations
regarding . . . the Relations of the Old World with the New."
This is a very guarded reference to the French occupation of
the Old Spain, and to the designs of the United States in the
New. Its obscurity is explained by a passage in the third
memorandum. This uses the French occupation as the main
argument for recognition, but mentions that it would be wise
" not to connect the proceeding [recognition] with the French
occupation of Spain; as it might appear that, by taking an
equivalent, we afforded a tacit sanction to that occupation."
In accordance with this advice recognition is, therefore,
represented in the Spanish despatch, " as a further advance in
measures already in progress, and in which we had already
sufficiently announced our intention to proceed." Canning's
private view was that the main motive was the French
occupation; the second, the designs of the United States;
the third, the completion of a process already far advanced.

8. The European Reception of Recognition
(January–February 1825)

Though some diplomats had reason for suspicion, no one
expected the step of recognition to be taken at this exact
moment. Canning broke the terrible news to the diplomats
on the 11th January 1825, and seems to have aggravated his
offence by summoning the ministers of the lesser Powers as
well. On the 7th February the public announcement was
made to Parliament in the King's Speech. The King refused

to deliver it; he had the gout, he said, and had lost his false teeth. So it fell to the Chancellor, Eldon, a bitter opponent, to announce recognition, which he did with a very bad grace and no enthusiasm.

The Neo-Holy Alliance was frantic, and five separate conferences were held in Paris to denounce Canning. Apparently the blow was unexpected, for the strong opposition in the Cabinet was known, and it had been hoped that Canning would fall. Spain protested at great length, saying she would never recognise the independence of rebels. Polignac lost no time in remonstrating on behalf of France, and Metternich thought that he should not have acted without his Allies. The three representatives of Russia, Austria, and Prussia made remonstrances separately on the 2nd, 3rd, and 4th March, one after the other. Canning disconcerted Lieven by refusing to hear his communication without a copy, and the others had to comply with a similar request. Lieven and Esterházy both protested, but in fairly courteous terms, against the departure from the principles of Legitimacy. Maltzahn, the Prussian, though of all Powers least interested in the question, was ' odious and offensive,' and seems to have exhausted Canning's patience. Canning therefore resorted to a game Wellington thought he played too often, and started ' quizzing the Allies.' Even in Canning's staid official account his design is evident, and still more so in his private letter. Baron de Maltzahn had informed Mr Canning " that the Court of Berlin disapproved of such an invasion of the Rights of the King of Spain," and that, " for its part, it was determined never to recognise the Independence of any portion of Spanish America, which had not been previously recognised by the King of Spain himself."

" I mean," wrote Canning to Stratford, " to have it understood that no such language is to be held to us, by either of the persons of the Continental Trinity. I had great pleasure in intimating as much, in somewhat plainer terms, to by far the most disagreeable of their 3 representatives, Baron Maltzahn,—worthy successor of the lover of Charlotte, though unluckily I could not think of a word for ' lectures ' and I am afraid I used ' lecturé ' coined for the express purpose : ' prêché ' would perhaps have done. But I hold that one has a right to coin words in French as well as in English, when the vocabulary of either tongue fails to furnish an exact expression of one's meaning, more especially if one is very angry, as I certainly was with Baron Maltzahn that day.

" I could wish that you had seen his disagreeable countenance when I proposed to him as a question for amicable discussion—a sort of academic exercise—' how the principles of legitimacy upon which his note turns, were to be reconciled with the disposition notoriously prevalent among the high Allies after the successes of 1814 and after the failure of all treaty with Buonaparte, to place some other than the Bourbons on the throne of France ' ; or when, after he had declined discussing that somewhat *épineuse* question, I set him the easier one, ' how those same principles were reconciled with the recognition of Bernadotte on the throne of Sweden, while the legitimate Sovereign of that country who had never, as far as I knew, abdicated his rights,[1] was wandering in exile and beggary through Europe ? '

" From the success of these galvanic batteries upon the physiognomy of Baron Maltzahn, I am persuaded that they offer the true antidote to lectures upon legitimacy, and if the three Powers shall ever be ill-advised enough to publish their lectures (as I believe Prince Metternich has more than once wished to induce them to do) I promise them that my ' *Questiones Legitimæ* ' shall obtain a similar publicity." [2] For once the three Powers were well-advised, and their remonstrance did not reach the public.

9. THE NEW WORLD IN EXISTENCE

The serio-comic aspects of the affair should not blind us to realities. The mulish Ferdinand of Spain could not be expected to approve any measure granting recognition to rebels. The French Government was angry because it might not have been displeased to follow suit, but could not break with the Neo-Holies. Polignac and the Ultras were furious— Corbière even said that the measure would result in war. The shrewder Villèle was sensible enough to see that England

---

[1] *N.B.*—Gustavus IV., though legitimate, was mad !

[2] *Strat. MSS.* *F.O.*, 352/10. George to Stratford Canning, Mar. 1825. Mr F. L. Paxson quotes the official record of the conference, *F.O. Prussia*, 64/145 ; *Austria*, 7|190 ; *Russia*, 65|151. *Cp*. Satow, i. 80–3.

could hardly avoid the step; he did not profess to like it. Metternich exaggerated his displeasure to gratify Alexander, who was now almost insane on the subject of Legitimacy. None the less the recognition of Spanish America was, and was intended to be, a severe blow to the Congress System. A congress or conference of all the great European Powers (except England) had sat at Paris during the whole of 1824, and frequently dealt with South American questions. It had entirely failed to delay England's action or to produce any result in America. Canning deliberately took the line that the Congress System and the Neo-Holy Alliance could be flouted and derided by England, and he publicly turned this ' rump ' of a congress into the laughing-stock of the world. He deeply injured their moral influence in Europe and destroyed it entirely in America. This was Canning's revenge for Troppau, for Laibach, and for Verona. These four Great Powers had had their way in Europe while one Great Power remonstrated, protested, or withdrew. Now one Great Power had its way in America, without heeding the protests or consulting the opinions of a Conference of Four in Europe. England had been ' at the tail,' now she was ' at the head,' of the European Confederation. Legitimacy, whatever its merits or influence, was never again to extend its arm across the Atlantic.

Canning summed up his view at a later date in the famous phrase: " I called the New World into existence to redress the balance of the Old " (12th December 1826). He expressed more soberly in private at the time the belief that the recognition of the Spanish-American States was the achievement on which he most prided himself. The use to which recognition was put, and the manner in which it was achieved, enabled Canning to secure both a diplomatic and a popular triumph over the Neo-Holy Alliance.[1] Whether the immediate motive of recognition—a desire to separate Spanish America from the French influence—was equally successful depends on the extent and reality of the designs of France in the New World and on her power to achieve them. On these questions opinions will differ, probably always. But, as French designs

---

[1] According to Stap., *P.L.*, ii. 2, Canning thought recognition of democracies and republics in the New World by England would console the advocates of freedom in Europe for the constitutions put down at Madrid, Naples, and Lisbon by the Neo-Holy Alliance or by absolutists.

in America did not altogether cease even after recognition, we may assume that they were potentially formidable before. On the whole, however, Canning's achievement here fell short of his belief. The danger of France to the New World and the importance of the New States in the world policy were neither of them as great as he believed or asserted them to be. Neither the troops, nor navies, nor policies of Latin America have ever had much influence on Europe, and the first time that ' The Balance of the Old World ' was effectively ' redressed ' by the New was in 1918, when American troops met Germans on the western front and arrived in Sedan. It is likewise true that the motive of increasing our prestige against the United States weighed in the decision, but at the critical moment that was the secondary, and not the clinching, argument of Canning. The despatch from Granville as to French intentions in Spain was the main theme of Canning's further memorandum which carried the day. The truth is given in Canning's own later words. " The French occupation was not the sole reason, nor perhaps in some quarters the most potential and reconciling reason . . . but it was emphatically *mine*." [1]

The expression ' calling the New World into existence ' has been criticised by many writers as ' false,' ' hollow,' ' bombastic,' and ' specious.' But, though rhetorical in sound and popular in its appeal, the statement is really one of fact. Recognition of a new state was not then, in practice, very common. Sometimes, as in the case of the Dutch Republic, recognition by the Mother Country in a public treaty had been delayed until some half-century after it had been achieved in fact. The recognition of the United States had been made by Great Britain in the Treaty which ended the war (1783), only some seven years after America had declared her independence, and some two years after she had really achieved it. But, in the case of Spanish America, independence had been substantially secured. By the end of 1824 they could repel Spain alone, and the Polignac Memorandum guaranteed that no other European Power would assail them. Buenos Aires had possessed independence for about ten years,

---

[1] Stap., *Corr.*, ii. 244, to Granville, Jan. 2/27. These italics are not in the printed version, but are in the original in the *Gr. MSS*. Liverpool seems to have been more desirous of checking the United States, *v.* his letter to Wellington, Dec. 8/24. *W.N.D.*, ii. 366.

Colombia for about six, Mexico for about three. Peru actually achieved it in December 1824, while Canning was writing his despatch. The independence of some of these Colonies had been recognised by Brazil and by the United States beforehand, but it appears that this recognition was not regarded by Europe as finally settling the question in either case. There was, however, no dispute among continental diplomats as to the fact that the action of Canning was decisive, and that the New States were henceforth fully recognised by one leading Power in Europe, which fact would bring other recognitions in their train, at a not very distant future. It is not recognition of one State by another that is decisive, but recognition by a State so powerful as ultimately to compel other States to follow suit.[1] Recognition of this decisive kind does mean, in the view of all authorities on modern international law, the admission of the recognised State into the Family or Comity of Nations, entitling it to full diplomatic privileges, to sovereign rights, and to equality with other States. Until a State has these rights it has no existence. When Canning said ' *I* called the New World into existence ' his colleagues did not relish the ' I,' and some subsequent historians seem to have carried their resentment beyond the personal pronoun. These objections seem in neither case sound. But for the threat of resignation his colleagues would not have yielded at the moment,[2] and but for its rhetorical setting no one would have questioned the truth of the phrase. A State may itself achieve its own existence, but it is for others to grant to it recognition. And, if Brazil and the United States have done something, Canning can surely have claimed to have done most, towards that end. At any rate, the Latin-American States ultimately thought so. And, in the last resort, they may be held to be the best judges.

---

[1] I think this view the most reasonable ; in which case Canning has the credit. Two other views may be held. If admission to the comity of nations depends on recognition being universal, that was not achieved until 1836, when Spain recognised Colombia. If the credit of recognition is due to the State which first recognises, that credit is due to Portugal and Brazil, which recognised Buenos Aires in 1821, anticipating the United States by a year.

[2] Cp. *W.N.D.*, ii. 365. Wellington to Liverpool, Dec. 7/24. " Excepting one [*i.e.* Canning] the former [the Cabinet] are either disinclined to stir farther in the [recognition] question, or are indifferent about the matter." This surely justifies Canning's ' I.'

CHAPTER VII

THE LATER AMERICAN POLICY

CANNING's round with Adams in the latter part of 1823 had not proved altogether successful. His redoubtable antagonist had evaded his overture, had proclaimed a separate policy on the part of the United States, and won much popular applause in the process for himself. So far as the Press was concerned he was the first in the field, the Monroe Message being published in December 1823 and the Polignac Memorandum not till March 1824. Canning had tried to break down the wall between America and Europe ; Adams had replied by adorning it with the machicolated battlements of the Monroe Doctrine. It was not for the moment recognised that the battlements were more imposing than substantial. The contest between the two men for the favours of Latin America was fought out during the years 1824–6.

1. COMMERCIAL RELATIONS (1823–7)

Canning's direct relations towards the United States were intended to be conciliatory, but he pursued a policy different from, and in some sense antagonistic to, them in his relations with the rest of the American Continent. Adams openly proclaimed that he wished America to be separated from Europe, Canning that they should be united. It is of much interest to watch the rapier-play of two men of such consummate ability. Adams conceived it to be vital to shut off the western hemisphere from European affairs, Canning was resolved to make it play its part in his scheme of world-policy. He did not deny to the United States the leading place on the American Continent, but he denied to them the right of making the other American States the satellites of their train, and of withdrawing them from the orbit of Europe. It was a simple question ; Adams wanted there to be two worlds in diplomacy, Canning only one.

" The avowed pretension of the United States to put themselves at the head of the confederacy of all the Americans and to sway that Confederacy against Europe [Great Britain included] is *not* a pretension identified with our interests, or one that we can countenance or tolerate. It is, however, a pretension which there is no use in contesting in the abstract, but we must not say anything that seems to admit the principle." [1] This instruction is the key to Canning's later policy. From the time of the proclamation of the Monroe Doctrine he was determined to hold out a friendly hand to the struggling States of Latin America, and, if possible, to bring them into connection with European ideas, European policies, and European forms of government, to which they were to be reconciled by the fact that England would defend them against armed intervention from Europe. He delayed recognition in order to see if Colombia or Mexico would adopt the monarchical form of government. It was due more to him than to anyone else that Brazil became an independent Empire, and he attached immense importance to thus preserving an island of monarchy intact amidst a tossing sea of republics. When he finally recognised the latter it was because he despaired of their adopting monarchy and wished to stabilise foreign property, to secure them against internal anarchy, and against any further danger of European intervention. He wished also to prevent their relying exclusively for support on the United States. " . . . an act which will make a change in the face of the World almost as great as that of the Continent now set free. . . . The Yankees will shout in triumph ; but it is they who lose most by our decision. The great danger of the time—a danger which the policy of the European System would have fostered, was a division of the World into European and American, Republican and Monarchical ; a league of worn-out Gov[ernmen]ts on the one

[1] *F.O. America*, 5/209. Canning to Vaughan, Feb. 18/26. This was first quoted in my article, " Later American Policy of Canning," in *A.H.R.*, July 1906, p. 795, and by several writers since without acknowledgment.

hand, and of youthful and stirring Nations, with the Un[ited] States at their head, on the other. *We* slip in between ; and plant ourselves in Mexico. The Un[ited] States have gotten the start of us in vain ; and we link once more America to Europe. Six months more—and the mischief would have been done." [1]

Canning had now to frame his Spanish-American policy. His aims were : to secure British property ; to protect the religious freedom of British subjects ; to abolish the Slave Trade ; and to obtain equal commercial privileges, though not denying the right of the Mother Country to preferential treatment.[2] The security of British property and of religious freedom were easily secured in principle, and one or two instances, in which Canning interfered with effect, taught the new States to respect it in practice. He had little difficulty in securing the abolition of the Slave Trade with Mexico, Colombia, or Buenos Aires, but had a long struggle with Brazil. Ratifications of a treaty to abolish the trade in three years were exchanged 13th March 1827, but it was not until half a generation after Canning's death that his pupil Palmerston finally secured it, a transaction always regarded by that boisterous minister as one of the most satisfactory of his life.

It has sometimes been maintained that Canning's recognition policy was of no importance, as commercial intercourse was already well established. This may be true of a relatively settled area like Buenos Aires, but is totally untrue of States like Peru, Chile, Mexico, and Colombia. Spain was impotent, and no redress could effectively be demanded of a revolutionary government until it was recognised or thought that it was going to be recognised.[3] The gloomy Dictator of Paraguay had kept a dozen British subjects

[1] Gabrielle Festing, *John Hookham Frere and his Friends* (1899), pp. 267–8. To Frere, Jan. 8/25, *cp.* a similar letter to Granville, Dec. 17/24. Stap., *G.C. & T.*, 411. I confess I agree with Professor S. E. Morison in thinking that Canning was too apprehensive as to the League of Republics in America. But, having regard to public opinion in England, it was not possible for Canning to despise this danger altogether.

[2] Canning used the expression ' most favoured nation ' in the sense of after the Mother Country. Both France and the United States used the expression ' most favoured nation ' basis in a different sense. They wanted to be on an equality with the Mother Country, *v.* W. S. Robertson, *Hispanic-American Relations*, p. 198.

[3] Vide *F.O. Chile*, 16/1. Planta to Mansfield, Mar. 23/23, *re* a case of injury to property of a British subject.

in prison for some years, but he released them in 1825, because he thought (wrongly) that this step would produce recognition. In other Latin-American States British persons were safer, but British property was not. Thus in Peru in 1821 certain British vessels were released only by the action of Sir Thomas Hardy (Nelson's Hardy) commanding a naval squadron. In 1822 the Patriots of Peru made one firm pay £8000 on goods imported from Spain, and confiscated four or five other cargoes. In that year a British naval commander dissuaded the Patriots from making a forced levy on British merchants, but in 1823 a number of traders found it safer to pay up.[1] In the same year certain British merchants in Mexico were forced to subscribe to a government loan " solely from the apprehensions of the consequence of a refusal." And again, " Duties on goods amounted to 27½ per cent." and were " lowered nearly one-half and raised again . . . in the space of two or three days, with the sole apparent object of favouring the introduction of a particular Cargo, not on British account." [2] In such cases the sole remedy was to apply to the ' precarious protection of the American Consul.' Matters improved somewhat with the arrival of British consuls during 1823-4, but it was not till recognition was announced and commercial treaties negotiated, that life or property were safe or customs duties equable.

The British trade to Spanish America had only recently been acquired. In eleven years (between 1814-25) the British export trade to Spanish America had actually become about as great as that to the United States, and the imports had been trebled in this period. The figures of this sudden expansion are startling. Annual average values of British goods from and to Spanish America (excluding Cuba) :—

1807-14. Exports, £444,773 ; 1822-7. Exports, £6,244,333.

Or, giving the figures in more detail :—

1822-4. Imports, £1,786,646 ; Exports, £5,883,397.
1825-7. Imports, £1,882,173 ; Exports, £6,605,269.[3]

[1] *History of A. & D. Gibbs*, London, 1922, pp. 397, 405-6, 422, *v. F.O. Peru*, 61/1 ; Aug. 9/23. The merchants say they were originally asked to contribute $230,000 out of a $400,000 loan, and that their obligation was ultimately reduced to $73,400.
[2] *F.O. Mexico*, 50/2. Petition of thirty British merchants, Sept. 12/23.
[3] L. A. Lawson, *Relation of British Policy to Monroe Doctrine* (1922), pp. 84-6. I do not think him right in saying " that the extension of

The values are only approximate, but there is no mistaking their general significance as to the enormous development of British trade since the war. The British export trade to Spanish America had been multiplied by fifteen times. Further, a comparison of British with United States figures shows also that the volume of British trade with Latin America was nearly thrice that of the United States to the same area.[1] So that, even if recognition did not increase trade, it was still an urgent necessity to conclude commercial treaties and thus prevent the United States from securing special commercial advantages by negotiation beforehand. Satisfactory commercial treaties were quickly negotiated with Buenos Aires and Colombia, ratifications being exchanged respectively on 12th May and 7th November 1825. The blunders of Canning's representatives in both Mexico and Brazil caused the rejection of their original treaties, but new and satisfactory ones were actually negotiated in his lifetime. The Mexican was ratified before his death, and the Brazilian shortly afterwards. The progress of the United States was slower, and even in 1829 she had commercial treaties signed only with Brazil, with Colombia, and with Central America. So that Canning had four treaties and the United States only three. One of them was with Buenos Aires, which was very important to England. Another was with Mexico, whose trade was most valuable both to England and to the United States. In negotiation with her, Canning had proved more skilful than the United States' representative.

It was an easier task to out-manœuvre other opponents. France was hampered by her pledge to the Neo-Holy Alliance not to recognise the new Republics. She, however, engaged in secret intrigues to obtain exclusive commercial advantages. In 1825 she recognised the independence of the French half

recognition . . . was not compelled by any immediate economic necessity," because the increase, 1825–7, was only 'slightly greater' than during 1822–4. There was a drop from £8,682,163 exports in 1825 to £4,531,094 in 1826, and to £6,602,163 in 1827. This was due, however, to the great financial crisis in England at the end of 1825, and could not have been foreseen at the moment of recognition.

[1] W. S. Robertson, *Hispanic-American Relations*, p. 197 (converting $5 into £1). Spanish-American *imports* into United States £1,152,756; *exports* from £2,604,152, 1825. The figures given in *B.F.S.P.*, xiv. 877–89, Oct. 1/25–Sept. 30/26, seem to work out differently. But such values are only approximate.

of San Domingo (Haiti) in return for a perpetual 50 per cent. preference in favour of French commerce. Canning instructed Granville to make no protest, because he considered a mother country had a right to exact a price for conceding independence.[1] About the same time, as will be mentioned (p. 223), France indulged in a discreditable intrigue to secure preferential commercial terms with Brazil.[2] Eventually she was compelled to connive at recognition of Spanish-American States. She issued exequaturs to the consuls of Brazil and of Mexico in 1825, and negotiated a commercial treaty with the first and a somewhat informal trade convention with the second (1827).[3] The smaller States of Europe—Bavaria, Würtemberg, the Netherlands, Sweden, Denmark, the Hanse towns—though much in dread of the Neo-Holy Alliance, also sent commercial agents and concluded similar surreptitious commercial agreements with most of the Spanish Republics, and more open ones with Brazil. Prussia indulged in similar negotiations *sub rosa*. Russia and Austria, who, having no transmarine commerce, could afford the luxury of political theory, did refuse all intercourse and continued to encourage Spain in her insane obstinacy. It was actually not until 1836, years after Ferdinand's death, that Spanish recognition was accorded. All that really happened was that other European States paid commercial penalties for not recognising the new States as quickly as England. Canning also secured commercial advantages over the United States, which had preceded him in recognition. In this direction, at any rate, England held the lead.

2. Latin-American Reception of Monroe Message and Polignac Memorandum (1823–6)

In more formal diplomacy Canning started with a grave disadvantage as compared with the United States. England was a monarchy and therefore suspect to the ardent disciples of liberty, the United States had formally recognised its sister Republics in 1822, and the Monroe Message had obtained

---

[1] *F.O. France*, 146/73. Canning to Granville, July 12/24.
[2] *Vide* on this point Notes to Chapter IX., p. 507.
[3] These steps were equivalent to recognition, though the French attempted to deny it in the case of Mexico.

publicity earlier than the Polignac Memorandum.   Canning was resolved to reduce this lead, and to counter the undue influence he conceived the United States had thus obtained. He therefore pursued a conscious policy of attracting Latin America with the magnet of England.

During 1824-5 Spanish-American opinion steadily veered away from Adams and the United States and in the direction of Canning.   Even if there was in fact no idea of European designs in the New World, the Spanish Republics believed that there was.   Their bugbears were Bourbonist France, the friend of tyrannical Spain ; and the Neo-Holy Alliance, ' that hypocritical federation of sovereigns.'   The declaration of Monroe was generally hailed in the Latin-American press as a definite pledge by the United States to defend the South American Continent by arms against a Europe which, as they thought, was threatening their liberties.   Even in February 1824, however, a Mexican newspaper, while briefly summarising the Message, suggested that recognition by England was in reality of more importance.   In Colombia gratitude expressed itself in flamboyant terms, ' The powerful and majestic rôle ' of Monroe was worthy of the ' classic land of liberty,' ' the policy ' was ' consolatory to the human race,' etc.   As they still were much afraid of French activities, the government of Colombia decided to bring the United States to action.   Their representative sent a note to Adams at Washington (2nd July 1824) asking for definite explanations.   After a Cabinet meeting and much discussion Adams replied on the 6th August 1824.   The attempt of Spain herself to reconquer her Colonies was no reason for the United States to interfere.   The President did not think that an intervention by other Powers now threatened ; if he did, he would recommend measures to Congress.   " As, however, the occasion for this resort could only arise by a deliberate and concerted system of the Allied Powers to exercise force against the freedom and independence of your Republic ; so it is obvious that the United States could not undertake resistance to them by force of arms, without a previous understanding with those European Powers, whose interests and whose principles would secure from them an active and efficient co-operation in the cause. This there is no reason to doubt could be obtained, but it could only be effected by a negotiation preliminary to that of any alliance between the United States and the Colombian Republic, or in any event coeval with it." [1]

There was no glow in this grey despatch. The United States was not at the moment prepared to fight at all. Before she fought, the crisis would have to be evident and real, the consent of Congress would have to be obtained, and the United States would have to secure " an active and efficient co-operation in the cause from certain European Powers." If this was what the Monroe Doctrine meant, it seemed better to turn to these ' European Powers ' at once.

Canning's declaration in the Polignac Memorandum had been absolutely unqualified. England had announced that she would fight, in case of an attempt ' by force or by menace ' by any European Power, other than Spain, to subdue Spanish America. But the Polignac Memorandum had only been circulated to diplomats in 1823. It was sent out confidentially to the British agents in Mexico, Colombia, and Buenos Aires in October 1823, and again in February 1824, so that some of its purport reached the ears of the governments of these countries. But it was not revealed to the world till March 1824, and the Latin-American Press did not hear of it till May or even July 1824. In fact, the moment was well chosen. For the words of Canning seemed as strong to the public as the explanations of Adams seemed weak to the diplomats. One Colombian newspaper, which perhaps was well informed, stated, in April 1824, that both England and the United States denied ' this pretended right of intervention.' Bolivar, who reviewed the Polignac Memorandum in Peru, commented thus : " The relations which Great Britain is desirous of establishing with America are worthy of her wisdom, and suited to ensure the destiny of the rising States of this hemisphere, which with a friend so powerful as Great Britain will be able to defy the rage of European tyrants." [2] Peru, as a whole, thought all danger from Europe over. Mexico was much impressed, for she had as good reason to

---

[1] W. S. Robertson, *Pol. Sci. Quarterly*, vol. xxx., March 1915, pp. 91–2; and also *Hispanic-American Relations with the United States*, [1923], pp. 50 *sqq.*

[2] *F.O. Peru*, 61/3. Bolivar to Rowcroft, Aug. 15/24. Rowcroft to Canning, Sept. 17/24.

dread French intrigues as had Colombia. An article in the *Sol* of Mexico, inspired by the British Commissioner, pointed to the manly declaration of England and denounced "the machinations of the Court of Versailles." The Mexican Foreign Secretary addressed the Assembly on the 11th January 1825, and drew attention to the Polignac papers and England's determination to repel armed intervention, other than that of Spain, in America. He added that the declaration of Monroe was of a similar character, but he evidently ranked it second in importance.[1] Very significant, too, was the action of the *Argos* at Buenos Aires. It began in February by printing Monroe's Message in italics. In June it published the Polignac correspondence and stated that they could *now* count on the friendship of England. The most enthusiastic welcome came from Chile. " One instance," wrote the British Consul, " will suffice for the fact. You, Sir, [*i.e.* Canning] are styled, even in the Senate, by all the Officers of State, ' The Redeemer of Chile.' " [2]

It certainly was not an accident that Colombia, Mexico, and Buenos Aires all applied to Canning before the end of 1824 [3] to mediate between them and Spain and to secure her recognition of their independence. As he was already acting in a similar capacity between Brazil and Portugal, he thus became the accredited mediator between Latin America and Europe. Finally, the decision to recognise Buenos Aires, Colombia, and Mexico on the last day of 1824 brought Canning again most definitely before the eyes of Latin America. For, while never concealing his preference for monarchy, he now announced his decision to recognise three Republics. It was a good start for the new year.

As matters became better for England, they became worse for the United States, in 1825. Bolivar, on the 11th March of that year, in considering how to defend South America, postulated a large native army ; a European policy ' to ward off the first blows ' ; the aid of England and of the

[1] This view is supported by W. R. Manning, *Early Diplomatic Relations between the United States and Mexico*, [Baltimore, 1916], pp. 68–9 and notes.

[2] *F.O. Chile*, 16/1. Nugent to Canning, July 30/24 ; in 1826 Chile expressed her disappointment that England had not recognised her.

[3] The Colombian and Mexican applications were official.

United States. It will be observed that he put England first.[1] Adams, who had just succeeded Monroe as President, appointed Henry Clay as his Secretary of State. He was called on at once by Brazil to explain the doctrine he had originated. The Brazilian Government appealed to him to sign a convention to preserve them against an attempt to reconquer Brazil by Portugal or by any Power, and suggested that the Spanish-American States should join this League of Defence against the Neo-Holy Alliance. Clay replied (13th April 1826) that the Monroe Doctrine was adhered to by Adams, but that it did not apply to the attempt of a mother country to reconquer her colony. (It will be seen that he omitted all reference to the other European Powers or to the Spanish-American States.) So Brazil was discouraged, and she finally owed it to British mediation that she secured her independence in August 1825.

Mexico also was disappointed. Poinsett, the American representative, tried to get her to give commercial advantages to the United States, by pointing to the Monroe Declaration that, " in the event of such an attempt being made by the Powers of Europe, we [the United States] would be compelled to bear the brunt of the contest." Clay answered this despatch diplomatically, showing that the United States had informed France over Cuba that " we could not consent to the occupation of these Islands by any other European Power than Spain, under any contingency whatever." But it was known that he did not extend this view to every part of the American Continent, and Poinsett himself had repudiated the idea that Monroe's Doctrine conferred on the Mexican Government " the privilege of demanding our interference as a right " (21st August).[2] Somewhat later he explained the Monroe Doctrine as a pledge binding on the Executive, but not on the nation, unless sanctioned by the Congress of the United States [3] (6th May 1826).

[1] Letter quoted by W. R. Shepherd, *Hispanic-American Review* (1918), p. 295.

[2] Debates in Congress arose on the point, and on the whole were in favour of disavowing Poinsett, *v. F.O. America*, 141/48. Vaughan to Canning, Apr. 3, June 6/26. For the letters quoted, *v.* Poinsett to Clay, Sept. 28 ; Clay to Poinsett, Nov. 9 ; Clay to Brown, Oct. 25/25 ; *B.F.S.P.*, xiii. 416–426.

[3] Poinsett to Clay, May 6/26; *B.F.S.P.*, xiii. 998. *Cp.* Manning, *Early Diplomatic Relations*, pp. 74–82.

The effect of these qualifications was soon seen. On the 23rd May 1826 the President of Mexico, in closing his Assembly, declared that the " Memorable promise of President Monroe " . . . " is disclaimed by the present Government of the United States " . . . " we have no longer any sort of Guarantee or Promise, on the part of that Government, to take part in the Contest, if a Third Power should become an Auxiliary of Spain." [1] His criticism was greatly enhanced by the eulogies he had poured on England a few months before. " The month of January of last year [1825] is deserving of eternal record, because of the announced British disposition to enter into friendly relations with, and recognise the Independence of, the New American States. This proceeding of the wise British Cabinet has strengthened our interests, and at the same time disconcerted the plans of external Enemies, surprising the Cabinets of the Allied Powers. . . . The latter have wished to waft across the Ocean the absurd principles of Legitimacy, and to smother liberal ideas in the New World . . . England has the credit of flying to the assistance of reason, justice, and liberty, and of rescuing America from the disasters of war, by the interposition of her Trident." [2] The allusion is plainly to the Polignac Memorandum confirmed by the recognition of England. And it is the more impressive as the Mexican President declared in May that the Monroe Doctrine was now disclaimed by the American President, who (incidentally) happened to be its author.

Colombia had also been moving in the direction of England. Bolivar's views on the Monroe Message are something of a mystery, for he received the first imperfect version of it while in camp when setting off to conquer Peru. Almost his only direct reference to it is in 1825, when he instructed the Peruvian delegates to the Congress of Panama to obtain such ' an energetic and efficient declaration ' as that of Monroe. Santander, Bolivar's vicegerent in Colombia, cannot have believed much in the Monroe pledge after the explanations of 1824. Bolivar himself, despite assertions to the contrary,

[1] B.F.S.P., xiii. 1068, Jan. 1/26, speech at opening of Mexican Assembly; p. 1082, May 23/26, speech at closing of Mexican Assembly.
[2] The Mexican President added that the fact, that Canning had forced the tyrants to disclaim their designs, proved that they had them, v. App. III. (b).

was not hostile to the United States, but he seems to have been more favourable to Great Britain. He was highly pleased with the Polignac Memorandum. He had recently showed leanings towards monarchy rather than to federal republican-ism ; he owed much to British soldiers and sailors, and he knew that British sea power was more valuable to Latin America than that of the United States. Moreover, he did not believe in the theory that America should be separated from the friendly part of Europe. It was due to Colombia, and probably to Bolivar, that England received an invitation to attend the congress which Bolivar now proposed to sum-mon at Panama. This invitation to England Adams did not expect, nor particularly appreciate. He would have appre-ciated it still less had he known that Bolivar dreamed of a league of American nations sanctioned by England. It is also of interest that the Colombian delegates at Panama stated that the United States were not to be members of the congress, merely observers or unofficial representatives like the Dutch or the British.[1] Even before the Congress of Panama met, England had begun to outstrip the United States in the favour of Spanish America. One great reason was that Canning had shown himself much more diplomatic than Adams in his discussions with Colombia and Mexico on the question of Cuba.

3. CUBA (1822–6)

" The island of monks and locusts, the police, ports without ships, troops without breeches, a brilliant priesthood, banditti, and an exhausted Treasury."
—J. M. CALLAHAN.

Cuba, as was aptly stated by a newspaper, was the ' Turkey of Trans-Atlantick politics,' apparently sick and tottering to her fall, an easy prey to an enterprising or adventurous Power, whether France, England, the United States, Mexico, or Colombia.

Canning's own view was clearly stated by himself : " We sincerely wish it [Cuba] to remain with the Mother Country. Next to that I wish it independent, either singly or in connec-tion with *Mexico*. But what cannot or must not be, is that

---

[1] *F.O. Colombia*, 97/115, June 6/26. Dawkins to Canning.

any great maritime Power [*i.e.* France or the United States]
should get possession of it." [1]

(a) *British Policy* (1822–5)

England was suspected both by the United States and
France of wishing to secure Cuba to England. Adams, indeed,
thought England was looking for territory everywhere, though,
when pressed by Stratford Canning, he had admitted that
she did not aspire 'to take a piece of the moon.' But these
suspicions were, in fact, unjust. When Canning authorised
British sailors to land in Cuba in December 1822, he informed
the various governments that we had no aggressive designs;
when he offered to guarantee Cuba to Spain in April 1824 he
took care to insert in this offer, and to point out afterwards
to diplomats, that his guarantee was purely maritime and did
not extend to the garrisoning of the island with British troops.
In October 1826, when hostilities became threatening with
Spain, he did contemplate occupying Cuba so as to bring the
Mother Country to reason, but apparently as an act of war
and not with any permanent design of annexation.[2] He would
never have forestalled any other Great Power in occupying
Cuba, but he might have sought to offset that annexation,
once accomplished, by some compensation to England. Thus
when in 1822 he thought (as it proved wrongly) that the
United States meant to annex Cuba, he suggested we might
have to annex Porto Rico to preserve the balance of power
in the Caribbean. But, in general, he held steadfastly to his
twin pillars of policy—non-intervention in the internal affairs
of other States, and preservation, so far as possible, of their
existing territorial integrity against external attack.

(b) *The French Démarche and Disclaimer* (1825)

During 1824 France increased her naval forces in the
Caribbean and began to cast longing eyes over Cuba. The
danger was more evident in 1825. It was the United States

---

[1] To Granville, June 21/25. Stap., *Corr.*, i. 276. Italics my own.

[2] To Liverpool, Oct. 6/26: " God forbid war ; but if Spain will have it,
ought not we to think of the Havannah ? Where else can we strike a
blow ? and what other blow would be so effectual ? " Stap., *Corr.*, ii. 144.

that moved first, but not along a good road. Adams, full of a recent successful negotiation with Russia, thought that he might get Alexander to persuade Spain to recognise the independence of her revolted Colonies on the basis of Cuba and Porto Rico remaining to the Mother Country. This step was taken on 10th May and a despatch sent accordingly ; with the intimation that, while the United States were " satisfied with the present condition of those islands . . . [they] could not, with indifference, see such a transfer to any European Power." Alexander replied politely, on the 20th August, that he could not negotiate without his [Neo-Holy] Allies, or without Spain.[1] Canning had not associated himself with this *démarche*, for he knew that no good result could come from it. He had predicted, even during the negotiation, that it must fail. Subsequently he remarked, with some scorn, that England would not have associated herself with a negotiation which had no chance of success. He knew already that Alexander was the last person likely to recognise the rebels of Spanish America.

In point of fact Canning had, in July, been engaged in a much more effectual protection of Cuba from ' European intervention.' Spain had sent out another expedition to Cuba, and her transports had touched at the French colony of Martinique, and were actually convoyed to Cuba under the escort of French ships supplied by the French Governor himself. Canning became very angry and at once demanded explanations at Paris. After much shuffling and tergiversation, Damas denied that the French Governor had been authorised in any way to act as he did. Villèle, however, in the midst of his protestations, indiscreetly disclosed the fact that, though the French Governor had not been authorised to convoy Spanish transports, he had been authorised, should occasion arise, to intervene with an armed force in Cuba in favour of Legitimist Spain and against the Revolutionists of that island.[2]

This disclosure aroused Canning, for it was a direct violation,

---

[1] *Vide* the correspondence in *B.F.S.P.*, xiii. 403–412.

[2] In fact, and it is a graver matter, the Neo-Holy representatives, in conference with Villèle at Paris in July 1824, had actually heard these instructions to Donzelot and had approved them, v. *A.H.R.*, Oct. 1924, p. 23.

if not of the Polignac Memorandum, at any rate of a special supplementary pledge given by Chateaubriand in November 1823 ' not to interfere ' between Legitimacy and revolution in Cuba.[1] Damas and Polignac both hinted to him now that armed intervention was necessary in Cuba, but his attitude became so formidable that neither ventured to propose France as the restorer of order. Finally, when Canning pressed for explanations, on the 15th July France gave an explicit pledge that French troops should not land in Cuba.[2]

As early as May 1825 the United States had become alarmed at the attitude of France towards Cuba. But, as has been indicated, she preferred to try to avert the danger by invoking the aid of Russia.[3] In August Canning approached the United States with a new overture. He proposed that, as the United States and England had most explicitly disclaimed aggressive designs, and as France had, though with less willingness, given pledges, the Three Powers should unite in a Tripartite Agreement with respect to Cuba. This arrangement was coldly regarded by the United States, not because they desired annexation, but because it would again have negatived all chance of incorporating Cuba in the Union.[4] France was compelled to decline owing to the connection she had with the Neo-Holy Alliance, which was opposed to any negotiation with England or with the United States. Towards the end of the year, as the French squadron was further increased in the West Indies, opinion in the United States became much alarmed. Remonstrances were at once made at Paris, and, to Canning's satisfaction, " as pert a paper as a

[1] *F.O. France*, 146/54. Stuart to Canning, Nov. 7/23. In March 1824 Canning had warned Cuban exiles in England that they would not be allowed to leave England to stir up revolution in Cuba, and this fact was known to Europe.

[2] *F.O. France*, 146/68. Granville to Canning, May 31, June 6, 14, and July 15/25.

[3] Brown, the U.S.A. Minister at Paris, appears to have made a communication on the subject to Damas in July (*v.* reference in his note to Damas, Jan. 2/26; *B.F.S.P.*, xiii. 444). He repeated this in October, but it does not appear to have been a remonstrance or to have produced a disclaimer. Granville says Brown was ' rather mild ' at this time, but ' excellent ' later. Gallatin (*Works*, 1879, ii. 353) says, Dec. 30/26, that when he was in France (1823 ?) he told Chateaubriand that England and France " could not take Cuba without making war on the United States."

[4] Adams apparently took this view. Gallatin was favourable to a Tripartite Agreement, Dec. 30/26 ; *Works*, ii. 353.

French Minister can desire to hear " [1] was presented to the French Government by ' Yankee Brown.' When, however, Rufus King, the new American representative in London, asked Canning to support these efforts, he met with a cold reception. Canning sourly remarked, " It is not Great Britain's fault that the Tripartite engagement was not arranged last year [1825], and that, if entered into, it would have spared France the American remonstrance and the United States the need of making it." As for Great Britain, he remarked, with conscious triumph, " we have long ago required and received ample explanations." [2] To renew them would only be to weaken their force. Here Canning had turned the tables on the United States. In the matter of the Monroe Doctrine he had been out-manœuvred. But now, so far as Cuba was concerned, it was England alone that had forced from France a disclaimer of aggressive designs, and when the United States intervened six months later, they could only give support to a cause already won. If anyone is entitled to the credit of preserving Cuba from France, Canning is that man.

(c) *Colombian and Mexican Designs* (1824–6)

The danger to Cuba was not only, as France thought it might be, from the United States ; or, as Canning thought it might be, from France ; or, as Adams thought it might be, from England. There was danger also from the now recognised and triumphant Spanish-American Republic. At the end of 1824 Bolivar had vanquished the last Spanish army in Peru and was able to turn his eyes towards the sea. The Colombian privateers had become more and more enterprising and successful. Not only did they swarm on the Spanish Main, they came over to Europe and snapped up Spanish prizes in the Mediterranean and in sight of Gibraltar. They had a small navy, consisting of one old 64 and fourteen smaller armed vessels. Now that the land war in Spanish America was over, it seemed natural to the Revolutionists to extend

---

[1] Anyone wishing to see ' the pert ' note will find it in *B.F.S.P.*, xiii. 444–5.

[2] *F.O. Spain*, 185/105. Canning to Lamb, No. 92, *cf.* Dec. 27/25 and Jan. 9/26. Granville to Canning, Jan. 2 and 5/26. Canning to Rufus King, Jan. 10/26.

their operations to the sea. Mexico, though with no naval resources, had a fair army, and was even more interested than Colombia. For Cuba was the arsenal of Spain in the New World and the base for Spanish descents upon Mexico. If the Spanish-American Republics once obtained possession of Cuba, they could hold it as a pledge, which even the obstinate Ferdinand might have been compelled to buy back at the price of recognising Spanish-American independence. On the other hand, if Spain refused to recognise their existence, they could add to their resources the harbours and wealth of Cuba.

These projects of Colombia and Mexico against Cuba, initiated in 1824 and openly voiced during 1825, caused great alarm in the United States. For they touched the sore, the sensitive spot in the American Union—the Slavery question. In Cuba there were slaves ; in Mexico and in Colombia all were free. Intervention by the two latter Powers in Cuba meant not only war but an invitation to slaves to rise against their masters, and the flame of a successful negro revolt might easily spread from Cuba to Georgia or to Virginia. A proclamation to negroes was actually prepared by Colombia and Mexico, and troops were massed at various points. Hence the United States deemed its special interests, if not its honour, involved in preventing any such outbreak or enterprise. Accordingly, in May and in December 1825, Colombia and Mexico were advised, in somewhat strong terms, by the United States to abstain from any expeditions they might design against Cuba, and, in any case, from arming or inciting the slaves.

Did Canning warn Colombia and Mexico not to attack Cuba ? England had had a slave-revolt in Demerara in 1823, which it had cost her some pains to suppress. It is stated that in October 1824 Canning pointed out to Michelena, the Mexican agent, the danger of a slave insurrection, and that in November and December 1825 he intimated to Hurtado, the Colombian agent, that the expedition would incur the displeasure of England. The evidence seems doubtful, and it is at least certain that his remonstrances were not as strong as those of Adams.[1] His own solution, of course, which had

---

[1] *Vide* J. M. Callahan, *Cuba and International Relations* (1899), pp. 144–51, and *Cuba and Anglo-American Relations*, Amer. Hist. Assoc. (1897), pp. 203–9. There is no trace of these interviews in British records. But Huskisson, speaking from recollection, seemed to think the story might be

already failed, was the Tripartite Agreement. This would have deprived the ' other Powers ' (*i.e.* France and the United States) of all pretexts for intervention. He had also proposed that the three guaranteeing Powers should also protest against such occupation by others (*i.e.* Mexico and Colombia). This move was intended as an inducement to Spain to grant a suspension of hostilities to the Spanish Republics. For, if that was conceded, it would be impossible for the Spanish Republics to attack Cuba, especially as Spain was protected against other Powers by the Triple Guarantee. Moreover, a suspension of hostilities by Spain would have been a step by her towards recognition.

This wise and statesmanlike move had failed, and, while the Mexican and Colombian designs against Cuba were still in the air, France suddenly sent a naval squadron to the West Indies on the pretext of collecting a debt from Hayti. This movement was ominous. The debt-collecting French squadron might soon become a landing party in Cuba. For it was remembered that the French Army had first been massed in the Pyrenees as a cordon against yellow fever and then transformed into an army which invaded Spain and suppressed constitutional principles. Adams and Clay were, of course, much more alarmed than Canning, for the latter had received pledges from France. The Washington Government prepared for action, Clay telling Vaughan, the new British representative, that " the occupation of Cuba by a French force would be just grounds of war on the part of the United States." [1]

At this interview Clay expressed alarm as to the designs of Colombia and Mexico on Cuba. On the 21st December 1825 Vaughan supinely suggested to Clay that the American Government should attempt to dissuade the two latter from the enterprise, and Clay said he was drawing up instructions

true, *v.* his *Speeches*, iii. 573, May 20/30. But Peel deprecated this view, Feb. 8/30, *Hans. Deb.*, N.S., xxii. 222. *If it is correct, Canning's tone was different in* 1826. The whole story looks doubtful, for even on Aug. 1/25 (*F.O. Spain*, 185/100. Canning to Lamb) Canning wrote that we " cannot exclude South America from Cuba," and it would have been unsafe to make any strong remonstrance after this. I am happy to say that Professor Callahan has very handsomely written to me, concurring with my views on this subject. The authority for the assertion is Sir R. Wilson, *v. Hans. Deb.*, N.S., xxii. 216, but he is not wholly to be trusted.

[1] *F.O. America*, 5/199. Vaughan to Canning, Sept. 30, Dec. 21/25, secret and confidential.

to that effect. Vaughan's suggestion proved welcome to
Clay. It excited very opposite sentiments in Canning, who
promptly disavowed him. " If it had been intended that
you should treat . . . in a matter so delicate, as the proposed interference of neutral Powers to controul the legitimate operations of belligerents against each other, You
would not have been left without instructions, upon a point
of as much novelty, as delicacy, and importance. If [went
on Canning] the United States think their interests likely
to be affected by the continuance of the war between Spain
and the new transatlantick States they are probably right,
and perfectly at liberty to employ their good offices to bring
about a pacification.

" We have long endeavored to do so but in vain ; and
Spain has been uniformly the recusant party. If the United
States think that particular interests of their own require
that a certain operation of war should not be undertaken by
one of the belligerents,—it is a question, and a very nice one
for them, . . . but it is manifest that we have not the like
interest either to induce or to justify us in so unusual an interposition. . . . If it is merely the interests of the United
States that are concerned, that ground of interference can
only belong to them, nor is there any obligation upon us to
share the odium of such an interposition." [1]

Canning's instructions to his representative appointed for
Panama did, in fact, finish the question of Cuba for his lifetime. He transmitted the correspondence over the Tripartite
Agreement, adding : " You will see how earnestly it is desired
by the United States, by France, and by this country, that
Cuba should remain a colony of Spain. The British Government, indeed, so far from denying the right of the New States
of America to make a hostile attack upon Cuba, whether
considered simply as a possession of a Power with whom they
are at war, or as an Arsenal from which expeditions are fitted
out against them, that we have uniformly refused to join
with the United States in remonstrating with Mexico and
Colombia against the supposed intention, or intimating that
we should feel displeasure at the execution of it.

" We should indeed regret it but we arrogate to ourselves

[1] *F.O. America*, 5/209. Canning to Vaughan, Feb. 18/26.

no right to controul the military operations of one belligerent against another.

" The Government of the United States, however, professes itself of a different opinion. It conceives that the interests of the United States would be so directly affected by either the occupation of the Havannah by an invading force, or by the consequence which an attack on Cuba, even if unsuccessful, might produce in the interior of the island, that the Cabinet of Washington hardly disguises its intention to interfere directly, and by force, to prevent or repress such an operation.

" Neither England nor France could see with indifference the United States in possession of Cuba.

" Observe, therefore, the complicated consequence to which an expedition to Cuba by Mexico or Colombia might lead, and let the States assembled at Panama consider whether it is worth while to continue a war, the only remaining operation of which (that is likely to be sensibly felt by their adversary) is thus morally interdicted to them by the consequences to which it would lead." [1] Colombia took the hint and put pressure on Mexico to abstain from interference, and as Colombia had the ships Mexico could send no men to Cuba.[2]

From this time forward Cuba became relatively unimportant. Suspicions of England's intentions were felt by the United States towards the end of 1826, and Gallatin approached Canning on the subject. Canning would give no pledge, because he thought at the moment that we might have to occupy Cuba if England went to war with Spain.[3] But then, as always, he had no designs on Cuba, for he held that England had too much territory, and that she must show an example of territorial disinterestedness to other nations. Gallatin was not very satisfied with this interview, but, in reality, the

---

[1] *F.O. Colombia*, 97/115. Instructions to E. J. Dawkins, Mar. 18/26. Dawkins to Canning, private, Oct. 15/26.

[2] Callahan, *Cuba and Anglo-American Relations*, Amer. Hist. Assoc. Report of 1897, p. 213.

[3] *Ibid.*, p. 214. Gallatin (*Works*, ii. 346) thinks Canning refused to give a pledge as to not annexing Cuba. But he confesses that he did not know of Canning's previous pledge to King in 1825 (p. 347). I infer that Canning refused to give a pledge not to *occupy*, which Gallatin misinterpreted as a refusal to give a pledge not to *annex*, Cuba.

question of Cuba was finished.   For the rest of Canning's life Cuba remained secure from all attempts upon it.[1]

4. THE CONGRESS OF PANAMA (1826)

" *The world of Columbus has ceased to belong to Spain.*"—BOLIVAR, 23rd November 1826.

The congress was based on a broad and statesmanlike idea of Bolivar's.   It was one which the ' Liberator ' had matured for ten years.   He wished to have a Congress of Liberty and to invite not only all the Spanish-American Republics, but the United States.   It was also to include the three constitutional monarchies of England, Holland, and· Brazil.[2]   It was to discuss the Confederation of Latin America, and more particularly to obtain the recognition by Spain of her independence. The papers of Bolivar show that he himself had seen visions of a League of American Nations sanctioned by Great Britain.[3] The idea was vague and splendid and yet statesmanlike, as were many of Bolivar's political conceptions.   From the first, however, it was doomed to failure.   It suffered much from the fact that Bolivar himself could not attend, more from the lack of enthusiasm which it evoked.   Holland and England sent representatives, but as unofficial spectators. The United States offered to send two representatives, but the disputes in the Senate over the matter were so fierce that their purpose was delayed.   Eventually one died on the way and the other arrived too late to take part in it.   Brazil feared the Neo-Holy Alliance and the Spanish Republics almost

[1] Poinsett, the United States Minister in Mexico, attributed the abandonment of Mexican and Colombian designs on Cuba at the congress, first to the warnings of Adams, and next to their inability to fit out an adequate expedition.   To Clay, Sept. 23/26, *B.F.S.P.*, xiii. 990.   A more substantial reason seems to have been Bolivar's desire to ingratiate himself with England.   He told the British Consul-General in Peru (for transmission to Canning) that ' he [Bolivar] did not much like the attack on Cuba,' *F.O. Peru*, 61/8.   Ricketts to Canning, Sept. 5/26.   W. R. Manning, *Early Diplomatic Relations of U.S.A. and Mexico*, [1916], is inclined to suspect Canning of designs on Cuba, *v.* pp. 159–62, but I think the evidence is unconvincing.

[2] This was the plan in 1815.   In 1824 he issued invitations to the Latin-American States ; in 1825 the United States were invited on the suggestion both of Colombia and of Mexico, but apparently not by Bolivar. England and the Netherlands received invitations apparently at his suggestion.

[3] W. S. Robertson, *Hispanic-American Relations*, p. 381 n.   For Bolivar's views on England, *v.* Appendix IV.

equally, and, though it agreed to take part, its representatives never arrived. Buenos Aires, from jealousy of Bolivar, refused to attend. Chile declined, probably for the same reason, but alleging that the island of Chiloe was still unconquered. So the congress actually consisted of Colombia, Mexico, Peru, and Guatemala. The latter was of no importance, the Peruvian deputies were extravagant even for South Americans, and Colombia and Mexico found that grave differences existed between them.

For our purpose the chief interest of the congress lies in its attitude towards British policy. The invitation was finally sent by Colombia in 1826, and contained the interesting comment that " Great Britain, situated as she is in a certain manner by the nature of her power and her policy between the Old World and the New, perhaps takes greater interest than any other Power, in the nature of the Equilibrium between the one and the other." [1] Canning accepted, and chose as representative Mr Dawkins. His instructions are dated the 18th March 1826, and inform him that the sole object of despatching him is to " obtain the most regular and correct information of its proceedings, and to assure the American States collectively of the friendly sentiments and the lively interest in their welfare and tranquillity " felt and expressed by the British Government. He considers the motive of summoning an English representative to have been " a due sense of the benefits which they [the American States] have derived and continue to derive from a friendly intercourse with Great Britain, and a very natural desire to increase the importance of that assembly in the estimation of the Old World."

Two subjects mentioned in these instructions may be speedily dismissed. Canning tells Dawkins to forward in every way the settlement of the dispute between Brazil and Buenos Aires, if it should come before the congress. Secondly, he tells him to represent, " not by direct official intimation, but you should not disguise the sentiments of your Gov[ernmen]t," [2] that Great Britain hopes the new States

[1] *F.O. Spain*, 185/105. Canning to Lamb, Feb. 15/26, enclosing Hurtado's invitation of Jan. 11/26.

[2] This method of representation was used by Dawkins throughout the congress.

will adopt those principles of maritime law on which she has uniformly acted. "And you will take care to have it duly understood that our determination to act upon these principles, as it has not been shaken by European confederacies, so it will not be altered by any Resolution or combination of the States of the New World." The old contention of the United States, that 'free ships make free goods' was, of course, directly opposed to this. If the Spanish-Americans agreed with the United States, therefore, there might be serious trouble. Despite all his liberal and conciliatory ideas, Canning was immovable as adamant when he thought the honour or interest of England really concerned. He evidently did upon this occasion, and the words above quoted show that exclusively English policy which Adams described as the characteristic of Canning. Here, then, were the beginnings of a serious dispute, which the differences in the congress, however, rendered harmless.

Canning proceeds to define the general attitude of England towards the Spanish-American Governments. He requests information about their feelings towards each other, and the degree of influence in their concerns which they may appear inclined to allow to the United States of North America. "You will understand that to a league among the States, lately Colonies of Spain, limited to objects growing out of their common relations to Spain, H[is] M[ajesty']s Gov[ernmen]t would not object.

"But any project for putting the U[nited] S[tates] of North America at the head of an American Confederacy, as against Europe, would be highly displeasing to your Gov[ernmen]t. *It would be felt as an ill return for the service which has been rendered to those States, and the dangers which have been averted from them, by the countenance and friendship, and publick declarations of Great Britain; and it would too probably at no very distant period endanger the peace both of America and of Europe.*" [1]

There were only two incidents of importance at the congress from the British point of view. They discussed the question

[1] The italics are my own. A passage of almost equal strength is to be found in further instructions of Mar. 18/26. Canning to Dawkins, *F.O. Colombia*, 97/115.

of obtaining recognition from Spain by offering a monetary compensation, England to act as the ' honest broker,' but this scheme soon dropped.[1] A curious incident then arose owing to the fact that some despatches from Everett, the United States Minister in Spain, became public. These suggested that England's efforts to obtain recognition for the Republic at Madrid were of a lukewarm character.[2] Gual, the chief Colombian representative, plainly showed his suspicions to Dawkins. The latter, who was an astute man, flatly contradicted the statement of Everett, and finally supplied Gual with copies of various British despatches from Madrid, which proved the exertions and sincerity of our attempts to secure recognition. English ascendancy at the congress was soon and completely recovered. Gual talked ' unreservedly ' to Dawkins " of the imprudence of the United States, of the errors committed by Mr Everett, and of the mischief which may be done by the indiscreet publication of his correspondance [sic]." Irritation between the United States and England was increased by the signing of a general confederative treaty between the Spanish-Americans on 15th July. That treaty was one arranging for a common army and mutual defence between Colombia, Mexico, Peru, and Guatemala. It contained the clause, " any American State may be admitted into the Confederation within a year after the signature of the treaty." Dawkins promptly inquired of Mr Gual whether this principle extended to the United States. His answer was, " Certainly if they will declare war against Spain." This was disquieting, but the matter dropped, as the United States had no intention of declaring war or of joining the league. Nor were even Spanish-American States enthusiastic. In the end Colombia alone ratified the treaty. The congress was adjourned to Tacubaya in Mexico, but in fact it never assembled there.

" The general influence of the United States," wrote Dawkins (15th October), " is not in my opinion to be feared. It certainly exists in Colombia, but it has been very much weakened even there by their protests against an attack upon Cuba, and by

---

[1] Vide *F.O. Colombia*, 97/115. Dawkins to Canning, private, Oct. 15/26. He says the purchase scheme would have gone through but for the opposition of Michelena of Mexico. Bolivar approved of it.

[2] Everett's chief despatch is Oct. 20/25, *B.F.S.P.*, xiii. 433–8.

the indiscretions they have committed at Madrid." [1] There were, however, other reasons for the decline of the United States' influence. Adams had been hard pressed by his own Congress and also by the Latin-American States to explain what means the United States intended to use to protect them against Europe. He felt obliged to answer this by a message to the House of Representatives, 15th March 1826. As regards the non-colonisation pledge, he merely suggested that the United States had free commercial intercourse with all parts of the Continent, and if a European Power founded a fresh colony she must encroach on these rights. This interpretation was new and unconvincing. A later passage brought the protection which the United States was asked to extend to other American Powers within the narrowest limits. " The purpose of this Government is to concur in none [*i.e.* no measures] which would import hostility to Europe, or justly excite resentment in any of her States. Should it be deemed advisable to contract any conventional Engagement on this topic, our views would extend no further than to a mutual pledge of the Parties to the Compact, to maintain the principle *in application to its own territory*, and to permit no Colonial lodgments or establishment of European Jurisdiction on its own soil." If there was " obtrusive interference from abroad " . . . " a joint Declaration of its character, and exposure of it to the World, may be probably all that the occasion would require. Whether the United States should, or should not, be Parties to such a Declaration, may justly form a part of the deliberation." [2] It is difficult to say what this singularly ambiguous utterance meant, but it certainly did not mean very much. Now everyone knew what Canning meant. England had obtained a public pledge from France

[1] *F.O. Colombia*, 97/115. Dawkins to Canning, June 6, July 5, 6, 7, 17, Oct. 15/26, private.
[2] The italics are my own. Adams' Message, Mar. 15/26, *B.F.S.P.*, xiii. 450–1. Mr Benton, Adams' opponent in the Senate, in *Thirty Years' View*, [N.Y., 1854], i. 67, commented severely. He thought it " incredible that Mr Adams could be deceived in his understanding; and according to him [Adams] this ' Monroe Doctrine ' . . . was entirely confined to our own borders. . . . The United States, so far from extending gratuitous protection to the territories of other States, would neither give, nor receive, aid in any such enterprise, but that each should use its own means, within its own borders, for its own exemption from European colonial intrusion."

that she would not attempt to use ' force or menace ' against
the new States.   If she or any Power, other than Spain,
did make the attempt, they knew England would fight.   It
was natural, therefore, that the prestige of the United States
should sink, and that of England rise, after the Congress of
Panama.

The only other indication of Canning's policy that need be
given is that in which he defines his view of the normal relations
of England towards a Latin-American State.   These are to
be found in his instructions to Lord Ponsonby, who was
appointed Minister Plenipotentiary to Buenos Aires, and
instructed to pass through Brazil on the way, to see if he
could avert the threatened war between the two countries.
On the 18th February 1826 he instructed him to communicate
the " anxiety of H[is] M[ajesty's] Gov[ernmen]t to restore and
reserve peace among the new States of America ; or the
deep interest which, in the opinion of this Government, those
States have, in avoiding to give room, by their differences with
each other, for the interference of foreigners in their political
concerns."   An embittered quarrel was in progress between
Brazil and Buenos Aires over the possession of Montevideo.
In a supplementary despatch of 18th March 1826, Canning
discusses the claims of the two governments.   Ponsonby is
to divert " the Brazilian Minister from any attempt to change
the practical question at issue [the possession of Montevideo]
into one of abstract legitimate right."   The Emperor of
Brazil had apparently thought of recognising the ' unextin-
guished rights of Spain ' to Montevideo, and thus depriving
Buenos Aires of any claim.   Canning therefore instructs
Ponsonby as follows : " Important as the question of Monte
Video may be to the Brazilian Gov[ernmen]t, it is scarcely
less important that the discussion of that question should not
be conducted on such principles, or supported on their side
by such arguments, as to array against the monarchy of
Brazil the common feeling and common interests of all the
Republican States of Spanish America."   Canning then warns
the Brazilian Government of trying ' too high ' the patience
of Bolivar, who is being incited to undertake a war against
Brazil, " for the express purpose of overturning a Monarchy,
which stands alone on the vast continent of America, and

which is considered by those enamoured of democratical forms of Government, as essentially inconsistent with the secure existence of the American Republicks." Canning suggests that Buenos Aires has the strongest claim to Montevideo and has, moreover, force to back it. But if Montevideo were transferred to Buenos Aires, it would still be reasonable " to secure to Brazil an uninterrupted enjoyment of the navigation of the river Plate." The British Government would guarantee the observance of such stipulations. And though " on the general principle of avoiding as much as possible engagements of this character," the British Government would prefer to stand aside, it would give this guarantee, " if it were desired by both parties . . . rather than that the treaty should not be concluded." Great Britain, " while scrupulously neutral in conduct " during the war, " cannot fail to be in favour of that Belligerent, who shall have shown the readiest disposition to bring that dispute to a friendly termination." A secret instruction accompanies the despatch, informing Ponsonby that in case of " any essential change . . . in the form of government his functions will be suspended," and that he is " studiously to keep aloof from all political intrigues and all contentions of party in B[uenos] A[ires]."

Ponsonby's efforts at mediation and his attempts to interpose the friendly office of Great Britain between Brazil and Buenos Aires ended in failure, and war began. Canning at once wrote (27th November 1826) : [1] " As to taking part with either side in the Contest, your Lordship cannot too peremptorily repress any expectation of that nature." He then proceeds to explain the failure of the negotiations. " There is much of the Spanish character in the inhabitants of the Colonial Establishments of Spain ; and there is nothing in the Spanish character more striking than its impatience of foreign advice, and its suspicion of gratuitous service." His original instructions had foreseen that the suggestion respecting Montevideo " was not unlikely to excite a jealousy of some design favourable to British interests. Such a jealousy has been openly inculcated by the publick press of the United States of North America, and no doubt secretly by their diplomatic Agents." He advises Ponsonby, therefore, ' to let

[1] *F.O. Argentine*, 6/13.

that matter drop entirely,' unless Buenos Aires itself should raise it. The best chance to suggest their doing so would be by " some slight manifestation of resentment at any such misconstruction of our motives." The last instruction of Canning on this point was to Ponsonby on 21st February 1827 : " Mr Gordon [the new ambassador] will press the many considerations which render peace essential to the interests and safety of Brazil . . . with all the means in his power short of that degree of importunity, which after the repeated refusal would become derogatory to the dignity of Great Britain." [1]

From this long survey the conclusion and the policy emerge compact and definite. Once a new State had been recognised, whether large or small, monarchy or republic, Canning accorded to it the full rights of statehood. When Damas suggested to him in 1825 that we should give facilities to the Spanish ships in European waters and refuse them to the Colombian, Canning replied indignantly that, though it was to our advantage to do so, it was not possible for England to discriminate between States because one happened to be a monarchy and the other a republic. Over the River Plate he went so far as to offer to guarantee the freedom of its navigation, if requested by both Buenos Aires and Brazil. But this was a limited, defensive, and maritime guarantee, which he could give. He made it clear that he would give no territorial guarantee.[2] Similarly, he rebuked Ponsonby for supposing that England advised the retention of the Constitution in Brazil. England had, he said, a predilection for monarchy, but her general principle was non-interference, and she had no more right to meddle in the internal affairs of Brazil than of St Petersburg.

Canning's attention was first turned to Latin America by our immense commercial interests. Yet he never aimed at obtaining exclusive trade privileges from them for England. Still less did he harbour any territorial designs, or dream of English princes on Latin-American thrones. The ascend-

[1] It is interesting to note that Canning's suggestion that the Monte-video problem should be solved, by its becoming independent both of Brazil and Buenos Aires, was ultimately adopted after his death.
[2] He disavowed and recalled Hamilton in 1824 for suggesting England would guarantee a loan to Mexico. In 1826 he refused to guarantee either loan, or territory, or succession to Brazil.

ancy he wished was a moral one, and he aspired to be their
leader, but not their controller, in the ways of policy. We
get one interesting hint of the use to which he thought they
might be put, in his instructions of 13th October 1825 to the
English Ambassador at Constantinople. The Sultan is to
be warned of insulting too grossly, by his acts, the moral
opinion of the world :—

" The recent events in the Western hemisphere have approxi-
mated, as it were, the different divisions of the world to each
other, and have brought new Powers to bear on every question
of political struggle or change, in whatever part of the globe
it may arise. The Porte cannot doubt that all the inhabitants
of both Americas to a man, are in their hearts favourers of
the Greek cause, and might at no distant period become active
co-operators in it. This is not the language of intimidation,
it is that of truth."

Though he would not have been sorry to make use of them
in Europe, Canning's idea was to leave the Latin-Americans
to work out their own destinies, to protect them against undue
influence either from the United States or from Europe, and
to indicate to them that England was a disinterested and
powerful friend. He succeeded to the extent that he obtained
the commercial hegemony, and a certain political ascendancy,
in Latin America. Further progress was restricted partly
by Canning's own principles, and partly by that moral law
which limits the success of revolutions by the capacity of the
peoples who make them. To stabilise the conditions of Latin
America would have required a perpetual interference or a
veiled kind of protection, to neither of which Canning would
ever have consented. His remedy was to facilitate their
commercial development in the hope that it would tranquillise
their politics. But he always refused to sanction their loans
or to give direct financial aid, for he knew that such financial
methods would bring political complications in their train.

Neither in internal development nor in external policy
did the new States fulfil the hopes of any of their admirers.
' I regard [Latin] America as in the chrysalis ' said Bolivar
in 1822, and he went on to prophesy anarchy or militarism in
Peru, Mexico, and Buenos Aires. Bolivar was right. Spanish
America has proved miraculously unstable, more unstable

even than the Balkans, and nothing could have tranquillised conditions in these countries at that time. " Against the theocratic peoples, who were seeking to overshadow the destinies of the earth," wrote a great South American, " he [Canning] evoked the opposition of these free democracies destined to establish the benefits of liberty on a firm footing. His hope was premature." It was, and yet his action was decisive in the impression it made on the New World. When Rocafuerte, the Minister of Mexico, talked of Canning's illness in August 1827, he ' could not refrain from tears.' About the same time Parish, the British Consul-General in Buenos Aires, was hoping that ' our old master Canning ' would not be displaced at the Foreign Office ; " no one but him (*sic*) will take the same interest in South American affairs." [1] The Spanish-American States have reverenced Canning as the States of the American Union have reverenced Chatham, and for the same reason. For they instinctively feel that he was the one statesman beyond the Atlantic who understood and sympathised with them at the great crisis of their destiny. And, whatever be the ultimate judgment of history, Canning's fame is not likely to diminish with Latin-Americans.

[1] *F.O.*, 95/591. Woodbine Parish to Staveley, Aug. 25/27. Parish knew of the ministerial crisis in England, but did not know of its outcome.

PART IV

PORTUGAL AND THE NEW WORLD

CHAPTER VIII

THE RESTORATION OF BRITISH INFLUENCE
IN PORTUGAL AND BRAZIL (1823–5)

CHAPTER IX

THE INDEPENDENCE OF BRAZIL

CHAPTER VIII

THE RESTORATION OF BRITISH INFLUENCE
IN PORTUGAL AND BRAZIL (1823–5)

I. INTRODUCTORY

FROM the first fortnight of his accession to power until the
very last of his life, Canning was occupied with questions
relating to Portugal and to Brazil. In these two countries,
during the years 1820–5, the whole of European and British
diplomacy was exhibited on a miniature stage. As elsewhere,
the revolution in Portugal was followed by the attempt of
the Neo-Holy Alliance to cause the Constitution to fail by
withdrawing their diplomatic representatives. Then there
was the revolt of Brazil, and the hardly concealed attempt
of France to interfere there by force of arms. In Portugal
itself there was a distinct threat of French interference of the
same kind during 1823–4. Combined with this went the
attempt of the Neo-Holy Alliance to intimidate the Sovereign
of Portugal and his rebel son in Brazil, through a conference
of Neo-Holy Ambassadors which sat constantly at Lisbon,
at Paris, and at Madrid. As a counter to this attempt Brazil
developed the germ of a Monroe Doctrine of her own, which
gave much anxiety to Canning. But every such attempt was
defeated, and by 1825 Canning had recovered British influence
at Lisbon, and had achieved the Independence of Brazil,
in defiance of the Old World. In this minor theatre of
operations the success of Canning was already great, but it
was not until 1826 that the affairs of Brazil and Portugal
achieved European importance, and it was then only that the
power of Canning was really exhibited. Men still differ, and
perhaps will always, as to what Canning did for Spanish

America, but there can be no dispute as to what he did for Portugal and for Brazil.

In 1820 Portugal resembled Spain in its anarchy and revolution, and also in being launched on a course which was bound to lead to the loss of splendid transmarine possessions.   In both cases, too, the mass of the people in Europe were brutishly ignorant, the democratic revolution was due to a mutinous and ill-paid soldiery, and the reaction to priests.   In both cases the fundamental cause of American revolt was the hatred of the Creoles, or natives, for misgovernment from over the sea, and a protest against the monopolising of power by Europeans.   There was, however, one important and fundamental difference.   In both Old Spain and New, revolt was headed by military adventurers or by ambitious generals.   In Portugal and Brazil the forces of reaction and revolution, alike, were headed by a son of the Royal House.   This fact touched the European diplomats.   They much preferred the coercion of a king by his sons to the coercion of a king by his subjects.

In both cases these revolutionary movements excited the exaggerated fear of contemporaries.   From their history, their old-time heroism, and their splendid dominions, these two countries had acquired a renown which neither folly, impotence, nor misgovernment could wholly tarnish.   The absurdities of the kings, the pronunciamentos of the generals, the violence of constitutionalists or of reactionaries did not really affect other lands.   For no countries (not even Naples and Piedmont) were at once so cut off from the rest of Europe, so futile in their policies, nor so semi-ludicrous in their agonies. The two kingdoms or kings were the ' tragic-comedians ' of Europe, at whom she should have laughed.   If she had regarded their constitutional experiments with the same scepticism or indifference that she now regards similar movements in the Balkans, she would have had a better measure of their value.   Yet it is true that, while the fear in Europe was exaggerated, the danger in America was real.   The Neo-Holy Alliance indeed feared and hated constitutions in Europe for their own sake.   But they feared also their reflex action upon the New World.   Wellington expressed what most of Europe thought when he wrote that, " no country in a modern constitutional state can keep a dependency." [1] Certainly the Constitutional Cortes of Lisbon could not.

2. CASTLEREAGH AND PORTUGAL (1820–2)

The situation of Portugal differed from that of Spain because the King had been absent from Lisbon for over a dozen years. Portugal hated the corrupt and incompetent Regency which he had left behind. The army, controlled by Marshal Beresford and his British officers, was miserably paid. Both soldiers and civilians were revolution-ripe. In April 1820 Beresford himself found the situation so alarming that he sailed to Rio to advise the King to return to Portugal at once, unless he wished to lose his Crown. In his absence revolution was practically inevitable.

Beresford found a singular Royal Family at Rio, for within its circle were the strongest dissensions. King John was agreeable, good-natured, enlightened, but terribly vacillating. He was feebly constitutional, his heir Pedro was flamboyantly so. Dom Pedro had many defects, ' educated by and with negro boys ' as a youngster, and consorting with light women, pimps, and horse-dealers since that date.[2] He was accused later of ' ferocity and cowardice,' but allowed ' energy and passion,' and these last qualities stood him in good stead when he had to strike out his own line for himself. The Queen, a sister of Ferdinand VII. of Spain, was even more absolutist than her brother, and therefore the opponent of her husband and eldest son in this, as in every other, way. Her infidelity was as notorious as her husband's morality. But she had energy, and infected with her ideas Dom Miguel, her second son, who was to develop ' cruel and murderous ' tendencies, and her granddaughter, the Princess of Beira. Beresford said all the daughters of the family had fits, though they did not seem to have any political views. But the eldest of them, Isabella Maria, a pretty girl, was to show unsuspected character, and to foil both her mother and her brother by proclaiming the Constitution in Portugal. John VI. wanted to go to Lisbon because the Queen preferred being at Rio.

[1] *W.N.D.*, i. 207, to Beresford, Dec. 14/21. He meant that Parliaments could not govern Colonies.
[2] Ponsonby to Bagot, Oct. 17/26. Bagot, *G.C. & F.*, ii. 310.

The Crown Princess wanted Dom Pedro to go to Portugal because Rio disagreed with his health. But none of them could take a resolution. Wellington said, coarsely, they were all timid, ' geldings in every sense of the word.' And, while Beresford implored them to take a decision in Brazil, the revolution burst in Portugal.

It was in August 1820 that disturbances first arose at Oporto, where the troops arrested their British officers. The revolution flamed along to the capital, uniting for a moment clergy and soldiers in demanding the Constitution, in praising the mutineers of Oporto, and in crying, " Religion for ever, the King for ever, the Constitution for ever ! " The Spanish Constitutionalist Ambassador " was seen [or heard] on horseback in the streets shouting for the new Constitution." One Junta arose at Oporto, and another at Lisbon. The latter began by transforming, and ended by suppressing, the hated Regency. In October the Oporto Junta joined the Lisbon one and indulged in fraternal embraces and in highflown oratory. The anti-British feeling swelled high. Beresford, who returned to Lisbon on the 10th October, was refused a landing and went back in dudgeon to England.

Castlereagh had thus a new care on his shoulders. British officers had been treated with contumely in Portugal, British interests were endangered, and the revolutionary contagion seemed to be spreading. He took up a moderate attitude in a despatch which he made known to the diplomats of Europe. He could not, he said, recognise the new regime, for the King of Portugal's views as to it were still unknown. And it was to him that England's envoy was accredited. But he was equally prepared to say that England would not " favour vindictive measures, or join with the King to attempt a system of unqualified reaction." At the same time, he sent off an urgent message to Brazil advising that the King should either come at once in person to Lisbon, or, if that was impossible, that he should despatch a member of the Royal Family. If he did not do this, Castlereagh hinted strongly that England might have to reconsider her ancient treaties which guaranteed the defence of Portugal.[1]

[1] *F.O. Portugal*, 63/231. Castlereagh to E. M. Ward, Nov. 8/20, enclosing instruction to Lord C. Stuart, sent to Vienna for Metternich. Metternich, with some disingenuousness, claimed this despatch as a proof (a)

3. England's Treaty Obligations to Portugal
(1373–1822)

What were the obligations of England to Portugal? It is well to settle this question here, for it was endlessly discussed in the next few years. The connection between the two countries had existed for nearly four centuries and a half. British troops had first landed to aid Portugal in 1380, and treaties of alliance were signed both in 1373 and in 1386; the countries arranging to give mutual aid if attacked. This treaty was renewed or confirmed nine times in the fifteenth century. When Philip of Spain conquered Portugal in 1580 England retaliated by attempting to rescue her in 1589. When Portugal at last successfully revolted in 1640, England made haste to conclude a new treaty of peace and commerce (29th January 1642), which preserved " alliances and Confederacies formerly made and contracted." Cromwell negotiated a new treaty, and in 1661 Charles II. confirmed all treaties since 1641. He bound himself to send ' ten good ships of war ' if Portugal were attacked, and, by a secret article, " to defend all colonies or conquests of Portugal." These arrangements were confirmed by the Methuen Commercial Treaty (1703), which introduced ' so much port-wine and so much gout ' into England, and by other instruments.

In two wars—that of the Spanish Succession and of the Seven Years—the defence, and even the existence, of Portugal was assured by the landing of British troops. In 1801 Portugal, though attacked, was not defended by England. In 1807 the British hurried the Regent (afterwards King John) on shipboard, just as Napoleon's troops entered Lisbon. This was done by Canning's order during his first Foreign Ministry in 1807, and the Regent was thus induced " to convey to the New World the hopes and fortunes of the Portuguese monarchy and the means of founding it anew in augmented strength and

that revolution was contagious, (b) that Castlereagh had declared that Portugal had ceased to be England's ally because she engaged in revolution, (c) that he refused to recognise revolution. Hence Metternich pretended that Castlereagh really agreed with him, V.S.A., Weisungen nach Russland, Bd. 2. Metternich to Lieven, Nov. 24/20. It is interesting to note in this connection that the members of the Neo-Holy Alliance withdrew their diplomatic representatives as a protest against the Constitution, but that the step did not lead to war.

splendour." Wellesley soon arrived and set Beresford to organise a Portuguese army, which combined with British troops to liberate their country. The bonds of alliance were naturally drawn more tightly than ever, though the main instruments were signed in 1810, after Canning's fall. The ports of Brazil were opened at once, and a treaty of commerce and navigation signed (19th February 1810) which was to endure till 1825. There was also a new treaty of alliance (19th February 1810) confirming one of 1807, and, in addition, binding Great Britain never to recognise as King of Portugal any but the legitimate descendant of the House of Braganza (Article 3). The settlement of Vienna by the treaty of the 22nd January 1815, however, annulled the special conditions of the guarantees of 1807 and 1810 (*i.e.* the British perpetual guarantee of the House of Braganza) and left the obligations on the pre-1807 basis.

It cannot be denied that the older treaties involved Great Britain in very extensive obligations. Article 3 of John of Gaunt's treaty of 1386 appears to bind her to aid in suppressing revolts or rebels in Portugal (*i.e.* to interfere in her internal affairs). The secret article of the treaty of 23rd June 1661 bound her to " defend and protect all Conquests or Colonies belonging to the Crown of Portugal, against all his Enemies, as well future as present." [1] But these almost unlimited extensions of obligation were held to have lapsed by time or disuse. At any rate, the British Government did not admit them. Castlereagh in 1820 stated that " our engagements were never intended to apply to combating revolutionary movements inside Portugal itself " ; though he fully admitted our obligation to defend her against ' ordinary invasion ' or external attack.[2] Canning took the same view in principle throughout, and it is the key to the whole of his policy. It is not clear that Castlereagh extended the territorial guarantee to the Colonial possessions of Portugal, but it is certain that Canning did not.[3]

---

[1] *B.F.S.P.*, i. 1812–14, p. 501.
[2] *F.O. Portugal*, 63/227.   Castlereagh to Sir E. Thornton, Nov. 15/20.
[3] *F.O. Portugal*, 179/28.   Canning to À Court, Jan 13/25, enclosing Jan. 13/25 to Chamberlain, Brazil.   Wellington thought the guarantee did extend to the Colonies, Mar. 5/25.   *W.N.D.*, ii. 423–4.   *Vide* Appendix II. (*c*).

4. Effects of the King's Return to Portugal
(1821–3)

By the beginning of 1821 even King John saw that he must do something if he did not want to lose the Crown of Portugal. If he departed from Rio, however, he was likely to lose that of Brazil. After first deciding to send Pedro, he finally agreed to go himself. He left Dom Pedro in charge at Rio, with the title of " Regent and Perpetual Defender of Brazil," with secret instructions to do what he could do to preserve the union of the two Crowns. The King sailed on the 26th April 1821 in a Portuguese ship, on which a British captain commented thus : " I never saw anything apparently more dirty or worse arranged . . . for a King's accommodation." On the 3rd July the watchers at Lisbon, for the first time for fourteen years, saw the Portuguese Royal Standard flying from a ship. On the 4th the prodigal King landed. He had no teeth, he made " a sort of grunting noise between each word," his deportment was ' apathetic ' but ' with an appearance of trepidation.' However, if there was ' no enthusiasm,' there was ' no opposition.' [1] The conduct of the Assembly had been extraordinary ; they had even questioned the paternity of the King's children, and their discussions were " rather like the debates of Bedlamites than of statesmen." None the less the King accepted everything and swore to the Constitution immediately after he had landed, while pathetically reproaching the Assembly for not having helped him to choose his ministers.

The Assembly now proceeded to the wildest and most extravagant decrees for the purpose of bringing Brazil under effective control, which naturally had the effect of deciding that colony in favour, of rebellion. The revolt of Brazil actually took place in September 1822, and Dom Pedro was proclaimed Emperor on the 1st December. Here it is enough to say that Canning heard of the revolt early in October 1822 and pronounced separation, in the *de facto* sense, to be inevitable.

During the last half of 1821 and the first half of 1822

[1] *F.O. Portugal*, 63/238. Capt. Duncan to Ward, July 3 ; Ward to Castlereagh, July 9/21.

Castlereagh had been gravely irritated by the insulting conduct of the Portuguese Government towards him, but he maintained his policy " to carry on our relations with that country, without reference to the state of its political institutions, and in the spirit of existing treaties." [1]   Before he had been a fortnight in office, Canning was called upon to make clear his policy and to meet a new crisis.

Portugal was much frightened by the threats of France against Spain. On the 25th September 1822 she invoked the treaty of 1810, and formally demanded that England should at once promise to guarantee Portugal against French attack. She stated that, if England did not do so, Portugal would make a treaty of offensive and defensive alliance with Constitutional Spain. In fact this treaty had already been proposed on the 14th September (*i.e.* ten days *before* the threat). Canning replied (1st October) that the alliance treaty of 1810 had been annulled in 1815, that England was ready to fulfil her old obligations in defending Portugal, but " that the signature of an *offensive* alliance with another Power to act against a third would prevent Portugal from having ' a right ' to call upon His Majesty for aid." [2]   Owing to this communication the project of an *offensive* treaty with Constitutional Spain came to nought. The treaty for defensive alliance and for mutual guarantee of political institutions collapsed because Spain would not ratify it. [3]   In a note of the 9th December Canning further explained that Portugal must not provoke the war by aggression, and that our obligations referred to defence against attack jointly or severally by France or Spain.

The French invasion of Spain, which began in April 1823, naturally caused alarm in Portugal as well as in England. Canning in his despatch of the 31st March 1823 made it quite clear that, so long as Portugal was not herself aggressive, England would defend her territorial integrity against France

---

[1] *F.O. Portugal*, 63/250. Castlereagh to Ward, Mar. 22/22, private. In January 1822 he had peremptorily refused to guarantee the political institutions of Portugal. *Cp.* Webster, 254 n.

[2] *W.N.D.*, i. 303-5, gives Sarmento's note, and Canning's reply, Oct. 1, pp. 335-6; copies of further correspondence, Dec. 9/22, Jan. 14 and 17/23, in *F.O. France*, 146/55, enclosed in Canning to Stuart, No. 5, Jan. 24/23.

[3] *F.O. Spain*, 185/91. Canning to À Court, Feb. 4/23.

or any other Power attacking it. To do French statesmen justice, they did everything in their power at this moment to abstain from any provocation. Their general line may be summed up in Villèle's advice to Angoulême (6th May) " not to get mixed up in the Portuguese affair," for, if so, England would intervene.[1]

Had it not been for the weakness of the King, the absurdities of the Assembly, and the growing strength of clerical reaction, Portugal might now have begun to settle down. But, though external enemies left her alone, internal ones did not. In October 1822 the termagant Queen had refused to take the oath to the Constitution. She was forced to quit the Court, and did so, loudly proclaiming that the King was utterly unfit to rule, and that it would be better for Lisbon to swim in blood than to have such a constitution. Reaction gathered in strength, and in May 1823 Dom Miguel won over some regiments to his side, frightened the King and forced him to leave the capital. The King felt compelled to issue a decree declaring the " Constitution illegal and incompatible with good government," promising, however, to grant another constitution in the future. John VI. returned to Lisbon on the 5th June, surrounded by the myrmidons of Dom Miguel, who received the title of Commander-in-Chief and assumed the functions of a military dictator. He arrested the Constitutionalists and kept the King practically a prisoner in his palace.

Three men influenced the King—Dom Miguel, Subserra, and Palmella—really corresponding to the three policies : Absolutist, pro-French, and pro-British. The Miguelites wanted to abolish the Constitution and make Miguel King. Subserra (Pampluna) was a Portuguese soldier who had fought on the side of the French against his own country and was now, with entire consistency, the leader of the pro-French party. Palmella, who had been Portuguese Minister in London, led the pro-British party and was an able and intelligent diplomat, but inferior in personality to Subserra. He became Foreign Minister in July 1823, and his first step was to invoke the

[1] Villèle, *Mémoires*, [1889], iii. 418-9. France explicitly gave assurances as to having no designs on Portugal, *v.* note of Canning to Sarmento, Mar. 7/23, in *F.O. France*, 146/55. Canning to Stuart, No. 25, of Mar. 11/23. Some of these assurances were published by Canning in April.

aid of England.   On the 15th July 1823 Palmella once more
formally requested Canning to send a British force to Lisbon
to maintain order there, and to repress the reactionaries.
Canning refused. Portugal had strained her neutrality
towards Spain by assisting France in the blockade of the
Spanish Constitutionalists at Cadiz, and by appointing an
accredited minister to the Franco-Spanish Regency at Madrid.
In any case, the British force was requested not for external
defence but for internal police measures, to which, as Canning
held, our treaty obligations did not extend.   True to his unchangeable principle of non-intervention, he refused a military
force, but sent a naval squadron to the Tagus.   This had
the great advantage that it could arrive suddenly without
its destination being previously suspected, and that while it
could not exercise a direct influence on internal affairs (which
Canning disclaimed a desire to do) its moral effect might be
considerable.   Moreover, in case of personal danger to the
King, it formed a refuge to which he could fly.[1]   A new British
Minister (Sir Edward Thornton) was sent out, taking with
him the Garter for King John.   If the King had not got the
redcoats, he had got the bluejackets, a blue ribbon, and a new
minister, all of whom contributed, though in different ways,
to his salvation.

5. Dom Miguel's Coup d'État (30th April 1824)

Canning had already thought it necessary to tell Palmella
that the " British Government could . . . [not] view without
jealousy the admission of a French force into Portugal "
(5th August), and that " our difficulty in the case of a French
advance [into Portugal] would not be to send troops but to
keep them away " (7th August).   His suspicions were justified,
for on the 10th August arrived a new French Ambassador who
was speedily to trouble the waters.   Hyde de Neuville was not
far from being a remarkable man.   A red-hot Clerical and
Royalist, he had at one time great influence with the King and
Monsieur, and also with Chateaubriand and in the Assembly.
Infinitely ambitious, and at all times ready to exceed his

---

[1] *F.O. Portugal*, 179/23.   Canning to Thornton, Aug. 5, 15, with note
of Aug. 7/23.

instructions, he was prepared to promise anything to Portugal provided he could depress British and exalt French influence. From the moment of his arrival he attempted to be the supporter both of Subserra and of Dom Miguel. Subserra was not able to divest himself of his old habits of fighting under French colours. But he was not a supporter of Dom Miguel. The pro-French and pro-Absolutist policies ultimately diverged, and de Neuville had to reject the Portuguese Prince in favour of Subserra.

At the end of August Canning received fresh assurances from Chateaubriand about Portugal, but they were of little use in view of the Ambassador France had sent. De Neuville brought the Order of the Saint-Esprit to King John, but it was noticed that he brought it also to Dom Miguel, and tried to force the latter into ' undue prominence.' All the Neo-Holies were now engaged in bullying King John in order to make him break his pledged word to reissue a constitution. De Neuville excelled them all, for, on the 27th October, he offered to King John an alliance, a guarantee of the House of Braganza, and armed aid to recover Brazil, if he would break his promise to grant a constitution.[1] The resistance offered to de Neuville by Thornton was weak, that of Beresford, who had returned in a private capacity to Lisbon, was stronger, but each was ineffective.[2]

The year 1823 ended in a kind of concealed revolution—King John timid and vacillating, Dom Miguel threatening, Palmella helpless, de Neuville imperious, Thornton feebly, and Beresford roundly, protesting. On the 21st February 1824 the King finally came to a decision, and issued a decree for the reassembling of the ancient Cortes by way of redeeming his pledge of a constitution. This Cortes was a feeble relic of the medieval estates-system. It had nothing democratic about it, and its assemblage could not, to all appearance,

---

[1] *F.O. Portugal*, 63/270 ; 273/21. Thornton to Canning, Oct. 31/23, No. 31, secret and confidential. Other acts adverse to England were de Neuville's persuading Portugal to send ships to assist in the blockade of Cadiz, a clearly unneutral act (*v. Mémoires*, de Neuville, [Paris, 1912], iii. 92–4). It was instigated by Chateaubriand, *ibid.*, iii. 86, 99. Canning believed de Neuville to act throughout under Russian influence, *v.* Stap., *Corr.*, Nov. 13/24, i. 195, but Thornton questioned this.

[2] Beresford's temper was much inflamed by the fact that he was continually being promised the command of the army without receiving it. He was on bad terms with Thornton.

have seemed dreadful to even the most violent reactionaries. None the less it was the signal for a *coup d'état*. On the 28th the Marquis de Loulé, the King's Master of the Horse, was found foully murdered, and suspicion pointed to Dom Miguel. Things went from bad to worse. The 30th April, the King's birthday, was fixed for a reactionary outbreak. On that day a number of arrests took place; Dom Miguel assembled his troops in the public places of Lisbon, the King's palace was surrounded and all entrance forbidden. Finally Beresford forced his way in, followed shortly afterwards by the whole of the diplomatic corps, who protested against any violence to the King's person. Dom Miguel hurried to the palace, and professed that no violence had been intended, but showed ' all the air of a guilty young man.' The King stated that all these things had been done ' without his knowledge.' De Neuville and Subserra now broke with Dom Miguel and supported his father.

There could be no doubt but that the ' Ultra ' party had been planning a reaction, with the aim of intimidating or kidnapping the King, and that this stroke had been averted only by the intervention of the Ambassadors. A few days of feverish excitement followed. Palmella, who had been arrested, was released, but no one felt safe from Dom Miguel and his bravos. During an anxious week the King conferred almost hourly with the diplomats, with Beresford and Palmella. Then Palmella got frightened again and sought refuge with Thornton, who hid him in his house, served him personally with breakfast, and finally hurried him off on board the British squadron. There, to his surprise, he met his old rival, Subserra, who had already taken refuge. The King gave no orders, Miguel gave many. He arrested a monk with his own hands, his officers made numerous prisoners, he fired on a British packet-boat, and interfered with the foreign shipping in the harbour. The King feared to go on a British ship because he would then no longer be on Portuguese soil, and might be declared to have abdicated by leaving the Kingdom. On the 9th May his timidity overcame his legal scruples, he put off in his barge under a British escort, and was received with due honours on board the British flagship, the *Windsor Castle*. He instantly issued decrees denouncing the recent measures and ordering Dom Miguel on board. Dom Miguel received the order while rowing in a boat on the river, and, after a moment's hesitation, obeyed the command. As he mounted the ship's side he saw his father on the quarter-deck surrounded by Portuguese guards and by British sailors. Still under the influence of fear, the unworthy son fell on his knees before his indulgent old father in an attitude of complete and humiliating submission.

His father advised him to travel abroad, and Miguel meekly allowed himself to be conducted to a cabin. There his spirits revived. He put his head out of the window and called out to passing boats, to which he threw papers. He stuck a poniard in the table and said he would strike it into his heart if he were compelled to go in a British ship. Finally, in the evening he was hurried on board a Portuguese frigate, and, under a British and French escort, conveyed out of the Tagus to the south of France, whence he proceeded to Paris and ultimately to Vienna. And such was the end of ' a complete military insurrection.'

6. The Blunders and Fall of Thornton
(June–September 1824)

According to Canning, Thornton ' bore the brunt of the day,' but Hyde de Neuville reaped the fruit of the victory, for he had promised the King French military aid, and actually ordered the French garrison of Badajoz to Lisbon, an order their commander was too prudent to obey. But this ' *beau geste* ' impressed everybody. Subserra returned to office along with Palmella. But Palmella was weaker, Subserra and the pro-French party stronger than ever, for Subserra had defied Dom Miguel and risked everything for the King. Thornton, while feebly endeavouring to counteract this influence, fell into several pitfalls. The Portuguese Ministry again demanded the despatch of a British force to Portugal. Thornton, aware of the credit which de Neuville had obtained for offering a French one, not only did not oppose the proposal but sent ' a reasoned opinion in favour of it ' to Canning. It reached him just about a week after he received the formal Portuguese demand to the same effect (29th June).

Thornton had already received the promise of a Marquisate and of wide lands from King John, and thought that similar rewards awaited him from his own country. His paradise was speedily disturbed. On the 20th July he received a trenchant despatch from Canning, severely reprimanding him for approving the Portuguese demand for troops. It was, said Canning, a plot hatched by Subserra and de Neuville, who knew that England had no troops to send, and, in any case, could not send them when Parliament was not sitting. They had counted on her refusal, he said. " Is it possible that you did not see the dilemma in which we were to be placed by such a demand as has been made to us, a demand equally embarrassing whether we granted or refused it?

" If we refused it we must consign an old and faithful Ally to ruin, or consent to an occupation of Portugal by France, *against* which (however you may have reconciled yourself to it) your Government is pledged in the face of the world.

" If we granted it we must either do so, *in concurrence* with France, and the Powers of the Continent; and then behold us associated with their schemes, and converts to the principles of the [Neo-]Holy Alliance, or we must do (as if at all we should do it) without their leave, and then who shall say to what this first step may lead? " [1] Thornton was at once to urge both the King and Palmella to retract their demands.

England had no troops to send, but Hanover came to the rescue. The Cabinet recommended the King to send his Hanoverians, and His Majesty had agreed to do so if necessary. [2] Fortunately, on the 12th July, Canning was able to write that it was not necessary. For, by a stroke of diplomatic *finesse*, he had already checkmated de Neuville. The Hanoverian preparations could not be concealed; they got out on the 3rd July in the British Press, and there was " a sensible depression in British and foreign funds." On the 8th July the *Times* hoped that the ministers would not be ' so besotted ' as to sanction interference in the internal affairs

[1] *F.O. Portugal* ,179/26. Canning to Thornton, July 10/24, private, received July 20.
[2] *V.S.A.*, Berichte aus England, 1824. Esterházy to Metternich, Aug. 15/24. George IV. defended his action to Neumann on July 29.

of another State. The French Government had already taken alarm, and had instructed Polignac to make inquiries of Canning. The British Minister at once complained to Polignac of Hyde de Neuville's proceedings. Polignac obtained from Paris an official statement admitting that de Neuville had ordered the French garrison from Badajoz to Lisbon, formally disowning his action, and giving a written assurance that the French Government had given no orders to that effect and had no designs on Portugal.[1] These circumstances caused Canning to decline to send the Hanoverian force, and Palmella subsequently withdrew the demand.[2] Canning thought this a great triumph, because he had destroyed the possibilty of French armed intervention in Spain and yet had not interfered in Portuguese internal affairs.[3] With a view of further safeguarding matters he reinforced the naval squadron, brought up the marines to the strength of 750, and instructed them to occupy the Forts of the Tagus if necessary. He also sent warm congratulations to King John from King George on his safety, granted his request to convert the British Ministry into an Embassy at Lisbon, but decided to recall Thornton.

The approval of the demand for a British force was not Thornton's only offence. He had informed Canning that he had attended a series of conferences with the Portuguese Ministers at which the Neo-Holies were present, and at which Hyde de Neuville's " rank and precedence gave him naturally the lead, as on most other occasions." [4] The conferences had been concerned with the purely internal affairs of Portugal, such as the methods to be adopted in coercing the termagant Queen.

To this singularly childish despatch Thornton received a reply on the 28th June. As regards the conduct of the Queen

---

[1] The assurance was authorised by Villèle (then acting Foreign Minister) on July 9. *A.A.E.*, 618, to Polignac, July 9/24.

[2] *F.O. Portugal*, 179/26. Canning to Thornton, July 12, Nos. 24–6. Thornton to Canning, *ibid.*, 273/23, private, July 24, says Subserra did *not* recommend the request for a British force.

[3] Wellington seems to have been in favour of sending the troops to Portugal (*W.N.D.*, ii. 276–84). The *Times* of July 8 abused the Ultras for influencing the Press in this direction.

[4] Cp. *F.O. Spain*, 185/96. Canning to À Court, July 20/24, No. 26. *F.O. Portugal*, 273/22. Thornton to Canning, June 19/24. Sept. 13, secret and confidential.

and the measures to be taken against her it " is not for Foreign Ministers to put themselves forward, or to allow themselves to be put forward as the advisers of them. . . . It is obvious that these Assemblies are got together for the purpose of covering the responsibility of Portuguese Ministers ; and of giving to the municipal acts of that Government what is called an European character.

" This is no part of the policy of your court.

" The actual intervention of the diplomatic corps on the 30th April was quite right, as that concerned the personal safety of the King and might be regarded as clearly exceptional. . . . But a standing council of Foreign Ministers, convened for no specific purpose growing out of previous obligations of Treaty, but constituted in a deliberative body for the guidance, in its internal details, of the conduct of the Government, to which they are severally accredited, is a thing unknown to the Law of Nations. The selection of certain Ambassadors and Ministers for this office, to the exclusion of those of other courts, makes such a council more objectionable ; as it assumes a species of superintending jurisdiction to the preponderating Powers to which your Government has repeatedly refused its acquiescence.

" We have heard with the greatest astonishment that other subjects, relating to the conduct and treatment of private persons, subjects of His Most Faithful Majesty [of Portugal], have been debated in these mixed Assemblies,—and that the countenance of the British Minister has been given, by his presence at the Council, at which they were decreed, to measures of individual punishment.

" This is wholly out of your province and entirely disapproved by your Court." [1]

Canning had determined to get rid of the ' Areopagus and all that in Europe,' and here was Thornton re-erecting it in Portugal. To do him justice, he admitted his fault : " I suffered myself to be diverted from [a] salutary line of conduct. You cannot think me on these occasions more wrong than I own that I feel myself."

Though France worked for her own ends, she was not wholly

[1] F.O. Portugal, 179/26. Canning to Thornton, July 19, No. 27, received July 28/24 ; ibid., 273/23. Thornton to Canning, July 28, No. 78.

independent of the Neo-Holy Alliance, which, under the influence of Russia, made every effort to intimidate King John and to prevent him from keeping his oath to grant a constitution or to summon the Cortes. Several Allied Conferences were held at Paris in the autumn of 1824 to remonstrate against any such design, and the pressure there decided on was transmitted to King John by the local Allied Conference at Lisbon. It is clear that Thornton injured the cause of England, therefore, by giving his support to some of these meetings. Poor, feeble, old King John confessed the truth just before his death. " You must know, as well as I do " he said to the Ambassador who replaced Thornton, " that if the country is not governed by a charter at this very hour, it was only because I was prevented by the interference of the Allied Sovereigns from executing that promise. . . . I have not seen the moment when I could execute them [it] without danger." It was in vain that À Court reminded him that England had promised to protect him against external aggression. " It was not an open aggression from without," said he, " that he feared. It was the encouragement of parties within this country." [1] So even by 1826 Canning had not got rid of the ' Areopagus and all that ' in Portugal. But the steps he was now to take were effective towards that end. The first step was one which no one could prevent him from taking, and that was to recall Thornton. " He has been cowed and cajoled till he forgot that he was Minister of England " wrote Canning on the 17th August. On the 22nd September he was succeeded by Sir William À Court, who had hurriedly been transferred from Madrid. The unhappy minister returned sadly from Lisbon, loaded with honours from Portugal's King, to find reproaches awaiting him from the British Foreign Minister.

7. THE FALL OF DE NEUVILLE AND SUBSERRA (1825)

The gravest consequences had been averted. Dom Miguel's attempt at a *coup d'état* was defeated, and that unfilial son was in exile. The armed interference of France had been officially disclaimed. But so long as the French Ambassador and the pro-French Minister remained, the influence of France was

[1] *F.O. Portugal*, 179/35. A Court to Canning, Mar. 4/26, No. 17.

still dominant in Portugal ; England could not permit her
influence to be overshadowed either by France, by Russia,
or by the Neo-Holy Alliance.[1]   In Canning's view England
would not secure her influence over Portugal, or exclude that
of other nations from it, until Subserra was dismissed from
office and Hyde de Neuville recalled to Paris.   For that result
he looked to Sir William À Court.

On the 22nd September À Court reached Lisbon and took
over from Thornton.   Both at Naples in 1820–1 and at Madrid
in 1823, À Court had shown great firmness amid almost
unprecedented difficulties.   This able and resolute man had
now even a harder task before him.   British influence had been
discredited in the persons of Thornton and Beresford : French
influence under de Neuville and Subserra ruled the wavering
and nerveless King : and the Neo-Holy Alliance exerted all
their influence to frighten Palmella and to prevent the Cortes
from being summoned.   But the resolute purpose that reigned
in London was now to be felt both at Paris and at Lisbon.

Fortunately de Neuville had committed blunders as bad as
those of Thornton.   ' Il fait des sottises,' admitted one French
diplomat.[2]   Villèle, hard pressed by Canning, had not only
disavowed him but had hinted he would recall him at the end
of July.   De Neuville had been unwise enough, from his own
point of view, to approve of King John's summoning the Cortes.
This fact became known, and it angered Villèle.   Spain and
the Neo-Holy Alliance were furious, and protested against
this traitor to the cause of Legitimacy.   Villèle sent him leave
of absence on 20th September 1824, but he did not take it,
and endeavoured to restore his reputation by pressing on
Portugal an ingenious scheme to declare Lisbon ' a free port,'
and thus deprive England of the advantages of her commercial
treaty.   But before this last intrigue had time to mature his
heart failed him.   On the 4th January 1825 he finally sailed
from Lisbon, only two days before orders arrived telling him
to remain.   He reached Paris in ignorance of this fact, and
accordingly had a warm reception from Villèle.[3]

De Neuville had fallen, but England's other enemy, Subserra,

---

[1] F.O. France, 146/59.   Sir C. Stuart to Canning, July 13/24, No. 357.
[2] A.A.E., 618.   Moustier to Polignac, July 20/24.
[3] F.O. France, 146/59.   Sir C. Stuart to Canning, July 23, No. 376.

remained. Even before the former's departure À Court had brought great pressure to bear on King John. À Court found him ' a very weak ' but ' a very cunning man,' and he now exhibited both qualities to admiration.[1] On the 17th December he promised À Court to dismiss Subserra within a month, but he said nothing about it to anyone else. Then, just about the time de Neuville was listening to Villèle's reproaches at Paris, the thunderbolt fell at Lisbon. On the 21st January 1825 the King issued a decree, dismissing every one of his Ministry. He named Subserra as Ambassador to London and Palmella to Paris. After much intrigue and negotiation these arrangements were again altered, Palmella sent to London, and Subserra to Madrid; the old Ambassador there, Porto Santo, being recalled and made Foreign Minister. A new Ministry of amiable and pro-British mediocrities was, meanwhile, installed in power.

Canning summed up the whole business as follows :[2] " With respect to Portugal, the point to which I particularly direct my communications to you is this :—to enable you to discountenance the rumours, which I know are circulated, touching an alleged overbearing interference in the affairs of this Portuguese Minister.

" Subserra may thank himself for all that has happened. On the explosion of the 30th April, he fled to a British frigate for the safety of his life :—while there his mind misgave him that he could never recover his power in Portugal again ; that the Nation would never tolerate him and that the King could not maintain him. In this state of things he saw no refuge but the Embassy in England." That he should have asked the question of Thornton as to whether he would be received here was " a plain proof of his own consciousness of the deadly enmity which he bears us." His request was, none the less, accepted by the British Government.

" After that time Subserra, having by Thornton's inconceivable mismanagement been removed from the frigate (in which he was happily separated from the King of Portugal) to the Line of Battle Ship in which H[is] M[ost] F[aithful]

[1] *F.O. Portugal*, 179/26. À Court to Canning, Dec. 17/24, separate, most secret, and confidential.
[2] *F.O.* 352/10. *Strat. MSS.*, George Canning to Stratford Canning, private, Feb. 23/25.

M[ajesty] was holding his Court, and there under the very nose of that henpecked diplomat, promoted by Hyde de Neuville to even a higher rank than he had before held in H[is] M[ost] F[aithful] M[ajesty's] favour, it became of absolute necessity that either Subserra's just and well-considered testimony of his own utter unfitness to govern should be accepted or acted upon; or that the British Squadron (the moral effect of whose presence in the Tagus was to keep such a Minister in Power) should be withdrawn.

" This is the only menace we have intimated and this has been directed only against Subserra."

The Portuguese ship had been guided through very stormy waters. By great diplomatic dexterity Canning had succeeded in preventing the despatch of a British force to Portugal, had damaged the Areopagitic system of the Neo-Holies, and destroyed the French influence at Lisbon. His action over Subserra is of great interest, as it is the only case in any country, except Greece, in which he departed from his principle of non-intervention in the internal affairs of another nation. À Court thought it more than justifiable, and Canning took the reasonable ground that Subserra had once been a French general, was now a French agent, and had himself asked to be sent as Ambassador to London, while the menaces of the French Ambassador supported him in power against the will both of the King and people of Portugal. Whether technically justifiable or not, the step was effective. The fall of the two arch-plotters meant the collapse of French influence and of the extreme Absolutist party. " We have undoubtedly struck *the great blow* " wrote À Court in justifiable exultation.[1]

8. The Last of the Three Plotters

The ninepins had fallen separately; first Dom Miguel, then Thornton, then de Neuville, then Subserra. A glance at the futures of three of them may be appropriate here. Subserra finally proceeded to Madrid, where he was received with great coldness by the Spanish Court. He committed a further indiscretion, owing to the fact that an enterprising tailor had sold him a Court suit with ' Long live the Constitution '

[1] *F.O. Portugal*, 179/30. À Court to Canning, Feb. 21/25, No. 9, private.

printed on its buttons. He seems not to have worn this costume at first, but when he finally appeared in it the sensation was great. The Spanish Court, cold enough before, now assumed that the arch-Legitimist was attempting to insult them. It was in vain for him to protest the purity of his monarchical principles and to denounce the wickedness of his tailor. Finally he threw up his Embassy in despair, and returned, without leave and on the pretence of illness, to Lisbon, where he was badly received.

De Neuville, who had resented his reception from Villèle at Paris, tried to offset his disgrace by intriguing with Chateaubriand and the Opposition. Then Canning had to protest, because he discovered that de Neuville was still carrying on a secret correspondence with King John at Lisbon. Charles X., furious at the first action, saw an opportunity to punish him for the second. He first placed de Neuville on half-pay and then actually struck his name off the list of Ambassadors. Ultimately restored to favour as Minister of Marine, he had the glory of administering the French Navy at the time of Navarino. He was soon again out of office, for he never could part company with Chateaubriand or with intrigue. He suffered, as he ingenuously said, ' for telling monarchs the truth,' an indiscretion for which he did not suffer with diplomats. After the fall of Charles X. he retired into private life and ended his days in great sanctity at his country estate at Lestang, where his chief delight had been to walk in a religious procession, to hold a cord of the canopy, and to wear his faded grand cordon of the Legion of Honour.

Miguel was to suffer an even worse lot. Cooped up for a time in Vienna, as a sort of ' bogus L'Aiglon,' he was compelled to marry his niece by proxy and to take an oath (characteristically with reservations) to the Constitution. In 1827 he was finally appointed Regent of Portugal, and again swore solemnly to the Constitution. He moved on slowly to Portugal, protesting the purity of his constitutional principles at Paris and at London. He arrived in Portugal as Constitutional Regent, broke all his promises at once, became Absolutist King on the 11th July 1828, and proceeded to massacre his opponents. He was disturbed in this congenial task by his exuberant elder brother, Dom Pedro, who, having been forced to abdicate the throne of Brazil in 1831, led an expedition to force his brother to abdicate that of Portugal. In 1834 he deposed Miguel, drove him into exile once more, and set his daughter Donna Maria on the throne. The whole chapter of events reads like a fable, but the most extraordinary part of it is that Miguel was popular while he reigned in Portugal, and was considered a saint by many after he had left it. However that may be, there was not one diplomat in Europe who approved his conduct in 1824, or thought that his exile in that year was undeserved. Whether it was approved by the majority of the people of Portugal is open to question.

CHAPTER IX

THE INDEPENDENCE OF BRAZIL

1. Brazil, Portugal, and the Neo-Holy Alliance (1820–3)

THE recognition of the independence of Brazil might be considered as akin to that of the Spanish-American Republics. In 1822 both Spanish and Portuguese Colonies were in successful revolt, and neither could have been subdued by the Mother Country alone. In reality the cases were very different. The Spanish Colonies at the beginning of that year were all avowedly democratic republics. They had no sort of recognised connection with England, for it was not till June 1822 that Castlereagh recognised the Spanish-American commercial flags, or till October 1823 that Canning sent consuls to them. Brazil, moreover, was not republican, and already had her commercial flag, in fact, recognised. She was monarchical in government, she had been until 1821 the seat of the King of Portugal, and though in 1822 she declared Pedro an Emperor and his dominion independent, she still obeyed a descendant of the House of Braganza. Further, the Emperor was the eldest son of the King of Portugal, and might (and did) ultimately inherit both crowns. The Brazilian trade had been legally, and not tacitly, open to British shipping for half a generation before 1822, and commercial intercourse, facilitated by the presence of a British Consul-General, could not be interrupted by Portugal. The British Consul-General remained after the declaration of independence, practically as a political agent. Lastly, while Spain had rejected English mediation between her and her Colonies, Portugal herself invited England to use her ' good offices ' with Brazil. In a quite peculiar way Brazil's destiny was bound up with those of Portugal, of Europe, and, above all, of England. For, while Spain had no claims on England, Portugal had a treaty-right to British protection. Canning did not admit that it extended to her Colonies, but he considered that it gave her a general moral claim upon England.

The revolution was due, first to the liberality of the despot who had ruled at Rio between 1808 and 1821, and next to the arbitrariness of his Constitutionalists at Lisbon, who tried to coerce both him and Brazil at the same time. The King had, however, already made coercion difficult. For, in Canning's words, he had granted to Brazil " a free trade and an independent Judicature. He made Brazil a Kingdom, from a colony. He founded a representative constitution. He gave into the hands of his son the authority with which that Kingdom was to be ruled." A kingdom thus endowed, not only with a sense of its importance, but with all the organs of government except an army, was not going to submit to the dictation of the Cortes of Lisbon. It met their absurd decrees and demands for submission by a revolution and a declaration of independence. Dom Pedro seems on this occasion to have acted with unusual prudence and dexterity. He does not seem to have wanted to betray his father, but was forced to yield to the storm. He decided (probably with sense) to adopt the title of Emperor and to retain the loyalty of Brazilians, if not for the Head, at any rate for the House, of Braganza. The situation was not an easy one for him ; Portuguese troops in considerable numbers garrisoned the outlying provinces, which only the internal disturbances at Lisbon prevented from being reinforced. Pedro himself, as a Portuguese, and as the son of his father, was not free from suspicion. His internal situation was precarious. He bore, indeed, an imperial title ; he wore a finer imperial robe than existed even in the treasures of Vienna, a mantle of deep rose-red, made from the breasts of toucans. But he was at the mercy of factions and of the army, and sat not on a throne, but on a rocking-chair.

Canning had anticipated independence as inevitable at the very first news of revolution. On the 21st November 1822 he promised to observe ' scrupulous neutrality ' in case of war between Brazil and Portugal, but intimated that we " may

find it expedient to acknowledge, more or less formally, the
de facto establishment of the new Brazilian Government." [1]
This suggestion marks a rather unusual eagerness to recognise
a newly revolted Colony, and was due to a special reason.
Brazil was the chief mart of the Slave Trade and the only
Latin-American State which continued it.   Canning therefore
instructed Lord Amherst, who was proceeding to India as
Governor-General *via* Rio, to negotiate with the Brazilian
Government for a declaration against it. [2]   In return for this
he actually promised the ' establishment of a cordial amity
and intercourse,' and a discountenancing of any aid to
Portugal ' to recover the Dominion of Brazil.'   He did also
(there can be little doubt) hold out the prospect of recognition
of *de facto* independence.   Had the negotiation succeeded,
Canning would have deserved well of humanity by stopping
this ' abominable traffic' at its fountain-head.   For during
1822, slaves to the number of 20,483 were embarked for
Brazil, of whom 1388 died on the way ; and during 1823 to
the number of 29,211, of whom 2499 died. [3]   But the negotiation failed, and Canning fell back on slower methods.

2. PORTUGAL ASKS FOR MEDIATION (1823)

Canning's early anticipation of the independence of Brazil
was, in any case, intelligent.   Lord Cochrane, that Ulysses
of the sea, who is even more famous in Latin-American than
in British annals, took command of the Brazilian fleet.   He
showed for the last time the real flashes of his naval genius,
and reduced province after province to the Emperor's sway.
By the middle of 1823 the issue was in reality decided, not
only at Rio but throughout nearly all Brazil, and on the
23rd September Villa Réal, the Portuguese Minister in London,
applied for British mediation.   But he tried to attach to it
the conditions that Great Britain should never recognise the
independence of Brazil by herself, and that she should not

---

[1] *F.O. Portugal*, 179/22.   Canning to E. M. Ward, Nov. 21/22, No. 14.
[2] *F.O. Austria*, 120/58.   Canning to Sir H. Wellesley, Aug. 19/23,
enclosing Amherst's instructions of Feb. 18/23, and to Chamberlain (Rio),
Feb. 15 ; and from Nov. 22/22 ; and to E. M. Ward (Lisbon), Oct. 18,
Nov. 21/22.
[3] *F.O. Brazil*, 128/2.   Figures given by Chamberlain, Jan. 4/25.

recognise Pedro's title as Emperor.   Canning offered to mediate, but would not accept these conditions.   Villa Réal then
said that the Allied Powers (*i.e.* other than England) might
mediate, and this suggestion led Canning to deliver one of
his tirades against the Neo-Holy Alliance.   " England would
never recognise rights in the Allied Powers to intermingle
[*s'immiscer*] in the affairs of the Colonies."   In such case
England would hold herself free to recognise them.   " If
England acted otherwise . . . it might be said that she
recognised the Tribunal the Allies had wished to set up to
direct the affairs of Europe, and she could not permit it to be
exercised in the New World, which had constantly pronounced
against a similar supremacy in Europe."

Villa Réal next suggested Prussia and Austria as mediators.
Canning objected to both, but was not disinclined to associate
Austria in the work of mediation, provided that the King of
Portugal knew of our communications, and that our recognition was not to be dependent on the Austrian.   And, in
such case, he would see " no difficulty in giving confidentially
to His Most Faithful Majesty [*i.e.* the King of Portugal]
the assurance of taking no new step on the independence of
Brazil." [1]   He added that such an assurance could, however,
not be indefinite or perpetual.

Austria had some reason to be associated with England, for
Dom Pedro had married a Hapsburg.   Metternich had given
his views to Canning earlier in the year, and they were of a
reasonable character.   He thought the revolt of a colony
against its mother country was justified in Brazil if ever or
anywhere, and that Dom Pedro, by taking the title of Emperor,
had " repressed and counterbalanced . . . the ascendancy of
democratic principles."   What he chiefly cared about was the
maintenance of the rights of existing families and of monarchical
principles.   It mattered very little to him, so long as these
were preserved, whether Brazil was governed by an Emperor
at Rio or by a Cortes at Lisbon.[2]   Indeed he preferred a single
ruler to an Assembly.   These views show the cynical realism

---

[1] *F.O. Brazil*, 128/1.   Canning to Chamberlain (Consul-General),
Nov. 5/24, No. 16, enclosing memo. of conference, Sept. 23, with corrections of Canning of Sept. 25/23.
[2] *V.S.A.*, Weisungen nach England, Feb. 13, 28/23.   Metternich to
Esterházy.   He said he hoped this would conciliate Canning.

of Metternich.   He did not really differ from Canning at all, but *pro forma* he was obliged to support the theory that the King of Portugal's consent was necessary to establish the independence of Brazil.   Canning, on the other hand, while preferring that solution, was prepared, if that consent was deferred too long, to recognise Brazil without it.   At a later stage the horror of Alexander was to force Metternich to insist on the consent of the King of Portugal,[1] but at the moment Metternich was sincere as well as sensible in not attaching much importance to it.

3. Austro-British 'Good Offices'; The London Conferences (1824)

Canning shortly afterwards explained to Chateaubriand (9th November 1823), in response to inquiry, that the principles of the Polignac Memorandum extended to Brazil, and that he had no aggressive designs.   But he thought that the use of force by Portugal would be a danger " which does not equally belong to Spanish America, that of risking the existence of a monarchical form of Government. . . . We attach great importance to its continuance in Brazil." [2] And a few days later he disclosed to Polignac that England had been invited to mediate between Portugal and her Colony.

Matters were made more difficult by the extravagant hatred displayed by the Brazilians towards the things and persons of Portugal.   While Villa Réal was conferring with Canning, Portuguese Commissioners had arrived at Rio. It was known, however, that they would not acknowledge the independence of Brazil.   So only one of them was allowed to land, their ship was confiscated, their communications left unopened, and themselves unceremoniously bundled back to Lisbon in a packet.   In November 1823 Dom Pedro, who had changed his Ministries like kaleidoscopes, decided to change his Assembly as well.   He led cavalry and artillery

---

[1] Vide *F.O. Austria*, 120/69.   Wellesley to Canning, Mar. 3/25.   Alexander styled Dom Pedro 'a rebel and a Parricide.'   The comment was strange, as Pedro was only the first, and Alexander had himself been both !

[2] *F.O. France*, 146/56.   Canning to Stuart, Nov. 9/23, No. 85.   *A.A.E.*, 617.   Polignac to Chateaubriand, Nov. 18/23.

against them in person and forcibly dissolved the Assembly. This body was next accused of perjury in a manifesto by the Imperial and ' Perpetual Defender of Brazil.' [1] The impression of these exciting events was not much allayed by the formation of a New Constitution, 25th March 1824, which was solemnly sworn to, as readily as the previous one had been abandoned. In point of fact it was quite a good and permanent constitution this time. But events looked bad both for the stability of Brazil and for the possibility of her coming to an agreement with Portugal. The whole circumstance only encouraged Lisbon to persist in their highest pretensions.

In December 1823 Villa Réal had renewed his proposals to Canning, who transmitted them to Brazil, with his own comments. He thought that ' we have gone too far ' to force Brazil to abandon her pretension to independence, that a Federative Union might perhaps be preserved, and that the sovereign might reign alternately at Lisbon and Rio, with a deputy sovereign at the other capital. The most essential thing was for the two parties to stop fighting, and for Brazil to relax her high-handed measures against Portuguese persons and property.

Canning was alarmed to find that the Brazilians had ideas of separating completely from Europe, on the lines of the Monroe Doctrine. " No State is altogether morally independent of the goodwill of its neighbours—and though the distance of Brazil from Europe may place her out of the vortex of European politics, yet connected as all States of the World, both old and new, are daily becoming with each other, it cannot be indifferent to any one of them to have the sympathies of others on their side, rather than arrayed against them. . . .   It would be of infinite advantage to Brazil that Her new rank among nations should be not merely arrogated by Herself, but confirmed to Her by the consent of Portugal, with the sanction of other Powers." [2] Here is revealed one of the leading ideas of Canning, to prevent the New World and the Old from becoming watertight compartments, and to introduce into the Family of European Nations the distant

---

[1] He finally explained away the charge of ' perjury,' but his manifesto was of the most extravagant character.
[2] *F.O. Brazil*, 128/1, to Chamberlain, Jan. 8/24, No. 1.

representatives of America, protected by England against the Tribunal of the Neo-Holy Alliance.

In April, however, Brazilian Commissioners arrived in London, and the first conference was held with Villa Réal on the 12th July, in the presence of Canning and Neumann, the Austrian *chargé d'affaires*.[1] It soon became clear where the difficulty was to lie. The ' Sovereignty of Portugal ' was the standpoint of one party, the ' Independence of Brazil ' that of the other. As this question was preliminary to all others, a deadlock was reached after five conferences had been held. Canning put forward a compromise scheme on the lines indicated to Villa Réal in December 1823, but received no support from the Austrian. For Austria now said that she must insist on the consent of the King of Portugal to Brazilian Independence. Canning then said he would carry forward his ' *projet* ' alone.

With this new *projet* he made a strong direct appeal to Portugal. The Neo-Holy Alliance " put forward a claim to interfere on the general principle of setting things to rights whenever they think them wrong. We renounce any such pretension, and consider it as essential to a legitimate inter-ference in the internal affairs of other countries, that our interests should have been, in some way or other, affected by their condition, or by their proceedings." The present conditions endangered the commercial interests of England. Four-fifths of the articles of the Portuguese Commercial Treaty with England, which was to expire in February 1825, concerned Brazil. If, therefore, there was not a speedy com-promise with Brazil, England might be forced to recognise her independence.

" Let M. de Palmella compare the frankness of this sort of communication, and the unpresuming nature of this advice, with the pretensions put forward in the Protocols of Confer-ences at Paris . . . in which Powers who have not a trans-marine Colony belonging to them, nor a single sail on the

---

[1] The words ' mediation ' and ' intervention ' were very loosely used at this time. It does not, in fact, appear at this stage that Portugal and Brazil submitted to the mediation of Austria and Great Britain. They discussed their difficulties before them and received from them ' counsel.' The situation is correctly described in the first Protocol (July 12), in which both parties accepted the ' good offices ' of England and Austria.

Ocean which washes South America, nor a bale of goods in
the ports either of Portugal or Brazil, discuss, very much at
their ease, the relation of a Mother Country to its Colonies,
and recommend perpetual war between them, by which both
may be destroyed ; rather than that any influence dangerous
to legitimacy should be drawn from a compromise by which
both may be saved.

" So far as the language of these Powers is doctrinal and
exhortatory, there is perhaps little to be said about it : but
. . . any attempt to enforce these doctrines and exhortations
by violence, would bring into instant operation the claim
which Treaty gives to Portugal upon the support of Great
Britain." [1]

Portugal was not convinced.   King John said : " I see the
Allies would deprive me of my authority here, while the
English would persuade me to resign my Brazilian Crown."
As he could rely on England to defend him against the Neo-
Holy Allies, he could afford to refuse her Brazilian *projet*.
So a *contre-projet* was submitted which was discussed on the
11th November at a sixth conference in London.   It insisted,
among other things, that the King of Portugal should be called
senior Emperor of Brazil, and so was bound to fail.   On the
20th Canning heard some grave news and suspended the
conferences altogether.   For the Portuguese Government
had been guilty of ' astonishing duplicity.'   The Portuguese
Government had just sent a circular requesting the other
Powers (France, Russia, and Prussia) to mediate between
them and Brazil, implying that Austria and England had
failed to do so.   But this had not been their only offence.

It now transpired that, in June 1824, the Portuguese
Government had sent out to Rio an obscure agent called
Léal, who was a tool of Subserra.   He had carried with him
proposals similar to the *contre-projet*.   Léal was thrown into
a dungeon and finally dismissed with a total rejection of his
proposals.[2]   Villa Réal (apparently in ignorance) brought
forward the *contre-projet* as new at London in the autumn,
and invited England to support it as new at Rio.   He has thus,

---

[1] *F.O. Portugal*, 179/26.   Canning to À Court, Oct. 9/24, No. 6.
[2] Canning got hold of a copy of Subserra's instructions to Léal, *v. F.O.
Portugal*, 179/28.   Canning to À Court, Mar. 23/25, enclosing Léal's
instructions, June 28/24.

wrote Canning, been " made the tool of a fraud, practised
through him, upon the Plenipotentiaries of Austria and of
England." [1] On the whole, Canning showed some moderation in suspending, and in not breaking off, the conferences.

4. BRITISH DIRECT NEGOTIATION ; THE INDEPENDENCE OF BRAZIL (1825)

Canning was now determined to have done with the whole
matter. He sent off the announcement of the British decision
to recognise the Spanish Colonies to Lisbon, with a strong hint
that she would do the same with Brazil if the King did not
mend his paces. He wrote privately to Villa Réal (16th
January 1825) : " Tell me, if you believe that any Government
here could throw away the trade with Brazil in order to avoid
the simple admission that *what is, is*, viz. that Brazil is
separated from Portugal." . . . " The King of Portugal has it
yet in his hands to decide whether Brazil shall be independent
by his act, or in spite of him." [2] Canning's position was very
difficult, and he had reason for annoyance apart from the
duplicity of Portugal. For there was danger in recognising
Brazil as independent without consent of Portugal. For,
as soon as he did so, Portugal, being still at war with Brazil,
could demand England's protection against her, and that would
be bad both for Brazilian liberty and for British commerce.

It was difficult, however, to use pressure with effect. For
the Conference of Allies at Paris was exhorting the King of
Portugal to stand firm on his inalienable rights, and the
contre-projet and the circular were the result of their pressure.
It was most opportune for Canning that Hyde de Neuville
left Lisbon early in January and that Subserra fell from power
three weeks later. For these events meant the end of Franco-
Russian influence at Lisbon and weakened the King's capacity
for resistance over Brazil. Even before the fall of de Neuville
and Subserra was known with certainty Canning resolved to
strike. The Neo-Holies had been invited to interfere, and as
their interest was in delay, and as reference back for instructions to Lisbon took three or four weeks, and to Rio

[1] *F.O. Portugal*, 179/26. Canning to À Court, Nov. 27/24, No. 18.
[2] *F.O. Portugal*, 179/28, to Villa Réal, Jan. 17/25, private and confidential.

five or six months, there was a fair prospect that the negotiation would last for ever. On the 12th January 1825 Canning
therefore proposed to send Sir Charles Stuart on a special
mission first to Lisbon, and next to Rio, where he was to
negotiate a treaty with Dom Pedro finally settling the matter.
The decision was a bold one, for Austria was politely ignored,
though she subsequently indicated that she desired to take
no further part in the affair. But various incidents favoured
Canning. On the 18th February the Brazilian Plenipotentiaries in London rejected finally the *contre-projet*, and declared
their negotiation ended. Subserra had already fallen and
John VI. acquiesced (though not without difficulty) in the
British negotiation—appointing Stuart his envoy on behalf
of Portugal.

On the 14th March Canning finally drew up his instructions
for Sir Charles Stuart. This classic despatch contains a
history of the whole previous negotiations and was written
with masterly ability. Even Metternich, who was in Paris
during March, intimated approval when he heard the despatch
and gave the mission his blessing.[1] He also instructed
Mareschal, his very able representative at Rio, to further
the negotiation.

Canning summed up the situation as follows: His own
projet and the Portuguese *contre-projet* both agreed that the
King of Portugal should recognise Dom Pedro's title as
Emperor, should acknowledge what had been done in Brazil,
and should grant that country a ' substantial and independent
administration.' The succession to Portugal likewise caused
no material difference. Canning had proposed that Pedro
should leave that question in the hands of his father ; the
contre-projet refused to impair Pedro's right of succession to
Portugal.

The *contre-projet* further demanded :

   1. That the King of Portugal should likewise assume the
      title of Emperor, allowing Dom Pedro that of Regent.

---

[1] Metternich seems to have been friendly throughout, but hampered
by fear of Russia, and the principles of the Legitimacy. His half-hearted
attitude in the autumn of 1824 was due to t e fact that " he is taxed [by
the Emperor of Russia] with departing from the principles of the Holy
Alliance." *F.O. Austria*, 120/66. Wellesley to Canning, Oct. 4/24, No.
96. In 1825 he lent Stuart's mission all the support he dared.

2. That there should be a common army and diplomatic service.

3. That the King of Portugal should retain the right of sanctioning by edict the laws of Brazil.

Canning declared that the first pretension was a point of punctilio ; the title of Emperor was new and had been conferred by a popular vote, and that it was far better for the King of Portugal to retain his old, indefeasible, hereditary, and legitimate title of King of Brazil, without putting in his cap a new-fangled imperial ' feather.' As regards the next two points he regarded both as having been already, in substance, surrendered by the King of Portugal by his old edicts in Brazil. The third proposal was particularly dangerous, for it was " an attempt to get back in detail what has been given in gross," and could be applied only, as Great Britain applied it in India and (formerly) in Ireland, to a dependency. It was an attempt to establish " a species of *suzeraineté* over independence " and could not, therefore, be accepted by Brazil.

Stuart started for Lisbon on the 16th March, and was finally accepted as the Portuguese representative for negotiating the treaty with Brazil, thus being technically no longer a British diplomat.[1] In July he reached Rio, only to find that a French representative—De Gestas—had anticipated him, and had offered to recognise Brazilian Independence if France received special commercial privileges. This discreditable intrigue was defeated by the firmness of Dom Pedro, who refused to negotiate with him until he had seen Stuart. But it strengthened Dom Pedro's hand, for, as he complacently said, he now had ' the two Tymbals ' of France and of England ' on which to play.' After several conferences Stuart obtained his treaty on the 29th August. By Article I. " His Most Faithful Majesty recognises Brazil as an Empire independent and separate from Portugal and Algarve ; and . . . Dom Pedro as Emperor, ceding and transferring, of his own free will, the

---

[1] King John issued a *Carta Patente* (Diploma) transferring to Dom Pedro full sovereignty over the Kingdom of Brazil, with the title of King of Brazil, reserving to himself the same title. This was on May 13, and Stuart carried with him the *Carta Patente* to Rio as something to bargain with. *Vide* E. Satow, *Diplomatic Practice* (1922), ii. 356–61, for a useful account.

sovereignty of the said Empire to His said son and to His legitimate successors ; His Most Faithful Majesty only taking and reserving the same title for His own Person." By Article II. the Imperial son agreed to permit his father to assume the title of Emperor in his own person. Article III. prohibited Pedro from accepting the proposals of any Portuguese Colonies whatever, to unite themselves with the Empire of Brazil. Article IV. arranged for oblivion of past dissensions, and "peace and alliance, and the most perfect friendship between the Empire of Brazil and the Kingdoms of Portugal and Algarve." The remaining articles stipulated for the equality of the nationals of both States, and the mutual restoration of sequestrated property, and arranged for a Commission for regulating these difficulties in the future.[1] The treaty was ratified at once by Pedro and sent off to Portugal on a British ship.

These were not ideal terms, but they were probably the best that could be got, and they represented a great diplomatic achievement on the part of Sir Charles Stuart.[2] The treaty reached Lisbon on the 9th November. On the 20th ratifications were exchanged and the separation and independence of Brazil were complete. Except for urging speedy ratification, Canning had no direct influence on the final stages. He objected to the King of Portugal assuming the title of Emperor, and John VI. added to his offence by making it precede, and not follow, his title of King of Portugal. The reception of the treaty at Lisbon was bad, and the opinion of Rio on King John's assumption of the imperial title was violent. But these were the clouds of smoke which still hang over a fire when the embers of strife are expiring.

The gravest criticism made by Canning was that the affair of the succession was not settled, and that, consequently, on John's death Pedro would inherit both crowns, and that death was not in fact far distant. For this event Canning had provided in the *projet*, but the question was left unsettled

---

[1] A convention, signed the same day, settled the financial arrangements. Brazil ultimately paid something over £1,000,000 to Portugal for claims of various sorts, *v.* Satow, ii. 361.

[2] Canning was annoyed at his consenting to the addition of the title of Emperor to that of King of Portugal, which was against his instructions. Stuart, from being a sort of Jacobin, had become an Ultra, and this made Canning think he had done it on purpose. *Cp.* Stap., *Corr.*, ii. 19, *sqq.*

in the treaty. The Portuguese Government answered his objection by saying that they could not regulate the succession, unless England was prepared to guarantee it. Canning refused, saying that he did not know what we were asked to guarantee. " We are really asked to make up Dom Pedro's mind for him " ; he was not going to do that, nor to be involved in any interference in the internal affairs of Portugal. The only guarantee he would give was that, if Brazil attacked Portugal or her remaining Colonies, England would defend either or both.[1]

None the less, despite irritation on both sides of the water, the great and main object was achieved. For this Canning deserves the chief credit. He had prevented the original negotiation at London from failure by persuading the Brazilians not to insist on a preliminary claim of absolute independence. He had proceeded with the conference despite the secret intrigues of Portugal and the final defection of Austria. France and Russia, by secret threats at Lisbon, and France by intrigues at Rio, had attempted, but in vain, to nullify his work. His *projet* was the basis of the treaty, which he finally carried to success by a direct negotiation first at Lisbon and then at Rio. He achieved the important object of a peaceful separation of the two countries, endorsed by the consent, if not by the approval, of the Mother Country, and in the teeth of the opposition of Russia and of France. It must have given Canning the greatest pleasure in the whole affair when that arch-Ultra, King George IV., referred to it at the end of 1825 in an interview with Esterházy. George IV. proceeded to eulogise Canning, who was present, for avoiding congresses. " When we see our way," said the King with sly humour, " and can employ our own influence, we can do anything. Who [turning to Prince Esterházy] could have done what we have just accomplished in Brazil ? " Prince Esterházy expressed his entire assent, and went into a panegyric of the instructions given to Sir Charles Stuart. So George was denouncing congresses and Esterházy praising

---

[1] *F.O. Portugal,* 179/32. Canning to À Court, Feb. 4/26, No. 7, enclosing memo. on guarantee of Feb. 3. It will be seen that Canning here engaged to defend the remaining Colonies of Portugal, though he did not admit that Portugal had a treaty-right to British defence of anything except the European Kingdom.

Canning for having opposed them! Even this was not enough. After leaving the King's presence, Esterházy met Canning in an ante-room and said that " he now comprehended and knew how to appreciate my policy, that I had everything in my hands, and was destined to play la plus grande rôle en Europe." [1]

The work was crowned by the ultimately successful negotiation of a commercial treaty and of a treaty on the Slave Trade with Brazil.[2] The immediate results were of great benefit to Brazil, which was recognised by, and signed commercial treaties with, almost every State in Europe during the next two years.

5. SUMMARY

Perpetually crossed by Portugal, by France, and by the Neo-Holy Alliance, Canning had achieved a triumph which was great and lasting. It was no less than to have planted monarchy for sixty years in Brazil. Metternich spoke truth when he said that monarchy would restrain extreme tendencies in the New World. Pedro himself had done a good deal to secure the success of this negotiation and had a real claim on the gratitude of his country. His unsuccessful war with Buenos Aires made them forget it and enforce his abdication in 1831; but the monarchy remained, first under a Regency, and then under his son. This institution rendered it the stablest of all Latin-American States, with an Upper Chamber admirably suited to the needs of the time, and a government more mild, more enlightened, and more just than that of any surrounding state. Without Canning it is probable that it would have had to choose between democratic anarchy and military dictatorship, the two recurrent and perpetual evils of South American politics. It was not his fault that there were defects in the structure; it was due to him, more than to anyone else, that the structure was preserved at all. Brazil did not proclaim a Monroe Doctrine of her own, and in 1826 and during 1832-4 her intervention exercised an

---

[1] Canning to Granville, Dec. 12/25. Stap., G.C. & T., 450-2.
[2] Stuart rashly negotiated two treaties on the subject, of which both had to be disavowed, v. Notes to Chapter IX., pp. 508-9. A new convention on the Slave Trade was signed Nov. 23/26, and subsequently ratified. The new commercial treaty ratifications were exchanged on Nov. 10/27.

active influence upon Europe. Apart from that, Canning's hopes were not realised for ninety years. The first time that the Brazilian Navy co-operated with the English (an event which Canning had always contemplated as possible) was when their united cruisers met the Germans in the autumn of 1918. Since that date the presence of Brazil on the Council of the League of Nations has enabled her to exercise an effective influence in the world's affairs.

PART V

CANNING AND ENGLAND

CHAPTER X
CANNING, THE MAN

CHAPTER XI
CONQUERING THE KING

CHAPTER XII
THE DAY'S WORK AT THE FOREIGN OFFICE

CHAPTER XIII
THE PRESS AND PUBLIC OPINION

INTRODUCTION

THE year 1825 is an evident and intelligible landmark in British foreign policy. For at that time Canning's personality became supreme at home, and powerful and triumphant abroad. In 1823 he had vainly tried to check the French invasion of Spain ; he had, indeed, forced Polignac to disavow French designs on America, but he had been outmanœuvred by Adams in the matter of the Monroe Message. During 1824 he had begun to gain in strength. He had given the *coup de grâce* to the Spanish-American Congress, he had forced his colleagues on the last day of the year to consent to the recognition of the New World. At the end of the year too he declined to join the congress on the Eastern Question. During 1825 he restored British influence successfully in Portugal, he established the independence of Brazil.

The Neo-Holy Alliance had been shattered over Greek affairs ; it remained to employ its individual members as instruments for England's advantage. This method was adopted during the last two years of his life, and the triumph of his policy and system became world-wide. The ascendancy which he finally won for England abroad was, however, only rendered possible by his ascendancy at home. For his full power was not felt abroad until he had dragged the wavering King and his reluctant colleagues with him by his influence over Parliament, the Press, and the People. It was in 1825 that he obtained this ' giant's power,' and this year forms a convenient dividing line between the foreign policy of his first period (1822–5) and that of his second (1826–7). In order to understand the situation it is necessary to analyse the characteristics of the man ; to know something of the secret struggle between him and the King ; of the prolonged

229

battle waged in the Foreign Office against older traditions and against stiff-necked diplomats ; and of the means by which the British Press and people finally gave to him a power in his own country as great as that which Chatham had once wielded.

GEORGE CANNING IN 1821
from a drawing by Chantrey

CHAPTER X

CANNING, THE MAN

" Canning's character is not a theme for prose."—HOOKHAM FRERE.

" He [Mr Canning] could hardly take his tea without a stratagem." *" I said of him ' that his mind's eye squinted.' "*—J. W. CROKER.

" Bright Spirit, Brightest of the Bright."—J. W. CROKER.

THERE are numberless portraits of Canning, but perhaps only three that reveal the authentic man. The first is an engraving of 1821 by Chantrey, the next a portrait by Lawrence of 1826, the last one by Stewardson of 1827. Chantrey's outline is pale and fine, the brilliancy of the eye, the exquisite delicacy of feeling and expression suggest a literary or intellectual character, with his faculties ground and polished to the finest edge, but without the toughness of moral and physical fibre so essential to the ' bull-fight of politics.' The Lawrence portrait shows Canning speaking in the House of Commons on the 12th December 1826. The arm is raised with a haughty gesture of command, the lips are uttering his famous boast ' of calling the New World into existence,' the face is full of passion and concentrated power, the eyes blaze. He has lost something of the keenness and fineness of 1821, but he has gained in strength. Stewardson's picture shows him as First Lord of the Treasury. He looks nearer seventy than sixty, his air is weary, the eye is less brilliant, the face coarsened and deeply lined. But the mouth is as firm as ever ; he is still able to set at naught sickness, care, and obloquy, but only by an effort of conscious will-power. In these three portraits the history of the last period of his life is summarised ; enforced leisure cultivating his intellectual side, realised power cultivating his practical gifts, achieved triumph bringing death in its train.

The ' vast orb ' Canning bore overwhelmed him as it had

done all his contemporaries. Pitt fell at forty-five, Castlereagh at fifty-three, Fox at fifty-four, Liverpool at fifty-six,
Canning at fifty-seven. The fever of revolution, the strain of
war or of its aftermath wore these men out before their time.
And perhaps Canning's work was more difficult than any of
them. Suspected at home by the Government and by the
Opposition ; suspected abroad both by Legitimists and by
Republicans, he returned to power with the memory of past
failure and the reality of present danger. He triumphed indeed
over all opponents, but only by efforts which destroyed first
his health, next his peace of mind, and finally his life.

His ascendancy over the King, over unwilling colleagues,
over sullen Ambassadors, over the British Opposition, over
Press, and over Public, was due to those same qualities which
enabled him to triumph over Metternich, over Alexander
and the Neo-Holy Alliance. Few would have predicted his
ultimate success in 1822, for, despite his long political career,
the man had remained an enigma to all except his nearest
friends.

The home side of Canning's life showed him in his most
amiable aspect. His love for his family was so proverbial
as almost to excite derision. Esterházy records, with some
amusement, that he once had an interview with him after the
death of an aunt, and that the great Foreign Minister frequently
interrupted the conversation with bursts of tears. To his
mother, thrice married and an ex-actress, he showed always
the warmest affection, thus silently despising the foul sneers
of pamphleteers and journalists. He settled on her his pension
and obtained a captain's commission for the son of her third
marriage.

His poor crippled eldest son was the object of his tenderest
care till his death, and the epitaph he wrote betrays his true
feelings :—

> " While I (reversed our nature's kindlier doom)
> Pour forth a father's sorrows on thy tomb."

His daughter—the beautiful Marchioness of Clanricarde—
was his favourite child, and to the end of her life retained a
love for him as undying as her hatred towards his enemies.
His wife Joan deserved and enjoyed both his love and his

confidence. She listened to rehearsals of his speeches, acted sometimes as his secretary, and helped him always with her sound judgment. Her capacity was certainly considerable, for her anonymous pamphlet on Portugal is written with great brilliancy, and gives a better idea of his policy and character in thirty pages than his secretary conveys in a thousand. It is at least significant that he seems to have given up India to please his wife and daughter, and that in his period of trial, when out of office, his spirits seem always undimmed and cheerful. One wonders whether the fame and power which he attained were well exchanged for the calm and peace of his own fireside.

It was remarked, at the moment of his greatest unpopularity, that no man had so many affectionate friends, and their influence was only less than that of his home circle. Frere— the wit of the *Anti-Jacobin*—Sturges Bourne, Charles Ellis, Lord Boringdon were his devoted admirers and, not seldom, the willing butts of his good-humoured wit. Bagot seems to have felt his loss as that of his dearest friend ; Granville threw up his Embassy rather than serve under Wellington. Opponents like Lord Holland, Sir Robert Wilson, and Mackintosh, irresponsibles like Sir Sidney Smith, or Lord Byron, surrendered to his charm. Even the hedgehog souls of Brougham and Rogers were touched by it. And though Canning's circle was, in one sense, a small one, it was in no way confined to the great. William Jerdan, a humble journalistic neighbour at Gloucester Lodge, tells a very touching story of how the great man was his neighbour and became his friend, and of how this intimacy became ' the pride of my life.' It is plain that Canning possessed, in a peculiar degree, the genius of friendship.

The wit of Canning was a legend in his own day, and explains both the affection of his friends and the resentment of his enemies. He had every weapon in his armoury, from fun to humour and to wit proper. He could play a rough practical joke, silence a friend with quiet humour, crush an enemy with the venom of epigram, or double up a dinner-table with a Rabelaisian story. The professional jester seems tedious at times, and some of his sayings wear thin in the twentieth century. In cold print we miss the careful baiting of the trap, the heavy fall of the victim, the humorous flash in the eye of the trapper as he seizes his spoil, and the ' table set in a roar.'   The sallies against Lord Folkestone, ' with the con-tortions but without the inspiration of the Sibyl ' ; or against Lord `Nugent, ' that most enormous breach of neutrality,' plumping his weight into the heavy Falmouth coach with his light horseman's equipment and his helmet as big as that in the Castle of Otranto, sent Wilberforce ' home crying with laughter.'   It was, perhaps, in the grave and dull atmosphere of the Commons that these violations of decorum were most appreciated.   Yet even his written sarcasms are not always effective to-day.   No one, indeed, can question the hard, metallic, and yet immortal brilliancy of the *Anti-Jacobin*. But the apotheosis of Sir John Sinclair, or the ridicule of Brougham's Committee of Education as ' *ego et committeus meus* ' in the *Quarterly*, strike us as a little drawn-out and too consciously studied.   Far better are the lines on Whitbread, which seem written as if in a flash, and partake of its lightness and brilliance.   So also with the change of the letter *w* to *f* which he once made with a pen in a pamphlet of Lord Sheffield's on the manufacture of British wool : " There can be no doubt that under a due system of protection, the supply of British *f*ools might be greatly increased, and that our domestic *f*ools might eventually be enabled to stand the competition of the *f*ools of the Continent."   This impromptu strikes us as a good deal more human than some more finished and elaborate attempts at wit.

The wit of Canning was on the surface.   The real tendencies of his inner life, in which he could sometimes forget his political ambitions, were towards literature.   It was in these pursuits that he found consolation and rest.   Marcellus illus-trates this beautifully by a story of a visit of his to Canning. During the stormy Spanish episode Marcellus sought Canning out and found him at Gloucester Lodge walking over the grass under the budding trees and reading Vergil.   " A truce," said Canning, "to politics to-day, . . . I am weary of them, let us read some Vergil.   In my little domain, like the old man of Galesius—

" ' *Cui pauca relicti iugera ruris erant* '—I was looking over the *Georgics*.   I was here—can anything be more touching than these verses ?—

' *Hi motus animorum, atque hæc certamina tanta*
  Pulveris exigui iactu compressa quiescent.'

. . . It must all end then in this little dust.   What have I
gained by so many battles, many enemies, a thousand
calumnies ? . . .   I can attempt nothing of that which an
inward and solemn voice appears to dictate. . . .   I am like
a bird which, instead of soaring to the cliffs and the precipices,
flies over the fens and skims the ground. . . .   How often have
I not been tempted to fly from society, and from power, to
the literature which was the food of my boyhood, the only
refuge which is impenetrable to the delusions of fate.
Literature is a consolation, a hope, a place of rest for me."
. . .   " Yet," he added, " still that desire of fame, which
cannot at my age be called ambition, drives me back to public
affairs. . . .   Human fame—mockery !   The ancients made
her a goddess—a woman to be more seductive, and dressed
her in the attractions of patriotism.   At this moment, when I
should so much like to dream of Vergil, I must go to encounter
Brougham in the Commons."   They passed quickly to the
Foreign Office and thence to the House of Commons.   As
they entered, Canning said roguishly to Marcellus, " What will
all these spectators, and even my own colleagues, think of
our long conference and open intimacy ?   They will send off
couriers, the Funds will rise—and yet we have discussed
nothing to-day but a few literary subjects, and quoted a few
melancholy verses." [1]

If Canning sought relief in books and in reflections, it was
because he was acutely conscious of the loneliness of his
position in the Cabinet.   There was in it political danger
as well as personal discomfort.   Huskisson was not in the
Cabinet until the autumn of 1823, Robinson carried no guns.
Wellington, Eldon, Westmoreland, Harrowby were always
hostile : Bathurst generally so.   Peel and Melville were doubtful, but often against him.   Liverpool—the head of the
Ministry—was, however, his firm supporter.   Their friendship dated from early days, when Canning's ascendancy had
been established over him.   On one occasion Liverpool came

---

[1] Marcellus, *Politique de la Restauration* (1853), pp. 15–17.   Marcellus
is not always exact, but I think the general impression of this scene is
correct.

into his rooms at Christ Church, found him surrounded by
friends, and said, " I am come to take tea with you." " No,"
said Canning, " you are going to the Pump," and to the
Pump he went, and not willingly.   During the years 1822–7
Canning dragged him along, though less boisterously, into
courses and policies which he would not himself have had
the boldness to adopt.   He complained that Canning worked
him with twenty horse-power, and never came to an interview
or to a Cabinet without bringing his resignation in his pocket.
Yet the support of this easy, amiable, straightforward man
was the true cause of Canning's success.   For Liverpool was
no supporter of the King nor of intrigue, and his loyal friendship and imperturbable ease and moderation met every
difficulty.   In the final crisis at the end of 1824, Liverpool
stood by Canning and offered his own resignation as well.
Canning was sometimes betrayed or secretly opposed by his
colleagues, but the loyalty of Liverpool was always unim-
peachable.   None the less, though he was assured of him and
would have fallen without him, this support alone was not
enough, and he felt deeply the enmity of other colleagues.

   The fact is that, in spite of his radiant and abounding
humour, Canning was acutely sensitive to coldness or hostility,
to criticism in the Commons or in the Press.   This sensitiveness bred a smouldering fire, a lengthened resentment towards
those whom he thought to have injured him.   In his latter days,
indeed, he triumphed both over his enemies and over himself.
Lord Holland, against whom he had long had a grudge ;
Brougham, whom he had savagely satirised, became friends
and colleagues.   Lockhart, whom he had unjustly suspected
of attacking him anonymously, received an acknowledgment
and a kindly message from him during his last month of life.
Even Hobhouse, one of his bitterest opponents, received evidence of his friendly feeling.   At the end of his life he was
turning old enemies into new friends.

   His over-sensitiveness led at times to displays of temper
which were often quoted against him.   The discreditable
scene between him and Brougham in the Commons satirised
by Dickens, his attacks on Lambton and Lord Folkestone,
displayed command neither of temper nor of taste.   In the
Cabinet Wellington said he was usually very silent, but that,

if he intervened, he argued with such heat and impetuosity that it was impossible to oppose him without great unpleasantness. The flash of his eye and the scorn of his lip were danger-signals that his colleagues in the Cabinet and his opponents in the Commons learnt to dread, and few diplomats cared to face the roused and furious Foreign Minister. Here again he sought (and with some success) to master himself in later years, and the temper and humour which he showed in the crisis of 1827 delighted his friends as much as they disappointed his foes.

The fact is that sensitiveness, as much as humour, was part of the man and even more of a defect. He was naturally nervous and easily stirred by friendship as by hostility. Before making some of his speeches he hesitated and blushed like a girl; he burst into tears when Addington offered him his friendship, or when his comrades congratulated him in the lobby on his speech defending his Lisbon appointment. When he listened to a sermon of Chalmers he wept like a woman with emotion.

Emotion, irritability, and sensitiveness disorganise the will-power of some men; they tempered and braced that of Canning. He was like a thoroughbred horse, all nervous and a-quiver, yet straining always to the goal, and spending his last strength in the effort. This great sensibility of temperament fretted him to decay at the same time as it fired him to effort. But the delicacy of perception gave him extreme quickness of thought and feeling and gave his will the resilience and fineness of steel. The man had often faced and converted hostile majorities by appeal now to argument, now to emotions. He bore down his colleagues in the Cabinet by another means. You could resist his graces, his charm, his eloquence, his tactics, his logic, his intellect, but there was no resisting the man. Even the iron of Wellington bent before the steel of that will.

Power, intellect, genius, few denied him in his own day, but there was something else that many denied him. Many diplomats questioned his sincerity, many opponents his bare honesty. His duel with Castlereagh, his fiery onslaughts on opponents, his wit, his haughtiness, explain much, but they do not explain all. Moreover, he did not, like Cavour

or Danton, willingly sacrifice his reputation to save his
country.   On the contrary, he claimed to seek power through
' character,' meaning that his character was not to suffer
by contact with the temptations of public life.   By that
test his character must be assayed.   A revolutionary age is,
indeed, the best time for the assaying process.   Wellington
and Castlereagh are generally, and on the whole justly,
acclaimed as men who held to truth and to honour in an age
of deceit and of intrigue.   Yet some of their practices are
not easy to defend.   Both men sometimes held positions in
which honour was impossible.   Castlereagh was the chief
agent in the shameless bribery which carried the Irish Union ;
Wellington, when Irish Secretary, administered corruption
as efficiently in London as he destroyed it in Spain.   Castlereagh suppressed some papers in order to justify to Parliament the case against Murat, and connived secretly at the
permanent negation of the Sicilian Constitution.   Wellington
praised his officers in public despatches and reprimanded them
behind the scenes ;   abused Canning in private to foreign
diplomats, and received from them despatches which he
showed to King George but withheld from the Foreign
Minister himself.

During his first tenure of the Foreign Office (1807–9) Canning
had not been blameless.   There was hastiness, pettiness,
perhaps intrigue, in his methods.   During his second Ministry
he was more sinned against than sinning.   Some of his
colleagues in the Cabinet attacked him at once in their Press
organs, and lifted their own voices against him in private.
Wellington used both the King and Madame Lieven against
Canning, till the latter turned the tables on the Duke, and used
both as agencies to defeat him.   It is certain that his colleagues
began by counter-working him, not he by counter-working his
colleagues.   On the whole, during his second Ministry, his conduct was more direct than theirs, because he appealed primarily
to the public and dragged things to the light of day.   He
really did try to square private action with public utterance,
and in the main he succeeded.   The courage, which he never
lacked, and his great intellectual gifts, taught him that
frankness and honesty were his best assets against the fraud
or trickery of others.   Such an honesty, based on intelligence

and experience, is less to be admired than one of instinct
and impulse. But it is not a quality to be despised. The
moral standards of State policy, in his or any age, do not accord
with those of individuals, and those with practical experience
of them will not lightly suppose that they either reach, or
aspire, to the ideals desired or entertained of public men by
the masses. The most that can be demanded is that statesmen who pursue a high moral standard should suffer inwardly
when they do not attain to it. The example of Cromwell
or Lincoln or Gladstone will illustrate the meaning. All
these men came to power imbued with a burning sense of
righteousness, but had to maintain themselves by acts which
their consciences cannot, at times, have approved. Gladstone
reconciled himself to his lot by laborious casuistry ; Lincoln
by a humorous half-tragic acceptance of the inevitable ;
Cromwell by the death-bed reflection, that, having once been
in a state of grace, he could not afterwards fall from it. With
such deep-souled men as these Canning cannot compare.
His religious faith, though strong and simple, did not separate
him from the world nor blind him to its attractions. Ambition
moved strongly within him. His intellect lured him on sometimes to an almost conscious casuistry. The true comparison
is not with moral giants, but with kindred parliamentarians,
as, for example, Peel.

Like Canning, Peel was ready at times to depart from party
principle, like him intellectual rather than religious in policy
and aim, like him eager to justify himself against opponents,
yet conscious sometimes of a partial failure to do so. There
was more courage, as there was more genius, in one man than
in the other. Canning boldly faced his opponents even when
he looked, and was, a dying man ; the assaults of Disraeli
reduced Peel to shamed silence. Yet, when all is said, what
Lord Rosebery has finely written of Peel, might be applied
with even greater justice to Canning. " For then, and now,
and for all time, above and beyond that Government and the
perished passions of the time, there looms the figure of the
great Minister, with feet perhaps of clay as well as iron,
but with a heart at least of silver, and a head of fine gold." [1]

[1] Rosebery, *Historical and Literary Miscellanies* (1921), i. 237.

CHAPTER XI

CONQUERING THE KING

I. The 'Cottage Coterie' and the 'Plot' (1822–4)

" Thy saddlegirths are not yet quite secure,
Nor royal Stallion's feet extremely sure."
BYRON to Canning, 1822.
" One of the cleverest men in Europe."—Sir W. KNIGHTON on George IV.

THE difficulties of Canning are nowhere more clearly seen than in his relations with the King, which seriously affected foreign policy. The first two Georges had indeed made British diplomacy difficult by their attachment to Hanover, but on the whole they were reasonable and straightforward men. George III., though he tried to bend all to his will at home, had been British enough when he looked abroad. But the fourth George, by his attachment to foreign diplomats and sovereigns and by his incurable love of intrigue, threatened gravely to complicate foreign relations. There was a real danger that a double system of foreign policy might be pursued, similar to that by which Louis XV. alternately outwitted or betrayed his accredited Foreign Minister. George was not indeed a Louis XV. any more than Lady Conyngham was a Pompadour, but he was a despot in Hanover and absolutely controlled Hanoverian diplomats. As Canning had no personal connection with Continental statesmen, the King had an opportunity of which he might make a dangerous use.

It is not indeed easy to credit King George with seriousness in anything. Even the sober Wellington said of him in 1818, " You never saw such a figure as he is." (Lord Folkestone had just written, " Prinney has let loose his belly, which now reaches to his knees.") " Then he speaks so like old Falstaff that, damn me, if I was not afraid to walk into a room with him." In 1820 the Duke pronounced him " degraded as low

as he could be already." There was a lower stage yet. In
1829 he said George had " the worst judgment that can be,"
and had " no idea of what a King ought to do." He certainly
had not ; he walked with his arm round Canning's neck in
public, and promised him he never would forgive Wellington.
Only a year afterwards he fondled ' Arthur,' shed tears over
him, and kissed the austere hero on the cheek.

Less trustworthy but still valuable authorities relate other
stories. In the later twenties he withdrew himself almost
wholly from the public gaze. He received ministers in bed
in his night-cap, and seldom rose till six in the evening. He
suffered from delusions, thinking he rode Fleur-de-Lis for the
cup at Goodwood, and led the Heavy Dragoons at Salamanca.
He asserted at a dinner before foreign diplomats that French
troops would beat British, that the British cavalry and the
Russian infantry were the best, and the Duke coldly denied
all three statements. " He was," said Greville, " not only
half-blind but half-mad." Finally he died in the odour of
sanctity, saying, ' Amen ' to prayers read by the Archbishop
of Canterbury. Countless tresses of women's hair lay in his
wardrobes, but a locket round his neck contained the portrait of one woman, and his will directed that it should be
buried with him.

While satirists and gossips can hardly exaggerate his
absurdities, they have done less than justice to his abilities.
Even Brougham admitted he had qualities far above medi-
ocrity. He was well informed on foreign policy, quick at seizing
a point, and still quicker at turning it to his advantage. He
was not easily defeated in an argument and made good use of
the one privilege every constitutional king retains—that of
having the last word. Moreover, he was by no means scrupulous. On his duplicity and even perfidy, Eldon agreed with
Canning, Wellington with Brougham, Lyndhurst with Peel,
Liverpool with Creevey, and such agreement may be reckoned
as decisive. A king who is both clever and perfidious is a
dangerous opponent for any British Minister. For while he
may overmatch his sovereign in cleverness, he cannot overmatch him in perfidy. For it is one thing to detect a king
in a lie or an intrigue, quite another to tax him with it.

The subject of foreign policy was one in which the King's

duplicity was specially dangerous.   For he exercised considerable influence, first through indiscreet revelation of secrets
to foreign diplomats, and next through his Hanoverian
ministers.   Under his control Count Münster directed the
Hanoverian diplomacy, so that he had a secret service and a
foreign policy of his own, with which no British minister could
interfere save by the royal permission.   Castlereagh had
managed to control the Hanoverian correspondence, but had
met with difficulties in his later years.   It was unfortunate
that George IV. selected a new mistress and chose the
Marchioness of Conyngham in place of the Marchioness of
Hertford (1819). For Lady Conyngham hated Lady Castlereagh,
and showed some interest in foreign policy and an interest
favourable to the Neo-Holy Alliance.   In 1820 Castlereagh
began to draw away from the Neo-Holy Alliance.   George IV.
had strongly objected to this move on his part, and naturally
strove to obtain more complete independence under Canning.

Canning's first move (as already related, p. 30) was judicious,
for he selected the son of the King's mistress—Lord Francis
Conyngham—for his Parliamentary Under-Secretary.   But
George, after a temporary outburst of enthusiasm in January
1823, when he sent him his picture, soon began to show his
dislike of the Minister's foreign policy, and cut him off from the
Hanoverian correspondence.   His differences with Canning
were played upon by the ' Coterie,' as it was called, that little
band of foreign diplomats who amused the King's private
moments and instilled their diplomatic news into his mind
during the process.   They met at the Cottage at Windsor,
usually for week-end parties.   First and most important were
Count and Countess Lieven, the ' two Russian Ambassadors '
as they were called, the latter being more important than
the former.   She was, at first, the mistress of the Austrian
Chancellor, then the friend of two British Foreign Ministers,
the close confidant of a British King, something more than
the friend of a British Prime Minister, and at length the aged
and Platonic Egeria of a French one.   It was no ordinary
woman to whom Metternich, Castlereagh, Canning, Grey, and
Guizot all at times deferred, and it is easy to understand that
the susceptible George felt her charm.   Without beauty, her
great attraction and fascination, her musical talents diverted

the 'Coterie,' just as her taste and elegance impressed British Society. Next to this formidable Russian influence came the Austrian Esterházy, grave and pompous, but liked by the King, with Neumann, his attaché, a wit and an amateur actor of repute, an avowed and special favourite. Late in 1823 Prince Polignac, the French Ambassador, was also introduced into the circle, so that George was surrounded by a body of as 'high-flying Ultras' as even Metternich or Alexander could desire. No English persons were usually present except Lady Conyngham, the King's mistress, and Sir William Knighton, the King's physician. The latter was important, for he managed the King's affairs, knew all his secrets, and was, until 1825, like all the others, a pronounced anti-Canningite. George IV. is reported to have once said, " I wish to God some-one would assassinate Knighton." But he feared him as much as he hated him.[1]

Wellington cannot fairly be called a member of the ' Coterie,' though he occasionally attended their meetings and seldom failed to express at them his antipathy to Canning. Like his colleagues in the Cabinet, Lords Harrowby and Westmoreland (the *sot privé*), he was an instrument rather than a prime mover in the intrigue. But the dislike of the King and the divisions in the Cabinet made both Alexander and Metternich think that Canning could be overthrown, provided that the ' Coterie ' played their cards well. The ' Coterie ' began definitely to work against Canning in February 1823. " It was," as Canning said, " a plot to change the politics of the government by changing *me*." Metternich resumed his secret correspondence with Wellington about the same time, in order to widen the breach. Esterházy read despatches to the King and to Wellington which he withheld from Canning ; secret letters from Alexander and the Emperor Francis, and one from Louis XVIII., found their way to the King, all encouraging him in his Legitimist views. There can be no doubt that the King answered, through his Hanoverian diplomats, to the

---

[1] It is unfortunate that the memoirs of this discreet personal adviser tell us nothing about the King which is not complimentary and common-place. The archives of Paris and Vienna reveal much about the King's relations with Polignac and Esterházy, but of Madame Lieven's influence we know little except that it was great. Knighton must have known the truth, and it is a pity he did not tell it.

effect that he agreed with these views, but could not at present force them on his English Minister.

Canning knew something, if not all, about these ' conspiracies.' His response to secret intrigue was the direct popular appeal of his speeches to the Commons of 14th and 30th April 1823. He evoked great enthusiasm, and the Press began to scent the intrigues of the Court. In May the *Times* reported that the King had wished success to France's invasion of Spain, and said that the King must be mad if this were the case. It was, at any rate, correct in suggesting that he had been indiscreet in his good wishes to the cause of Legitimacy.

But George went even further than this with the French representative, Marcellus, at a ball at Carlton House on the 11th July.[1]

" ' They claim,' said he, ' that Ferdinand has again recalled, as Ministers at Cadiz, those who deposed him at Seville. That is a weakness I shall never imitate. They wished here recently to make me pass for mad, and you know the pretext better than anyone ' [the *Times*], added the King, smiling. ' At the time I told Lord Liverpool to take care. If my ministers one day declared I was mad I might take back my senses, but I should never take back my ministers.' "

Shortly afterwards Canning began to talk to Marcellus. George approached :—

" ' What are you speaking about to the representative of France ? ' said he jestingly. ' Sire,' answered Canning in the same tone, ' I spoke to him of the excellence of the representative government and of forced labour in the Commons.[2] M. Marcellus cannot be an orator at home, and he is an auditor abroad.' ' I see,' interrupted the King, ' this year, M. Marcellus, you have been an auditor under painful circumstances. I have made a complaint to you that it was necessary you should hear, and if you had not kept your mouth shut, and if Parliament could have heard you, you would have

[1] *A.A.E.*, 617, July 11/23. Marcellus to Chateaubriand. The version here given is that in the despatch. It differs only slightly (there are some omissions) from that printed in *Politique de la Restauration*, pp. 24–6.

[2] This was a reference to the fact that, on becoming Foreign Minister in 1822, Canning wrote to Chateaubriand, saying, "he was restored to the labouring oars for life."

had great difficulty in answering.'   Mr Canning was very disconcerted by this language.   ' Sir,' said Marcellus, ' the sailor
forgets the storm when the calm returns.'   ' Very good,'
said the King, ' but don't be carried away by our system of
government which is said to be so reasonable.   If there are
advantages, there are inconveniences, and I have never
forgotten what a witty king once said of it to me.[1] " Your
English Government," he assured me, " is only good to protect
rascals [*les coquins*] and intimidate honest men." [2] What
do you think of that, Mr Canning ?   Is there not a great fund
of truth in it ? '   The minister, embarrassed, hesitated to
answer.   ' We are still alone,' said the King, ' in our kind of
government, and for the good of the world we ought not to
desire our institutions for any other people.   What is almost
good with us would not be so with others.   Every land has
not the same fruits above, or minerals below, its surface.   It
is thus with nations, with their manners, and with their
character.   Remember this, M. de Marcellus, it is my opinion
fixed and unalterable.' "

After the King had moved away Marcellus says that Canning
added bitterly :   " Representative government has still one
advantage that His Majesty has forgotten.   Ministers have
to endure, without answering back, the epigrams by which a
king seeks to avenge himself for his impotence."

The last sentence in this remarkable interview is not in the
official despatch and may have been invented by Marcellus.
But he says something similar in another official despatch just
afterwards.   " Canning is not devoted to the King nor to
the royal family (he knows that in England this is not the first
of duties).   He says proudly that he came to power without
them and will not fall because of them.   He wishes to be
monarchical without ceasing to be popular." [3]   It was quite

[1] Apparently Louis XVIII.
[2] In the printed version Marcellus uses the word ' *aventurier* ' instead of
' *coquin*.' This is to show that Canning, who was sometimes called ' an
adventurer ' (*cf.* p. 31), was aimed at. This seems clear anyhow, without
introducing a wrong word.
[3] *A.A.E.*, 617. Marcellus to Chateaubriand, July 22/23. It should
be noticed here that Marcellus (with whom Polignac agreed) thought that
Canning's popularity was too great for him to be overthrown, and that the
only chance was to cajole him. Here they judged more correctly than the
' Coterie.'

true. Canning was a convinced monarchist, but he meant the monarch to be English and popular and not to be influenced by foreign intrigues.

The ' plot ' languished during the latter part of 1823. Early in 1824, however, hopes revived. The extraordinary persistence of foreign diplomats in pressing the project of a congress on Spanish-American affairs after Canning's formal refusal (30th January 1824) must be ascribed to the ' Coterie ' and to the fact that they thought Wellington and the King would support them. Here they were wrong, for Wellington was against a congress, and without him the King alone could not prevail against Canning. But on the general question of not recognising the Spanish Colonies, or at least of delaying that recognition as long as possible, both King and Duke agreed, so that a field for intrigue was open. On the 30th May the well-informed Neumann wrote to Metternich that the Cabinet was divided on the question, there was a right kind of party (*saine partie*) in it, and that the King had shown more energy of late, so that there was a chance of displacing Canning. The King was reported as approving of a plan in a secret letter to Metternich written by Count Münster.[1] It suggested that Metternich should give Canning's colleagues ' weapons against him.' Metternich was delighted, and wrote a long letter on the 14th June to work on Wellington, the sense of which was that Canning's plan to remain independent of the Neo-Holy Alliance meant the ruin of Spain.

Wellington was furiously angry at the Cabinet decision on the 23rd July to negotiate with Buenos Aires. An explosion seemed imminent. The King had already (1st May) remonstrated to Lord Liverpool about Canning's speech at the Mansion House, which, he said, marked a separation between him and his colleagues. The fact is, Waithman, the Mayor, had been a defender of the Queen, and George thought Canning should have abstained from the banquet in consequence. Liverpool and Wellington had tried to concoct an apologetic letter to George in reply, stating that Mr Canning had not intended ' to give him pain.'

---

[1] *Vide* above, p. 141. *V.S.A.*, Berichte aus England, Bd. 222. Neumann to Metternich, May 30/24, *v.* also Stap., *Corr.*, i. 258. This letter is probably the one of which the contents were known to Canning, and which he describes as containing some ' incredibly ill-advised expressions.'

At this stage a still more unfortunate personal incident occurred. With the King's knowledge and connivance, Wellington wrote a letter to Canning on the 5th October, saying that he had heard " from the King's Equerries " that " you [Canning] proposed paying a visit to Paris," and that it would result in " inconvenience to the public and annoyance to yourself." Canning replied tartly that " another member of the Cabinet " (Lord Westmoreland) had just come back from Paris and had had a conference with the King of France on the recognition of Spanish America, but had omitted to give the Foreign Secretary the results of that conversation. An angry correspondence ensued, in which Wellington was forced to admit that Charles X. had advised Lord Westmoreland against the recognition of the Colonies. Canning then sent the correspondence to Liverpool, stating that he knew the King had concocted the letter of 5th October with the Duke, though the latter had not admitted it. " Now this I hold not to be fair . . . it is high time to look about one, and to beware of what Burke calls ' traps and mines.' " [1] Liverpool tried to pour oil on the waters, but a copy of Canning's letter found its way to the Duke, who did not see his way to continue the correspondence. On 17th October Metternich told Esterházy to tell the King that Canning ' was no statesman,' and that ' the hope of the better policy of England was beginning to disappear.' [2]

2. The King Surrenders at Discretion (1825)

The King's bitter opposition to Canning over the South American question has already been told, but the aftermath must be treated here. Canning triumphed in the Cabinet and defended his position to the King with vigour on the 1st February 1825. One of the points on which he specially dwelt was the leakage of secrets to Foreign Powers and the consequent danger of corresponding confidentially with them. The King seems to have been frightened, perhaps because he

[1] *W.N.D.*, ii. 325. The collusion of the King in the letter of Oct. 5 is proved by Esterházy to Metternich, Oct. 12, *privé. V.S.A.*, Berichte aus London, 1824.
[2] *V.S.A.*, Weisungen nach London. Metternich to Esterházy, Oct. 17/24.

scented a reference to his own intrigues. Wellington even warned him that there might be a *coup d'état* if Canning revealed the matter to Parliament. At any rate, he sent Canning a ' decidedly conciliatory ' reply. In March Metternich came to Paris, and Canning discouraged his visit to England in a well-known letter to Granville.[1] " I have evidence which I entirely believe," that [this] intrigue had been proceeding "for the last twelve months at least, perhaps longer." Metternich was at the bottom of it, and Madame Lieven was the ' organ.' The aim was " to change the politics of the government by changing *me*." " Now you shall know what I would have done if this intrigue had gone on, and if fortunately the intemperance and miscalculation of the King had not brought it to a premature *dénouement*, and so been obliged to give in— I would have resigned upon the S[outh] A[merican] question and I would have declared openly in the H[ouse] of C[ommons] —taking care to keep safe my sources of intelligence—that I was driven from office by the Holy Alliance, and further, that the system, which I found established of personal communications between the sovereign and Foreign Ministers, was one under which no English Minister could do his duty. If, after such a denunciation, the L[ievens] and Esterházy did not find London too hot for them, I know nothing of the present temper of the English nation."

As regards a visit which Metternich proposed to make to England, Canning went on to Granville, " Do not encourage him. But as Esterházy is going to meet him at Paris, I trust that he has given up the notion of a visit to Windsor. He would have come to triumph, I would not advise him to come to intrigue." Metternich learnt enough from Esterházy, and prudently declined the King's secret invitation. George then wrote expressing his regret at his inability to come, and Metternich coldly replied to the effect that the line of policy England was now assuming was so different from that of Austria that his visit would have been misinterpreted.

The ' Coterie ' had already been aware of their loss of influence. Esterházy thought the game lost in January, as

---

[1] Stap., *Corr.*, i. 258, Mar. 11/25. Canning to Granville. He says Esterházy told ' a person about it, who has reported to me.' It seems likely that this person was Lady, or perhaps Lord Francis, Conyngham. The latter seems to have been devoted to Canning.

did Wellington.[1] Canning wrote to Granville on the 29th
March : " I presume the plot is at an end, and that the several
actors in it are desirous of making it up and having no more
said about it." " With all my heart ! " George seems to have
been thoroughly frightened by Canning's veiled threats and
by his open popularity, so, though he sulked for a time, he
finally decided to come to terms.   On the 27th April he sent
Sir William Knighton to Canning, who was ill in bed, ostensibly
to inquire after his health, in reality to surrender at discretion.
The astute Sir William, seeing in what quarter the wind sat,
improved the occasion by offering his own services to Canning,
whom he had hitherto counter-worked and exposed.   Canning
did not stand on ceremony, and the interview of the 27th
April marked a new era in his relations with the King, and in
his control of future foreign policy.

The interview is vividly and briefly described by Joan
Canning in a letter to Granville, with whom she has just been
staying.   " This illness of Mr C. has produced one rather odd
circumstance—a visit of about two hours' continuance from
the person who did *not* leave his name at your door in passing
through Paris last January.[2]   The ostensible cause of his visit
was particular enquiries after Mr C.'s health at the express
command of his Master—but the result was a long detail
amounting, in fact, to an offer of himself body and soul to Mr C.
in any way that he could be useful, and an implied refutation
of being party to any intrigues or participating in any attempts
to Mr C.'s disadvantage—and describing the present state of
his Master's mind as being very much changed in respect to
his dislike of the S. American recognition, as well as come
round very much from the predilection for the Continental and
S[ainte] Alliance policy—perfectly satisfied that all was going
on well for the advantage of England and content to enjoy
his popularity in peace and indolence.

" In the course of the conversation . . . without any *à propos*
to lead to the assertion [he] said that Metternich's hostility

---

[1] *V.S.A.*, England ; *Varia*, 21. Münster to Metternich, Mar. 18/25.
Weisungen nach Russland, 1825. Metternich to George IV. and to
Wellington, both of Mar. 27 ; Weisungen nach London, 1825.   Metternich
to Esterházy, Apr. 7.

[2] Knighton had visited Paris (Jan. 1825), and had, doubtless by the
King's direction, omitted to call on Granville.   The slight was certainly
intentional, as Granville was known as Canning's friend.

to Mr C. came entirely from jealousy—that he [M.] wished to be considered the chief ruler of the destinies of Europe and could not bear to find that Mr C.'s fame and power exceeded his own—but that he was now convinced that all efforts to overthrow him would be of no avail—and was therefore disposed to submit and make the ' *amende honorable.*' " [1]

Canning was surprised and delighted at this overture, and characteristically seized the opportunity to end the double system of correspondence. He got the King to make the change in his sentiments known to foreign diplomats through the medium of the Hanoverian correspondence.

On the 10th May Münster, under the King's direction, wrote a letter to Metternich attempting a mild defence of Canning and of the British policy of isolation, and stating that it was necessary to yield sometimes to public opinion in England, and therefore to Canning who represented it.[2] Metternich instructed Esterházy on the 7th August to answer Münster by a reassertion of the principles of the Neo-Holy Alliance, and by a violent attack on Canning, who was ' inflammatory ' as regards Catholic Emancipation, Greece, and South America. Esterházy was directed to show this despatch secretly to the King, to Wellington, and to Münster. If shown, its effect was useless, for Canning was daily improving his position with the King.

On the 13th October 1825 Canning wrote to Granville that the King had begun showing him all his secret Hanoverian correspondence. ' *Comprenez-vous ?* ' he added significantly. It was, in fact, the end of the ' Coterie' influence and the intrigues of the Cottage. Not only was this Hanoverian correspondence most important as giving Canning excellent information, but as preventing the King from pursuing a Hanoverian policy separate from the British. Münster, under Canning's direction, was therefore now compelled to bring the Hanoverian diplomats to heel. This he did in a highly important circular to them of the 8th November. He plainly stated that England, without treason to her constitution,

---

[1] *Gr. MSS.* Mrs Canning to Granville, Apr. 29/25. There is a longer and less indiscreet account in Stap., *G.C. & T.*, 437-44.

[2] *V.S.A.*, England, *Varia*, 20, May 10/25. Münster to Metternich ; Metternich's reply, Aug. 7/25, is in Weisungen nach England, Bd. 227 ; Aug. 7/25, to Esterházy. *Vide* Appendix V. for further documents.

could not agree with ' other Courts ' if they " lay it down as
an axiom that they are called upon unconditionally to interfere in every quarrel between Governments and their subjects,
to lift their swords on behalf of the former." He admitted
that " some of the sentiments uttered in the course of these
transactions were not perhaps to be approved." But he
concluded with a vigorous attack on the Neo-Holy Allied
policy over Greece, and the futility of their conference idea,
and strongly defended Canning's right to recognise the Greeks
as belligerents.[1] The answer of one Hanoverian diplomat
showed that the double system was at an end and the change
of policy complete. " I must confess that the twofold
character of our most gracious Monarch has often excited
in me doubt and perplexity, when drawing up my reports, as
to the nature of many terms I have employed. But your
Excellency's most important despatch of the 8th of this month
has rendered my task perfectly easy."

Canning attached the greatest importance, and rightly, to
this despatch. He could have objected to only one phrase—
that deprecating " some of the [*i.e.* his own] sentiments
uttered in the course of these transactions [relative to
Spain] which are not perhaps to be approved." But this
small effort of the King's to preserve his consistency was a
cheap price to pay for the despatch as a whole. It definitely
marks both the end of the influence of the ' Coterie,' and the
end of the independence of the Hanoverian Foreign Office.
The new situation becomes even more clear a little later.

In November Sir William Knighton was sent on a secret
mission to Vienna, and in January 1826 he returned *via* Paris,
taking care this time to call upon Granville and to have an
interview with him. Sir William began by inquiring, with
some anxiety, if Canning was suspicious. Granville tactfully
suggested that Canning was very anxious to please the King.
Knighton said that " the Queen *Business* had been the misery
of the King's life, that when Canning became His Minister
His Majesty had therefore much to get over, much to blot
out of his Recollection ; that the dining with Waithman

---

[1] *F.O.*, 360/3, *H. de W. MSS.* Münster to Count Grote at Paris, Nov.
8/25, translation. Philipp to Münster, Nov. 21/25. Canning sent a copy
of the Münster despatch to Granville, Nov. 13 (Stap., *Corr.*, i. 322), but
insisted on his returning it, *v.* Appendix V.

at the Mansion House had brought back circumstances to
H.M.'s mind, which he had been endeavouring to forget, that
the King was ' of a forgiving temper,' and that his forget-
fulness of injuries had been misinterpreted into caprice and
insincerity, but that, without doubt, the King's cordiality
with Canning was every day increasing. He spoke of the
Coalition of the Powers of Europe having had the effect of
strengthening in the King's mind the prejudices which
belonged to the Brunswick family, and fortified his inclination to connect England closely with the Continent ; from
which connection Sir W. K. thought we had better keep
ourselves disentangled. When I [Granville] spoke of the
graciousness of the reception which Hurtado (the new Mexican
Minister) had experienced, at his audience of the King, Sir
Wm. said, ' Oh all the feeling of last year upon that subject
is wholly gone by—the King is quite satisfied that the right
course of politics has been adopted' ; I [Granville] said that it
was impossible that the King could not be proud of the
commanding station which his Kingdom occupied among the
nations of the World, far beyond that of any former reign
in the History of England. He assented to this." . . .
Sir William " asked me [Granville] what were the motives of
the rapid journey Mad. Lieven made to and from Russia—he
thought her *intrigante*, and cautioned me strongly against
Esterházy as very intrigant and hostile to English interests."
He added, "that the King looked on Metternich as the cleverest
man he had ever seen, and that he [Sir W. K.] was persuaded
of the great advantage that would be derived from Canning
and Metternich meeting—that Canning had the finest mind
in the world, he would not say he was violent and quick in
his temper, but that he was subject to transitory sensations." [1]

It was amusing, but significant too, that Knighton should
warn Granville against the intrigues of Esterházy and Madame
Lieven. It meant, indeed, that the influence of the ' Coterie '
had faded. The climax was reached when Canning was
present at a farewell audience which George gave to Esterházy
in his presence on the 20th December 1825. At that ceremony

---

[1] *Gr. MSS.* Draft of Lord Granville's interview with Sir W. Knighton
sent to Canning and returned thus endorsed by him Jan. 9/26—" Many
thanks, I have burnt your accompanying letter." For the motives of
Madame Lieven's journey, *v.* pp. 340, 344.

the King and Esterházy vied with one another in praising
Canning for refusing to commit England to conferences![1]
and George described Metternich as a ' very clever ' but
' very prejudiced man.' It is characteristic that the King,
while giving a formal farewell audience to Esterházy, had
previously, through Count Münster, privately asked for his
retention. Metternich granted the request in December 1825,
making some strong remarks on the King's double-dealing.[2]
The King, wrote Metternich, had real knowledge, and his
principles were very correct (' *d'une grande correction* ').
Since 1815 his faith in Austria ' had risen to the height of a
religion.' It was now all changed. But Wellington was
' *dépourvu de tout talent politique*,' and had lost his control
over the King.[3] The *grande déviation* had begun, and was
due to Canning.

In one word, by the end of 1825 the ' Cottage Coterie ' had
broken up. Metternich despaired both of the Duke and the
King. One reason was that Russia was now unfriendly with
Austria, and the two Lievens were cultivating friendly relations
with Canning. Sir William Knighton was Canning's, ' body
and soul,' and the King, though he still indulged in petty
duplicity, was now well under control in large matters. The
best proof of this is that Canning now began showing to the
King the private letters he received from British diplomats
abroad. He would not have done this unless he was sure that
their contents would not be revealed to the ' Coterie.'

During 1826 Canning still further increased his ascendancy
over his frivolous Master. In 1823 George had sent a secret
message to Metternich that he had selected Sir Henry Wellesley
for Vienna as his minister. In April 1826 Canning refused to
permit George to send a message to the Czar that the Duke of
Devonshire, who was to attend the Coronation at Moscow, was

---

[1] Stap., *G.C. & T₁,* 448–52. Memo. by Canning, Dec. 21/25. This
memo. was not reported by Esterházy to Metternich.

[2] Treble-dealing would be a more correct term. For the King got
Münster to write on Nov. 25 to Metternich, and yet on Dec. 20 accepted
Canning's offer to make a private overture to Metternich without informing
him of Münster's effort. Metternich, in fact, agreed to Münster's request
on Dec. 22, before Canning's overture reached him. This seems to have
been a last flicker of the King's duplicity.

[3] *V.S.A.,* Weisungen nach England, Bd. 227. Metternich's secret
instructions to Apponyi, Dec. 1825. Apponyi was intended as Esterházy's successor, but finally went to France.

' his personal nomination.' " It was quite impossible for me to acquiesce in the notion," wrote Canning to Granville (7th April), though he was prepared to consult the royal wishes " both in appearance and in reality." He also insisted on being present when the King interviewed foreign diplomats. Further, he controlled the Hanoverian correspondence, and finally, in November 1826, got Münster to write a despatch to Metternich explaining (much on the lines of his circular to Hanoverian Ministers of 8th November 1825) the limitations imposed on the King by the constitution, and once more praising Canning. Metternich returned an angry reply which betrayed his consciousness that the ' plot ' had failed.[1]

3. THE KING AND HIS MINISTER (1826–7)

George IV., though inclined to deprecate Canning's action in October 1826 in recalling the British Minister from Madrid on his own authority, supported him at the Portuguese crisis in December. On the 18th he told Esterházy that he advised Metternich not to make a personal enemy of Canning. He (the King) himself had had Canning, in some sort, forced on him. " But he has shown great talents, much cleverness, and is one of the most active and vigorous members of my govern-ment." Esterházy gravely suggested that it was due to Canning that Russia and England were good friends and left Austria out in the cold. The King (with heat), " No, that is not so. Appearances deceive you. I attest it on my honour. I will speak of it to Canning . . . I am not a [pro-]Greek—God knows ! I send the whole nation to the Devil ! But I share the opinion of my Cabinet that the Ottoman Empire is tum-bling into ruin," and Russia cannot be left to herself ! The King told him to tell Metternich of his good wishes. " Sire," said Esterházy, " I do not doubt your power." " Ah well, I answer for the good-will," said George.

Then he spoke of the Portugal question, justified the action of his Ministry, spoke of its pacific intentions, and their excellent relations with France.[2] A little later George got

---

[1] *Vide* Appendix V.
[2] *V.S.A.*, Berichte aus England, Bd. 229. Esterházy to Metternich, No. 23, Litt. B., Dec. 18/26.

Count Münster to write a strong letter to Metternich defending
the Portugal policy, and stating that, although not necessarily
prepared to defend Canning's speech, any criticism of the
action would be regarded as criticism of the King.   Thus
George still refused whole-heartedly to support his minister, or
to avow that he had separated from his old Legitimist friends.
But Metternich, at last, came to see that the King had, in
reality, deserted them, though too timid or too double-faced
to admit the fact.   At any rate, he suspended all further
private relations with Münster.

The King's personal relations with Canning improved as their
ideas on diplomacy began to harmonise.   There is a pleasant
tale of how the King conspired with him in 1826 to surprise
Canning's old friend Charles Ellis with a peerage (under the
title of Lord Seaford).   " Never," wrote Canning to Granville,
" was a secret so well kept.   For six weeks or nearer two
months—it has been settled between the K[ing], Liverpool,
and me.   Three other persons only [one of them Mrs Canning]
were in the confidence—and not a human being without that
circle had a suspicion of it—and less if possible than any other
human being Charles himself, till he learnt it through a letter
delivered to him by Mrs C. on Saturday last.

" It is impossible to describe the kindness of the K[ing] on
this occasion.   If H.M. had been at C[hrist] C[hurch] with us,
and full of the recollections of those times, he could not have
entered more cordially into all my feelings.   Everything since
C[hrist] C[hurch] H.M. seemed to know as well as myself." [1]

The fact is that George could be very good-natured and
fascinating when he wished, and even Canning occasionally
submitted to his charm.   But he had to pay for such favours
by granting others of a less innocent kind.   For instance, Sir
William Knighton went over to Paris in June 1826 with a
letter from the King on business of a personal and secret
nature, and Canning recommended Granville to assist him in a
transaction which is unlikely to have been of a creditable kind.
He lent his aid in another matter.   Lord Ponsonby, who had a
small post in the Ionian Isles and was returning to England,
was a very handsome man, with whom the King's mistress,
Lady Conyngham, had once been in love.   Canning apparently

---

[1] *Gr. MSS.*   Canning to Granville, May 30/26.

visited the King in November 1825, found him in low spirits, rather in the style Keats has described :—

> " He (the Emperor) shrunk back in his chair,
> Grew pale as death and fainted—very nigh !
> ' Pho ! nonsense ! ' exclaimed Hum, ' now don't despair,
> She does not mean it really.' "

Canning, at any rate, effectually revived the King's spirits by suggesting the appointment of Lord Ponsonby to Buenos Aires, a post remote enough to separate him from Lady Conyngham. The appointment was made late in 1825,[1] but, as it involved Ponsonby's return to England, precautions were necessary. Canning arranged that Bagot should stop him in Holland, and there sent him his instructions " which I could not give. Among other things it is very difficult for me to say, ' Be as little in England as possible before your departure.' But I wish it said—or at least I wish the thing so to be. There are *pourquois* first *qui ne s'expliquent pas*—I wish him only to come here to kiss the King's hand, and to embark with as little delay as possible." [2] ' Poodle' Byng moralised thus to Granville : [3] " Does Ponsonby's appointment surprise you ? What eternal recollections women carry, and, in spite of any ill-usage, how kind they are to those they have loved." Ponsonby and his wife arrived in England " highly delighted at the thoughts of going to B[uenos] A[ires]," and were promptly hurried off there. Their misfortunes at once began. Ponsonby complained that his wife had ' lost all her fine gowns ' on the way, " and what is much worse, . . . I have lost in the said damned case all my black neckcloths." He implored Bagot to buy him some more. On arrival things went no better. " Let nothing induce you to visit this *bepraised* country. It is the vilest place I ever saw, and I should certainly hang myself if I could find a tree tall enough to swing on. It is a beastly place ! " [4] In fact, Ponsonby was much attached to

---

[1] Lord Dalling, *Historical Characters* (1900), pp. 452–3, quotes the story as an anecdote. It was more than that. Canning saw the King on Nov. 11–12. From *Bag. MSS.*, Planta to Bagot, Dec. 23/25, I find Ponsonby's appointment ' had only been settled six weeks before.'
[2] *Bag. MSS.* Canning to Bagot, Dec. 2/25; *G.C. & F.*, ii. 305.
[3] *Gr. MSS.*, Jan. 1826. ' Poodle' Byng was a clerk at the Foreign Office.
[4] *F.O. Argentine*, 6/13. Ponsonby to Lord Howard de Walden, Dec. 4/26. In 1791 he had been caught in Paris and had been swung *à la lanterne*. The French women promptly cut him down, as being *un trop joli garçon pour être pendu*.

his wife, and the danger, on his side at least, seems to have been imaginary. But Canning had rendered a service in the value of which the King at least believed.

It is perhaps unfair to George the Fourth to suggest that these personal services counted as much with him as the great strokes of policy his minister achieved. In spite of his selfishness and pettiness he was too astute a man not to see further than that. His dread of losing his throne had led him to side with the Neo-Holy Alliance, in the belief that a trades union of kings might intimidate the "Jacobins of the World (now calling themselves the Liberals)." He evidently feared that a separation from his brother monarchs, as evidenced over the recognition of the Spanish Colonies, might endanger his throne. When he found that it was welcomed with enthusiasm by the solid merchants of the Kingdom, he realised the advantage of his Canning's popularity. If you had a lion it was better to ' have him under the throne,' and it was easy to place him there. For the price of Canning's support was that the King should act in a constitutional way, and George was quite willing to surrender his independence in foreign policy so long as the minister never failed to give him the credit for any success that might be achieved. In a word, the ideal of Canning was realised. He became more monarchic in proportion as the King became more popular.

On one point there can be no doubt. George IV.'s secret intrigues with foreign Courts were a real danger. Canning was absolutely right in trying to put an end to the secret correspondence and secret negotiations of the King with foreign sovereigns and diplomats. And, by whatever means he achieved it, he rendered a notable service in forcing him to act like a constitutional monarch.[1] The service did not go unrewarded, for in the great crisis at the beginning of 1827 the King did, in fact, support his Foreign Minister against all opponents, and most notably of all against the Duke of Wellington.[2]

---

[1] The struggles between Queen Victoria and Palmerston, though important, were by no means of so serious a character as this. For George IV. had, through Hanover, an authorised diplomatic channel by which he could circulate his personal opinions throughout Europe; Victoria had not, and could only do so at her peril. Canning's achievement was to use that channel for the promotion of British views and interests.

[2] It was not, of course, possible for the King to refrain from complaints about Canning in private in 1827, but he gave Canning the reality of support.

CHAPTER XII

THE DAY'S WORK AT THE FOREIGN OFFICE

I. GENERAL

" Within whose hot brain's hammering purpose whirled
A thousand busy wheels untired."

MEREDITH.

CANNING brought to the Foreign Office the impulse at once of
a fresh mind and of a giant energy. " What you have heard
of Mr Canning's intense application is true. It was such as
to surprise the clerks at the F.O." [1] And it was an energy
which was sustained as well as enormous. On his visit to
Paris in 1826 he kept the clerks there writing twelve hours a
day, and, when he lived at the Foreign Office in his last two
years, the work of his subordinates was as unending as his
own. " His habits of industry," wrote Lord Dudley, " must
appear quite incredible to those that did not know him. I
met him once at a country house where he went *for what he
was pleased to call his holidays*. He had his secretaries about
him soon after eight (a.m.), had despatches ready before
breakfast, then wrote all day till six (p.m.). At tea-time he
established himself in a corner of the drawing-room to write
his private letters—and this every day—only now and then
with the exception of a ride, and even during that he talked
eagerly and fully upon public affairs or any other subject that
happened to present itself." [2] He noted, too, that while
Wellington was ' as quick as,' Canning was ' quicker than,'
lightning. Though severe, in some sense, to subordinates,
because exacting and at times irritable, Dudley ' never knew
a more kind-hearted and affectionate man.'

[1] Sir G. H. Rose to Bagot (Oct. 1822). Bagot, *G.C. & F.*, ii. 149.
[2] *Letters to Ivy*, [1905], pp. 326-7. Italics my own.

2. THE ESTABLISHMENT AND PERSONNEL AT THE FOREIGN OFFICE

The Foreign Office establishment consisted, in 1822, of a parliamentary under-secretary, a permanent under-secretary, a private secretary to the minister, a chief clerk (responsible for internal economy), a librarian and sub-librarian, and a staff of some seventeen clerks, together with a précis writer, translator, collector, and two office-keepers—twenty-eight in all. To these Canning had added, by 1827, five clerks, one library clerk, one assistant translator, and assistant office-keeper, making thirty-six in all.[1] There was no legal adviser. Many legal questions were settled in the Office ; others, and these only the most important, were referred to the King's Advocate or the Law-Officers of the Crown. Lord John Russell said that, under Canning, not only was all important business transacted by him at the Foreign Office, but that diplomats abroad did not dare to act except upon instructions sent by Canning himself, who " considered all the contingencies of a case and all the arguments that might be used." [2] Such a concentration of power was only possible in the hands of a man of great ability and industry, like Castlereagh or Canning, and the immensity of their labours certainly shortened both their lives. The mass of business, which began with the telegraph, has indeed of later years forced even the most energetic of foreign secretaries to devolve much business upon other shoulders. But Canning bore the whole burden till the end. Even when Prime Minister, and when overwhelmed with other business, his last strength was exhausted by composing ' a very long and very able state paper ' on Portugal. " Then he had Herries with him for three hours ; then at five o'clock he called for Stapleton and desired to see his state paper again to revise it." This was his last effort, and he died shortly afterwards.

[1] *Parliamentary Returns*, Jan. 5/22, and Jan. 5/27.
[2] *Report of Select Committee on Diplomatic Service*, 1861, sec. 3501, p. 308. A return in 1859 of despatches shows that in 1821, 1659 ; in 1822, 1506 issued from the Office ; in 1823, 1989, and from that time onwards they never fell below 3000, reaching 3846 in 1826, or over 10 a day ; the despatches coming into the Office were about double the number, or over 20 a day in 1826. Of these in each case about one-quarter were consular. It will be apparent why Canning had to obtain more clerks and an additional translator.

The organisation of the interior of the Office and the laying down or enforcement of rules and regulations, was the first, though not the most important, task of Canning. Planta, as permanent under-secretary, was really the head under Canning; the parliamentary under-secretary, Lord Francis Conyngham, holding a position inferior to him, just as is the case to-day. But some of the business arrangements with foreign Legations (accounts, ciphers, etc.) were shared between Planta and Lord Francis. Planta interviewed foreign diplomats in the absence of Canning, and dealt with most of the consular business. He was an excellent permanent official, a prudent diplomat, a kindly and humorous man, and an old and devoted friend of his master.[1] Lord Francis Conyngham was amiable, and of service to Canning in his relations with the King. Subsequently Lord Howard de Walden and the Marquis of Clanricarde (Canning's son-in-law) were also parliamentary under-secretaries. Canning had been a parliamentary under-secretary himself in the nineties, under the cold and haughty Grenville, when the pompous Hammond was permanent under-secretary. The Foreign Secretary then sat in his room alone in almost Oriental state. He summoned the parliamentary under-secretary and the permanent under-secretary from their rooms by a bell, the latter often having to break off an interview with a diplomat to answer it. Castlereagh had maintained this state even with his friend Clanwilliam and with Planta. Canning, with his usual humour, determined to abolish one of these ' acts of subordination.' He told Granville that he would retain for his parliamentary under-secretary " the coming at verbal calls (as he must do) [made] through office-keepers and messengers, and the bringing papers into the Cabinet room—and *standing* while Wynn and Lord Bathurst [*i.e.* Cabinet Ministers] perhaps are reading them.

" The *Bell*, into *his* room (with which you may remember Frere and I used to ring such peals in old Hammond's ears,

---

[1] *Vide* C. N. Crawley, *Cambridge Historical Journal*, No. 2 (1924), pp. 209-13, for an instance of his views on Greece. He had a kindly feeling for the clerks, whom he called my ' owliculi' or little owls, and wrote of himself with " the cloven foot of Diplomacy more than ever placed on my broad and ingenuous Heart." To Stratford Canning, May 12/21 ; Jan. 14/22. *Strat. MSS. F.O.*, 352/8.

whenever we learnt that he was engaged with someone before whom he wished to appear particularly grand), I will abolish." [1] It is more dignified to answer a call than a bell, and affords some consolation for being obliged to stand in the presence of a Cabinet Minister. Etiquette had become less rigid. The great Lord Chatham allowed no secretary to sit in his presence, Canning only made them stand when another Cabinet Minister was reading a despatch.

The office of ' Librarian and Keeper of the Papers ' was already of old standing in the Foreign Office, and its most famous occupant had already held the post since 1810, and added to it that of Superintendent of King's Messengers and Controller of the Accounts for the three Secretaries of State (Home, Foreign, and Colonial Offices). Hertslet originated and compiled the monumental series of *British and Foreign State Papers*, and also that of *Commercial Treaties*. These comprehensive and exhaustive works were the most exact and accurate accounts of diplomatic and commercial transactions then extant in the world. They were first printed privately for the use of the British Diplomatic and Consular Staff, and the first volume (1812–14) appeared in 1826 ; some years later (1839) they were issued for sale to the public. It does not appear how far they were a private venture and how far the expenses of printing were borne by the government, though Hertslet ultimately (and rightly) reaped a handsome reward by their sale to the public.[2] But it seems difficult to suppose that Canning, with his passion for accuracy and diffusion of knowledge of state papers, did not encourage the venture.[3] Ultimately, in view of his immense knowledge, Hertslet extended the activities of the librarian, and, not seldom, exercised a powerful influence on policy. But this develop‑ ment was not conspicuous in Canning's time.

In addition to the higher officials, Canning imported his own private secretaries and placed them in the Foreign Office. He also brought Backhouse from an office stool in Liverpool,

---

[1] *Gr. MSS.* Canning to Granville, Sept. 26/22.

[2] For a general account, see E. Hertslet, *Recollections of the Old Foreign Office*, 1901, pp. 144–8. It is unfortunate that his memories do not extend farther back than 1840.

[3] At any rate, he sanctioned the appointment of an assistant clerk to Hertslet at this time, who was employed on this task.

made him director of the Consular Department in 1825, and Permanent Under-Secretary in 1827, when Planta went to the Treasury. Of three or four others, the most important was Stapleton, his personal secretary and subsequent apologist. So far as the Office was concerned, private secretaries and clerks were merely registers of the will of the Foreign Minister. Their chief (almost their sole) function was to act as copyists and to practise ' a good round hand.' Some of them seemed to have been needy men of fashion or younger relatives who had been given posts by the influence of powerful patrons. They tended to be idle and troublesome.[1] Of these, the most conspicuous was a certain Mr S., who began by plaguing Castlereagh, and continued to plague his four successors, by various claims for money, particularly his expenses at Calais in 1818, and about an allowance for service in another depart-ment. Canning dismissed the latter claim on the ground that a rule refusing to allow it had been laid down by Order in Council in 1809, and ' as I am the author ' (he had been Foreign Secretary then) ' he ' (Mr S.) ' cannot expect to *persuade* me.' Accordingly, Mr S. was refused an interview. When he complained that Castlereagh had given him one, Canning wrote : " That could not but operate against an interview, when I found a conversation with His Lordship (at which there were no witnesses) referred to by Mr S. to invalidate a receipt in writing " (9th November 1822). Mr S. next threatened Planta with legal proceedings, and Canning thereupon " dispensed with your attendance at office pending proceedings " (8th February 1823). Mr S. remained a supernumerary clerk, and continued to persecute Canning with his letters.[2] Finally, he had an altercation with another Foreign Office clerk in public, and appears to have refused ' an affair of honour.' For the other clerk wrote to him (25th February 1826) : " I have already stated to you personally that I considered you a scoundrel and a disgrace to the character of a gentleman. . . . I am now compelled in addition to denounce you as a *coward*." Mr S. applied to

---

[1] *E.g.* on Mar. 22/25 Canning had to warn Granville about a certain man in Paris who had ' formerly been in the Office,' but had found it convenient to leave England.

[2] The S. case is in *F.O.*, 95/591. I am indebted to Mr Gaselee, librarian of the Foreign Office, for information as to when his pension ceased.

the Court of King's Bench for protection and sent all the papers to Canning, who commented drily : " It does not appear to me that I have anything to say—It is sufficiently manifest that there is no danger of that sort of issue to this contest, against which it would be incumbent on the friends of the parties to interfere.—G. C." Shortly after this Mr S. was again dispensed from attendance at the Office. He continued to protest against this and other arrangements, and was finally placed on the retired list, with a pension of £272, 10s., in 1830. This action gave him an opportunity of calling for a review of his whole case, and Palmerston had to read all the records, which mighty task occupied him apparently till June 1831. ' Pam ' allowed the pension, but closed the discussion and Mr S.'s official career. His pension and life ended on the 31st January 1853, at the age of sixty-four.[1]

While we cannot judge all clerks by Mr S., the system was radically bad, and the practice of supernumerary clerks was open to abuse. For that reason Canning was " most adverse to the arrangement, criticised it very severely," and ultimately abolished it.[2] There does not seem to be much to be said for the system, but some were good like Lenox Conyngham and ' Poodle ' Byng, the latter celebrated for attending the King of the Sandwich Isles on his visit to England. Both owed their appointments to influence, but justified them by merit and hard work.[3]

3. DIPLOMATIC METHODS AND RULES

(a) *The Regulations for Correspondence*

No special reforms were required in the Foreign Office itself, except the stopping of the leakage of diplomatic secrets. This was a most serious matter, and it cannot be said that

---

[1] Mr S. revealed his case and identity to the public in two pamphlets in 1830—*Memoirs of an Employé*, and *Statement of Facts to His Majesty's Ministers*, by E. Scheener.

[2] *F.O.*, 95/591. Planta, to a correspondent, ' confidential,' undated, in answer to a letter of Jan. 6/24. The correspondent had applied for a supernumerary post. The *Return* of Jan. 5/27 shows no supernumerary clerks; there are three on that of Jan. 5/22.

[3] Between 1822 and 1826 the number of despatches written was doubled. To provide for this, Canning increased the clerks by five and the total establishment by eight, but the salaries at the Foreign Office were only increased by £2000 a year.

Canning attained complete success, though he let it be known in 1824 that he would dismiss any clerk found guilty of disclosing office secrets to the Press. The Russian circular of January 1824 got into the Press but probably from a French source, and there were two leakages in 1826, one from the Paris Embassy in that year and a disclosure of Wellington's protocol of the 4th April in 1826. The last seems to have been due to Russia. In each case Canning complained bitterly, as this might cause unjustifiable suspicion to be thrown on his own clerks at home. In the case of the treaty of the 6th July 1827, which was revealed in the *Times*, there was more ground for suspicion that the leakage had been in the Foreign Office, but Canning appears to have thought that France was the culprit.

The regulations for out- and in-correspondence were of importance and were systematically laid down in a circular of Planta's on the 23rd November 1824. Despatches were to be numbered, and on the 1st January a return was to be made from each diplomatic centre of the number of despatches in the preceding year, together with a list of diplomatic representatives, and a collection of all the state papers published by the foreign government. Each diplomat was to write on folio paper, in " a large legible hand, . . . docketting all your letters on the back thereof," with minute directions as to what the docket should contain. " You will be punctual in confining each despatch to one subject." " You will be careful that there shall be no blots or erasures in your correspondence." No instructions were to be shown to foreign Courts except on order from the Secretary of State. Diplomats were kept strictly to this circular. For instance, Sir Edward Thornton was reproved for ' the slovenly penmanship ' of his despatches, and informed that he must not pack up tea in his despatches, as one packet had burst and defiled an autograph letter from ' His most Faithful Majesty of Portugal.' Granville was told to write " a little more legibly and carefully in your private letters " as Canning wanted to show them to George IV.

Canning was exceptionally careful that private letters from diplomats should not be included in their official correspondence, and that undesirable details should not appear in despatches.   Castlereagh had been much less strict, and the historian must deplore the prudence of his successor.   Canning apparently destroyed the record of a private conversation he had with Hurtado, in which he is thought to have warned Mexico not to attack Cuba, and thus left a baffling problem to posterity.   Similarly there is a private interview with Gallatin in 1826, of which the American has preserved a record. But Canning's version does not exist, and the two together would have given a priceless comment on his American policy.[1]

(b) *The Attachés*

The regulations as to in- and out-letters, dear to the devotees of red-tape, were rendered necessary by the lack of system which prevailed in the British Diplomatic Chanceries abroad. Each diplomat took out his staff of young men, personal friends whom he treated as his family, who were frequently unpaid, who often remained a short time and showed little interest in their official duties.   " A couple of dozen of young men," wrote Canning, " scattered over Europe ; owing no allegiance and taking diplomacy only as subsidiary to amusement."   He reproved Granville on account of the inefficiency of his Chancery.   " Remember it is not my fault, for I am always ready to make a change at your smallest suggestion," wrote Canning ; " but do not be induced, if ever you do make such a suggestion, to accompany it with a recommendation for promotion ; for such recommendations I make a point of disregarding.   It was hard enough to find thirty younkers already chosen for me, but I will not further be hampered in *my* choice *among them*.   It is a bad system, but there is no getting rid of it in my time." [2]   Almost the only

[1] Even his conversations with Rush were destroyed as being private, but were fortunately preserved by Rush in his Diary.   We owe to Rufus King, his successor, the fact that two valuable private letters from Canning to him, of Aug. 7 and Sept. 15/25, are preserved.   King sent them to his government, much to Canning's annoyance, and the latter, therefore, preserved them in the official records.   Vide *F.O. America*, 115/45.   Canning to Vaughan, Oct. 8/25.

[2] *Gr. MSS.*   Canning to Granville, May 9/26.   It was even the custom for young men to be attached during their summer vacations to Embassies, *e.g.* on May 31/25 Canning recommended the son of Sir John Gladstone to be attached for the vacation to the Paris Embassy, " a youth of good parts and blameless character," apparently not W. E. Gladstone, but his brother.

able member of Granville's Chancery was Henry Fox, the efficient man, who " never alters a despatch without improving it," but " he seldom goes to bed before daylight and lies in bed always till an advanced hour of the day." [1] He was called ' Black Fox,' inheriting the hair of Charles Fox, who was called ' Niger ' in his youth. The sharp eye of Canning noticed his ability and he became Secretary of Legation at Naples, where his cousin inherited, and heartily despised, the mistress of Byron, ' La Guiccioli.' [2] Lady Holland, thinking doubtless that Henry's promotion was done out of friendship, wrote in gratitude to Canning. The Foreign Secretary austerely replied : " I promoted Henry Fox because he had been doing very well " (1st September 1826). He justified his promotion, and in 1836 became the British Minister at Washington. Much of this work was done in the twilight, but, on one occasion, in 1823, it attracted public notice. On the 4th and 7th October 1823 the *Star* pointed out that a city merchant, Alderman Fox, had been appointed by Canning to be a British Commissioner for the claims of British subjects on Spain. It said that this was unusual ; it " might have been a provision and reward for an immediate personal friend." Efficiency was thus the reason for promotion. There was, indeed, no other road to it in Canning's eyes.

(c) *The Reform of the Messengers*

One source of great evil lay in the service of messengers. These persons were " indiscriminately taken from the class of gentlemen's servants," and in carrying despatches from abroad were open to all sorts of undue influence. Sir Charles Stuart was promptly instructed by Canning, in 1822, to see that no private letters of non-official persons should be sent through his diplomatic bag, as the practice had been abused by suspected characters. It was well that he took this step, for a question came on in Parliament in 1823 which showed that an enterprising tailor had sent Canning's Court-dress,

---

[1] *Gr. MSS.* Granville to Canning, Oct. 14/24. Planta thought it worth while to assure Lord Strangford in 1825 that he was sending out to him at St Petersburg "a real hard-working paid attaché, not a Dandy." *F.O. Russia*, 181/65, Dec. 19/25.

[2] *Journal of Henry Edward Fox*, [1923], pp. 338, 377. Henry Edward was cousin of Henry, Fox.

together with those of two other diplomats, to Paris to get French embroidery, and then evaded the British duty, getting them smuggled back in a diplomatic bag.[1] Canning was furious, and repeated his orders. He kept a sharp eye in the future, and on the 21st March 1826 Lord Granville was informed that " Mr Canning has intimated that, if messengers again carry private letters, they will be dismissed."   By this time he had reformed the system.   For on the 5th July 1824 his circular gave Hertslet, the librarian, complete control over the messenger service.   The reform struck at the root of the evil, and altered the character of the messengers.   Military and naval officers were, in future, selected, and this measure, as Mr Hammond said (7th April 1870), " was certainly a great improvement," not only in efficiency but also in economy. The actual methods of carrying despatches was also altered. In previous times messengers carried despatches from and to all the Courts of Europe.   But at the end of 1823, ' in view of the great expense,' diplomats at the nine minor Courts were instructed to use the ordinary post in general, and cipher when necessary.   It is certain that Canning knew the ordinary post was tampered with in most countries, for Mr Watts reported on ' the perfidy of the post ' in France in 1823, and Disbrowe from St Petersburg in 1825, where a conference was sitting, related that in order to find out their views, " the [Russian] Emperor directed that, until further orders, the Post Office should read every letter directed to the *corps diplomatique*, not omitting even their family letters, which used to be respected, also to read one letter in 6 instead of one in 20, which previously was the rule observed." [2] Special British messengers still went to Paris and St Petersburg.   But despatches were sometimes carried from Constantinople to Vienna and thence to London by the carriers either

---

[1] *Vide* the *Times* of Apr. 22/23, which remarked that this event will " go far to ' eclipse the gaiety of countries.' "

[2] *F.O. France*, 146/62. Barnes to Planta, Feb. 21/24. *Vide* also *H. de W. MSS., F.O.,* 360/2. Lord Charles Stewart to Planta, Mar. 9/21, complained that his despatches going *via* Paris had been opened ' not the first time.' *F.O. Russia*, 181/66. Disbrowe to Canning, Apr. 20/25, says he was ' credibly informed ' that despatches had been opened. No one who knew Vienna's police methods could doubt that letters there would be read. This proves, therefore, that French, Russian, and Austrian Governments all endeavoured, and sometimes with success, to read British despatches.

of Austria or of the great financier Rothschild.[1] In the
former case, at any rate, they were usually read. Wellesley
from Vienna warned Strangford at Constantinople. " You
must be aware that all your despatches are read, if not copied,
before they come into my hand." He relates amusingly how
Metternich, for once, had betrayed himself by declaiming
against the prolixity of the Austrian Internuncio (representative) at Constantinople ' long before I even read your
enclosure.'[2] Canning knew this well enough, and at the
autumn of 1825, when it became important to preserve
secrets from Austria, he instituted a special service of
messengers from Constantinople to London *via* Vienna,
insisting that they should not stop on the way. Metternich,
thus deprived of a source of information, at once vented his
annoyance. Austrian customs officials, doubtless under
instructions, stopped the despatches on the Turkish frontier
and endeavoured to obstruct their passage, or even to open
them, under the specious pretext of ' fumigating them.'
Wellesley had to make more than one sharp remonstrance
before Metternich accepted his defeat. Even the cipher was
not necessarily a protection if the despatch was liable to be
opened, and one of Canning's last acts as Foreign Secretary
was to direct the destruction of cipher U which he thought
had been discovered.[3]

(d) *The Secret Service*

In one department, that of the Secret Service, there was a
financial increase, because a new continent was open to
diplomacy. In 1820 Mr Hume, that inveterate pruner of
extravagancies, called attention to the fact that £80,000 had
been spent in two years.[4] It was pointed out that it " was
applied for, not merely for the foreign, but for the home
department also," as also for the Department for War and

[1] Canning had his suspicions of Rothschild. " I hope you will contrive
to establish some communication with the F.O. at Paris that shall prevent
Rothschild from getting official *papers* (*news* you cannot help) before
you," Dec. 20/26, to Granville. Stap., *Corr.*, ii. 173.
[2] From an undated and mutilated private letter of Wellesley to Strangford in cipher of 1823 or 1824 in *F.O. Austria*, 120/61.
[3] *F.O. Russia*, 182/2. Canning to Disbrowe, Mar. 6/27.
[4] Some of this was exceptional, and due to the Milan Commission to
investigate the conduct of the Queen.

the Colonies. In 1822 Castlereagh, with unwonted but appropriate humour (the date being April the first), declined to give details. " It was rather an Irish proposition, for it would then be secret service money no longer." For the historian the fact is unfortunate. It was suggested in Parliament at this time that the expenses were always largest during the years of general elections. In such case the Home Secretary could not be responsible, for the total amounts, expended by Peel, in the Canning period were under £4000. In the year 1826, when there was a general election, the total amount expended by the Foreign Secretary at home was £35,000, which was less by £4000 than his normal expenditure. Probably, therefore, the money was used either for domestic espionage or really for diplomatic purposes. We happen to know something of the care with which Canning watched over its administration. He laid down the rule that he alone was responsible for it, but that the Permanent Under-Secretary should keep the account, no other person, not even the Parliamentary Under-Secretary, having access to the books.[1] He insisted strictly on the rule of payment by results and was prompt to disallow any latitude in its use. Thus Mr Ward—acting Minister in Mexico—proposed to charge £400 to this account, partly for a book and a map he had had printed on ' United States designs on Texas,' and partly ' for dinners and parties.' He was informed that the merits of the book and the map would be considered, but that no part of " Secret Service can be appropriated to the expenses of Balls or Fêtes ; the oath which you will be required to take respecting money disbursed for Secret Service would of itself have averted the erroneous notion . . . respecting the application of the Fund." And, as a useful reminder, the money for dinners and parties was charged to his private account.[2]

With a view to attacking Canning, the embittered Lord Londonderry called for a return of Secret Service Money for

[1] E. Hammond, Mar. 21/70. *Select Committee on Consular and Diplomatic Services*, July 25/70, pp. 58–9.

[2] *F.O. Mexico*, 50/19. Planta to Ward, June 20/26. The oath is in 22 Geo. III.: Act for regulating Payments of Civil List:

" I, A.B., do swear, that I have disbursed the money, intrusted to me for Foreign Secret Service, faithfully, accordingly to the Intent and Purpose for which it was given, according to my best Judgment for His Majesty's Service."

1819–22 and 1823–26. This disclosed the fact that the total sum in the latter four years was £203,000, an increase of £58,000 over the first period.[1] The Marquis promptly suggested that this increase was due to payments for influencing the Press. Lord Dudley, who had investigated the documents personally, expressed " the strongest conviction that not one shilling had been applied (from the Secret Service) for the purpose of influencing any portion of the Press of this country." He declined, however, and significantly, to give the amounts expended respectively abroad and at home. Lord Strangford gave evidence as to its administration abroad—" He had served His Majesty under nine different Secretaries of State," and Canning in five different diplomatic posts ; " he felt himself bound to aver, that he had never known any Minister exercise over the particular branch in question, a more scrupulous and vigilant control, or surround it with more efficient safeguards than the right hon. person who lately presided over the Foreign Department [Canning] . . . no administrator of the fund could be more cautious in its employment . . . or more alive to the principle that the public money ought never to be expended on such occasions without a *quid pro quo*." [2] The testimony of Strangford to the merits of Canning in this or any other particular may be accepted as decisive.

We know the allocations of Secret Service money in the countries of Europe, but the total amount spent on them was small. Castlereagh spent £8399 as against Canning's £3770 in France ; £5348 as against £1823 in Spain ; £1178 as against £4398 in Constantinople ; £687 as against £1589 in Russia. But the largest increase was in Naples, where Canning spent £3856.[3] The Secret Service in America was paid for

---

[1] There seems to be some serious error here in the figures which is due, I suppose, to the fact that the return was provisional in character, Secret Service accounts never being balanced annually to date. The accounts given in *A.O.* 1/2129–30 do not permit me to distinguish between the years, but only between the total periods, Jan. 1/16–Aug. 12/22, and Sept. 16/22–Apr. 30/27. The results are : Castlereagh *at home*, £252,214, 3s. 4d. ; Canning, £195,832, 17s. 2d. Castlereagh *abroad*, £25,483, 9s. 2d. ; Canning, £25,149, 19s. 4d. Taking an approximate yearly average, we get Castlereagh *at home*, £35,802 ; Canning, £39,166. Castlereagh *abroad*, £3902 ; Canning, £4229. In each case expenses went up yearly.

[2] June 7/27, *Hans. Deb.*, N.S., xvii. 1138–9.

[3] Vide *A.O.* 1/2129–30. The accounts given in Parliament are misleading. The money spent at home was roughly ten times that spent abroad. But, in point of fact, there is only one item, £255, for Secret

from the home account. The latter also bore the expense of intercepting despatches. The machinery of decipher has been preserved in the British Museum, and there is no con-cealment possible of the fact.   Castlereagh left a whole mass of ' intercepted letters from Foreign Courts ' behind him in the Embassy at Paris in 1818, where they were found sewn up in a sofa in 1824. Canning was certainly not behind him in this practice. He knew, for instance, that the King had sent a letter, personally attacking him, to Vienna ; he knew, he said, as much about the French agents in Latin America as Villèle ; he obtained copies of several secret conferences of the four other Great Powers at Paris in 1824 and in sub-sequent years. In the same year a correspondent wrote to Zea at Madrid : " To give you an idea of the preponderance of England I will just tell what the Ambassador À Court had the weakness to say to a member of the *corps diplomatique,* ' *we have got money and by means of that we know whatever passes in this country, and whatever is intended, and even what is said to the King : in this way I am not ignorant of what some of the foreign Ministers represented to His Most Faithful Majesty last night.*' " [1] For Canning the Secret Service was specially necessary, because he found, to his regret, that the despatches of Hanoverian diplomats frequently contained much more information than the British ones.[2]   So that the secret reports of informers were essential to amplify the information of his Ambassadors. This dark traffic, in what diplomats call ' *le cabinet noir,*' is not a pleasant subject on which to dwell.[3]   But

Service abroad, in America, and this is not in Canning's time. We know that Canning had secret agents in Latin America, and that he paid them money (*e.g.* in Mexico). These items (which may have been very large) can only have come out of the home account.

[1] Yet Canning spent only £502 in Portugal. Our paid informant was an Englishman in the service of the King.

[2] The following Secret Service money was spent in Germany, *v.* *A.O.* 1/2129–30, but, as indicated, the results were poor :—

	1816–22.	1822–7.
Frankfurt (out of Empire) .	£700	£1200
Dresden	25	200 Berlin.
Hamburg	100	
Vienna	1450	1785

[3] Professor Webster (*Leaflet* No. 56 of Hist. Assn.) (1923), p. 16, condemns the Allies at Paris, in 1919, for " spying on one another's confidential communications." Mr Lloyd George, *Daily Chronicle,* Sept. 4, 1924, tells how at Paris, in 1919, he directed his secretary to telephone in Welsh to London, and says " the others at the Conference were, of course, furious."

there can be no doubt that all diplomats dealt then in it, as they are likely to do until the end of time. There is equally little doubt that Canning used this means to exalt ' the preponderance of England.'

4. Canning's Diplomatic Innovations

(a) Copies and Lectures

Canning's own methods at the Foreign Office, as distinguished from those which he laid down for his clerks, were of great importance. Castlereagh had transacted much of his business by friendly, informal, and verbal conversations with foreign diplomats. As the separation with the Continent grew, this method became impossible for Canning. He distinguished between private conversations, of which he destroyed all record, and official ones, which he noted down. For his words were liable to be misrepresented or misunderstood, and the foreign diplomats were likely to give accounts different from his own. For instance, when representations were made to him by Esterházy and Lieven as to speeches in Parliament in July 1823, both men seemed to have represented their remonstrances to others as much more formidable than they really were. Canning, therefore, adopted other methods. Polignac was invited to hold conversation with him as to the intentions of France in America (October 1823), and was astonished to find that he sent him a memorandum of these talks which he was reluctantly compelled to authenticate. Henceforward all important interviews were treated thus, so that record of the original conversation could be produced if any doubt arose as to what had occurred. A similar method was adopted when the Neo-Holy Representatives called to remonstrate with him on his recognition of South America in March 1825. The three representatives had decided in each case to refuse a copy of their remonstrances. Lieven (the Russian) saw him first and proposed to read his despatch. Canning refused to hear it unless he received a copy. Lieven, according to Canning, was ' confounded '; according to himself, ' in no way disconcerted.' To Esterházy, who saw him next, Canning said he had heard that a state paper of Metternich's, denouncing England's conduct in strong terms, had been

circulated to foreign Courts, though not to England, and had
since been recalled.   If he once consented to *hear* a despatch
on the same subject, of which he received no copy, he could
not, six months hence, contradict it from his own recollection,
" whatever it might suit the policy of any foreign Power,
or Foreign Minister, to quote as the contents of that despatch."
Mrs Canning more freely explained this position in private.
Lieven's communication " being a sort of lecture made up
reasonings and objections.   To hear that without having the
means of answering it would be interpreted into acquiescence
in the truth of all the objections made, however absurd they
might have been.   He did not, however, refuse to listen to the
reading of the despatch until his demand of an assurance that
the written document would not be given to others was declined,
because, in fact, copies had been sent to every Minister (except
the British) at every other Court in Europe." [1]

With a view to getting over the difficulty Canning finally
said he would, in each case, receive a *verbal* communication,
and subsequently make a résumé which each diplomat would
authenticate.   The three Neo-Holies ultimately consented,
though with an ill grace, to do this.   " The result is that I
have a document in spite of all their contrivance."   Also he
could insert his part of the dialogue, which had advantages.
When ultimately corrected, the remonstrances did not appear
as severe as they might have been represented if no copy
had been obtained.   " I think," added Canning, " I shall teach
the Holy Alliance not to try the trick of these simultaneous
sermons again." [2]

This same method produced great effects with Esterházy
in July 1826.   For, by refusing to hear a despatch on Portugal
read without receiving a copy, Canning elicited a very important fact which Esterházy had intended to suppress.
Metternich perceived that he was dealing with a master in

---

[1] *Gr. MSS.* Mrs Canning to Lord Granville, Mar. 22/25.   There is
another graphic and unpublished account in *F.O.*, 352/10.   *Strat. MSS.*
George to Stratford Canning, private, Feb. 23/25.   " It would not be the
first time by many that, after having read me a long lecture, he [Lieven]
has put the textbook in his pocket ; while his Court was circulating its
contents through all the Govts of the Alliance, and calling upon them
to observe what home truths it had told, to which it had received no
answer."

[2] Stap., *G.C. & T.*, 428.   Canning to Granville, Mar. 4/25, private.
Sir E. Satow, *Diplomatic Practice*, i. 80–2.

the diplomatic art, who allowed no rash phrase or strong expression to pass without ' taking note.' The Neo-Holies were, therefore, reduced to making diplomatic remonstrances under conditions in which every word was weighed and measured. Under these circumstances they lost their value, and, after Canning's speech on Portugal of 12th December 1826, Metternich mournfully confessed that remonstrances were useless. For indignation can be expressed by word of mouth, and be conveniently forgotten afterwards, but it may create a serious diplomatic incident if it is recorded in a formal document.[1]

(b) *The Use of English in Diplomacy*

Another direction in which Canning was influential was in promoting the influence of English as a diplomatic language. As Under-Secretary with Granville as Foreign Minister he had a hand in enforcing the use of English, instead of French, in communications with foreign diplomats in England. In 1823 he instructed Thornton at Lisbon, and in 1824 À Court at Madrid, to communicate with their respective Courts, not in French but in English ; a practice already adopted since 1814 by Castlereagh at The Hague and Paris, though there was evidently a danger of its becoming disused.[2] In 1826 a serious controversy arose with the Court of Berlin, as Bernstorff refused to receive a despatch from the English *chargé d'affaires* because it was in English. Canning instructed him to tender his note again in English, because " the rules of Count Bernstorff's office govern the correspondence of Russia, but they have no authority over that of England." This time it was accepted. As a compromise, however, and in view of the difficulties at Berlin because the King could not read English, Canning eventually agreed to send notes in English with a certified translation in French. He threatened, if this was not accepted, to answer all notes at Berlin with notes addressed in English to the Prussian Minister in London. The controversy was prolonged after Canning's death.[3] It

---

[1] Satow, i. 83.

[2] Thornton in reply, while promising to obey the instruction, stated that he had used French at Hamburgh.

[3] *Cp.* Satow, i. 76–8.

may fairly be claimed that he was the stoutest champion of the use of English in diplomacy, and that it has never been displaced from the eminence in which he set it.[1]   The highest point it has reached is in the Treaty of Versailles (1919), in which the instrument is in both English and French, both versions having equal validity.   But the man who secured this triumph was an American, not an Englishman, and the policy has been since abandoned.

(c) *Interviews*

In dealing with other persons less distinguished than foreign diplomats Canning was equally strict.   The conversations of agents, such as those from South America before recognition, were strictly noted down, unless the interviews were purely informal.   In other cases, as in that of a dangerous firebrand like Iturbide, the pretender to Mexico, he refused to see the man at all.   He wrote to a friend of Iturbide's to explain the reason.   He would have been glad to see him " had it been possible for me to do so, as a private individual, or without leading to inferences, which it was my duty to avoid ; inferences not only relating to important publick questions, but likely to affect the pecuniary interests of large classes of British subjects.

" This latter consideration is one which I have felt myself bound to keep constantly in mind, having had occasion to know that interviews in the Office have been sometimes causes of sudden fluctuations in the price of foreign securities ; that they have been sometimes sought and sometimes (I am sorry to say) feigned with that view." [2]

With such persons Canning was willing to hold intercourse in writing, but, once that began, he refused to see them, " knowing by experience that nothing but confusion arises from the intermixture of personal conference with detailed written correspondence." [3]   The man to whom he wrote this was Sir Edward Codrington, destined to be his fellow-worker in the glorious task of freeing Greece from the Turk.   It appears that, in consequence, the two never met.   To the

---

[1] *Cp.* Satow, i. 83.
[2] *F.O. Mexico*, 50/8.   Canning to M. J. Quin, May 17/24.
[3] *F.O. France*, 146/62.   Canning to Sir E. Codrington, Sept. 6/24.

modern diplomat these precautions may appear elementary or excessive, according to taste ; in the amateurish world of that day they were essential.

(d) *General*

Canning was probably the most learned diplomat of his generation. He had studied Grotius, Vattel, and Bynkershoek, and knew the general principles of international law as well as any man, certainly much better than Castlereagh before, or Palmerston after, him. But he was not impeccable, and the study of international diplomacy becomes simpler when we recognise that statesmen are frequently ignorant of some of the subtler distinctions of international law. Canning himself sought to distinguish between ' congresses ' and ' conferences,' and though he could see the difference between ' good offices ' and ' mediation,' he sometimes loosely used the word ' intervention ' to imply the latter. Yet these small technical slips do not impair the value of his contributions to the science and art of English diplomacy. In certain respects his work remains unapproached and is unapproachable. No other English diplomatic despatches can bear comparison with his. They have the hardness, the clearness, and the brilliancy of a diamond, and illuminate every point which they touch. The despatches are equally striking, whether they lay down details of organisation, or grapple with technical problems, or state the broadest principles. As models of instructions we might cite those to Sir Charles Stuart of the 18th March 1826, or those to Wellington of the 10th February 1826.[1] But it was in definition of principle that he most excelled, and in that the ' Guarantee ' despatch to À Court has never been surpassed. Almost equally brilliant, though obscure and forgotten, is his lengthy study on the Oyster Fisheries, which illustrates most of the principles of maritime right, and the despatch to Metternich which lays down, in respect to Greece, the classic doctrine for recognition of belligerency. The marshalling of the arguments, the logic,

---

[1] For instructions to Sir C. Stuart, Mar. 14/26 (*v.* pp. 220–1) ; for those to Wellington, Feb. 10/26, *v. W.N.D.*, iii. 85–93. ; for the ' Guarantee ' despatch, *v.* App. II. (*a*) ; for the oysters, *v. F.O.*, 97/173 ; for the belligerents, *v.* pp. 326–7.

the illustrations, and the cumulative force of the conclusion, in each case, are truly astonishing. The faults, if there are any, in these noble state papers, are that their logic is too merciless to be diplomatic.[1] It is, however, on the South American question that his chief fame as an exponent of political principle must rest. The principle of recognition was then new, and it was applied by him in a peculiar manner. He does not seem to have seen that appointment of consuls with exequaturs might be held to imply ultimate recognition, and he had difficulties with Spain over her ' tacit agreement ' not to interfere with British trade with her Colonies, and with the distinction between *de facto* and *de jure* recognition. But his main thesis was triumphantly right. Recognition was not to be accorded partly for sentimental reasons as by the United States, or totally refused on that ground as by the Neo-Holy Alliance. It was " an assertion of a fact, or rather of an opinion of a fact." And the doctrine of the necessity of recognition in such cases has now been universally accepted. The Neo-Holy Alliance were wrong in asserting that the consent of the Mother Country or of a king must be obtained before a rebel province is independent, for in fact it often becomes independent before that consent is obtained. England preferred to obtain such consent, and did obtain it from Portugal in regard to Brazil. But she could not perpetually subordinate commercial and diplomatic interests to the caprice of a Spanish tyrant who refused to acknowledge facts. Anarchy cannot be eternal, and the recognition of achieved independence is the surest method of healing wounds and repairing disorders. In fact, Canning's action in Spanish America legalised something like a quarter of the habitable globe. The contention advanced by the Neo-Holy Alliance that it sanctioned ' revolution ' seems to us now merely a piece of delusive pedantry. The arguments Canning used to demolish it are as clear and as irresistible to-day as they proved in his own time. They are, in fact, universally accepted.

[1] This specially applies to two despatches to Gallatin on commercial questions in 1826. They have the air of special pleading ; *v. B.F.S.P.*, xiv. 462–86. For Spanish despatches *v. B.F.S.P.*, xi. 58–63 ; xii. 909–15.

5. The Organisation of the Consular Service

(a) *The Reform of the System*

The consuls were important in this period, for in many cases they had to assume diplomatic functions, and also because the service was in urgent need of reform. That reform had far-reaching financial effects, and resulted in a great improvement of efficiency in the procuring of accurate commercial information. Hence the reform of the Consular Service is the prelude to that of the Diplomatic Service.

The whole Consular System was in need of drastic revision and was systematically remodelled by Canning and Huskisson during the years 1823–6. The consuls themselves were a miscellaneous and often undesirable set, sometimes merchants pursuing their own objects, sometimes worn-out men of fashion, like poor Beau Brummel at Caen, escaping the debtors' prison by holding government offices abroad. The systems of appointment, as well as of payment, being the reverse of uniform, were open to all sorts of abuses. By a careful selection of new consuls, and by a rigid control over the old, many of the former abuses were removed. But the methods of payment were more difficult to regulate. There had been in fact complete chaos, which resulted in extravagance and perplexity. Sometimes a consul had no salary, sometimes he had only fees, sometimes he had both salary and fees. The scale of fees and the principle upon which they were levied were equally various. Sometimes the consuls got very little, sometimes enormously too much.[1] The Levant Company had the absurd anomaly of a private Consular Service of its own. In fact what happened was that the shipping and trade of the country was taxed with fees to the amount of at least £60,000 to £70,000 a year to pay indirectly the salaries of consuls, whom the government refused to pay. Canning seems to have believed that the fee-system could have been remodelled, and that it was quite right that the trade

---

[1] The *Times*, July 12/22, made some severe comments on the papers laid before the Commons in that year. It was disclosed that the Consul-General at Brazil had made £57,567 in six years, of which he admitted £43,000 to be clear profit ; the Consul at Bahia, in the same period, made £14,000 ; and the total receipts by our Consuls in Brazil (1815–20) were £90,274, 13s. 4d. Cp. *Hans. Deb.*, N.S., vii. 1658–60.

of the country should pay for the benefits they received. Huskisson held the opposite, and probably the sounder, view. The question had been raised in 1822 while Castlereagh was still minister, and Canning, admitting that the general sense of the House and of the business world was with Huskisson, carried out that decision, though he said it was ' no system of his.' He instituted the system in October 1823 when appointing new consuls to Latin America, and had applied it throughout the whole service by 1825. He claimed that his method of carrying out the measure resulted in a clear saving of £12,000, and even the ' penny-wise ' Mr Hume expressed ' high gratification ' at his efforts. The principle actually adopted was to give moderate and remunerative salaries to consuls, to confine their fees to purely notarial ones, and to prohibit them from engaging in trade. Various anomalies were got rid of. The private Consular Service of the Levant Company was now transferred to the government. In two cases only, one of which was at Rotterdam, the consuls, because they were ' eminent merchants,' were not displaced. But the general principle, despite these exceptions, of making the office of consul a professional and official post was strictly carried out.[1]

(b) *The Carrying out of the New System ; Mr Mackenzie*

Consuls, though more amenable to discipline than ministers, were also, from the circumstances of the case, more likely to overstep official etiquette. In 1825 Backhouse was made Director of the Consuls, though the rod had already been used without mercy. Barnes, the Consul at Nantes, wanted to come to London and give Canning verbal information about the Slave Trade. He was told curtly to confine himself to his regular duties, and to remain in his post, with an intimation that he would not remain there very long if he did not amend his ways. The Vice-Consul at Boulogne was removed on

---

[1] Vide *F.O.*, 95/591-2, *passim*. More brief outlines of the views of Huskisson are given in the speech of Mar. 25/25, *Hans. Deb.*, N.S., xii. 1218-20. Those of Canning and Hume may be found in the debate of Mar. 17/26, *Hans. Deb.*, N.S., xiv. 1400-1410. Canning's are given at length to Huskisson in *F.O.*, 95/592. Memo., Jan. 1824. Canning's economy appears to have been that £30,000 had previously been appropriated for consuls from the Civil List, and this amount was, in future, reduced.

account of 'frequent inebriety.' The Consul at Oporto was suspended for refusing to answer letters with promptitude. In Latin America it was easy to find applicants for consulates, but the successful candidates were not always suited to their posts or reconciled to their exile. Mr Charles Mackenzie, Consul at Vera Cruz, no sooner arrived there than he complained first of not being allowed to supplement his official income from anything but notarial fees, and then of everything else. The reply was direct.[1] " As to all other inconveniences which you mention—the climate—the unhealthiness of the place—the distance from Home and imperfect civilisation, Mr Canning presumes that you were apprised of all these circumstances [as all the world was] . . . and Mr Canning cannot listen now to any representations founded upon circumstances, essential to the destination which you have sought and inseparable from it. Should they prove more inconvenient in effect than they appeared in contemplation, you can resign. Let me know your reply without delay as Mr Canning is beset with applications for consular appointments." Mr Mackenzie hastily replied, by a separate note to Planta : " The resignation of my office, before I know whether or not it will afford me the means of living with decency and respectability, would be an act of insanity."

Mr Mackenzie was not happy in other respects. He reported that he had presented his credentials and was informed that ' a consul has no credentials.' He retired himself to the health resort of Xalapa, and proposed that a vice-consul should be appointed to the fever-haunted Vera Cruz. As, however, he unfortunately added there was " absolutely nothing for a consul to perform at Vera Cruz, except to maintain the communication between H.M.'s Commission and Government," these ' grounds ' appeared ' insufficient for Mr Canning to consent.' So Mr Mackenzie had to come to do official business to Vera Cruz, and, as he complained, risk catching yellow fever, because there was no vice-consul to catch it for him. But Canning was not without heart, for he granted him leave home to consult a

[1] F.O. Mexico, 50/2. Planta to Mackenzie, Apr. 8, July 23. Mackenzie to Planta, Aug. 30/24.

surgeon, though it must have seemed to him doubtful whether this was not a mere excuse for absence.

(c) *The Dismissal of Mr Staples* (1825)

Apart from the salaries, notarial fees brought in little. Mr Mackenzie earned only £9, 16s. in notarial fees in a year, and it was doubtless for a similar reason that Mr Staples, the Consul for Acapulco, tried to supplement his regular income from other sources. But one condition of his acceptance was that he should ' absolutely renounce all trade.' On the 18th January 1824 he accepted this condition in a letter and took up his appointment. On the 22nd July a thunderbolt was launched. " It has been communicated to H.M. Government that, subsequent to that letter, you have *entered* into a contract for a loan to the Mexican Government. . . . It is not to be supposed that you embarked on this transaction without some view to benefits, justly the objects of a commercial man, but entirely unbecoming of H.M.'s Consul." So " there was no further occasion for his services." [1] The sequel throws an even more interesting light on Canning's methods. Staples had married Lord Ormond's sister and was favoured by Canning's great friend, the Marquess Wellesley. Both influential noblemen solicited further employment for him in 1826. Canning inflexibly refused, informing Staples that his former conduct ' precluded ' him [Canning] " from again recommending you to His Majesty for employment." [2]

(d) *The Castigation of Mr Watts* (1826)

Other consuls in both worlds received lessons as to the difference between diplomatic and consular functions. Mr Watts, Consul at Cartagena de Colombia, wrote a letter to his Consul - General at Bogota, complaining that " this comfortless place is the plenitude of dulness and insipidity." He was soon to be enlivened. For he had been maladroit

---

[1] *F.O. Mexico,* 50/2. Planta to Staples, Oct. 10/23 ; July 22/24. Canning had avowed it as a principle that he would let no persons with consular appointments engage in trade, and appears to have removed others who did so. *Vide* his speech, July 5/25. *Hans. Deb.,* N.S., xiii. 1485–7.

[2] *F.O. Argentine,* 6/14. Canning to Staples, May 22/26.

enough to introduce by letter an Englishman to the Colombian Government, without mentioning the fact to the British Mission or Consul-General at Bogota, though he complacently informed the Secretary of State of his action by direct letter. Planta wrote to the Consul-General of Bogota enclosing a copy of his letter to Watts (8th July 1826). " Mr Canning apprehends that this is the first time that a consul has taken upon himself not only to act exclusively upon his own impressions of a case brought before him without the knowledge of his Government but to report to the Secretary of State for his information, not the particulars of the case itself but merely the fact that he [the consul] highly approved of it. . . . But that you should think yourself authorised to address yourself directly to the Ministers of the State at one extremity of which you exercise a subordinate function (there being at the Capital of the said State a British Mission and Consul-General) is a degree of irregularity and presumption which, I am directed by the Secretary of State to say, has incurred his severe displeasure. The circumstances you mention in extenuation of this act (or rather in your own view as an enhancement of its merit), namely, the ' intimate friendship ' you say subsists between you and the Colombian Ministers to whom you address yourself, so far from extenuating your fault, makes it more inconvenient to the public service, and, unless checked, of more evil example. Your business as His Majesty's Consul is not one of private friendship but of public duty." [1] Mr Canning was very sorry to have to circulate this letter, as he had hitherto performed his duties well. In these rebukes, and actions, in spite of their sharpness, there is a sort of severe magnificence, which evinces a lofty conception of public duty.

6. Canning's Financial Reforms in the Diplomatic Service

(a) *Tightening the Financial Reins*

Canning was anxious that diplomats abroad should have the means of maintaining a proper state, but he took care

---

[1] Correspondence in *F.O. Colombia*, 135/1. The phraseology of the letter is obviously that of Canning.

that such indulgences should not exceed proper limits. Thus he directed repairs and new furniture to be made to the Ambassador's house in Paris, for he thought it ' very well ' that the Embassy in Paris should be " fitted up in as splendid a style as any house in London." But, owing to his inter-vention, the total expenses were reduced from £23,100 to £12,000. Again, services of plate and a picture of the King had formerly been given as personal perquisites to all Ambassadors. He directed that both should remain in the Embassy as a permanency. Granville's service of plate, as issued to him in 1825, consisted of 24 oval table dishes; 16 oval and 16 round dishes and covers; 4 tureens with royal crest; 48 soup dishes; 18 salt-cellars; 12 sauceboats; 12 bed-chamber and 12 table candlesticks; 12 dozen dessert knives (6 dozen with silver blades); 1 coffee-pot; 4 teapots; 4 Grecian pattern ice-pails; 6 ice-spoons; a spoon ' to take out flies with.' In all, he received 14,051 ozs. 8 dwts. of silver. Inventories were to be kept, and everything was regulated with meticulous care. The Paris service was the most expensive and cost £8500, 15s. 11d. Table services with Chapel services were provided at Paris, St Petersburg, Vienna, and The Hague; while at Madrid, Berlin, and Constantinople, Ambassadors were permitted plate but no Chapel service. Special missions, as for congratulating monarchs on their succession and the like, were always most expensive. Hence a peer, often a duke, was selected, who was lordly enough to pay his own expenses. The Duke of Northumberland, who went to Paris to the Coronation of Charles X., received a diamond sword worth £10,000 from the government as a present, to remain as an heirloom in his family. The gift was magnificent, but the bargain was advantageous for the government, for he had incurred expenses estimated at over four times that sum. And, as Canning explained to the House of Commons (17th March 1826), " It was not thought right that the public and the sovereign should be served entirely gratuitously."

Castlereagh had initiated various important reforms by a committee in 1816, but there had been much waste of public money, as always in war periods, and the improvement was slow. The whole system was revised with the utmost care by Canning in person in 1825. He had in fact put most of the reforms into practice before that date. The house rents had been reduced below the level of 1815–6. Then Sir Charles Stuart was informed that Great Britain " cannot allow reimbursement of sums for interest on advance of money, brokerage and commission, salaries are nett." [1] The principle was established definitely in 1825. Other means were taken to prevent ministers from carrying off perquisites. Castlereagh's foolish brother—the new Marquis of Londonderry—seems to have been the last Ambassador who carried off a service of plate as well as a picture of the King. He succeeded also in passing an inordinate quantity of wine through the Customs free of duty—no less than 2 tuns or 504 gallons. When some hesitation was shown at permitting it, he made furious protests, but was informed that his wine was passed only as ' a special indulgence,' and Canning laid down as an allowance ' never to be departed from ' in future, " 1 tun to Ambassadors and half a tun to Ministers and Envoys." [2]

Pensions to ex-diplomats amounted to £52,000 a year at this time, and were another item which was carefully scrutinised. Under the circumstances it was ill-advised of Londonderry to apply for one. Canning very wisely handed on his petition to the Prime Minister, " not wishing to take upon himself the responsibility of deciding on such an application, or of setting a value on the services of the noble marquis." Liverpool, at first, disregarded the application; but, on its renewal, sent the papers back to Canning endorsed, 'This is too bad.' [3] The sentiment must have appealed to Canning. During thirty-four years of public service he received some £60,000; while during ten years of diplomatic service Londonderry had received £160,000!

Though he was well aware that his two representatives at

[1] *F.O. France*, 146/56. Planta to C. Stuart, Oct. 28/23. Planta's letter to Secretary of the Treasury, Sept. 18/25.
[2] *F.O. France*, 161/56, to Stuart, Aug. 4/23. There is an amusing correspondence in *B.M. Ripon MSS.*, iii. 1821–8. Robinson to Londonderry, July 18/23, in which the latter is convicted of all sorts of blunders and told he had had ' every consideration.'
[3] June 26/27. *Hans. Deb.*, N.S., xvii. 1404–5. Tom Moore wrote on this:

" I doubt if e'en Griffinhoofe could
(Though Griffin's a comical lad)
Invent any joke half as good
As that precious one '*this is too bad*!'"

Paris had to supplement their official incomes from their private purse, Canning never hesitated to reprove them for unnecessary expenditure of public money.[1]   Thus, Sir Charles Stuart was brought to book for having allowed his house expenses to go unreported and unpaid for a year and a half. In 1826 Lord Granville learnt of " Mr Canning's regret that he spent 1120 francs more on stationery than last quarter." It was, however, Mr Ward in Mexico who incurred the most Olympian of rebukes when he subscribed $1000 (about £250) to alleviating calamities and epidemics in Mexico.   He was informed that " Mr Canning considers the sum extraordinarily large.   He must again and again urge upon you the absolute necessity of economy in expenditure.   You are not to consider it as either incumbent on you or as expedient to take every opportunity of purchasing the good will of the People among whom you are placed by ostentatious liberality.   You are to recollect that your example will be pleaded against all future Ministers of His Majesty in Mexico and that largesses on such a scale would soon exhaust any allowance likely to be made to an established mission."   Further, he deducted from his submitted expenses $500 for half a year's salary to Dr Wilson ; $328 for plate purchased ;   and $51 for a pencil-case.   Mr Ward did not learn much from this lesson, for in the next quarter he was informed that there was ' so extraordinary a difference ' between his expenses and those of the British Minister in Colombia, where ' every article of consumption and demand ' is, ' so far as is known, of equal price.'   By this standard his stable charges and servants' wages were about double, his house-rent yearly triple, and his housekeeping more than quadruple, those of Colombia.[2] In ordinary circumstances in South America, as Canning explained to an amused House of Commons (17th March 1826), it was difficult to fix a scale of prices " in a country in which a man might buy a horse for a dollar which would cost him 2 guineas to get shod."   Where comparisons were possible, however, it will be seen that economy was rigidly enforced.

Canning was the first to consider the hardship due to slow-ness of promotion among those persons abroad, like secretaries

---

[1] *Vide* his remarks, Mar. 21/25.   *Hans. Deb.*, N.S., xii. 1093.
[2] *F.O. Mexico*, 50/19.   Planta to Ward, Feb. 14, 15, June 8/26.

of legation, who were diplomats by profession. Finding that the promotion between secretary of legation and secretary of embassy was slow, he laid down a principle afterwards known as 'Mr Canning's rule.' The secretary of legation was to have £250 a year extra, after a service of ten years. When he got promoted to be secretary of embassy, however, he lost this extra amount, and, though gaining in promotion, might even be slightly reduced in salary. This anomaly was pointed out to Mr Hammond in 1870 by the Select Committee, but he regarded a change as almost blasphemous. " Mr Canning was a great man, and a rule which he laid down was no doubt well considered."

(b) *Comparison with the Castlereagh Period*

In general it may be said that the whole financial aspect of the diplomatic service was revised and examined, and plain and intelligible rules laid down for the future. As a result of all this careful scrutiny important economies were achieved. Hoping to contrast his brother's economy with Canning's extravagance, the second Lord Londonderry called for a return of the years 1817–21 and 1822–6. This return is, in reality, favourable to Canning.[1] The return showed a total increase of £100,000, or, in other words, that Canning had increased expenditure by an average of £25,000 a year. But this was due to expenditure that was exceptional and non-recurrent, such as the appointment of new Ambassadors and the provision of their outfits ; to special missions on the death of sovereigns ; and finally to extraordinary special commissions, as those to Spanish America. Under Castlereagh the first two items were £18,136, under Canning £109,732. The third item, that of special commission, came to £33,000 more under Canning.[2] Apart from these, the average annual expenditure was reduced.

[1] *Parliamentary Return* of May 18/27. For purposes of comparison I take the years 1818–21 and 1823–6. The year 1822 is excluded as Canning was only three and a half months in office. If one averaged the proportions of this year, and counted in the year 1817 for Castlereagh, the comparison would be more unfavourable to the latter. The chief saving effected by Canning at home was on the Messenger Service and on contingent expenditure, and abroad on the salaries of Ambassadors.

[2] It is perhaps fair to note that a new Foreign Office was built in 1825 at a cost of £30,000, and that Canning henceforth lived there (the only Foreign Secretary who ever did), and, by doing so, probably added to government expenditure. He took up his residence there at the end of 1825, giving it as his address ' for mutton as well as letters.'

On the home establishments Canning, despite an increase of
staff at the office, saved about £5000 a year, on Ambassadors'
salaries about £11,000 a year, and on the total of all expenses
(excluding consuls and special non-recurrent items) about
£8000 a year. Thus real economies were actually effected,
and the economy was actually greater than appears, for the
normal expenses, which tend to creep up gradually in all
public service, were actually cut down.

7. Canning's Relations with British Diplomats Abroad

(a) *General*

It was comparatively an easy task to organise the Foreign
Office and to introduce efficient methods at home. Abroad
it was possible to regularise the methods of correspondence
and to reduce the financial extravagance. It was easy to
coerce or control inferior officials like consuls. But it was
difficult to bend to the new master and to the new policy
the will of distant, sullen, haughty, ignorant or pleasure-
loving diplomats. The men of the Castlereagh school, like
Wellington, Londonderry, Stuart, À Court, and Henry
Wellesley, did not always understand, or appreciate, or obey
their instructions. Others, like Thornton or Cathcart, were
weak men. Three men were entirely devoted to Canning—
Granville and Bagot, and his cousin, Stratford Canning. But
the last of these, the greatest diplomat England ever had in
the East, was the only man who perfectly understood and
executed, or sometimes judiciously exceeded, his instructions. The British diplomats of this age were better than
those in the eighteenth century, whom a French writer calls
" dissipated diplomats not infrequently met with in English
Legations abroad ; whither they are bound . . . as fit for
the looser ways of the continent." But it is certain that
Canning thought the Hanoverian diplomats superior to the
British in the production of information, and equally certain
that some British Ministers had a very amateurish notion of
diplomacy. They usually owed their appointments to personal
or political influence and sometimes resigned on the advent
of a new Ministry or of a new man.

Canning did not shrink from strong measures when

necessary. Vaughan at Washington was censured for ex-
ceeding his instructions with a severity that surprised him.
Sir Edward Thornton was recalled from Lisbon "because he
forgot that he was Minister for England." Sir Charles Stuart,
after blunders at Paris and a great success at Rio, had two
treaties disavowed under painful circumstances. Of the
Special Commissioners sent to Mexico one was disavowed,
a second made to ' kiss the rod ' for giving imperfect and
misleading information, the acting *chargé* censured for
extravagance, and the commercial treaty refused ratification.

Lamb, in Spain, was an excellent diplomat, who rendered
great services in 1826, and who was, noted Canning, " a source
of much more accurate information than we had before."
À Court, whom he succeeded in Spain, had shown at Naples
in 1820–1, at Madrid in 1823, and at Lisbon in 1825–6, the
firmness and address of a really great diplomat, and won in
all three capacities unstinted praise. His defect was that his
information was not always adequate, and he committed two
grave faults. Through his maladroitness the secret offer to
guarantee Cuba to Spain became known to other governments,
a very serious error, if not worse.[1] Again, though he had
himself suggested the independence of the Spanish Colonies
in 1823, he criticised Canning before several diplomats at
Lisbon for having established it in 1825. The second indiscretion became known to Canning through intercepted
letters, but he generously disregarded it, and defended him
stoutly in Parliament. These errors are the sole blot on the
fame of this resolute diplomat who lived to become Lord
Heytesbury, to be nominated, but not to become, Governor-
General of India, to win fresh diplomatic laurels in Russia,
and to end as Lord-Lieutenant of Ireland.

(b) *The Chastisement of Strangford*

The case of Lord Strangford was even more painful than
that of Sir Charles Stuart, in so much as he was a more
brilliant man, who had received both an Irish and an English

[1] *V.S.A.*, Berichte aus Frankreich, Bd. 357. Vincent to Metternich,
May 8/24, No. 22 B, enclosing a despatch from Royer (Prussian Minister
at Lisbon) to Maltzahn, of Apr. 28. Royer says À Court referred to the
Cuba guarantee of Apr. 2. The secret was apparently unknown to France
till 1825, and Canning, though aware of the leakage, did not suspect
À Court.

peerage for distinguished services. When Canning was fresh
at the Foreign Office in 1807, it was Strangford who had carried
the Regent of Portugal almost by force off to Brazil in a British
ship, just as the ragged and weary French troops entered
Lisbon. He won an Irish viscountcy for this act. It was he
who, by much diplomatic finesse and patience, averted war
between Russia and Turkey during the stormy years of 1823–4.
Canning recalled him to London, and rewarded him with
the English title of Lord Penshurst in the middle of 1824.
Strangford proceeded to irritate him by voting against Catholic
Emancipation in the Lords, a step which caused Canning to
'cut him dead.' But Canning had other reasons for suspicion.
The brilliant Strangford was ambitious and vain, something
of an intriguer, and at heart a supporter of the Neo-Holy
Alliance, of congress policies, and of European intervention
in Turkey, all of which were now odious to Canning. He
suspected, and with truth, that Strangford had had secret
correspondence with Metternich, and that he was now in
very close confidential relations with Esterházy in London.
Strangford actually showed his secret despatches to Esterházy
and deplored with him the policy of the Foreign Secretary.
Canning had decided to send him as Ambassador to St
Petersburg, but refused to admit him to his confidences, and
only sent him his instructions just before he was leaving
England. Canning was sending his cousin Stratford to
Constantinople, but he refused to tell Strangford the objects
of his mission or to give him any verbal advice. The
irritated Strangford told the tale of his last interview with
Canning to Esterházy, who thought it 'too comic' not to
report it to Metternich.[1] Strangford lunched with the
Foreign Secretary in the presence of Stratford, but could
not touch on serious topics till 7 p.m., when the following
conversation occurred. Canning seated on sofa :—

CAN.—Ah—when are you going ?

STR.—As soon as necessary ; I have nothing, not even my
instructions.

CAN. (*yawning*).—Oh, you don't need them ; I'll send them
in a couple of days from the country.

---

[1] *V.S.A.*, Berichte aus England, Oct. 8/25. Esterházy to Metternich.

STR.—But I have still to speak to you on so many subjects. I know nothing of France, Spain, Portugal, Brazil; I don't know any of your views on all that.

CAN.—Oh ! that is not necessary for the moment.

STR.—But finally for Russia—what style of attitude (*quelle nuance*) have I to adopt to the Emperor ?

CAN.—Just keep him in good humour—that's all. Good-bye. Adieu.

His instructions (drawn 12th October) reached him just before he sailed (18th October). They remark on the ' extreme difficulty ' of working either with France or Austria over Greece, and told him it was " desirable that the Russian Government should know the grounds on which our sense of that difficulty is founded." Strangford was thus clearly intended not to commit us to joint intervention with Austria or France, but to welcome or transmit Russian overtures, and was intended, in reality, to do nothing. He was too vain a man and too much a pro-Metternichian to accept the rôle of a cipher or of a telephone receiver.

When he got to Russia Nesselrode began making overtures as to a joint intervention of England and Russia. Strangford, on his own authority, suggested that France, Russia, and Austria should be asked to join in the intervention. He went straight off to the French and Austrian Ambassadors and drew up a project for a collective *démarche* of the Five Powers at Constantinople. His *projet* suggested that, if the Turks refused, the other Powers ' *reconnaitraient à la Russe* ' the right of making war on the Porte. Lebzeltern, the able Austrian Ambassador, objected to the last phrase. Strangford saw the danger, and cut out the phrase from his despatch to Canning. But, unfortunately for him, Nesselrode had already ' taken note of it,' and sent off a copy to Lieven in London, instructing him to tell Canning.

On the 17th December Lieven read his government's despatch. Canning professed incredulity and forced Lieven to reread, three or four times, the passage about Strangford having recognised the right of Russia ' to go to war in case of failure.' Canning wrote sharply to Strangford the same day. " I really want words to express the astonishment which

I felt," as one of your instructions was " the absolute stipulation against force." He bade him sharply to clear up
' this extraordinary and unaccountable confusion.' Strangford replied by ' a deliberate denial ' that he had ever used the
phrase about war, said his opinion had been personal, and
tried to justify his policy of non-intervention. On the
31st December Canning totally disavowed him, told him to
make this disavowal clear to all diplomats concerned at
St Petersburg, and ended with what he called ' a padlock.'
" The instructions which I have now to give Your Excellency
are comprised in a few short words, *to be quiet*." [1]

Strangford replied by a complaint against ' this unexampled
severity of reprimand,' protesting that he had received
inadequate instructions, and had not seen those of Stratford.
Canning replied sternly that, if his instructions were inadequate, " the fault is with me. . . . But I am not prepared
to commit to any Foreign Minister [*i.e.* British diplomat], or
suffer to be assumed by him, the discretion of taking a step
which is to change the whole policy of his country and for
which I am to be responsible." As to Strangford's suggestion
that his overture was personal only, " I should have thought
it unnecessary to point out to me, who had been so long
versed in Diplomatick Affaires, the utter futility of such an
inference.

" ' To try the ground ' professedly from himself without
committing his government is one of the most hackneyed
institutions of diplomacy." But it was unlikely to be believed
that he did not speak from authority, and it was obvious that
the situation was no longer the same after a disavowal. " To
conclude this unpleasant subject entirely, I have only to repeat
now to Your Excellency the positive direction that, in any
similar case, you will prefer the declaring frankly at once,
that you are, if you are, without instructions, and expressing
your readiness to refer Home for them, to the taking upon

[1] *F.O. Russia*, 181/65. Canning to Strangford Dec. 1, 8, 31/25. *Ibid.*,
182/2. Strangford to Canning, Nos. 5–6, Dec. 9/25; No. 4, *cf.* Jan. 17;
No. 16, *cf.* Feb. 14. Strangford's denial cannot be accepted. Nesselrode
gave Lebzeltern ' his word ' that Strangford had used the phrase, and
this was accepted by both Lebzeltern and Metternich, *v. V.S.A.*, Berichte
aus Russland, Bd. 9. Lebzeltern to Metternich, Feb. 4/26, and see some
notes of Metternich, 1827, on a despatch of Canning to Strangford, Dec.
1/25.

yourself to act, as you have done on the present occasion, in the faith, that, if you happen to guess wrong, your error will be entirely cured by a disavowal." [1] Canning intimated privately he did not, in fact, want to recall him. But Strangford's pride could not stomach such a rebuff, and on the 9th May he obtained leave of absence from Russia and soon ceased to be Ambassador there.

His fall was great, and he was vocal enough. He wrote to Bagot : " I have had a jobation and such a jobation . . . Mr C. will find it hard to make folks believe that I am *quite* such a noodle as he makes me out to be " (19th January), " our classical and choleric chief. . . . Happy man that you are to be out of all this mess ! " After twenty-four years of service " it is hard to be treated . . . like a troublesome child, with a thump on the back and a peevish ' Be quiet ! ' " (4th February). The genial Bagot replied : " I cannot find a syllable to say against the manner in which you have received the thundering castigation with which you have been belaboured by Busby [Canning] before the whole diplomatic sixth form." Others saw more truly. The American, Christopher Hughes, his former colleague at Stockholm, wrote to Strangford, " you allowed yourself to be *betrayed by a Cossack kiss*." [2] Canning had written severely, " if Strangford will play false I shall have no remedy but to show him up." Canning spoke true ; it can be shown that he had played false. In March 1826 Canning sent a confidential despatch criticising the Prussian policy to him, with instructions to convey it to Russia. [3] Strangford, smarting with irritation, violated the confidence and, ' under seal of secrecy,' showed it to the Austrian Ambassador at St Petersburg. [4] Here is revealed a gross and indefensible violation of confidence, even worse than his

[1] *F.O. Russia*, 182/68. Strangford to Canning, Feb. 4/26, No. 16 ; 181/68. Canning to Strangford, Mar. 4/26.

[2] This correspondence is in Fonblanque's *Lives of the Lords Strangford*, p. 148 *et seq.*, and in Bagot, *G.C. & F.*, ii. 313–14, 326, 329–33.

[3] Canning's despatch is in *F.O. Russia*, 181/68, to Stratford, No. 8 of Mar. 17/26.

[4] *V.S.A.*, Berichte aus Russland, Bd. 9. Lebzeltern to Metternich, Apr. 3/26. Schiemann, *Geschichte Russlands*, Berlin, [1904], i. 348, quotes Lieven, Oct. 5, 30/25, as suggesting that Strangford had been, or could be, bribed by Russia. I confess it seems to me that this accusation goes too far and the evidence seems ambiguous. But the suggestion could not even be made of a man above suspicion of intrigue.

previous secret revelations to Esterházy in London.   Further,
his ' deliberate denial ' of having used the phrase about
recognising the right of Russia to go to war was not only
disbelieved by Canning, but also by Metternich, by Lebzeltern,
by la Ferronays, and by Nesselrode.   On such a man and on
such methods sympathy is wasted.   Strangford's fall was
due to himself, to his tendency for intrigue and to his incurable
vanity.   It is seldom that so brilliant a man has merited so
stern a condemnation.

(c) *Granville and Bagot*

Canning's personal friends did not always escape correction,
and they seem sometimes to have deserved it.   Of these,
Lord Granville was Ambassador at The Hague (1823–4), and
then at Paris (1824–8) ; and Sir Charles Bagot Ambassador
at St Petersburg (till 1824) and subsequently at The Hague.
Both men corresponded with him upon terms of intimacy
and affection.   Neither of them always understood his policy.
Granville, though an able and conciliatory diplomat, was too
fond of aristocratic ease.   His despatches are very short,
his information often defective, his office-work poor.   Once
there was a serious leakage at the Paris Embassy in 1826 ;
often his information was late.   On the whole he was handled
with humour and with much gentleness.   He answered one
reproof by saying that he was always interrupted in his
despatches by dinner.   " The perpetual recurrence of dinner,"
answered Canning, " is exceedingly distressing.   But did it
never enter your mind that you might evade the force of that
not unexpected impediment by beginning to write at a time
of day when it does not usually present itself ?   Try that
device."   On the whole, Granville bore his chastenings with
good humour, doubtless because he knew they were deserved.
In fact, though indolent in detail, he handled large questions
with ability.   One fancies such a letter as this from his Chief
must have atoned for much.   " In order that you may be
as fine as your colleagues at the Coronation [of Charles X.]
I have asked the King to give you Lord Whitworth's Red
Ribbon [Order of the Bath], which His Majesty has graciously
consented to do." [1]

[1] *Gr. MSS.* Canning to Granville, May 17/25.

The amiable and generous Bagot was almost as close a friend as Granville, and his correspondence with Canning has an indescribable charm. Though more businesslike he was less far-sighted than Granville, and on one occasion committed a serious diplomatic error. At St Petersburg in 1824 he committed the British Government to a joint conference for intervention in the East, and incurred, and with justice, the wrath of Canning.[1] " I was sorry," wrote Canning privately (29th July), " to have to *snub* or *snouch* you in your old age (the old age of your Embassy) for disobedience of your instructions : but that disobedience . . . might have done a world of mischief." The incident in no way disturbed their friendship, or Bagot's easy amiability. Canning had privately suggested to Bagot that he must have been drinking ' *usquebaugh*,' and concluded matters by an instruction to bring him ' some tea . . . black tea not green ' on his return to England.

(d) *The ' Rhyming Despatch '*

" Happy man, that you are ! " wrote the aggrieved Strangford (4th February 1826) to Bagot, now comfortably installed at The Hague, " to swig your curaçoa in peace, and to be able to open your despatches without the fear of their actually exploding in your face." This was on the 4th February 1826, when the curaçoa-swigging Bagot had just received a despatch most disturbing to his nerves. The story is already known, but is too characteristic of both men to be omitted. On the 23rd December 1825 Canning had instructed Bagot that, in consequence of the obstinate attitude of Falck, the Netherlands Foreign Minister, a 20 per cent. duty would be levied on Dutch shipping. On the 31st January 1826 Canning sent him official intelligence of this duty having been imposed by two Orders in Council, accompanied by an enclosure in

---

[1] *Vide* Bagot, *G.C. & F.*, ii. 259–74. Captain Bagot very candidly (p. 258) admits his ancestor to have been somewhat at fault. Bagot was not, however, recalled on this account ; he had applied already for permission to go to The Hague, as he did not think St Petersburg a suitable place to educate his children. Stap., *P.L.*, ii. 419–23, curiously enough, is ' very tender ' to Bagot. In fact he misses the point. Russia wished to hold the conference, in order to avoid sending Ribeaupierre to Constantinople. *Vide* Canning to Wellington (*W.N.D.*, ii. 340) of Nov. 10/24. This point was divined by Canning at the time, and subsequent events proved him in the right.

cipher marked ' separate, secret, and confidential.' Bagot
replied in some alarm on the 3rd February that he had not the
cipher in question, and hoped the " circumstances will not be
productive of any public inconvenience." Canning replied
gravely and formally ' regretting the circumstance,' and
forwarding the cipher (6–7th February). The rest may be
told in Bagot's private letter of the 13th February :—

"The Hague, *Febry.* 13, 1826.

(Private)

" MY DEAR CANNING,

" You have fretted me to fiddlestrings, and I have
a great mind not to give you the satisfaction of ever knowing
how completely your mystification of me has succeeded. It
was more than you had a right to expect when you drew
from me that solemn and official lamentation which I sent
you of my inability to decypher His Majesty's commands ;
but, as the Devil would have it, your success did not end here.
The post which brought me the decyphers arrived at eleven
o'clock at night, when I had only time before I sent off the
other messenger to read your grave regret at what had
occurred and to acknowledge the receipt of the mail. The
next morning Tierney and I were up by cock-crow to make
out ' *la maudite dépêche*,' and it was not till after an hour
of most indescribable anxiety that we were put ' out of our
fear ' by finding what it really was, and that ' you Pyramus '
were not Pyramus, but only ' Bottom the weaver.'

" I could have slain you ! but I got some fun myself, for I
afterwards put the fair decypher into Douglas's hands, who
read it twice without moving a muscle, or to this hour discovering that it was not prose, and returned it to me, declaring
that it was ' oddly worded ; but he had always had a feeling
that the despatch must relate to discriminating duties.'

" C. BAGOT.

" The Right Hon. the Foreign Secretary."

The decipher in Sir Charles Bagot's own handwriting runs
as follows :—

" Decypher, Separate, Secret, and Confidential.

" Foreign Office, *January* 31, 1826.

" Sir,

In matters of commerce the fault of the Dutch
Is offering too little and asking too much.
The French are with equal advantage content,
So we clap on Dutch bottoms just 20 per cent.
(*Chorus*) 20 per cent., 20 [per] cent.

(*Chorus of English Customs House Officers and French Douaniers*)

(*English*) We clap on Dutch bottoms just 20 per cent.
(*French*) *Vous frapperez Falck avec* 20 *per cent.*

" I have no other commands from His Majesty to convey to your Excellency to-day.

" I am with great truth and respect, Sir,

" Your Excellency's most obedient humble servant,

" George Canning.

" His Excellency The Rt. Honble.
Sir Charles Bagot, K.B." [1]

Some writers have suggested that the ' rhyming despatch ' was an instance of the incurable and incorrigible levity of Canning.[2]   Our sketch has shown the rigidity of Canning's methods, the severity of his economy, and the inflexibility of his disciplinary system.   It is certain, at least, that Vaughan, Thornton, Strangford, Stuart, Wellesley, Granville, or Bagot himself, would have been happier if he had been less unbending.   Yet perhaps the most genuine and unforced tribute to his work at the Foreign Office comes, as it always does, from one who had worked in closest touch with him.   ' Alas ! poor Mr Canning,' wrote a clerk at the end of 1827 ; ' how we miss him.' [3]

[1] Owing to the fact that an inaccurate version was given in *F.O. Holland,* 147, I got this wrong in my *Life of Canning,* 1905, pp. 192–3.   I am happy to have been corrected from the Bagot papers by my friend Sir Harry Poland, in *Trans. Royal. Hist. Soc.,* [New Series], 1906, xx. 49–60.   The material parts of this paper are reproduced in Bagot, *G.C. & F.,* ii. 317–25.

[2] The modern Foreign Office, with a happier sense of proportion, has purchased this unique despatch and preserves it among its most valued records.

[3] *F.O.,* 95/591.   F. S[tavely] to Parish, Dec. 29/27.

CHAPTER XIII

THE PRESS AND PUBLIC OPINION

1. THE BRITISH AND FOREIGN PRESS (1820–7)

" He [his Lordship] sometimes wondered what public opinion was. It was a nice point how public opinion was created, and whether public opinion represented the views of busy working folk, or whether it represented the views of those who owned or conducted newspapers."—JUSTICE M'CARDIE, *Times*, 6th June 1924.

THERE is nothing in which Canning's attitude was so peculiar and unique in his own day, as in his policy towards the Press and the public in his own and in other countries, a policy different from that of his colleagues and of all the diplomats of Europe.

He had once been a brilliant journalist himself in the days of the *Anti-Jacobin* and of Addington. But he abjured connection with the daily Press ' for ever ' in 1804, though in 1806 he forgot his vow.[1] Afterwards he wrote several articles, not indeed for the Press, but for the staid *Quarterly* (the last in 1818). This journal, whose editor, Gifford, was a personal friend, remained faithful to him during his second Ministry, but neither it nor its famous rival, the *Edinburgh,* appeared often enough to influence the temporary gusts of opinion.

Canning was no favourite with the Press in 1822. He had concurred in muzzling it in England during 1819–20, and few men knew that at the same moment (*v.* p. 40), he had refused to restrict it in India. His bold attitude in defending ' the Six Acts ' had greatly galled the journalists. On one occasion, in June 1819, the *Times* had reported Hume as say-ing that Canning " had risen above the sufferings of others by laughing at them." Canning raised the matter in the

---

[1] Stap., *G.C. & T.*, to Boringdon, Dec. 7/06, p. 116.

Commons and forced Hume to deny that he had used the words. He then had the editor (Bell) summoned to the Bar and the reporter (Collier) committed to the custody of the Sergeant-at-Arms. It was even moved that Collier should be sent to Newgate, though he eventually escaped with a reprimand and a small fine. The step was probably a grave error. With one exception, the *Times* had the largest circulation, and double the influence of any other paper. It never forgot the insult. It went into transports of fury when Canning took office, and nearly always attacked him. Even after his great triumph in 1826, when it grudgingly supported him, Canning wrote, " It must never be forgotten that the *Times*, though borne away on this occasion by the tide of public opinion, is at bottom as inimical to me personally as ever." [1] This fact again is interesting because the *Times* was subjected to other ministerial influences, as Croker himself confessed.[2]

Canning had supported the government policy of direct suppression of some journals in 1819. But he appears to have disapproved of their other attempts to influence the Press. Their policy of high postal rates and heavy paper duties was intended to hamper the Press. Hume declared that the former had reduced newspapers from 383 in 1810 to 271 in 1816 and to 206 in 1821. Government advertisements supported the feeble life of some papers and directed their policy. Four of these obtained £1358 in 1816. Of these indirectly subsidised organs, three died in 1823 and the last in 1824.[3] I do not think we shall be wrong in attributing the cessation of such subsidies to Canning. In the same year newspapers, as a whole, revived to 281, and those who did not benefit by government subsidies increased in vigour and freedom of criticism.

Marcellus, the clever young French *chargé d'affaires*, gave

---

[1] Stap., *G.C. & T.*, 556. Canning to Granville, Dec. 29/26.

[2] *Croker Papers*, ii. 22–3. He says that he himself " conveyed to the public articles written by Prime and Cabinet Ministers," they supplying the fact and he the tact.

[3] *The British Neptune, National Register, National and Provincial Gazette* died in 1823, the *Weekly Guardian* in Apr. 1824. Papers in Ireland seem to have had a good deal of money from the government, *v.* H. R. Fox Bourne, *English Newspapers*, [1887], i. 385 ; and *Melbourne Memoirs*, [1890], 161–2 ; and Hume, *Hans. Deb.*, N.S., vii. (May 7/22), 366 ; x. (Feb. 26/24), 501–2 ; he points out there were 581 papers in the United States ; *cp.* xvi. (Dec. 13/26), 400–1.

an interesting foreign view of the British Press in 1823. The *Times*, he said, ' is most to be feared,' and attacks us (the French). The *Morning Herald* and the *Sun* are the echoes of the *Times*. The *Morning Chronicle* (a Whig paper) is ' less dangerous,' but violent and cynical. The *Star* is ' Mr Canning's organ ' ; the *New Times* and the *Times* ' are for us.' He recommended that they should be fed with news. For " here a newspaper hardly yields to money ; one manages it by getting it a greater number of subscribers (by getting it good information). Every other means of influence is almost without result." [1] This sketch is not wholly correct. The *Morning Herald* was at times under the influence of ' Ultra ' Tory Ministers. Even the *Times* and the *New Times* occasionally received articles and inspiration from Ultra sources,[2] and sometimes, apparently, both news and gold from France.[3] He does not mention the *Morning Post*, an Ultra-ministerial organ, or state that it, like the *New Times*, had a dwindling circulation and importance. He says nothing of the two Radical weeklies, Fonblanque's *Examiner* and Cobbett's *Political Register*, the licensed free-lances of the Press. Their opinions were widely read, but not always accepted, by their readers. For extreme violence attested their honesty but destroyed their influence.

The *Political Register*, like the *Courier*, seems to have profited by French information, perhaps by French gold. On 5th March 1823 Cobbett wrote a letter to Chateaubriand, and added longer articles in the *Political Register*, defending the French invasion of Spain. One of the proprietors of the *Courier* objected to the attacks on Canning, and had some fierce discussions with the editor (Mr Mudford) in May 1823. Ultimately Mudford agreed that ' Mr Canning should never be attacked,' but complained very bitterly that " Mr Canning had been an enemy of the paper all the winter, refusing any communication with it," and admitted that was the reason of his attack. It was also evidently the reason of his defence of France,

[1] *A.A.E.*, 616. Marcellus to Chateaubriand, Mar. 11/23 [also printed].

[2] Fox Bourne, ii. 19–21 ; and *v.* the *Times*, Apr. 25/23. Vide *F.O.*, 97/169. Darby, June 22/24, said he had information that Villèle had bought the *New Times*.

[3] *F.O. France*, 97/169. Goldsmith, Oct. 5/24, quotes Corbière to the effect that the French Government paid the *Times* money for two years under Decazes.

though he denied that the ' *Courier* was in the pay of any Government.'[1] Canning thought so too, for in July 1823 he wrote to Bagot: " Your sagacity was not astray. The villain [Mudford] was sold to France and took his lessons partly from the French Embassy, partly from our own Ultras . . . whether the rogue now repents, I know not nor care."[2] In October 1824 Granville reported : " I think I can assure you, on authority not to be disputed, that the private corre-spondence in the *Courier* and the *Morning Chronicle* is written under the direction of the agents of the French Government."[3] It seems deeply discreditable to the British Ultras that organs, which they at any rate partly controlled, were employed in the French interest and to attack Canning during 1823, and the *Times* commented severely on this on the 25th April of that year. The Whig *Morning Chronicle* found a source of inspiration in Austria, as well as in France. For Metternich early in 1822 directed Esterházy to insert an article in it.[4] The result was not quite what either expected. Black, the editor, was a man of unblemished character, little in-fluenced by information received, though, being a journalist, he would be less than human to have refused it. Metternich got little for his pains. Black continued his liberal policies, and warmly praised Canning's famous Plymouth speech (28th October 1823).

Canning seems to have impartially and strictly refused private information to any newspaper ; any that he gave was official and public, and given to all of them. In 1822 he

---

[1] Stap., *Corr.*, i. 122–3.

[2] Bagot, *G.C. & F.*, ii. 183. To Bagot, July 14/23. The following extract proves Ultra influence in 1820. "The *New Times* will, I think, have shown you that I have acted upon your hints. I really believe that we are doing with the Press all that is possible. And I am sure that both the *New Times* and the *Courier* have been full of able writing. I am doing all I can also to get this good writing circulated. The *New Times* is sent to friendly papers in the country, with the best articles marked with red ink to have them inserted. We are getting several pamphlets written under the eye of the Att[orney] and Sol[icitor]-General ; and we shall circulate widely Lord Liverpool's and Lord Lauderdale's speeches. In short, I think that in this way every effort is made, and I will take care that it shall not slacken." Charles Arbuthnot to Lord Bathurst, Nov. 29/20, *Bathurst Papers*, p. 489.

[3] *F.O. France*, 146/60. Granville to Canning, Oct. 11/24. Goldsmith, *F.O.*, 97/169, Oct. 25/24, said the *Courier* received 2000 francs a month from France ' ever since the Restoration,' with two short interruptions.

[4] *V.S.A.*, England, *Varia*. Metternich to Esterházy, Jan. 31/22.

said he ' rarely read the evening papers,' but had remonstrated (though without much effect) with the *Courier*.   " But I should a little doubt the policy of interfering with his political speculations.   The distance between the telling of these gentry what they ought not to say is so small to the demand from them what they are to say, that I rather dread opening even this negative road to the office." [1]

On one occasion, in 1825, Canning gave some private information to a newspaper.   A copy of his despatch to the Spanish Government of the 25th March 1825 got into the French and German Press in a garbled form.   Dr Stoddart of the *New Times* asked leave to compare the translation with the original text ' in order to correct the one by the other.' Canning permitted this, but the result was unexpected.   " The rogue begins by announcing that he has an authentic copy, etc. etc., and in effect tells the world that he has got it from my office.   This is scoundrelly—if it had been harmless, but it is mischievous into the bargain. . . .   The publication is annoying in a high degree, and would be offensive if it were intentional.   Pray be beforehand in assuring Damas and Villèle that it was not so . . . the most mortifying thing is the destruction of my system (hitherto persevered in and with tolerable success) of abstinence from communication with the newspaper writers . . . I am cured of this sort of liberality and have done with *hoc genus omne* for good and all." [2]

In a despatch to Russia in 1826 Canning quoted the *Courier* as ' having the reputation ' of being in the confidence of some Departments of the British Government.

" I think it right, therefore, to direct you to give to Count Nesselrode the most positive and unequivocal assurances that neither that nor any other newspaper is admitted to the confidence of the Foreign Office in London, nor is it possible for that office to be answerable for the speculations in which newspapers may think fit to indulge, respecting political events in any part of the World." [3]   The same denial was repeated by Lord Goderich in the House of Lords in May 1827,

---

[1] *Gr. MSS.* Canning to Granville, Oct. 7/22.
[2] Stap., *Corr.*, i. 328–9. Canning to Granville, Nov. 14/25. This is hardly an exception to the rule of refusing information.
[3] *F.O. Russia*, 181/69. Canning to Disbrowe, Sept. 24/26, No. 13.

on Canning's direct authority, and during his brief Premiership he rejected at least one opportunity of influencing the Press through the government.[1]

Some further light is thrown on government policy by a letter of Dudley's in January 1828, in response to Metternich's complaints about the British Press. " There was one newspaper, and one only, over which government exercises not indeed an absolute control but that sort of influence which is occasionally derived from giving to it a priority of information." The editor had been sent for and told that information would be refused in future unless his language was more ' becoming.' " We have no demi-official newspaper. The most friendly journals look more to the people than to the government. Sometimes, and to a certain degree, they accommodate their language to the wishes of those they profess to follow, but we by no means exercise over them such an influence as should render us answerable for their indiscretions." [2]

It will be noticed that Canning denied that any newspaper received information from the Foreign Office, but did not, and apparently for good reasons, deny it on behalf of ' other departments.' Though refusing information, Canning did influence at least one newspaper and two newspaper men in another way, by paying for information received. Goldsmith of the *British Monitor* received money during 1824 for forwarding French news. He was not modest, and proposed a scheme by which he should be head of a Passport Office. He added, " I should then give up my paper. In that case I shall not publish my memoirs." Canning rejected this polite blackmail in a very emphatic manner. Shortly afterwards he got Planta to prevent Goldsmith from attacking Metternich. Finally, Planta wrote to Canning, 6th December 1824, " What do you say to trying Goldsmith at Paris with £200 a Quarter? We give him almost as much here, and his

---

[1] Stap., *Corr.*, ii. 370. A. G. Stapleton to Jerdan, May 5/27.

[2] *V.S.A.*, England, *Varia*, 1827–8, private. Dudley to Sir H. Wellesley, Jan. 8/28 (apparently an intercepted letter). The paper he alludes to may be the *Courier*, but is probably the *Standard*, a newspaper started in May 1827, with which Wellington was connected, v. Fox Bourne, ii. 23–4. The evidence in Canning's Premiership, quoted in preceding note, suggests that not even one newspaper, in his time, was under government influence.

paper is a *discredit* to us rather than an advantage." ' Try
him,' minuted Canning.   So Goldsmith went off to Paris ' to
write to us anything he can pick up.' [1]   In reality, Goldsmith only succeeded Darby.   The latter was an agent who
had for nine years picked up private information at Paris and
communicated with French newspapers, but whose activities
became at last so well known that it was deemed better to
recall him at the beginning of 1823.[2]   He arrived in England
and was employed in a similar capacity at home, where he
obtained valuable information from Foreign Embassies.

One newspaper, the *Star*, which Marcellus and Esterházy
both pronounced to be ' Canning's organ,' offers some difficulties.   It began by criticising him on hearing of his probable
accession to office, as not having enough ' solidity.'   But the
magnificent speeches of April 1823 effected a conversion, and
from this time forward the *Star* was his enthusiastic supporter.
It seems difficult to suppose that someone closely connected
with Canning did not occasionally give it information.   On
the 28th April 1823 it made some unfavourable comparisons
between Lord Grey's attitude towards Spain in that year
and in 1807, which appear almost *verbatim* in Stapleton.   An
attack on Sir Robert Wilson (11th August) is almost in the
very spirit of Canningesque raillery.   It is at least curious
that an article on the resources and population of Spanish
America appeared on the 17th October 1823, the day that the
circular appointing consuls was actually issued, but *one day
before* it was communicated to the Press.[3]   Similarly, the
attack on the Monroe Doctrine on the 27th December 1823
is very much in the vein of Canning.   The mystery is a little
difficult to solve.   Perhaps the simplest explanation is the
best.   Canning liked dropping into the Lobby of the Commons
to hear the talk of Back Benchers, and he probably gave them
some information in return.   One of these must have transmitted this ' Lobby gossip ' to the *Star*, and Canning could
hardly have been unaware of the fact.[4]   Public information

[1] *F.O.*, 97/169. Goldsmith, *Secret Correspondence*, Feb. 14, 20, Dec.
6, 10/24.   *Gr. MSS.*   Planta to Granville, Dec. 20/24, private and secret.
[2] Vide *F.O.*, 97/168, which gives Darby's correspondence of 1822 from Paris.
[3] The *Times*, for instance, had no information till the 18th.
[4] Sturges Bourne, a devoted friend, is a likely man.   He had been
actually used by Canning in earlier days for communicating with the Press,
v. Stap., *G.C. & T.*, 116.

he gave to the whole Press, but the best reports of his speeches are in the *Star*. So also are the best expositions of his policy, though Canning took care that these should not be, in any way, authorised directly by himself.

With the Foreign Press Canning had some relations, and the indications, though few, are not faint. The newspapers of Germany, of Austria, and of most of Italy were controlled and gagged by Metternich, those of Russia by Alexander. Apart from these, the only papers that counted were those of the Netherlands, of France, and of America. Over the latter Canning exercised no control, though he studied them with great attention as he considered them a key to government policy in the United States.

In France the Press was subjected to alternating doses of intimidation, freedom, purchase, or corruption—the latter system being even extended to the Opposition Press.[1] But, throughout, some organs remained independent. The following extract from letters to Granville show Canning's methods in 1825.[2] " Pray send Granville half a dozen (or more) copies of the Brit[ish] Press—and tell him that if he has any means of insinuating it into French papers this is the Report from which I wish it to be taken " (4th April). " Put a notice in Galignani's paper " [the *Messenger*] (1st July). " Follow up the overtures of the *Constitutionnel*." We do not know what these overtures were, but in 1824 Sir Charles Stuart reported this paper as bought by the French Government for 18,000 francs followed up by 50,000 more.

In 1824 the British Commissioner in Mexico inserted an article in the *Sol* denouncing the intrigues of the Court of Versailles, and praising Canning's share in the Memorandum of the Polignac Conference.[3] In 1826 À Court got an article inserted in the *Lisbon Official Gazette*, explaining some indiscretions on the part of the Regent. These efforts, and there were similar ones on other occasions and in other countries, amounted to direct inspiration of certain Press-organs abroad,

[1] *F.O. France*, 146/57. Sir C. Stuart to Canning, Jan. 22/24.
[2] *Gr. MSS.* Canning to Planta, Apr. 4; Canning to Granville, Apr. 4, July 1/25. The *Constitutionnel* was at this time receiving secret communications from the Kings of Würtemberg and of the Netherlands, both Liberals. *V.S.A.*, Berichte aus Frankreich. Apponyi to Metternich, Mar. 9/26, enclosing a French police report.
[3] *Bag. MSS.* Canning to Bagot, June 4/27.

MS. IN CANNING'S WRITING.
CORRECTED PROOF OF A SPEECH DELIVERED AT LIVERPOOL
ON THE 15TH MARCH 1820 AT THE CANNING CLUB.

but they were approved by Canning. A more direct method was to see that accurate copies of state papers and speeches were inserted in the foreign Press, and this was done, and with marked effect, in the case of Canning's famous speech of the 12th December 1826.

It will be seen that, despite all his efforts, even Canning occasionally failed to withhold information from astute or unscrupulous journalists. It is certain that no Foreign Minister could withhold private or confidential information from Press-organs to-day. But Canning can claim to have been more scrupulous in the matter than his colleagues or than foreign diplomats.

2. Canning's Personal View of the Power and Use of the Press

Canning was not an enemy of the Press; he was a discriminating supporter of it. " I acknowledge its power," he said in 1816, " I submit to its judgment, but I will not be summoned to its bar!" This utterance seems to mean that, while he allowed it a sphere of power, he did not think it necessary to defend himself against any personal attack a paper might make upon him.

None the less, he fully recognised the great importance of the new power that had arisen. He compared the Fourth Estate to another new power which had arisen upon the earth, and urged the public to "take into account other powers extrinsic to the two Houses of Parliament, which are at work in the political world and require to be balanced and counter-poised in their operation.

" What should we think of that philosopher, who, in writing, at the present day, a treatise upon naval architecture and the theory of navigation, should omit wholly from his calculation that new and mighty power,—new, at least, in the application of its might,—which walks the water, like a giant rejoicing in his course;—stemming alike the tempest and the tide;—accelerating intercourse, shortening distances;—creating, as it were, unexpected neighbourhoods, and new combinations of social and commercial relation;—and giving to the fickleness of winds and faithlessness of waves the certainty and steadiness of a highway upon the land? Such a writer, though he might describe a ship correctly ; though he might show from what quarters the winds of heaven blow, would be surely an incurious and an idle spectator of the progress of nautical science, who did not see in the power of STEAM a corrective of all former calculations. So, in political science, he who, speculating on the British Constitution, should content himself with marking the distribution of acknowledged technical powers between the House of Lords, the House of Commons, and the Crown, and assigning to each their separate provinces,—to the Lords their legislative authority,—to the Crown its *veto* (how often used ?)—to the House of Commons its power of stopping supplies (how often, in fact, necessary to be resorted to ?)— and should think that he had thus described the British Constitution as it acts and as it is influenced in its action ; but should omit from his enumeration that mighty power of Public Opinion, embodied in a Free Press, which pervades, and checks, and, perhaps, in the last resort, nearly governs the whole ;—such a man would, surely, give but an imperfect view of the government of England as it is now, modifies, and would greatly underrate the counteracting influences against which that of the executive power has to contend." [1]

Canning recognised public opinion as the steam driving the government engine, and in the last resort he seems to have viewed public opinion as a more important influence than the Press itself, which it ultimately controlled. Thus it came about that he trusted to bring public opinion to his side first and to leave the Press to follow it. The *Courier*, for instance, was important if it represented England, worthless if it represented France. The *Times* could be defied, for if he won public opinion, it would be borne along with the stream. Some of his methods have already been indicated (pp. 303–4). His view seems to have been that the Press ought not habitually to receive private information, nor be encouraged to comment upon foreign affairs when undesirable. The Press was not like the sun, which could lighten every dark place : it had the more limited power of throwing a beam of light on one or other dark corner. Hence, at one time it was as inconvenient as at another it might be useful. When Canning considered the moment ripe he gave an open and

---

[1] Aug. 30/22. *Liverpool Speeches*, [1825], pp. *xiv–xv*.

frank exposition of policy in the Commons or on the platform, and made the most careful effort to see that accurate reports of his speeches reached the public. Every speech delivered was corrected for the Press, revised, and frequently almost rewritten with the most meticulous care, so that every word could be weighed and balanced. A revised and corrected report of a speech nearly always followed the jejune or malicious extracts which were given on the morning after delivery. But, whenever he considered the crisis delicate or the time inexpedient, no one was more careful to refuse all information. Some statesmen had been wont to transmit correct public information to the Press, and others to send to them private communications. Canning did not, as has been seen, entirely escape from some indirect connection with it. His peculiarity was that he eschewed this connection and preferred direct communication of documents to private communication of information. He used the Press to enlighten the public, but looked, as it were, beyond the Press to the people at large. He wished to make the Press the instrument of public opinion, not public opinion the instrument of the Press.

3. Secret *versus* Open Diplomacy

This policy of popular appeal quite confounded con-temporaries, and particularly the diplomats. It was novel, it was alarming, it was successful. Castlereagh had displayed a lofty contempt for public opinion : why did not Canning do the same ? He did not, in fact, believe that it was right or expedient to do so. His strength, as he wrote to Sir Henry Wellesley in 1823, lay in making foreigners believe that he said the same things in public as he did in private. When he broke loose from the Neo-Holy Alliance he had, indeed, no other resource than an appeal to the public. If he could not influence foreign States in conference he must influence them first by British public opinion and next by the infection which that influence spread to other countries. He was, in short, compelled to adopt the method of ‘ open diplomacy,’ and pleaded the Parliamentary system as an excuse for doing so. But, in reality, he was always looking beyond the walls of Parliament to the people outside.

This method was one which no foreigner and few British Ultra-Tories understood or approved. The *Times*, for instance, commented on Canning's speeches to Liverpool in August 1823, suggesting that such attempts to win favour with the public were unworthy of a minister. George IV. complained to Wellington of Canning's attendance at the Mansion-House dinner in 1824, because this attitude separated him from his colleagues; " the King will never consent that his government shall be degraded by such attempts to acquire popularity " (1st May 1824). And the Duke agreed with his master.

Foreign diplomats were unanimous in their condemnation. " He tries," wrote Chateaubriand, " to compel himself to find a support which his predecessor disdained." [1] Metternich wrote, " He flatters revolution and is a Radical " (20th March 1823). " The fatal divergence of principles which is anew displayed in all its deformity . . . Mr Canning has no other aim than to sacrifice to the opinion of the day, to flatter the pride of some, the blind cupidity of others, and to impose silence on the factions. It is not far-sighted for the future, but it seems that the present moment is constantly the only one which this Minister consults " (30th January 1824). " His strength consists only in a certain popularity " (30th May 1824). " The basis of the erroneous policy of Mr Canning is to be found in the search for a personal popularity which is unattainable " [2] (11th December 1824).

Metternich's views on the subject were unquestionably sincere, for on the accessions of two genuine Legitimists— Charles X. of France and Czar Nicholas of Russia—he rejoiced at their autocratic tendencies but deplored their attempts to win popularity. " For a number of years I have heard so much of public opinion that it is the duty of men entrusted with the first interests of society, to examine the worth of this phrase. I doubt very much if there is anyone, placed above the mists of illusion, who knows what real public opinion is, and what is represented under the colours attached to it by

---

[1] *A.A.E.*, 617, to Polignac, Oct. 11/23.
[2] *V.S.A.*, Weisungen nach England. Metternich to Esterházy, Mar. 20/23; May 30, Dec. 14/24. England, *Varia*, 1824, Jan. 30/24; *ibid* to *ibid*.

parties, and often by men [*e.g.* Canning] who should know it to be their duty not to falsify it." [1]

In Metternich's view, a search for popularity was a risky experiment. Public opinion was unstable, dangerous, and could not be foreseen or controlled. But Canning knew very well whither he was going, and saw that he could ' ride the whirlwind.' He had shown often enough that he could brave public opinion, now he was to show that he could lead it. He was determined to show the public what British policy really was, and to drag it from the Chanceries into daylight. Thus in April 1823 he published the recent correspondence relating to Verona, which proved that we had then broken off from the Continent, in spite of the heated protests of Wellington and Metternich. He published also the letters between him and Chateaubriand, which revealed his immediate protest against the doctrine that kings alone could grant popular institutions. But he did more than this. He published extracts from the famous state papers which showed that, even as far back as the 5th May 1820, Castlereagh himself had held a similar doctrine, though he had not then revealed it to the world. [2] It was not the divisions in the European concert that distressed the diplomats ; it was the revelation of them in public documents to the world. Canning knew that papers, if so published, would affect public opinion in his favour and against the Neo-Holy Alliance. He knew, too, that if he did publish them, he could proclaim that he was simply carrying out the aims of Castlereagh. That was true, but his methods of pursuing that policy were different.

The attitude was one which astonished old-fashioned diplomats. When they protested, he replied : " I am only saying in public what we long ago said in private." When they said these views should not be public he replied that publication had been rendered necessary by the attempts of Chateaubriand to quote isolated passages from these documents, and that step rendered full publication necessary. He could not discuss the matter in Parliament with mutilated documents as his text. England had a Parliament, and he

---

[1] *V.S.A.*, Weisungen nach England, Bd. 227. Metternich to Esterházy, Feb. 10/25, No. 2.
[2] The public knew nothing till the famous circular of Jan. 21/21.

could not resist its demands and inquiries. He was too diplomatic to add that he did not want to. For neither Alexander nor Metternich hesitated to reveal documents secretly to the Press when it suited their purpose. Canning preferred to anticipate secret leakages by open publicity.

Thus he outraged old etiquette in July 1823, when he published correspondence showing that he had refused to recognise the Spanish Regency (installed under French protection) in Spain. Parliament had a right to know, he said, in reply to protests. The famous Polignac Memorandum was another case. In deference to protests of the Allies he deferred publication from November 1823 till March 1824; but he explained to them that it had become necessary because President Monroe had already published his Message, and that England's resolution as to attempts on Spanish America ' by force or menace ' must be made known. On the 4th March 1824 Canning published the Polignac papers, together with a letter to the Spanish Government declining to enter a congress on Spanish affairs, of so late a date as the 30th January 1824. Wellington indignantly protested against this action to Liverpool. " The moment the government lay papers before Parliament on any political question the decision is no longer practically in their hands. Whatever may be the consequence in point of form, the decision of the government in point of fact cannot be independent." He complained further that foreigners " aware of the caution and reserve with which we are in the habit of communicating papers of this description to Parliament, will see in this act a desire to throw it out of our own hands . . . that it is our wish to see it " [the recognition of Spanish America] " settled one way." [1] This statement is entirely true. Canning had got the assent of the Cabinet to his declaration that England would fight if a European Power (other than Spain) attacked the Spanish Colonies, and their refusal to enter a European congress on the question. Decisions communicated in secret could be modified, those announced in public could not. That was just what Canning wanted. Publication served the double purposes of tying the hands of the Cabinet and of impressing foreigners. Here we see the new method at work.

---

[1] *W.N.D.*, ii. 228–9, to Liverpool, Mar. 5/24.

Revelations had formerly been extracted ; now they were calculated, and made at the moment Parliament was sitting or just before it met, and not in the safe solitude of a parliamentary vacation. As soon as a policy was laid down, public interest was aroused to endorse it. Some despatches published in April 1823 were not ten days old, some of those published in March 1824 were barely a month old. His method is revealed well enough in a private letter about the results of the recognition of Spanish America. He says he hopes it will not disturb the ' good understanding ' with Russia. " But if it should be so (and we must be prepared for everything in this mortal world) *there are nice papers for Parliament* whenever an account of our transactions with the [Neo-]Holy Alliance shall come to be rendered." [1] This shows precisely the difference between Canning and Wellington. The Duke regarded papers as dangerous explosives, never, except when inevitable, to be exposed to the light or the flame ; Canning saw that they were thunderbolts to be launched against his enemies at convenient moments.

It would be a mistake to think that Canning was the slave, though he was the enlightener and director, of public opinion. He jestingly alluded to himself ' as a Liberal, yes a Radical, Minister,' but he was not a Democrat in any sense that we now understand. He had the Whig idea of conciliating public opinion ; but where he thought it necessary, he was prepared to resist it. Thus over the South American question he made a skilful use, with his colleagues, of the combined pressure of commercial interest and popular appeal to obtain recognition. But over Greece he resisted the popular feeling for some years. Ultimately he gave way to it, but only under circumstances which he deemed to be greatly to England's advantage. The public were kept in the dark, or introduced to the light, just as it suited his purpose.

In certain directions, small as well as great, Canning intervened to secure redress of grievances before the public got to know of them. The threat of publicity was, of course, always behind such intervention, and it was usually successful. He failed, indeed, on one occasion, to get Metternich to release

---

[1] *F.O.*, 352/10. *Strat. MSS.* George Canning to Stratford Canning, Feb. 23/25, private.

a young Italian nobleman imprisoned for a trivial offence, but his allusions to British public opinion seem to have caused Metternich to pardon some of the Milan conspirators. In 1825 Canning remonstrated vigorously with Spain for arresting a Piedmontese emigrant, who had resided in Spain since 1821, and forcibly deporting him to England, where he arrived with a wife and three children in a state of complete destitution. " Lose no time in remonstrance with the Spanish Government upon such an undue exercise of authority. You will inform them that, if they take upon themselves to send individuals to this country, not subjects of Great Britain, His Majesty's Government will have no other resources than to send back again to Spain, not only such individual but others [*i.e.* Spanish exiles] whose presence there may be much more inconvenient to the Spanish Government." [1] The threat was effectual. In another case he inquired if it was true that they had burnt a man alive for heresy at Valencia. " Such a spirit, revived at the present moment, might have justly no small influence on the relations of foreign governments with Spain." In 1823 he went to great lengths in Portugal to obtain the release of a British sailor arrested for carrying letters from Portuguese exiles in London. In 1825 he discovered that the English inhabitants of Malaga were buried standing up on the seashore, and that the Catholic public polluted these poor tombs. He at once sent a strong remonstrance against such ' degrading and indecent acts,'. and the Spanish Government took measures to repress them.

On the 15th October 1822 Canning sent a pamphlet to Wellington which described the sufferings and persecutions of the Vaudois in Piedmont. The Duke was to inquire into the " grievances inflicted on this harmless and meritorious people," and on finding their truth to make representations. " Your Grace is to express the interest His Majesty takes in the welfare of this Protestant community and to endeavour to obtain assurance for their good treatment in the future, for toleration for their worship and respect for their privileges, as the British Government have in former times thought it their right and their duty to require." These last words show that Canning was thinking of that glorious time when the

---

[1] *F.O. Spain*, 185/106. To F. Lamb, Sept. 24, Oct. 5/26.

strong arm of Cromwell was uplifted in righteous indignation to stay the persecution of these same poor Vaudois, and when his famous Latin secretary penned the noblest of his sonnets against the ' bloody Piedmontese and the triple tyrant ' who had slaughtered the saints of God.

All the efforts, thus indicated, were concealed from the public, but the power that lay behind the remonstrances was the fear that they might not be. The enthusiasm that was aroused, when such efforts became known, proves this fact clearly enough. Thus he took up vigorously the cause of Bowring who was imprisoned, and of Sir Robert Wilson's daughters who were maltreated, in France ; and of General Devereux who was arrested in Italy. Feeling in Parliament was enhanced when it became known that in each case he had sent off a despatch of remonstrance ' within less than an hour ' of hearing the first news of the outrage. On the question of the Slave Trade his enthusiasm showed itself with a flame almost as fierce as that of total emancipators, such as his friend Wilberforce himself. ' The Slave Trade requires no comments,' wrote Castlereagh in his instructions to Verona. Canning felt that comments were urgently needed, and wrote a lengthy despatch to Wellington immediately to press on the congress the question of ' that scandal of the civilised world.' The restrictions had not been all for good, as " the dread of detection suggests expedients of concealment productive of the most dreadful sufferings to a cargo of which it hardly ever seems to occur to its remorseless owners that it consists of sentient beings. . . . The probable profits are notoriously calculated only on the survivors, and the mortality is accordingly frightful to a degree unknown, since the attention of mankind was first called to the horror of this traffic." [1] And he took care that this despatch should be published. All the difference between Castlereagh and Canning is here expressed. The one worked as hard as the other, but the second brought his efforts to the direct knowledge of the public. The history of his attempt to ameliorate the condition of slaves in the Colonies, and to abolish the Slave Trade throughout the world, is one of the noblest passages of his life. He negotiated several treaties and he wrote more than a

[1] My *Life of Canning*, [1905], pp. 155-6.

thousand despatches over it ; most of them saw the light in his own day.[1] The effect of this policy was most striking on the vast mass of the people and is one of the explanations of their confidence in him.

4. GENERAL ATTITUDE TOWARDS PRESS AND PUBLIC OPINION

Thus it will be seen that Canning represented a new influence and a new power—the power of propelling and forcing public opinion along courses and in directions which no Foreign Minister had yet essayed. As the years rolled by and as the outlines of the policy became clear Canning met with a reward such as no Foreign Minister, not even Palmerston, ever obtained. Even at the beginning of 1824 the *Morning Herald* could write : " It strikes us that no Minister, since the Revolution, excepting only the great Lord Chatham, has acquired the same national popularity which is at this moment possessed by Mr Canning." [2] The people recognised that he really did believe in popular influence, that he was proud of England's Parliament, and did not ' apologise for England's institutions.' They were, indeed, his glory and the instruments of his power. Monarch and people, Parliament and Ultras, were swept away in the tide of his popularity. Besides the *Star* and *Quarterly* he never had any real supporters, if we except the short-lived *Representative*.[3] Yet in 1827 he was able to win the almost unanimous support of the Press. In these critical days he made an astoundingly frank declaration to Princess Lieven. " He had," he said, " been the first to inaugurate the power of the Press by letting it influence affairs. He governed it." [4] If he did so it was only because he also governed public opinion.

The result of his power over public opinion extended beyond

[1] He reprinted the despatches on the Slave Trade from other diplomatic correspondence by an order in 1823, and took care to publish most of them : *e.g.* in 1825–6 he published 262 ; in 1826–7, 255.

[2] *Morning Herald*, Jan. 28/24. Yet this paper had been, and perhaps still was, under ' Ultra ' influence.

[3] Started by John Murray, editor of the *Quarterly*. It lived for six months, ending July 1826. H. R. Fox Bourne, *English Newspapers*, ii. 22. It cost the promoters £15,000, and enabled Disraeli to exercise his eccentric originality, this time in finance and to everybody's disadvantage.

[4] *Lie. MSS.*

his own country. It is enough to recall Metternich's
characteristic dictum (*v.* p. 88), that a desire " to acquire a
sort of popularity " was " a pretension that is misplaced in
a statesman." Against this we may put the words of Joan
Canning.[1] " While *he* was at the helm there was not one
of the European governments who dared to provoke the
vengeance of England, because they well knew that a war
with England would be a measure *too unpopular* to hazard.
Thus Mr Canning was enabled to hold language and to carry
measures in defiance of the principles and prejudices of some
[*i.e.* the Tories], and contrary to the orders of the Governments
of the Great Continental Powers. By these means he
obtained over these governments an influence which he
employed not only to promote the interests of England, but
the general prosperity of the world."

Within his own country his aims were less pure, though
his influence was no less. For, though he used his power
over opinion abroad for English ends, he used his power at
home for his own. His methods, indeed, came as a surprise
to contemporaries. The *Times* commented on his tour in
Lancashire (30th May 1823), to the effect that he was
' flattering ' the commercial body outside London, and
boasting that he sought and sometimes took their advice.
These methods were, doubtless, " a masterpiece in the art of
maintaining and improving his political system *out of doors*."
Clearly the *Times* regarded such proceedings as unusual and
to be deprecated.

" Mr Canning is, so far as our recollection serves," wrote
the editor of his *Liverpool Speeches* in 1825, " the first British
minister who has valued himself upon maintaining a constant intellectual intercourse with his constituents, and has
seized every opportunity of personally inculcating . . . those
political opinions . . . which he had invariably advocated
in the Commons." He published state papers at critical
moments, instead of long after the event. He made speeches
on foreign policy not only in Parliament, but he introduced
the striking innovation of addressing the public direct outside
the walls of the Commons. Here is the real line dividing him

---

[1] Lady Canning's anonymous pamphlet, 1830, *An Authentic Account of
Mr Canning's Policy*, etc. Italics my own.

from Castlereagh. At the end of his life that unfortunate minister was thoroughly unpopular, unable alike to bend before, or to ride upon, the storm. At the request of his friends, said the papers, he carried pistols and kept two fierce mastiffs in his house to protect himself. He could not appear in public to give his vote at the hustings without being jeered at and hissed. As his coffin sank from view in the Abbey, a crowd of ruffians raised a yell of brutal exultation. How different were the closing years of Canning! When he visited Brighton or Chiswick or the Lakes the Press chronicled his every movement with solicitude; his utter-ances at Harwich, at Plymouth, at the Mansion-House, or at Liverpool, never failed to win tumultuous applause, and were events quite as important in themselves as a debate and division in the Commons. His accession to the Premier-ship caused more popular sensation than any event since Waterloo. During his last illness a hundred thousand bulletins were circulated daily throughout London. His funeral, despite its private character, was attended in a storm of rain by an innumerable and silent multitude. That was the result of a popular foreign policy.[1] Whatever judgment may be passed on the two policies or on the two men, no one can question the profound revolution that Canning had effected in public opinion.

---

[1] Yet he resisted certain obviously popular demands for the protection of foreign revolutionaries (Speech on Alien Bill, May 22/18. *Hans. Deb.*, xxxviii. 907. " What man, who loved the glory of his country, or valued the liberty of the world, would consent even to the chance that it might become the unsuspecting prey of secret and foreign enemies ? ").

PART VI

GREECE, THE NEO-HOLY ALLIANCE, AND
THE DIPLOMATIC REVOLUTION

CHAPTER XIV
THE AWAKENING OF GREECE (1821–4)

CHAPTER XV
THE GREEK PROTOCOL OF THE 4TH APRIL 1826;
AND THE DIPLOMATIC REVOLUTION

CHAPTER XIV

THE AWAKENING OF GREECE (1821–4)

1. INTEREST OF THE GREAT POWERS IN GREECE

THE real crisis of foreign policy for Europe proved to be in Greece, and Canning committed England eventually to a policy of far-reaching and even revolutionary character. For in the last two years of Canning's life this fire, which had smouldered fiercely for five years, threatened to become a prairie-fire sweeping over the Continent. The uprising of the sturdy Serb peasants against the Turks, and their achievement of practical independence between 1807 and 1817, had barely rippled the diplomatic waters. Yet within twelve months of the similar Greek revolt in 1821 one Great Power came to the brink of war with Turkey, and the clouds gathered ever more darkly over Europe for seven years, till they burst at last in liberating thunder at Navarino. To Europe the Serbian revolt seemed merely local and Balkanic, the Greek distracted her for eight years, split asunder the Neo-Holy Alliance, brought Russia to the gates of Constantinople, and finally lopped a limb off the Turkish Empire.

On the difference between the two revolts sentiment was at one with diplomacy. Only Goethe knew that the Serbs had created poems not greatly inferior to that of Homer, and that there were rude peasants among them whose exploits surpassed those of the heroes of the *Iliad*. But the European Liberals, to whom the Serbs were unlettered barbarians, thrilled to the memory of Greece and compared the exploits of their savage guerrillas to those of Leonidas and Epaminondas. Some went to serve under Odysseus of Ithaca or Kolokotrones ; others despatched money to the more pacific, but no less enterprising, brigands who directed the finances of Greece. Frederic

North went to Corfu to found a university, to wear a purple robe, and to compare himself to Plato; Colonel Stanhope edited a paper which he forgot that the majority of Greeks could not read; the young Gladstone appeared at an Eton Montem in the petticoats of a Greek mountaineer. But the meetings of enthusiasts in Paris, in London, in Switzerland, or in the United States—even the support of men like Erskine or Chateaubriand or Byron—did not affect the diplomats at once. Enthusiasm of that type takes time to develop before govern-ments are impressed. It was not for that reason that the Chanceries were ruffled in 1820, and most deeply agitated in 1821. The revolt of Serbia affected neither the trade interests nor the sea-borne commerce of any State. That of Greece touched at least four. Austrian ships carried most of the Turkish commerce, the Russians carried their own and much that was Greek, the British impartially carried both, and were exposed alike to the fierce corsairs of Greece and to the no less fierce admirals of Turkey. The vital interests of the Ionian Isles were touched, for the British Governor ('King Tom of Corfu') had to restrain the eagerness of the in-habitants, and to be constantly on the watch to repel raiders or disturbers of the peace. Austria, timid as ever, was not desirous to interfere; her interest, like that of Walpole, was not to stir the sleeping dog; but she wished to secure immunity for her trade, and, above all, to prevent Russia from annexing fresh territory to her already enormous Empire. The ambition of Russia was active and imperialistic, and contemplated ultimately the end of European Turkey and the shifting of her capital to the Bosphorus. That was her age-long dream and purpose, however Alexander himself might hesitate to avow or attempt to resist it. The vital interest of Great Britain was touched by this design, which a Russian war with Turkey might achieve. Her interest was not only commercial, but naval in the strategic sense. In the Black Sea lay the Russian Navy, formidable in itself, dangerous if joined to that of any maritime power in the Mediterranean other than England. For she would have a secure base once she could operate from the Dardanelles. Constantinople, therefore, was the Turkish sentry who barred the back door to the Black Sea and the front gate to the Mediterranean.

It was England's interest to keep that sentry both strong and armed. Pitt had taken this view in old days, Canning had held it strongly during his first Ministry, Castlereagh had defeated Russia's designs on the Ionian Isles, and rejected her projects for an international navy which would have diminished that of Great Britain. Wellington and the majority of the Cabinet remained strongly pro-Turkish through the whole of this period. Canning agreed with their views for some years. He only changed them on becoming convinced that the persistent attempt to repress the Greeks was actually producing a danger greater than the recognition of their qualified independence. And the change in his view brought with it a revolution in the British Cabinet, in Turkey, and in Europe.

2. FIRST RESULTS OF THE RISING; ATTITUDE OF RUSSIA AND TURKEY

In 1821 a revolt against the Turks broke out in the area now called Rumania and then termed the Principalities (Moldavia and Wallachia), under the lead of Demetrius Ypsilanti, and aided unofficially by Russian influences and by Russian gold. Quickly suppressed to the north of the Danube, it disappeared, like an amphibian, to revive elsewhere. The revolt of a Turkish pasha in Albania, the veteran Ali, stirred up Greeks to imitate his example. Suliotes sprang as of old to arms, the Greeks of the Morea rose and massacred 6000 of the Turkish inhabitants. War ensued—to the death, terrible, internecine, relentless. Kolokotrones stormed Tripolizza and rode his horse over corpses till he reached the centre of the town, 'without once touching the ground.' Turks impaled Greeks in the historic pass of Thermopylæ; Greeks set a line of crucified victims on the roads along which a Turkish army advanced. Not to be outdone in the policy of 'frightfulness,' the Sultan nailed hundreds of pairs of human ears to his Seraglio-gate, and hung the Patriarch 'as high as Haman' in his robes above it. Finally, in the harbour of Chios the Turks, in the full view of neutral observers, fired on and massacred thousands of men, women, and helpless children. Even Castlereagh, no agitator, raised his voice then and declared no 'human offences justify such actions.'

He did not want to encourage the Greeks to resist,[1] but the Turkish massacres, and the popular resentment which they evoked, told even on his cold serenity.

Popular sentiment stirred in England; in Russia it burst into flame. The Russian officers, though often liberals and free-thinkers, thirsted for war; their men and the masses were stirred by the tales of the spitting on the Cross, of the desecration of churches, and of how the Patriarch's body was defiled and cast into the Bosphorus, there to be rescued by a miracle and decently buried. For Russian merchants on the Black Sea there was loss, interruption, delay, damage. At Constantinople the Russian colony and Ambassador (Stroganov) could not go out in the streets without seeing signs of the persecution of their co-religionists, without beholding the insults to their Church, and without endangering their own personal safety. Stroganov raved and addressed the Porte in language of 'no ordinary vehemence,' and finally handed in his papers and left for St Petersburg. Thus the breach between Russia and Turkey was complete. Alexander himself was much moved, susceptible as ever, despite his arbitrary instincts, to popular feeling in Russia, and to the religious appeal of the persecution of fellow-Christians; yet impressed by hatred of rebels and love for the moral union of sovereigns, he was torn this way and that by all sorts of different passions.

The Turkish attitude throughout was simple and characteristic. The combination of Christian powers under the banner of the Neo-Holy Alliance excited their deep suspicions. Russia was their age-long enemy and must therefore have instigated the revolt. The first outbreak had come from Russian influence, and it was widely believed by the Turks that Alexander himself was a member of the Greek Society of Conspirators, the *Hetairia Philike*. Ypsilanti, who first raised the standard of revolt, had been a Russian officer; Capodistrias, a Greek born and an ardent Phil-Hellene, was Alexander's chief diplomatic adviser. No denials convinced the Turks that Russia was not the stimulator of conspiracies and the friend of rebels.[2] So pressure, whether collective

---

[1] *Vide* Webster, p. 379 and n.

[2] According to Gordon, Metternich held the view that the Greek Revolution was 'entirely the work of Russian agents.' *F.O. Austria*, 120/55. Gordon to Canning, Jan. 23/23.

by the Powers, or individual by Russia, was equally to be opposed. The one thing the Turks never would, or could, admit was that their own rayahs, these inferior beings the Christians, had the right to rebel, or that any government or sovereign had the right to sympathise with them or to support them. Mahmud, the only great personality among Sultans since Suleyman, recognised, however, that war with a great Power might be dangerous. He was in the midst of reorganisation and wished to exterminate his own rebellious janizaries, as well as the Greeks. So his policy was to avert war by all those arts of dilatoriness, by those infinite subtleties of negotiation in which Orientals excel. When absolutely inevitable he would make illusory concessions, which he would recall as soon as he was strong enough to do so. And, then, he always hoped that his arms would subdue the Greeks before Europe could interfere.

3. AUSTRO-BRITISH GOOD OFFICES (1821-2)

With Russia so powerful, Turkey so crafty, and the Greeks so successful, Castlereagh and Metternich might well be alarmed. Neither of them was in a position to make war or even to threaten any other Power desirous of making it. There was, however, one string on which they could play. Alexander, despite every other emotion, had no love for rebels even against the Turk. War meant the dissolution of his life-dream, of the reign of peace and Christian brotherhood which he had proclaimed in the Holy Alliance and had sought to develop in the Neo-Holy Decrees of Troppau and Laibach. He could not dissipate that noble vision without heart-searchings. He could not go to war without the approval of a congress, and that approval he hoped that England and Austria would give. Metternich and Castlereagh knew their man, appealed to his vanity and allowed him to believe that they shared his professions.

At the Hanover interview in November 1821, Metternich and Castlereagh coolly concerted their plan. Castlereagh wrote off a long despatch to St Petersburg, full of the most windy sentiments of trust in the moral union of European Powers.[1] Metternich followed it up with all sorts of instructions

[1] *Vide* Webster, pp. 360-1.

on the same lines, which Lebzeltern, his able representative at St Petersburg, artfully insinuated into the ears of
Alexander. Finally Castlereagh, not quite consistently with
his late attitude, spoke of the Greeks as the counterparts of
the Carbonari in Italy, of the Constitutionalists in Spain, and
of the Radicals in England, and let it be known that he would
not oppose a congress on the East. Congresses were things
which Alexander loved, partly because they exhibited a moral
union of sovereigns, partly because he thought that he would
tower against a background of lesser sovereigns, as Napoleon
had towered above the kings and princes at Erfurt. The lure
was the more dazzling because it had looked, at the beginning
of 1821, as if Castlereagh had abjured congresses for ever,
and at the end of it he was actually suggesting one. Alexander swallowed the bait, stayed his hand, suppressed the
murmurs of his generals, of his priests, and of his peoples,
and looked forward to renewed harmony and glory at
Verona. Austria and England were, in effect, to mediate
between Russia and Turkey, and for this purpose a dis-
guised conference met at Vienna early in 1822 to smooth
the way for the larger assembly at Verona at the end of
the year.

The Congress of Verona was, however, a disappointment to
the Czar in all ways. It was Spain, not Greece, which loomed
largest on the canvas, and the Duke of Wellington was by no
means conciliatory. Alexander strongly encouraged the idea
of intervening with an armed Neo-Holy Alliance force in Spain,
in the hope that this might set the precedent for his own
intervention in Greece. But Metternich's attitude in supporting intervention in Spain was unsatisfactory, and over Greece
he was very disappointing. Finally, Russia formulated
certain demands and handed over the Greek negotiation to
the British Ambassador at Constantinople, the brilliant
Strangford. He had already done much service in the thank-
less rôle of a mediator between Muscovite and Mussulman.
He was not indeed wholly satisfactory. Wellington had
differences with him at Verona ; Gordon reproved him in
private letters from Vienna for suspicions of Canning as ' a
revolutionary ' ; Wellesley thought Strangford had an undue
fear that Metternich wished to take the negotiation out of his

hand ; Canning thought he had reason to deplore Strangford's undue intimacy with the Neo-Holy Alliance.[1] But he was, none the less, very able and adroit.

4. STRANGFORD'S NEGOTIATION WITH TURKEY; THE 'THREE POINTS' (DECEMBER 1822–SEPTEMBER 1823)

The year 1823 marked three important developments in the Greek question, due to three Englishmen : Strangford, Canning, and Byron. The first removed most of the difficulties remaining between Turkey and Russia ; the second recognised the Greeks as belligerents ; the third by going to Greece as a volunteer enlisted the popular sympathy on their side. The first action tended to make it difficult for Russia to interfere, the second and third made it easier for the Greeks to resist, and went some way towards strengthening their position.

To take the work of Strangford first. It was admitted that, under the Treaty of Kutchuk Kainardji (1774) Russia had a right by treaty to interfere in matters of religion. Metternich himself admitted this,[2] and Canning qualified it by saying that Russia had a special right of friendly advice on this subject in peace time, but he doubted whether this " right extended to interference on behalf of subjects of the Party who had thrown off their allegiance." [3]

Russia had already presented an ultimatum known as the ' Four Points.' These need not be discussed here, for they were in substance conceded before the congress met at Vienna.[4] But Russia was still dissatisfied and formulated new demands, which we may call the ' Three Points,' which Strangford was instructed to secure. There were (1) guarantees by the Turks to the Greeks of future good government or ' a series of facts ' showing that these guarantees were unnecessary ; (2) reduction of Turkish armed forces in the Principalities (Moldavia and Wallachia) to a pre-1821 standard ; (3) removal of the

[1] Vide *F.O. Austria*, 120/59. Canning to Wellesley, Sept. 15/23, No. 11. Canning instructed Wellesley to stop Strangford from accepting Metternich's ' extraordinary proposition ' to visit the Russian and Austrian Emperors at Czernovitz, when he (Wellesley) was not asked. Wellesley stated that he had not been invited.

[2] *F.O. Austria*, 120/67. Wellesley to Canning, Dec. 28/24.

[3] *F.O. Russia*, 181/58. Canning to Bagot, Jan. 15/24, No. 1.

[4] *Vide* Webster, pp. 378–82, 387–400.

obstacles placed by Turkey in the way of Russian Black Sea commerce. By the 22nd September 1823 Strangford had obtained satisfaction on the third point. He considered that satisfaction on the first had been fairly given and that the second would not be long in being conceded. On the 4th October 1823 Canning praised him for ' his extraordinary address and ability.'

5. CANNING RECOGNISES THE GREEKS AS BELLIGERENTS (MARCH 1823)

Meanwhile Canning himself had taken an important step which tended to separate British policy from that of the Neo-Holy Alliance. Pursuing his usual line of deference to British commercial interests, he recognised the Greeks as belligerents in March 1823. Such a step was, however, offensive both to Russia and to Austria. The former had at the moment (March 1823) no commercial access to the Ægean, the latter's commercial marine was employed in serving the Turkish fleet. Neither recognised that England's commerce was at the mercy of both Turks and Greeks. The measure was not new and not revolutionary, for it had been clearly contemplated by Castlereagh in his instructions for Verona as possibly imminent. The fact that Canning took it, however, awakened violent protests from Metternich, who talked of the measure as a dangerous acknowledgment of revolution and as a departure from the principles of Castlereagh. Canning replied by a reasoned statement. " Belligerency was not so much a principle as a fact." The Turks could not protect British commerce, and so we must treat the Greeks either as pirates or as belligerents. As they had acquired ' a certain degree of force and stability ' the latter course was obviously preferable. Metternich had violently protested in the name of Legitimacy for the benefit of Alexander, but he had more material reason for his wrath. Much Turkish commerce was borne in Austrian ships, and the Greeks would now be in a better position to injure it. Canning's view was that, as British commerce was borne by both Greeks and Turks, he was bound to treat each party with the same neutrality.

The decision was, in the main, a practical one, but he was

probably also influenced by the growth of popular sentiment. Phil-Hellenic meetings had been held both in London and Paris, and at the latter centre the Duc d'Orléans was discussed as a candidate for the throne of Greece. Volunteers and money came from both France and England, subscriptions were raised and meetings held by enthusiasts, loans were discussed by business men, who proved even more quixotic than the sentimentalists.   In reply to all remonstrances from the Neo-Holy Alliance that he had not suppressed these demonstrations in England, Canning replied, with irritating conservatism, that the same manifestations had been made in favour of Corsica in 1768 and of Poland in 1792, and that the British Government had not then intervened.[1] He did, however, go so far as to strike off the active list all military or naval officers who enlisted on the side of Greece.[2] It was, however, unfortunate for Canning that his protestations of the perfect neutrality of the British Government were made difficult by the action of the one private man then living, who could make his voice heard in every corner of the world.

6. Byron Intervenes (1823–4)

" Fling him from you as unworthy of England . . . and he will go to die for Greece, and will have for country all Humanity."—Castelar.

The adventure of Byron in Greece was the last and most glorious phase in the pilgrimage of Childe Harold. Towards the end of 1823 he raised his head from his sordid seclusion at Venice, left La Guiccioli to weep and to become the mistress of Henry Edward Fox, and embarked with a crew of shady and reckless adventurers for Greece. The entourage was not impressive, but the gesture was. Its effect was electric. Byron was received with the honours of a king, a position he might have attained had he lived. He was given a body-guard of cut-throats from Suli, he was welcomed with the wildest enthusiasm. The Greek Loan was subscribed in London, the newspapers of the Continent spoke of nothing but Greece. From his retreat at Corfu and at

---

[1] *F.O. Turkey,* 78/113.   Canning to Strangford, July 12/23.
[2] He did not prevent officers leaving England to serve as volunteers, which fact Metternich regarded as a breach of neutrality.

fever-haunted Missolonghi he laboured strenuously, and, on the whole, wisely, in a cause in which he hardly believed but would not desert, and on behalf of men whom he could not trust, but whom he would not disavow. Harassed by intriguers, haunted by delusions, worried and torn on all sides, his strength began to fail him. He read, with delight, a warm letter from Goethe. He wrote the noblest and tersest of his poems upon Greece, and then lay down on the bed from which he never rose. At the last moment letters came to him from England to say that the cause was progressing, that the loan was successful, and that Canning was more favourable to Greece. But to Byron, dying as living, came always fame but no true comfort. His senses failed before his life ebbed, and the glad tidings were never made known to him.

On the morning of the 14th April Hobhouse was roused in London by a knocking at his door. In a few hours the whole city heard the tremendous message, ' Byron is dead.' His corpse was carried to England amid a demonstration of sorrow such as Europe had seldom witnessed. All men felt that a spirit had passed from the earth—almost Napoleonic in its power, the spirit of rebellion and defiance incarnate.

Byron had caught up Greece in the whirlwind of his fame and inseparably associated her with his memory. The poet, who had died in Greece, did more to bring her before the eyes of Europe than all the dead singers of her own land. The Greeks themselves, who have never wanted in imaginative sympathy, were nerved by that inspiration to die at Missolonghi, as he had died, with a heroism that echoed through the world. Their sympathisers in all lands drew inspiration from the same mighty source. The bed on which he died, the sword which he bore but never used, the wreath which lay on his coffin, are still objects of sacred veneration, and his statue has been erected near the Parthenon, as though to enrol him among the heroes or demigods of Greece.[1] The waves that Byron set in motion never ebbed again, and he did more service to Greece by his death than he could have done by his life. And

---

[1] Mr Harold Nicolson thinks that the bed preserved at Athens is *not* the one on which he died. When Constantine ambushed British sailors and marines from the shadow of the Parthenon in Dec. 1916, a Greek, who seems to have had an eye for effect, bandaged the eyes of Byron's statue, that he might not look on the slaughter of his countrymen!

those who may now think otherwise, do not know what Byron meant to his own age, and still means to-day, to Greece.

7. ALEXANDER PROPOSES A SETTLEMENT AND DEMANDS A CONGRESS (JANUARY 1824)

Canning had known Byron well; he was the only statesman whom the poet admired. Yet the message borne to Byron's unconscious and dying ear that Canning was more favourable is not perhaps a true account of his attitude at the moment. Nor do we know anything of his thoughts on the death of the man who had as large a share as he in giving freedom to Greece.[1] At the moment of Byron's death her freedom was indeed threatened as much by Russia as by Turkey, and Canning had to guard against both dangers.

Though no one had a better knowledge of Greek literature and thought, and though he had written a youthful poem on the misery of Greece under Turkish tyranny, and expressing the hope of their freedom, Canning had no high opinion of the modern Greek. " There is no denying they " (the Greeks), wrote he, " are a most rascally set." And again, the war had been marked, on both sides, ' with the most disgusting barbarities.' Anyhow, England would ' not dream of incurring ' war for the sake of protecting ' Epaminondas and St Paul.' The whole secret of Canning's policy until the end of 1825 is that he entirely disclaimed the use of force for England, and had neither the desire nor the intention of intervening if it could be avoided. He sought to get all other Powers to adopt the same view. He had no regard for the Turk as such, but he did not mean to excite the millions of Mohammedans in India by a display of partiality. Moreover, he wished to maintain the Turkish Empire, if that were possible, in order to protect Constantinople, for he held that, if war occurred, Russia would gobble Greece at one mouthful and Turkey at the next. Hence, while he would not use force,

---

[1] There is only one reference to him. Canning is referring to the export of money or loans from England to Greece, and its relation to neutrality. " The supply [of money] said to be administered by Lord Byron is of an amount perhaps more serious [than £1000], but neither Law nor Government can interfere with the voluntary sacrifice by an individual of his own unquestioned Property." *F.O. Turkey*, 195/46. Canning to Strangford, Apr. 24/24.

he wanted, so far as possible, to temporise, in order to prevent Russia from using it. Here he was in agreement with Metternich. Where he differed from him was that he wanted to avoid a congress, while Metternich was willing to have one. Alexander had always liked congresses, and he now wanted a new and particular congress on the Turkish question, to contribute to the greater glory of Russia and to entrust him with a mandate against Turkey, just as the Neo-Holy Alliance had supported Metternich in his reduction of Naples by arms, and had encouraged France in her attitude towards Spain.

Alexander began by issuing (January 1824) a circular inviting the Powers to unite in a congress which should *force* the Turks to accept a scheme for the settlement of Greece. He proposed to form three Principalities out of Greece and to obtain the guarantee of the five Great Powers to this settlement by treaty. The intention was clearly to make all dependent upon Russia. Alexander already had a recognised influence in Wallachia, in Moldavia, and in Serbia. If he attained it in the three new divisions of Greece, six meagre and divided Balkan Principalities would revolve as satellites round the Russian sun. The scheme was so obviously drawn in Russia's interest that no other Power could look on it with favour.

For the moment, however, it was dangerous to dissent. Metternich, who could not favour so open a Russian predominance in the Balkans, did not venture on open disapproval.[1] He played as always, for time and favoured a congress as the expedient for wasting it. He trusted to lure the Russian fly into the congress parlour and there enwrap him gently in the silken mesh of his diplomacy. Canning was perplexed and doubtful. He hated congresses on principle, but a congress might here be the only means of averting war. Moreover, there were less objections to a congress on the Near East than elsewhere, for Turkey had been excluded from the engagements of Vienna. It could, therefore, be maintained that the Eastern question was

---

[1] Vide *F.O.*, 352/9. *Strat. MSS.* Memoir of Stratford Canning's interview with Metternich, Dec. 1824. The latter expressed himself ' unfavourably ' as to it.

particular and special, and that a congress on it would not commit England to any general support of the Neo-Holy Alliance policies. Canning's aim was, however, to hold it off as long as possible, and only to consent to it as a last resource.

8. CANNING OPPOSES A CONGRESS (JANUARY– DECEMBER 1824)

Before entering upon Canning's attitude towards the congress, we may conclude the account of the negotiation of Strangford. He finally obtained the last of the three points —the military evacuation of the Principalities on the 23rd June 1824. Immediately after this success Minciacky was appointed as Russian *chargé d'affaires* to Constantinople (which he reached on the 14th February 1824) and entrusted with the care of her commercial interests. Alexander was promptly pressed by Canning to nominate Ribeaupierre as minister, and thus to resume full diplomatic intercourse. In view of his memorandum on pacification and his desire for a congress, he did not find this demand very convenient, and he began to raise further difficulties. He made use of the fact that the military evacuation, though conceded, had not yet been completely executed. He demanded the restoration of the civil *status quo* in the Principalities, as well as the military, a demand Strangford denied he had ever been instructed to press.[1] Alexander's general attitude was disquieting, and it is obvious that he was trying to make excuses to hold a congress, in order to act forcibly against Turkey. This was marked by the fact that though, on the 6th August 1824, he at length nominated Ribeaupierre as Ambassador to Constantinople, he made all sorts of excuses for not despatching him there at once.

Meanwhile Canning had been almost as tactful and conciliatory at St Petersburg as Strangford had shown himself at Constantinople. On the 15th January he had shown objections to a conference as to whether St Petersburg were a prudent place for it. He thought, however, a con-

---

[1] *Vide* his despatches summarising the whole question, *F.O. Turkey*, 195/55. Strangford to Canning, Sept. 3, 22/25. Later incidents show that Russia profited by the Turkish evacuation of the Principalities to intrigue in them, *v.* Schiemann, *Geschichte Russlands*, ii. 187, n.

ference might be 'inevitable,' but insisted that it could not be held until diplomatic relations between Russia and Turkey were re-established, *i.e.* until Ribeaupierre arrived at Constantinople.[1] On the 24th April, however, he withdrew his objection to the place being St Petersburg. Then at the end of May the Russian Memorandum of January was published to the world in a Paris newspaper.[2] Canning was secretly perhaps not displeased, for it revealed Alexander's ambition to control Greece, and was thus equally annoying both to Turkey and to Greece. It also gave him a pretext, of which he made good use. He instructed Bagot that 'the mischief' is extreme, and that this publication "made it impossible to think of taking any further step towards the opening of the conferences on Greece." [3]

Before he received this despatch Bagot had made a *faux pas*. He attended two conferences of Allied Ambassadors at St Petersburg, which dealt with Greece, on the 17th June and the 2nd July. Canning was angry that Bagot had thus exceeded his instructions and committed England to the conference scheme. He promptly disavowed him and 'snubbed him well.' Meanwhile Russia had nominated Ribeaupierre as Ambassador (6th August) but unaccountably refused to send him to Constantinople. So Canning, who saw objections to the transfer, still adhered to the view that Ribeaupierre must be at Constantinople before the conference opened.

In September Canning was making new arrangements for diplomatic representation both at St Petersburg and at Constantinople. For Bagot was exchanging Russia for Holland. Strangford was returning home in a blaze of glory from Turkey, and was destined to be made a peer of England and to succeed Bagot at St Petersburg. Stratford Canning (the cousin of George) was designated for Constantinople, and meanwhile was to go on a special mission to St Petersburg, in order to be present at the conference, " if conference there is to be, and then to proceed to his post [Constantinople] with the result of that deliberation." In

---

[1] *F.O. Russia.* Canning to Bagot, 181/58, Jan. 15 ; 181/59, Apr. 24/24.
[2] Some thought Canning himself had revealed it. Schiemann thinks it was not he, but Metternich, and I incline to that opinion.
[3] *F.O. Russia.* Canning to Bagot, 181/58, Jan. 15 ; 181/59, Apr. 24, June 29.

addition, he was sending to St Petersburg a new secretary
of the Embassy, Michael Ward, " my predecessor's [Castle-
reagh's] brother-in-law; consequently acceptable to the Holy
Alliance : and he is further peculiarly qualified for the cold
and the glare of a snowy clime, by wearing a large brown wig
and spectacles, probably green. He will have nothing to
do . . . but to wear them in the manner most agreeable to
the Emperor." All this, he hoped, would conciliate Russia.

In October he was still desirous of avoiding a conference.
Had Ribeaupierre been promptly despatched to Constantinople, he would, however, have been obliged to consent to
one. But the departure of Ribeaupierre for Constantinople
was always a *sine qua non* of his consent. While he was still
waiting for this event he received a communication from the
Greeks. Though dated the 24th August it was not actually
received until the 4th November. Greece complained bitterly
of the January Memorandum of Russia as ' unjust and cruel,'
as deciding her fate by the will of a foreign Power. She
appealed to England, which had shown sympathy with South
America, for her help to constitute herself a nation. Canning
replied diplomatically on the 1st December. He declared
that the Russian Memorandum had been published without
authority, but was, of course, unable to deny its authenticity.
He added that it had been equally condemned by the Turks
as by the Greeks. But he indicated the policy of Russia
as one of suspending hostilities. He suggested that the
memorandum (if genuine !) contained the elements of pacification. For it laid down that " the sovereignty of the Turks
was not to be absolutely restored nor the independence of
the Greeks to be absolutely acknowledged." As, however,
both parties had refused this or any compromise, " any hope of
successful intervention at the present moment " is ' utterly
vain.' England had been neutral as regards South America,
and intended to be equally so towards Greece. She was
connected with Turkey by ancient treaties, which the latter
had not violated, and, if she took part with the Greeks in their
struggle for independence, would " engage in unprovoked
hostilities against that Power in a quarrel not her own." On
the other hand, the Greeks might be assured that Great Britain
would not be concerned in any attempt (if such attempt were

in contemplation) to force upon them a plan of pacification contrary to their wishes. But she would undertake the office of mediation with Turkey, if asked by the Greeks, and, if accepted by Turkey, would " do our best to carry it into effect, conjointly with other Powers." [1]

Thus Canning had now determined not to enter a congress or conference, on the ground that neither Turkey nor Greece would accept its rulings. Thus the intervention of the Powers could only be effected by force, and to that Canning was still entirely opposed. Hence, if there was to be a congress at St Petersburg, England would not be represented there.

Stratford Canning, who was proceeding to St Petersburg *via* Vienna, therefore, received instructions on these lines. On the 8th December, Metternich, who had made a frantic appeal to Canning on the 16th October, received information to this effect on the 5th December. He was told that England could not, as he suggested, join a congress to impress the Russian people and save the face of the Czar by exhibiting moral solidarity of Europe against war. " We must either assign to the Parliament and people of this country reasons for our conduct by which in fact it is not actuated, and must express hopes of success which in fact we do not feel ; or, by declaring frankly our real motives . . . must betray the secret . . . and therewith destroy the illusion by which the Emperor of Russia has to be fortified against the warlike impulsion of his people.

" In the silent recesses of a Cabinet it may be possible to employ arguments which you do not openly avow. . . . But in the broad daylight of Parliament, no British Minister could venture on a declaration by which the truth should be knowingly either altered or concealed." [2]

Such a communication was not likely to please Metternich. He received Stratford on Christmas Eve with the undiplomatic remark, " You have a bug on your sleeve." He went on to suggest that Canning was a Jacobin, which Stratford

---

[1] *B.F.S.P.*, xii. 899-903.

[2] *F.O. Austria*, 120/66. Wellesley to Canning, Oct. 16 ; 120/67. Canning to Wellesley, Dec. 5/24, No. 28. Stratford's conversations with Metternich are in two memos. of Dec. 1824 and Jan. 1825, *Strat. MSS. F.O.*, 352/9.

promptly denied. And he then implored Stratford, almost with tears, to get his cousin to abandon his position.

Metternich and Alexander both desired a congress, but for exactly opposite reasons. Metternich desired a congress, hoping that he could again cajole and hoodwink the Czar into staying his hand against Turkey. Alexander thought that he would obtain from a congress a mandate for force against Turkey. Canning, by refusing to enter a congress, called down the wrath of both parties on his head. But, while Metternich was tearful and tactful, Alexander was wrathful and explosive.[1] On the 30th December he sent this curt message to England : " the Cabinet of London will easily understand that His Imperial Majesty on his side regards all further deliberation between Russia and England on the relations with Turkey and on the pacification of Greece as definitely closed." [2] " He was damned," said Canning, " if he would speak Greek to us." And for nearly nine months Lieven never opened his lips about Greece to Canning. The Englishman was not at all disturbed. He compared Alexander in private to ' silly Mr Tomkins ' in a popular song, and Metternich to ' cruel Polly Hopkins,' who would ' step between him and his desires.' The quarrel between ' silly Mr Tomkins ' and ' cruel Polly Hopkins ' ' would cause the congress to fail.' Then Russia and Austria would have to apply to England separately, and the game would be in his hands. It was a bold game to play. He had now reached a definite separation from the Neo-Holy Alliance over Greece, as over everything else, and isolation is dangerous in diplomacy. He had done what none of them had done : he had recognised the Greeks as belligerents and had corresponded with the Provisional Government of Greece. Yet he was not committed, like Alexander, to an anti-Turkish attitude, nor, like Metternich,

---

[1] It is hardly possible to suppose that Alexander was acting in good faith. On Nov. 11 the Turks evacuated the Principalities and thus deprived Alexander of his last excuse for not despatching Ribeaupierre before the congress opened. As Canning pointed out, Lieven spoke in one of his letters of the "awkwardness of M. Ribeaupierre's situation if he should arrive at Constantinople while war was still raging." " Indeed ! then it would appear that it *was* in contemplation to suspend his departure, until some way had been made in the conferences," v. *F.O. France*, 141/64, Dec. 8/24

[2] Nesselrode to Lieven, Dec. 30/24 ; copy in *F.O. Austria*, 120/68. Canning to Wellesley, Feb. 26/25.

to a pro-Turkish one. As regards the two belligerents, therefore, he had the chance of becoming their mediator. And
he calculated that, in the end, Russia or Austria would have
to act with him. When the congress failed (as he knew it
would), its *disjecta membra*, as he called them, could be employed as he desired. He was still, however, determined that
he would have nothing to do with any mediation to which
" the disavowal of force was not an indispensable condition."
On every other point Canning was correct in divining the
future. But an event had just occurred which was to cause
him in ten months to contemplate the use of force. For a
new and formidable Power was coming to the aid of Turkey,
and the advent of that Power was to change the whole
situation.

9. THE PASHA OF EGYPT INTERVENES (1824)

Mehemet Ali—
 " *Wary, astute, neither a fanatical Mussulman nor a devoted servant of
the Porte, guided almost entirely by his personal interest and ambitions.*"—
DUDLEY, 14th July 1827.

In the middle of 1824 everyone thought that the Greeks
were at last securing their *de facto* independence, and that
Sultan Mahmud was at the end of his resources. The Greeks
were more successful than ever, Russia was threatening war,
the Neo-Holy Alliance had done little to restrain her, Canning
had actually received overtures from the Greek rebels.
Mahmud could not rely on his own efforts or on his own
forces. He wanted to massacre his turbulent janizaries and
to replace them by a more regular force, but he could not
do this while his best troops were in Greece and the insurgents were gaining ground. So he looked over the sea for
aid to Egypt where Mehemet Ali reigned as Pasha, owing only
a nominal allegiance to the Sultan. Mehemet was an Albanian
of genius, as forceful and as cruel as Mahmud, but with more
enlightenment and ability. He was congenial to Mahmud
because he had already massacred his own janizaries (the
mamelukes) and had formed a new army on the European
model. While Mahmud had failed to subdue the Greeks,
Mehemet had crushed the Arabs. He had seized Mecca and
Medina and penetrated to Khartum. Mahmud now summoned
him to aid him in Greece. Mehemet sent the Egyptian Fleet

at once, and promised to send Egyptian troops under his son
Ibrahim. Some preliminary successes were at once obtained,
but it was the arrival of Ibrahim that was ominous. No
diplomat nor politician like his father, he was actually his
superior as a warrior. He promised to bring the Egyptian
Army by the spring of 1825, and that army was to upset all
diplomatic calculations.

CHAPTER XV

THE GREEK PROTOCOL OF THE 4TH APRIL 1826; AND THE DIPLOMATIC REVOLUTION

I. THE RUPTURE BETWEEN ALEXANDER AND METTERNICH (JANUARY–AUGUST 1825)

" I am not a [pro-]Greek, God knows. I send the whole nation to the Devil!"—GEORGE IV. to Esterházy, 18th December 1826.

IN February 1825 the terrible Ibrahim landed in the Morea, and made war in a fashion that was new. Probably he was no more cruel than other Turkish generals; it was his efficiency, not his ruthlessness, which increased the danger from Russia. For Alexander was now in wrathful mood. He had clearly summoned his congress to authorise him to use force against the Turks, as Laibach had authorised Metternich to use it against Naples, and as Verona had encouraged France to use it against Spain. Canning, for that very reason, declined to enter it. Russia, in great wrath, broke off all relations with England on the Eastern question. So the conferences began at St Petersburg, with representatives only from France and the Neo-Holy Alliance. Their meetings were not harmonious. In order to avoid sanctioning the use of force, Metternich started off by the bold proposal to recognise the independence of Greece.[1] He thought that Alexander would have to choose between the absolute submission or absolute independence of the Greeks and that he would refuse to accept either. Metternich was right in thinking this, for Alexander declined the idea of independence,

---

[1] This bold *tour de force* by the arch-priest of Legitimacy was apparently a desperate effort to 'side-track' Alexander. As such it failed, and it was unfortunate for Metternich. He never heard the end of it from Canning, who reminded him that he was the first to proclaim the freedom of Greece.

and thereupon France and Austria opposed any kind of forcible intervention. What Metternich had not foreseen, when he impaled Alexander on the ' independence horn ' of the dilemma, was that he would thus awaken Alexander's furious resentment. By March it was clear the conference could not agree ; by May it was suspended altogether. Nesselrode, normally a mild and cautious man, expressed himself with extraordinary bitterness against Austria. Metternich added to his offences by a visit to Paris (March–April), where he boasted inordinately of his ascendancy over Alexander. It only needed that news to come to the Czar's ears (which it very soon did) to make the wound too deep to be healed. In June and July the split in the Neo-Holy Alliance could not be concealed. Nesselrode told Lebzeltern he could not trust himself to speak to him about the congress. On the 18th August Alexander addressed a circular to his diplomats to the effect that he would no longer work with Metternich. His Allies had not supported him over the Greek question and, in other matters as well, there was not " that reciprocity of services which he had a right to expect." [1] So the rifts in the Neo-Holy Alliance yawned wide, while the ruthless Ibrahim advanced to the conquest of Greece.

Canning had played his game with nerve and skill. He had foreseen the failure of the conferences, and he knew enough of their transactions to see that his forecast had been fulfilled. He took pains in private to prepare the way for Russia by cultivating the Russian Ambassador in London. Thus he wrote to Stratford, then on a special mission to St Petersburg, that he did not want Lieven, who was doing his best, to be replaced.[2] " In the present state of our relations and in the ticklish temper of the world, a great, rough, staring, whiskered *owski* on the one hand or a fine intriguing *ozzo* on the other (of which species the Russian diplomacy is generally composed) might easily snap the thread, which is quite strong enough to hold if it is not strained too hard, and may hereafter be twisted into strength again." [3] Canning had indicated also privately to Lieven (who remained dumb

---

[1] Schiemann, *Geschichte Russlands* (1904), i. 608–10. The date given is the 6th, but this is old style (*v.* i. 346) and therefore the 18th.

[2] *F.O.*, 352/10. *Strat. MSS.* George to Stratford Canning, Feb. 23/25.

[3] *Ibid.*

about Greece), that he understood his position, and he took
care to make both him and that more important diplomat,
his wife, feel that England would be ready at the right time
to resume discussion. Madame Lieven heard, and saw, and
understood. She went off in June 1825 on a visit to St
Petersburg, hoping to bring about a diplomatic *coup* by her
feminine arts. Her hopes were not to be disappointed. This
amazingly clever lady had only recently desisted from her
intrigue with King George to overthrow Canning.[1] She now
recognised that the quarrel with Metternich necessitated a
rapprochement with Canning. She was willing to be this
friend, and hoped to make him her tool. Her venture seems
to have been undertaken entirely on her own responsibility,
and is certainly one of the most remarkable pieces either of
unofficial or of feminine diplomacy. Alexander stood in a
position of isolation. He had broken with Metternich and
had refused to ' speak Greek ' to Canning. Madame Lieven
decided to loosen his tongue.

2. Ibrahim's Successes

While Madame Lieven was whispering delicately in the ear
of Alexander, and while Canning was predicting the failure
of the conferences, Ibrahim was settling the question of
Greece in a manner which no one had foreseen. He had a
well-disciplined army and was himself an admirable soldier.
To these two features, new on the Turkish side, he added
a third, and used sea-power, for the first time, to the Turkish
advantage. Instead of passing his troops through the
dangerous defiles of Thessaly, or the narrow way of Corinth,
where Turkish armies had been ambushed and shot down,
Ibrahim ferried them safely over from Candia and Egypt to
the Morea, taking the Greeks in reverse. He soon had
11,000 first-class troops at his orders. Thus firmly and
securely based on the Morea, he commanded the situation.
He captured Navarino (May). Desperate bands of Greeks
held out in isolated areas, and the corsairs still harassed
his sea communications. Kolokotrones, who had been imprisoned by his countrymen, was brought from the gaol to

[1] *Vide supra*, pp. 250–3.

make head against him. Ibrahim was momentarily checked in front of Napoli di Romana and Patras, but he devastated or occupied the rest of the Morea. He prevented all communication between it and the hard-pressed garrisons at Athens and Missolonghi, and it soon became clear that in the end he would reconquer the Morea. Once he had done that, all Greece would be at his mercy, and all resistance over. The most horrible stories were told of his cruelties, and there was soon to be attributed to him the monstrous plan of depopulating the Morea and colonising it with Turks or Egyptians. This sinister ' depopulation project,' whether deemed true or false, whether invented by Greeks or Russians, proved eventually stronger than the soldiers or victories of Ibrahim.

Victory had divided the Greeks, the sword of Ibrahim at length brought some semblance of unity to their councils. They looked round for support in June. Alexander had just disavowed Greece, now he seemed either unable to help, or ready to betray, her. England, therefore, seemed the only resource. She, at any rate, was the land of Byron ; she had recognised them as belligerents ; she was supreme on that sea which Ibrahim was beginning to command. She had refused to coerce them or to join that conference, now expiring in empty words and bitter recriminations at St Petersburg. The despatch of a Greek delegation to London, well trumpeted in the Press, might revive interest in their sinking cause, aid the British Phil-Hellenes to work on their government, and persuade or compel Canning's intervention.

3. THE GREEK DELEGATION ; CANNING'S INSTRUCTIONS TO STRANGFORD AND STRATFORD (OCTOBER 1825)

The delegation arrived and laid their proposals before Canning (29th September 1825). They demanded the protection of Great Britain, and offered to accept ' a supreme chief ' (*i.e.* ruler or king) from her. They suggested either Prince Leopold or the Duke of Sussex. Canning said such a proposal, if accepted, would be inconsistent with neutrality, and he gave them no hope that it would, or could, be accepted. He reiterated to them the arguments of his letter of the 1st December of the previous year. He added that, " while preserving scrupulous neutrality, England would promote any compromise between the Greeks and their late masters, not for the entire independence of Greece . . . for that could not form the subject of a compromise (if they could conquer it [independence] it was well, and it was their affair), but for anything short of independence, which might form the basis of an arrangement with the Porte." The Greek Delegation was disappointed, but Canning had already gone further than any other Power to meet them.

Canning had been diplomatic and discreet, but he was now formidably armed. He was, if not the mediator, at any rate the favourite and the hope of' the Greeks ; he was more acceptable than Alexander to the Turks. For Strangford had achieved considerable success even with these most slippery of negotiators. By September Canning had already received tentative overtures from Austria and France. But in France Canning had little faith, and in Metternich none at all. If he negotiated in joint concert with him it was with ' the certainty of being betrayed ' ; if he entered a congress he would injure himself in British opinion by adopting a method that was ' delusive and outworn.' By the end of September he was ready to negotiate between Turkey and Greece single-handed and at once. And he was prepared to consider co-operation with Alexander, whenever that worthy was ready to ' speak Greek.' Madame Lieven arrived back from St Petersburg at the end of September, but she went off to Brighton, and did not see Canning for nearly a month. She thought it better ' to raise the question by slow degrees,' for she knew the majority of the Cabinet favoured the Turks, and did not know whether she could get Canning to favour the Greeks. During this period Canning took steps to negotiate with Turkey, direct and alone.

Canning had two ambassadors to send out : one of them greatly distinguished at Constantinople in the past, the other to be still more distinguished in the future. Stratford Canning had now returned from St Petersburg, where Strangford was to replace him. On the 12th October Canning gave Stratford his instructions and sent him off to Constantinople on the 13th.[1] They show that he was intended to forestall any Russian designs of war by working on Turkish fears for the benefit of Greece. The Turks were to be informed that, " To suppose that Greece can ever be brought back to what she was in relation to the Porte is vain. With how much less than complete independence Greece herself would be satisfied we have not the means of pronouncing ; but, if it is wished, we would endeavour to ascertain. We do not obtrude our services. We do not insist that they should be exclusive ; [2] but we are at present free from all engagements with other Powers, direct or constructive, with respect to the affairs of Turkey and Greece." Canning, in effect, offered British mediation, and the Porte was strongly recommended to take advantage of this offer at once. The line of argument is purely British, and is plainly an offer of British mediation to Turkey over Greece, to avert a Russian declaration of war.

While he had entire confidence in Stratford, Canning had none in Strangford. The latter had offended him by voting against Catholic Emancipation, and still more by private consultations with Esterházy, to whom he showed his secret despatches, promising to play Metternich's game. Canning knew that Strangford favoured conference policies and probably suspected these intrigues. So he did not show him Stratford's instructions, nor even give him his own at his last interview with him. Strangford pressed him hard but Canning yawned, said he would send them before he left, and told him " just to keep him [Alexander] in good humour— that's all. Good-bye. Adieu." Strangford's instructions, finally drawn on the 14th October, reached him on the 18th, just before he sailed. They remark on ' the extreme difficulty ' of working either with Austria or France over Greece, and say that " it was desirable that the Russian Government should know the grounds upon which that difficulty is founded." Clearly Strangford was meant to avoid all joint intervention, but to flatter Russia and to welcome and transmit any over-tures from her. But Canning's farewell had been delivered

---

[1] *W.N.D.*, ii. 530–5. To avoid confusion I refer to Stratford Canning as Stratford, and to George Canning as Canning.
[2] Canning did not really want joint-mediation. " To do any good we must make it [Stratford's overture] *alone.*" To Granville, Nov. 8/25. Stap., *G.C. & T.*, 467.

in cavalier fashion. Strangford was much displeased. He
was too vain to believe that " doing nothing is as often a
measure, and full as important a one as the most diligent
activity." He sought to negotiate on his own, and in a sense
adverse to that of his superior, and was soon to be disavowed
under painful circumstances.[1]

This pair of instructions makes it absolutely clear that
even in mid-October Canning had not yet received any message
from Madame Lieven. He was, in fact, expecting an overture
from Russia, and meanwhile was trying to forestall her action
by direct negotiations at Constantinople.

4. THE ' GRAND SECRET ' OF MADAME LIEVEN

At this moment Madame Lieven, who had always had a
great place in England's society, acquired one in history
and in foreign policy. For she brought a message direct from
the Czar, and of the highest diplomatic importance. Her ex-
periences at St Petersburg had more than realised her hopes.
Her success had been extraordinary, and the message with
which she was charged on her departure was equally so. She
had found that the Court of the Czar-Mother at Pavloffsky
was as brilliant as ever, but that Alexander remained a hermit
at Tsarskoe-Selo. Living apart from his wife ' by a sort of
reciprocal expiation,' he had fallen into a kind of religious
coma, very suspicious, very mystical, looking everywhere for
inspiration and for a sign. Attending no ceremonials, and
seeing his ministers only for business, he spent most of his
time aloof and alone in his fine gardens reading the Bible or
walking about with it under his arm. He received Madame
Lieven more than once, but, as often in moments of difficulty,
was vague. And the mystery and obscurity of his attitude over-
shadows the whole negotiation. The lady insinuated delicately
that it was time to break with Austria, that Canning was not
a Jacobin, and that, at any rate, he was an enemy of Metternich. Alexander listened but did not reveal his thoughts.
To Nesselrode she was less guarded, and doubtless her hints
reached Alexander in an intelligible form. A fortnight before
she left, Alexander had taken the decisive step of sending out

---

[1] *Vide*, for a further discussion, pp. 288–93.

to his diplomats his circular of the 18th August, and that circular announced his breach with Metternich. Madame Lieven professes ignorance of this step in her *Diary*. She was not ignorant, however, that ' the moment of a great resolve was near,' and that Alexander was contemplating a breach with Metternich. On the night before her departure she was fully enlightened. The Czar knew she was leaving for England on the 31st August. At 10 p.m. on the 30th, Madame Lieven received an urgent message from Count Nesselrode to the effect that he must see her the next morning so as to give her " an urgent communication on behalf of His Majesty the Emperor." Madame Lieven sent a message in reply that she would see Nesselrode at ten the next day, before leaving. He arrived and informed her that it was " a conference in due form. He would speak as minister to minister, and that for better comprehension he would give me word for word the dialogue he had had the evening before with the Emperor " : [1]

" *Alexander*.—' Madame Lieven goes to-morrow ; have you seen her much during her stay here ? ' ' Several times, Sire ' (Count Nesselrode's precautions went so far as to conceal his frequent visits to me. The Emperor was very suspicious).

" *Alexander*.—' Ah, well ! if you have spoken with her you will have been satisfied. I have found her sensible on all questions. She judges fairly and without prejudices. An idea has come to me which I have been working out for some days. Could we not profit by her return to England to re-approach that Cabinet ? She knows the influential persons in that country, she enjoys great consideration, she well knows the means to use her position to render the service I ask of her. This is what you must tell her is my opinion on the present situation. The Turkish power is crumbling ; the agony is more or less long, but it is stricken with death. I am still here, armed with all my power, but strong in my known principles of moderation and disinterestedness. How will it not profit me, with my aversion from any project of conquest to reach a solution of the question which is in-

[1] *Lie. MSS.* These extracts published in *E.H.R.*, Jan. 1924, pp. 60–2.

cessantly disturbing Europe? So long as I follow them [my principles], they [Metternich] try to profit by it. I cannot remain in this position for long.

" ' Affairs become daily more complicated. I am pushed, urged on, by all my entourage. My people demand war ; my armies are full of ardour to make it, perhaps I could not long resist them. My Allies have abandoned me. Compare my conduct to theirs. Everybody has intrigued (*tripoté*) in Greece. I alone have remained pure. I have pushed scruples so far as not to have a single wretched agent in Greece, not an intelligence agent even, and I have to be content with the scraps that fall from the table of my Allies.[1] Let England think of that. If they grasp hands [with us] we are sure of controlling events and of establishing in the East an order of things conformable to the interest of Europe and to the laws of religion and humanity. That should be the foundation of the instruction to Madame Lieven. In addition, she must understand well that we cannot make the least advances to England. That would not suit my dignity after what passed last winter. But we can make the Cabinet of England understand that, if it takes a step, it will not be repulsed, that we shall always be ready to welcome its ideas. The sending of Lord Strangford will serve as a pretext ; his arrival here will form a new epoch in this question. He must be furnished with instructions to take it up on a new basis. Finally, these are the ideas which I wish you to make Madame Lieven clearly understand. You will listen attentively to her observations and objections and you will report them to me. . . .' " [He ended by telling Nesselrode to get into touch with her before she left, and to preserve complete secrecy.]

The flattered lady describes herself as amused and disturbed: " Here was the most cautious and discreet of ministers compelled to entrust the most confidential, the most intimate, and most bold political projects to a woman. It was new and something to laugh at." She observed that all

[1] I am indebted to Mr C. N. Crawley of Trinity College, Cambridge, for the following note as well as for some other advice. In the Record Office, *C.O. Ionian Isles*, there are a good many intercepted reports from the Russian Consul, Sandrini, at Corfu. Later there was a Greek (Vlassopoulos) in the Russian service travelling in Greece before the first accredited agent was sent.

the [British] Ministers were pro-Turk and had a horror of Greek revolutionaries, " the King sharing all these prejudices, the public very cold . . ." ; on the other side, Canning was " *fort capable d'exaltation*, and one who easily took up an idea that was great and new. But how arrange it when we had shut our mouths in England ? " " A woman," said Count Nesselrode, " knows how to make people speak, and that is precisely why the Emperor considers you have a unique opportunity, and your presence here has been for him like a revelation " (here was revealed in its entirety the mystic faith of the Emperor).

" But what an incredible idea ! The Emperor then wishes to break the Alliance. He desires a separate engagement with England, and, in agreement with her, to drive the Turks from Europe. To erect in their place a Christian power ; in a word, to overthrow everything.

" The Count de Nesselrode seized himself by the head and looked fearfully at the door. ' My God ! if the Emperor heard you ! ' Then, very low : ' Ah, well ! it is possible that that is what he dreams of,' and shoving his spectacles up over his forehead, he gave way to a movement of lassitude and despair."

Madame Lieven, after some more *badinage*, demanded instructions in writing.

The prudent Count de Nesselrode confined himself to writing :

" ' Believe all the bearer tells you,' and ten minutes after he led me to my carriage. The Emperor had doubtless enjoined this piece of politeness, which agreed with his caution not to see me till the moment of my departure." [1]

This, then, told as nearly as possible in her own words, is Madame Lieven's story. Her statement is clear. She was, said Nesselrode, ' a living despatch.' She says that she was instructed with a mission to give Canning the verbal information that Alexander was ready to break with the Neo-Holy Alliance and to work separately with England over Greece. She was to hint that his dignity forbade him to make an overture himself, but that if England initiated proposals

[1] *Lie. MSS.*

in the sense indicated they would not be rejected. Of the Czar's message to Madame Lieven she complacently records, " the last act, the last word, I would even say the last political *thought* of his reign was, then, the mission he entrusted to me."[1]

On the 13th September Alexander left for the Crimea practically *incognito*, without a minister but significantly attended by a general, and on the 1st December he died at Taganrog. It is known, almost with certainty, that he had decided on war with Turkey in the spring, if he did not obtain satisfaction from the Turks on the question of the Principalities.[2] But he hoped to stop at the Danube. There was nothing in all this to prevent him co-operating with England over Greece. It was England whom Madame Lieven was intended to induce to co-operate with him.

5. The Lieven-Canning Overture and the Death of Alexander (1st December 1825)

Lieven undoubtedly received a message, too important to be trusted to paper, direct from that ' living despatch,' his wife. Nor does there seem any reason to doubt that its purport was that Canning was to be informed that he would not meet with a refusal if he made overtures to Russia as to Greece. Alexander, it was to be understood, could not compromise his dignity by lisping the first syllables of Greek. The real difficulty does not consist in the purport of the ' great secret ' but in the date at which Canning actually received the message. It is even possible that he did not know it until December, but he cannot have doubted that some overture was afoot at the end of October. For, on the 24th, Lieven (and apparently Madame also) came over from Brighton

---

[1] *Lie. MSS.*

[2] The evidence is overwhelming, see *F.O. Russia*, 182/2. Strangford to Canning, No. 4, Jan. 17/26. Strangford seems to have got his information from the very able Austrian Ambassador at St Petersburg. Lebzeltern reported this determination as ' not certain ' (Jan. 6/26, *V.S.A.*, Russland, Berichte, Bd. 9) to Metternich, but a week later said that he had been mistaken. See *ibid.*, Bd. 10, to Metternich, Jan. 13/26, *lettre particulière*. Also (*ibid.*, Bd. 9, to Metternich, Feb. 4), he says Nicholas told the French Ambassador, ' Il [Alexander] allait enfin le terminer.' Canning expressed the same view derived from other and no less correct sources. So also did the Prussian envoy, General Schöler. See Schiemann, i. 495–6.

to Seaford, where Canning was staying, and had an interview with him of decisive importance.

Lieven, in ' entire personal confidence ' and ' without the orders of his Court,' showed him two Russian despatches.[1] One of these seems to have been the circular of the 18th August breaking with Metternich. The other was a résumé of the points of difference between Russia and the Allies at the Conference of St Petersburg. This showed clearly that Alexander had proposed to employ force against Turkey, that Metternich had refused to do so and made the counter-proposal of recognising the independence of Greece. Canning recorded of these, " it is impossible for ill-humour to be expressed more strongly than in the whole tenor of these documents."

Lieven's last communication was : " The Court of Russia has positive information that before Ibrahim Pasha's army was put in motion, an agreement was entered into by the Porte with the Pasha of Egypt, that whatever part of Greece Ibrahim Pasha might conquer should be at his disposal ; and that his plan of disposing of his conquest is (and was stated to the Porte to be and has been approved by the Porte) to remove the whole Greek population, carrying them off into slavery in Egypt or elsewhere, and to re-people the country with Egyptians and others of the Mohammedan religion."

This was a masterstroke. For Canning knew that the British public would never tolerate the ' depopulation,' or, as he called it, ' the Barbarization ' project. And, if it was revealed to them, England would be forced to take some drastic kind of action.

It appears also that, at the same time, Lieven or Madame communicated the ' great secret ' that Russia would receive favourably overtures from England. This last piece of information was verbal and personal, and could, of course, never be avowed.

Canning excelled in divining the hidden meaning of an opponent's words. Even if he had not heard the ' great secret,' he could not doubt that this communication, though personal and unauthorised, indicated that Russia was prepared

---

[1] *Vide* Canning's summary, Oct. 25/25. Stap., *Corr.*, i. 314-5.

to negotiate with him. Doubtless also, if he disregarded the communication about the depopulating of the Morea, Lieven would see that the British public heard of it. Canning knew what that would mean. " I begin to think," wrote he to Liverpool the next day, " that the time approaches when *something* must be done." [1]   The knowledge of a project, so monstrous and horrifying as the ' Barbarization project,' supplied him with a motive for action.   In the second week of November he asked the British Admiralty if the present British naval force in the Mediterranean was " sufficient to enforce an armistice between the belligerent parties " (*i.e.* Greece and Turkey), and, if not, whether it could be speedily and adequately reinforced.[2] He had another motive for action too.   A fortnight after his last message to Madame Lieven, Alexander had left for the Crimea (13th September). His armies were beginning to concentrate towards the Principalities, and Canning guessed (as it proved accurately enough) that he meant war on the Danube in the spring.   If there was a Russian army on the Danube it would be well to have a British fleet off the Morea.   Thus two motives—one fear of possible popular sentiment, the other, fear as to the balance of power—were causing Canning to contemplate the possibility of using force in the East.   He was clearly moving away from the position that he had upheld for over three years, that force should *never* be employed.

Madame Lieven's ' grand secret ' had brought him knowledge of the most vital importance, and the possibilities of co-operating with Russia had to be carefully explored.   While he was flattering the Lievens and considering his plans, two most unfortunate incidents suddenly intervened.   They were the indiscretions of Strangford and the death of Alexander.   Either seemed enough to break the fine-spun web of Canning's plans. Strangford's indiscretions are related elsewhere (pp. 288–93). It need only be said here that, when Nesselrode suggested an overture with England direct, Strangford tried to bring Austria and France into the negotiation, and suggested a formula which would give Russia ' the right to go to war,' if a last effort at joint intervention with the Porte failed.

[1] Stap., *G.C. & T.*, Oct. 25/25, to Liverpool, pp. 465–6.
[2] Canning to Sir G. Cockburn (between Nov. 2 and 5/25). Stap., *Corr.*, i. 321.

Canning heard of this first from Lieven on the 17th December and refused to believe it, until the despatch had been read several times. The same day he sent a furious despatch to Strangford, demanding explanations. On the 31st December, having received further information, he totally disavowed Strangford, telling him to make this disavowal known, and adding, that he was ' *to be quiet.*' Beneath this ' padlock ' Strangford was henceforward dumb.

Alexander's death took place on the 1st December and became known in England on the 18th. It was followed by an amazing contest between his two brothers for the throne, and by mutiny and revolution in St Petersburg. Finally, by the end of December, the young and vigorous Czar Nicholas seated himself firmly on a throne whose steps were awash with blood.

Most men would have been unnerved by this chapter of accidents, but they acted as a stimulus to a statesman so supple and resourceful as Canning. Even Madame Lieven cannot refrain from expressing her admiration at this juncture, though she thought him ' not all sincere ' as to Greece. " ' Old people ' . . . hesitated to put confidence in his [Alexander's] successor. It was not the same with Canning. It was just the novelty of the person and the situation which nerved his mind and made him imagine and hope for a policy more conformable to his views." He knew now pretty well that Alexander, ' in a spirit of gloomy abstraction,' had resolved upon immediate war. He guessed that Nicholas would have been thoroughly disillusioned as to the Neo-Holy Alliance, and would pursue a ' more purely Russian policy ' and might not be so ready at once to engage upon it. So Canning thought that the proposed overture with Russia might still be promising. Nicholas might be ready to honour Alexander's overture, and he knew the Lievens well. They were obviously the instruments through whom Canning and he could work.

6. THE SIGNATURE OF THE PROTOCOL (4TH APRIL 1826) ; THE DIPLOMATIC REVOLUTION

In a spirit, half of friendship, half of suspicion, the Lievens and Canning laboured together for a *rapprochement* in

January. Canning only saw Lieven once, apparently in December, and that was over the Strangford affair (17th December), and was doubtless confined to that sole issue.[1] But on the 12th January Canning informed Lieven that he intended to send the Duke of Wellington on a complimentary mission to St Petersburg to congratulate the new Czar. " The Duke not only accepted but *jumped* at the proposal." " Lieven received the information first with astonishment, and then *literally* with tears of pleasure." It was a proof that the confidences of October were bearing fruit. Canning's explanation of the choice of Wellington was that, as ' the ultra system ' was ' dissolved,' " the elements of that system " (*i.e.* Wellington and Russia) " have become agreeable for good purposes. I hope to save Greece through the agency of the Russian name upon the fears of Turkey without a war, which the Duke of Wellington is the fittest man to deprecate. . . . *De plus*—the Duke of Wellington is the only agent by whom I could suppress, and extinguish Strangford." [2] Canning added he had no fear that " he [the Duke] will dream in his own head, or put into the autocrat's, any chimera of a new Holy Alliance." Madame Lieven says Canning's idea was ' *bouffonne et grande* '; " besides the salaam [to Nicholas] he [the Duke] would have to make an understanding on the question of Greece, he [Canning] would [thus] compromise him and dupe him at the same time—a double pleasure." [3] She goes on to say that the Duke's absence assured Canning's ascendancy in the Cabinet at home, a point that was noticed by other observers, including the Duke himself, who took care to avoid the Russian coronation ceremony and return home as quickly as possible.

It is clear that, by mid-January 1826, an agreement between the Lievens and Canning was, at any rate, imminent. The arrangement seems to have got into actual working order between 31st January and 2nd February, when the Lievens and Canning stayed at Windsor with the King. Madame

[1] He says he did not see him at all between Dec. 1 and Jan. 12. Canning to Granville, Jan. 13/26, in Stap., *G.C. & T.*, 471. This is a slip. He probably means he said nothing to him about Greece. As he heard of Alexander's death on Dec. 18, he had every reason for not wishing to hurry matters for the moment.

[2] Canning to Granville, Jan. 13/26, in Stap., *G.C. & T.*, 471-2.

[3] *Lie. MSS.*

Lieven states that she brought the King and Canning together, and that the latter was grateful for her display of social tact. The King's letter to Nicholas is dated 7th February, and the instruction for Wellington 10th February, so that any private arrangement with the Lievens must have been reached before those dates. That there was some understanding is evident, for, in his own abstract, Canning lays stress on the alteration in Russia's disposition shown in the communications with Lord Strangford and "*in those of Prince Lieven with Mr Canning.*"[1]

Canning's instructions to Wellington were clearly intended to avert the possibility of war.[2] The Duke was to reveal Stratford's instructions to Nesselrode, *i.e.* the proposed single intervention of England between Russia and the Porte and Greece. If that was a failure, he was to prepare to renew to Nesselrode that offer of intervention in conjunction with Russia. He was not to admit that a failure, in either case, would confer on Russia the right to make war. He was to defeat any proposal for a renewal of conferences of the Five Powers by proposing impossible conditions, as, for instance, including the Netherlands as a member of the conference, and insisting on London as the seat of it.

He was, in the case of Turkey's rejection of single British or joint Russo-British intervention, to communicate to Russia England's intention " to prevent, if necessary by force, the accomplishment of the plan imputed to Ibrahim Pasha," *i.e.* of depopulating and transplanting the inhabitants of the Morea. His grounds for this were that, ' supposing the fact to be true,' he did not think " it would be possible for us to justify to the country a continued abstinence from all inter-position." Nor, if we so abstained, could we " hope hereafter to interpose, with the consent of the country, any effectual resistance to whatever enterprise Russia (alone) might under-take at the impulse, and under the pretext, of so enormous a moral as well as political provocation." He was " to express the willingness of the British Government " to co-operate with Russia in negotiating any arrangement between the Porte

[1] The italicised part is not in Wellington's instructions, but is in Canning's " Abstract of Proceedings of Wellington's Mission to St Petersburg." This is in *F.O. Greece*, 32/26.

[2] Text in *W.N.D.*, iii. 85–93, Feb. 10/26.

and Greece, and "its readiness to place that arrangement under the guarantee of Russia, jointly with that of Austria, of France, and of Prussia," but not of England. He was to disclaim any idea of territorial aggrandisement by Great Britain or jealousy of Russia. "In the union of the two Powers the best chance of success was to be found."

That was Canning's policy : co-operation with Russia, with the possibility of force being used against Ibrahim, but nowhere else. Wellington, when he arrived, was completely deceived. Nicholas pretended that he was, for the moment, not occupied with Greece, as he regarded them as rebels. He admitted that he was pressing demands, of the nature of an ultimatum, on Turkey for satisfaction as regards the Principalities and the Serbian question. The Duke went off on the false trail, and his remonstrances proved useless. Indeed, the Czar sent his ultimatum before Wellington was informed of the fact. However, it did not eventually lead to war.[1] Wellington, alarmed and bewildered as to the ultimatum, almost forgot about Greece. Canning was much annoyed on learning the situation, and sent off a despatch, which dissected, with veiled irony, Wellington's arguments. It did not reach the Duke in time to affect events, and, owing to his protests, was eventually withdrawn. But it is of great value as indicating that Canning held that Wellington was not fulfilling the object of his mission, which was, in brief, to minimise other alleged Russian grievances and to magnify Greek claims on Russia and therefore secure Russo-British agreement.[2] Probably, in fact, the whole negotiation would have failed but for the arrival of Lieven in St Petersburg.[3] Then, by various methods, the Duke was induced to sign a protocol on Greece on the 4th April, of which he did not recognise the true import.

[1] The Turks accepted *pourparlers* on May 25, and all outstanding difficulties between Russia and the Porte (except the Greek question) were settled in the Convention of Ackerman (Oct. 6/26).

[2] See *W.N.D.*, iii. 290–6. Canning to Wellington, Apr. 11/26. The last despatch he had then received from Wellington was dated Mar. 16; see *ibid.*, pp. 172–96.

[3] Canning's "Abstract" states that the Greek question remained in abeyance " until the arrival of Prince Lieven, when the Duke of Wellington observed an increasing anxiety in Count Nesselrode, and also in Prince Lieven, upon the subject," *F.O. Greece*, 32/26. He confirms the outline of Madame Lieven's argument.

Madame Lieven writes :

" He [Canning] relied on us and the vanity of the Duke of Wellington to get the Greek question pushed on at St Petersburg, but always within prudent limits. My husband, summoned by the Emperor, arrived at St Petersburg a few days after the Duke [in fact on 21st March, nineteen days after Wellington]. By us the question was presented to the Duke in a new light. It was not the revolution that we patronised ; we wished to stop the insurrection, to control the move-ment ; we wished to establish in Greece the conservation of order ; for it was proved that the Turks were powerless, that we desired a regular state of things, a hierarchical discipline, all of which sounded well in the ears of the Duke of Wellington. He entered under full sail into this order of ideas, and on 4th April he signed at St Petersburg with the Count de Nessel-rode and M. de Lieven the first protocol which prepared for the emancipation of Greece. Canning, when he received this document, was not quite sure whether to congratulate himself on a success or to complain of a snare, for it had gone much beyond his instructions and his wishes. England found herself irrevocably engaged. He showed to me, naïvely enough, his hesitation and even his regret. However, once done, he consoled himself with thinking of the dislike Prince Metternich was going to conceive and of the mystification practised on the Duke of Wellington, and he said to me, ' if the Duke had been more acute (fin) he would have played his cards better on his side.' We were too prudent to laugh." [1]

For the moment we need not concern ourselves with any-thing but the fact that the Protocol was signed.[2] It seems to be certain that Wellington did not recognise the importance of what he had signed, and probable that he had been cajoled into it by Lieven. He spent much time later in trying to explain it away, and certainly did not understand its im-portance. For the signature, implying as it did Russia's separation from the Neo-Holy Alliance and co-operation with England, was a diplomatic revolution in itself.

[1] *Lie. MSS.*   [2] For the terms, *v.* pp. 390–1.

7. THE EUROPEAN RESULTS OF THE DIPLOMATIC REVOLUTION

The responsibility for the Protocol is divided between the Lievens and Canning. The Greek aspect of the question can be treated later, for it was not at first the most important one. Such a total change as the Protocol brought with it, was felt, and felt immediately, throughout Europe. Owing partly to the calculated indiscretion of Russia,[1] partly to loose talk on the side of Wellington, it was speedily published in the papers. Canning was much annoyed, not because he had conceived it possible to withhold it for long, but because he wished to negotiate first with France and Metternich, and to prepare the public for the new orientation of policy. Immediate publication forced his hand and made wide the breach between Russia on the one hand and Austria on the other. Canning had no objection to shattering the Neo-Holy Alliance, nor to acting with Russia alone. But he would have preferred to get Russia to act with him, after having disavowed Neo-Holy Alliance principles. And immediate publication made this difficult.

Even before the Protocol was signed the Prussian Minister in Portugal had acutely perceived that a change in European politics was imminent. He reported as ' certain ' that " the new Emperor (Nicholas) will renounce the Alliance in so far as it demands any special action or intervention, or influence in the internal affairs of other governments. The motive for this modification—so important for the States whom this intervention has saved—was the disgust and annoyance finally caused to Alexander.

" But at first if there have been disgusts and annoyances the fault is not in intervention itself, but in the deplorable manner in which it has been conducted.

" England will rejoice with the dissolution of the Alliance by one of those fatal errors which so often force us to choose for our ruin and against our safety. Pitt and Castlereagh thought in this way, otherwise is it with Mr Canning." He

---

[1] Nesselrode told Lebzeltern on Apr. 6. *V.S.A.* Berichte aus Russland. Lebzeltern to Metternich, Apr. 7/26. This made it the common property of European diplomats. For this despatch, *v.* Appendix VII.

was substituting for a true aristocracy, one " of *Banques des Comptoirs, des Tribunes et des Orateurs*, fine fellows, who by that and their newspapers excite passions which they use to forward their ambitions. Already this aristocracy overwhelms the great English aristocracy." [1]

If this was the situation even before the Protocol, the news of its signature was certain to impress Europe. The King of Naples declared this Protocol " highly disagreeable, because the powerful influence England must thus acquire must greatly contribute to support and propagate the diabolical principles of Liberalism." [2] Certainly ever since Castlereagh's state paper of 5th May 1820 co-operation between England and Russia had been difficult. Now the Russian autocrat's influence tended in a liberal direction, in Portugal, in Spain, and in America. Russia's views on the Colonies had ' entirely changed,' and, though still declining to recognise the Spanish-American Republics, she made it clear that she would place no obstacle in Canning's way in negotiating for recognition on their behalf with the Mother Country. Her attitude indicated she was giving England ' some support ' in this matter.[3] As regards Spain, Nicholas was even more amiable. Madame Lieven at once began writing to her husband about the ' absurdity ' of the Cabinet of Spain.[4] The Russian agents, who had perpetually intrigued in that country, now promptly ceased from troubling. Even Dom Pedro's grant of a constitution to Portugal did not shake Russia's loyalty or provoke her remonstrances. Metternich got no encouragement for his plan of instigating opposition to Dom Pedro's Constitution from Spain, and for his idea of summoning a new conference. Russia refused to adopt either suggestion. Even when the *casus fœderis* occurred in December, and Canning sent troops to Portugal, Russia did not withhold her support, though both Pozzo and Lieven objected to the phrases of Canning's famous speech of 12th December.

[1] *F.O.*, 360/4. *H. de W. MSS.* Royer (Lisbon) to Maltzahn (Paris), Feb. 21/26.

[2] *F.O.*, 360/4. *H. de W. MSS.* Girardi (Naples) to Cte. Ludoff, May 18/26.

[3] *V.S.A.*, Weisungen nach Frankreich, Bd. 372. Metternich to Apponyi, May 31/26.

[4] *F.O.*, 360/5. *H. de W. MSS.*, June 1/26. Madame Lieven to M. Lieven.

Without the Protocol it is reasonably certain that Russia would have maintained a hostile attitude on all these subjects; with it Canning was enabled to enjoy a great triumph. It was ultimately crowned by the adhesion of France to the Protocol. England, instead of being isolated, was associated not only with Russia but with France. At the end of the year Metternich sat forlorn amid the ruins of his Neo-Holy Alliance, with only Prussia to give him comfort and aid.

8. The Shattering of the Congress System; The Temple Despatch (19th September 1826)

The destruction of the Congress System was, in fact, avowed by Canning as the aim of his co-operation with Russia. When Prussia was being approached over the Protocol, Count Bernstorff suggested that " the course now adopted by the British Government is that which has been for the last three or four years recommended by the Continental Allies, and by none more frequently and more earnestly (it must be confessed) than by Prussia." He expressed his regret that it was not adopted earlier. Canning did not mean to allow such a statement to pass unchallenged. He at once addressed a despatch to Mr Temple, the *chargé d'affaires* at Berlin, to point out that the policy of the Protocol was totally different from, and indeed opposed to, that of the Neo-Holy Alliance. His line was that England recognised the advantage of co-operating with one or more Powers. To do so without a Congress System was preferable to isolation. But, in any case, isolation was preferable to a Congress System.

" The objections which we have always stated to those suggestions have been : (1) That neither the Porte nor the Greeks having shown the slightest disposition to depart from their respective extreme pretensions—the Porte from that of a complete restoration of its unqualified sovereignty, the Greeks from that of total independence—the attempt to mediate between them *unasked* was utterly hopeless of any useful result. (2) That such an attempt was not only likely to be useless, but was, in *our eyes*, improper, as assuming a right, on the part of the Alliance, to interfere in the concerns of nations, as if in virtue of some inherent authority of supervision and control ; a pretension which we have never sanctioned in principle, which we denied after Laybach (*sic*), and at Verona, and which we could not be induced to counten-ance even by all the topics and adjurations derived from the peculiar nature of the struggle in Greece, with which the Russian Cabinet repeatedly endeavoured to shake our resolution.

" The third objection which we felt to engaging in any scheme of intervention hitherto proposed to us, was, that we never before could succeed in extracting, from the Powers proposing it, a direct answer to the very natural and not unimportant questions : ' Do you mean to go to war with Turkey, or with Greece, whichever may be the recusant party ? or, with *one* of them only in case of such recusancy ? and with which ? '

" To these questions it was generally answered, that it would be time enough to discuss them when once an inter-vention was decided ; that, in fact, they were the questions to be discussed at the Conference to which we were invited.

" As if, after Laybach (*sic*) and Verona, it was likely that we would go again into a Conference, at the risk of appearing to lend the authority of the British name to principles which we might be (as after Laybach) under the necessity of disavowing, and to measures against which we might protest, as at Verona, in vain.

" Now, in the present instance, all these three objections are obviated.

" First, it was declared to our ambassador to the Porte, on his way to Constantinople, by certain leaders of the Greeks, speaking in the name of their compatriots, that they desisted from the claim of unlimited independence, and were prepared to accede to some arrangement on the basis laid down in the protocol.

" On these intimations the protocol was framed. There was at least a hope of success which had never been presented before, when one of the two parties consented to lower its extreme demands.

" Secondly, before the protocol was acted upon, the inti-mations received by Mr Stratford Canning on his way to his post, were converted into a direct and formal application from the Greek Government to his Excellency, to mediate for them in the name of his Government with the Porte. Here is a direct authority for intervention, not growing out of a self-assumed right in any Power, or combination of Powers, to dictate to both of two belligerent parties, but in the solicitation of one of those parties for a mediatorial intervention according to the wholesome and established usage of nations.

" When so solicited, however, we grasped not at the request of our single mediation. No such thing. Our answer to the Greeks was, indeed, affirmative for ourselves. But we declared, at the same time, our determination to defer carrying that assurance into effect until we should have consulted our Allies, and invited their co-operation. We do so ; and we are desirous of acting with our Allies cordially and confidentially in what is now in our eyes, as well as theirs, a legitimate intervention.

" Thirdly, the protocol disposes of the question of *war for Greece* in a way which must satisfy the apprehensions of those Powers (not Prussia), who were thinking of separate combinations and undertakings against the consequences of such a war (if it should arise), as a necessary sequel or accompaniment to a joint intervention with Russia in the affairs of Greece and Turkey. Upon this point it is not necessary to enlarge, nor would it be seemly to do so after the hard and self-denying obligations which the signing parties to the protocol have voluntarily imposed upon themselves." [1]

Temple was instructed to communicate " the substance of this despatch " to Count Bernstorff " in the most amiable manner." [2] He was not very discreet, because he allowed him to take a copy, which eventually came under the eyes of Metternich, and sent him into transports of fury.

9. METTERNICH MORALISES (17TH OCTOBER 1826)

" It is a question," wrote Metternich on the 17th October, " neither more nor less of the foundations of the law of nations recognised up to this hour. *Le droit des convenances* [the law of expediency] has to replace that of respect for real

---

[1] Austria and France are meant.
[2] Canning to Temple, Sept. 19/26. Stap., *G.C. & T.*, 481-4.

independence. Everything of which Mr Canning accuses the Alliance is false ; what he admits as his *right*, is that of which he accuses the Allies. It is only necessary to change the point of departure. Legitimate oppressed authority cannot be rescued without a manifest violation of the independence of States ; insurrection (provided it declares itself a government) becomes a *Belligerent Power* ; it establishes by its appeal a *right of intervention*, in favour of that into which it wishes to change itself ; the intervening Power has the right of *declaring itself a mediator between the two parties recognised as equal in rights*. Such is the new Evangel preached to Mr Tempel (*sic*) ! There is not a factious person in Europe who will disavow it. We who are not of their number, we shall *never* recognise it.

" What would be the fate of Europe—that of civilisation if the doctrine of the *dédoublement des États* were ever admitted by the last supporters of the peace of nations ? How can a man of sense advance so subversive a contention, or at least permit himself the attempt to advance it ? Is England then ready to *regard as a Power equal in rights to that of the* [*British*] *King* the first Irish Club which declares itself the *Insurgent Government of Ireland* ? To regard as *fondée dans son droit* the French Power which would accept the office of mediator, by reason of the sole fact that the invitation had been addressed to it by *the Irish Government*—to regard finally as conformable to the law of nations, the menace of compulsory measures, or even of those furnished by France, or of those she should find means to combine with other Powers.

" The Ambassador of France will none the less continue his diplomatic functions, French commerce will suffer no prejudice in English ports. Whither does this absurdity not lead us ? " [1]

There is some ingenuity in Metternich's reasoning, but it seems permissible to remark that England was not Turkey, nor was Greece Ireland. Further, at the beginning of 1825 Metternich had himself proposed the Independence of Greece, and was objecting to Canning because, over a year later, he proposed that Greece should submit to a species of suzerainty, which saved the face of Turkish Legitimacy. It was not

[1] *V.S.A.*, Weisungen nach Frankreich. Metternich to Apponyi, Oct. 17/26. Italics in original.

really on the particular question, but on the general policy of congresses and of the Neo-Holy Alliance that Canning and Metternich joined issue. If that system meant anything, it meant a policy of intervention in the internal affairs of other States. Yet in January 1827 Metternich had the face to object to the Protocol, or at least to " some of its principles, particularly that of intervention in the internal concerns of other Sovereigns !!!!!! " [1] The fact that he was driven to such inconsistencies shows that he was conscious that Canning, and not he, was at last dominating, not only Russia but Europe. Gone was the enormous influence exercised by Metternich over Russia through the Neo-Holy Alliance system for four years. In August 1826 Russia refused a congress on Portugal and declined to attend the Conference of Ambassadors. In September, Pozzo di Borgo, Russia's Ambassador, that former ' hot-gospeller ' of the Congress System, was walking about arm-in-arm with Canning in the streets of Paris. That was the end of the Neo-Holy Alliance and Congress System. And the results were soon to be seen, and disastrously for Metternich, first in Spain, next in Portugal, and last in Greece. It will be well to trace the results in the first two, before approaching the last. But it is on this tripod that Canning's system was built.

[1] *F.O. France*, 146/85. Granville to Canning, Jan. 19/27, No. 24. The notes of exclamation are Granville's.

PART VII

THE RESULTS OF THE DIPLOMATIC REVOLUTION

CHAPTER XVI
CANNING'S TRIUMPH IN PORTUGAL (1826)

CHAPTER XVII
THE FREEDOM OF GREECE

CHAPTER XVI

CANNING'S TRIUMPH IN PORTUGAL (1826)

1. The Death of John and Accession of Dom Pedro

BEFORE the new Protocol was a month old, the effects of its signature were felt in Portugal. On the 10th March 1826, good-natured, feeble, fat old John VI. died at Lisbon. In his last hours, realising his danger, he had appointed a Council of Regency to protect the kingdom against the excesses of his termagant wife and his embittered absolutist son, Dom Miguel, now sulking in enforced exile at Vienna. Both were excluded from the Regency which, for the moment, held the field. Villèle made the unwise suggestion that the Queen Mother united in herself the Crowns of Portugal and Brazil, and was therefore the fittest representative of Legitimacy. Pozzo di Borgo went even further, and said no king could alter the hereditary succession without the consent of the other kings of Europe.[1] But for these robust doctrines even Metternich was not prepared. He issued a circular on the 27th March suggesting that the Regency was the only true authority in Portugal, that Dom Pedro, the Emperor of Brazil, was the legitimate sovereign of both countries, that his will must be obeyed and his pleasure awaited, though Austria conceived that the separation of Brazil from Portugal was inevitable. Dom Pedro had a surprise in store for the Legitimists of Europe. On the 22nd June the dreadful news of his pleasure was known. He renounced for himself the Crown of Portugal, which he devolved on his eldest daughter, Donna Maria, a child of eight, whom he proposed, after proper

---

[1] This doctrine, if correct, ought to have applied to Russia at the end of 1825. Alexander died, having altered the succession in favour of his younger brother Nicholas. But he did not consult Europe first, nor did Nicholas subsequently !

dispensation, to marry to his younger brother, Dom Miguel. He left the Council of Regency (which did not include Dom Miguel) to govern during the new Queen's minority, and he made his pretty sister, the Infanta Isabel, the Regent. So far, so good. But the second part of his decision horrified Metternich. He, a crowned monarch, and the son-in-law of the Austrian Emperor, did what monarchists thought impossible. He endowed Portugal in the very act of his abdication with the *funeste et fatal cadeau* of a brand-new constitution.

2. DOM PEDRO GRANTS A CONSTITUTION (29TH APRIL 1826)

In the Foreign Secretary's room at Rio hangs a large picture portraying the British diplomat, Sir Charles Stuart, in a pink uniform, kneeling at the feet of the Brazilian Emperor, and receiving from him that constitution which was to light the fires of discord in Portugal and in all Europe. Yet he had not inspired it. On the contrary, when he came to Lisbon, he said that he had tried to persuade the Emperor not to grant it. He returned to Europe, not as an English but as a Portuguese Minister, he was divested of all diplomatic capacity as soon as he had presented the charter. Baron Mareschall, the Austrian representative at Rio, had done more even than Stuart to dissuade the Emperor from this step. But it is not always easy to dissuade emperors. Dom Pedro was a curious character, very boastful and very self-confident, who thought that he alone had given peace to Brazil by revolting against his father and by proclaiming a constitution for that country. Would not the same expedient give peace to Old Portugal as it had done to New ? At any rate he thought so, and he prided himself on his constitutional knowledge and capacity. Without consulting Mareschall or Stuart, without caring much for more than one of his own advisers, he compiled in his own palace the instrument of fate. It issued from his head alone, and did not altogether do credit to that organ.[1] But as a

---

[1] Lord Ponsonby to Bagot, Oct. 17/26. Bagot, *G.C. & F.*, ii. 310, gives a lively account of the incident. " He [Pedro] hates liberty . . . as much as Sir Toby Belch did water, but he is vain of his political science." He consulted his private secretary, ' his pimp,' and the book of Benjamin Constant. " And so, one morning they sat them down after breakfast, and at dinner-time (they dine early too at Rio) out came the Constitution . . . of such facile parturition."

diplomatic *coup* it was for the moment unsurpassed. It divided Portugal, angered Spain, and astonished Europe.

The message reached France on the 22nd June, and the serious part of it—the news of the grant of the constitution—was withheld for a time from the Press. À Court reported that his colleagues at Lisbon were in a state bordering on 'insanity.' Metternich was frantic, and by the 4th July had addressed a circular despatch to Paris, Berlin, St Petersburg, but not to London. The Emperor Francis, Pedro's father-in-law, was, he announced, *vivement affligé.* Even a king must not introduce ' violent change,' and inaugurate " a destruction of the fundamental laws of the kingdom." There must be a conference or a congress at Paris to discuss what to do. " It threatens with death and destruction the social order, for it would be difficult not to regard the revolution sanctioned in Portugal as a true unchaining [of forces]." It would, he said, have its " reaction on Spain, and the influence of that reaction would be felt on France, Italy, and all Europe." Meanwhile he laid special stress on the danger of this moral contagion to Spain. If, he said, His Majesty of Spain protests against the Constitution of Portugal " *as incompatible with the security of His Kingdom,*" His Austrian Majesty " *would feel himself called upon to lend support to any step [démarche] His Catholic Majesty [of Spain] should take to produce this effect.*" [1]

In a more secret despatch he stated that, speaking as a publicist, he did not himself think that Pedro had a right to overthrow the fundamental laws on which rested permanent order, " the special authority of all laws, and the guarantee of all properties as of all existences." Even more severe was his criticism on " a Prince who abdicates and destroys the State at the same time." But, as he lugubriously confessed, it was a very delicate matter for diplomats to ' touch the rights of sovereigns ' at conferences.[2] To agitate such questions was ' idle and dangerous.' He must first make a *démarche* and find out what Canning thought.

[1] *V.S.A.,* Berichte aus Frankreich, Bd. 372. Metternich to Apponyi, July 4, circulated to Berlin and Petersburgh.   Italics my own.
[2] He had never thought it ' delicate ' to touch the rights of people at a congress.

3. ATTITUDE. OF CANNING (MARCH–JULY 1826)

Canning was, in fact, much annoyed at Pedro's *coup*. Huskisson, who was present when he heard the news, said that the vexation he expressed was extreme.[1]   Canning did not wholly trust Stuart; he did not trust Dom Pedro at all. He told Damas later that he 'thought very little of him [Dom Pedro],' he even called him " a *fou* on whom you could reckon for nothing, the plaything of treacherous counsellors." [2] He had no belief in ' paper constitutions ' as such, particularly in the more democratic ones.   But his conscience was clear ; England had not inspired Pedro's Constitution and had done nothing to promote. it.   But she certainly would do nothing to injure .its chances of success.   She would not oppose constitutions, for she possessed the oldest in the world. Moreover, she had proclaimed the doctrine of non-intervention in the internal affairs of other States, and was therefore doubly bound not to interfere.   But could anyone else interfere ?   The Despotic Powers had " put down the Constitutional Systems, however little worth maintaining, of Naples and Spain, not on the ground of their intrinsic worthlessness, but simply and solely because they were not *octroyées* by the Sovereign." [3]   Now whatever the defects of Pedro's Constitution it certainly was *octroyée* by the sovereign and of his own free will.   Even the late King of France had said a " king was free to give institutions to his people which they cannot hold but from him."   How then could any Legitimist State object ?

Certainly Esterházy, when he sought him out on the 26th July, found it difficult, for he wrote with much indignation : " It would appear to hear him [Canning] that there has never been a more zealous defender of the free exercise of the rights and prerogatives of sovereigns, since misfortune willed that he, whose acts cause so much embarrassment, has so strangely neglected the monarchical interests, whose existence he so strongly compromises in the States of Europe and America. The arguments in favour of absolute power in the mouth of

[1] *Hans. Deb.*, N.S., xxiii. 143, Mar. 10/30.
[2] *V.S.A.*, Berichte aus Frankreich, Oct. 7, 28/26.   Apponyi to Metternich.
[3] *F.O. Portugal*, 63/306, June 28/26.   Canning to À Court.

Mr Canning are not naturally such as to demand serious attention ; and he even only uses them, I am sure, from a spirit of derision by which this Minister is sometimes led away." [1] In private, the Countess Lieven enjoyed seeing her new friend, Canning, thus deride her old lover, Metternich. " Esterházy chokes at this constitution because of the effect it will have on his chief. This chief [Metternich] will find himself that he has established the dogma that there is nothing legal except what emanates from the sovereign . . . and how could Metternich ever allow a constitution ? I think people are much amused at that. In truth, it is the only thing which makes me laugh at this moment." And again, " Mr Canning has been to see me." . . . " He is particularly droll in his reflections upon the dilemma in which a certain unknown person is going to find himself." [2]

But the great master of diplomatic irony was having more than his joke, he was having his triumph as well, for the argument was in strict logic unanswerable.

On the 11th July Canning had addressed a circular despatch to Paris, Vienna, and Berlin.[3] He denied totally Sir Charles Stuart's participation in the grant of the constitution. " The Emperor, indeed, thought fit to impose upon His Excellency a large share of His Imperial Majesty's confidence, in the course of His Imperial Majesty's deliberations upon those important matters ; but His Imperial Majesty decided and acted in every respect for Himself, and in very many instances the decision upon which His Imperial Majesty finally acted, was materially different from that which had been confided by His Imperial Majesty to Sir Charles Stuart." This denial, like every other statement of Canning's, was for a time distrusted by Metternich, but he seems ultimately to have accepted it as made in good faith.[4] Canning further

[1] V.S.A., Berichte aus England, Bd. 228. Esterházy to Metternich, July 26, No. 11. Litt. B.
[2] F.O., 360/5. H. de W. MSS. Comtesse to Cte. de Lieven, Paris, July 14, 18/26.
[3] F.O. Prussia, 244/19. Canning to Lord Clanwilliam. The despatch to France of same date is No. 63, and to Austria, No. 23.
[4] V.S.A., Weisungen nach Frankreich, Bd. 372. Metternich to Apponyi, July 20/26, accepted the denial. But he commented with suspicion on a despatch from Esterházy of July 26, received Aug. 3. Berichte aus England, Bd. 228. Esterházy to Metternich, July 26, No. 11. Litt. A. Later on he abandoned these suspicions.

acted with great correctness. For, with the view of preventing Sir Charles Stuart from influencing the internal affairs of Portugal, he recalled him from Lisbon.

Canning went on to demonstrate, in words similar to those already quoted, that a constitution " which had emanated from the benevolent disposition of a Sovereign " offered no objection even to Legitimists, and still less to England. He concluded by a warning, which the future was to make prophetic. " Tremendous would be the responsibility that any government would take upon itself, which should either advise the rejection of the constitution, or should stir up the interest or the passions of any part of the Portuguese nation to resist its Introduction." This despatch of 11th July at once gave England the initiative and the preliminary success.

4. THE ALLIED CONFERENCE ACCEPTS CANNING'S VIEWS

In Portugal, England held the force as well as the logic, and on the 24th July the Conference of the Four Ambassadors met at Paris to ' regret ' that there was no evidence that the Portuguese Regency had remonstrated against the constitution, and that it was clear that England intended to execute the decrees of Dom Pedro. Thus neither Neo-Holy Alliance nor France could take action in Portugal; all that could be done was to advise Spain to keep quiet.[1]

So far the resolutions of the conference were peaceful enough, but they closed on a bellicose note. Portugal must keep quiet within her own borders and not attempt to extend her revolutionary propaganda to Spain. " If ever Spain is touched with it, France and the Alliance will fight it à toute outrance, and it will be in the interests of their own safety, attacked and menaced by the revolutionary hydra, that they will be forced to take this part." [2] Portugal, thought both Pozzo and Villèle, would thus be isolated, would fall into civil war, and the constitution would perish of itself.

[1] V.S.A., Berichte aus Frankreich. Apponyi to Brunetti, July 28/26.
[2] This was approved by Metternich, as we see from V.S.A., Berichte aus Frankreich, Bd. 369. Apponyi to Metternich, No. 1 of Aug. 28/26.

5. SALDANHA ENFORCES THE CONSTITUTIONAL OATH
(31ST JULY)

In his interview with Esterházy on the 26th July Canning had extracted one very important fact by refusing to hear his remarks without receiving a copy. Esterházy was then obliged to disclose what he had designed to omit, viz. the ominous passage about Spain which closed Metternich's circular of the 4th July to the other Powers. This bound Austria to Spain in case her internal security was menaced from Portugal, a clause, thought Esterházy, by which his own government was very imprudently and seriously committed. Canning answered to this observation, merely that " the Treaties of this country were known to all the World ; that we were bound by that obligation to resist any attack upon that Kingdom ; and that he had no doubt Spain would bear that fact in mind, and would avoid any occasion for bringing the Treaties into operation." [1] This warning was a grave one, and it would have been well had Austria and Spain borne it in mind. There was now an end to open defiance though not to secret intrigue. This was the more discreditable to Spain, because Canning lost no time in warning Portugal against any agitation or propagandist " attempt to carry their new constitutions out of their own country and to stir up commotions in Spain." [2]

Canning's action secured the result for the time being in Europe. He was now supported by the one man in Portugal herself. The Infanta Regent was a pretty, spirited, and way-ward girl, inclined to be despotic and much under the influence of her foolish doctor, Abrantés. As always, in this period, the ministers were weak, the bureaucracy corrupt, and the army demoralised. But the Governor of Oporto was a strong man, General Saldanha, the grandson of the famous Pombal, the only respected and successful commander in Portugal. While the dotards at Lisbon were wavering, he acted. He wrote to the Regent pointing out the last clause of the charter, ordered all authorities to swear to it and to cause it to be sworn

---

[1] *F.O. Austria*, 120/78. Canning to Wellesley, July 26 ; Wellesley to Canning, Aug. 9/26, *v.* also *F.O. Portugal*, 179/33, to À Court, No. 6, July 27.

[2] *F.O. Portugal*, 179/33. Canning to À Court, Aug. 11/26, No. 63.

to. He stated that he had delayed out of respect for her to execute this provision, but that, if the oaths were not taken by the 31st July, he would take them himself and would cause all the Northern Provinces to take them. He concentrated his military forces, and informed the Minister of War, at the same time, that he would march on Lisbon if the charter was not sworn to by the 31st July.[1] This unconstitutional way of maintaining the constitution prevailed. Without it the Queen ' would have remained Princess of Grand Para,' wrote Saldanha later. On the date named, the oath was taken at Lisbon by the Regent and a great gathering, with a *Te Deum* and a *Magnificat* ceremony, and the *pronunciamento* General found himself Minister of War on the 1st August. Saldanha, not for the last time, had thus exercised a decisive influence, but Oporto did not represent the nation, and Saldanha declared that discipline had been unknown in the army for years. He immediately set to work as " a heavy-handed surgeon, purging and letting blood." One success had been gained, but the situation both in the army and in the State was still serious. None the less, by the end of July foes both within and without were compelled to turn from open defiance to secret intrigue. And the fruits of the latter speedily appeared.

6. THE CASE OF THE PORTUGUESE DESERTERS

Early in August some of the discontented members of the Portuguese Army (Miguelites, of course) passed over into Spanish territory, led by a brigadier, one whole regiment (the 17th) with ' drums beating and colours flying.' At the same time some Spanish deserters entered Portugal and were speedily disarmed. So long as these Portuguese deserters remained intact on Spanish territory they could be used (and ultimately were used) as a Miguelite force to invade Portugal and to overthrow the constitution.

The question of these Portuguese deserters was, in fact, to be the crucial point of the whole question. It was a flagrant breach by Spain, not only of neutrality but of an express treaty stipulation (1st March 1778) by which Spain and Portugal

[1] For Saldanha's action, *v. F.O. Portugal*, 179/33. À Court to Canning, July 22, No. 76, and Carnota, *Memoirs of Saldanha* (1880), i. 99–117.

respectively agreed not to receive nor to harbour deserters. Portugal could, in fact, have insisted on the deserters being restored to her. Under the influence of Canning the Regency put forward the much more moderate demand that the deserters should be dispersed in Spain, and their horses, arms, and equipment only restored to Portugal. On the 18th August, Damas, the French Foreign Minister, assured Granville that there had been a conference of the Four Powers at Paris that very morning, and that they had all agreed to urge the Spanish Government to disperse the deserters.[1]

This was stating only half the truth. In point of fact, the Ambassadors' Conference, in this, the last decision it ever took, recommended Spain not to give up the deserters, but do not appear to have recommended her to disperse them.[2] The consequence must have been a great encouragement to Spain to persist in her attitude, and there can be little doubt that it also encouraged her to proceed by stealth to arm and to organise these deserters for a filibustering attack on the hated constitution. That was to enter on a course Canning was determined she should be made to abandon, if necessary, by actual war.

This was, however, the very last time that the Ambassadors' Conference at Paris, or, indeed, any conference of these Four Governments, was to have power either for good or for evil in Canning's day. Metternich had appealed for a conference to settle the whole matter, but Russia, now under Canning's influence, replied by a blunt refusal to attend any congress or conference at Paris. Metternich knew that Canning would not attend one. He still grumbled and shuffled ; he had not meant, he said, a real congress with crowned heads. The Paris Conference was already at hand. " It was not then a question of making a special conference, of exciting public attention, of provoking questions of jealousy and pre-eminence, not at all—we must love, and advance, and understand one another." This refusal of a congress was all due

---

[1] *F.O. France*, 146/106. Granville to Canning, Aug. 18/20. It is perhaps fair to add that Spain denied that the treaty covered the case of a collective body of deserters. But she could not deny the obligations of neutrality.

[2] *V.S.A.*, Berichte aus Frankreich, Bd. 369. Apponyi to Metternich, Aug. 24, enclosing Apponyi to Brunetti, Aug. 28/26.

to Russia's ' fear of offending England.' Amid Metternich's protests this last project of a congress had the *coup de grâce* administered to it by Russia at the bidding of Canning.

On the 19th September Apponyi reported. " There is no more question of conference on which he [1] [Pozzo] formerly insisted with unexampled heat."

7. CANNING IN PARIS (SEPTEMBER–OCTOBER 1826)

On the 19th September Canning arrived in Paris in person, a day late, because his wife Joan insisted on arriving, not on a Sunday but on a Monday. She could not bear to be seen in Paris for twenty-four hours without a French costume. The Austrian Ambassador, Apponyi, wrote that Canning set all the cooks of Paris agog, that he enjoyed ministerial fare good and bad, and ' made shake hands ' with everybody. Canning said that he came on a personal visit to Granville, and *incognito*. But few believed him. For he came in the fullness of his fame, indisputably as much the master of English policy as Castlereagh and with a popular renown his predecessor had never possessed. His popularity had just won a general election. He had " all the giddy young men, the dandies of London, at his feet," he shared " the principles of the liberal majority," and had " no longer an opposition to fear." All the diplomats flocked to see one who had already exercised so great an influence on the world, who had emancipated South America, defied France, and separated Austria from Russia. Apponyi, a high-bred aristocrat, thought him *gauche* in society, and little accustomed to the world, but said that his manners were ' gentle and engaging,' that his face often showed ' benevolence and *bonhomie*,' though the expression is " soon effaced by one of his searching looks, or by a smile that is evil and mocking." The lips, so famed for eloquence and wit, uttered nothing but compliments ; they were dumb on politics, at any rate in public. But he was closeted all day with Granville and drove the pens of his subordinates at the rate of twelve hours a day. He was doing something clearly —but Apponyi did not know what. He noticed only that

[1] *V.S.A.*, Berichte aus Frankreich, Bd. 369. Apponyi to Metternich, Sept. 19/26.

Pozzo di Borgo had, after a painful struggle, overcome his deep antipathy to England, and appeared to be the bosom friend of her minister.[1] In secret Canning held meetings with Villèle and Damas and Pozzo, and brought them over to his policy over Portugal. At length he struck, and struck hard. Spain was clearly violating neutrality ; the Portuguese deserters were being pushed up to the frontier, with the connivance and active support of the Captains-General of adjoining Spanish Provinces. On the 3rd October he deemed the crisis so serious that, without consulting the Cabinet or the King at home, though in concert with Pozzo and Villèle at Paris, he sent a despatch to Lamb at Madrid ordering him to quit the Spanish capital if the Spanish Government did not disperse the deserters in time for the fact to be announced at the opening of the Portuguese Cortes (*i.e.* by the 30th October). On the 7th October, finding the latest news a little more encouraging and having more confidence in Pozzo and Damas, he revoked this step and suspended Lamb's recall.[2] But to those who knew, alike in Spain, in Russia, and in France, he had shown that he would not shrink from any measures needed to defend the integrity of Portugal or the honour of England which was bound up with it. Well indeed would it have been for Spain and for France if the warning he gave had been heeded. For he was not one who threatened in vain. As he once wrote : " A menace unaccompanied by means of action is an engine which England would never deign to employ." There would be no more threats. If Spain did not submit, there would be action soon.

8. CANNING FORCES MIGUEL TO TAKE THE OATH ; ITS EFFECT IN PORTUGAL

Austria did not know of these resolutions, nor of the consent of France and Russia to them. Pressure was now to be applied to Austria to use her influence to quiet Spain and to allay unrest in Portugal. The position of Metternich was

[1] These details are in *V.S.A.*, Berichte aus Frankreich. Apponyi to Metternich, Sept. 19, 21, Oct. 7, 19, part^re.

[2] *F.O. Spain*, 185/106. Canning to F. Lamb., Oct. 3, Nos. 45-6 ; Oct. 7, No. 49, 1826.

important, because he retained Dom Miguel at Vienna, and could let him loose to destroy the constitution. Metternich had announced unctuously that Dom Miguel would be left perfect freedom of choice, though everyone knew that he would take the advice of the Emperor Francis. The Emperor Pedro had written Miguel a letter in which he ordered him to do three things : to take the oath to the constitution ; to obtain a Papal dispensation and marry his, Pedro's, daughter, Maria Gloria ; and lastly, to repair to Brazil. The command as to taking the oath was an awkward one, and Metternich, as he confessed, would have liked to have some preliminary explanations. But throughout September Canning pressed Metternich hard. Why did not Miguel take the oath ? It was only with reluctance that Metternich and Miguel surrendered, and even after Miguel had taken the oath, Metternich concealed the fact for some days. On the 13th October it was announced to diplomats, but not published, that Miguel ' some days ago ' had taken the oath verbally and in writing. " Necessities," whimpered Metternich, " are often greater than the means within the reach of human faculties." [1] When there was ' no categorical concurrence ' in the Courts of Europe, Russia and the ' *insistance de Canning* ' were bound to carry the day. Canning was indignant at the attempt to keep secret the taking of the oath. He told Villèle that " The Prince Metternich undertakes a great responsibility by his fatal silence, and he will answer for the distressing results that may come from it."

The news that Miguel had taken the oath reached Canning at Paris on the 19th. Within an hour he had forwarded the information to Madrid by a trusty messenger, who was instructed to proceed hot-foot from thence to Lisbon. He arrived there in time, but only just in time. " By a most fortunate chance," wrote À Court, " the messenger . . . with your despatch of the 19th instant from Paris . . . reached Lisbon at 7 o'clock yesterday, the very morning of the opening [of the Cortes], notwithstanding the extraordinary impediments he experienced on the road." The news was

---

[1] *V.S.A.*, Weisungen nach Frankreich, Bd. 373. Metternich to Apponyi, Oct. 13/26 ; Berichte aus Frankreich, Bd. 370. Apponyi to Metternich, Oct. 20/26.

in time to be inserted in the Regent's opening speech, and produced a profound sensation. The Infanta read her speech herself, and, when referring to the support of England, " she was pleased to address herself to me," writes À Court com- placently, " honouring me with a profound inclination of the head." . . . " The oath of Dom Miguel, arriving at such a moment, was everything to the Government . . . a sufficient guarantee against future desertions or rebellion or any rash proceedings in the Chamber." [1] " *Viva, Viva !* " wrote Canning, " Thus the *benevolent* intentions of Prince Metternich towards Portugal are happily frustrated. If the messenger had arrived twenty-four hours later, who could declare the consequences which might have resulted from the belief in which the members of the Chamber were—that Dom Miguel was hostile to the Constitution." [2]

The intrigue was even more discreditable than Canning knew. Not only had Villèle and Metternich plotted in common to induce Dom Miguel to delay taking the oath,[3] not only had Metternich delayed the announcement of the fact, but on 30th October, the day after Dom Miguel's marriage by proxy at Vienna, Metternich revealed to the Great Powers that Dom Miguel had reserved certain rights in taking the oath.[4] This last concealment worked against Metternich for the moment, as it had been announced by Isabella that he had taken it without conditions. In the end, however, Miguel's reservations became known, and encouraged disorder in Portugal and interference from Spain.

9. The Spanish Intrigue against Portugal

What followed is obscure. In October and November Metternich was still intriguing to obtain the revocation of the

---

[1] *F.O. Austria*, 120/81. Canning to Wellesley, Oct. 20/26, enclosing À Court to Canning of Oct. 31.

[2] To Palmella, *Memoirs of Saldanha*, i. 117-8.

[3] *V.S.A.*, Weisungen nach Frankreich, Bd. 372. Metternich to Apponyi, No. 2, Sept. 7/26. Villèle's suggestion for delay is in Berichte aus Frank- reich, Bd. 369. Apponyi to Metternich, Aug. 26/26. The Regent Infanta in her speech to the Cortes of Oct. 30, said, " Dom Miguel had . . . simply and *unconditionally* taken the oath." Wellesley had warned Canning on Oct. 1 that he thought the oath would be conditional, but did not state it in his despatch of the 13th.

[4] *Ibid.*, Oct. 24/26, *ibid.*

Portuguese Constitution; Russia was supporting England; France seems to have hovered uncertainly between the two. Her representative at Madrid (de Moustier) was still more uncertain, and his rebukes and remonstrances to the King of Spain were of the mildest kind. At the last moment he was recalled in disgrace, but too late to avert disaster to Spain and humiliation to France.[1] There was no doubt what Spain was doing. She was pursuing a policy familiar to Balkan States in the nineteenth century. In order to create dis-turbance or to provoke incidents, *comitajis* and brigands are armed and sent across a neighbouring border to overthrow an unstable government or to provoke international interference. In this case, instead of raising their own *comitajis*, the Spanish Government proceeded to arm, to clothe, and to organise the Portuguese military deserters whom she had promised to disperse. The idea was ingenious, for such persons could be disavowed, though the fact that they had Spanish arms and equipment could not be. Spain doubtless hoped that the Portuguese Government would be provoked to attack her openly, in which case France might intervene. If she did not, the weak government and the detestable constitution of Portugal would be destroyed by the incursions of the deserters. Neither Lamb nor À Court doubted that high Spanish officials, from Ferdinand downwards, were deep in the plot, though, ostrich-like, they thought themselves quite unobserved. But then, as Metternich once genially said, " there is not a man of sense in the whole of Spain." In this case, whatever we know of their wisdom we cannot doubt their guilt.[2] Yet these methods of covert warfare might have succeeded. Portugal was in a state of great unrest, the constitution was a mere name, and the government might collapse at a touch. It was only the resolution of Canning which caused the Spanish aggression to fail of success.

---

[1] *F.O. Portugal*, 63/310. À Court to Canning, Nov. 25/26. " The possibility of the arrival of an auxiliary corps of British troops has been the *principal stimulus* to the more explicit and direct instructions sent to the Marquis de Moustier." Canning underlined the italicised passage and wrote in the margin ' *the only one.*'

[2] Certainly À Court did not, *v. F.O. Portugal*, 63/310, Nos. 138–9, Nov. 27/26. On this the main British case was founded, but there was plenty of other evidence from Madrid. *Vide* also À Court, No. 151, Dec. 11, and No. 153, Dec. 13.

10. THE *CASUS FŒDERIS* OCCURS (8TH DECEMBER 1826)

Canning returned to England on the 25th October, and found he had to face bitter opposition there on account of his high-handed action in recalling Lamb. He had, said Wellington, committed us to possible war on his own authority, and the King professed to agree with the Duke. But Liverpool replied firmly to Wellington that Canning's measures had been taken in concert with France and Spain, that they were necessary to avert war, and had in fact succeeded. Canning's action was soon to be justified. On the 14th November he wrote to Granville that Portugal had appealed to him for help against Spain, but that he did not think that the circumstances even yet justified intervention. Spanish aggression had clearly increased, despite the strong warnings recently sent her. His part was, however, taken. " Whatever might be the risk," he wrote on the 27th November (and it was considerable), " of introducing a representative constitution into Portugal, the danger of retracting it after it had been introduced would have been tenfold more formidable." [1] The Portuguese Constitution was not, at any rate if he could help it, to be assailed from without. On the 3rd December, Palmella once more wrote to Canning and gave evidence as to fresh incursions into Portuguese territory from Spain, and formally claimed Portugal's right to British assistance under the treaty. Canning still doubted whether the evidence was good enough, but on the 8th he was convinced. On the 9th he wrote to Granville, ' The *casus fœderis* has occurred.' Spain had furnished the Portuguese deserters with arms and equipment, who were attacking in the north, and there were now details of a second attack on Portuguese territory from the south.

11. CANNING'S PARLIAMENTARY TRIUMPH
(12TH DECEMBER 1826)

Action was seldom more prompt. Canning came down to the House with a message from the King on the 12th, and spoke as follows : " It was only on last Friday night [8th December]

---

[1] *F.O. Argentine*, 6/13, to Lord Ponsonby, Nov. 27/26.

that precise information arrived.[1] On Saturday His Majesty's confidential servants came to a decision. On Sunday that decision received the sanction of His Majesty. On Monday it was communicated to both Houses of Parliament, and this day [12th December] that I have the honour of addressing you— the troops are on their march for embarkation. . . . Let us fly to the aid of Portugal by whomsoever attacked ; because it is our duty to do so ; and let us cease our interference where that duty ends. We go to Portugal, not to rule, not to dictate, not to prescribe constitutions—but to defend and preserve the independence of an Ally. We go to plant the Standard of England on the well-known heights of Lisbon. Where that Standard is planted, foreign dominion shall not come ! " As he uttered these words he looked upwards. A beam of light streamed through the windows and smote on him, and his face seemed as if inspired.[2]

The effect was profound, but it was even surpassed in his reply, a reply in which he showed how closely Portugal and Spain were involved with the New World. He was taunted, as so often before, with having shown pusillanimity in per- mitting a French occupation of Spain. To this reproach he was sensitive, for he held that Villèle had tricked him by promising to evacuate and then recalling his words. If so, he took an ample vengeance. " It would be disingenuous indeed not to admit that the entry of the French Army into Spain was, in a certain sense, a disparagement—and affront to the pride—a blow to the feelings of England. . . . Was nothing then to be done ? . . . What, if the possession of Spain might be rendered harmless in rival hands—harmless as regarded us— and valueless to the possessors ? Might not compensation for disparagement be obtained, and the policy of our ancestors be vindicated, by means better adapted to the present time ? If France occupied Spain, it was necessary in order to avoid the consequences of that occupation—that we should blockade Cadiz ? No—I looked another way—I sought

---

[1] *F.O. France*, 146/83. Canning to Granville, Dec. 9. The ' precise information ' was in a despatch of Sir Wm. À Court of Nov. 27, which reached Canning on Dec. 8, at 8.15 p.m. *F.O. Portugal*, 63/310. À Court to Canning, Nos. 138 and 139, Nov. 27.

[2] This story was told by Lord John Russell in after days to the late Master of Trinity, Dr Montagu Butler, from whom I had it.

materials of compensation in another hemisphere. Contemplating Spain, such as her ancestors had known her, I
resolved that if France had Spain, it should not be Spain
'WITH THE INDIES.' I CALLED THE NEW WORLD INTO
EXISTENCE TO REDRESS THE BALANCE OF THE OLD." [1] For
a moment the daring of this utterance imposed a profound
silence, there was even a titter ; and the stroke seemed to have
failed. Then the House grew electric, and rose at him, as an
audience rises at a theatre. The storm broke, cheer on cheer
re-echoed to the rafters, and in one delirious moment Canning
reaped the reward for five years of labour and self-sacrifice.
" If I know anything of the House of Commons from thirty-
three years' experience," wrote he to Granville on the 14th
December, " or if I may trust to what reaches me in report of
feelings out of doors, the declaration of the obvious but unsuspected truth, that ' I called the New World into existence
to redress the balance of the Old,' has been more grateful to
English ears and English feelings ten thousand times, than
would have been the most satisfactory announcement of the
intention of the French Government to withdraw its army
from Spain. . . . Nor will it escape Villèle's observation that
the decision of the House of Commons is quite as enthusiastic
for active exertion now, as it was in 1823 for passive
neutrality." [2]

12. CANNING, FRANCE, AND METTERNICH

Great oratorical successes are not always, perhaps not ever,
great diplomatic triumphs. For, as Canning once himself
said, appeals to public opinion are an internal question, but
their results may be external. He had caught and gauged
English opinion exactly, and enlisted the whole strength and
power of his country in the cause of Portugal. But outside

[1] *Speeches*, [1836], vi., No. 1. The original version is much shorter
(*Star*, Dec. 13/26). "Was it necessary to blockade Cadiz, I say, to restore
the situation of England ? No; I look at the possessions of Spain on
the other side of the Atlantic : I look at the Indies, and I call in the New
World to redress the balance of the Old."
[2] Stap., *G.C. & T.*, 547. Madame Lieven heard this speech from the
ventilator (a hole then used as the Ladies' Gallery). She had to be
released from it, as she was in a hurry to attend a dinner. Stapleton
released the fair captive, who complained, as she went, ' *mon mari me
battra.*'

England the story was a different one.   France was naturally mortified. Villèle and Damas were now reminded in direct fashion of their aggression on Spain of four years back, and of the measures taken by England to defeat its effects. Canning seems to have felt that they deserved this rebuke, though he had perhaps gone too far in his expressions. As Wellington wrote, with a world of concentrated bitterness, " We are now explaining away the effect of our speeches at Paris and Madrid." The nervous strain of delivering his speech had brought back " all the rheumatics [I] had been bleeding and blistering away during the preceding week." Yet he found time to write frequently to Granville. He circulated a revised version of his speech, he praised the moderation of the reply of Damas, " Whatever he may finally think of my speeches, nothing can alter my opinion of his." He was sorry to have ' cuffed and rubbed ' Villèle, but he had really supported the moderates and weakened the bigots of France by the strength of his language. Finally, on learning that they accepted these explanations in good part, he pronounced Damas ' a saint ' and Villèle ' an angel ' (29th December).[1]

One thing, however, can hardly be denied.   France, whatever her good intentions, had been remiss in action.   She had shared in the advice to Spain to refuse to give back the Portuguese deserters in August, and Villèle had tried to get Miguel to delay his oath in October. He had recalled de Moustier, indeed, but too late. The French troops in Spain, if vigorously handled, could at any time have stopped the Spanish aggressions. Apponyi wrote, ' France *a gâté tout* ' ; and Metternich agreed with him.[2]

As regards Spain, Canning's speech was not undiplomatic. He might, and with justice, have publicly said a great deal more than he did say of the perfidious and unneutral acts which had been instigated from Madrid. He told Esterházy privately on the 11th : " The aggression of Spain was evident, and, as for its effect, it was to be considered as if made against England herself. It is as though they had gone into Plymouth," added he, cutting short the conversation. On the

---

[1] Stap., *G.C. & T.*, 545–56. Damas, in his *Mémoires*, [1890], relates the affair with dignity and candour, ii. 92–103.

[2] So also did Brunetti, Austrian Minister in Spain, v. *V.S.A.*, Berichte aus Frankreich, Bd. 374. Apponyi to Metternich, Jan. 6/27, particulière.

same day he wrote to Polignac : " It is not our fault. Treaties are sacred things, and the longest *longanimité* can finally be exhausted. It is not war with Spain. It is simply the defence of Portugal." [1] In the King's Message and his own speech the jealous susceptibilities of Spain were considered. Further, the recall of England's Minister from Madrid, which had again been ordered, was suspended on the 12th December to avoid any appearance of war. Esterházy admitted that the language as to Spain appeared ' calm and moderate,' though he thought there was much menace and irritability beneath the surface.

But there was a European as well as a Spanish and French side to the speech. The phrase used in what some called the *corrigé*, and Canning the ' authentique,' version was that " in the case of war England could not avoid seeing ranked under her banners all the restless and dissatisfied of *any nation* with which she might come into conflict." The original version was : " All those who—whether justly or unjustly—are dissatisfied with the present state of *their own countries*." There was a world of difference between the singular and the plural. [2] Villèle thought the phrase meant that, in such case, Canning would arm Spanish constitutional refugees and send them to capture the Balearic Isles. Others interpreted it as an incitement to revolution in every country. Esterházy deplored this utterance ; even Lieven shook his head sadly, saying, it " will produce the most serious effect on us, and I shall have much difficulty in presenting it in a less unfavourable light." [3] Pozzo di Borgo suddenly revived all his old hatred of England and of Canning. He wrote characteristically : " He [Canning] conjures us to take care not to put him under the necessity of opening the cataracts of his furies, if we do not wish to be their victims." There was no dissentient voice

---

[1] Both in *V.S.A.*, Berichte aus England, Bd. 329. Esterházy to Metternich, Dec. 11/26. In point of fact, Canning decided to recall Lamb from Madrid on Dec. 3, but suspended it again on the 5th. On deciding to send troops he instructed him to remain (Dec. 14), as " your coming away now would be *almost* tantamount to a declaration of war," *v.* Canning to Lamb under dates cited. *F.O. Spain*, 185/106.

[2] *Vide* Appendix VI. for text of the two versions of the speech.

[3] *V.S.A.*, Berichte aus England, Bd. 229. Esterházy to Metternich, Dec. 18/26.

in the Commons when he said this [there were really three or four], so we must " avow a sad and terrible truth, that is, that there is a revolution in England in the minds opposed to the tranquillity of the monarchs of the Continent, and that if any struggle were to break out between England and any other Power, the man who presides over the Cabinet of London and the nation as a whole, would have recourse to the blackest means to accomplish their aim, that is to satisfy their pride and their insatiable rapacity." [1] Metternich, viewing the speech more calmly, thought it most serious. In sending troops to Portugal, wrote he on the 25th December, " Canning gains the revolutionary party and goes to moral war with us." [2]

But there was wisdom in Canning's appeal as well as rhetoric and passion. By the confession of his foes the whole British public opinion was on his side. He appealed also to moderate opinion in other countries. Villèle, Pozzo, and Metternich really were afraid that such words would excite many of their own Liberals to protest against all hostile action against a constitution defended by Great Britain. The possibility of a split between despotic governments and their peoples was one the rulers were not prepared to face. It was just because the Great Continental Powers thought Canning a ' revolutionary ' appealing to their ' revolutionaries ' that they decided to take no action in the matter.

Yet Canning was not a ' revolutionary ' on this or on any other occasion.[3] Even Wellington had to admit this. " We pass in Europe for a Jacobin Club but at present we have done nothing to justify this," *i.e.* by action. The policy of action was pursued in deference to treaty rights. Castlereagh himself had approved it, for he had promised in 1820 and in 1821

---

[1] Pozzo di Borgo, Dec. 22/26. *Portfolio*, 1836, i. 277–8. The letter is undoubtedly authentic.

[2] *V.S.A.*, Weisungen nach Frankreich, Bd. 373. Metternich to Apponyi, Dec. 25/26. It is characteristic of his duplicity that he told Wellesley on Dec. 22/26, and again on Jan. 4/27, that Canning's action was ' completely justified,' *v.* under these dates *F.O. Austria*, 120/83 and 84.

[3] The following extract from Hobhouse's *Diary* is of great importance, Dec. 18/26. " Lord Ashley told me that Canning had made his strong attack on the Ultra-Legitimates purposely to assist Villèle in his struggle with that party in the French Cabinet. He told me that he knew Canning well, and that Canning was, in fact, very much afraid of revolutionary power, and would never, except in cases of indispensable necessity, assist it in any country." Lord Broughton (Hobhouse), *Recollections of a Long Life* (1916), iii. 160.

to defend Portugal against territorial aggression from without, and Canning had explicitly repeated this pledge several times during every year of his Ministry from 1822 to 1826. All he did now was to honour the pledge by ready and prompt action when the necessity occurred. What the Neo-Holies really objected to was that Canning, in defending the territory, defended also the Constitution, of Portugal. He actually had had the temerity to say, " May God prosper this attempt at constitutional liberty in Portugal ! " But could any British Minister say otherwise ? The deserters—instigated by Spain —had attacked the territory of Portugal as the best means of subverting the constitution. To give moral support to a constitution thus assailed from without seemed natural and right, but the material aid had not been sent either to establish or to preserve it.[1] In point of fact, Canning remonstrated with the Regent for issuing a proclamation without counter-signature, and advised her not to allow parliamentary debates to be public, thus moderating arbitrariness and constitutional-ism at the same time. His advice was not authoritative, for he thought that any nation should experiment in political science as it liked. But he was prepared to say that he would not countenance Portugal (or indeed any other nation) in extending her political propaganda outside her own borders. France and the other Allies had all said, in fact, that they would fight if she did. Canning while at Paris had heard something of this from Villèle, and he not only in no way objected to this point of view, but had already remonstrated strongly with Portugal on the subject. Owing to his advice, the Portuguese Government, after one or two provocative utterances, eventually assumed a most rational and moderate attitude. They would have been within their rights in insist-ing on a restoration of their deserters to Portugal, not on a dispersion of them in Spain, and in demanding from Spain a complete, instead of a qualified, political recognition for the Regency. But they did neither, and by this studied modera-tion greatly contributed to a peaceful solution of the whole question. The whole is a valuable illustration of Canning's peculiar conception of nationality. He did not think that any

---

[1] It is quite clear that Canning had faint hopes of the survival of the constitution, but supported it, once granted, as the least of evils.

nation could afford to be 'chivalrous and romantic,' and he defended Portugal by arms, not because he was a political Don Quixote championing the rights of a small nation, but because treaty obligations bound England to defend her territorial integrity.

In truth, and it is a fact of considerable interest, it can be shown that Metternich himself in reality approved of the principle. In 1824, when the idea of sending Hanoverian troops to Portugal was discussed, Metternich approved the action in these words : " Everything in the matter has the stamp of legality. The King of Portugal had the right to claim aid [from England] when he judged it well and useful to do so. Any objection on the part of the Allies appears to me compromising and a sheer loss." Not only so, but Metternich brought the matter before the German Diet, which unanimously approved " the right of His Hanoverian Majesty to accede to the demand of His Most Faithful Majesty " (the King of Portugal).[1] Why then did Metternich think differently in 1826 ? The reason is interesting ; it was simply and solely that in 1824 Portugal had a monarch with a relatively strong prerogative, but that in 1826 she had a constitution. Metternich approved of sending troops to defend an arbitrary king, and disapproved not so much of sending them to defend the territory of Portugal but of the support thus lent to constitutionalism. Here he was clearly inconsistent, and on strict grounds Canning was absolutely right. He held that the constitution was an accident (which incidentally he turned against the Neo-Holies with happy effect), but that was no reason for refusing to come to Portugal's aid when the *casus fœderis* occurred. And that the *casus fœderis* did occur in 1826 Metternich himself admitted.[2]

The position then is that Metternich, the failing champion

---

[1] *V.S.A.*, Weisungen, etc., nach Russland. Metternich to Lebzeltern, July 14, Aug. 11/24. In the last despatch he somewhat modified his view because he did not think that information showed that the *casus fœderis* had occurred. Here Canning agreed with him, and for that reason refused to send troops in 1824. On the question of right, if the *casus fœderis* occurred, Metternich agreed throughout with Canning.

[2] Metternich expressed great disapproval of Canning's speech, but that was because of its appeal to Liberals, etc. He twice said that the 'measures' (*i.e.* sending troops) were completely justified, *v. F.O. Austria*, 120/83. Wellesley to Canning, Dec. 22/26, No. 134 ; and *F.O. Austria*, 120/84, *ibid.*, Jan. 4/27, No. 1.

of the Neo-Holy Alliance, preferred the maintenance of strong monarchies to the maintenance of treaties. As Canning once wrote to Wellington (30th November 1824), " I have no doubt in my own mind that Mett[ernich] *does* undervalue treaty, *because* he prefers authoritative interference." [1] This instance proves that he was right, for Metternich wished, as did Pozzo and Villèle, by discrediting to destroy the constitution. There was one reason why he particularly wished this con- stitution to be destroyed. After the Polignac Memorandum and the Monroe Doctrine, Europe, no longer able to influence, had tried to ignore, the New World. The American Continents were left to mismanage their own affairs and to discredit their own constitutions. But Metternich thought it in the highest degree improper that a New-World potentate should introduce a constitution into the Old World, turn a strict monarchy into a limited one, and be supported by Canning, the foremost champion of constitutional liberty in both worlds. That was bringing the New World into the Old with a vengeance. Where was the process to stop, and how could it be justified ? To these questions the forebodings of the Neo-Holy Alliance gave but gloomy answers. France, too, though not particularly fond of her Allies, had her grievance. England now had troops in Portugal, as France had troops in Spain. Hence England had a lever in the future to obtain French evacuation such as had been so often promised and deferred. For she was unlikely to agree to leave Portugal unless and until France agreed to leave Spain.

13. Effect of Canning's Despatch of Troops to Portugal

On the 11th December even Metternich admitted that the incursion into Portugal was " one of those events which place things on a slide, the rapidity of which seems to be impossible to calculate." In point of fact, the southern incursion, reported to Canning on the 8th December, was an actual threat not only to the constitution but also to the government and the capital itself. Sir William À Court wrote from Lisbon on the 19th December, " it would be

---

[1] *W.N.D.*, ii. 359.   Italics in original.

difficult to describe to you the joy and enthusiasm with which the intelligence of the speedy arrival of our troops was received by the Publick," and spoke of the " most extraordinary promptitude with which execution followed acknowledgment." On the 23rd he wrote, " no one is afraid to be a Constitutionalist now." On Christmas Day he described how the white sails of the fleet were sighted and how the banks of the Tagus were thronged with shouting crowds. " We are perfectly tranquil now. England has spoken, and some of her troops have already arrived. The lion's awakening (*ce réveil du Lion*) has been majestic." [1] The supporters of Miguel in Portugal went back home at once, the deserters in Spain were disarmed and dispersed, even the invincibly obstinate Ferdinand bowed his stiff neck to the yoke, recognised the Portuguese Regency and forebore from covert or open attacks on their territory. And to whom was all this due ? About that there could be but one opinion. Even Lamb, who wrote privately to Granville that Canning's speech had ' done infinite mischief at Madrid,' felt constrained to write to Wellington : " What I said to-day finishes the affair, and never was a more desperate one saved." [2] And even Wellington would not have denied that it was Canning who had saved it. The vigour of the action, like the vigour of the speech by which he justified it, positively electrified Europe.

When a diplomat takes up arms, even though, as in this case, the results are bloodless, the effects go far beyond the immediate incident in question. Before this date the language used by his detractors suggested that Canning was a man of words and expedients, a vain seeker after popularity, a diplomatic demagogue. Such language was never used again. Canning had made himself and England feared, because he directed a public opinion irresistible in England and powerful throughout Europe. It was now seen that he had not hesitated in this case, and would not hesitate again to support words and policies by vigorous and resolute action.

---

[1] *F.O. France*, 146/89. Canning to Granville, Jan. 1/27, enclosing Sir William À Court to Canning, Dec. 19, and also Dec. 25/26. Two private letters of À Court to Lord Howard de Walden of Dec. 3 and 25, in *F.O. Portugal*, 63/311. The second speaks of ' *Ce réveil du Lion.*'
[2] *Gr. MSS.* Lamb to Granville, Jan. 5/27, and to Wellington, *W.N.D.*, iii. 554, of Jan. 21.

And behind his action loomed the new and terrible power of his opinions. It is certain that the prestige of Canning never stood higher than at the end of 1826, and it is doubtful if that of England ever did.[1]

Neither the judgment of diplomats nor of the public Press is always that of posterity, but there was one man in Europe who was fitted to anticipate it. Goethe, with sage and serene detachment, had always praised the things and the men that he thought great and wise. Despite everything, he had admired Napoleon when the Allies condemned him, and the 'Holy Alliance' when Liberals condemned it. Now he admired Canning when the 'Holy Allies' condemned him. The speech he thought was ' excellent ' and even ' sublime.' Those who objected to it were simply objecting to the statement of facts. They must have something great that they may hate it. " . . . He " (Canning) " feels very well the extent of his power and the dignity of his position, and he is right to speak as he feels. This . . . [they] cannot understand . . . greatness disturbs them ; they are not so constituted as to respect it and cannot endure it." [2] Clearly the sage of Weimar had in view the stately image in which Canning described England's position :

—— " *Celsa sedet Æolus arce,*
Sceptra tenens ; mollitque animos et temperat iras ;
Ni faciat, maria ac terras coelumque profundum
Quippe ferant rapidi secum, verrant que per auras."

[1] *Cp.* Sir J. Mackintosh, June 8/27. *Hans. Deb.*, N.S., xvii. 1190. " Looking to the recognition of the independence of the South American States— looking to the succours that had been sent to Portugal—considering the good which, he hoped, was silently but surely working for Greece, he came to this conclusion when he cast his eye over the page of history, that no three preceding years could be compared with the three which had [just] elapsed . . . in point of brilliant, beneficial, and successful policy."

[2] Conversations with Eckermann, Jan. 3/27.

CHAPTER XVII

THE FREEDOM OF GREECE

1. THE TERMS OF THE PROTOCOL (4th APRIL 1826) [1]

THE first phase of the Greek question lasted from 1821 to the 3rd April 1826. It was marked by the fact that every Power, except Russia, declined to sanction the use of force in settling the problem, by the failure of Metternich to retain the Congress System or his hold over Alexander. Scarcely less important was the separate action of England in upholding the right of both Greeks and Turks to be heard in the settlement. More important still was the decision of Canning to contemplate a limited use of force, and to co-operate with Russia to the exclusion of Metternich. That goal was not reached till the Protocol was signed, and the result was to place the whole Eastern question in an entirely new position.

The Protocol of the 4th April 1826 contained the following important provisions :—

1. That mediation should be offered to Turkey over Greece. If accepted, Greeçe was to be a dependency of the Porte and pay tribute. She was to have liberty of conscience and commerce, and complete power of managing her own affairs, but Turkey was to have a share in nominating officials.

2 and 3. England was to try a single mediation between Greece and the Porte, and between the Porte and Russia. Joint Anglo-Russian mediation was to take place if English mediation was refused.

4. The conduct of these negotiations and the boundaries of Greece to be arranged by Russia and England with Turkey.

[1] For text of Protocol see Appendix VII.

5. Both Powers disclaimed, for their part, any special territorial or commercial designs on Turkey.

6. The other Great Powers—Austria, France, and Prussia—were to be asked to accede to the Protocol and to join with Russia in guaranteeing the settlement. England would not give such guarantee.

The Protocol was claimed by Madame Lieven, as by some later writers, as a victory for Russia. It was certainly a victory over Wellington. Villèle, Metternich, and Lebzeltern thought that Canning had really triumphed both over Wellington and the Lievens. It does not seem correct that Canning disapproved of the Protocol as a whole, or thought that it went too far. He objected, indeed, to Article 6 as ' not very artistically drawn,' and thought it unfortunate that Austria, and France, and Prussia were asked to guarantee ' we know not *what*.' [1] But he admitted that the Duke took care " to go no further, under any circumstances, in support of the Greeks, than the British Government thought proper." [2] So his objections to the Protocol extended not to substance, but to form.

Czar Nicholas claimed that the Protocol had prevented separate action by Canning over Greece, but that he had none the less delivered his ultimatum over the Principalities to Turkey.[3] But the Russians did not understand that Canning did not want to soften the ultimatum ; he thought threats from Russia, in her own special interests, might be salutary, and help both England and Russia to settle the Greek affair. In his view it was a gain, and not a loss, that the use of force in Greece was not, as such, prescribed in the Protocol. Canning had indicated, indeed, that he would stop Ibrahim by force from depopulating the Morea. To that he might be compelled by public opinion. But he hoped still to get, and did

---

[1] Stap., *G.C. & T.*, 478, to Granville, Aug. 8/26.
[2] *F.O. Greece*, 32/26. Canning's Abstract of negotiations.
[3] Schiemann, *Geschichte Russlands*, ii. 138. Nicholas had deliberately deceived Wellington as to the ultimatum to Turkey, and as to the numbers of the Russian Army, and, perhaps intelligibly, thought he had done so over other things too. His explanations to his old Allies (France and Austria) were probably not sincere, and were certainly not taken by them as such. He claimed that he could bring England into line with other Allies; cf. Nicholas's explanations to Ferronays in *V.S.A.*, Russland, Bd. 9 (1826). Lebzeltern to Metternich, Apr. 3/26, No. 173.

ultimately succeed in getting, a practical, though not formal, disavowal of the project from the Turkish Government. As soon as he had this he was free from all promise of force, and he obtained it by the end of August.

The declaration of disinterestedness was indeed of more questionable policy. Russia, together with England, was most unequivocally pledged (Article 6) " not to seek in this arrangement any increase of territory nor any exclusive influence, nor advantage in commerce for their subjects, which shall not be equally attainable by other nations." The danger of this clause was that it simply depended for its efficacy on the good faith of Russia. In the end she sought to explain it away. But, even at the worst, it was better to make Russia sign such a declaration of disinterestedness than not to do so. Madame Lieven certainly believed that she had entangled Canning with Russia. But Canning had at length made up his mind to be entangled. Russia was likely to make war on her own account. It was better for England to act with her than to remain isolated and powerless. Metternich had failed to restrain Russia by a policy of doing nothing ; Canning, therefore, could only restrain her by doing ' something.' [1] His view was that Russia might act alone over the Principalities, but that she must act with England over Greece. Thus he left a free hand to Russia over her separate negotiation with Turkey, which ended successfully at Ackerman (6th October).

Canning made himself very agreeable to Madame Lieven pending the return of her husband to London. " He made a great exclamation of joy " when he heard Lieven would return soon. He flattered the young Russian *chargé d'affaires* Potemkin, took him by the arm and walked in with him to the table at a grand dinner he gave to diplomats. He and Madame Lieven saw one another when even the Duke of York was denied her door, and stayed at the Cottage together with King George. Each cleverly professed to be persuaded by the other. M. Lieven did not hurry over his return, and passed

---

[1] Lebzeltern, than whom there was no better judge, said that Canning had detached ' the preponderant Power' from the Alliance and made it ' adherent to his plan.' Metternich commented that Canning would try to paralyse Russia and ' will prevent war.' *V.S.A.*, Russland, Bd. 9. Lebzeltern to Metternich, Apr. 7/26.

slowly through Europe, taking Paris on his way, where Villèle found him *inabordable*.[1] He found at London and in Canning a negotiator more subtle than the Duke.[2]

2. ATTITUDE OF GREEK, FRENCH, AND AUSTRIAN GOVERNMENTS

Good news had arrived from Greece. Stratford reported that, for the first time, the Greeks, disheartened by their reverses, showed themselves willing to be content with something short of complete independence. They offered to recognise the suzerainty of the Porte, and to pay either tribute, or a lump sum as indemnity, to Turkey. But they demanded a 'bag and baggage' expulsion of Turks from Greece, a wide extension of her boundaries, and complete control of their own internal administration. So far so good, for they had approached nearly to the terms of the Protocol. Their further demands for an immediate armistice and for a guarantee by Great Britain offered more difficulty. Otherwise, Canning was a little dissatisfied. Wellington had no sooner returned than he began to repent of his action, and most of his colleagues were frankly Turcophile. British public opinion, though friendly to Greece, was hostile to Russia. Canning's method of conciliating it was to work up feeling over the increase of piracy in the Ægean—to 'press the Turks hard' over this. Externally things were more satisfactory. In August the French Government was approached, like the others, and seemed conciliatory, while Prussia did not appear to be hostile. Metternich had in private expressed violent opinions. He wrote '*quelle folie*' on a despatch from St Petersburg giving the first news of the Protocol; '*faux*' on one from London giving Wellington's defence of it. He informed Esterházy on the 4th June, "All in this system is absurd, and of an incontestable absurdity."[3] On receiving the official

---

[1] The matter had been mentioned by Canning to the French Government on May 4. *F.O. France*, 146/80. Canning to Granville, May 4, and formally on Aug. 15/26.

[2] The Duke was entirely mistaken as to Greece. So late as Sept. 7/26 he wrote his "opinion that the Emperor of Russia cares little about it." He relied "not only upon what I saw and learnt at St Petersburg, but upon what has passed here." *W.N.D.*, iii. 405. That is surely proof enough.

[3] *V.S.A.*, Weisungen nach England, Bd. 230. Metternich to Esterházy, June 4/26, No. 1, *reservée*.

news he replied in a more discreet, but highly oracular, tone. He hoped the peace of Europe would not be troubled, but he said that Austria reserved her attitude, in view of the fact that England did not seem to wish to give a guarantee.[1]

3. CANNING AND LIEVEN (SEPTEMBER–NOVEMBER 1826)

Immediately on Lieven's return to London, Canning sent him an official note as to communicating the Protocol to Turkey. He stated to him on 29th August that both the Turkish Government and Ibrahim had given a positive verbal denial of the 'Barbarization Project.' It would have been better to have it in writing, but he conceived that this matter was ended. If the Ackerman negotiations ended in war, he stipulated that Article 3 of the Protocol, providing for single English mediation between Turkey, Greece, and Russia, was still binding, as well as Article 5, by which England and Russia agreed not to obtain territorial advantages. But the war cloud was lifted on the 6th October, for on that day Turkey signed the Convention of Ackerman with Russia. By that instrument the local and particular grievances of Russia were settled and danger of war on that account removed. Only the question of Greece, which was indeed the *pierre de touche*, remained. And Canning was not bound to use force now that the ' Barbarization Project ' seemed to be at an end.

Canning had made up his mind that it was no use delaying action too long. But he had to be cautious. Lieven wanted to go too fast, Wellington too slow, and " I have had to accommodate my pace to both, like a man walking between two companions, lame of opposite legs." During his visit to Paris of September–October he spoke to Villèle frankly on the subject. He found Villèle would adhere to the Protocol, but wished to turn it into a treaty. In referring to the Russian ultimatum to Turkey over Ackerman, Canning said, " by these means alone " are " we able to finish with the question." . . . " The Porte, unless they count on the miraculous protection of the Great Prophet, will have to yield to save its existence." This utterance was thought " to throw a great light on the probable *dénouement* of the Greek question," and he said again, if the

[1] *F.O. Austria,* 120/80.   Wellesley to Canning, Sept. 23/26.

Ackerman Conference succeeded, ' all the Powers should unite.' [1] When, in fact, the Ackerman Conference succeeded (6th October), he sought to bring all the Powers into line with the Protocol.

On his return to London (4th November) he suggested that pressure might be put on Turkey to accept mediation by threatening to withdraw the Allied Missions from Constantinople. He spoke of the possibility of declaring Greece independent if Turkey proved recalcitrant. The proposal for the independence of Greece was his *ultima ratio* with the Turk, and intended to be used if all other means failed. But he said that a mere rejection by Turkey of mediation would not justify war. Lieven wrote anxiously on the 19th that there would be need of concerted measures if Turkey rejected the mediation. Canning replied on the 20th, in a confidential letter, that he wished concert with the Allies first, but that he was, if necessary, prepared to go forward with Russia alone. This utterance seems to mean that he was still not prepared to use force, but that he was prepared to recognise the *de facto* independence of Greece as a last resort.

4. The Russo–British Overture to France

On the 22nd November Canning finally communicated the Protocol to France and to the other Allies. He instructed Granville that England did not admit that Russia had a right to go to war if mediation were rejected, but that there was no objection to converting the Protocol into a treaty. Villèle, who considered these proposals on the 1st December, in the presence of Granville and Pozzo di Borgo, showed himself favourable. Of course he wanted a treaty because that was necessary to the dignity of France. Instead of adhering to a Protocol she proposed to negotiate a treaty, which the three signed as equals. But Villèle went farther than this ; he demanded that the signatory Powers should bind themselves to guarantee the integrity of the whole Ottoman Empire. Pozzo at once looked ' very grave ' at this suggestion, and Granville suggested that Article 5 (the self-denying ordinance)

---

[1] *V.S.A.*, Berichte aus Frankreich, Bd. 369. Apponyi to Metternich, Sept. 21, part^re ; Sept. 24/26.

was quite sufficient. After Villèle left, Pozzo, with unconscious humour, protested to Granville that a guarantee
of the whole Turkish Empire " would be laying the ground
of unceasing congresses." [1] On the 8th December Granville
repeated that Villèle had acceded absolutely to the Protocol,
but that he demanded also a treaty with general guarantees.
If Austria and Prussia concurred, he was willing to withdraw
the French Mission from Constantinople.

Much had thus been gained. France was practically
detached from Metternich, and her complete support could
be won at the price of a general guarantee. Canning was, in
principle, almost as opposed to general guarantees as he was to
general congresses. He found Polignac ' in a humour to spoil
all ' and, for that reason, had kept the negotiations away from
London and in Paris.[2] On the 22nd December he instructed
Granville to push on with the Treaty project. The refusal of
England to give a guarantee was " occasioned by the separate
application of the Greeks for a guarantee addressed separately
to England." He did not care about a guarantee, but, if the
Five Powers agreed, he might reconsider the matter. In any
case, he must know what the guarantee meant. In a private
letter of the same. day he told Liverpool he " would never
guarantee the Turkish Empire (which I suspect to be in
Austria's head) ; but the guarantee of our own work in
Greece [*i.e.* a guarantee limited in object], with five or six
auxiliaries, I think we *may* venture ; though, you see, I do not
promise even *that*." However, he thought it difficult to be
inflexible, and that, if all Powers concurred, this limited type
of guarantee might be given.[3] The limited guarantee would,
however, only be given if Austria and Russia concurred. So
far as England was concerned, Canning was to have his way
about the guarantee, but he was to be compelled to consent to
coercive measures. Indeed, ever since the signing of the
Protocol, he must have thought that an eventual, though
undesirable, possibility.

[1] *F.O. France*, 146/78. Granville to Canning, Dec. 1, 8/26.
[2] The Treaty would have been signed at Paris but for the fact that
full powers were sent from Russia to Lieven at London, not to Pozzo at
Paris.
[3] Stap., *G.C. & T.*, 486. Canning to Liverpool, Dec. 22/26.

5. THE NEGOTIATIONS OF 1827 AND THE SIGNATURE OF THE TREATY OF LONDON (6TH JULY 1827)

The real interest of the Treaty negotiation depended on the concord between Russia and Canning, for while France would hedge over details, she would have to accept their joint decision. The first step, however, was with France, which had been asked to draw up the *Projet* of the Treaty. Damas produced his *Projet* on the 10th January.[1] It contained a preamble, which omitted all reference to the previous Protocol and suggested that the Treaty would be signed and executed by the Allied Powers (*i.e.* including Austria and Prussia). Article 1 laid down that simultaneous mediation should be offered to Turkey ; Article 2 that the mediation, if accepted, would give the Greeks a limited independence, stipulating for payment of a tribute to Turkey, but giving them the administration of their own affairs, and liberty of religion and of commerce. The third stipulated for the fixing of the boundaries of Greece by conference later between Turkey and the Allies (again including Austria and Prussia). By the fourth the contracting Powers arranged for the possibility of a collective guarantee of the Treaty to Greece. The fifth arranged that, in the case of refusal by Turkey, the Powers should accredit commercial agents to Greece. The sixth included a declaration of commercial, political, and territorial disinterestedness by the Powers on the lines of Article 5 of the Protocol. The seventh provided for ratification of the Treaty.

Granville and Pozzo objected to this *Projet* on the ground that the preamble did not mention the Protocol, and that it implied that Austria and Prussia would have to sign and agree to it. They therefore corrected these two points in a new draft, and forwarded both versions to London on the 19th January. Canning agreed with both suggestions, especially as he was convinced by the 19th February that Austria might not come into the Treaty. He objected to Article 4 (the collective guarantee) ; while Lieven thought that more pressure must be put on Turkey than by the appointment of commercial agents to Greece (Article 6), there was still

[1] *Vide* Appendix VIII. for these drafts and text of Treaty.

absent, even from the Pozzo-Granville draft, that element of coercion on which Russia was now prepared to insist.

The Emperor Nicholas had at last thoroughly determined to end the matter by strong measures. During 1826 he had shown great activity in reorganising his army and, what was still more significant, his navy. On the 21st February 1827 Lieven presented four different despatches from his government to Canning. The net result of these was that the Emperor did not think a recall of Ambassadors would be any use unless it was simultaneous and quintuple (*i.e.* including Austria and Prussia), that he was not anxious for the recognition of the complete independence of Greece, and preferred the accrediting of consular agents to this step. Last of all, and most important, he demanded a secret clause, or addition to the Treaty, by which the Powers, in the case of Turkish obstinacy being prolonged beyond a certain time limit, would reunite their naval squadrons in the Mediterranean, with the view of preventing " all aid of men, arms, or ships, whether Egyptian or Turkish, from reaching Greece or the Archipelago." [1]

Canning was thus, at last, brought face to face with the prospect he had long been expecting—the demand for using force. In the Protocol he had only agreed to a restricted use of force to prevent the 'Barbarization Project' of Ibrahim, and as this had been disavowed, he had considered himself released from that limited obligation.

It was pretty clear now that, unless he consented to use force, Russia would go forward alone.[2] It seems likely that Canning had now made up his mind that force might be necessary, though he hoped it would not be. In any case, he had tried to prevent Russia from using it.

But, if force was to be used, England must act with, and restrain, Russia.

---

[1] *F.O. Russia,* /168. According to Martens, xi. 350, Lieven was to urge Canning, if he proved reluctant, by pointing out that under Article 3 of the Protocol Russia could act against Turkey ' *soit en commun soit séparément.*' But Lieven does not seem to have used this argument.

[2] Lieven, on Feb. 26, wrote to Canning refusing to accept British mediation with Persia. This stiff refusal had been preceded on the 24th by a very friendly communication from Lieven that Russia would support England in any measure to settle Portugal, *v. F.O. Russia,* 65/168, under dates mentioned.

To the use of force Wellington and the majority of the Cabinet were opposed, and on the 17th February Canning's best supporter, the Prime Minister Liverpool, had been struck down with paralysis. He was himself ill during most of February, and could do little in March as the question of the Premiership was unsettled.

Russia drove as furiously as Jehu. And on the 22nd March Canning and Lieven had a conference on the final form of the Treaty. On the 23rd, Lieven submitted to Canning the joint product of their labours, with the significant observation that "I have exhausted all the latitude the instructions of my Court reserved for me." [1] On the 12th April Canning became Prime Minister, but he was unable to settle his Cabinet till the end of the month. On the 23rd April he promised Lieven he would do his best to hurry on matters. On the 6th May Lieven submitted further despatches from St Petersburg and became more insistent than ever. Canning wrote to him saying that he had submitted all the papers to some of the Cabinet. But "the day failed us before we had got through them. Many of us had *all* to learn." The process of instruction lasted a fortnight longer. The new Treaty draft was discussed by the Cabinet some time in the second week of May, and on the 22nd it was adopted and forwarded to Paris. It corresponded substantially to the Russian proposal and to the final form of the Treaty. The only serious change Canning made in the Russian draft was to insist in the preamble that the Greeks had asked for British mediation. He substituted ' *les Grecs* ' for ' *les sujets* ' in Article 1, which perhaps indicates his desire for the ultimate independence of Greece. Canning settled another point by limiting the collective guarantee to the question of Greece alone, and by making such guarantee optional on the contracting Powers. England was thus exempted from the necessity of guaranteeing, though further discussion was promised on the point. Lieven secured the main Russian point by obtaining Canning's consent to the secret article, agreeing to the use of force, if necessary.

The reception of the Russo-British draft by France was disappointing and suspicious. Damas rejected the project of simultaneous recall of Ambassadors from Constantinople.

[1] Martens, xi. 352.

He pressed for the guarantee on the 28th May but gave way on the 30th.   Finally he offered to sign the Treaty if it was submitted first both to Austria and to Prussia.   This was a pretext for delay of which Metternich was only too delighted to make use.   But pressure was now applied both by England and by Russia, and Austria was finally compelled to decline acceding to the Treaty on the 16th June, Prussia following suit.[1]

6. The Terms of the Treaty (6th July 1827)

The Treaty, as finally signed, did not refer to the Protocol in the preamble.   Article 1 demanded the consent of both Turks and Greeks to an immediate armistice.   Article 2 placed Greece under the suzerainty of Turkey, made her liable to a fixed annual tribute, gave her freedom of internal administration subject to a certain Turkish control.   It omitted the clause about freedom of religion and of commerce, and provided for the ' bag and baggage' deportation of Turkish proprietors from Greece with adequate compensation for their property.   Article 4 pledged the Powers to immediate negotiation with the Turks at Constantinople.   Article 5 contained the avowal of mutual disinterestedness.   Article 6 that of optional guarantee of the settlement.   Article 7 provided for ratification of the Treaty.

The secret article pledged the contracting Powers, if the Turks did not accept the armistice within one month after the Treaty was presented them, to take the following steps immediately.   (1) To accredit consular agents to Greece.   (2) If either Greeks or Turks did not accept the armistice, the contracting Powers would interpose between the two contending parties, in order to prevent all collision between them.   Apparently on the initiative of Canning himself, the period of grace of one month was shortened to a fortnight; an indication that he, at least, had no desire for delay.

The Treaty was signed on the 6th July, but certain forms of communication had to be settled.   There were the instructions to the Ambassadors at Constantinople who were to deal with

[1] *F.O. France*, 146/90.   Dudley to Granville, June 20/27.   He says Prussia would have acceded if Austria had.

the Turks, and the instructions to the Allied Admirals who were to deal with the Greeks, and to interpose between the two contending parties if necessary. These were not concluded until the 13th July, and it was not until the 20th that Polignac consented to shorten the period of grace from one month to a fortnight.

7. THE LAST VIEWS OF CANNING

It was well that the Treaty was signed, for on the next day (7th July) a despatch reached London from Stratford Canning reporting the failure of his attempt to get Turkey to accept the single mediation of England between her and Greece on the basis of the Protocol. Turkey, after much vagueness and shuffling, replied in a sort of manifesto, compounded of ' insolence and obstinacy,' which was, in effect, a total refusal of the Protocol. As will be seen, the Treaty provided for means to overcome that obstinacy.[1]

Greece was at the last gasp. Athens had fallen, Ibrahim with his well-disciplined army was devastating the Morea, his fleet was threatening Patras. Intervention, if it was to come at all, must come soon. The period allowed to Turkey to comply with the demands of the Allies had been now shortened to a fortnight, and the Treaty reached Constantinople on the 8th August, a date memorable for that, and for another, reason.

In point of fact, Canning can have been under no illusion that the use of force might lead to hostilities, for the law officers had pointed this fact out to him. But he trusted to avert its use altogether by an ingenious expedient. Towards the end of 1826 Mehemet Ali had been hinting, through various sources, that his heart was not in the Greek business. Canning therefore got hold of Major Cradock, a British official at the Paris Embassy known to Mehemet Ali, and despatched him on the 14th July to Alexandria on a secret mission to secure the neutrality of Egypt in the coming crisis.[2] He instructed him to point out to the Pasha the danger from the rashness of Turkey and the great advantage he would derive from keeping clear of the complication. He was to be

[1] *F.O. Turkey,* 78/151. George to Stratford Canning, Feb. 19/27.
[2] Vide *F.O. Turkey,* 195/66, for instructions to Cradock, July 14/27, and also *F.O. Egypt* 142/2. The suggestion was first made by Damas.

reminded that the Allies " do not mean war, while they talk of mediation, yet any rash and violent determination on the part of the Divan might, in the progress of the transaction, produce some hostile collision in spite of their earnest and anxious desire to avoid it. In that case, the Allied Powers would instantly appear in those seas with a force sufficiently formidable."

This overture is of great interest, as it was the last definite diplomatic step undertaken by Canning. Cradock reached Egypt on the 8th August, but he failed to gain Mehemet Ali and departed before the end of the month. That astute ruler perhaps felt himself too deeply committed to consent to the proposal.[1] But he seems to have secretly, though fruitlessly, advised the Turks to give way. For, on hearing the news of Navarino, he said, " I told them what would be the consequences. Did they think they had to deal with Greeks ? " These words seem to show that Canning's overture had made a strong impression upon him.[2]

One last vexation awaited Canning. The Treaty, together with its secret article, was published in the *Times* on the 13th July. There was, naturally, an immense sensation. Polignac tried to blame Canning, and Canning Polignac,[3] and the question has never been settled. But the views of Canning, both on this event and on the overture of Cradock, are preserved in his final letter to Granville.

(*Private and confidential*)

" Downing Street, 13*th July* 1827.

" I was very glad to receive your letter by Cradock as Sir F[rederick] A[dam] had written to Goderich in the same strain as to you ; and had created an uneasiness respecting the designs of the French, which your further information has dissipated.

---

[1] French officers were in the Egyptian Navy, and French interest in Egypt was great. Canning, writing to Granville (*Gr. MSS.*), June 22/27, intimated that the French gave ' the *appearance* of crooked policy, and contradictory engagements ' with Egypt.

[2] Codrington thought de Rigny had influenced Mehemet Ali in the wrong direction. *Memoirs*, i. 443–7. *Vide* Stern, *E.H.R.*, April (1900), pp. 277–8 *sqq.*

[3] Polignac was opposed to the Treaty, and Canning was not. Russia, which was always blurting out secrets, was not suspected on this occasion, *v.* Notes to this chapter, pp. 518–9.

" Cradock turns out to be an old acquaintance of the Pasha of Egypt ; and therefore the fittest person that could have been selected for the Commission. If the Pasha's fleet has not sailed before Cradock reaches him I flatter myself it will remain in port.

" The Treaty is, after all its delays and difficulties, satisfactorily adjusted. Its premature publicity is, however, very unfortunate : I am inclined to suspect Polignac's Chancery of the breach of confidence ; in great part from the eagerness which, Dudley tells me, Polignac shows to throw the blame upon this Office. The misfortune is, nevertheless, not without its consolation. The notoriety of the provisions of the Treaty baffles misrepresentation, and leaves Austria only the choice to join or not to join, in the face of all the world, a concert which all the world generally approves.

" Greece thus disposed of—we shall come next to the Peninsula. But I must take a few days' rest between for I am quite knocked up. I go to Chiswick for that purpose to-morrow.   " Ever affect^ly yours,   " G. C." [1]

The Treaty reached Constantinople on the 8th August, and Stratford received a private letter from Canning at the same time, informing him that the " spirit of that agreement was peaceful interference, recommended by a friendly demonstration of force." He remarked in the letter a " tone of depression quite unlike the usual elasticity of his [Canning's] mind," [2] and on the day he received it, the news flashed on the world that his great cousin was dead.

8. CODRINGTON AND THE INSTRUCTIONS TO THE ADMIRALS

" *L'épouvantable catastrophe de Navarin. L'évènement du 20me Octobre commence une nouvelle ère pour l'Europe.*"—METTERNICH to Apponyi, 13th November 1827.

" *I have sent him [Codrington] a riband, but it ought to be a halter !*"— GEORGE IV., end of 1827.

It was perhaps due to Canning's illness that the instructions for the British, French, and Russian Admirals, who were to

[1] *Gr. MSS.* Canning to Granville, July 13/27.
[2] This letter is quoted by Lane-Poole, but does not appear in the Stratford Canning MSS. in the Record Office.

enforce the armistice, were not drawn with complete precision. The result was that Codrington, the Allied Admiral-in-Chief, found himself in some perplexity. "He wrote," says Stratford, "privately to me professing an uncomfortable uncertainty as to what he was to do," and requesting some information which might enable him to see his way more clearly. "Neither I nor the French Admiral can make out," wrote Codrington on the 12th August, "how we are by force to prevent the Turks, if obstinate, from pursuing any line of conduct which we are instructed to oppose, without committing hostility. Surely it must be like a blockade ; if an attempt be made to force it, by force only can that attempt be resisted." Stratford replied on the 1st September that he had consulted with his colleagues. "On the subject of *collision*, for instance, we agree that, although the measures to be executed by you are not adopted in a hostile spirit, and although it is clearly the intention of the Allied Governments to avoid, if possible, anything that may bring on war, yet the prevention of supplies, as stated in your instructions, is ultimately to be enforced, if necessary, and when all other means are exhausted, *by cannon-shot*." [1] The substance of this communication was embodied by Codrington in a General Order to the British Squadron, which he dated the 8th September, the day on which he received it.

Stratford afterwards regretted that he had written thus to a man of Codrington's fiery temperament. Codrington was indeed an old captain of Nelson, ardent, brave, and generous ; one of those men who did not fear to bring the enemy to battle. On the 'glorious First of June' he had earned the praise of Howe for his gunnery. At Trafalgar he had caused a French ship to strike by the discharge of a single broadside, and the deadly accuracy of his gunnery was soon to be terribly proved. He was clearly a Phil-Hellene, and seems to have assumed that the Treaty was to settle the freedom of Greece. [2] His blood boiled at the massacres and cruelties of the Turks. On the 28th July he wrote the ominous words that war might be " a more humane way of settling affairs here than any other.

[1] Lane-Poole's *Stratford Canning*, i. 448–9 ; *Memoirs of Codrington*, by Lady Bourchier (1873), i. 416–7, 451–2. Last italics my own.
[2] *Vide* his letter of July 21 on hearing the news that the Treaty had been signed. *Memoirs of Codrington*, i. 393–4.

One strong act of coercion would place the Porte at our mercy."
Yet it is not easy to see that he could have acted otherwise
than he did. Even Stratford's powers of persuasion and
intimidation failed to wring any other answer from the Porte
than that they would " resist the mediation to the last man
and to the last drop of their blood." The Greeks accepted
the armistice, but, as the Turks refused it, held that they were
at liberty to go on with hostilities.[1] At any rate, Codrington
alone had the means of persuading the Turks. He had his
technical justification, and no lover of freedom or of Greece
(and perhaps even a historian may be both) can be sorry that
he used it.

9. First Interview with Ibrahim (25th September)

The chief defect lay, not in Codrington's instructions, but
in loss of time. He lay off Smyrna, and it was not till the
11th August that he received an official copy of the Treaty,
nor till the 7th September that he learned that the Turks
had refused its demands, and that the fortnight's grace had
expired. He was therefore instructed to ' impede further
hostilities ' between them and the Greeks. On the 9th,
4000 fresh Egyptian troops were landed in the Morea, and
the Egyptian Fleet entered Navarino and united with the
Turkish Fleet there. Had Codrington been able to intercept
them on the way (and he seems to have thought the French
Squadron could have done so),[2] it is probable that hostilities
would have been averted. As it was, he arrived off Navarino
on the 11th, but too late. On the 19th, he communicated to
the Turkish Admiral a copy of the Treaty and his intention
to enforce it. On the 21st, regardless of this fact, some of
the Turkish Fleet put out to sea. Codrington, reinforced in
the nick of time by the French Squadron, forced it back into
the harbour. On the 25th September Codrington and the
French Admiral, de Rigny, landed and had a conference with
Ibrahim. That great warrior received them with hospitality.
He refused to do business until they had drunk coffee, out of

[1] *Memoirs of Codrington*, i. 464. Sir Frederic Adam (Governor of the
Ionian Isles) to Codrington, Sept. 19. This judgment of Adam's is important.
[2] *Ibid.*, i. 462. To Lady C., Sept. 13. Canning also had his suspicions
owing to French connections with the Pasha of Egypt. *Gr. MSS.* Canning
to Granville, June 22/27.

china cups in gold filagree stands, and sweetened as a special concession to European tastes. Each Admiral was forced to smoke a chibouque, with a stem ten feet long, encrusted with diamonds and jewels. They seated themselves on the end of a sofa on which Ibrahim was heavily sprawling. He was " a man of about forty years old, not at all good-looking, but with heavy features, very much marked with the smallpox, and as fat as a porpoise." He had large blue eyes, a high forehead, and a reddish-brown beard, and was plainly dressed, while his officers stood behind him ' covered with gold and embroidery.' [1]

As always in Turkish negotiations, Ibrahim attempted to evade the issue by a mixture of bluff, dilatoriness, and superficial geniality. The two Admirals remained inflexible to these blandishments, and finally induced him to promise to suspend hostilities for twenty days, until he had heard from Constantinople. Ibrahim " put his hand on his heart and said it [the promise] was sacred." Immediately after concluding the agreement Ibrahim learnt that the Greeks, on the 26th September, had made a descent on Patras. He therefore sent to the British Admiral requesting permission to break the armistice and put to sea. Codrington met this demand at once with a peremptory refusal, and Ibrahim for the moment acquiesced.

10. THE PRELUDE TO NAVARINO (1ST–19TH OCTOBER)

On the 1st October Codrington, temporarily abandoned by de Rigny, had to face a new crisis. A Turkish Admiral came on board his flagship, the *Asia*, to say that he (Codrington) had given permission to a Turkish division to go to Patras, and that it was now moving out. Codrington denied this and replied sternly, " having broken their word of honour, I would put no faith either in Ibrahim or any one of them hereafter ; and if they did not turn about willingly I would make them." The Turkish division putting out consisted of 7 frigates and 28 corvettes and brigs, with nearly a thousand guns. Codrington had only 4 ships and 172 guns. But a single shot from the *Asia* decided the matter, and the Turkish division put back.

[1] *Memoirs of Codrington*, ii. 15-6. H. J. Codrington (son) to his sister Jane, Sept. 25/27.

On the next few nights Turkish ships again stole out of the harbour. As Codrington put it, " in the night, inspired by the dirty weather, the *dirty dog* edged away for Patras." [1] On the 5th, like a shepherd collecting his sheep, Codrington caught up with them, turned them round and drove them before him back to Navarino, firing several shots to accelerate their progress. Thus he had four times (and twice wholly unaided) enforced the Treaty of July against the Turks by judicious measures, and in two cases by cannon-shot without provoking hostilities. " There is no solid foundation," he wrote, " for the prevalent belief in either Turkish honour or Turkish bravery." These incidents seem to show that Ibrahim must have known that any action on his part, in resuming hostilities with the Greeks, might provoke them with the Allies as well.

On the 13th October Codrington was again joined by the French under de Rigny, and on the 14th also by the Russian Squadron under Admiral Heiden. Ibrahim, foiled in his efforts to get to Patras, now revenged himself by devastating the Morea. He slew the men and women, burned the houses and cut down the fruit trees in the neighbourhood of Navarino. From their decks the Admirals watched the smoke and flames from the burning houses, which told of Ibrahim's insolent defiance of his promise. On the 17th the three Admirals sent a peremptory warning that these devastations would not be allowed to continue. On the 18th they demanded an interview with Ibrahim, but were answered that he was ' absent they knew not where.' This answer was a characteristic Turkish subterfuge, and accordingly the Admirals informed Ibrahim that they intended " to take a position with the Squadrons in Navarino," and there renew their propositions to him. The only alternative for the Admirals would have been a blockade which would have been slow in operation and hazardous in execution, for their ships might at any time be dispersed by a storm. Moreover, there would have been no certainty that Ibrahim would not have continued to conceal his whereabouts and to pursue his devastations. Even de Rigny, who was friendly to the Egyptians and hostile to the Greeks, concurred with Codrington in his proposal, while the Russian Admiral, Heiden, heartily supported him. Ibrahim

---

[1] *Memoirs of Codrington*, ii. 39–40. To Lady Codrington, Oct. 6.

must have understood the grave nature of the demonstration ;
he had, in fact, the unexpected advantage of a day's grace,
for the winds were too light to carry the ships into the
harbour on the 19th.

Codrington issued his final instructions on the 19th. No
shot was to be fired by the Allies without a signal from the
flagship, but if any Turkish ship fired it was to be destroyed
immediately.   Certain features indicate that Codrington's
demonstration was not absolutely hostile, though he thought
that hostilities might occur.   His ships entered the harbour
with decks cleared for action and with the tompions out of the
guns.   But he gave two signs of his pacific intention.   His
lower-deck ports were kept square with the decks and not
hauled flat against the sides ; and his advance was in two lines,
not in battle formation.   Further, the Turco-Egyptian Fleet
was arranged in a crescent, with fireships on the flanks, adjoining the land-batteries at the end of the bay.   The design was
evidently to catch the Allied Fleet in a trap by decoying it
into the centre. . Had Codrington attempted a manœuvre by
" breaking a way between the upper end of their line and the
shore and thus taking them in reverse," his hostile intention
would have been evident.   As it was, he headed towards the
centre of the crescent, posting himself parallel to the Turkish
Fleet, and thus placing the Allied Fleet at a relative disadvantage.   The Allies had 24 ships of war, of which 10 were
line of battle, 9 frigates and some smaller craft.   The Turks had
89 ships of war, of which 3 were line of battle, 17 frigates and
69 smaller craft.   They had also a great superiority of guns.

11. The Battle of Navarino (20th October)

The advance of the Allied Squadron into the bay on the
20th was majestic but ominous.   They approached in perfect
order and in perfect silence, Codrington anchoring the *Asia*
opposite the Turkish and Egyptian flagships.   In a few
moments a dispute between boats' crews brought on a general
action.   For a time the fighting was very fierce.   At one
period Codrington, though the tallest man on his own quarter-
deck, was the only one unwounded.   The mizzen-mast fell
and missed him by a hair's-breadth.   Four bullets pierced his

hat or his clothing, and a fifth smashed his watch. His own gunners of the *Asia* made the Egyptian flagship a wreck in ten minutes ; and in three-quarters of an hour they sent the Turkish flagship drifting mastless out of the battle with five-sixths of the crew disabled ! Many Turkish ships were soon dismasted or shattered, and, as night fell, the sound and sight of ' 37 beautiful explosions ' showed the Turks themselves were destroying such ships as had escaped Codrington. His general order ran the next day, " of the Turkish Fleet there remain only one frigate and fifteen smaller vessels in a state ever again to be put to sea." [1] Even Nelson could not have desired a more complete victory for his old captain.

On the morrow the sea, in Æschylean phrase, ' flowered with the dead.' Such Greeks as remained alive in the neighbourhood gazed over the sea, reddened for some distance with blood, on which tossed the shattered wrecks and the floating bodies of their oppressors. Four hours of battle had done more than seven years of diplomacy. The pride of Ibrahim was humbled in the dust, and the freedom of Greece was thunderously proclaimed amid the roar of Codrington's guns.

Whether Codrington acted according to the spirit of his instructions is a secret buried in the grave of Canning. But all contemporaries agreed that he would not have acted like his successors, in showing a chilling disregard to a gallant sailor for winning a great victory. This incident, even had he not foreseen it, would have given him a unique opportunity for enlisting popular interest in the Greeks. It seems likely, too, that he would have sent the fleet to the Dardanelles. On these points no man can be sure. But it is certain that Canning had decided to protect Greece against Turkish oppression in future, that he contemplated her independence as possible, and that, but for him, there would have been no intervention. Some have held that it was Byron, others that it was Codrington, who liberated Greece. Yet there are some, and among these be the Turks, who say that ' the two Cannings ' were the men who tore Greece from their grasp. If this be so, the freedom of Greece was George Canning's legacy to the world.

[1] Schiemann, on Russian authority, gives it at two frigates and twenty smaller craft, ii. 205.

PART VIII

THE TRIUMPH AND LEGACY OF CANNING

CHAPTER XVIII
THE HUNDRED DAYS OF CANNING

CHAPTER XIX
MR CANNING'S 'SYSTEM OF POLICY'

CANNING AS PRIME MINISTER

from the painting by Stewardson (1827)

CHAPTER XVIII

THE HUNDRED DAYS OF CANNING

" Even I can praise thee—Tories do no more ;
Nay not so much ; they hate thee, man, because,
Thy spirit less upholds them, than it awes."
BYRON, " Age of Bronze " (1823).

1. THE PROLOGUE

" He who had toiled thirty years to attain this dizzy height ; he who had held
it for three months of intrigue and obloquy, and now a heap of dust, and that is
all."—SIR WALTER SCOTT, *Journal*, 10th Aug. 1827.

THE last struggle in which Canning engaged was perhaps the
fiercest, as it was certainly the most triumphant, of his life.
It was called by Metternich ' The Hundred Days ' of Canning,
and in that brief space were crowded all sorts of intrigues
and counterplots which ended in a tragedy. It witnessed the
grapple of old prejudices with new parties ; the appearance
of a new Prime Minister, opposed by factions and by old parliamentary hands, but, like the two Pitts, visibly called to office
by the voice of the nation. His advent not only signalised
the end of old combinations at home ; it also had a message
and a meaning for the world. After three months of strife
and uncertainty he adjourned Parliament with a triumphant
majority. Within a fortnight the nation was applauding a new
and epoch-making phase in foreign policy. A fortnight more
and sinister rumours began to flit about, and a week later the
new Prime Minister was dead.

2. THE DIVISIONS IN THE CABINET AND LIVERPOOL'S ILLNESS (17TH FEBRUARY 1827)

The outlines of the drama are simple ; the details infinitely
complex. It is a tragedy in two ways, for it lowered the fame
of Wellington and hastened the death of Canning. The crux

lay in the Catholic question. On this the Cabinet had agreed on division, the Whips being withdrawn, and both Ministers and Members voting as it seemed good on the question. When Canning had entered the Cabinet in 1822, there were only three Emancipationists besides himself, of whom Castlereagh was one. Canning, as the most ardent of Emancipationists and the most brilliant of speakers, had done much to encourage their cause. There were still only four so-called ' Catholics ' in the Cabinet—Canning, Huskisson, Melville, and Robinson ; the ' Protestants ' were eight—Wellington, Bathurst, Harrowby, Westmoreland, Bexley, Eldon, Peel, and Liverpool himself. When the latter fell, most of the ' Protestants ' refused to have a ' Catholic ' for Premier ; some were determined to exclude Canning altogether from office. The attempt had been actually begun before Liverpool's incapacity was made known.[1]

It is not quite fair to suggest that this was the sole motive of the ' Protestants,' and that they had no other grounds for opposition. Since 1825 Canning had had his own way in the Cabinet, and been supported, through thick and thin, by Liverpool. As soon as Liverpool was gone, the Ultra section of the Cabinet saw an opportunity for recovering their lost control of foreign policy. An Ultra Prime Minister might hold Canning in check ; one of his own kidney would only lend him further support. The cause subsequently assigned by Wellington for refusal to serve under Canning was that he had had previous relations with the Whigs.[2] In the strict sense this statement was apparently incorrect. Canning had had friendly relations and private correspondence with Lord Holland and Sir Robert Wilson ; he had intimated through friends to Brougham that he appreciated the tone of his speeches and the support he had lent to his foreign policy ; he had sent the Dukes of Devonshire and Northumberland on complimentary missions to St Petersburg and to Paris. Beyond this he had not gone, though his general sympathy with some of their ideas was clear. The fact is that ' the real Opposition

[1] The Duke of York, a most ardent anti-Catholic, and heir to the throne, died on Jan. 5/27. Shortly before this he had written to the King, demanding a uniform anti-Catholic Ministry, a demand really aimed at Canning. Stap., *P.L.*, iii. 299–300 ; Yonge's *Liverpool*, iii. 432–7.
[2] *Vide* Notes to Chapter XVIII., pp. 521–30.

sat on the Treasury Bench.' They consisted, wrote Palmerston breezily, 21st October 1826, " of old women like the Chancellor [Eldon] . . . ignoramuses like Westmoreland [the sot *privé*], old stumped-up Tories like Bathurst ; how such a man as Peel, liberal, enlightened, and fresh minded, should find himself running in such a pack is hardly intelligible." Like Canning, Peel leaned in the direction of relaxing the Navigation Acts, of modifying the Corn Laws, of abolishing the Slave Trade, and he seems to have favoured a liberal foreign policy. The Ultras forgave all these faults to Peel because he was a ' Protestant,' and none of them to Canning because he was a ' Catholic.' Canning was as suspect to the Ultras in the Cabinet as he was agreeable to the Whigs in opposition.[1] Here again the disablement of Liverpool rendered it almost inevitable that the two sections of the Cabinet should fly apart. Canning's head was not that of the cherub behind which the two wings of the Cabinet could unite. Some of them, indeed, thought his countenance anything but cherubic.

The true causes pierced deeper than principles to personality. Wellington had forced Canning on the King in 1822, trusting to have an obedient and grateful Foreign Minister, and relying on the King and the majority of the Cabinet to keep him in check. But the Foreign Minister had displayed unexpected independence, and the Duke discovered at the end of 1824 that neither he, nor the majority, nor the King could prevent the recognition of the independence of Spanish America. He complained bitterly of the fact to Esterházy. Fresh humiliations followed. Canning settled the question of Brazil in 1825, and of Portugal in 1826, on his own lines, and induced Wellington himself to sign the April Protocol as to Greece. The Duke was dismayed at the dissolution of the Congress System, furious at the popular success Canning achieved over Portugal. His pen flowed with vitriol. Canning is " certainly a most extraordinary man. Either his mind does not seize a case accurately ; or he forgets the impressions which ought to be received from what he reads, or is stated to him ; or knowing or remembering the accurate state of the case, he

---

[1] Hobhouse notes the feeling thus in his *Diary*, Feb. 12/27 : " He [Canning] has been very ill indeed, and some of his colleagues had been *congratulating* themselves on *the probable event*. Shame ! " *Recollections of a Long Life*, ii. 168. Italics my own.

distorts and misrepresents facts in his instructions to his ministers with a view to entrap the consent of the Cabinet to some principle on which he would found a new-fangled system." . . . " In respect to the negotiation itself with the Porte I have never in my life known anything half so confused as Mr C.'s ideas." [1]

Just about the same time Arbuthnot (the Duke's henchman) informed Liverpool that Wellington had been dissatisfied with the conduct of foreign policy ever since Castlereagh's death, that he would be ' no party ' to war, and might resign from the Cabinet.[2] These communications took place *before* Canning recalled our Minister from Madrid on his own respon-sibility, and *before* he made his famous Portugal speech of the 12th December 1826. From January to March 1827 the Duke continued to write Canning letters protesting against the steps he was taking as regards Greece, and attempting to prevent the conclusion of the Treaty on the lines he evidently desired. This matter was much more important to Wellington than the Catholic one, for he was a political, rather than a religious, ' Protestant.'

One thing is clear from first to last. The Duke's great fear was that the Whigs, whom he suspected of intriguing with Canning, might join the government. In that case they would carry the Greek Treaty, which he abhorred. He was resolved never to admit Canning as Prime Minister, but thought the government too weak to go on without him in the Cabinet. Canning, on the other hand, was resolved either to be the acknowledged Prime Minister, or to serve only under a ' dummy ' who would carry out his wishes. He was quite aware, however, of the distrust many of the Ultras entertained for him. Hence he was resolved to give them no occasion for saying anything against him. Until his actual accession to office it was therefore much to his interest to act with

---

[1] Wellington to Bathurst, Sept. 7/26. The passage here quoted is *suppressed* in *W.N.D.*, iii. 403, but printed in *Bathurst Papers*, [1923], p. 615.
[2] Arbuthnot to Liverpool, Sept. 5/26, *v.* Yonge's *Liverpool*, [1868], iii. 395. A little later four peers were made without Wellington's knowledge ; two of them, Seaford (Charles Ellis) and Clanricarde, being Canning's nominees, *v. Gr. MSS.* Lord Morley to Granville, Nov. 16/26. Owing to Canning's influence, and against Wellington's views, Sir Charles Stuart was refused a peerage. *Cp.* Colchester Diary [1861], iii. 500.

extreme candour as well as with prudence. He could not afford to do anything else.

From January onward Canning had been at Brighton (where the King was), suffering from brow-ague. His condition was serious and alarmed his friends, and during the first fortnight of February he was quite incapacitated. On the 17th February Liverpool was found insensible in his breakfast-room clutching in his hand a letter from Stapleton which gave him a bad report of Canning's health. He had been struck by apoplexy, and was henceforward politically incapable. His friends believed there was a hope (though it must have been a faint one) that he might recover, and Peel, who sought out Canning and the King at Brighton on the 19th February, agreed with both of them to do nothing until more was known of Liverpool's condition. Thus action, though not speculation, was suspended. Canning saw the King on the 22nd February and advised him not to go to meet difficulties by acting prematurely.[1] The situation was embittered by the imminence of a bill reducing the Corn Duties (which disturbed the landlords) and of the annual motion for Catholic Emancipation. Canning returned to town on the 27th February, and on the 1st March he carried the Corn Bill. The Catholic Debate on the 5–6th March was conducted with unusual acrimony. There was a fierce argument between Canning and Copley—the Attorney-General—who objected to his legal opinion being quoted. Canning protested his right to do so, and covered his opponent with ridicule by insinuating that he had inspired a well-known Protestant pamphlet by Bishop Philpotts. He added the well-known lines from a popular song :—

" Dear Tom, this brown jug, which now foams with mild ale,
    Out of which I once drank to sweet Nan of the Vale
        Was once Toby Philpotts." ![2]

But this good-natured banter did not calm the stormy waters. The debate went on fiercely, and ' Orange ' Peel drew down on him the thunders of Brougham and the lightning of Plunket. Finally, amid intense excitement,

---

[1] Parker, *Peel Papers*, [1891], i. 450.
[2] This is not in Hansard, but is quoted by some authorities as having been uttered. Others say that Canning sent this squib round the Lobbies.

the motion was lost by four votes. Canning's position was certainly not improved by this defeat. Planta, who was a good judge, wrote, just before, that a large 'Catholic' majority would have put Canning in power,[1] that a large 'Protestant' one would have ruined his hopes, but that a small majority, either way, left the whole situation in doubt. Thus the Corn and Catholic Bills, by inflaming the fires of political life, rendered the solution of the burning question more difficult than ever. For the 'Protestants' had only a majority of four in the Commons.

3. CANNING'S TALK WITH MADAME LIEVEN (FEBRUARY 1827)

Sometime during February, but after Liverpool's seizure, Canning revealed his views to Madame Lieven at Brighton. She often took out the sick statesman in her carriage, and, one day, he broke silence. He intimated that he governed the Press, that the moderate opposition supported him in both Houses, and that his liberal economic policy secured public opinion. He claimed that " for some years the Ministry owed its success to him alone. He could then, with good reason, look on himself as master of the situation and pay little attention to the hostile sentiments borne to him by the old Tory aristocracy. . . . He added that his resolution was taken ; he had decided to become the head of the Cabinet or to leave the party. The whole difficulty, according to him, lay simply in the prejudices of the King, whose imagination remained struck by the danger run by the Protestant Church if the Cabinet had an advocate of Catholic Emancipation as its chief—for he formally engaged to let the question sleep. If the King made him first Minister, he would neither make it a Cabinet question nor a subject of discussion. In a word, Emancipation would not pass, and he had the right to count on his own power to keep that promise, for the whole liberal part of the Lower Chamber and of the Country was his . . . he ended by telling me that the most complete inertia was the only conduct which suited his situation and that he had

---

[1] Peel confirms this, for he wrote to Canning later (Apr. 17) that he would have resigned had Emancipation passed by a large majority.

resolved not to say a word to the King on the actual crisis.
I understood the meaning of his confidences, and I knew the
whole part I could play in respect to Lady Conyngham
[the King's Mistress]. . . . I reported to her these confidences of Canning so as to make much impression on her." [1]
This account is not quite correct, but it is quite likely that
that astute lady said something on her own responsibility, in
her communications with the King.   Canning cannot have said
more to Madame Lieven than that he would keep Catholic
Emancipation as an open question in the Cabinet, and would
not adopt it as his official policy.   Canning's later interview
with the King and the King's report to Esterházy make that
quite certain.   And another proof of it is that Peel expressed
his entire disbelief in any rumour to the contrary.   Had he
felt any such doubts he would have joined the Ministry.   It
soon became the King's turn to take a hand.   With a view of
settling existing differences, he finally summoned Wellington
and Canning to the Cottage at Windsor on the 28th March.
The Lievens and the Granvilles, the new and the old friends
of Canning, were already staying with King George.

4. WELLINGTON'S VIEWS (FEBRUARY–MARCH 1827)

Canning's views are thus clear.   For him it was all or
nothing, now or never.   But the Duke's are less easily
discerned.   On the 18th February Wellington talked with
Croker and seemed to assent to the suggestion that Canning,
of whom he 'spoke handsomely,' should be Premier, but
demurred to Canning's friend, Robinson, going to the Foreign
Office.   He must have known that Croker would carry this
message to Canning.[2]   Yet on the 21st February Colchester
reported that the Duke and Peel had both declined to serve
under Canning, and on the 22nd reported a rumour that
Wellington was to have the first place.[3]   On the 27th February
Charles Arbuthnot (the Duke's confidant) wrote to Bathurst
intimating that " it would be worse if the whole patronage
and the elections were in that person's [*i.e.* Canning's] hands,"

---

[1] *Lie. MSS.* This conversation must have taken place before Feb. 27.
[2] *Croker Papers*, i. 364, Feb. 18. Croker is not wholly convincing, but
the Duke said something like this, 19th March. *Colchester Diary*, iii. 469.
[3] *Colchester Diary*, iii. 463–4.

and that he thought Peel would take the same view.[1] On the 10th March Arbuthnot addressed a still more remarkable letter to Peel, some three days after the Duke had had an interview with the King. He discreetly indicated that the Duke saw only three possible rivals for the Premiership—Peel, himself, and Canning ; and that he was willing to serve under Peel. But the Duke " cannot bring himself to put trust in Canning," for there was ' much of trickery ' in him, and he suspects direct or indirect understandings with the Whigs. Wellington himself could have headed the government had the Duke of York lived (for then he would not have been embarrassed by the command of the army). " The time has been when the King would not have heard of any other successor to Lord Liverpool " (than the Duke). But the fact of his holding the command of the army was a difficulty. Arbuthnot expressed a ' strong belief ' that the Duke would like to discuss with Peel the arguments for and against his (the Duke's) Premiership.[2] What Peel said we do not know, except that he refused to stand for the Premiership himself. But it is singular that, on the 16th March, Croker, who dined with Peel, records that " he [Peel] would like to see the Duke, or Bathurst, or Melville as Premier " [3] (i.e. to exclude Canning, to whom he had previously been favourable). Croker said Peel had changed his views since he spoke with him in February, and that he never knew why. Arbuthnot's letter of 10th March seems to be the explanation.

On the 17th Arbuthnot wrote to Bathurst that the Duke was " quite miserable. Everybody, he says, takes part against him " (for the Premiership?) " I do intreat you to go along with him and to get some of your party to do the same." [4] On the 19th Colchester reported the Duke as expressing fears that Canning might secure the first place. It is therefore

[1] Hist. MSS. Commn., *Bathurst Papers*, [1923], pp. 630–1.

[2] C. S. Parker., *Peel Papers*, i. 452. It is perhaps fair to say that Arbuthnot was not necessarily the mouthpiece of the Duke, but as nearly all his letters of this period were written while he was in attendance upon him, it is probable that he was.

[3] *Croker Papers*, i. 365 ; *Colchester Diary*, iii. 466.

[4] *Bathurst Papers*, pp. 631. These statements directly contradict those in Wellington's memo., Apr. 14–16. " That he [the Duke] had prevented the formation of . . . a faction or a combination of the Protestant members of the Cabinet and others for the purpose of opposing Mr Canning's appointment to the head of the Government."

proved (though the Duke denied it in his memorandum of the 14th–16th April) that Wellington was trying to exclude Canning from the Premiership. His conduct, in any case, was open to criticism. For, if he did not trust Canning, he should have refused to act with him at all. But, as the next overture shows, he wanted to include him in the Cabinet but to exclude him from being its head. As Canning wrote later, he wished :

> " To make the drudging Goblin sweat
> To earn his cream-bowl duly set."

On the 20th March the Duke of Buckingham, who knew Wellington was going to Windsor, wrote to him in the name of Lord Londonderry and of other peers. " There exists in the minds of many persons, who think differently upon the Catholic question . . . a strong disposition to afford to his Majesty their best assistance and support should his Majesty contemplate the formation of a balanced government without Mr Canning's assistance." The Duke wanted Buckingham's ' assistance,' but not Canning's exclusion from the Cabinet, and thought it prudent to return the letter as ' *non avenue.*' [1] The ' Protestants ' seem to have brought further pressure on the Duke in a separate and later overture in which they offered him the Premiership.[2] For, in a statement to his brother Wellesley, he writes that he discouraged attempts of Protestants *and others* to make him Premier, as he did not think himself qualified for the position. But he admits that he said to them " circumstances might . . . be conceived under which it would be his duty to accept the situation if he were called upon by the King to do so." [3] This extraordinarily important admission is the clue to the Duke's whole attitude. Against Canning's premiership he was unyielding, but he was willing to be pressed to take the post himself in the last resort.

---

[1] *W.N.D.*, iii. 611–2.

[2] The unpublished *Bath. MSS.*, [xvii.], have a letter, also of the 20th, from Buckingham to Bathurst, in which he suggests that Bathurst will be Premier and that he (Buckingham) will accept the Governor-Generalship of India. So Buckingham's overture to Wellington on the same day was *not* an offer to Wellington of the Premiership. That must have come later.

[3] *B.M. Add. MSS.*, 37, 297 ff., 272–91. The statement is dated Apr. 14 and 16, and was made by Wellington to Colonel Shawe. It was sent, *via* Canning, who refused to comment on it, to the Marquess Wellesley on May 24. [Published in *Wellesley Papers* (1914), pp. 164–9.]

5. THE KING'S CONFERENCES AT WINDSOR
(25TH–31ST MARCH)

On the 19th the King heard from Lady Liverpool that her husband was incapacitated *en permanence* ; on the 22nd he saw Wellington. On the 24th or 25th March the Ultra (and ducal) party decided to attack the King direct at Windsor through the Duke of Newcastle. This blustering ' Protestant,' who controlled five parliamentary seats himself, and had promises of a hundred from the boroughmongers, exercised his right of audience as a peer. He told the King that he could promise him the support of a large body of peers for a wholly ' Protestant ' administration, thus clearly indicating the exclusion of Canning. The King assured him he was ' a Protestant heart and soul,' and that he would choose a ' Protestant First Minister.' He closed the interview by inviting him to come and fish at Windsor in the summer, and by ' talking to the Duke about his *tailor*.' [1] Despite this amicable farewell the King had been deeply wounded by this interview, and afterwards complained that " the Duke conversed with me in a very unbecoming manner." [2]

Madame Lieven claims that she improved this occasion. " When I saw the King again later I neglected no suitable opportunity to prepare his mind for a great change. I made much of that remarkable circumstance that Canning never spoke to him of the great crisis in which the Cabinet was, that the Duke of Wellington ceaselessly intervened about it —thus there was respect and deference on one side, importunity and bothering on the other ; Canning waiting the orders of his Master, Wellington mounting to the assault to force him to decide—the great Tories—insistent—insolent— the Dukes of Rutland and Newcastle, loaded with the favours of the Court, had dared to address remonstrances to the King. The King, naturally very proud, but a dissembler like all kings, listened to all this, felt it all without letting it be seen, though I was enabled to divine it.

[1] *Diary of Lord Colchester*, iii. 472–3, Mar. 26–7.
[2] *Vide* his conversation with Lord Londonderry, Apr. 13. Wellington, *W.N.D.*, iii. 634. Stap., *G.C. & T.*, 582, says Newcastle threatened the withdrawal of support if Canning became Premier, and spoke of him in ' a most undecorous ' manner.

". . . On the 28th March, the King commanded the Duke of Wellington, Peel, and Canning to the Cottage. They arrived . there early. The King usually came down for breakfast (*le premier déjeuner*). This day we met without him. Peel was also absent ; he was conferring with the King.[1] Not long after they came to summon the Duke. We remained in the reception-room. The conference was prolonged ; it lasted two hours. People went and came, took up books and laid them down ; all thoughts were fixed on where the King was. The faces friendly to Canning visibly lengthened, like his own. At 2.30 the King came to lunch, followed by the Duke of Wellington smiling. Canning showed little mastery of himself, his face looked drawn and agitated. The King noticed it but did not put him quite at his ease. He addressed himself to Wellington more often and more familiarly than to Canning. These symptoms were unimportant to one who understood the King's mischievous spirit, but they did not appear thus to the interested parties. When the carriages were announced the King began to arrange their distribution. We went out in pairs in little low chaises drawn by ponies. The King always took out Lady Conyngham. He began by turning to me, in a mood of finest malice, and said quite loud, ' I am sure that you and the Duke of Wellington would like to go out together.' He knew that we had not the least desire to do so. We had chatted alone long enough, the Duke and I ; we had nothing sincere to say to one another. The other arrangements for the carriages were made. Canning was not in them. He put on his greatcoat awkwardly. I thought him quite ready to explode when, at the moment of my keenest anxiety, the King, suddenly getting up, asked my husband to take Lady Conyngham, and himself squeezing Canning by the arm, said to him : ' I want to talk with you ; I shan't go out.' There was a great change of expression on everybody's face.

" The excursion lasted long. I will relate briefly my dialogue with the Duke. We had exhausted every topic, our boredom became very great.

[1] This is a mistake. Peel did not go to Windsor till the 29th. Madame Lieven was still there, but Canning and Wellington had gone. Madame Lieven's evidence, that the King saw the Duke before Canning, is confirmed by the King's statement of Apr. 13 to Londonderry, and, later, to Esterházy.

" ' Ah well, M. le Duc, you have talked for two hours with your Master. What news ? Has he taken his stand ? '

" W.—' Devil take me, if I know ! '

" L.—' But have you explained to him the situation and your decision ? '

" W.—' According to the King's mode of conversation. He talks all the time himself.'

" L.—' Ah well, has he named you First Minister ? '

" W.—' Listen, Madam Princess, let us be frank. You know the difficulties well. I will be wholly frank. The difficulty is with one man.'

" L.—' Canning. But you must have taken your part, to remain with him, or to have him against you.'

" W.—' To have him against us ? The Cabinet would not remain for a week if he left it.'

" L.—' In that case are you resigned to having him as head ? '

" W.—' Never.'

" L.—' Then it is really very difficult, for he wants to be it.'

" W.—' My word, we shall see.'

" The excursion began at 3.30, we returned at 6.30. As we were getting down from the carriage they told us Canning was still with the King. It was the Duke of Wellington's turn to pull a long face.

" Before dinner Canning took me aside with a troubled air to ask me if I knew anything. I answered, much astonished, by putting the same question to him. ' It is impossible for me,' said he, ' to understand what the King means,' and we remained one as wise as the other.

" Never did I have as curious a dinner with the King as on that day. All observed and sought to understand the King. He was impenetrable. He took a special pleasure in teasing me. I willingly gave him this little satisfaction, for I felt sure of my achievement. M. de Polignac had been asked to dine that day, and the King said a few words to him about France, on the obsessions of the Ultra party and of the Jesuits on the side of Charles X., handling this party roughly enough. It was evident that the Rutlands and the Newcastles weighed on his mind. I spoke of it to

Canning and informed him that he would see himself Prime Minister." [1]

Madame Lieven relates her story with inimitable art. She is herself the dupe of one of the impish humours of George in which it pleased him to impress the Court circle and to mystify his ministers. He decided nothing till the 6th, when he came to town. Otherwise her account agrees with what we know from other sources, except for the mistake about Peel. Wellington subsequently said that, in his interview with the King, the latter proposed that the Cabinet should choose the Prime Minister. The Duke replied that he ought to exercise his prerogative as a personal act. The King then said that the Prime Minister should be a ' Protestant,' though the Cabinet should be of both opinions, and that Canning was essential to the government.[2] Probably the Duke agreed to this, for it secured the exclusion of Canning from the chief place. In any case, Madame Lieven was right in saying that he intended not to have Canning as Premier. Her suggestion to Wellington that he might be Premier was not directly contradicted. He did, in fact, accept, within nine months from this date, that post to which, he said in May, he would have been ' worse than mad ' to aspire.

Canning's interview with the King on this occasion has been described by himself at some length. After his Majesty had entertained him by a long historical survey of his own views, Canning replied by advising him to choose an anti-Catholic administration. The King replied that he could not part with him. Canning answered that, if he remained in the government he must be ' free as air ' to vote as he always had done on the Catholic question. Further, " he felt bound honestly to tell his Majesty, in plain terms, that the substantive power of First Minister he must have, and what is more, must be known to have," or he must resign.[3] George remained unconvinced, and on the 29th asked Canning to

---

[1] *Lie. MSS.* In fact Madame Lieven's memory is slightly at fault. The King knew of Rutland's views, but had not seen him yet. It was not till Mar. 31 that the Duke of Rutland and his brother made a similar communication to that of the Duke of Newcastle, though ' of a most conciliatory and respectful description,' *v. Colchester,* iii. 473–6.

[2] Speech, May 2. Letter to Canning, May 6. *W.N.D.,* iv. 7, 25.

[3] Stap., *G.C. & T.,* 582–6. Peel saw Canning and the Duke on the 29th, in London, before leaving for Windsor.

summon the Cabinet and to submit to them the proposal that they should agree on a First Minister. Subsequently Peel saw the King, and brought back a message giving Canning power to withhold this suggestion from the Cabinet at his discretion. Peel himself agreed that it was wiser to withhold it, and the King then dropped the proposal (31st March). The Cabinet met on that day, but did not discuss the succession at all.

6. THE KING DECIDES FOR CANNING
(31ST MARCH–12TH APRIL)

At the interview of the 29th, Peel and Canning had spoken very frankly to one another. " Mr Canning's declaration was in substance, ' I will be head of the Government or nothing.' Mine [Peel's] was, ' I will be content with things as they are ; but if you are head of the Government, I will not act under you.' But then Peel did not want the Premiership, and Canning knew it. So both men knew exactly where they stood, and neither seems, in any way, to have objected to the other's declaration. Further, Canning disclosed to Peel that he had received overtures of support from the Whigs." [1] The King now knew that the Cabinet would not choose a Premier for themselves, and that Canning might remain under a ' dummy Premier,' but not otherwise. It seems certain also that he knew that Wellington would not accept Canning or his nominee as Premier. On the 31st Rutland visited the King with demands for a 'Protestant administration,' suggesting Lord Bathurst as Premier. He was graciously received, and presented with the Duke of York's ' George.' Newcastle and other peers were now proposing to move a motion in the Lords in favour of ' a wholly Protestant administration,' and of this Wellington cannot have been ignorant. But it is not fair to suggest that either he or Peel ever favoured any project other than that of a balanced administration.

Between the 31st March and 6th April Canning saw nothing of the King but much of Peel and Wellington. On the 3rd April Canning saw Peel, and subsequently the Duke, and the

---

[1] Parker, *Peel*, i. 457. The disclosure about the Whigs was perhaps on the 31st, *v. ibid.*, 463, quoting Hobhouse's *Diary* of May 12/27.

latter was a lengthy interview.[1] What happened there seems to be disputed. Stapleton says Canning gave the Duke the fullest details of his audience at Windsor. If so, Wellington must have heard that Canning claimed the ' substantive power ' of First Minister, but would submit to a ' dummy.' The Duke denied later that he had received this impression, but admitted that Canning proposed Robinson as the Premier with a seat in the Lords, and that he (Wellington) refused to accept this suggestion. As Robinson was a personal friend of Canning's and a ' Catholic ' he was as good a ' dummy ' as could be wished. Doubtless for that reason the Duke would not agree to him. The Duke said later that there was no evidence that he had refused to serve under a ' Catholic ' Premier. But it is significant that he never asserted that he then proposed either a ' Catholic ' or ' Protestant ' peer as a substitute for Robinson, or indeed any substitute at all,[2] in spite of the fact that the interregnum was already six weeks old. He had objected to every name put forward, and suggested none himself. Had he proposed the ' Catholic ' Melville, he would have prevented Canning altogether from making the assertion that it was invariably put to him that he should submit to a ' Protestant ' Premier. And it was on this principle of excluding a ' Catholic ' from the Premiership that Canning took his final stand.

On the 5th April, however, after a further long interview with Peel and a short one with the Duke, Canning recorded his impression. " My belief is, that he [the Duke], and perhaps P[eel] too, hoped the explanation between me and the D[uke] would end in *my* begging *him* to take the Government. I mention this, because it is contrary to the *belief* which I had before stated to you, that the Duke never thought of himself for that post. Further light has changed that belief entirely." [3]   It cannot be said that he was wholly

[1] Wellington says the 2nd, Canning leaves the date blank in his letter of May 5, but Stap., *Corr.*, ii. 284, shows the correct date was the 3rd, as stated also by A. G. Stapleton, *G.C. & T.*, 588.

[2] The Duke says in his memo of Apr. 14–16 that he would have accepted the ' Protestant ' Lord Bathurst, or the ' Catholic ' Lord Melville. But he did not say this to Canning. By not doing so he certainly gave Canning grounds for thinking that he would accept only a ' Protestant ' peer as Premier, which was, in fact, the King's proposal.

[3] Stap., *G.C. & T.*, p. 589, Apr. 5/27. The letter is Canning's, but it does not appear to whom it is addressed.

wrong about the Duke, and he certainly was right about Peel.

Canning's mind had really been made up after the interview of the 3rd. He had never offered to accept 'a dummy Premier' except one who was a 'Catholic'; he knew that that fact carried with it Peel's resignation, and almost equally certainly that of the Duke.[1] He began, therefore, on the 3rd April (after the interviews of that day), to contemplate (and for the first time) a practical coalition with those Whigs who had already offered to support him at the end of March. He seems to have thought that the resignations of Peel and the Duke would not involve those of their colleagues. His correspondence with Croker of the 3rd April is illuminating. That expert Tadpole and Taper submitted to him details as to "the number of members 'returned to Parliament' by some of the Peers," giving 96[2] as returned by Tories and 54 by Whigs. Canning replied that he did not believe the King was " as completely in the hands of the Tory aristocracy as his father, or rather as George II., was in the hands of the Whigs. If so, George III. reigned and Mr Pitt (both father and son) administered the Government in vain. I have a better opinion of the real vigour of the Crown . . . and I am not without some reliance on the body of the people. . . . I will not act (as I have never acted) as the tool of any confederacy, however powerful; nor will I submit to insult (without resenting it according to the best of my poor ability) from any member of such a confederacy, be he who he may.

" These are my opinions. They are purely *defensive* ones, but there are limits beyond which defence cannot be purely passive."[3] The reference to the Duke is obvious, and equally so Canning's resolve not to give way.

On the 5th, Colchester riding in Hyde Park saw " an elderly looking gentleman wrapped up in a greatcoat (*the day very warm*), pale-faced, but with a sparkling eye . . . I found it was Canning." On the 6th the King came to town and saw Canning again, but no progress was reached. On the 8th

---

[1] It is particularly curious that neither he, nor the King, appears to have anticipated that of Lord Eldon, *v.* his speech, May 3/27. *Hans. Deb.*, N.S., xvii, 522.

[2] Subsequently he made it 116. *Croker Papers*, [1885], i. 367–71.

[3] *Ibid.*, i. 368.

the King received Bathurst and later Eldon, the great
' Protestant ' Chancellor.   Eldon was commissioned to call
on Peel and to report the result of the interview.[1]   After a
conversation with Eldon on the 9th, Peel visited Canning, by
the King's command, to place before him " the name of an
individual whose appointment as Premier Mr Peel conceived
likely to solve all difficulties."   The name was that of the
Duke of Wellington, and it seems to have been the joint
suggestion of the King and Peel, in which Eldon, and perhaps
Bathurst, acquiesced.[2]   Peel says he thought that the overture offered prospects of success, perhaps because it was supported by the King.   But Peel knew Canning's terms and that
the Duke was not a ' Catholic,' and would not be ' a dummy '
of the type Canning demanded.   The effect was therefore
most unfortunate, for it finally convinced Canning that the
Duke was himself aiming at the headship.   This view was
not very far from the truth.   Had Canning accepted Peel's
proposal he would not have been Prime Minister, and the Duke
would have been.

On the 10th the King received Canning in audience.
Knowing the failure of the Peel overture, he was now compelled
to accept Canning.   " No one," he complained three days
later, " would take the responsibility of this arrangement
but Mr Canning, and this is the predicament I am placed in."
He instructed Canning, therefore, to prepare, with as little
delay as possib e a p an for the reconstruction of the Administration.   With some astuteness he did not actually
designate Canning as Prime Minister, and the omission had
serious consequences.

[1] *B.M. Ripon MSS.*, i.   Peel to Robinson, Apr. 12.   Two extremely
guarded letters of Peel to Eldon of Apr. 9 (reporting the result of their
conversation) are in Twiss, *Eldon*, [1844], ii. 589–92.

[2] Wellington denied that he had ever suggested himself, but Peel had
received Arbuthnot's letter of Mar. 10, which amounted to a suggestion,
though it cannot be positively said to have been authorised by the Duke.

7. The Quarrel of Wellington and Canning
(April–May 1827)

" M. Canning a pour lui ce que les cent mille trompettes du jour appellent SA FORCE ; *cette force est le. fait incontestable* QUE CE MINISTRE EST LE REPRÉSENTANT VÉRITABLE DE L'ESPRIT DU TEMPS.*"*—METTERNICH to Count Zichy, 30th April 1827.

Canning at once addressed letters to, or made calls upon, the other ministers, offering to continue the Government on the principles of Lord Liverpool. Wellington objected to the tone of his letter as stiff and unfriendly, and replied by asking who was to be Prime Minister.[1] Canning answered on the 11th : " I believed it to be so generally understood that the King usually entrusts the formation of an administration to the individual whom it is His Majesty's gracious intention to place at the head of it, that it did not occur to me, when I communicated to your Grace yesterday the commands which I had just received from His Majesty, to add that, in the present instance, His Majesty does not intend to depart from the usual course of proceeding on such occasions.

" I am sorry to have delayed some hours this answer to your Grace's letter ; but from the nature of the subject, I did not like to forward it without having submitted it (together with your Grace's letter) to His Majesty."

Wellington saw in this second letter a ' rebuke ' covered ' with His Majesty's sacred name and protection.' He resigned office at once. On the 12th he threw up the command of the army as well (a step even his admirers found it difficult to defend), alleging as his ground not only ' political differences ' but the ' tone and temper of Mr Canning's letters.' In May a further angry correspondence ensued in which both men lost their tempers and misinterpreted one another's arguments. The Duke contended, and with some justice from the precedents, that it did not follow that the man who made the plan for administration necessarily became the Premier. In a tactical sense the Duke scored a point here. But the true answer of Canning, which he indicated in public, was, of course, that at this stage of the proceedings he would

---

[1] If Wellington knew (a fact which cannot be proved) of Peel's overture of the 9th to Canning, both this question, and his subsequent anger, are intelligible.

not have written the letters at all, unless he was to be head.[1] For Peel and Wellington had both already declined the ' dummy ' compromise.

It is melancholy to see two great men thus at variance. The readiness with which Wellington had acted with difficult colleagues or allies in the past, together with his massive integrity, is certainly *a priori* in his favour. But it cannot be said that his behaviour at this crisis added anything to his fame. For some years he had complained of Canning secretly to foreign diplomats and received their criticisms of him with complacency, and during 1826 his personal dislike of the Foreign Secretary had become almost an obsession. He was, in the last resort, prepared to become Premier, but was throughout resolved not to admit Canning, or his ' dummy,' to that office. His complaints as to the tone of the correspondence in April are therefore entirely beside the point, for he would have resigned from any Cabinet headed by Canning or by his ' dummy.'[2] He evidently felt the difficulty of resigning his command of the army. For on the 15th May he told Colchester, " If the King (as may be) should desire me to resume the command of the army, I do not see how, as a soldier, I could refuse it."[3] Within less than a week he was offered the command by the King, but he refused it on the 22nd, stating that the ' reasons ' already stated on the 12th April and the 6th May ' still continued in force.'

This action, like so many others, is inconsistent with his usual conduct and previous utterance, and the vehemence of his letters can only be explained by a personal hatred of no ordinary kind. On the 14th April he wrote to Londonderry, " The King believes, or thinks he believes, everything Mr C. tells him—for believe him with sense he cannot—and he takes the chapter of accidents and the advice of this charlatan. God send that this chapter may not turn out fatally."[4] On

[1] In the unpublished *Bathurst MSS.*, xvii., there is a letter from Bathurst to the Duke, of Apr. 10, which says that he has heard Canning had seen the King and that everything was settled. The Duke acknowledged the letter, and said he had received one from Canning. There is no suggestion that he thought Canning would not be Premier.

[2] In his memo of Apr. 14–16 he admits " other considerations which (without reference to the letter) would have rendered it difficult for him " to accept Canning as head. He said the same to Esterházy.

[3] *Diary of Lord Colchester*, iii. 502, Apr. 15.

[4] Alison, *Lives of Lord Castlereagh and Sir C. Stewart*, [1861], iii. 250, n.

the 15th May he told Colchester " he [Canning] had long intended to get rid of me," and spoke of the " foolish, insulting, and indecent manner of his behaviour to me." Even the event, which came so soon, did not alter him one jot. " I hear," he wrote to Bathurst on the news of Canning's death, " that Dr Farr says that it was Canning's temper that killed him." [1]

Canning was, of course, not blameless in the controversy. His secret message to the King through Madame Lieven was a little incorrect, though he seems to have behaved quite honourably in respect to the Whig negotiation. Croker's information, even if inaccurate, led him at first to think that the Duke would not object to his being Premier and had no desire for further promotion for himself. Wellington may have been technically correct in saying that he never proposed himself for the Premiership, nor had it proposed to him by the King. But in the face of Arbuthnot's letter of 10th March, of Peel's overture of 9th April, and of his own memorandum to Wellesley of 14th–16th April, the Duke's denial is more technical than convincing. Canning's conclusions on the 2nd and 5th April were correct enough in the sense that the Duke would accept the Premiership, and only incorrect in so far as the Duke would not take the initiative himself, but was waiting to have the prize offered him by the King, with the assurance of a strong backing in the Cabinet. It is impossible, in any case, to accept the Duke's further statement in his letter to Canning of the 6th May : " I did not know that you claimed to be First Minister as a *sine qua non*." This is mere quibbling, for the Robinson proposal meant nothing else, and the Duke never made any counter-suggestion to Canning himself.

The King bears the main responsibility, and acted a double part up till the 9th. Probably he encouraged the Duke to think that he might ask him to be Premier. He said himself he had actually offered the Premiership to him twice, but the Duke said he never did actually propose it. Certainly the King must have thought he had grounds for supposing the Duke would accept, when he commanded Peel, and probably Eldon, to make that proposal to Canning. Wellington complained later that the King had ' misrepresented ' the facts, for, he said, there was " a moral twist in him, which made it quite

[1] *W.N.D.*, iv. 76, Aug. 10/27.

impossible to believe in what he said at the moment, and still less to depend upon his promises." [1] This was true enough. Even after he had decided to support Canning, George could not be loyal to him in speech. At dinner on the 15th April with Gallatin, the American Minister, he said suddenly, " Canning is a damned old woman." . . . " I could see," writes his son, " that father could hardly dissemble his disgust." [2] On the 23rd April Canning explained to Gallatin at dinner, that England was not an aristocracy but (he said emphatically) ' a Monarchy.' If so, the monarch was not easy to serve.

The fact is that, while from the first Canning held himself to be master of the situation, Wellington thought that he was. He seems to have believed to the last that the King would support him, or at any rate exclude Canning from the highest place. On the 15th May he told Colchester that he had forty times reconciled Canning to the King, and added : " Canning, I know, would give half his tenure of office to have me back in his Cabinet, *i.e.* instead of ten years of power without me he would be content with five years of power. . . . His colleagues, I know, urge him to press my rein-statement, but he fears what may follow." [3] (Plainly Canning is to fear that the Duke would recover the ear of the King.) The Duke was entirely mistaken. Canning felt so sure that he could dominate the King and be supported by the people that, in the beginning, he was not unwilling to work with Wellington. But for that same reason he did not fear to do without him. It is upon this miscalculation, and upon the personal feelings of the Duke, that much of the responsibility must be laid. There can be no doubt that Wellington showed lack of judgment, and that his hatred of Canning (and it is painful to make such a statement) led him into regrettable

---

[1] Gleig, *Personal Reminiscences of the Duke of Wellington*, [1904], p. 107.

[2] *Diary*, James Gallatin, [1914], p. 269 ; *Life*, A. Gallatin, [1879], p. 626 ; *v.* also Buckingham, *Memoirs of the Court of George the Fourth*, [1859], ii. 345–7, which gives some further abuse of Canning by the King in July.

[3] If this be so, the Duke's contention in his letter of May 6, that Canning's invitation on Apr. 10 was ' a very cold ' one, is absurd. Wellington asks us to believe that Canning wanted his support, but used terms which ensured his refusal. The unpublished *Bathurst MSS.* give a letter of Wellington to Bathurst of Apr. 15, which is very violent in tone, and suggests that Canning did not want him in the Cabinet because then the King would have the truth told him. As seen above, on May 15 the Duke told Colchester that Canning *did* want him in the Cabinet.

statements and manœuvres. One can only grieve that so great a man should, on this occasion, have shown something of a petty spirit. Of one thing there can unfortunately be no doubt, in the light of the facts now known. Canning's manners may have been bad, but Canning's public explanations were more straightforward than those of Wellington. It is the only occasion in the Duke's life on which his statements suffer by comparison with another's.

8. THE COALITION GOVERNMENT (APRIL)

By the morning of the 12th Canning had received nine replies from the rest of the Cabinet. Lord Harrowby, Huskisson, Robinson, Wynn elected to stand by him. Wellington, Westmoreland, Melville, Bexley, and Peel had resigned. So Canning was left with only four colleagues out of nine, while two had not yet answered. He went off to the King and, while actually conferring with him, received the resignations of Bathurst and Eldon, making seven in all. He did not flinch. He told George that Parliament adjourned that day, and that a new parliamentary writ for himself must be moved that afternoon, if he was to take office as Prime Minister. The King doubted if he had enough support, but Canning pulled a letter out of his pocket, showing the Whig offer. " Sir," said he, " your father broke the domination of the Whigs. I hope your Majesty will not endure that of the Tories." " No," said the King, " I'll be damned if I do." [1] He gave him his hand to kiss, and Canning rose up First Lord of the Treasury, Chancellor of the Exchequer, and Prime Minister.

Canning struck at once. On the 13th it was announced that the ' Sailor Prince,' the Duke of Clarence, would enter the Ministry as Lord High Admiral. Even enemies admired the boldness of this move, while friends declared it to be a ' coup de maître.' Its effects were immediate. It brought the Whiggish and reluctant heir of the throne into the Ministry, and proved that the King meant to stand firm. Bexley withdrew his resignation, indicating at once his belief

[1] Greville, *Journals*, Sept. 23/34, quoting Melbourne, to whom Canning told the story. Esterházy quotes King George to a similar effect.

in the sincerity of Canning and in the new government's chance of survival. Sir John Copley, to whom Canning offered the Chancellorship, *Philpotto non obstante*, accepted the seals, as Lord Lyndhurst. Canning even wrote privately to Bathurst asking him to return, but without effect. Plunket was 'peered but not placed,' the English Bar objecting to an Irishman becoming Master of the Rolls and the King objecting to his becoming Irish Chancellor. The recognition of the fact that any other government but Canning's would destroy the hopes of liberal foreign policy finally converted the Whigs. Sir Robert Wilson conducted the negotiation. They failed to agree on the 19th April as to entering the Cabinet. But the great Whig chieftain, Lord Lansdowne, indicated support, as did Tierney and Brougham. Lord Holland gave a magnanimous approval and used all that influence with the Whigs which the nephew of Fox could wield. Another great Whig magnate, the Duke of Devonshire, the brother-in-law of Lord Granville, accepted the office of Lord Chamberlain (28th April). Even the firebrand Burdett lent active support, and Brougham carried a motion at the Whig Club of "Brooks" in Canning's favour. Althorp, together with Lord John Russell and Hobhouse, at first stood aloof but ultimately gave independent support. Only Canning's old enemy, Lord Grey, remained irreconcilable.[1]

The public was enthusiastic over the change, and, for a moment, the popular tide ran so strongly that hardly any paper could refrain from approval.[2] The Press expressed itself in characteristic fashion. In those days, when even reputable journals had a likeness to the *Eatanswill Gazette*, the shafts were always barbed. This time, they were dipped in venom. Universal ridicule greeted the retreat of the 'seven sages.' The *Courier* (once Arbuthnot's organ) declared they had attempted to dictate to the King. It added, "a more extraordinary attempt to fetter the King's choice, to circumscribe his authority . . . is not to be found, we believe,

---

[1] It appears that Grey, always a difficult man, was not adequately consulted in the negotiation. Lord Grenville, his old ally, was consulted, but preferred 'his rhododendrons and azaleas' to further politics.

[2] Stap., *Corr.*, ii. 320. It seems quite certain that, while Premier, Canning not only did not influence the Press, but refused opportunities of doing so.

in the history of this country " ; " Mr Canning enjoys the
entire confidence of his sovereign and of the country." " No
borough interest," wrote the *Morning Chronicle*, " can stand
against the contempt of the nation," and it implored the
Whigs to defeat " men inflamed with hostility to all that is
good." The *Times* pronounced the whole affair a ' conspiracy,'
and said the retreat of the seceders " is such a blessed relief
from a whole bundle of nuisances as in our time, and through
natural means, we had scarcely ever hoped to see accomplished." Tom Moore, as usual, contributed the comic note :

> " Why, why have ye taken your flight,
>   Ye diverting and dignified crew ?
> How ill do three farces a night
>   At the Haymarket, pay us for you ? "

The *Examiner*, formerly no friend to Canning, now belaboured
his enemies. " Whatever may be the merits of Mr Canning,
the country must despise these men." They were ' insects '
and " the Sovereign ought to crush them under his nail for
their audacious enterprise." " The Seven have been brought
to a just and painful sense of the estimation in which they
are held." Mr Canning was not ' a political Messiah ' but
the substitution of his rule for that of " his late bigoted (*sic*)
and despised colleagues " was " a comparative benefit of great
value obtained by the nation. He is not all that we wish—
they are all that we hate. He has the merit of casting out
these devils. . . . The unclean spirits have rushed in their
swinish shapes and manner on destruction, and we thank the
purifier for his signal service, but refuse to acknowledge,
like our contemporaries, his divinity on the score of it. . . .
[Yet] he [Canning] is far, very far, from insensibility to honest
fame, and the whole world rejoices in the ascendancy of his
genius, and regards it—we stop not to enquire with what
rationality—as the star of promise."

Wellington was assailed, to the dismay of his friends, with
extraordinary vehemence, as a stanza from Tom Moore
shows :

> " Great Captain, who takest such pains
>   To prove—what is granted *nem. con.*,
> With how moderate a portion of brains
>   Some heroes contrive to get on. . . ."

The extraordinary thing is that even the most liberal and popular journals vied in upholding the royal prerogative, and in praising the King for his firmness in refusing to be bound by the ' iron circle ' of prejudice.   Even George Canning was, for the moment, no more popular than King George.   The choice of the King was undoubtedly the choice of the nation. Some of the Press changed their tone later, but till the 1st May they were practically unanimous.[1]

It was fortunate for Canning that Parliament did not meet till the 1st May.   On the 27th April he ' went out riding,' having completed all the arrangements he could.   They were gazetted on the 30th.   Huskisson, Harrowby, Bexley, and Wynn resumed their old places.   Robinson became Secretary of State for War and the Colonies, and went to lead the Lords as Viscount Goderich.   The other posts were filled by Canning's friends and admirers.   Ward (Lord Dudley) became Foreign Secretary, the Duke of Portland (his brother-in-law) Privy Seal, Sturges Bourne Home Secretary.   Palmerston entered the Cabinet for the first time ; Lord Anglesey, as a military hero, was secured as Master of the Ordnance.   The Whigs were in support, but only one or two in office, for Canning in a conference with them on the 19th April found himself unable to give them the lead in the Lords, and refused to pledge the Government to Catholic Emancipation or to form " the Government of Ireland " out " of individuals not opposed to the removal of the Catholick .Disabilities." Negotiations were, however, resumed by Sir Robert Wilson and Brougham, in defiance of Lord Lansdowne, on the 21st, and it was clear that some arrangement would eventually be made.

9. The Parliamentary Struggle (May–June)

On the 1st May Canning went down to the Commons in the late afternoon.   A young journalist saw " his radiant face, as he rapidly mounted the old staircase " . . . and heard

---

[1] Peel deplored the unanimity of the Press on Apr. 22 ; Gallatin, on Apr. 28, could only find ' one pamphlet on the other side.' Gallatin, *Works*, 1879, ii., 372.   Later Canning was attacked in pamphlets, which declared his mother had received a state pension, and published the handbills of her performances as an actress.

' whispered blessings on many lips.'   " I was an enthusiast then. . . . Now, a generation later, . . . I may look back on that occasion and soberly say, ' Nor did he seem insensible to the best of all earthly rewards, the love and admiration of his fellow-citizens. Hope elevated, and joy brightened his crest.' " [1]

At 5 p.m. Canning took his seat on the Treasury Bench. Behind him sat the unfamiliar Whig figures of Brougham, Tierney, Sir Robert Wilson, Sir Francis Burdett.   Opposite were some of his old colleagues in the Cabinet.   Peel led off with a long speech justifying his resignation ; after an interval Brougham followed with an equally long one justifying his support of the Government.   Canning, ' under evident emotion,' rose to pay a sincere tribute to the candour and rectitude of Peel.   He then proceeded to justify his own conduct in terms, which awakened thunders of applause.

" Now, what was it I proposed ?   What was it I had in command to do in the reconstruction of the government ? To form a ministry upon the principle of Lord Liverpool's administration.   That the government should even consist of the very same individuals, I am sure I had no objection. But, what was proposed to me ?   That I, having his Majesty's commands to form a government upon the very same prin- ciples as those of my lamented predecessor, should place at the head of that government another person, holding upon the subject of the Roman Catholic claims Lord Liverpool's opinions ?   [hear, hear].   Now, what was it I was desired to sanction by the adoption of that course ?   What principle is it I was called upon to admit ?   Why, I was desired plainly to say, that I, holding the opinions I have repeatedly avowed myself to hold upon the Catholic question, am thereby dis- qualified from being placed at the head of the government [cheers].   I was called upon to acknowledge, in the face of the country, that I, forming an administration upon the principles of Lord Liverpool—that is, of divided opinions on the Catholic claims, was from the very holding of a different and divided opinion disqualified from taking the highest office in that

[1] Charles Knight, *Passages from a Working Life* (2nd ed., 1873), pp. 51-2. The quotation is from Burke, on American Taxation, 1774.

government [*cheers*]. I will retire altogether and for ever from
public life ; I will betake myself to the furthest boundary
of the earth, and into perpetual banishment ; I will resign
any and every hope of office—for I care nothing for office—
but I will not disgrace myself, by consenting to sanction a
principle which could only bring degradation to those who
must become the subject of such an exclusion upon account
of their opinions [*hear, hear*]. To that principle, Sir, I repeat
I could not submit. I would rather have quitted office a
thousand times—I would rather be proscribed and persecuted
by all who are disposed to proscribe and persecute for opinions
—than live to be execrated to all futurity, for having, in my
person, fixed such a blot upon the cause of those who thought
that every man was free to hold opinions, although he might
not be able to persuade others to adopt them " [*cheers*].[1]

On the 3rd May, Dawson interrupted the debate by asking
if any arrangement had been made for filling up the offices
of Master of the Mint, Judge-Advocate, and Surveyor of Woods
and Forests. " The answer was the monosyllable ' yes,'
but pronounced in such a tone of mingled scorn, anger, and
grief that it seemed as if the heart of him who uttered it was
breaking with grief and disappointment." [2]

When he came to speak, however, Canning was himself
again. He told Dawson he had received no hint of his purpose,
" and even now he could not imagine how the production of
the patent for appointing the judge-advocate, and laying
it on the table, could have the effect of satisfying *his anxiety*,
unless it were, upon the old Cambridge principle, by taking
the masts and guns of the ship and dividing by the men, you
can get at the name of the captain " [*a laugh*]. Questioned
as to his attitude towards Reform, he answered he meant
" to oppose it to the end of my life," as also the Repeal of
the Test Acts. Gladstone afterwards referred to this as an
instance of ' great parliamentary courage.' In view of
Canning's precarious relations with the Whigs at the moment
it certainly was so.

[1] *Hans. Deb.*, N.S., xvii. 432, May 1/27.
[2] Earl Russell, *Recollections and Suggestions* [1875], 63. He adds : " I remember nothing like it but Kean's answer to Iago. ' You are moved,'
when he replied, ' not a jot,' in a voice of the deepest anxiety and emotion."
The *Star* merely says it was uttered ' in the loudest tone.'

The Lords' debate began on the 2nd May, and was prolonged for days. That august assembly beheld the most virulent exhibitions of temper and of language. All the ex-ministers justified their resignations and denied that they had concerted them. Wellington spoke with some bitterness ; Newcastle was violent ; Londonderry plainly accused Canning of having intrigued for the highest place since 1822, and of having betrayed the principles of Castlereagh. He displayed the worst possible taste and temper, and laid himself open to some humiliating rebuffs. He alluded to the connection with the Whigs as 'a state of disgusting concubinage,' and described the Ministry as composed of 'a sort of rubbish.' Lord King neatly replied that "Any person who was practically acquainted with building houses must know, that what was sent away was rubbish."

Subsequently Lord Dudley covered Londonderry with ridicule by disclosing the sordid story of his unsuccessful attempts to obtain a pension.[1]

Newcastle or Londonderry could be despised, but a more important antagonist now entered the arena. On the 10th May the Whig Lord Grey, who regarded " the son of an actress [*i.e.* Canning] as being *de facto* incapacitated " for the Premiership, delivered a most damaging attack on him. It is analysed elsewhere,[2] and it is enough to say here that he represented Canning as a mere boastful impostor and his foreign policy as a series of ingenious tricks. The speech was based largely on misquotations and misrepresentations, but it was one of those great parliamentary masterpieces, which are so near the truth, and yet so far away from it. And its acid bit deep. Stapleton afterwards said that Canning had cared little for the taunts of the Commons or of the Press, but that this attack had cut him to the quick. He debated seriously whether he should take a peerage to answer it. Goderich was wretched in the Lords, and had replied even to Londonderry with a burst of tears. A month later Sir James Mackintosh made a stately eulogy of Canning's foreign policy in the Commons, but even this did not console the new Prime Minister. Joan Canning believed that Grey's speech shortened

---

[1] P. 284, n. 3.   [2] *Vide* pp. 449–50.

her husband's life. So it was in the Lords that ' the hart was bayed.' [1]

A further mortification awaited Canning in the Lords. There Wellington carried an amendment to the Corn Bill, an amendment which, as Tom Moore said, ' made matters *worse*.' On the 18th June, the anniversary of Waterloo, Canning commented on it truly in the Commons by saying that the Duke had wrecked the whole purpose of the Bill, and bitterly by asserting that he had been ' made an instrument in the hands of others.' In the Commons, as in the country, Canning was still secure. On the 30th June he introduced the Budget himself, handling figures and finance with as much ease as he expounded principles of foreign policy. He concluded by declaring himself a disciple of Adam Smith and of Pitt in finance, and an advocate of applying the principles of philosophy to politics.[2] It was of this speech that Disraeli wrote : " I never saw Canning but once—I remember as if it were but yesterday the tumult of that ethereal brow. Still lingers in my ear the melody of that voice."

10. THE LAST MONTH

Canning was free of Parliament at the beginning of July, but his difficulties were not yet over. His temper was sorely tried by the Whigs, as one contemporary tale illustrates. A great Whig dignitary called upon him to give him counsel. After he had withdrawn, Canning said : " He comes to me with advice " (and his imperious voice and vehement gesture accorded, as he spake, with the animation of his angry eyes) ;

---

[1] Yet the Peers, except Lord Grey, had much the worst of the encounter, *cp.* :

> " Ah ! where is that dear House of Peers
> That, some weeks ago, kept us merry ?
> Where, Eldon, art thou with thy tears ?
> And thou, with thy sense, Londonderry ?
>
> Then come again, come again, Spring !
> Oh haste thee, with Fun in thy train ;
> And of all things, the funniest, bring
> These exalted Grimalkins again ! "
> *Dogday Reflections* (TOM MOORE).

[2] This was the last time Canning spoke in the House except in reply to a question.

" it is not advice that I want.   I want tools ! tools ! tools ! " [1]
The proud Whig nobles did not care to be the tools of a
parvenu, and Canning, between them and the King, was
forced into a series of vexatious compromises which fretted
his proud spirit. [2]

It is only necessary to allude to the arrangements here.   In
July three Whigs—Tierney, Lords Lansdowne and Carlisle—
entered the Cabinet.   Lord William Bentinck became Governor-
General for India, and this part of the Empire reaped lasting
benefit from Canning's appointment.   Other details are
needless, for the Ministry faded with Canning's life.   As soon
as the session was ended the Treaty over Greece was signed
(6th July), and the last letter Canning wrote to Granville
(13th) expressed the hope that there would be time to save her.
Though he knew it not, his own life was more imperilled than
that of Greece.

Canning cared little for doctors and less for his own health.
Earlier in the year, however, alarming signs had already
appeared.   At the funeral of the Duke of York he contracted
a severe chill, which brought on his illness of February.   On
the 1st March he had had, for the first time in his life, " a
completely sleepless night " . . . " I felt as if every limb,
from top to toe, was alive like an eel ; and I lay all night,
not tossing or tumbling, but as broad awake as if it were
midday."   Knighton, to whom he wrote this letter, might
have seen grave symptoms in the incident.   The labours
and cares of the Session increased Canning's weakness.   One
observer reported him as ' very ill and feeble ' at its beginning,
and even as ' looking a dying man ' towards its end.   A
doctor summoned suddenly to the Privy Council Board asked,
" Who is that individual with such a fine eye, who is so near
his end ? "   He was horror-struck to hear that it was Canning,
for he was one of the great man's admirers.   Yet his spirits
and courage were such that he rose superior to his weakness.
" He was," wrote Dudley, ". . . to the very last, gay and
playful."   Even so late as the 26th June he thought his
illness had passed and that rest would restore him ; his

---

[1] *Quarterly Review* (1831), xliv. 283.
[2] The Plunket incident has already been mentioned.   Another vexation
for Canning was having to break his promise to Palmerston to make him
Chancellor of the Exchequer, as the Whigs wanted that post.

closest friends seem to have been deceived. On the 11th July Stapleton could write to Stratford, there was 'every chance' that his cousin would "keep his health, for he is delightfully well now." On the day before this letter was written, Canning had contracted the chill which ultimately proved fatal.

On the 18th July, Huskisson, who was going abroad, paid his last visit to his friend. He told him he was looking ill and pale, but Canning gaily replied it was only the reflection of the yellow lining of the curtains. "Ill as he was," Huskisson told the Commons afterwards, weeping while he spoke, "his enthusiasm for his country knew no bounds . . . and he sacrificed himself as truly in the service of his country as Nelson, to whom alone for patriotism and devotion he could be compared."

The Duke of Devonshire had offered Canning his country house at Chiswick as a place of rest. "Do not go there," said Lady Holland. "Why?" asked the Premier. "Oh, I have a presentiment; you know Mr Fox died there." Canning laughed gaily, but even the hardened Lady Holland could never repeat the story without emotion. On the 20th he went to Chiswick; on the 30th he returned to Windsor, where he had his last audience with the King. There a stranger, who viewed him driving from the Castle gates, saw death in his looks.

On the next day he returned to Chiswick. On the 1st August he 'looked very ill but was very cheerful,' and worked away at a despatch on Portugal. On the 2nd he dealt with Treasury business and signed his name for the last time on two warrants. He then wished to revise his Portugal despatch but seemed so ill that Stapleton persuaded him to rest. That evening he was seized with violent pains. On the 3rd, Knighton saw him by command of the King, and diagnosed his case as that of inflammation of the liver. Three doctors attended him, and pronounced him to be 'in great and imminent danger.' A hundred thousand bulletins were issued daily from Downing Street. The voice of controversy was hushed; England and Europe watched expectantly at the bedside of the sick man. He was suffering from internal inflammation; his pains were of the most agonising character and his groans were heard even beyond the garden of Chiswick House. On the 5th his appearance was ' quite altered,' and he said faintly that all the pain he had suffered in his life " would not amount to one-hundredth part of the pain which I have suffered these last three days." On the 6th he slightly rallied and attempted to give Stapleton instructions, ' but they were not coherent,' though the word Portugal was uttered frequently.

An old friend recorded some other of his dying words. " The Country," he murmured, " has had the best of me. I think it will do justice to my publick character—I regret not the few years which might have remained to me, except for the dear ones whom I leave behind me."

"When Mr Blackburn was repeating the words in the Lord's Prayer—' Forgive us our trespasses as we forgive them that trespass against us '—he said, in a distinct voice, ' That I do most heartily, and I declare that I have not the slightest feeling of illwill to any human being.' " [1]

Late on the 7th he rallied, and spoke gently with his wife. She, observing the signs of dissolution in his face, fainted and was borne from the room, not recovering consciousness till after his death. Canning never spoke again, and became insensible towards night. At dawn on the 8th ' the flame of life went wavering down.'

The letters sent by his various relatives and friends to Stratford Canning tell the story, and are full of a tender pathos.[2] For they make it clear that Canning was beloved by his own circle, not as a statesman of genius and renown, but as an ideal husband, father, kinsman, and friend. Even now it is impossible to read the letters from his relatives without deep emotion at such unaffected sorrow. Those of his friends are equally moving. The distress of Frere, of Planta, of Granville, of Seaford, of Bagot, of Sir Robert Wilson, of Addington, could not have been greater had he been their own brother. Even an enemy like Grey thought " there is something awful and striking in the premature extinction of great talents in the very moment of successful ambition."

---

[1] *Gr. MSS.* Lord Morley to Lord Granville, Aug. 14/27. Several other utterances are given in Stap., *G.C. & T.,* 604.

[2] *Strat. MSS. F.O.,* 352/16.

II. RESULTS OF THE DEATH OF CANNING

" The praise of Kings is after their death,
And from the mouths of their enemies."
GIBBON.

The formation of the Ministry had been a great personal triumph for Canning, and its destructive effects were lasting. The spectacle of a parvenu minister supported by King and people, and defying the Tory Lords, was decisive. It portended the greater triumph of 1832. Canning's success discredited the old Tory party and machine, and formed a combination between its more progressive members and the Whigs, which proved fatal to the old régime. Even Wellington and Peel, backed by all the influence of the peers and the Treasury, could not avert Catholic Emancipation nor delay Reform for more than a brief space, nor prevent the Tory party from suffering its greatest eclipse during the century. But whether Canning could have fashioned a constructive policy, and continued for long to direct his strange coalition, must always be doubted. His death, at any rate, made the attempt impracticable, and ultimately converted the Canningite party to that Parliamentary Reform to which their leader had always been opposed.

Whatever may have been the result of his death on internal affairs, there can be no doubt of its profound effect on the world. As with Cromwell, the fame he had at home was " but a shadow of the glory he had abroad." Certainly the death of no British Foreign Minister ever produced so great an effect in a time of peace. " Now foreign Powers," wrote Russell, " will fear no longer." " He had given laws and encouragements to rising States," wrote Mary Bagot, " his name was re-echoed from every quarter of the globe. Such he was at the commencement of that week whose close saw him restored—ashes to ashes—dust to dust ! " [1] " His name," wrote Fonblanque, " was the very watchword of liberty, and oppression quailed at its ascendancy." " I confess." wrote Hobhouse, " I was overwhelmed. He was no friend of mine, yet I knew his name was the terror of tyrants." And he thought sadly of who might take the seat " from

Mrs Charles Bagot, *Links with the Past* (1901), p. 251 ; *Diary*, Aug. 18.

which the great orator had lately poured forth his thunders and shaken the thrones of superstition and despotism. I would have given my right arm to save him." Huskisson, who returned from Austria, said the peoples in the countries through which he passed, " felt as if mankind had lost a benefactor." Mackintosh, " attempting the temper of the historian of future times," wrote : " It was an event in the internal history of every country. From Lima to Athens, every nation struggling for independence or existence, was filled with sorrow and dismay. The Miguelites of Portugal, the Apostolicals of Spain, the Jesuit faction in France, and the Divan of Constantinople raised a shout of joy at the fall of their dreaded enemy." The greatest tribute came from the men who had hated and opposed him most. It is " an event which may transform the whole policy of Europe," wrote Gentz. " C'est un évènement immense," wrote Metternich, "for the man was a whole revolution in himself alone." He rejoiced, and thanked a merciful Providence for thus delivering Europe from ' this malevolent meteor' and ' this Scourge of the World.' Even four years later he could write : " The Ministry of Canning has marked an era in the history of England and of Europe." [1] Could Canning himself have wished any better epitaph than this ?

[1] *V.S.A.*, Weisungen nach England, Aug. 12/31. The Ministry referred to is that of Canning, and the measures which marked ' the era ' are the coalition with the Whigs and the Treaty over Greece, *v.* text, p. 607.

CHAPTER XIX

MR CANNING'S 'SYSTEM OF POLICY'

1. CASTLEREAGH AND THE 'SYSTEM'

STAPLETON always declared that 'Mr Canning' had 'a system of policy,' and that in this consisted both his originality and his greatness. 'A policy' has been defined as " a blackmail levied by the Fool on the Unforeseen " ; and ' systems ' have always been viewed with suspicion by Englishmen. They are particularly open to criticism in the sphere of foreign affairs, which is so often a shifting kaleidoscope coloured by the passions and interests of a dozen conflicting States. Yet the age in which Canning lived, not only favoured, but actually demanded, the existence of policies, theories, and systems. The French Revolution propounded a new theory of foreign relations, in the form of a levelling gospel and of an invocation of the rights of peoples against kings. Napoleon preached this gospel with his sword, until he broke his weapon against the united strength of Europe. Thereafter, for it was necessary to combat ideas with ideas, diplomats propounded counter-theories. Talleyrand championed Legitimacy, Alexander the Holy Alliance, Metternich acquiesced in the perversion of it into the Neo-Holy Alliance. All these theories, whether of revolution or of reaction, were intended as an appeal to opinion. Napoleon and the Jacobins failed because they sought to force opinion too far on new courses ; Alexander and Metternich because they sought to restore too much that was old. Canning succeeded because he popularised ideas, which were to spread throughout Europe in a generation. And these ideas were comprised in his system.

It would be wrong to suggest that Canning was the inventor of his system. As he himself said, more than once, he was

447

carrying out the ideas propounded by Castlereagh in his state paper of the 5th May 1820, and in this sense Castlereagh and Canning were at one. The respective merits of the two men, that problem, which so agitated contemporaries, is now well on its way to solution. Castlereagh is no longer the combination of 'goose and vulture' which satirists depicted, nor the idol of High Tories, nor the scorn or scandal of Whigs. As a serene and strong statesman his place in history is secure. No one now denies his immense services to the Coalition which overthrew Napoleon ; and the title of 'the most European' of English Foreign Ministers, which he gained in his later years, has given him a measure of well-deserved fame. Canning's place is less easy to estimate. Some are apt to sneer at a phrasemaker and to suppose that great popularity among contemporaries produces a surplus, which historians are called upon to reduce. Castlereagh has had certainly less, Canning perhaps more, than his meed of praise. But they remain, none the less, associated and inseparable. They form, indeed, a pair of statesmen to whom there is no parallel in English foreign policy. Towards the end of his life Pitt pursued a policy which Fox carried on, but their combination was in war time, not in peace settlement. Canning and Castlereagh both indeed conducted a war policy, but their most important combined work was in peace, when old principles were abandoned and new ones proclaimed, when a world was emerging again out of chaos, and when it had, 'for weal or for woe,' to be fashioned anew. Beside them the brilliance of Palmerston, the emotion of Gladstone, and the legerdemain of Disraeli, is the mere sheet-lightning of history. None of their successors have wielded such great power, achieved such permanent results, or attained such lasting renown. It is, in fact, true to say that their successors received the principles of these great men, and continued, consciously or unconsciously, to imitate either the one or the other. It was not until a half-century after Vienna that those forces began to be shaped which were destined to plunge the world into a chaos as great as that of the French Revolution, and to disturb the relative permanence and tranquillity bequeathed by the policy of Castlereagh and Canning. Certainly their successors at the Peace of Versailles in 1919, and in its aftermath, have achieved nothing as lasting as the settlements that followed upon Vienna.

2. THE WELLINGTON POLICY

It is, of course, vain to speculate upon what Castlereagh would, or could, have done had he lived. But by 1820, and still more by 1822, his great idea was already worn out. The Congress System was becoming a menace to England, and the European method of regarding English policy had become difficult, if not impossible, to continue. At any rate, it cannot be denied that some new orientation of policy was necessary, and that at the moment of his death Castlereagh had not been able to complete it nor to win the British people to his support. After Verona, even Wellington made up his mind that the Congress System was discredited, that advocates of it would be misrepresented by ' *ces habitans de Westminster*.' " We stand alone, and we do so by choice," he wrote to Metternich. He was definitely as opposed to the summoning of new congresses as Canning, though his method of deprecating them was by private letters, and he remained fixed in the idea that the less Parliament and the public knew of foreign policy, the better. His policy then was to avoid both congresses and publicity ; not to act, and yet not to break, with the three great military monarchies of the Continent. It is possible that this system might have been pursued by Castlereagh. But it would be doing less than justice to his memory to suggest that he would have adopted the views that Wellington put forward as to Portugal and Greece. Castlereagh's policy would almost certainly have been different ; in any case, it could not have been less popular or less successful than the Duke's.

3. THE WHIG ALTERNATIVE

If Wellington's policy offered less prospects of success than Canning's, it is fair to ask if the Whig or Liberal policies would have been more successful. These are best stated by Lord Grey in his famous attack upon Canning of the 10th May 1827.[1] He denounced him on the ground that he should have

---

[1] *Hans. Deb.*, N.S., xvii. (May 10/27), 727–30.

threatened France with war before she invaded Spain in 1823. This charge hardly seems sound. Threats to France over Spain were clearly dangerous, for the plain reason that we had not enough troops to prevent the invasion of Spain ; and the fact that the policy of neutrality was approved by a huge majority in the Commons does not suggest that the nation would have been in favour of war. Canning's recognition of Spanish America, Grey declared, had been too long delayed, as she had already achieved her independence. He accused Canning of declaring in one breath that he had called ' the New World into existence,' and in another that he had done nothing to promote her independence. The confusion of thought in this argument has already been pointed out (pp. 155–6). Grey's last point was that our succour of Portugal in 1826 had been ' too tardy.' Here he was plainly in the wrong. To aid Portugal, before the *casus fœderis* had occurred, would have been to agitate Europe unnecessarily. In fact, both aid and justification proved adequate to the occasion. Two other Whig arguments were that Canning should have liberated all slaves by a stroke of the pen, and should have intervened earlier than he did with armed force in Greece. All these arguments rest on the assumption that England should act without reference to other Powers, without particular regard to treaties, and should aid oppressed nations in the crusading and romantic style, a policy which regarded little either the chances or the consequences. When he was in office, Grey, by emancipating the slaves, produced a veiled rebellion in Jamaica and an open one in South Africa. His crusading efforts on behalf of Poland resulted in a humiliating diplomatic defeat. These events suggest that Canning made the right compromise between the policies of Wellington and Grey ; now holding back in deference to European diplomats, now going forward in harmony with national sentiment and with popular opinion. Here, as elsewhere, he held the balance with a steady hand. And it was in the preservation of this balance between democratic and despotic policies that his system consisted.

4. THE PERSONAL SIDE OF CANNING'S POLICY

While, therefore, it is contended that Canning's policy was the one best adapted to his own period, it must not be suggested that it had no defects. Castlereagh was supreme in the adroit and tactful execution, Canning in the intellectual conception, of policies. And the genius, which enabled him to formulate ideas and to divine movements, did not always help him in the management of men. His tongue and pen were sharp, and he used both sometimes to his own disadvantage.

Castlereagh had excelled in the handling of men, and Adams and Gallatin and Monroe all testified to the wisdom and firmness of his touch. None of them liked Canning, Adams least of all. Rush admired his ability, but did not succumb to his influence. Only Clay felt his charm and said he was ' quite in love ' with him. And the comparative failure of Canning in North America was not much more than counterbalanced by his triumphant success in the South.

With the statesmen of France Canning had serious disputes. Yet even the serenity of Castlereagh had been sorely tried by Richelieu and by Decazes, and Canning found Villèle more aggressive than the first, and Polignac more perfidious than the second. Yet, despite sharp contests in 1823 and in 1826, Canning ultimately won France to take part in the Treaty of the 6th July 1827, and thus made possible friendly co-operation in the future.

Canning's methods of negotiating with Metternich and Alexander can be criticised. Metternich, though in principle friendly to England, particularly on the question of the Colonies, was forced to choose between Castlereagh and Alexander, when their policies diverged in 1820. Metternich naturally had to choose Alexander, and for a time danced a decorous minuet to the sound of the imperial flute, though inwardly detesting the music of Troppau and deriding the author of the ' Holy Alliance.' This ' inharmonious music ' made Castlereagh threaten to break with Metternich, and gave Canning an opportunity to do so at Verona, which fact he announced openly enough in Parliament. Perhaps Castlereagh could have handled the two men better, but even this must be regarded as doubtful. Wellington himself broke with Metternich in 1822, and Canning carried on the feud in 1823, when the Duke was anxious to make it up again. During 1824 Canning managed to work with Metternich over Brazil and, to some extent also, over Greece. By 1825 Canning had come to the conclusion, which he frankly expressed to Ester-házy, that the principles of Austria and England were so different that they could not work together. It is true that there were personal reasons as well. He knew that Metternich had intrigued with the King, with the Duke, and with some members of the British Cabinet to overthrow him, and he called him " the greatest rogue and liar in Europe, perhaps in the civilised world." In 1825 Canning certainly believed that he could not work with Metternich without being betrayed. It is at least singular that by August of that year Nesselrode and Alexander, over whom Metternich had long exercised unrivalled ascendancy, had come to the same conclusion.

Here was Canning's chance. It has already been related how he made friends with the two Lievens, and seized the opportunity to dash the Neo-Holy Alliance in pieces with the aid of the brother of its founder. Whatever defects Canning may have shown in dealing with Russian statesmen in the earlier period of his Ministry, there can be little doubt of his masterly handling of them during the last two years of his life. Here the dash, the quickness, and the boldness of his method succeeded, where those of caution and discretion would have failed. Metternich hit the mark, when he wrote of English policy in 1828 : " It is going on a dangerous course, and more dangerous, because *less bold*, than that of Mr Canning."

5. England's Obligations to Europe

Though Canning allowed his personal feelings to deflect his policy, in some degree his main ideas were based upon principle. And one of these principles was that it was important to defeat the Congress System and discredit the Neo-Holy Alliance. Like Wellington, Castlereagh, and like all men who had contended against Napoleon, Canning was determined to uphold the territorial settlement of Vienna and to exclude the Napoleonic dynasty from the throne of

France. There, however, he stopped; for he refused to
extend the obligations to general guarantees, and to approve
any other interferences with the internal affairs of France
or of any other nation. " There are," he said to Damas in
1826, " three treaties in my view which rule the politics of
to-day. The first is the Quadruple Alliance directed against
France, and of which you [France] consequently do not form
a part. The second is the 'Holy Alliance,' *absurdité*, from which
we are excluded. The third is the Quintuple Alliance, of
which England and France form a part, which I always
recognise, and from which I have never departed, and in
which you will constantly find me.   In my letter to Mr Temple
I tried to prove to Prussia, who claimed that we had abandoned our first opinions on the Greek question and had re-
entered the 'Holy Alliance' in this matter, that it was not so ;
that the circumstances, that the position of the question had
wholly changed, and that if we spoke of agreement, of co-
operation of the Powers, it was only in the sense of the
Quintuple Alliance, the fruit of the Congress of Aix-la-
Chapelle." [1]   Thus he stood by both Quadruple and Quintuple
Alliances, but rejected the extension of those obligations by
arguments from the 'Holy Alliance' (from which we were shut
out) and from the Neo-Holy Alliance which we had never
joined. This reasoning did not suit Damas, who declared that
" Canning had the air of wishing to arrange a policy applicable
only to England, without any consideration for the general
interest." Metternich was still more furious, and said that
he did not regard a union of the Five Powers as ' practicable.' [2]
So there was the paradox that Canning supported France
and wished to co-operate with the Powers in a Quintuple
Alliance, which Metternich disdained.

In all this Castlereagh would have agreed ; he supported
both Quadruple and Quintuple Alliances ; he denied the
extensions of them proposed by the Neo-Holy Alliance. He
said the latter ' had moved away from us, not we from them.'

Canning believed that the Congress System not only offered
grave disadvantages to England, but that public opinion

[1] *V.S.A.*, Berichte aus Frankreich, Bd. 370. Apponyi to Metternich,
Oct. 28/26, No. 34 E., reporting a conversation with Canning.

[2] *V.S.A.*, Weisungen nach Frankreich, Bd. 373. Metternich to Apponyi,
Nov. 9/26.

would not any longer allow us to continue it. He compared the position of England to that of a character in the *Arabian Nights*. " Do you remember the story of Barber's brother, who, to oblige a neighbour, gets into his mill-wheel, and consents to turn it for half an hour ; but being once in, is whipped on, every time that he attempts to pause ; the miller, in the meantime, turning his thoughts to his other business ? " [1] The mill was the Congress System, the neighbours the Neo-Holy Alliance, and the Barber's brother was England.

6. THE ATTACK ON THE NEO-HOLY ALLIANCE

Canning had not been a fortnight in office before he took steps to break loose from this system. And he took such steps because he saw from evident signs that the Spanish question would be the supreme one at Verona, and that the collective pressure of the Powers would be exerted to whip England along, and to grind out the corn for the benefit of others.

Canning's attack on the Congress System began on the 27th September 1822, when, in his famous ' come what *may* ' despatch, he instructed Wellington to refuse to be a party to any project, by force or by menace, urged by the Congress at Verona. That ended the Congress of Verona, and made the break between Europe and England evident. The next stage was the despatch of the 31st March 1823, when he indicated, plainly enough, that England refused to accept the French doctrine of intervention in Spain, and was likely to recognise the Spanish Colonies at her own time and dis-cretion. The conference with Polignac on the 9th October 1823 forced a disclaimer from France as to the Spanish Colonies, and indicated England's probable refusal to attend a congress on the question. That refusal was made definite on the 30th January 1824. In November of that year Canning refused to attend a congress on the Eastern question, and on the last day of December he recognised three Spanish Colonies without reference to Europe or to the Congress policy.

[1] To Bagot, Jan. 22/24. Bagot, *G.C. & F.*, ii. 215. In this application he refers specifically to Russia, but he quotes the story again in 1825 to Stratford, referring to the Neo-Holy Alliance.

These were the chief stages in the grand attack on the Congress, but side by side with them went similar refusals to co-operate with the other Powers of Europe in conferences. At the end of 1822 Russia and Austria made great efforts to continue the system of the Conference of Ambassadors at Paris, and to inaugurate similar gatherings at Madrid, Petrograd, and Lisbon, and these sessions continued until 1826. Canning never permitted his representative to attend one at Madrid, and reprimanded his diplomats at Lisbon and Petrograd for attending two or three of them. Out of sixty-six conferences at Paris during the years 1822–6, Canning permitted England to be represented only at five, all of them purely formal and connected with the execution of the Treaty of Vienna.

The result of this policy of abstinence both from general congresses and ambassadorial conferences was seen in 1825 and in 1826. In May 1825 the Eastern Congress broke up in mutual recriminations, and in August Alexander refused to co-operate longer with Metternich and began to approach Canning. That was the end of Congresses. The ambassadorial conferences lasted longer, but in August 1826 Russia, under the influence of Canning, abandoned the system of ambassadorial conferences, and refused Metternich's invitation to a new congress on Portugal. That was the end of the Neo-Holy Alliance altogether.

These examples illustrate Canning's methods. What was peculiar in them was not his refusal to participate in congress or conference. That Castlereagh might have done, or Wellington. Canning not only abstained from such gatherings but informed the public that he had done so, and described the principles on which he took his stand. The instructions of the 27th September 1822 and of the 31st March 1823 were published in April of the latter year. The Memorandum of the Polignac Conference (9th October 1823), and the despatch refusing a Congress over Spanish America (30th January 1824), were published in March of that year. The despatch of March 1825, asserting the right of England to recognise the Spanish Colonies on the ground of their *de facto* independence, was published before the end of the year.

Such boldness in action, and such frankness in declaring it openly, were almost wholly new. While they inspired the

European diplomats with alarm, they took the British people, and Liberal opinion throughout the world, by storm.

Canning was successful, for he touched a chord to which public opinion responded. He ultimately made it clear even to foreign statesmen that they would lose and not gain by admitting England to a seat in their councils, and that a parliamentary country could not associate itself with vague and general theories, or with mutual insurance companies which guaranteed every monarch his throne, and which menaced all constitutions and constitutionalists with the bayonets of three military despots. In Europe he had to be diplomatic; beyond it he could defy the Neo-Holy Alliance. To the attempt to extend the Neo-Holy Alliance over the ocean he opposed the fleet of England which rode upon it. "We ought never to forget," he said once, "that the field of our native glory is that sea, which disjoins other countries from each other, but which unites them to England." The power of the Neo-Holy Alliance ceased at low-water mark in Europe. The ocean was to maintain the liberty of the New World. This was revolutionary doctrine to Metternich, who declared that Canning had "flashed like a malevolent meteor through Europe."

Connected with the attack upon the Congress System was the discredit he sought to bring upon the theory of Legitimacy. He horrified Maltzahn by asking why its advocates had permitted the mad King of Sweden to wander an exile over Europe, and a French Marshal to sit on the throne of the Vasas. He pointed out in a published despatch to Spain that "the principle of the imprescriptible rights of a legitimate sovereign, and the obligation of all foreign Powers to respect those rights," was not supported by the recent practice of Spain herself. For she had not only acknowledged the governments *de facto*, which dethroned the Bourbons, but had concluded an alliance with Napoleon "against whom his unrestrained ambition, and not a principle of respect for the rights of legitimate monarchy, had armed all the Powers of Europe." He reminded her that England herself had negotiated with the usurper, and that other Powers had been prepared to see a ruler, not a Bourbon, succeed to the French throne which Napoleon had vacated. In fact, England in recognising the Spanish revolted Colonies as States could be defended by "abundant examples of the recognition of governments *de facto* by Great Britain, which in this respect was always more tardy than the other Powers of Europe, and especially Spain, which gave them the example." This public defence of the principle of recognition dismayed the advocates of Legitimacy almost more than the act of recognition itself. It was after the publication of this despatch that a Whig paper wrote : " a new era has dawned in diplomacy. . . . Instead of cunning, over-reaching, trickery . . . the quibbling of the lawyer . . . dubious verbiage . . . confusing language . . . Mr Canning dares to appear the man of talent and the scholar . . . [this] vigour of style, and open manly reasoning, consonant to the elevation of his office, to the intellect of his country, and the established opinion of his own powers." [1] It is certainly true that what England wanted was a man who would tell all the world the principles and the policy on which he acted, and that man she found in Canning. Castlereagh found it necessary to say in 1821 that he was as sincere a friend of freedom as any man. No one thought it necessary for Canning to make that statement in 1827. Yet, as sometimes happens, public opinion, though it had plenty of information, did not always understand Canning's policy towards constitutions and towards democracy.

7. Attitude towards Constitutions ; Non-Intervention

The policy towards constitutions in other countries has, to some extent, been misunderstood by the champions of Canning : first by the Whigs who wished to see in him the constitutional Don Quixote, next by his own nearer intimates who ought to have known better than to try to hide the truth.[2] But we have an authentic witness in Stratford

---

[1] *Constable's Miscellany* (1827) speaks of Canning's ' resistless arguments ' in this connection.

[2] *E.g.* Stapleton mutilates one despatch (*F.O. Portugal, 179/35*). Canning to À Court, June 28/26. Canning refers to the Neo-Holy Alliance as having " put down the constitutional systems of Naples and Spain, *however little worth maintaining*, not for their [own] intrinsic worthlessness, but simply and declaredly because they were not *octroyés* by the Sovereign." Stapleton omits the passage in italics, and is followed by Lady Canning in her anonymous pamphlet of 1830, p. 15. The omission is evidently designed.

Canning, whose private papers detail an interview with his great cousin in 1824, when George Canning delivered to him a discourse on *General Politics*. " Great Britain maintains a policy of her own, suited to her position and constitution. She will be no party to a general interference in the concerns of other States ; though prepared to interfere on *special* concerns in her opinion justifying such interference. Why should the Governments, forming the [Neo]-H[oly] A[lliance] be looking continually to parties in foreign States, and not to their Governments in their relations with those States ? G[reat] B[ritain] is ready to live on terms of amity with arbitrary Governments, why should they not do the same with respect to free States ? So long as nothing be done by the latter to violate their rights or to prejudice their just interests. The principle of British policy is shown in nothing more than in abstaining from controlling the interference of the Allied Sovereigns with Spain and Naples, when she could not herself take part with them. G[reat] B[ritain] in communicating with despotic Governments does not complain of their principles of government ; why then should they complain of her free institutions and the spirit of her nation in dealing with Her ? NOT ON THE OTHER HAND, A BRITISH INTEREST TO HAVE FREE STATES ESTABLISHED ON THE CONTINENT. MUCH BETTER AND MORE CONVENIENT FOR US TO HAVE NEIGHBOURS, WHOSE INSTITUTIONS CANNOT BE COMPARED WITH OURS IN POINT OF FREEDOM.[1] The principle of all this [is] a middle course between *Jacobinism* and *Ultraism*, with a view particularly of preventing extreme parties from coming to an open rupture." [2] Here, if ever, is a political testament from one diplomat to another as able and masterful as himself, from the first to the ' third great Canning.'

The view, thus stated, is a priceless comment on Canning's attitude. He was the assailant of the European Areopagus ;

---

[1] *Cp.* Apr. 30/23, *Speeches* (1836), v. 125. " The principle which for centuries has given ascendancy to Great Britain, is that she was the single free State in Europe. The spread of the representative system destroys that singularity, and must (however little we may like it) *proportionately enfeeble our preponderating influence*—unless we measure our steps cautiously, and accommodate our conduct to the times." Italics my own.

[2] Italics in original ; capitals my own. *F.O.*, 352/9. *Strat. MSS.* Memoranda of conversation with the Secretary of State and Mr Planta on leaving the Foreign Office, Dec. 4/24, and previously to setting out for St Petersburg and Vienna.

he was the preserver of the European system, as he under-stood it ; he was not the chivalrous and romantic defender of constitutions. He preferred constitutional monarchy to any other form of government because it was the *via media* between despotism and democracy. He expressed some alarm at the progress of constitutions, especially when ultra-democratic, as in Spain, Naples, and Portugal. " The general acquisition of free institutions is not necessarily a security for general peace. I am obliged to confess that its immediate tendency is the other way." He blamed the French Chamber, and not the French King, for the war with Spain in 1823, and he pointed out, with reference to ' the democrats of the ancient world,' that ' their existence . . . was in war.' [1]

In regard to constitutions of a moderate and not ultra-democratic character, he was more favourable. " I would not prohibit other nations from kindling their torches at the flame of British freedom." But even so, he was cautious in approval and showed no eagerness to recognise even moderate and limited constitutions. Authoritative lecturing in the Palmerstonian style formed no part of the master's policy ; non-intervention was, indeed, the corner-stone of his whole system. He did not hesitate to depart from it in Portugal in 1825 when the particular interest of England was affected by the continuance in power of Subserra. Similarly, during 1823, he tendered friendly advice to the Spanish Constitution-alists to moderate their institutions, not because he wished to interfere with their constitution, but because they them-selves had admitted defects in it, and because a remedying of those defects might avert war with Bourbonist France. The support he gave to Portugal in 1826 was primarily due to treaty obligation to defend her against attack from outside, and his support of her new and moderate constitution was not because of his love for it, but because he thought it the only solution of both internal and external difficulties. In fact, though supporting the new constitution, he did not hesitate to call attention to defects and to give advice, though in neither case authoritatively, as to moderating its character. His main policy, therefore, was to support England's honour

[1] Apr. 30/23. *Speeches* (1836), v. 124–5.

and interests, but to adjust both to public opinion in his own country and to the spirit of the times.

While it is true that he was an avowed opponent of the Neo-Holy Alliance as a collective body, it is not true that he defied these powers in their individual capacity, or that he provoked opinion in their own countries, or in his own, against any one of them by itself. Though strongly disapproving of Metternich's ' smelling out traitors ' at Milan, or of his Emperor's stinting the rations of his state-prisoners, he deprecated all formal remonstrance. But he did not conceal from these governments that he thought their policy provoked unrest in their own countries, and that, in their own interests, they would be wise to adopt other methods. From England's point of view despotic institutions in other countries were to be preferred, for liberal unrest demoralised the army and weakened the State. It was, as he conceived, a fact which he did not hesitate to announce in public, that, in a war with a despotic country, England could not " avoid seeing ranked under her banners all the restless and dissatisfied of any nation with which she might come into conflict " (12th December 1826). If that was the result of Neo-Holy Alliance doctrines, England had no reason to complain for her own sake. But, for the sake of the world, she deprecated " exaggerated and violent doctrines on both sides."

For England, then, Canning was not afraid. He had " a source of confidence and security in her giants' strength," which consisted in the support of her public opinion. He held in utter contempt Alexander's favourite doctrine that the discontented in all countries were in league with one another, that the Carbonari in Italy, Sir Robert Wilson in England, Bolivar in America, and the Jacobins in France were the leaders in that international militia of rebels which could only be suppressed by an international army organised and led by the despots. There was something " in the constitution of the English mind that . . . would repel the aid of foreign treason and would not inoculate itself with any infection that was not at least of native origin." The continental suggestions that his recognition of the revolted Colonies of Spain would cause the rebellion of Jamaica, or the loss of India, aroused his scorn. The informal offer of the Emperor

Francis to send Austrian troops to suppress revolt in Ireland fired his utmost wrath. "Naples, Piedmont, Spain, Ireland! Who shall draw the line if the principle of European intervention be once admitted?"[1]

"Dearly as he valued the ties by which European nations were held together, there was not a connection that he would not sever at once, rather than allow any measure brought forward in that House to originate from a foreign Source."[2] Compared with England, the Neo-Holy Alliance counted but as dust in the balance, and the chief evil of that system was just that it encouraged interference from outside with the Press, with the people, or with the institutions of independent countries. What he attacked was not Austria, Russia, or Prussia, but their unholy, or Neo-Holy, Alliance acting on general principles, from which England dissented, and which she thought would lead to perpetual interference in the interests of Legitimacy. What he defended was the European States System, the Quadruple and Quintuple Alliance, and the territorial settlements of Vienna.

8. Negotiations with Individual States; The Small Powers

Provided they were prepared not to insist on their collective principles, Canning was quite ready to act with any individual member of the Neo-Holy Alliance. He rejoiced in 1822 at direct negotiations with France, "between Kingdom and Kingdom in the old intelligible European form," and, had she been able to separate herself from the others, he was prepared to act with her over Spanish America. He did again act with her in the matter of Greece. During 1823–4, despite great difficulties, he acted with Metternich over Brazil, and only parted as Metternich insisted on the preliminary recognition of her independence by Portugal. And, even after this separation, Metternich continued to co-operate with him privately over Brazil. When Metternich sought to bring him into the council over Greece at the end of 1824, he declined, because that meant attendance at a congress at

---

[1] Dec. 12/24. Canning's memo. to the Cabinet. Stap., *G.C. & T.*, 407.
[2] Mar. 17/26. *Hans. Deb.*, N.S., xiv. 1405.

which England would have been compelled to dissent from her Allies. But that refusal did not prevent him from acting separately with Russia in 1826, and that separate action confirmed the break-up of the Neo-Holy Alliance System. Similarly in regard to the Transatlantic Republics, he made the boldest overture of his time when he offered to co-operate in a joint declaration with Monroe. But it is characteristic that, when that overture failed, he sought to prevent the United States from heading a league of Republics in the West, succeeded in erecting a monarchy in Brazil, and cultivated the individual suffrages of Latin-American Republics. For, while he was quite willing to act with either monarchy or republic alone, he had no intention of entering an alliance in which one or other principle was exclusively proclaimed.

Canning's attitude towards the small Powers was much affected by his attitude towards the great. England ought to manage her own internal affairs, and every nation, great or small, should do the same. He recognised that at the moment it was the small which were in danger. He defended his care for them in an interesting way. It had never, he said, been the principle of this country to neglect the minor independent governments of the Continent—he did not believe that the time would ever have to arrive when this country would regret that she had held up those heads "which circumstances had contributed to lay low. On the contrary, he was more disposed to think that these governments contained in themselves the seeds of future prosperity, perhaps of future glory." [1] The small States were of use to him in his policy. Thus he declined one congress on the ground that the United States (then a small Power in European eyes) was left out, another because the Netherlands was not consulted. He took care, when he announced his intention to recognise Spanish America, to summon representatives of the small Powers, a step which seriously annoyed the Neo-Holy representatives. Yet he was not prepared to carry his championship of small Powers to quixotic lengths. Such Powers as the Netherlands, the Scandinavian States, and the Hansa Towns, gave way to the threats of the Neo-Holy

[1] Mar. 17/26. *Hans. Deb.*, N.S., xiv. 1405.

Alliance, and feared to recognise Spanish America unless backed by England's support. Canning did not consider it safe to give it, for these small States were in reach of the armies of Europe. With the Spanish Republics and the United States the case was different, for they could be pro-tected by the navy of England. They were therefore encouraged to defy the Neo-Holy Alliance. " I do not say (God forbid I should !) that it is no part of the duty of Great Britain to protect what is termed the balance of power and to aid the weak against the strong. I say, on the contrary, that it is her bounden duty ; but I affirm also, that we must take care to do our duty to ourselves. The first condition of engaging in any war . . . is that the war must be just ; the second, that, being just in itself, we can also with justice engage in it ; and the third . . . that we can so interfere without detriment or prejudice to ourselves." [1] These precepts, publicly proclaimed on the 14th April 1823, were strictly carried out in future years. War did not, in fact, extend to Spanish America and to Portugal ; but these countries would not have been left alone, had not Canning made clear that in certain contingencies England would actively assist or protect them.

In his general relations with the smaller Powers Canning was really triumphant. He certainly improved British relations with the Netherlands and with the Scandinavian States. And, while he was necessarily never on good terms with Spain, he seems to have been at least as successful as were the Neo-Holy Alliance, who professed to be the active sympathisers and co-operators of Ferdinand. Portugal and Brazil were petted and fussed over, but were not permitted to be spoiled. When Palmella had the temerity to demand undue advantages in a commercial treaty, he was reminded sharply that " it was not the custom of the British Govern-ment to negotiate within the circle traced by Popilius." The reminder proved effective enough. With states and states-men struggling into recognition, like the Brazilians and Spanish Americans or the Greek delegates, Canning assumed, with great adroitness, the attitude of a temperate, friendly, but occasionally stern, elder brother. Those who know either

[1] Apr. 16/23. *Speeches*, v. 48.

the politics or politicians of small states well, know also that they can learn lessons of gravity and responsibility from great states and statesmen. On the whole, Canning's method of friendly admonition, combined with a firm upholding of the dignity of England, was the best method that could have been applied to such states, and was entirely justified by results.

9. NATIONALISM; THE PUBLIC LAW OF EUROPE; THE BALANCE OF POWER

Though not advocating the British or any free constitution as a model for other lands, Canning was in a sense the champion of national independence. But the Treaty settlement of Vienna confined that support within limited bounds. Two principles, usually confounded in his own day, were, in his view, entirely distinct. The adoption of free institutions or the retention of arbitrary government was the affair of each individual State; but the assertion of national independence might affect other States as well. It was therefore an international concern, and regulated by treaty. In his earliest days, Canning had conceived that the French had a right to dethrone Louis XVI. and to proclaim what doctrines they liked, so long as they kept within their own borders and indulged in no hostile acts beyond them. In his first Ministry he had recognised the peoples or nation of Spain as having a right to rebel against Napoleon; he had made an alliance with them; and the results of that alliance fixed their lasting impression on his mind. For, while he utterly despised and ridiculed Spain's Constitution of 1812, he greatly admired and stimulated the heroism of their national and patriotic uprising. Similarly during 1814 and 1815 he spoke of Germany as ' no longer a name but a nation '; he took deep interest in the national movement in Poland; and he strongly condemned Castlereagh's policy of forcibly blockading Norway until she submitted to an unnatural union with Sweden. Had Canning been in power at the Congress of Vienna, he might have tried to remedy some of these evils. But he was not, and, once Vienna had issued its fiat as to territorial arrangements, he accepted it as binding for his own generation. " I was—I still am—an enthusiast for national independence ; but I am not—I hope I never shall be—an enthusiast in favour of revolution " (20th April 1823). And one of the worst kind of revolutions was an attack—of open power or secret influence—against the boundaries set by the Congress in 1815.

Let us see how he applied the principle. The settlement had placed Germany in the power of Metternich, and when that statesman proceeded to gag the Press and imprison so-called conspirators throughout the Confederation, Canning made no formal remonstrance. In the still more extreme case of constitutional Würtemberg, which protested against the exclusion of small States from the Congress of Vienna, he declined to interfere. Metternich set Alexander on to bully the King ; the Neo-Holy Alliance and France withdrew their diplomatic representatives, and forced the King to insert a newspaper paragraph explaining away his circular. Canning would not suspend diplomatic relations with Würtemberg, but he publicly declared in Parliament that he would make no formal remonstrances to those Powers who did so. He thought the principle of interference was ' bad,' but the territorial settlement of Germany at Vienna forced him to admit that " it was not fair to call [this] application of it a flagrant outrage." . . . " A single spark flashing unhappily from the hasty zeal of England, might light up a conflagration on the Continent which no after-exertions could extinguish." [1] They could not form another world " of one entire and perfect chrysolite." Connection with despots had overthrown the colossal despotism of Napoleon, and it was not our business to separate too much from them, or to inquire too minutely into " abuses which may exist in foreign governments." He regarded, indeed, Metternich's police-raids in Germany, and Alexander's hunts after Liberals in Poland, with the same contempt that he looked upon the crazy orgies of Constitutionalists at Naples, Madrid, or Rio. As he denied to the Neo-Holy Alliance the right of interfering on behalf of despotism, he denied the exercise of

---

[1] Feb. 3/24. *Hans. Deb.*, N.S., xi., *v. F.O. Stuttgart,* 163/16. *Vide* Wynn to Canning, June 23/23, No. 8, he had expressed regret at the behaviour of the Neo-Holy Alliance, but not committed Canning. " I had no orders from you, nor was it likely I should have on a subject where it was impossible for England to interfere with any effect." Canning subsequently approved.

the same right to himself or to the Whigs in England on behalf of constitutional or national liberty, or to the United States on behalf of triumphant democracy. Sentiment and opinions ought not to cause the breach of territorial treaty rights.

England's duty was to keep treaties, whatever the cost, for thus alone could confidence in their sanctity or in the public law of Europe be justified. Treaty rights were stronger than Legitimist or Liberal ideas ; and his chief objection to both was that they aimed at upsetting the sovereignty or boundaries of independent States. He feared equally intervention in the internal affairs of a State or the disturbance of treaties, whether by the system of general control asserted by the Neo-Holy Alliance, or in deference to general sentiments as asserted by the Liberals. He maintained, in fact, that he alone followed the true middle course and viewed treaties as civil contracts.

For diplomatic purposes, he knew of no nations save those whose boundaries as States were settled of old time or revised at Vienna. Of course that settlement was, if not disturbed, at any rate changed by events in the American Continents, where more than half a dozen States were constituted *de novo* in his time. On them he sought, however, to impress the need of regarding treaty rights, and did his best to confine the new Spanish-American Republics within the clear administrative boundaries laid down by Old Spain. He was unsuccessful in preventing a war over Montevideo between Brazil and Buenos Aires, but it was probably owing to him that the formidable Bolivar was dissuaded from engaging in it. As regards the United States, he used every effort to get her to observe towards Mexico the boundaries laid down with Old Spain, and to dissuade her from incursions into Texas.

Definitely settled territorial boundaries were, in his view, the best guarantee of the existing balance of power, and any questioning of them a sure sign of its disturbance. But the ' balance ' was not " a fixed and unalterable standard. Is it not a standard perpetually varying, as civilisation advances, and as new States spring up and take their place among established political communities ? " The invasion of Spain by France and her continued military occupation of

Spanish territory produced disturbances of the balance. To 'redress the balance' he called in 'the new States,' recognised the New World, and thus separated its resources from those of Old Spain. In this way England acquired a moral influence in Spanish America comparable to the material influence of France in European Spain. Similarly, when Russia threatened Turkey and set the balance rocking, England decided to act with her in order to restrain her, and brought France in to 'weight the scale.' This was intervention of a sort, but it was undertaken to avert a far worse kind of intervention—that of Russia alone.

Another method of preserving the balance in certain areas was not to make a multi-lateral treaty, but to give a special English guarantee by treaty to the Power affected. This limited territorial guarantee existed in Portugal and was recognised and applied by Canning. But he refused to extend this guarantee to the defence of monarchical institutions in Portugal, or of democratic institutions in Spain. He seems also to have been unwilling to admit that we had given any guarantee to the internal constitution of Poland, a position not upheld a few years later by his exuberant pupil, Lord Palmerston. Existing territorial guarantees, as in Portugal, he was prepared to uphold. But even such limited guarantees he thought it dangerous to make or to offer. He refused a territorial guarantee to Brazil and to Greece. He offered a guarantee of Cuba to Spain, and a guarantee of the navigation of the Rio de la Plata to Buenos Aires and Brazil, but these were strictly limited to their application. Both were maritime and not territorial, and were not only defensive in their nature, but a species of guarantee which could be enforced against all comers by England's fleet. The New World, and the ships which furrowed the Atlantic, concerned England more than Europe.

The third method of preserving or restoring the balance of power was by regulating the balance of opinion, and this was Canning's most original and characteristic contribution to diplomacy. Opinion could only be enlisted on England's side by publicity, and it therefore was to this method which he appealed.

10. THE POLICY OF PUBLICITY

The charge has been frequently made that Canning was impulsive and reckless. Such a charge was certain to be applied in that age to a man who did not hesitate to appeal to the people, and it is unquestionably true that no speech in or outside Parliament can ever have the caution and restraint of a note or of a conversation in private. But a man who governs by the aid of Parliament has sometimes to appeal to it for support. The system of publicity was part of his policy, inseparable from it, and the chief source of his strength and influence. The criticism to be made here is not as to what he said, but as to whether he should have abandoned the private intercourse method of Castlereagh for the *rostrum*. Some, at any rate, will think that the results of the new system justified its adoption.

Even Wellington, who declared Canning spoke like ' a Jacobin ' at the end of 1826, admitted that, as yet, he had not acted like one. In fact, with two exceptions, none of the great decisions he took appear to have been ones which could, in any degree, be called sudden. It is possible that he showed too much anger against France in 1823, and his overtures with Rush in the same year, which resulted in the Monroe Doctrine, were perhaps too impulsive. On the other hand, the order to recall Lamb from Madrid in October 1826 is not to be so described. It was issued without consulting the British Cabinet (as Canning was staying at Paris) but in conjunction with French and Russian representatives, who approved. And it was successful both in impressing them and Spain. Liverpool subsequently defended it on that ground against Wellington and the King, and maintained that the measure had been effective for the time being.

To no other acts of Canning can the description of impulsive be justly applied. Contemporaries often brought forward the accusation, because they were bewildered by the popular enthusiasm which his great decisions produced. Yet these decisions were in no way sudden. The recognition of the Spanish Colonies had been foreshadowed as imminent by Castlereagh in July 1822 ; it had been suggested to Europe as a possibility by Canning in October and November of that

year ; again on the 31st March and the 9th October 1823 ;
yet again in January and May 1824.   The final decision was
only taken after the reports of the Commission of Enquiry
had been received, after Spain had repeatedly refused all
offers of mediation, and when France herself, together with
half a dozen small Powers, thought recognition desirable,
and were only restrained by the Neo-Holy Alliance.   A
decision, seven times indicated as possible, cannot be called
sudden.

Similarly with Portugal the resolution to defend her against
any external attack had been formally announced to the
diplomats by Castlereagh in 1820 and 1821, and by Canning
in 1822, and publicly in 1823.   He repeated the same resolution privately in 1823, in 1824, in 1825, and at every stage
of the crisis of 1826.   The decision finally taken at the end
of 1826 was only made after a dozen warnings, and after all
the world knew that the *casus fœderis* had occurred.   To blame
him for the rapidity with which it was acted upon, as the
European diplomats did, is like blaming a man, who has
determined after long deliberation to fight, for attempting
to get in the first blow.   He himself has given the answer :
" If England does not go *promptly* to the aid of Portugal,
then Portugal will be trampled down, and England will be
disgraced, and then war will come, and come too in the train
of degradation." [1]   Similarly in Greece for three whole years
he steadily deprecated all employment of force.   At the end
of 1825 he began slowly to move in that direction.   Yet the
Protocol of the 4th April 1826 contemplated only a special
and limited application of force, and it was not until much
further consideration that it was decided on as a means of
terminating hostilities in July 1827, and in that decision
France, as well as Russia, concurred.   What is surprising, on
the whole, is not his impulsiveness but his deliberation.   He
would not have wanted supporters had he recognised the
Spanish Colonies in 1822, or advocated war against France
in 1823, or in defence of Portugal during 1824–5, or of Greece
in 1826.   It is true that his colleagues might have been
against him, but he himself was of their opinion in each case
except the last.   In fact, he contrived to restrain public

[1] Dec. 11/26.   Italics my own.

opinion for years, even on the most exciting topics, until he
was sure it was overwhelming and would support a diplomatic
decision, which had long been assured and prepared, and of
which the consequences had been carefully thought out. He
had, in a peculiar degree, the knowledge of the appropriate
time for an announcement of a change in public policy. When
it came the moment seemed golden, and his words fire. Thus
it was that the public rallied to him, when he called ' the New
World into existence,' or defended the liberties of Portugal.
If the Pyrenees had fallen, was it not right that England would
maintain the Atlantic ? Were the liberties of Portugal to
be ' utterly trampled down,' when England's word had been
given to protect them ? The effect thus produced was
so profound, just because it was so calculated. Diplomats
might protest and colleagues complain of his ' incendiary '
methods, but they knew that England was behind him, and
that at such moments he wielded a power that neither could
resist. He had indeed at such moments ' a giant's strength,'
and thus illustrated his own doctrine that England should
only intervene occasionally on the Continent, but ' then with
a commanding force.' In similar crises Palmerston was able
to call to his aid flamboyant patriotism, and Gladstone
generous emotion. But in neither case do we feel sure that it
was not sentiment first and statecraft second. In the case of
Canning we see the statesman's brain directing the orator's
appeal.

11. The ' System '

The real key to Canning's policy is that, though emotional
on the surface, it was intellectual in its aims and design. It
was, in truth, ' a system of policy ' profoundly matured in
time of enforced idleness, fortified by knowledge of history
and international law, and practically applied to the conditions of the time. And these principles, he considered, were
sufficient for the time being. Their nature may be indicated
in a few words : no Areopagus, non-intervention ; no
European police system ; every nation for itself, and God
for us all ; balance of power ; respect for facts, not for
abstract theories ; respect for treaty rights, but caution in
extending them. Provided it is sovereign and observes

diplomatic obligations, a republic is as good a member of the comity of nations as a monarchy. ' England not Europe '; " *Our* foreign policy cannot be conducted against the will of the nation "; " Europe's domain extends to the shores of the Atlantic, England's begins there." England's function is " to hold the balance between the conflicting principles of democracy and despotism," to mediate between two hemispheres, and to bring the New World (*pace* Monroe) into connection with the Old.

Castlereagh differed from him in insisting less upon principle, and more upon the politics and negotiations of the moment. Canning certainly conceived that his system covered the facts of his own age, but it is idle to suggest that he conceived his principles to be eternal. During his later years his policy showed signs of change. ' Non-intervention,' he once, if not twice, abandoned; the balance of power was modified; he involved England in extensive obligations by his Greek Treaty. Had he lived in Palmerston's day it is even possible that he might have modified the principle of non-intervention, which he described as ' unchanged and unchangeable.' All we can say with certainty is that he would only have done so after profound reflection on the consequences of such a step. He lays down his doctrine clearly as follows : " Cases must arise upon facts which it is utterly beyond the powers of human foresight to combine and calculate beforehand." And again he warns him, " You will therefore be very careful not to lay down beforehand fixed resolutions for eventual probabilities." [1]

In fact, Canning's non-intervention dogma, together with most of his other principles, have stood the iron test of time. England still deprecates interferences in the internal affairs of States. She is still a mediating power between the New World and the Old. Though a monarchy, she occupied up till 1914 a middle position between the democratic republics and the less democratic kingdoms. Canning's doctrine of guarantee has laid down for succeeding generations a rule for guidance from which they have never departed, without subsequently acknowledging the truth of his principle. His view of the maritime code of England has indeed been

[1] *F.O. Mexico*, 50/19. Canning to H. G. Ward, No. 6 ; July 8/26.

modified, but not so far as to destroy its essential conception. Certain positive statements of his, such as the question of neutrals supplying arms to belligerents, or the position of diplomats in a besieged capital, have been accepted as the permanent rules on the subject. Though no man could have been more opposed to general congresses than he in his own day, it would be unsafe to suggest that he would have denounced them in this. In laying stress upon the doctrine of national individualism in his own day he foresaw the future, but at the present time he might not have viewed the frenzied developments of nationalism as a good, or a reformed and constitutional ' Areopagus ' as an evil.

12. Summary

The large outlines of his policy are now clear. He was no believer in the Divine Rights either of despots or of democrats. He was no believer in congresses of few, or public meetings of many, behind which lurked threats of coercion. He did not believe in the application of stiff general principles to fluid and shifting facts. He believed in a minimum of obligation, but in a rigid adherence to such ' public law ' as was really that of Europe ; that is, in adherence to treaties and to the proper and accustomed forms of diplomatic intercourse. It is true that he introduced new elements into diplomacy, by settling the basis on which new States should be recognised, by allowing alike to the commercial, to the journalistic, and to the popular elements a weight and a power which they had never before enjoyed. Yet none of these elements were introduced to upset the old system, but to conserve and to maintain it. Extensive publications of state papers and speeches in Parliament were not more new than the Congress System, nor more revolutionary than the theory of Legitimacy. On the contrary, by enlightening the public mind, they tended to allay popular discontent.

Again, in his view, non-intervention was an old policy, and the doctrine of intervention a new one. This curious conservative vein is seen in his reply to the protests against a subscription being raised on behalf of Spanish Constitutionalists. He quoted the precedent that one had been

raised for Corsican patriots in 1768, and for Poles in 1792.
Even his intense interest in the New World might be
explained by saying that the Colonies were the chief pre-
occupation of England in the eighteenth century, for which
she sacrificed hopes of aggrandisement in Europe. Then
again, the balance of power and the separation of Spain from
the Indies were ideas as old, though not as dead, as Queen
Anne. Even the liberty which he demanded for States, that
freedom of which he was the champion, was of that limited
and balanced character dear to the disciples of Locke and
the Whigs of 1688. He had nothing in common with the
flamboyant democracy of Jefferson, or of the Spanish Constitutionalists of 1812. Nor in theory, at least, would Castlereagh have dissented from any of these views, though he
might have objected to their publication.

Yet, when all is said, there was a difference between him
and any who preceded him, a difference recognised by all
those who followed him. For he was, or conceived himself
to be, ' a new man,' and he was also a bold one. His frank
words, his open addresses to the public, sent a wind stirring
through diplomatic Chanceries such as had never whistled
there before. He broke the rules of secrecy and reserve,
but those who complained that he broke the rules, found, as
did the young Napoleon, that to break the rules is sometimes
the best way to beat the enemy. His principles were not new,
but his methods were, and they astounded and impressed
contemporaries. The man, in the phrase Metternich approved,
' was a revolution in himself.'

There have been few men, who effected a revolution, who
proceeded on such moderate principles. What he did, indeed,
was not to change the principles but to bring Parliament
and public to support them. The old diplomatic machine
ran on fixed lines; what Canning did was to charge it with
new electric forces, to awaken public interest, to rely on
public support. Such a lesson could never be forgotten either
in England or in Europe. This masterly management of the
the public gave him an unknown power, and forced despots
to tremble at his name. The hatred or praise of contemporaries was so great that it is difficult to understand. To
Apponyi he was an ' Attila,' to Metternich " an immense

phantom, who operated as such on all minds." Yet he earned
the admiration even of the sage Goethe. And to Liberals he
was ' the great, the noble, the adored,' the hero of Freedom
and of light. Mackintosh said that he could apply no better
compliment to England than to call it ' the land of Canning ' ;
Chateaubriand thought him a man, whose discoveries in
diplomacy rivalled those of Newton in science. At the news
of his death the governments of the Old World rejoiced,
but the peoples of both worlds were in sorrow.

Whatever estimate history may form, it cannot reject this
extraordinary tribute of the moment. It may say, and
perhaps with truth, that it was exaggerated. Yet certainly
the man had done much. To the Liberals of the world the
Neo-Holy Alliance was a monstrous portent in 1822 ; it was
a thing of contempt in 1827. The work thus done was
permanent. Such a system might and did threaten Eastern
and Central Europe again ; it never threatened the West
of it or the lands beyond the Atlantic again. Nor did England
ever again enter a congress in which the Great Powers of
Europe asserted the right of general intervention. The
diplomatic formulæ of Canning ruled English diplomacy for
a generation and a half, and behind them was the ' giant's
strength ' of public opinion. Under Palmerston, an exuberant
pupil of a more prudent master, public opinion veered steadily
towards constitutional monarchy in Europe, and was taught
to accomplish revolutions without disturbing tranquillity,
and to set up constitutions without evoking armed protests
from military despots. The security which England enjoyed amid the storms of 1848 is due more to Canning than
to any other man. For he had made a bridge between the old
and the new, not only in Europe but in England. He had
reconciled the Whigs to his more conservative foreign policy,
he had grouped the Parliament and the people in support of
the throne. It was this passionate love for his country, his
pride in its institutions, in its renown, which reconciled men
to the policy which he pursued. It was this control of the
currents of public opinion which Canning was the first to
establish. For the tide did not overwhelm, it actually
supported, the Ship of State. The revolutions of 1830 and
of 1848 proved that the world could be ' made safe for

constitutional monarchy.' And it was Canning who had foreseen its moderating influence in the twenties. By 1848, the ideas of the Neo-Holy Alliance and their system were dead, those of Canning were more powerful than ever. It was not, indeed, until Bismarck introduced the age of 'Blood and Iron' that the mighty tide of opinion, that Canning had directed, spent its force.

No man in his own age had wielded public opinion as a diplomatic weapon with as consummate a mastery, and with as close an adherence to the iron realities, as Canning. It is that fact which renders his career unique, and makes a survey of it indispensable to all those who study foreign policy as the permanent expression of national characteristics. There will always be some who will think Castlereagh superior to his great successor in character, in diplomatic method, and in achievement. There will be others to whom Canning will remain as the supreme type of a diplomat who made foreign policy popular without ceasing to make it effective. It is more likely, however, that the future historian will pronounce that Castlereagh and Canning both wrought greatly for England, and that both rendered service to the world. For without Castlereagh the world might not have been saved, and without Canning it might not have been freed.

NOTES TO CERTAIN CHAPTERS

NOTES TO CERTAIN CHAPTERS

1 GENERAL

BIBLIOGRAPHIES may be found in vol. x. of the *Cambridge Modern History* and the *Cambridge History of British Foreign Policy*, vol. ii. No attempt has been made to compile a complete Bibliography. Such lists are not usually complete unless a separate volume is published on the subject. It seemed better to give some references in the text, and further references in the notes to certain chapters, to such books and articles as bore specially on each problem as it appeared.

2. NOTE ON THE LEADING SOURCES

EXTERNAL AFFAIRS

For *Russian Archives*: F. de Martens, *Recueil des Traités* [Petersburg, 1874–1909], is chiefly useful for documents.[1] *Madame Lieven's Diary* and other unpublished papers, and Lebzeltern's despatches from St Petersburg, preserved in the Vienna Archives, are very important. There are Russian papers in the unpublished *Howard de Walden MSS.*

The *French Archives* contain despatches that are very strictly official, the private letters having disappeared. We find traces of them only in the memoirs of the period. This is not the case with the *Vienna Archives*. Much secret correspondence exists, and there is much valuable information as to the intrigues against Canning in the English Cabinet, as well as to diplomacy proper. The London despatches from and to Metternich are the best example of the first, those from and to Lebzeltern at St Petersburg of the second.

The *British Archives* tend to exclude all matter not strictly official. That was the aim of Canning, and, unfortunately for historians, it was largely successful. By contrast, the despatches of the Castlereagh period have a good many private letters in them.

Most of Canning's private letters to Bagot at St Petersburg and the Hague are in *George Canning and his Friends*, by Captain Bagot (1900), vol. ii. Others unpublished are in the *Bagot MSS.* (v. pp.

---

[1] As indicated (pp. 485, 517–8), the comment is not always accurate.

256, 304, 507). A number of Canning's private letters to Granville at the Hague and at Paris are in A. G. Stapleton, *George Canning and his Times* (1859), and in E. J. Stapleton's *Political Correspondence of Canning* (1888). The former is carelessly edited and contains inaccuracies of dates at times. The latter, however, is very correct and has useful comments.

The unpublished *Granville MSS.* give very valuable papers, which Stapleton omitted for reasons of discretion. The most important are here quoted, pp. 129, 249–53, 273, 388, 402–3, 485 n. 2.

The *Stratford Canning MSS., F.O.* 352/8–16, are very valuable, though many of them have been printed in Lane-Poole's *Stratford Canning*. Indications of important unpublished letters are given here, pp. 152–3, 207–8, 273 n. 1.

There are a few private letters from and to À Court quoted in the text, pp. 208, 388 n. 1, but not the whole series. The present Lord Heytesbury informs me that he has not found any for this period in his ancestor's papers.

The private letters of Sir Charles Stuart to and from Canning have not been found. Some of his other private correspondence, in which he abuses Canning roundly, is in the *Howard de Walden MSS., v.* pp. 508–9, 515–6.

The private letters of Planta, the Permanent Under-Secretary of the Foreign Office, to various persons are sometimes of value. They are scattered through various records, the most important being quoted here, pp. 48 n. 1, 260 n. 1, 280–1.

The other private letters of British diplomats have either not been published or have perished. The most important would be those of Sir Henry Wellesley at Vienna, who was not friendly to Canning. One or two are quoted, *v.* p. 324.

A miscellaneous collection of the private and official correspondence of foreign diplomats, both European and American, are in the *Howard de Walden MSS.* Some of these are quoted, pp. 357–8, 369. The evidence concerning King George and Hanoverian policy is in the same collection and is quoted here, pp. 250–1, and in Appendix V.

Stapleton's *Political Life of Canning*, 3 vols. (1831), is too much of an apology and too prejudiced against Castlereagh and Wellington to be good history. It quotes documents without dates and not always ingenuously. (I give an instance, p. 457 n. 2.) Lady Canning's *Anonymous Pamphlet* (1830), though biassed, is brilliant and informing.

INTERNAL POLITICS

Some authorities are equally valuable from both points of view. This is strikingly the case with the Stapleton volumes, and the correspondence of Esterházy with Metternich in the Vienna Archives, which has just been mentioned. The same applies to

Wellington's *Despatches, Correspondence, and Memoranda* (1867–71), vols. i.–iv.

This immense collection has the advantage of giving not only Wellington's letters, but those of his correspondents. It is a wonderful survey of his activities. The letters are not always correct as to details and dates, and sometimes important omissions are made (*v.* p. 416 n. 1). I think it certain that, for reasons of discretion, the editor omitted some letters altogether during the crisis of 1827. Thus his Memorandum to the Marquess Wellesley (quoted here, pp. 420–1) is not printed by the editor.

The *Bathurst Papers*, Hist. MSS. Commission (1923), give an excellent selection of the papers of Bathurst, who is important because he had much correspondence with both Canning and Wellington. The unpublished portions, to which I have had access, add a few details which are quoted here on p. 421. Mr Trevelyan informs me that there is nothing in the Grey Papers not indicated in his *Life of Earl Grey*.

A. G. Stapleton, in *Macmillan's Magazine*, xxxi. (1875), criticises the evidence of Greville on the period.

The papers of the other members of the Cabinet already published do not give much help. Those of *Peel* (C. S. Parker) (1891), vol. i., are the fullest. Twiss' *Eldon* (1844), vol. iii., and *Liverpool* (1868), vol. iii., are disappointing. Some material can probably be found in the unpublished papers of Huskisson. The *Ripon MSS.* in the British Museum (papers of Robinson, afterwards Viscount Goderich and Marquis of Ripon), *v.* pp. 284 n. 2, 428–9, are very scanty. The *Vansittart MSS.* (*B.M. Add. MSS.*, 31,237) contain almost nothing except a valuable memorandum on the recognition of the Spanish-American Colonies (printed in Appendix III. (*c*)).

Lord Colchester's *Diary*, 1861, vol. iii., and the *Croker Papers* (1885) give sidelights, as do the *Wellesley Papers* (1914), vol. ii.

The *Memoirs* of the Opposition in Parliament are not very helpful. Those of Sir Robert Wilson (*B.M. Add. MSS.*, 30,111, 30,132, etc.), with his printed *Narrative* of 1827, edited by H. Randolph, 1872, are the most useful, but these contain serious omissions. Hobhouse (Lord Broughton's *Diary*) is the most important printed source.

Lord Brougham's *Memoirs*, 1871 (like many of his statements), are almost worthless.

3. PUBLICATIONS OF THE AUTHOR ON THE PERIOD (1822–7)

The following publications and articles in periodicals give more detailed evidence, to which I can only allude in the text of this volume :—

Life of George Canning. 1905. [The opinions expressed here have been revised in this volume.]

" Documents illustrating the reception and interpretation of The Monroe Doctrine in Europe, 1823–4," *English Historical Review*, October 1924.

" French Designs on Latin America," *English Historical Review*, January 1925.

" The Later American Policy of George Canning," *American Historical Review*, January 1906.

" Canning and the Conferences of the Four Allied Governments (1823–6)," *American Historical Review*, October 1924.

" Princess Lieven and the Protocol of 4th April 1826," *English Historical Review*, January 1924.

" Canning, Wellington, and George IV.," *English Historical Review*, May 1923.

" British Policy in the Publication of Diplomatic Documents under Castlereagh and Canning " (with C. K. Webster), *Cambridge Historical Journal*, No. 2, October 1924.

Chapter II. in *Cambridge History of British Foreign Policy*, vol. ii., 1923, with Appendix containing suppressed parts of Polignac Memorandum, pp. 633–7.

PART I

No references are given to Chapters I. and II. The authorities for the first are fully given in Webster's *Foreign Policy of Castlereagh* (1924). The authorities for the second are printed sources quoted in the text.

PART II

FRANCE AND THE CONGRESS OF VERONA

NOTES TO CHAPTER III

1. The Congress as a Whole

MSS.—The Congress of Verona still contains some unsolved problems. The *British* papers are in *F.O. Continent*, 92, and also in *F.O.* (Archives), 139/49. Practically all these have been printed in *W.N.D.*, i. 284–672. Some illustrative comment may be found in *F.O. Russia*, 181/48, and *F.O. Austria*, 120/54.

The *Austrian Archives* give the formal documents in *V.S.A.*, Congress Akten, 43, 45, 50, and some comments in *Weisungen nach England*, Bd. 218 (1822) ; *nach Frankreich*, Bd. 350 (1822) ; *Russland, Varia, und Berichte*, Bd. 1 and 2 (1820–2). As, however, Metternich was himself at the Congress much valuable information is unrecorded.

Printed Sources.—F. de Martens, *Traités conclus par la Rusie*, xi. 306 *sqq.*, gives the Russian side. His commentary, based on unpublished papers, is, however, inaccurate and misleading in this instance, as in others.

The printed despatches of Nesselrode, *Lettres et Papiers* (Paris, 1908), tome vi., are too meagre to be of value.

General accounts may be found in Bardoux, ' *Le Congrès de Vérone* ' (*séances et Travaux de l'Académie des sciences moraux et politiques*), tome 147 (1897), 405–24. Stern, *Geschichte Europas seit*, 1815 (Berlin, 1897), Bd. 2. Phillips, W. A., *Confederation of Europe* (2nd ed., 1920).

2. THE ATTITUDE OF FRANCE

MSS., British.—Apart from *W.N.D.*, some information of value is in *F.O. France*, 146/48, Stuart to Canning; and 146/50, Canning to Stuart. Some useful information as to the Press, etc., is in *F.O.* 97/168, by Thomas Darby, a British publicist and agent in Paris.

The *Austrian* sources are in *V.S.A.*, Berichte aus Frankreich (1822), but Vincent was neither a very well-informed nor an acute observer.

The *French* Archives have been explored by Mr J. E. S. Green, but they are meagre. The MSS. account of Bois-le-Comte exists, but he was not in the inmost secrets, and Montmorency's MSS. defence has perished. It was used by Nettement in his *Histoire de la Restauration*.

Printed Sources.—Chateaubriand's *Congrès de Vérone* (*Œuvres complètes*, tome xii., 1912) relates his own side of the story from an amazingly egoistic point of view. There are a number of documents, but the account is not wholly trustworthy.

Villèle's more authentic, but also more discreet, version is in his *Mémoires* (1889), tome iii.

Marcellus, *Politique de la Restauration* (1853), is a highly coloured work, with documents, but it deals chiefly with 1823 and with the London end.

Pasquier, *Mémoires*, v. (Paris, 1894) 439–95, is ingenious and suggestive, but not always accurate.

Duvergier de Hauranne, *Histoire Parlementaire* (1865), vii., is good on the French Parliamentary side. Neither they, nor the manuscript sources, disclose the true springs of French policy.

A careful study of the French newspapers of the time is illuminating, particularly of the *Journal des Débats* and the *Constitutionnel*. Darby's comments on the French Press at the critical period in 1822 in *F.O.* 97/168 are of much value.

The French problem may be stated as follows :—Montmorency appears to have been cajoled by Metternich and to have been converted to the Neo-Holy Alliance point of view. This the French Government were, for a time, inclined to accept, but were compelled by public opinion ultimately to reject. Chateaubriand endeavoured to reconcile the ' European ' or ' Neo-Holy Alliance ' point of view with the ' French ' policy, but, after Montmorency left

Verona, he agreed with Alexander that war must come. Louis XVIII. and Villèle, regarding the matter from a purely French standpoint, appear to have been the decisive factors. Their dismissal of Montmorency resulted in the instruction to de la Garde of 25th December 1822, and in the appointment of Chateaubriand. But it seems that they had not then resolved upon war, though they recognised that this might be the result of their action. Chateaubriand had, however, committed himself to Alexander, and was resolved to make war, as was Pozzo di Borgo. But Louis XVIII. and Villèle do not seem to have known this when they made him Foreign Minister.[1] In January, partly as the result of Chateaubriand's influence, partly owing to diplomatic difficulties and to popular pressure, war became certain. But Villèle may be said to have 'muddled' into it.

Villèle clearly has something to conceal, for there are significant omissions in his correspondence between January and March 1824. The best explanation seems to be that Villèle was determined to assert the dignity of France and her independence of the Neo-Holy Alliance, and that he ultimately found that he could not do this without declaring war upon Spain. But it does not seem that he was anxious to do this, or contemplated this result as inevitable even in the early part of January 1823.

Canning's account to the Commons (14th and 30th April 1823) of the transactions at Verona, and just afterwards, has been criticised by Fyffe and J. E. S. Green as misleading and disingenuous. I do not think this is the case. His statement with regard to Castlereagh's instructions, not emphasising Spain as the chief topic, is indeed a little misleading, but as Webster (p. 478) points out, 'he was . . . entirely unaware' of Castlereagh's conversations with Lieven and Chateaubriand in June and July 1822 (v. p. 476). Fyffe, *Modern Europe* (1924), i. 525, is in error in saying that Canning denied that he had offered to mediate between France and Spain. He affirmed it in the Commons (v. *Speeches*, v. 15–6).

The only point in which Canning seems to be in error is in saying that 'Montmorency was . . . notoriously the adviser of war against Spain,' 30th April 1823. This is probably incorrect, but Canning was not in a position to know this.

3. THE RELATIONS BETWEEN WELLINGTON AND CANNING

The most sensational problem of the Congress of Verona is thus propounded by Lord Acton. " While Canning was straining all his resources to stay the invasion of Spain, the Duke showed his fidelity to his colleague by exhorting the French Government to push on boldly and defy him."

[1] Pasquier, *Mém.*, v. 459–62, 464–5. Pasquier claims to have had confidential information at first hand. If he is right, the whole difficulty is explained.

Martens expands this story farther by suggesting that Wellington, while pretending to disapprove of the invasion of Spain, not
only urged it on France, but even communicated secretly a military plan by which it could be made to succeed. If this story is
true, Wellington was guilty of deliberate treachery to Canning.[1]
It does not, however, appear that this charge is true. Wellington
doubtless allowed it to be seen that he did not entirely approve of
his Government's attitude, but there is every indication that the
Congress as a whole believed that his protest of the 30th October
was sincere.

During this Congress, Wellington, Metternich, and Nesselrode
were all assiduous worshippers at the shrine of Madame Lieven,
and she lends testimony to the view here indicated. "The Duke,"
she writes on the 9th November, "is in a better state of health,
but not in a good humour; he is bored, they vex him, and I am
truly pained that things go so little as I had hoped. . . . He
sighs for the moment of his departure, and I love him so much that
I would sigh also if that would give him pleasure, but it would
not, in any way." [2] The view of this frivolous, but acute, lady is
important, for the date (9th November) is one which gives time
for the results of Wellington's protest of the 30th October to have
been considered both by him and by his opponents. Subsequently
Metternich reported that Wellington left the Congress ' discontented with us all,' and showed his displeasure by suspending his
normal correspondence with the Duke for some months.

The Duke, however, was not always discreet, and he probably
did say at the Congress in private that, if France wanted to do
anything, she must act quickly. This view was apparently repeated
by him on the 3rd January 1823 to Marcellus, the French *chargé
d'affaires* in England. He then told him that the French Army
could go to Madrid ' without delay and without danger,' but that,
once it got there, it could not remain without exacerbating Spain
and ultimately endangering French interests.[3] That he had
previously given the same advice to Villèle is confirmed from
the British Archives eighteen months later. "He [Villèle] said
that before the commencement of the Spanish War the Duke of
Wellington, with the view of convincing him of its impolicy, had
described the embarrassments in which France would be involved,
even after success had attended her military operations."[4] And
Villèle stated that the Duke's opinion had proved the true one.

[1] Martens, *Recueil*, xi. 306 ; Marcellus, *Politique de la Restauration*,
Brussels, 1853, throws a strong but biassed light on the question. His
authenticity is examined in my article in *E.H.R.*, Apr. 1923, p. 209, n.
He invented details and altered dates, but was not, *au fond*, a romancer.
[2] *Gr. MSS*. Madame Lieven to Lady Granville. Verona, Nov. 9/22.
[3] *A.A.E.*, 616. Marcellus to Chateaubriand, Jan. 3/23.
[4] *F.O. France*, 146/64, Dec. 8/24. Granville to Canning. I can find
no more authority than this for the allegation that the Duke disclosed
secretly a military plan to the Allies by which France could conquer Spain.

The question which is bound up with the Duke's general attitude, has been examined by Mr J. E. S. Green (*Transactions Royal Historical Society*, 3rd ser., vol. vii., 1913, "On the Instructions for Verona"; 4th ser., vol. i., 1918, "Wellington, Bois le Comte, and the Congress of Verona"; and again in *E.H.R.*, vol. xxxv. (1920), "Wellington and the Congress of Verona"), 200–13. It was answered by Miss Lackland, *E.H.R.*, xxxv., 1920, 574–5, on the basis of Austrian records supplied by Professor Webster, and I think the answer is convincing.[1]

The difference between the Duke and Canning was that Wellington did not wish to break with the Congress, if he could help it. But he did show that he disapproved strongly of the Neo-Holy Alliance move, and he did advise France against invading Spain. It was a mistake to tell France to 'go quickly,' if she went at all. It would have been more discreet not to show that he was executing his instructions with reluctance. But there is no evidence for the charge of betraying or of deliberately counterworking Canning at this time, though even at this stage an estrangement between the two began. There can be no doubt that the breach Wellington made with the Neo-Holy Alliance in October 1822 not only produced a strong effect, but led for some months to a suspension of friendly relations between him and Metternich. Somewhat later the Duke's notorious disapproval of Canning led to foreign attempts to overthrow him, to which the Duke unwisely lent some countenance. But this development was produced not by the Congress of Verona, but by Canning's attempts in February and March to stop the French invasion by appealing to British public opinion, and by his vigorous denunciations of French policy in his speeches of April 1823.

NOTES TO CHAPTER IV

MSS. sources from the British records and *V.S.A.* are quoted in the text.

GENERAL

Baumgarten's *Geschichte Spaniens*, Bd. 2, 3 (Leipzig, 1868-71), is still worth reading.

Two English works have merit, H. Butler Clarke's *Modern Spain* (Cambridge, 1906), and G. F. White, *A Century of Spain and Portugal*, 1909.

Villanueva, *Fernando VII. y Los Nuevos Estados*, [1913], is meagre but valuable. This book is, of course, only concerned incidentally with European Spain (*v.* p. 490).

[1] *Vide* Webster, p. 478 n.

SPECIAL

Villèle's *Mémoires*, vols. iv., v., and Chateaubriand's continuation of the *Congrès de Vérone*, *Œuvres*, xii., give a number of documents, but omit others equally important.

Stap., *Pol. Life*, is fairly full on 1823, but, as usual, does not give the dates of the documents he quotes.

H. D. Perkins, *A.H.R.*, January 1922, has some useful information from Russian records on the years 1823–4.

F. Rousseau, *Revue des Questions Historiques*, xc. 86–116, " La mission de Talaru " (1823–4), is of value.

My own article in *A.H.R.*, October 1924, gives a full account of the attempt to control Spain by the Neo-Holy Alliance from 1823-1826. Some of this information had been published before by Leland and Jameson in *A.H.R.* Many French and English documents are published in *B.F.S.P.*, x.–xii., and in the French *Annuaire Historique* of 1823 and 1824.

NOTES TO CHAPTER V

THE POLIGNAC CONFERENCE AND THE MONROE
DOCTRINE

For *Russian aspect*, *v.* 6 (*a*), at end of these notes.

1. PRELIMINARIES OF THE MONROE DOCTRINE

The philosophic preliminaries of the Doctrine, reaching back to the days of Washington, are well worked out in J. H. Kraus, *Monroe Doctrin, in ihren Beziehungen zur Amerikanischen Diplomatie und zum Völker-recht*, Berlin, 1913.

This book is concerned with the more purely British aspect. Two points only may be mentioned in the early part of 1823 as anticipating the Declaration. Adams spoke to Stratford Canning on the British attitude in the Spanish crisis on the 27th March 1823, talking of the great principle of national independence which he seemed to consider as brought into immediate danger by the impending conflict ' between Autocracy and Parliamentary Government.' He indicated friendliness towards Great Britain and surprise at the liberality of her policy. And on the 3rd May he remarked on the ' similarity ' of the English and United States policies.[1] In private letters to his cousin, Stratford reported that both Adams and Clay were favourably disposed to us with regard to Cuba, and were inclined to work in harmony with us. On the 6th May he reported Adams as favouring a sort of triple *entente* of England, Mexico, and the United States

---

[1] *F.O. America*, 5/176. Stratford to George Canning, Mar. 27/23.

against Alexander's pretensions on the North-West Coast. And he added these important sentences : " The course which you [Canning] have taken in the great politics of Europe has had the effect of making England almost popular with the United States. The improved tone of public feeling is very perceptible, and even Adams has caught a something of the soft infection. The communication of your correspondence with France has also had its effect. On the whole, I question whether for a long time there has been so favourable an opportunity, as far as general disposition and goodwill are concerned, to bring the two countries nearer together. France for the moment is quite out of fashion. It may possibly be worth your while to give this hint a turn in your thoughts." [1] Canning had therefore something to go upon when he approached Rush in August.

2. THE AUTHORSHIP OF THE MONROE DOCTRINE

The *Memoirs* of Adams and of Rush are of prime importance. Stapleton's account in the *Pol. Life*, ii., chapter viii., is not very good. The modern view, which was first put forward in Reddaway's brilliant sketch, *The Monroe Doctrine*, 1898, has been confirmed by the later researches of W. C. Ford among the Adams Papers, *A.H.R.*, vii., July ; viii., October 1902. It is unfortunate that his edition of the writings of J. Q. Adams has not yet reached the end of 1823.

There has been an attempt to revive the claims and credit of Monroe by W. A. MacCorkle, *The Personal Genesis of the Monroe Doctrine*, 1923. His thesis is interesting, but not entirely convincing. A conversation of Monroe, recorded by Addington, 30th April 1824, has been published by me in *E.H.R.*, October 1924, p. 593. It supports the view of Reddaway and Ford.

A despatch, No. 18, of early November 1823, from Addington to Canning, dealing with an interview with Adams at the crisis of 1823, is missing from the British records. Canning considered it too confidential, and told Addington to turn it into a private letter, and to renumber his despatches accordingly (*F.O. America*, 5/177, Canning to Addington, 8th December 1823). But the renumbering was done differently by Addington at Washington and by the Foreign Office in London.

The following table will explain what happened.[2] The solution is due to the ingenuity of an anonymous friend of mine.

[1] *F.O.*, 352/8. *Strat. MSS.* Stratford to George Canning, Feb. 7, 15, Mar. 19, and May 6/23.
[2] The solution can only be made by comparing *F.O.* 5/177 (the Office copy) with *F.O.* 115/41, the Archives copy. It is not quite grasped by Paxson and Paullin in their admirable *Guide to the Materials in London Archives for the History of the United States since* 1783, p. 54. No. 2. Washington, 1914.

Original Number as given by Addington.	Numbers as Altered in Embassy Archives, 115/41 (including first words of despatch).	Numbers as Altered in F.O. 5/177.
18	Cancelled and removed.	Cancelled and removed.
19	18 (Nov. 3. ' I have been able.')	18.
20	— (Nov. 20. ' Since I sent off ') cancelled by A, but original 22 (*v. below*) renumbered as 20.	20 retained with original number ; but F.O. retained original 22 also, renumbering it as 20, *v. below.*
21	19 (Nov. 20. ' I have the honour.')	19.
22	20 (Nov. 30. ' At an interview.')	20, *v. above.* Retained as a 2nd No. 20, but so badly altered that it looks like 22.
23	21 (Dec. 1. ' After the repeated.')	21.
24	22 (Dec. 1. ' The turn which affairs.')	22, but F.O. has renumbered a duplicate as 24.
25	— (Dec. 1. ' As a sequel to my despatch No. 18 ' (as above noted, this was cancelled). Addington cancelled this and substituted a formal despatch of Dec. 30 dealing with Consuls, numbering it 25.)	25, F.O. did not cancel No. 25, retaining original number. This was probably due to error.
26	23 (Dec. 2. ' I have the honour ' *re* Congress.)	23 (but F.O. has renumbered a duplicate of this as 26).
27	24 (Dec. 2. ' The President, having returned.') *N.B.*—Addington's numbers, as altered, end for the year with 25 ; and his 25 (as above stated) is different from the F.O. one.	27, remains as in original. *N.B.*—F.O. numbers, as altered, extend to 27, as they include two duplicates, which they renumbered as Nos. 24 and 26.

The original No. 18 has therefore disappeared. But we may thank the clumsiness of some Foreign Office clerk for retaining 20 and the original 25, which is a ' sequel ' to 18. The original No. 18 was quite rightly cut out by Addington in his *Archives*. This No. 25 despatch is so lengthy and important that we need hardly regret the missing No. 18, especially as the F.O. retained No. 20, which Addington cancelled. Both are quoted in the text (*v.* p. 122 nn. 2–3).

3. The United States and the Monroe Doctrine

Vide H. Dexter Perkins, " Europe, Spanish America, and the Monroe Doctrine," *A.H.R.*, January 1922.

R. H. Dana, *Notes to Wheaton's International Law*, 8th ed., 1866.

A. B. Hart, *Monroe Doctrine*, Boston, 1916; and my own article, *A.H.R.*, July 1906, " Later American Policy of George Canning."

4. The French Aspect

The question of French designs on Spanish America is an important one.

C. A. Villanueva, *La Monarquia en América ; Fernando VII. y los Nuevos Estados*, 1913 [based on French, Spanish, and British records], takes the view that there was no design to establish Bourbon princes *by force*. He is followed by H. D. Perkins, *A.H.R.*, xxvii. 208, and by Professor S. E. Morison, *Revue des Sciences Politiques*, January–March 1924, pp. 70–84. The latter is a trenchant critic of Canning, and a milder one of myself.

The question is a very complicated one, as so much of French policy was concealed and tortuous, and there were so many undercurrents. My conclusions, on a survey of all available evidence, is that there was, at any rate, a party in the French Cabinet which desired to use force, *v.* my article in *E.H.R.*, January 1925, " French Designs in Spanish America." I do not see how anyone can say that there was no such design. All they can say is, that the evidence is inadequate.

If, however, there was no such design, Canning would show himself as a still greater diplomat. For, in this view, Polignac did not object to giving the pledge at all, and yet Canning managed to obtain a great popular success at the cost of absolutely nothing ! For the use to which he put it, *v.* chapter vi., pp. 133–40, *passim*.

5. Reception of the Monroe Doctrine

The view held by Mr Perkins, *A.H.R.*, xxvii., January 1922, is that the Monroe Doctrine had no effect at all at the time in Europe, and he is supported by Professor S. E. Morison, *Revue des Sciences Politiques*, January–March 1924, " Les origines de la Doctrine de Monroe." This view is, I think, incorrect with reference to Europe till mid-January, or even perhaps till June 1824. It was only in that month that European diplomats became finally convinced that Canning did not like the Monroe Doctrine and had not inspired it. The best examination is still W. S. Robertson's, " The Monroe Doctrine Abroad in 1823-4," *American Political Science Review*, November 1912, pp. 546–63. I have published some extracts from Austrian, French, and British records, additional to his, in *E.H.R.*, October 1924, and I think I am in agreement with this distinguished student.

Some additions can be made to Professor Robertson's account of the reception by the British Press and public. He quotes (*loc. cit.*, 547–50) only the *Times*, the *Courier*, and the speech of Brougham, 3rd February 1824. But the *Star*, 27th December, contains an attack on the Monroe Message, interpreting it as meaning that the United States intended to prevent Spain from recovering her Colonies. It also attacks the prohibition of future colonisation by European Powers on lines which are the authentic reproduction of Canning's thought, and look very much like his very words.

" The plain Yankee of the matter is, that the United States wish to monopolise to themselves the colonising of that [*i.e.* the North-West Coast] and every other part of the American Continent in a similar condition. . . . To attempt to give a shew (*sic*) of *right* to a mere arbitrary assumption partakes little of the simplicity and integrity which are said to be elements of the Republican character."

This jarring note is the more remarkable as every other newspaper and politician, not in the Cabinet, seems to have assumed that the Message would be acceptable to England. The general interpretation was that the United States had announced that they were prepared to repel intervention by force of arms.

6. Canning's Policy towards the United States (1824–7)

It has been thought better to summarise this policy here, rather than to introduce it in Chapters VI. and VII. The negotiations, here dealt with, were mostly abortive and did not affect Latin America. The first of them, however, affects the Monroe Doctrine, and the remainder are of some interest, as illustrating the clash of wills between Adams and Canning.

(a) *The Settlement with Russia* (1824–5)[1]

The situation up to 1823 has been described (*v.* pp. 104–5). Canning had delayed the negotiation because the United States had shown some desire of jointly negotiating with England to induce Alexander to withdraw his *mare clausum* ukase.[2] Canning seems to have doubted whether it was wise to co-operate, as Russia was likely to be more impressed by single and separate negotiations. At any rate, after the Monroe Message, he declined to act with the United States. This decision was probably right, and is defended by Canning in a despatch of the 15th January 1824.

---

[1] There is a general account in Martens, *Recueil*, xi. 304–22, from the Russian side. *Cp.* Schafer, *A.H.R.*, Jan. 1911, xvi. 273–89.

[2] *F.O. Russia*, 181/55. Canning to Bagot, July 12/23.

There were two questions which directly concerned England, and only one which directly concerned the United States. The first was the boundary between Russian and English territory in the Alaska area as raised by the Russian Ukase ; the second was the old dispute between England and the United States as to the Oregon territory. In the first question the intervention of the United States ' could be necessary only as an umpire.' And it did not seem she was likely to be a very impartial umpire. For Russia and the United States both concurred in bringing the Russian boundary down as far as 55°.[1] " This coincidence certainly argues either a foregone understanding between Russia and the United States, or a disposition on the part of the United States to promote what they knew to be the desire of Russia.

" When to this statement I add that the United States propose, according to the aforesaid memorandum of Mr Rush, to draw the line of demarcation between themselves and Great Britain at latitude 51°—the point at which the Russian pretension, as set forth in the Ukase of 1821 terminated,—it does not seem very uncharitable to suppose that the object of the United States in making a selection, otherwise wholly arbitrary, of these two points of limitation of British Dominion, was to avoid collision with Russia themselves, and to gratify Russia at the expense of Great Britain. There is obviously no great temptation to call in such an arbiter, if the partition between Russia and ourselves can be settled, as no doubt it can, without arbitration. By admitting the United States to our negotiation with Russia we should incur the necessity of discussing the American claims to latitude 51°—at the same time that we were settling with Russia any respective limits to the Northward."

The Monroe Message, with its ' extraordinary doctrine,' . . . " supplied another reason at once decisive in itself, and susceptible of being stated to Mr Rush with more explicitness, than those which I have just now detailed." [2] For these reasons, then, Canning decided on a separate negotiation as regards Alaska. But Canning, though acting in separation, told Bagot to be friendly to his American colleague at St Petersburg, and quoted the language of Titania :

> " ' Be kind and courteous to that gentleman,
> Hop in his walks and gambol in his eyes,
> Feed him with apricots and dewberries,' [3]

as I did with Mr Hughes."

The American negotiation with Russia proved a simple one. Alexander regarded Adams as a sincere republican who negotiated

---

[1] It ultimately proved to be 54°/40.

[2] F.O. Russia, 181/58. Canning to Bagot, Jan. 15/24, No. 2. In this case the Monroe Doctrine was used by Canning as a pretext to decline joint negotiation.

[3] Canning to Bagot, Jan. 22/24. Bagot, G.C. & F., ii. 217.

with Monarchists, Canning as an insincere Monarchist who negotiated with Republicans. He differed with Adams only over America, with Canning over everything in Europe. Moreover, he thought that if he showed favour to the United States he would raise up a rival to the commercial marine of England. Hence he was more amiable to the one than to the other. Few difficulties were made by him with Adams, and a convention between Russia and the United States, giving the United States free commercial intercourse to the Russian possessions for ten years, and limiting the Russian Boundary South to the 54/40 line, was signed on the 17th April 1824.[1] It was ratified in January 1825, before Canning had obtained any satisfaction from Russia. It was not till a month later that Stratford Canning managed, with great difficulty, to extract from him a similar convention (28th February 1825) on behalf of England.

Stratford's convention was based on a draft instrument of Canning's forwarded to St Petersburg on the 12th July 1824. This shows the points in this negotiation to which Canning attached importance. He took pains to understand the question, consulting both the Hudson Bay Company and the Whalers, 'the furry and the finny tribes.' He was determined to gratify both, and to secure to British fishermen access to the Behring Straits. " There is very nice ' bobbing for whale ' they tell me, *ipsi Behringi in faucibus*, which must be guarded." [2] But he was resolved to confine Russia to her fisheries, and to within ten maritime leagues of the coast. He was resolved also to prevent her from extending to the Rocky Mountains, and to preserve the course of the Mackenzie River to England so that the fur trade of the Hudson Bay Company might have access to the coast. He aimed also at securing free British commercial access *for ever* to the Russian port of Sitka (Novo Archangelsk), and free navigation of the Pacific.[3] Canning obtained all these points except that the free access to Sitka was limited to ten years. Thus the Russian Ukase was effectively disposed of, and the navigation, fisheries, and coast of the Pacific lay open to British commerce. But joint American and Russian pressure had brought the boundary line of Russia to as far south as 54/40. This first raised difficulties in another direction, for the American chauvinists wished to extend the boundary of the United States to that parallel.

---

[1] Even as early as Dec. 14/22 Nesselrode had shown willingness to come to an agreement with the United States, *v. A.H.R.*, July 1913, p. 541.
[2] Canning to Bagot, July 29/24. Bagot, *G.C. & F.*, ii. 266.
[3] *Vide F.O. Russia*, 181/58. Canning to Bagot, Jan. 15, Mar. 29 ; 181/59, Apr. 24. The most important paper of all is Canning's Draft Project of the Convention, July 12/24. This last was drawn up by Lord St Helens, who had settled a dispute with Spain over Nootka Sound (in this area) in 1790. Bagot, *G.C. & F.*, ii. 266.

(b) *The North-West or Oregon Boundary Dispute with the United States* (1824–7)

We are now in a position to see the British aspect of the Oregon question. Chauvinists in the United States claimed the whole Pacific coast northwards as far as 54/40, which would have excluded England altogether from the Pacific. Castlereagh had treated the matter in a conciliatory spirit, and signed a convention in 1818 which arranged for a *condominium* in the disputed territory until an agreement was reached. But in doing this he surrendered part of the claims and definitely admitted that the Fort of Astoria should become American. Canning discovered to his dismay that he had been a member of the Cabinet when ' that unlucky transaction ' took place. He commented upon it bitterly to Liverpool as follows : . . . "think what a task it will be to justify this transaction to Parl[iamen]t, if upon this transaction we rest our justification for abandoning the whole N.W. Coast of America to the Yankees. *I feel the shame of such a statement* burning upon my face by anticipation." [1]

The real point in dispute was the Colombia River triangle, which was south of the 49th degree and which Adams would not give up. In any case Canning announced his intention of taking his stand immovably upon the 49th parallel of latitude. The English boundary was to extend to that degree on the south, and no consideration would induce him to recede from this position. He was induced to this course by what he conceived to be the just claims, the honour, and the interest of England. He saw " that the ambitious and overbearing views of the [United] States are becoming daily more developed, and better understood in this country, and he was determined to check them. Also he saw the advantages England would gain from an eventual " immense direct intercourse between China and what may be, if we resolve not to yield them up, her [England's] boundless establishments on N.W. Coast of America." [2]

Finally a new arrangement for continuing the *status quo* was patched up on the 6th August 1827, two days before Canning's death.[3] But it is interesting to note that the final settlement, twenty years later, conceded the British claim to the 49th parallel of latitude, and thus preserved to her the Pacific coast. The Canadian steamers and captains that now plough the sea from Vancouver to China, do so all unconscious of the man who maintained their rights and foresaw their future a century ago.

---

[1] Stap., *Corr.*, ii. 73. Italics my own. On Astoria, *v. F.O. America*, 5/129, 165–168, on Oregon, 191 and 192. There is not much on Oregon not indicated in *B.F.S.P.*, xiii. 498–520, or Stap., *Corr.*, ii. 58, 62, 71–115.

[2] Stap., *Corr.*, ii. 74.

[3] *Cf.* G. L. Rives, *Mexico* (N.Y., 1913), ii. 6–7.

(c) *The Slave Trade*

There was no question to which Canning attached more importance than the Slave Trade. The chief difficulty over this was the
mutual Right of Search or Visit on the High Seas, to which the
United States had never yet consented. Canning had not been
in office a month before he urged this measure on the United
States: "There can be no disparagement of National Dignity
in equal and reciprocal concession. Great Britain desires no other
than that any of Her Subjects, who so far defy the Laws, and
dishonour the character, of their Country, as to engage in a trade
of Blood, proscribed not more by the Act of the Legislature, than
by the National Feeling, should be detected and brought to justice,
even by foreign hands, and from under the protection of a Flag,
whose guarantee was never violated with impunity." [1] The
negotiation was pushed during 1823–4. Finally, on the 20th
March 1824, Canning transmitted a copy of a Convention on the
Slave Trade, signed by Rush and the British Plenipotentiaries,
and asked for immediate ratification, as he wanted to present the
completed instrument to Parliament before it rose. Canning, like
Adams and Monroe, reckoned without the Senate, and the strong
Southern element in that body, which proved adamant. They
modified the Convention, admitting the Right of Search on
the coasts of Africa and the West Indies, but striking out the
words 'and America' (*i.e.* the Continent). This modification
Canning refused to accept, and though negotiations continued in
1825, they eventually came to nothing.

Addington attributed the defeat to three causes: (1) disinclination
to give up the right of search, (2) fear of ulterior objects of England
for total suppression of the Slave Trade in all countries, (3) 'Party
Spirit.' Canning's disappointment was extreme. He had been
rejoicing in the "triumph of sheer straightforwardness over that
scoundrel Adams," and now the cup was dashed from his lips.
He was less than just to both Adams and Monroe, who were not
only sincere but 'distressed' at the failure. It was one of the
first occasions when the Senate showed initiative and independence.
Canning summed up the difficulties which the American Senate
opposed to successful ratification of Treaties, and recorded a
permanent truth: "The knowledge that the Constitution of the
United States renders all their diplomatic compacts liable to this
sort of revision, undoubtedly precludes the possibility of taking
exception to any particular instance in which that revision is
exercised, but the repetition of such instances does not serve to
reconcile to the practice the feelings of the other Contracting
Party, whose solemn ratification is thus rendered of no avail,
and whose concessions in negotiation having been made (as all

[1] *F.O. America*, 115/40. Canning to Stratford Canning, Oct. 11/22,
No. 5.

such concessions must be understood to be made) conditionally, are thus accepted as positive and absolute, while what may have been the stipulated price of these concessions is withdrawn." [1] These wise words are confirmed by the record of some seventy treaties rejected or amended by the Senate, and they state an eternal principle, which all European diplomats should bear in mind in negotiating with the United States. It is a statement which they would do well to embroider on their phylacteries and to hang about their necks. Had it been regarded by Mr Lloyd George, or for that matter by President Wilson himself, the Peace Conference of 1919 might have been conducted on different lines and had a different issue.

(d) The Commercial Disputes

The last internal dispute with the United States in which Canning was engaged was of a commercial nature, and connected with the Navigation Laws. In this instance, Canning would appear to have been in the right. For Adams practically attempted to intervene in the commercial intercourse between England and her West Indian colonies. The result was an acrimonious correspondence and, at the end of 1826, a suspension of commercial intercourse in these regions. The publication of the Canning-Gallatin Correspondence, however, worked much in favour of England, and one famous despatch of Canning's made the United States Government unpopular in their own country. It was not until after Canning's death, and, as some said, because of it, that the matter was satisfactorily adjusted on lines favourable to England. Temper was unfortunately shown on both sides, but even Gallatin admitted that "Great Britain certainly does not wish to be at war with us." [2]

It must be admitted that Canning's policy towards the United States was not always fortunate. Neither he nor Adams was the most patient of men, and each had a great patriotic instinct, approaching sometimes to the limit of chauvinism. It has been suggested that the silken smoothness of Castlereagh would have effected better results. It is certainly true that Canning spoke contemptuously of ' the Yankees ' in private,[3] and that the Star,

[1] F.O. America, 115/44. Canning to Addington, Aug. 27/24, No. 17. Most of the story is told in B.F.S.P., xii. 827–58.

[2] The correspondence is in B.F.S.P., xiv. 462–608 ; 976–1008. Gallatin [Life, N.Y., 1879, p. 343] went so far as to say that Canning declared the United States' language in this connection was ' almost tantamount to a declaration of war.' And Adams commented bitterly upon it. The main results lie outside our period, and have not been worked out fully from MSS. sources. There is a useful study by F. L. Benns, The American Struggle for the Carrying Trade, 1815–30 [Indiana University], 1923.

[3] E.g., to Liverpool, Aug. 6/25, Stap., Corr., i. 283. " The Yankees may be just the rogues we have always hitherto taken them to be, but which I was willing to hope they might have resolved to be no longer."

the newspaper which most nearly expressed his views, sometimes attacked them. But these expressions should not mislead us too much. He seems to have been hurt and angered that his frank overtures had been regarded with suspicion and his real desire to remove outstanding difficulties had been frustrated. His resentment was on the surface, but his policy within had a brighter side. Henry Clay, a man of impulse though also of genius, proclaimed that he had fallen ' quite in love with Canning,' and his instinct was not deceived. Canning's *beau geste* in his interviews with Rush in 1823 was the most friendly overture that the United States had ever received from England. And even its failure was not without some good fruit. ' Our flirtation,' said Canning, ' went off, but it left a tenderness behind it,' and a tenderness which has endured. Canning had done more than most English statesmen to assert the true importance of the United States in the eyes of Europe, and to inaugurate that ' era of good feeling ' which succeeded to one so full of bitter memories.

NOTES TO CHAPTER VI

CALLING THE NEW WORLD INTO EXISTENCE

I. GENERAL

Mr Paxson's revised edition, Phil[a.] 1916, is most useful and informing, as is W. S. Robertson's *Hispanic-American Relations with the United States*, Carnegie Endowment, 1923.

Mr Paxson takes me to task, p. 251, for denying that the British ' Ministry ' was ' legitimist in its real sympathies to the end.' The view is, to some extent, true of ' the Ministry,' but not of Canning. And Wellington said that, but for one man (*i.e.* Canning), there would have been no recognition in December 1824. So Canning's view, which was not sympathetic with Legitimacy, prevailed. The *nuances* between Canning's attitude and that of the rest of Europe have been sketched by me in the text of this chapter. It is quite true that Canning had no desire to promote revolution or democracy, but he had also no desire to bolster up despotism, and never failed to speak of ' Legitimacy ' with the utmost scorn. Canning equally objected to the ' natural law ' doctrine of Adams that all nations ought to be free who wished to be, and to the Legitimist doctrine of Alexander that no nation could ever be free without the leave of a monarch. Canning's doctrine was the *via media*, with a moral preference for monarchy, and a regard for existing treaties, and for existing institutions, whether monarchical or republican. His main point, throughout, was that a *de facto* government ought eventually to be recognised, and that England's commercial interests ought not to be sacrificed to vague political theories, whether despotic or democratic, nor to be submitted to a European Congress.

For the English recognition policy consult Colonel E. M. Lloyd, " Canning and Spanish America," *Trans. Roy. Hist. Soc.*, N.S., xviii. pp. 77 *sqq.* His view is based almost wholly on printed authorities, and he assumes erroneously that the views of George IV were imposed on the Cabinet. It is plain from the MSS. sources that the King, though he did not ' concur,' was forced to acquiesce in Canning's measures. His bitter complaints on this subject to Esterházy are alone enough to prove this. He told him that he had consented to commercial measures, but had intended to exclude political recognition.

Some information as to the reception of Recognition by Foreign Powers will be found in my article in *A.H.R.*, October 1924, pp. 25–6, 35, 38 ; and in Mr Leland's, *A.H.R.*, April 1917, pp. 595–616; and in Robertson's *Hispanic-American Relations*, pp. 40–59.

2. The Authorship of the British Memoranda on Recognition (Text in App. III. (*c*))

Much mystery prevails on this subject. The first, of 30th November 1824 (*W.N.D.*, ii. 354–8), was, technically at any rate, by Liverpool, with touches by Canning.[1] It has eight points, of which six deal with the question between Spain, her Colonies, and England, the seventh with the danger from France, and the eighth with the danger from the United States. Liverpool apparently produced a further Memo on the 8th December, of the text of which I have found no trace (Stap., *Corr.*, i. 212, 11th December). It was in existence on the 8th December, but circulated *after* Villèle's refusal to give a time-limit to French occupation in Spain had been reported to the Cabinet, and seems to have been altered accordingly. The third Memo is to be found in Vansittart's papers in *B.M. Add. MSS.*, 31, 237 (*v.* App. III. (*c*)). It is unsigned and undated, but Canning says he was recasting his paper (a new one) on the 14th December (Stap., *Corr.*, i. 213). It has eight heads, whereas Liverpool's second Memo appears to have had ten,[2] and it bears strong traces of the hand of Canning, *e.g.* the reference to Guatemala.

The chief argument in it is that, as Villèle's answer is unsatisfactory, it is necessary to play for safety and to counteract the power of France by " a separation of the resources of South America from those of Spain."

---

[1] *W.N.D.*, ii. 354–8. C. D. Yonge, in his *Liverpool* [1868], ii. 297–304, claims the Memo for Liverpool.

[2] Stap., *Corr.*, i. 212. Canning to Liverpool, Dec. 11/24. " I return your paper "; he says he has divided it into heads, ' of which there is one more than Hydra had,' *i.e.* 10. Of course the second and third Memo may be the same document, but I do not think so.

The two other arguments are the magnitude of the British commercial interests involved, and one, stated to be ' more important ' than that, viz. the opposing of a barrier to the United States, as head of a Trans-Atlantic League, by recognising Mexico.[1] The Memo concludes by saying that it would not be wise openly to " connect the proceeding with the French occupation of Spain," though that is clearly the strongest argument advanced.

The Memo seems to answer Canning's description of his own arguments. " The French occupation was not the sole reason, but perhaps in some quarters the most potential and reconciling reason . . . but it was emphatically *mine*." [2]

This Memo appears to have convinced the Cabinet. The Minute to the King was drawn up by Canning, but though dated the 14th, was not sent till the 15th. It was accompanied by Liverpool's Memo of the 30th November, but not by Liverpool's second Memo, nor by Canning's (the third) Memo. The Minute, however, contains a discussion, in very guarded language, of the effects of the refusal of Villèle to give a date for the evacuation of Spain. In addition there was a note on the Irish question as affecting recognition by Canning circulated 12th December (Stap., *G.C. & T.*, 406-7).

3. BRITISH RECOGNITION OF SEPARATE SOUTH AMERICAN STATES (1824-5)

(a) *Buenos Aires*

The recognition here was rather different from the others. Canning already knew that Buenos Aires was independent and republican. He therefore made some attempt to induce the different provinces of the Rio de la Plata to combine into one State. When this result appeared to be attained, the treaty was signed on 2nd February 1825. Ratifications of the commercial treaty were exchanged on 11th May 1825, thereby completing recognition, *F.O.* 118/5. This was the first recognition of a Spanish Colony by England. The Argentine side is in E. Ravignani, *Correspondencia Generales de la Provincia de Buenos Aires relativas a relationes exteriores* (1820-4), Buenos Aires, 1921, xiv. ; *v.* Paxson, pp. 225, 234-41 ; and Papers of Sir J. Woodbine Parish (1910), which print Canning's instructions, 10th October 1823, pp. 420-33. These latter are, in fact, extracts from *The Woodbine Parish Papers* in *F.O.* 354/1-4. They add little or nothing to the official records in *F.O. Argentine*, 118/1-6 ; i. 119/1.

[1] *Cf.* Festing, *J. H. Frere and His Friends* [1899], p. 267-8. " The Yankees will shout in triumph, but it is they who lose most by our decision. . . . *We* slip in between ; and plant ourselves in Mexico. The [United] States have gotten the start of us in vain, and we link once more America to Europe," etc.

[2] Stap., *Corr.*, ii. 244. To Granville, Jan. 2/27. The italics are in original in *Gr. MSS.*

(b) *Colombia*

Generally, *v.* Paxson, p. 209 *sqq.* For the negotiations preceding 1823, *v.* Webster, pp. 405–436. From Hamilton we learn that the Colombian Government refused exequaturs to British consuls, on the ground that the Government of Colombia was improperly described in their commissions (Hamilton to Canning, *F.O. Colombia*, 18/3, 14th April 1824). Hamilton's despatch of 5th July 1824 [1] (received 23rd October) told Canning that the Colombian Government conformed to all the tests he had laid down as essential to recognition. They (i) had notified its independence by public acts ; (ii) possessed the whole country ; (iii) had reasonable consistency and stability ; (iv) had abolished the Slave Trade. Canning accepted this opinion, though (8th November) he complained that Hamilton had *not* supplied ' detailed information.' Ratifications of the commercial treaty were exchanged on the 7th November 1825. Canning then made out new commissions for the British consuls, to whom Colombia granted exequaturs. But recognition was complete with the exchange of ratifications.

(c) *Mexico*

For the interpretation of the Polignac Memo as applied to Mexico, *v.* App. III. For the United States side, *v.* the careful study of W. R. Manning, *Early Diplomatic Relations between the United States and Mexico*, Baltimore, 1916. Generally, *v.* Paxson, pp. 213–6.

F.O. Mexico, 50/3, contains the instructions of 10th October 1823 and correspondence of 1824. 50/4 contains the correspondence of 1825.

The Commissioners, who arrived on 12th December 1823, reported 18th January 1824 in favour of recognition of Mexico as a republic. Canning received this on 20th March. He was still hoping for monarchy, and reprimanded them sharply for reporting so soon, but hardly saw his way to contest their conclusions.

Hervey—the chief Commissioner—was disavowed for informing the Mexican Government he would " endeavour to procure the guarantee of your Government for [the] eventual repayment " [of a loan]. He was succeeded by Morier, *v.* Canning to Hervey, 20th July 1824.

From *F.O.* 97/270 we learn that the immediate cause of decision to recognise Mexico appears to have been two interviews of a Mexican agent (Michelena) with Planta, 22nd September, 11th October, 1824, in which the former detailed the Mexican resources and asked Great Britain to mediate between his country and Spain.

The first Mexican Commercial Treaty, signed 6th April 1825,

[1] *F.O. Colombia*, 18/3.

was disavowed (*F.O. Mexico*, 50/18, gives Huskisson's objections to it, 3rd August, 8th September, 1825). Recognition was, therefore, technically deferred till ratifications for the new treaty were exchanged (19th July 1827). But H. G. Ward was joint Commissioner to negotiate the treaty with Morier, and on the latter's departure for England with the treaty, was instructed to present himself as *chargé d'affaires*. This he did to the Foreign Minister on the 21st May and to the President on the 31st May 1825 (one day before the United States Minister was received). This was stated by Canning himself to be "in fact the result of a treaty for which they [Mexico] are naturally most anxious." [1]

(d) *Peru and Chile*

Canning did not recognise these States in 1824 because there was still a struggle in Peru and little information about Chile. It is not clear why he did not do so subsequently, when he knew more of Chile and when the Royalists had been crushed in Peru. After 1826 both seem to have been as qualified for recognition as they have ever been since. But Canning seems to have objected to Peru repudiating her loan.

(e) *Guatemala*

Canning was much exercised on this subject because Guatemala had shown a desire to be incorporated with the United States, which Adams had not rejected. *F.O. Guatemala*, 152/182, shows that Canning sent a consul to Guatemala, who arrived on 24th June 1825. He also sent an agent from Mexico (G. A. Thompson), *F.O. Central America*, 15/1–3. But both were unable to procure the information demanded, and during the latter part of 1826 and 1827 Guatemala fell into a state of anarchy, which rendered recognition impracticable.

4. SPANISH ATTITUDE TOWARDS RECOGNITION

Vide W. S. Robertson, *Hispanic-American Review*, February 1918, pp. 70–91. "Recognition of Spanish Colonies by the Motherland."

C. A. Villanueva, *Fernando VII. y Los Nuevos Estados* (1913), is valuable, and is based on French, British, and Spanish sources. *B.F.S.P.*, xiii. 909–15, prints Canning's reply to Spain of 25th March 1825 *re* recognition.

---

[1] *F.O. Mexico*, 204/4. Canning to Ward, Sept. 9/25. The only difference between Mexico and Colombia was that the appointment of a minister was made in the latter case, when ratifications were exchanged, but delayed in the former because the treaty was disavowed. But the residence of a *chargé d'affaires* amounted to recognition.

5. The United States and Recognition

Generally, *v.* Robertson, *Hispanic-American Relations*, pp. 30–42 ; Paxson, pp. 163–79.

This, though made in 1822, was preceded in time by that of Portugal, one important fact. W. S. Robertson's *Hispanic-American Relations*, p. 30. It was not very impressive. Monroe, *Works*, vi. 211 (12th March 1822), said he did not want to make too much *éclat*, and Wellington thought it had produced 'little effect.' *W.N.D.*, ii. 277, 12th June 1824.

6. The Technical Aspects of Recognition

(a) *The Effect of Accrediting Consuls*

So far as I can discover, Adams alone held the view which is now considered correct in international law and practice. He held that the despatch of a consul to a new country, and the according by that country of an exequatur, implied ultimate recognition.[1] This is the doctrine accepted by Oppenheim.

Canning, in accrediting his consuls to Mexico, Colombia, and Buenos Aires in 1823, directed them to apply for exequaturs.[2] He described them to À Court as " commercial agents with no other than a consular character . . . the question of political recognition being thus suspended for a time." [3] Hall tries to argue that, as these consuls were not gazetted, they were not really consuls. I do not think this argument holds, because the appointment of the consuls to the various towns was officially notified to the several European Powers. Also the British consuls duly received their exequaturs from the Governments of Buenos Aires and of Mexico, that of Colombia being refused on a pure technicality.

The fact is that most European Powers at that time thought that accrediting of consuls, whether they were granted exequaturs or not, had no political implication. France held this view (*v.* below), as did the Netherlands. Prussia nominated consuls to Mexico in 1826, but explained that she was prevented from political recognition by " her relations and engagements towards Spain and the [Neo]-Holy Alliance." [4] Owing to the protests of the latter she eventually did not send even consuls.

It was asserted by Esterházy to Metternich that " the establishment of [British] consuls [in Mexico] is not a political act, they are not of a diplomatic character—they represent no English

[1] Paxson, pp. 155, 159.
[2] His instructions are quoted in *F.O. France*, 146/56, Oct. 13/23.
[3] *F.O. Spain*, 185/92. To À Court, Dec. 2/23.
[4] *F.O. France*, 146/81. Canning to Granville, Jul. 18/26 ; *F.O.* 360/4, *H. de W.*, Rocafuerte to Mexican Government, Mar. 4/26.

sovereignty, they attest no acknowledgment of the Mexican sovereignty." [1] This view was not apparently contested by Metternich, who was a great stickler for diplomatic technique.

The modern British and general practice when it is desired to establish commercial relations with a newly formed State, but not to imply or suggest political recognition, is to send either a commercial agent, or a consul *without* asking for an exequatur. The former is more probably the correct course, but the omission of the request for an exequatur in the latter case shows clearly that the intention to refuse any political implication is conveyed by both methods. The importance attached to an exequatur to consuls is shown by the British action in 1920 towards Montenegro. That State had no diplomatic representative in England, and the British Minister accredited to King Nicholas had been withdrawn. England made a statement recognising Montenegro as absorbed in the Serb-Croat-Slovene State. She terminated her political recognition of Montenegro by cancelling the exequaturs of Montenegrin consuls throughout the British Empire.

(b) *Commercial Recognition*

Adams held the view that a grant of exequatur to the consul of a new State implied political recognition. Canning differed from this view in thinking that the recognition of the commercial flag of a new State and the accrediting of consuls had no political meaning. But he held that the exchange of ratifications of a commercial treaty conferred full diplomatic privileges on a new State, and that the accrediting of a *chargé d'affaires* practically amounted to political recognition.

France, however, held that full commercial recognition could be granted without any political implication. She distinguished four stages. (i) In 1824 she sent and received consuls from Brazil, Mexico, and Colombia. (ii) In 1825 she issued exequaturs to the consuls of Mexico, and defined this act as ' public recognition ' of Mexican consuls.[2] (iii) On the 18th October 1826 the *Moniteur* published the fact that France had recognised the commercial flags of Mexico and Colombia.[3] (iv) On the 8th May 1827 France exchanged ' declarations ' with the United States of Mexico to regulate ' provisionally ' their commerce on ' the most favoured nation ' basis. This seems to have been, in effect, political recognition, though France still denied the fact. At any rate, as regards the first three stages, there can be no question that France thought no political implication was given by their action.

---

[1] *V.S.A.*, Berichte aus England. Esterházy to Metternich, July 6/25.
[2] *F.O. France*, 146/69. Granville to Canning, Dec. 29/25. He says Villèle overruled the scruples of Damas in this matter.
[3] At the same date she accorded full political recognition to the Emperor of Brazil.

(c) *Principles of Political Recognition*

Canning held that his despatch of 31st December 1824 inviting Mexico, Colombia, and Buenos Aires to negotiate commercial treaties with him was not recognition. That only occurred when the treaties were ratified, and the ratifications exchanged ; or a *chargé d'affaires* accredited. In this he was probably incorrect. The mere intimation of willingness to negotiate, provided that the new State is formally named as a government, is probably recognition. " Any act is sufficient that indicates recognition," and you can hardly offer formally to negotiate a treaty with a State, without addressing it as an independent Power, and thus practically recognising it.

Similarly it is difficult to draw Canning's distinction between *de facto* and *de jure* recognition. He held the view that his recognition ' determined no question of right,' and that legal recognition depended upon independence being acknowledged by the former sovereign (in this case Ferdinand VII). This is hardly tenable. Here again the doctrine of Adams, " to consider the *de facto* government as the legitimate government for us " is, in reality, sound. It is, at any rate, the usual practice. In 1920 the Allied Powers obtained the recognition by Turkey of the independence of Syria, Palestine, etc., by the Treaty of Sèvres. This was a *de jure* recognition of their independence, but it never materialised because the Treaty of Sèvres was never ratified. None the less in 1922, before Turkey gave any formal consent, the Council of the League gave France the mandate for Syria and England that for Palestine. This is clearly a *de facto* recognition, and it is the more significant because the preambles of the mandates had to be altered to conform with the fact.[1] The truth is that the law does not always fit the facts in such cases.[2] Canning's general doctrine, however, that you cannot go on indefinitely delaying the *de facto* recognition of a State, because the *quondam* monarch refuses to grant it, is essentially right.

[1] *Vide* my *History of the Peace Conference*, [1924], vi. 37 n. The general practice of the recognition of new States from 1913 to 1919 is stated by me in the *History*, [1921], v. 157–60.

[2] The British Government, by its commercial agreement with the Soviet Republic, recognised the latter as a *de facto* Government in 1921, and in Feb. 1924. The difference is supposed to be that *de facto* recognition is the recognition of a fact ; *de jure* that of a legitimate position. The analogous case is that of an illegitimate baby. Every one recognises its *de facto* existence, but the law can legitimise or refuse to legitimise the infant. But, of course, municipal is very different from international law.

NOTES TO CHAPTER VII

THE LATER AMERICAN POLICY

1. GENERAL

C. A. Villanueva : *La Santa Allianza (passim)*. 1913. W. S. Robertson : *Hispanic-American Relations*, Carnegie Endowment. 1923. *Rise of the Spanish-American Republics as Told in the Lives of Their Liberators*. N.Y., 1918. " South America and the Monroe Doctrine," *Pol. Sci. Quarterly*. March 1915.

And my article : " Later American Policy of Canning," *A.H.R.*, July 1906.

2. MEXICO

Sir H. G. Ward (formerly British *chargé d'affaires*) : *Travels in Mexico* (1825–7). 1830.

G. L. Rives : *The United States and Mexico*. 1913. Vol. i. is useful and careful.

Rives admits the ' amazingly imprudent ' conduct of Poinsett, the United States Minister (i. 163–5). He sought apparently to favour Masonic Lodges with the view of discouraging aristocratic and monarchical institutions.

Canning, *F.O. Mexico*, 50/19, commended Ward, 7th January 1826 " for watching and counteracting of the intrigues . . . of Mr Poinsett." Further information is contained in *Mexico and Mr Poinsett* : Reply to a British pamphlet on the conduct of Mr Poinsett. N.Y., 1829. Poinsett also annoyed Mexico by protesting against her giving a commercial preference to Colombia. His indiscretions seem to have caused the failure of the United States Commercial Treaty (*v.* Rives, i. 168–70). For a few points *v.* C. J. Stillé, *Life of Poinsett*, Philadelphia, 1888, and J. H. Smith, " Poinsett's Career in Mexico," *Am. Antiquarian Soc.*, xxiv. [1914], pp. 77–92.

3. CUBA, ETC.   *B.F.S.P.*, xiii. 402–33, 439, 452–83, 490–2.

C. A. Villanueva : *La Santa Allianza* [1913], pp. 163, 195, 237, etc.

J. M. Callahan : *Cuba and International Relations*. Baltimore, 1899. " Cuba and Anglo-American Relations," *Am. Hist. Assoc.* [1897], pp. 195–215.

L. S. Rowe : *The United States and Porto Rico*. N.Y., 1904.

The chief points are brought out in the text. The essential one seems to be that Canning obtained a disclaimer from France as to designs on Cuba in July 1825, whereas the United States did not remonstrate vigorously with her till the end of the year. There is a curious letter of Adams on this subject of 11th August 1837, published by E. Everett, *The Monroe Doctrine*, Loyal Publication Society, New York, 1864, pp. 12–15.

4. Bolivar and the Congress of Panama [1]

As indicated in the text, there was a difference between the Colombian Government and Bolivar as to the Congress of Panama. Bolivar was a Venezuelan and suspected of monarchical leanings, and therefore not always popular with the Colombian Cabinet. And it seems to have been his pressure which secured the invitation to England. On the 5th September 1826 he is reported by Consul Ricketts (*F.O. Peru*, 61/8) as hoping to apply the Bolivian (*i.e.* monarchical) system to Colombia, and as disapproving the proposed attack on Cuba. Neither view could have been welcomed in Colombia. He also stated then that he was ' pleased with the Congress,' and its transfer to Tacubaya in Mexican territory. Later on, in 1826, when it had ended in such a fiasco, he changed his view and declared that from the origin the Congress of Panama was ' a piece of bravado ' (*fanfarronada*) and that he had no hopes of bringing Mexico to the aid of Colombia.[2] It will be seen that his contemporary evidence does not support this view.[3] Extracts from his conversations, exhibiting his peculiar doctrines of monarchy and relationship to England, are quoted in Appendix IV.

PART IV

NOTES TO CHAPTER VIII

The Recovery of British Influence in Portugal

Section 2. *Castlereagh and Portugal*, 1820–2.—In addition to the MSS. authorities in the text, *v.* Webster, *Foreign Policy of Castlereagh* [1924], chapter v., section 3.

Section 3. *England's Treaty Obligations to Portugal*, 1386–1822.— The text of the whole series of treaties is in *B.F.S.P.*, i. (1812–14) 470 *sqq.*

The chief MSS. authority is *F.O.* 97/301, which is a statement drawn up by an official in the Foreign Office for Canning's use in April 1823. References to other MSS. are given in the text. Wellington has a Memo (5th March 1825), *W.N.D.*, ii. 421–5, on the subject, in which, as usual, he differs from Canning.

For an article on " The Beginnings of the Anglo-Portuguese Alliance," by Violet Shillington, *v. Transactions Royal Historical Society*, N.S., vol. xx. [1906] ; and for one on " The Beginnings of the Oldest European Alliance : England and Portugal " (1640–

---

[1] W. R. Shepherd, *Hispanic-American Review* (1918), pp. 270–98, has a useful article on "Bolivar and the United States," with a select bibliography.

[2] W. R. Shepherd in *Pol. Sci. Quarterly*, Mar. 1924, p. 41.

[3] *Cf.* also a letter of Bolivar's of Aug. 11/26, which appears to contemplate an alliance with Mexico, just *after* the Congress of Panama. O. Learey's *Bolivar*, ii. 645–6, Madrid, 1916. Vide *infra*, p. 561.

61), by Guernsey Jones, *Report American Historical Association for* 1916, i. 405–18. [1919.]

Both of these are general accounts, and I am aware of no treatment from the strictly diplomatic point of view.

Sections 5–8. *Miguel; de Neuville; Subserra.*—The MSS. authorities are very fully quoted in the text, and there is enough in the French Archives to show that Villèle strongly disapproved of de Neuville's policy. There are some interesting comments from Polignac in *F.O. Library*, Notes on Spain, 1824–5.

The chief printed authority consists of the *Mémoires et Souvenirs du Baron Hyde de Neuville* [Paris, 1912], vol. iii. It is a prejudiced and untruthful performance. He conceals the fact that he ordered up the French garrison from Badajoz, which was admitted by Villèle. He also omits the detail of his desperate struggle against À Court in the autumn of 1824. It seems probable that Neuville was secretly intriguing with Chateaubriand and Polignac. Inspired by them, he summoned the French garrison from Badajoz and promised to defend King John by arms, if he would forsake the English alliance. But there seems no reason to doubt the pacific nature of Villèle's policy, and that was one reason why de Neuville threw up the Embassy in disgust on the 4th January 1825.

Other sources show that de Neuville was a man of violent temper, *e.g.* on 15th January 1822 he accused Stratford Canning at Washington of insulting him without any justification, *v. Bag. MSS.*

NOTES TO CHAPTER IX

THE INDEPENDENCE OF BRAZIL

1. *Brazil, Portugal, and the Neo-Holy Alliance* (1820–3)

The MSS. authorities from the British records are fully quoted in the text.

The most important works on this period are Oliveira Lima, *Dom Joao VI. No. Brazil*, 1808–21 (Rio de Janeiro, 1908–9, 2 vols.), and *O Movimento Da Independencia*, 1821–2 (San Paulo, 1922), two works founded on documentary sources and of great value. J. Armitage, *History of Brazil* (1808–31), 2 vols., 1836, is a useful contemporary account, quoting from what were then unpublished documents.

On *French Policy*, *v.* de Neuville, *Mém.*, iii. 124–31, 135, 143. The circumstances of French policy towards Brazil are suspicious, and Thornton's assertion that de Neuville offered to recover it by force of arms (*v.* p. 199) has not been disproved. I know of no other direct proof, but Thornton, through a paid spy, was in a position to know all the secrets of the Portuguese Court.

2, 3, 4. *Negotiations Establishing the Independence of Brazil*

The British MSS., together with extracts from the intercepted despatches of Foreign Ministers, are fully quoted in the text. For an admirable account of the whole, *v.* Oliveira Lima, *Historica Diplomatica Do Brazil Reconcimento do Imperio* (1822–7), Rio and Paris, 1902. This gives the texts of the protocols of the London Conferences. Sir E. Satow, *Diplomatic Practice* (1922), ii. 356–63, gives some useful diplomatic hints. The text of the Constitution of Brazil, with brief comment, is in H. P. James, *Constitutional System of Brazil*, Carnegie Endowment, 1923.

5. *The Later Career of Sir C. Stuart in Brazil*

Stuart had made some blunders while at Paris (*v. F.O. France*, 146/56, Canning to Stuart, 19th September 1823), and was told that he would be recalled on the death of Louis XVIII. He was involved in various intrigues with the King on his recall in 1824, which Canning deprecated, Stap., *Corr.*, i. 155–59, 166–9, 172–3. He thought that ' a king should act like a gentleman ' (i. 200–1).

When he went to Brazil, *via* Lisbon, his relations with Canning were already strained. The Brazilian delegate in England wrote in a despatch to his Government on 16th March 1825: " His [Sir C. Stuart's] travels will be very extensive. After finishing the business which takes him to Rio de Janeiro, *he is to go to Colombia and Mexico.*" A copy of the despatch got into Canning's hands, who underlined the last words and added in the margin the grim pencil-note, ' *Not he !* ' [1]

Stuart justified his suspicions, for, though once a Liberal, he had now suddenly become a legitimist Ultra. He no sooner got to Lisbon than he began denouncing to foreigners ' the false system ' followed by Mr Canning relatively to the Spanish Colonies. " We have got into a real crisis . . . of which the shipwreck will be the shipwreck of our public fortune. Mr Canning has let himself be dragged away by it." He also " demonstrated the error of endeavouring to separate from the Continent." [2] Canning, who learnt of this privately, must have been furious. In addition to this, Stuart appears to have meddled with Beresford in the internal politics of Portugal. With these not very promising beginnings, he started off to Rio and there achieved a considerable success, obtaining on the 29th August 1825 the signature of the definitive treaty in which Portugal recognised the independence of Brazil.

This signal triumph was marred by his later actions in negotiating two treaties, one commercial and one dealing with the Slave Trade between England and Brazil. The points to which

---

[1] *H. de W. MSS., F.O.* 360/3.   Brant to Brazilian Government, Mar. 16/25.

[2] *H. de W. MSS., F.O.* 360/3.   Royer au *Roi de Prusse*, Apr. 2, May 14/25.

Canning objected were technical and need not detain us, but they would have had a bad effect in the pending negotiations with Mexico. Canning was, however, prepared only to instruct him to revise them, when they unfortunately appeared in a newspaper at Rio. Canning therefore had to disavow him and formally refused to ratify the treaties. " This comes," he wrote, " of a man thinking himself cleverer than all the rest of mankind, and believing himself to be protected by the King against the responsible Minister under whom he is acting. He set out, as you may remember . . . while the K[ing]'s mind . . . was alienated from me in the highest degree. S[tuart] reckoned upon the continuance of this temper. . . . His enmity to me need not be accounted for to you, who are one of the causes of it." [1]

The disavowed Sir Charles vented his spleen in various epistles, all of which came under the eyes of Canning. Thus to his wife : " The person who ill-uses another never forgives his victim. . . . Mr Canning seems determined to make Rio as odious to me as possible " (9th February). And this to À Court (12th February) : " He orders me home and sends no ship. . . . I suppose, therefore, I shall be kept here a mark to shoot at, or rather to vent ill-humour upon in bilious despatches for the next six months."

6. *Recognition of Brazil by the United States*

Vide W. S. Robertson, *Hispanic-American Relations*, pp. 34–5. It was on 9th March 1825, and produced a ' passionate ' protest from Portugal ; and W. R. Manning, *Hispanic-American Review*, May 1918, pp. 123–45, " An Early Diplomatic Controversy between the United States and Brazil."

7. *General*

For two admirable cultural and general studies, see again Oliveira Lima, *Formation historique de la Nationalité Brésilienne*, Paris, 1911. An even more valuable work has been published by the same author, annotated by Professor P. A. Martin, the *Evolution of Brazil compared with that of Spanish and Anglo-Saxon America*, Stanford University, U.S.A., 1914.
For the crisis of 1826, *v.* Notes to Part V. Chapter XVI.

No references are given to Chapter X., as this is based on authorities quoted in the text. Unpublished authorities are quoted for Chapter XI. in the text, and some others will be found in App. V.

[1] Stap., *Corr.*, ii. 16–19. Canning to Granville, Mar. 6/26. Of course, because Granville had succeeded Stuart at Paris. For Sir Charles' later and unfortunate experience in Portugal, see notes to Chapter XVI., 515–6. Stuart was quite wrong in attributing the disavowal of his treaties to the ' spite ' of Canning. They were reported against, both by the Law Officers of the Crown and by Huskisson at the Board of Trade, before Canning took action.

PART V

NOTES TO CHAPTER XII

THE DAY'S WORK AT THE FOREIGN OFFICE [1]

Diplomatic Service—MSS. Sources, Printed Official Papers, and Parliamentary Debates

1. *General.*—Most of the official MSS. dealing with the organisation of the office have perished. *F.O.* 95/591 contains some scattered information on various subjects, chiefly the case of Mr S. Much sporadic information has been collected from various MSS. sources, to which references are given in the text.

The Foreign Office Library has a volume, *General Correspondence and Memoranda* (1799–1867), which has some useful miscellaneous information chiefly on the Library and Office Rules.

Unofficial Printed Sources.—Professor C. K. Webster's chapter i., in the *Foreign Policy of Castlereagh* (1924), is valuable up to 1822. There is nothing between 1822–7. Sir E. Hertslet's *Recollections of the Old Foreign Office* (1901) begins at 1840, and Algernon Cecil's brilliant chapter viii. in the *Cambridge History of Foreign Policy*, vol. iii. (1922), practically begins there.

2. *Establishment and Personnel.*—This can be built up from the printed return to the House of Commons, 1797 (in *F.O.* 95/591) ; the printed return of 1807 (23rd July) in *F.O. General* (Foreign Office Library), 1801–59, and the printed Parliamentary Papers, *6th Report of Public Committee on Finance*, 23rd July 1817. The printed returns of 5th January 1822 and 5th January 1827 are in *General* (Foreign Office Library), 1801–59. Curiously enough, these returns deal with the three separate periods when Canning himself was at the Foreign Office.

The total figures of establishments and salaries abroad and at home from 1817–1826 inclusive are given in a Parliamentary return of 22nd May 1827 (v. *F.O.* 95/592). These afford a basis for comparison between the administration of Castlereagh and of Canning.

3 (*c*). *Messengers.*—*F.O. Misc.*, 95/589–90. These exhibit the situation up to 1824, and described the reforms then instituted, *v.* also *Select Committee on Diplomatic and Consular Services* (1870), 1841–6.

3 (*d*). *Secret Service*, v. *Select Committee on Diplomatic and Consular Services* (1870), §§ 639–67, 3894–3899 ; and *Hans. Deb.*, N.S., i. 1127–8 ; vi. 1430–2 ; xvii. 1136–9. None of these are entirely satisfactory. The full totals over the periods 1816–22 and 1822–7 are given in *A.O.* 1/2129–30. As is pointed out in the text, the amounts spent at home are ten times those spent abroad. And,

---

[1] References here are to sections in Chapter XII.

in Canning's time at any rate, there is strong reason to suppose that the Secret Service in America was charged on the home fund. *Intercepted Despatches.*—For this, *v.* for this period *Howard de Walden Papers, passim, F.O.* 360/1–5 ; and *F.O. Misc.,* 95/6, for Prussia (1782–1837).

4. *Canning's Diplomatic Innovations.*—(*a*) *Copies and Lectures, v.* Satow, *Diplomatic Practice* (1922), i. 79–83. (*b*) *Use of English Language, F.O.* 183/127. Hammond in *Select Committee on Diplomatic Service* (1861), § 671 ; Stap., *G.C. & T.,* pp. 48–54, for the controversy in 1800. Canning instructed Thornton at Lisbon (1823) and À Court at Madrid (1824) to write in English. The controversy with Prussia in 1826 is in *F.O. Prussia,* 244/19, 10th October 1826, Canning to Temple and following despatches. This discussion, as well as other changes in diplomatic formulæ and procedure, may be found in Sir E. Satow, *Diplomatic Practice,* 2 vols., ii. (1922) ; i. 76–9.

4 (*d*). *General.*—For distinction between congresses and conferences, *v.* Satow, ii. 1–211 ; between " good offices " and mediation, ii. 326–95.

5. *Consuls.*—The genesis and result of the Canning-Huskisson consular reforms is in *F.O.* 95/591–2. More general sketches of the situation are found in *Hans. Deb.,* N.S., vii. 366–71, 1658–60 ; xii. 1217–21 ; xiv. 1400–1410. A great deal of valuable information is in various *F.O.* records, to which references are given to the more important in the text.

There were numerous Parliamentary papers and reports on this subject, but all just beyond the year 1827. They throw little light on the previous period.

6. *Finance.*—*Vide F.O.* 146/56 for Planta's circular to Secretary of Treasury, 18th September 1825 ; giving the general financial reforms for ' Mr Canning's rule,' *v. Select Committee on Diplomatic and Consular Service* (1870), §§ 1539–41, 1747–52. " Parliamentary Debates " *Hansard,* N.S., vi. 1279 *sqq.* ; viii. 692–5 ; xii. 1090 *sqq.* ; xiv. 1399–1409 ; xv. 70 ; xvii. 774–9, 1399–1407.

Some information is in the following *Reports of Select Committee on Diplomatic Service* of 1861 (and of 25th July 1870), but they deal chiefly with matters subsequent to 1827, and are not always correct in regard to the period 1822–7.

The *Report of Select Committee on Foreign Office Reconstruction* (1858), vol. xi., session 1857–8, has information of the building of the new Foreign Office in 1825. Valuable information on all subjects is scattered through the various diplomatic records, and references to the more important of these are given in the text.

General.—Algernon Cecil's chapter viii. in *Cambridge History of British Foreign Policy* (1923), vol. iii., relies solely on printed sources before 1840, and these are very few. Generally speaking, the whole history of the Foreign Office before 1840 is obscure and fragmentary, and depends on the piecing together of minute details from dozens of different manuscript sources.   The results are presented in the text of this chapter.

NOTES TO CHAPTER XIII

The Press and Public Opinion

Two general accounts of the Press have merit for this period: H. R. Fox Bourne, *English Newspapers*, 2 vols., 1887, and James Grant, *The Newspaper Press*, 3 vols., 1871-2 (includes weeklies, monthlies, and provincial press).   Lucy M. Salmond, *The Newspaper and the Historian* [1923], is too general to be of much service.   But W. Lippman's analysis of *Public Opinion* [1922], particularly chapter xxiii., is valuable.

No subject is more difficult on which to find accurate information in detail.   For the purposes of this work the files of the *Times, Courier, Morning Chronicle, Star*, and *Examiner* have been used; on the whole, the five most important organs.   A number of details as to ownership, policy, influences (domestic, foreign, and financial), are quoted in the text from MSS. sources, private papers, and published works.

The secret correspondence of what were practically two British publicity agents in France is in *F.O.* 97/168, Darby, 1822-5; 97/169, Goldsmith, 1824-5.   Some use has been made of the French Press, *e.g. Journal des Débats* and *Constitutionnel*.

Scattered references are found in the British, French, and Austrian Archives, and in various private MSS. and in printed memoirs, of which use has been made in the text.   For Parliamentary Debates, *v. Hans. Deb.*, N.S., vii. 366; x. 501-4; xvi. 400-3.   For the general policy of publication by the Foreign Office from 1812-27, see an article by Professor Webster and myself in the *Cambridge Historical Journal*, No. 2 [1924], entitled " British Policy in the Publication of State Papers under Castlereagh and Canning."

Canning's Speeches Outside Parliament

It may be of interest to tabulate these as, except at the Lord Mayor's Banquet, extramural speeches by Cabinet Ministers were most unusual at this time.   Those marked (X) were of considerable importance as expositions of policy.

1822
Aug. 23, 30.   (X) Liverpool.   On his political position.
Nov. 9.   Lord Mayor's Banquet.   General.
1823
Feb. 11.   (X) Harwich.   On attitude of England in Spanish
                        crisis.

1823

Aug. 25. (X) Liverpool. Advocating co-operation with the United States.

Oct. 28. (X) Plymouth. On the Spanish crisis and British sea power.

Nov. 9. (X) Lord Mayor's Banquet. Hints at Polignac Memorandum.

Nov. 25. (X) London. Reception of, and reassuring speech to, Merchants' Deputation on recognition of Spanish America.

1824

Jan. 27. London. Speech at annual dinner of Shipowners —on British sea power.

Nov. 9. (X) Lord Mayor's Banquet. On the Country's support of his Liberal policy.

1825

Jan. 12. Bristol. Speech on receiving Freedom of City with Lord Liverpool.

1826

Nov. 9. Lord Mayor's Banquet. In praise of Polignac and of France.

NOTES TO CHAPTERS XIV AND XV
GENERAL

Austrian.—A. V. Prokesch-Osten, *Geschichte des Abfalls der Griechen* (Bd. i., iv., 1867), gives many Austrian documents.

Les Rapports diplomatiques de Lebzeltern Ministre d'Autriche à la Cour de Russie (1816–26), St Petersburg. This is a selection from Lebzeltern's despatches to Metternich, and of high value. Others are quoted in the text from *V.S.A.*

English.—Stap., *Pol. Life*, chapters xii. and xvi., is meagre; *W.N.D.*, vols. iii. and iv., is illuminating at many points. W. Alison Phillips, *The War of Greek Independence*, [1897], is a brilliant summary based on Prokesch-Osten. Lane Poole's *Stratford Canning* (1888), vol. i., is indispensable, as some of the documents quoted are not in the *Strat. MSS.*

French.—Isambert, *L'Indépendance de la Grèce*, Paris, 1900, based on French records. For the letters of de Ferronays, see under Russia. The French *Annuaire Historique* is valuable for the years 1824–7.

Russian.—T. Schiemann, *Geschichte Russlands*, i.–ii. (1904–8). Vol. i. deals with Alexander ; the second with the beginning of the reign of Nicholas. It is an excellent and judicial survey, based on Russian and German Archives. There are a few instances of errors in detail.

The best work on Alexander is *L'Empereur Alexandre*, par le Grand-Duc Nicholas Mikhailowitch, St Petersburg, 1912, 2 vols.

This contains letters of de Ferronays, and throws some light on French policy. It is a great pity that the other collection published by the Grand Duke (Letters of Ambassadors from and to Russia) stops at 1820. There are, however, a number of letters of Pozzo di Borgo in *V.S.A.*, which have been used, and also some in *F.O. Russia*, 65/168. Martens, *Recueil de Traités conclus par la Russie*, [1895], xi., is valuable for documents printed, but his introductions and selections from despatches are, in some cases, incorrect or misleading.

Jorga, *Geschichte des Osmanischen Reiches (Gesch. der Eur. Staat)*, Gotha, 1913.

NOTES TO CHAPTER XIV
The Awakening of Greece

1. *The Castlereagh Policy* (1820–2), *v.* Webster, 347–400.
2. *The Strangford Negotiation for the Three Points*, 1823–4. This offers little difficulty, and full references are given in the text.
3. *Byron, v.* Harold Nicolson, *The Last Year of Byron* (1924). An admirable and discriminating account.
4. *Canning's Opposition to a Congress*, 1824. The account in the text, based on British and Austrian records, shows, I think, clearly the facts. Canning held to two points: (1) the despatch of Ribeaupierre to Constantinople, (2) previous disavowal of force by those entering the Congress. The protest of the Greeks completed his reasons for refusal.
5. *Mehemet Ali's Intervention*. Of this we do not know very much.

NOTES TO CHAPTER XV
The Greek Protocol of 4th April 1826 and the Diplomatic Revolution

1. *The Conference at St Petersburg and its Rupture (January–August* 1825)

This is described in Prokesch-Osten and Schiemann, and more fully in Lebzeltern's despatches in *V.S.A.* Metternich's suggestion of the independence of Greece was a last desperate effort to avert the use of force. Alexander was determined to obtain the consent of the Congress to such use. When that was refused, he practically ended the Neo-Holy Alliance system.

2. *The Instructions to Strangford and his Disavowal (October–December* 1825)

These are treated fully, with references to Austrian and British records, on pp. 288–93 and pp. 350–3. One of two conclusions alone is possible. (1) Strangford was deliberately trying to tie Canning up with the Congress System, *or* (2) he made inconceivable blunders. For reasons quoted in the text, I believe the first interpretation to be correct. It involves serious reflections on his good faith, for which reasons are given in the text (pp. 291 n. 1, 292). In this connection, however, it is well to note that he was accused by a member of his own Embassy at Constantinople of having intrigues with Foreign Powers, *v*. Lane Poole's *Stratford Canning*, i. 412–3.

3. The 'Grand Secret' of Madame Lieven and the Protocol (4th April 1826) (For text, v. App. VII.)

This revelation comes from Madame Lieven's own unpublished Diary. The case is more fully argued by me in an article in *E.H.R.*, January 1924, pp. 55–78. My conclusion is that Madame Lieven did bring a verbal message from Alexander to Canning, to the effect that British overtures over Greece, if made to Russia, would not be refused. This knowledge enabled Canning to make the change in British policy which led to the Protocol.

It rests on the word of Madame Lieven alone, and her narrative, written some time later, has some inaccuracies. But the main points of her contention are nowhere contradicted, and, in certain important instances, actually confirmed by Martens and Schiemann.

It is the only satisfactory explanation of this remarkable change in foreign policy. Canning's difficulties, once he had this information, were confined to his colleagues and principally to Wellington. These come out fully in the *W.N.D.*, vols. iii.–iv.

It is clear that Wellington did not realise what he was signing. I think it is equally clear from the British sources and *Lie. MSS.* that Canning did. He must, further, have recognised that the Protocol, while not actually implying the use of force, except over the 'Barbarisation Project,' did make it an eventual possibility. That, however, he was not ready to admit to the more recalcitrant of his colleagues until the last moment.

PART VII

NOTES TO CHAPTER XVI

Canning and the Defence of Portugal

1–6. Death of John VI ; Dom Pedro's Constitution

Apart from the MSS. quoted in the text, the only general account is Armitage, *History of Brazil* (2 vols., 1836). M. de Lima has a forthcoming volume on this subject.

Palmella's *Despatches e Correspondencia* were edited by Holstein Sousa, 1851–69. Saldanha's *Mémoires*, ed. Conde da Carnota, i. 1–202 (English translation, 1880), are flamboyant but useful.

The Action of Sir Charles Stuart

Under the circumstances Canning did not blame Stuart for carrying the Treaty to Portugal. He did so as a Portuguese, not as a British, representative. But his situation was ambiguous, and Canning took an early opportunity of recalling him. It was time to do so, for he was again meddling in the internal affairs of Portugal, and in any case would have been suspected of doing so. He had, in fact, no longer any diplomatic status. The circumstances are correctly given in Lady Canning's anonymous pamphlet.

Just before his recall Stuart again sent violent letters to his wife. After complaining of his enemies, he wrote (15th July): "I believe after all Mr Canning is the worst of them. He is a hearty friend or a hearty enemy, and I would rather have my neck wrung by the latter than be humbugged by one who is not the former." To Lord Lowther he wrote, just before leaving Lisbon on the 23rd July, "My measures have been the salvation of the country." . . . "I saw my name put down in the list of new Peers. I was of course kicked out, as I always shall be so long as the present people continue to persevere in their present animosity."[1] In view of the fact that Canning knew of all these acrid sentiments, it is not surprising that he refused to recommend him for a peerage, especially as that honour would, under the circumstances, have been considered by the Neo-Holy Alliance as a reward for instigating Dom Pedro to grant a Constitution. But most people will think that Canning, in spite of much provocation, acted with fairness, for it would certainly have been defensible to disavow his action in bringing the Constitution to Portugal. It was too much to expect the Foreign Minister to reward him for embarrassing his policy. It was characteristic that after Canning's death he received a peerage from Wellington, and returned for two years to his Embassy at Paris as Lord Stuart de Rothesay.

7–15. *Canning's Despatch of Troops to Portugal*

The Austrian and Russian attitudes are fully illustrated in the MSS. in the text. The Parliamentary papers of 1826 give a good deal of information on the British side. The actual incident is treated in a good many text-books of international law, but by very few with nicety and precision. The anonymous pamphlet (by Lady Canning), *An Authentic Account of Mr Canning's Policy with Respect to the Constitutional Charter of Portugal* [1830], is a reply to a pamphlet by Mr Lamb (not F. Lamb). It is a brilliant and spirited account, but not quite ingenuous as to Canning's constitutional policy; otherwise accurate and convincing.

The following pamphlets, though some of them deal with later developments, are all useful :—

W——r. *The Rights of Don Miguel Incontrovertibly Established,* 1830.

[1] These quotations are from *H. de W. MSS., F.O.* 360/3. A few details may be found in J. A. Home, *Letters of Lady Louisa Stuart* (1903), pp. 31, 36.

Anon. *Observations to the Author of Portugal, Their King and Constitution*, 1829.
English Civilian. *Reply to Two Pamphlets by a Portuguese Lawyer.*
Capt. W. White. *A Warning Voice to the British Nation on the Affairs of Portugal*, 1833.
A volume by J. M. Browne on *An Historical Review of the Revolutions in Portugal* [1827] is worth reading.
The French side is given temperately, but too briefly, in Damas, *Mémoires* [Paris, 1923], ii. 92–103. Villèle's *Mémoires* [1890], v. 239–47, give two letters of De Moustier, but otherwise throw little light.

NOTES ON CHAPTER XVII

THE FREEDOM OF GREECE

1. *The Negotiations Preceding the Treaty of 6th July* 1827
(v. *App. VIII.*)

It is possible to construe Canning's letter to Lieven of 20th November 1826 as implying that England had accepted the policy of force, but I do not think myself this is correct. At that stage he still believed that the recognition of independence, or the simultaneous recall of Diplomatic Missions, might be effective. Of course, he may have given verbal assurances to Lieven, but on the whole I think this improbable.

Early in 1827 Canning seems to have come to the view that forcible intervention by peaceful means (if possible by blockade) would be necessary. After 19th February he no longer believed that Austria or Prussia would come in, and this fact prevented a simultaneous recall of missions. The notion of using force was opposed by Wellington so late as the middle of March, and Canning might have found difficulty in carrying it in the Cabinet.

But there seems no reasonable doubt that he was personally favourable to the secret article enjoining the use of force, if necessary. And he was strengthened in his view by the disasters which befell Greece in the spring of 1827. But the complaints of his delay or hesitation by Madame Lieven, Nicholas, and Nesselrode took no account of his illness in February or the extreme delicacy of his position in March. An official despatch from Canning of the 20th February to Granville, who was to visit England in March, shows that he expected to give Granville the Treaty to carry back with him to Paris. And he was due to return at the end of April or early in May.[1] The political crisis made it impossible for Canning to do this, or to send the Treaty draft to Paris before the 22nd May.

The final Treaty arrangements were delayed by the French,

[1] *F.O. France*, 146/89. Canning to Granville, Feb. 20/27.

and by technical difficulties as to their doctrines of maritime law. But, if it is correct that Canning proposed the shortening of the period of grace to a fortnight, he must have been as anxious for speedy action as Lieven.   Martens, xi. 354, says Lieven obtained this clause.   But Dudley says: " His Majesty's Government have thought it right to make [this proposal] to France and Russia." [1] The account given by Martens, xi. 347–55, of the negotiations of Canning and Lieven in 1827 is of high value.   In the instance just quoted, Martens appears to be in error.   I doubt also if it is true (xi. 352) that Canning promised, on the 3rd April, to sign the Treaty as soon as he became Prime Minister.   Otherwise, so far as his narrative can be checked, Martens appears to be correct.

2. The Signature of the Treaty and its Disclosure to the Press (v. App. VIII. for text)

From a comparison of the Canning-Lieven draft with the Treaty, it appears that, at the last moment, Russia triumphed.   She secured the omission of the reference to British single mediation, and that relating to the liberty of the religion and commerce of the Greeks.   Whether this was done with sinister meaning it is hard to say.   Russia was certainly hostile to the absolute independence of Greece, for she wished to control and influence her.   Until early in 1827 Canning did not wish independence, but suggested a relation of suzerainty equivalent to that which the Republic of Ragusa had once had under Turkey.   But there is just enough to suggest that he changed his views towards the end of his life, and was feeling his way towards absolute independence.   His change of the phrase from ' sujets ' to ' Grecs ' indicates this, and it is significant that Russia objected to it.

Schiemann, in Geschichte Russlands (ii. 178–195), gives a good account of the negotiations.   He makes one curious slip.   On p. 194 he says that the Treaty was really signed on the 13th, and predated till the 6th.   He founds this on a misinterpretation of a letter of Lieven to Nesselrode of 13th July, which he quotes in full (pp. 429–30).   Lieven says he has just signed ' the pieces complementary to the Treaty.'   The ' complementary pieces ' are not the secret article, but the Instructions to Ambassadors and Admirals, which took till the 13th to complete.   They arise out of the Treaty and secret article, but were not part of either as such.   It is possible that Lieven waited to complete them before sending a copy of the Treaty to St Petersburg.   Dudley did this in the case of Constantinople, but on the 6th July he forwarded a complete copy of the Treaty, including the secret article, to Granville at Paris (F.O. France, 185/90).   Further, the Treaty was published in the Times with the secret article on the 12th July, and must have been known to them on the 11th.   But the ' complementary pieces ' were not

[1] F.O. Turkey, 195/66.   Dudley to Stratford, July 14/27, No. 12.

signed till 2 a.m. on the night of the 13th–14th July. Canning and Polignac each accused the other, in private, of the indiscretion. The Treaty reached Granville on the 9th, and the *Times* stated its information came from a correspondent in Paris on that day. There certainly often were leakages from the French Foreign Office. If Canning or Granville were the culprits, they showed a refinement of art in waiting for this date, for it could have been revealed in England either earlier or later. Dudley, in an extremely acrid circular of 30th July 1827, denied that there was any more evidence that the copy was made from the English draft than from the French one. Russia seems not to have been suspected on this occasion, but Lieven thought Canning had revealed it. Appearing as it did on the 12th, it was calculated to embarrass and to delay the signing of the 'complementary pieces.' Delay was what Polignac wanted to have, and Canning to avoid. But there is not enough evidence to settle the question either way.

3. *French Policy* (1826–7)

French policy seems as mysterious at this date as in Spanish America. Villèle seems to have been reluctant to push the matter of the Treaty, and Damas did not count.

If Apponyi, the Austrian Ambassador at Paris, is to be believed, Villèle's views were as follows : He thought the Anglo-Russian union indissoluble. The only way " to diminish the dangers of that Alliance, to paralyse it, perhaps to neutralise it, to watch over and restrain its evil action, to work secretly for its dissolution, and to facilitate opportunities for that end, was to join ourselves to it for the moment, to be always at their side, to place ourselves, so to speak, between England and Russia, to spy out (*épier*) the moment, and to profit by it, at which the true interests of these two Powers, so essentially opposed to a union, would prevail over a forced, artificial, and monstrous state of things." France wanted the preservation of the Porte and was against Greek independence,[1] etc. If this report is correct, it would be fair to assume that Villèle published the Treaty surreptitiously, and worked against the Cradock attempt to neutralise Mehemet Ali.

Isambert (pp. 295–6), who quotes most of this passage, doubts the value of Apponyi's evidence. But it is, to some extent, supported by that of Pasquier (*Mémoires*, vi. 68). If the conversation is correctly reported, Villèle comes out badly either way, for he was either a complete Machiavelli or asserted himself to be one. In the first case his morals, in the second case his intelligence, would be at fault.

It seems most probable that, in this as in other negotiations, Villèle tried to pursue the straight path, but was hindered by the

[1] *V.S.A.*, Berichte aus Frankreich, Bd. 375. Apponyi to Metternich, June 5/27.

Ultra section of the Cabinet. Polignac was bitterly opposed to the Treaty, and he was becoming more and more influential with the French King.

The Cradock Mission to Mehemet Ali was suggested by Damas, and its failure causes a suspicion of French double-dealing. But their whole attitude is difficult to understand. Even the newspapers under the control of the Government were not consistent in their view. The *Moniteur*, in its non-official part, said that speedy action was essential; the *Constitutionnel* said the Allies must delay till the consent of Austria was obtained. The fact is that the political situation was very disturbed, Villèle was tottering to his fall, and probably swayed this way and that as circumstances dictated.

4. *Austrian Policy* (1827)

About this there cannot be much doubt. Dudley afterwards drew up a Memo (*H. de W. MSS.*, 360/1) to show that Metternich had done all he could to delay the Treaty, and had secretly encouraged the Turks to resist it. The behaviour of the Austrian Internuncio at Constantinople in August and September suggests the same conclusion, and Stratford had certainly no doubt about it.

5. *Codrington at Navarino* (*20th October* 1827)

The whole question of Codrington lies beyond the scope of this book. He was ultimately recalled on account of actions subsequent to Navarino. But in the matter of his instructions it does not seem possible to meet his argument that, if the Turks tried to break his blockade, he would have to use force. Schiemann (ii. 199) makes the point that Ibrahim never thought, when he promised Codrington to abstain from hostilities for twenty days, that he would be prevented from re-provisioning Patras. But it is easy to see how the men could misunderstand one another. Codrington knew of the movements of the Greek Fleet, and did not mean to allow the Turkish Fleet to move out and thus risk a conflict. Probably Ibrahim did not know, and therefore took the other view. At any rate Codrington's accounts, 26th October and 9th December 1827 (*Memoirs*, 1873, i. 91–100), are a great deal more correct than Ibrahim's of 29th October 1827 (*W.N.D.*, iv. 141–2).

Schiemann (ii. 206) says that Codrington, in his despatch of 9th December, ' against all truth,' states that he ' used my utmost endeavours to avoid the collision.' Schiemann's is too strong a statement. For, as Codrington states in his letter of the 26th October, the formation he gave to the Allied Fleet was not favourable to hostile action and placed him at a relative disadvantage.

The only point in favour of the Turks is that they did not fire on the Allied Fleet from their land-batteries as it entered the harbour. Had they fired they would have done considerable execution, but would at once have produced a general conflict. Codrington held that the Turks thought that they had him in a trap, as they believed from French renegades that the French squadron would not fight (*Mem.*, ii. 93). Hence they allowed him to enter the harbour, hoping to surprise him with their fireships at night. It seems in fact that, once the harbour was entered, conflict was practically inevitable. Codrington decided on this step (ii. 134) because " a blockade of the port of Navarino was physically impracticable." The Duke of Clarence, as Lord High Admiral, considered him justified. The Duke of Wellington and Dudley publicly ' acquitted him of all blame,' and he received decorations from the Emperor of Russia and King of France as well as from George IV. The latter, however, said in private that Codrington deserved a rope, not a riband !

PART VIII

NOTES TO CHAPTER XVIII

THE WELLINGTON-CANNING CONTROVERSY : CANNING'S NEGOTIATIONS WITH THE WHIGS

The following are the chief MSS. authorities : *Stratford Canning MSS.*, *P.R.O.*, 352/16 (useful) ; *Private Lieven Diary* (very valuable) ; *Ripon MSS.*, British Museum (a few letters only) ; *Private Wilson MSS.*, British Museum Add. MSS., 30, 111, ff. ; 36, 282–4 ; 30, 132 ;[1] *Granville MSS.* (very slight, as Granville was in England at the crisis).

V.S.A., Berichte aus England, 1827 (valuable), iii. 299–497.

Mention may be made here of a little-known article by A. G. Stapleton, *Macmillan's Magazine*, xxxi. (1875). It has a useful criticism both of Greville and Arbuthnot. The *Quarterly Review*, vol. xliv., of 1831, is interesting.

Bathurst Papers (1923), Hist. MSS. Commission (some unpublished letters in vol. xvi. and xvii. have also been used).

Stapleton, writing in 1875, said that enough documents had been published to reveal the facts. This is true on the Canning side, the only further ones being in Stap., *Corr.*, ii. 284 *sqq.*, indicating the negotiations with the Whigs, of which the substance was already known.

But the *Peel Papers* (1891), vol. i. 452–3, have revealed Arbuthnot's letter of 10th March to Peel, the *Bathurst Papers* (1923) that of 27th February (pp. 630–1), and the *Wellesley Papers* (1914) the Memorandum of Wellington, 14th–16th April (ii. 164–8).

---

[1] These are fragmentary and disappointing, but are supplemented by his printed Narrative of the crisis, written in 1827, and edited by H. Randolph in 1872.

None of these publications is favourable to his case. A critical examination of all the material available is now possible. Of secondary authorities the most recent and judicious, but too brief, is M. E. Halévy's *Angleterre* (1923), ii.; Spenser Walpole, *Hist. of England* (1900), vol. ii., is useful, but assumes incorrectly that the King was against Canning. Mr F. H. Hill's *George Canning* (1887) contains a spirited and fairly accurate account. E. J. Stapleton's account is also useful (*Corr.*, ii. 302–9).

It is important to establish that the Duke had been contemplating measures against Canning while Liverpool was still Premier. On the 9th November 1826, the Duke of York proposed an entirely 'Protestant' administration in a Memo sent to Liverpool to be transmitted to the King. Obviously in connection with this, Wellington prepared a memorandum of his own (20th November). The real aim of this Memo was to get the King to put pressure on Canning to " induce him to avoid proposing measures for further concessions to the Roman Catholics," although he would have to vote for them, if 'proposed by others.' [1] Ultimately he was wise enough not to send this letter, but, if he wanted to put pressure on 'Catholic' Ministers in the Cabinet, he can hardly have wanted a 'Catholic' Premier. He denied indeed, on 6th May 1827, that any evidence could be adduced that he was unwilling to accept one. But he refused the 'Catholic' Robinson, and never suggested the 'Catholic' Melville, for the post.

Further, when the King stated that he wanted a 'Protestant' Premier on the 28th March, Wellington certainly did not oppose the suggestion, and, by discouraging the election of a Premier by the Cabinet and by encouraging the King to make his own choice, he in effect concurred in it. Further, it is at least singular that the Duke never proposed or suggested the 'Protestant' Bathurst, though he says (14th–16th April) that he would have accepted him for the post. This fact is the more remarkable as he was in touch with Bathurst. It seems difficult therefore to resist the inference that, while not proposing himself for the post, he left the door open for that possibility until the very last moment.

Wellington's statements in his speech of the 2nd May are partly incorrect and partly misleading. He says that, having attained the command of the army, " I could not be desirous of leaving it in order to seek to be appointed to be the head of the Government, a situation for which I am sensible that I am not qualified ; and to which, moreover, neither His Majesty nor the Right Honourable

---

[1] Vide *W.N.D., passim*, and iii. 462–3. If Greville, *Journal* (Jan. 4/31), is to be believed, the Duke of York got ' a rap on the knuckles ' from the King. This would account for Wellington's withholding his Memo. In Maxwell's *Clarendon* (1913), i. 50–1, there is a letter from Bagot to Villiers (Feb. 6/27) accusing Wellington of desiring to turn out Canning and head ' an ultra and anti-Catholic ' Ministry. This is incorrect, and an unpublished letter from the Duke to Bathurst shows him as thinking only of the army. Liverpool's illness changed his views.

Gentleman (Canning) nor anyone else wished to see me called. . . . His Majesty never offered to make me His Minister." [1] This is not ingenuous. For, on the 9th April, the King and Peel both wished him to be Premier, and only dropped the proposal on Canning's refusal. The Duke states that such a proposal " was not made in concert with me, and still less at my suggestion " (letter of 6th May) ; but he did not deny he was aware of it. In his Memo of 14th–16th April to Wellesley he states that he told those who pressed him that " circumstances might . . . be conceived under which it would be his duty to accept the situation if he were called upon by the King to do so." And on the 10th March he had asked Peel, through Arbuthnot, to discuss with him the arguments for and against his being Premier. To say therefore, as he did on the 2nd May, that " I was, and must be, totally out of the question," and " I should have been worse than mad if I had thought of such a thing," was to say something which, even if technically correct, was practically misleading. Even if he, never knew of the 9th April proposal, there is no getting away from Arbuthnot's letter to Peel of 10th March and his own statement of 14th–16th April. Arbuthnot's letter to Bathurst of 27th February tends in the same direction.

This case is therefore one of a concealment of fact. His state-ment of 14th–16th April adds that it was ' particularly unjust ' to accuse him [the Duke] " of encouraging a faction or a combination of the Protestant members of the Cabinet *and others* for the purpose of opposing Mr Canning's appointment to the head of the Govern-ment. . . . On the contrary, he had prevented the formation of such a faction." Unfortunately for the Duke, Arbuthnot's letter of the 27th February to Bathurst, of the 10th March to Peel, his own statement to the King on the 28th, prove that he was trying to exclude Canning from the Cabinet and to get others to do so. The statement of the 14th–16th April is, in this particular, not only incorrect but plainly untrue.

On the other hand, the Duke was genuinely for a ' balanced administration,' wishing to retain Canning in it, but not as head. He had no direct connection, therefore, with the Newcastle-Rut-land-Londonderry intrigue to get rid of Canning altogether by forming an exclusively ' Protestant ' Cabinet, nor had Peel. The fact is that neither thought the Government would survive without Canning.

The action of Peel, indeed, differed from Wellington's in that he would not under any circumstances have accepted the Premier-ship nor submitted to Canning's doing so, and Canning knew this at an early date. But Peel knew Wellington's views, and in the

---

[1] It seems only fair, however, to say that the King told Buckingham on July 13 that the Duke had twice refused to be Premier before Apr. 9, when the King concurred in Peel's suggestion on the subject, *v.* Duke of Buckingham, *Private Diary* (1862), i. 12–3.

last resort (9th April) was prepared to support, and did support, the idea of his heading the Ministry. What we do not know is whether he informed Wellington of the proposal beforehand or let him know, before the 10th April, of Canning's refusal to accept it. As Arbuthnot was in close touch with Peel, it seems difficult to suppose that he did not. Peel appears to have had no confidential interviews with anyone but the King, the Duke, Canning, Eldon, and perhaps Bathurst. His conduct throughout was marked by much prudence and more discretion.

Eldon was an old enemy of Canning's, but his conduct does not appear to have been incorrect on this occasion. He appears to have taken no active part in the events until his interview with the King on the 8th April, and, though he concurred in the proposal of the 9th, the King and Peel seem to have been the prime movers. Bathurst is known to have had conversations with Wellington and also relations with him *via* Arbuthnot. He was asked by Arbuthnot to mobilise the ' Protestant ' section of the Cabinet to exclude Canning, and he had an audience with the King on the 8th, so he probably concurred in the proposal of Wellington as Premier on the 9th. Bathurst showed some hesitation on resigning, and only did so, as he said, not to separate himself from his friends. He declined a further overture from Canning on the 15th April. Of the views and actions of Melville, Westmoreland, Bexley, and Harrowby we know nothing. Melville declared in the Lords that he had had no communication with anyone.[1] His resignation caused much surprise, and was explained by him on the excellent Scotch principle, that the new government seemed too weak to last. Melville saw Canning on the 9th, but, in view of his denial of having talked with anyone on the Ministry, we must suppose that his conversation dealt only with naval matters.

The only part that remains to be cleared up as regards the evidence is as to Canning's negotiations with the Whigs. Canning always denied that he had had any such previous to Liverpool's illness, or that he had himself solicited them. The Duke in private sometimes averred that he had. A sensational disclosure was made on the subject by Arbuthnot in 1831,[2] and the veracity of this story has been recently supported by the high authority of Mr H. W. C. Davis on the ground that the story was specific, and that the Duke was usually accurate in statements of fact. In this particular case, however, it has been shown that the Duke was inaccurate in one of his dates (2nd for 3rd April) and not wholly ingenuous in his public statements. And Greville (not always a trustworthy authority) does not report the Duke's own words, but only Arbuth-

---

[1] On Mar. 28 Melville gave a dinner to the whole Cabinet, except Wellington and Canning. It seems very difficult to suppose that some of them did not talk of the succession.

[2] Greville, *Journal*, July 31/31 ; H. W. C. Davis, *E.H.R.*, Oct. 1923, pp. 544–6.

not's version of them.   As will be soon seen, that version is very inaccurate, or, as Greville said, 'a very loose conversation.'

Arbuthnot's contention in brief is this.   The Whigs had made overtures to Canning *via* Sir Robert Wilson, who told Huskisson in the autumn of 1826, who repeated it to Canning.   He does not assert that Canning sent any reply.   He does say the affair took place before Liverpool's illness, *i.e.* before 17th February 1827.[1] He further says that Canning confidentially disclosed to the King that he ' was sure of the Whigs ' at his interview on the 28th March, and that the King indiscreetly repeated this to Wellington whom he saw ' immediately after.'   The Duke thereupon declared against Canning, saying that he had known already of the Whig intrigue. There is an error here, because the Duke saw the King *before*, and not *after*, Canning on that day.[2]   Arbuthnot says that he was then visited by Knighton, who regretted the King's indiscretion, and tried to patch up things between the Duke and Canning.   Arbuthnot then came to see Canning about it, and arranged a meeting with the Duke.   This was on the 2nd, the Duke came on the 3rd (not the 2nd, as he himself says), and Arbuthnot says " not a word passed between them about the formation of a new Ministry."   This statement is doubly contradicted by Wellington himself.   In their correspondence he and Canning both subsequently admitted that they had discussed the question of making Robinson a ' dummy Premier.'   The Duke added that this was the only conversation ' on the formation of the government ' he ever had with Canning. Arbuthnot is therefore in error.   He further says that, in the interval " between his [Arbuthnot's] leaving Canning and the Duke's going to him, Peel had been to him [Canning] and proposed that the Duke should be Prime Minister."   This proposal was not made by Peel on the 2nd or 3rd.   It was made on the 9th, and the terms in which he proposed it show clearly that it was then actually put forward for the first time.   So Arbuthnot misdates the proposal by six days.   Arbuthnot also omits to note that the Duke saw Canning himself for a short time on the 5th.   It was then (and not, as he suggests, on the 2nd or 3rd) that they " talked of a variety of matters, but not a word about the formation of a new ministry."   Here are four plain errors of fact and a complete confusion of dates and circumstances, of which some could have been refuted by the published documents accessible to Greville himself.   Greville has, therefore, either misrepresented Arbuthnot or the latter's facts are not only untrustworthy, but actually at variance with the Duke's own statements, as well as with those of others.

Arbuthnot's disclosures took place four years after the event.

---

[1] Huskisson had no part in the negotiations of 1827, as he was ill.

[2] It is conceivable that the King saw the Duke on the 29th, and then disclosed Canning's secret.   But there is no evidence that he did, and the King did see Canning on the 29th.

But we have his contemporary evidence upon them, for on the 10th March 1827 he wrote a letter to Peel, at the Duke's instigation, charging Canning with having intrigued with the Whigs before Liverpool's illness. But he then brings forward no specific evidence such as he quoted to Greville, only vague suspicions. It is improbable that between the 14th and 28th March 1827 he or the Duke received any fresh proof of a verbal arrangement made at the end of 1826, so that, on the 28th, the Duke had no evidence at all except suspicions. Further, in letters of Arbuthnot, seen by Greville on 9th August 1827,[1] the charge is that " Canning was negotiating with the Whigs [*i.e.* in March or April 1827] while he was pretending that he wished the old Government to go on." At that date, therefore, Arbuthnot does not appear to have known of the alleged Whig overture of 1826.

A further indication of Arbuthnot's inaccuracy may be given from these letters (9th August 1827). He says the Duke was ' miserable at the idea ' of being Premier. " However, the Peers, meaning all the Lords who had made such a stir, applied to the Duke to put himself at the head of the Government, but he hardly sent an answer to their application, he would not hear of it." This either refers to the Buckingham overture of the 20th March (which did not offer the Premiership), or to a later one of which we know nothing except that it did. Arbuthnot omits all reference to the fact that the Duke wanted to argue the case as to his premiership with Peel on 10th March, and also to the Duke's own statement (Memo of 14th–16th April) that he replied to such proposals that he did not wish the premiership, but that " circumstances might . . . be conceived under which it would be his duty to accept that situation if he were called upon by the King to do so." The Duke returned Buckingham's letter as *non-avenue* on the 21st March, so this must refer to the second overture. And if so, Arbuthnot's description is incorrect, for the Duke did not absolutely refuse to be considered.

Therefore Arbuthnot's letter of 10th March is contradicted in some particulars by his letters seen by Greville on 9th August 1827, and both are contradicted by some of his statements of 31st July 1831. The two latter also contain errors of fact, of which some are established by the Duke's own statements. Plainly no reliance can be placed on any statement of Arbuthnot's made to Greville, which is unsupported by other testimony.

Mr Davis thinks that Arbuthnot's story of the Whig overture of 1826 was ' probably true.' But it was flatly denied by Stapleton when it appeared, who added that Canning had had no negotiations with the Whigs till ' upwards of four weeks ' after Liverpool's illness.[2] It is highly interesting that this statement is borne out

[1] Greville, *Journal,* Aug. 9/27.
[2] *Macmillan's Magazine,* xxxi. [1875], 211. Even if the negotiation of 1826 were true it would not amount to much. Arbuthnot says: " He

by Mr Davis, who has discovered a letter of Brougham to Wilson of the 18th March. This proves that the question was then being discussed, but does not assert that Canning, if approached, had given any answer.[1] Even on the 24th March, when Lord Erskine took up Canning's cause, he had to ask Lansdowne and Wilson what were the bases of the negotiation, and these were indicated by Lansdowne on the 25th in a letter to Canning.[2] By the time Canning went to Windsor on the 28th he was assured of a measure of Whig support, but even then it was not of a very definite character. It has not, I think, generally been noticed that Lord Granville, who was a Whig in principle, and related by marriage to the Duke of Devonshire and in touch with Lords Holland and Brougham, was also at Windsor at this time. Madame Lieven also, though she does not mention it in her *Diary*, was active with the Whigs in private.

It is at this point (and at this point only) that Arbuthnot's evidence may be correct. Stapleton gave in full Canning's interview with the King on the 28th, but he did not later deny Arbuthnot's assertion that Canning had disclosed to the King on the 28th the offer he had had of Whig support. Canning did actually disclose it to Peel on the 29th. But the evidence shows that Canning did not seriously contemplate the inclusion of Whigs in the government until the 3rd April, *i.e.* after the Duke had refused the ' dummy Premier ' project, and caused him to suspect he was playing for the Premiership. So it may be that, if he said anything to the King before the 10th April, it was on the 6th of that month.

Canning appears to have been perfectly consistent throughout. He always intended to be the real master even if he wore a ' dummy's ' mask. He never intended to commit himself, and did not commit himself with the Whigs, until he found it impossible does not know what answer Canning sent to this, nor whether he *did* anything on it." The only thing it would really prove is that the denials made at the time by Canning, and later by Stapleton, were untrue. The Fazackerly negotiation of Feb. 21/27 (*v.* next note) was apparently unknown to Stapleton, but not to Canning. It is not asserted that Canning replied to it, and the later negotiations do not suggest the meeting was of importance. For instance, Lord John Russell, though alleged to promise to support Canning in February, refused to do this in April, and the Lansdowne group took the same line. The Whigs, as a whole, continued divided even after Apr. 19.

[1] Nor does Grey, who wrote to Holland on Mar. 13, on the question, Trevelyan's *Grey* (1920), p. 375. A new discovery, reported by Mr Davis to me, has been made by Mr Arthur Aspinall in the *Hatherton Papers*. A day or two before Feb. 21, but after Liverpool's illness, a "numerous and respectable Whig meeting discussed the situation and decided unreservedly to support Canning." Lord J. Russell, Fazackerly, and Abercromby (the last two connected with Lansdowne) were present. Brougham, who was not present, indicated sympathy. Littleton, a friend of Canning's, heard the news on the 21st and wrote to Canning about it.

[2] E. J. Stapleton, *Corr.*, ii. 301–2. The date is correct, though the Editor thinks it is not. Brougham's foolish letter of the 26th should be placed after it.

to go on with his colleagues. He did not intend to be excluded from the Premiership because he was a ' Catholic,' and therefore advised the King on the 28th to form a wholly ' Protestant ' Ministry.

Until the 2nd or 3rd of April it is certain that Canning believed Croker's report (18th February) of the Duke's assurances that he did not want the Premiership himself, or necessarily object to him (Canning) having it. The different (and substantially correct) impression of the Duke's views he then obtained, together with the proposal made by the King-Peel-Eldon proposal on 9th April, are quite enough to explain his final irritation. It may perhaps be argued, therefore, that Canning's letter of the 10th April to Wellington was intended to produce a refusal. It is probable that it was not, but his indignation at the Duke's attitude may have made him word the invitation more coldly than was prudent. But as he knew that Peel, who was closely connected with the Duke, would resign, he probably did not think that the Duke would stay in the Cabinet. He did not, however, expect the Duke to throw up the army command, nor did Wellington perhaps mean to do so. That was the result of the correspondence and of the long-smothered mutual irritation.

Of the King's attitude it is difficult to speak. If Arbuthnot's story is correct, he comes out even worse than he was previously supposed to do. Wellington said (2nd May), " His Majesty never offered to make me his Minister." The King told Buckingham on 13th July that he offered it him twice.[1] His statements were always loose and sometimes untruthful. But it is pretty clear that he wanted to prevent Catholic Emancipation and yet to keep Canning in the Cabinet. The threats of Newcastle (26th March) frightened him into promising him to appoint, not a wholly ' Protestant ' Ministry, but a ' Protestant ' Premier. To cause the Cabinet to elect their chief would, he thought, perhaps produce that result and coerce Canning into accepting that solution. The refusal of Peel and Canning to accept election of the Premier by the Cabinet on the 31st March coincided with a visit to him from the ' Protestant ' Rutland, to whom he showed much consideration. By the 6th at any rate he must have known that Canning was inflexible, but as no one else was ready to serve, he must have been much embarrassed by his promise to have a ' Protestant ' Premier. As a last desperate effort he permitted Peel to ask Canning to accept the Duke on the 9th.[2] When that failed he was faced with the fear of what Canning might do in opposition, and also with the fear that he might not be able to form a government without him. When on the 10th April Canning revealed (or again asserted) that he had Whig support the King's last doubts were removed. He

---

[1] Duke of Buckingham, *Private Diary*, [1862], i. 12–3.
[2] Buckingham makes the King say Wellington had twice previously refused to let the King propose him as Premier. George said the same to Esterházy.

did not like the Whigs, but it amused him to think that he was breaking up parties, and acting as a King in deed as well as in name.   In spite of appearances to the contrary, it seems true that he really wanted Canning all the time; for he was very susceptible to personal influences, and Canning had definitely superseded the Duke in his favour long before the crisis.   The real difficulty for the King lay in the pledge given to Newcastle to have a 'Protestant' Premier.   After the 10th April his intrigues to secure a 'Protestant' administration in Ireland, his abuse of Canning in private, and the 'Protestant' declarations which he caused the bishops to make public, need not be considered seriously.   They are plainly attempts to save his face and to cover up the fact that he had broken his promise to Newcastle.   It was not in the man's nature to say the same things to different people.   But, subject to that limitation, he appears to have supported Canning throughout his Premiership.

To sum up, the assertion that Canning negotiated with the Whigs previous to Liverpool's illness remains unproved, and is probably incorrect.   The other chief question is whether Wellington knew that Canning claimed to be Prime Minister *sine qua non* on the 3rd April.   Stapleton says that Canning then disclosed to the Duke all his conversation with the King on the 28th March. This was denied in substance by the Duke on the 6th May.   But it has been shown that Arbuthnot's statements are many of them misleading, and that some of the Duke's were incorrect.   On the other hand, Stapleton's evidence, where capable of being checked from other sources, remains absolutely correct.   The only thing of which he was ignorant was the Fazackerly negotiation.

These four persons must have known the truth between them. There were only five others who may have done.[1]   The King's evidence is without much weight, but he did ultimately support Canning.   Bathurst's attitude does not suggest that he condemned Canning, though he decided to resign.   Peel appears not to have disapproved of Canning's attitude up till the 10th April; after that he seems to have objected to the tone of his correspondence with the Duke; but there is no suggestion anywhere before that date that he thought Canning had acted unfairly.   Two foreigners knew a good deal: Madame Lieven and Prince Esterházy.   It was the former's interest to support Canning, but, though her judgments of him were not always favourable, she seems, in this case, to think that he acted with perfect straightforwardness, and she is rather unfavourable to Wellington.   Esterházy, on the other hand, was no friend to Canning.   He saw the correspondence and heard versions of the facts both from the King and the Duke.[2]   He does not say that Canning had

[1] The King, Esterházy, Madame Lieven, Bathurst, Peel.

[2] *V.S.A.*, Berichte aus England.   Esterházy to Metternich, Apr. 18, 27 ; June 2, 22; July 21/27.   The three points that emerge are: (1) The King

negotiated with the Whigs in 1826. But he doubted whether Wellington was wise in resigning at all, and undoubtedly condemned his throwing up the command of the army. Finally, the Marquess Wellesley, who received several accounts both from his brother the Duke and from Canning, supported the latter. It is fair to add that he was a friend of Canning's and not on particularly good terms with his brother, the Duke.[1]

admitted that Canning had insisted on the Liverpool, or balanced, policy for the 'Catholic' question. (2) The Duke admitted that, in fact, he did *not* wish to serve under Canning in the Cabinet. He never told the King so, but George observed it and informed Canning. Hence the quarrel. (3) The Duke made no specific allegations as to Canning's dealings with the Whigs, and never referred to 1826.

[1] Sir Herbert Maxwell, *Life of Wellington*, [1900], ii. 169–207, plainly deprecates the action of his hero.

APPENDICES I–IX

APPENDIX I

METTERNICH AND CANNING ON THE HOLY ALLIANCE AND NEO-HOLY ALLIANCE

(a) *Metternich on the Holy Alliance*

V.S.A., Weisungen nach Frankreich, Bd. 361, No. 3, Metternich à Vincent, 8 *October* 1824

Objects to protocols, 31 août, at Paris re evacuation by French troops of Spain, for containing the term ' Ministres de la Sainte Alliance ' (des Cours Alliés) and says it is ' déplacée ' and ' un abus de mots.'

" L'Alliance est une, indivisible *de droit*, ses organes ne doivent pas souscrire à des divergences de fait ; aussi souvent que les Représentans des cours se rassemblent à Paris pour prendre en considération des objets d'intérêt Européen, ils se réunissent au nom de l'alliance fondé en 1813 à Toeplitz, confirmé à Chaumont en 1814, sanctionée de nouveau et publiée à Paris en 1815, consolidée par l'adhésion de la France à Aix-la-Chapelle en 1818 et subséquemment mise en pratique tant à Laibach en 1821 qu'à Vienne en 1822. Admettre dans un tel état de choses une subdivision des Ministres de la Sainte Alliance, ce seroit en quelque sort donner acte d'une défection ou d'une scission dans la grande Alliance.

" Cette observation pourroit peut-être paroître minutieuse, il n'arrive cependant que trop souvent que l'abus dans les mots surtout, lorsqu'on les laisse passer en usage dans des pièces officielles, conduit à accréditer des idées erronées dans les choses. Cette conséquence est d'autant plus à craindre dans le cas présent que les représentans des Trois Cours en ne recusant pas la dénomination particulière de Ministres de la Sainte Alliance, semblèroient acquiescer aux restrictions dans lesquelles le Ministère actuel de la Grande Bretagne s'est retranché et vers lesquelles le Cabinet de Tuileries a témoigné en plus d'une occasion vouloir également se ménager une position isolée.

" En effet, si l'on considère que dans les derniers temps les trois Cours de concert avec le gouvernement français ont jugé conven-

533

able d'insister près le Cabinet de St James, tant par leurs dé-marches directes que par les insinuations de Sa Majesté Catholique sur la nécessité de conférences préalables au sujet de l'affaire des Colonies Espagnoles, il est dans les conséquences d'une telle marche de conserver à toute delibération rélative à l'état de l'Espagne le caractère et le nom de conseils de l'alliance Euro-péenne et d'eviter soigneusement de lui donner la couleur de vœux particuliers de la Sainte Alliance. . . .

" L'Acte auquel va uniquement la qualification de Sainte Alliance est un acte abstrait dans sa partie morale et particulier dans sa forme. Il a été passé entre les Monarques et il n'appartient pas à leurs Cabinets ni par son origine ni par sa rédaction. Aussi jamais n'a-t-il été cité par ces derniers dans aucun de leurs relations diplomatiques. C'est le public seul et nullement les Cours par aucune de leurs documents, ni même que par aucune de leurs paroles, qui a prêté à l'amalgame des stipulations positives qui s'attachent à leur alliance politique avec cette union toute morale qui porte le nom de la Sainte Alliance. Le nom de celle-ci est cependant généralement répandu ; il est pour ainsi dire la cheville d'une grande somme d'attaques que les révolutionnaires ont dirigé depuis 1815 contre les Monarques et contre leur Cabinets en même temps, que les hommes de la Monarchie et les defenseurs des droits positifs ont essayé de s'en rendre forts. D'où vient un fait aussi extra-ordinaire ? Je recherche l'origine dans le *vague* auquel doit prêter tout acte du genre de celui connu sous le nom de Sainte Alliance. Le vague sert toujours aux fins des partis et c'est tout juste par cela que les gouvernemens doivent ne point fonder sur lui une attitude quelconque. Nous ne reconnaissons et ne recon-naîtrons dans notre langage diplomatique jamais autre chose que *l'Alliance.* Son esprit, ses règles et ses stipulations, telles qu'elles se trouvent renfermées dans les actes diplomatiques cidessus mentionnés. Il y a une grande et notable différence entre les idées qui s'attachent *à la morale* et celles qui se lient à la *réligion.* Les actes regulièrement rédigés forment le Code de *notre réligion politique* ; la *Sainte Alliance* ne forme que sa partie morale. Je crois que cette distinction vous mettra en entier au fait de notre pensée et vous prouvera les raisons sérieuses que nous avons pour ne jamais confondre ce qui se trouve placé sur des domaines séparés." [1]

---

[1] In consequence of this remonstrance the protocol was altered and the term *Ministres de la Sainte Alliance* replaced by *des Cours Alliés.*

(b) *Canning's Statement to Neumann (Austrian Chargé in London),
24th June 1824, on the Neo-Holy Alliance*

V.S.A., Berichte aus England, Bd. 223, No. 25, Litt.B., Londres,
4 *juillet* 1824

Neumann to Metternich

MON PRINCE,

Le Courrier Schiller arrivé ici le 20 juin m'a remis l'expédition dont Votre Altesse m'a honoré en date du Johannisberg le 14 juin.

Conformément à la dépêche No. 1, ayant rapport à l'office de Mr d'Ofalia je me suis empressé à demander une audience à Mr Canning qui m'a reçu le 24. L'ayant prévenu que j'avois une communication à lui faire de la part de Votre Altesse, il me dit qu'il ne pourroit la recevoir que dans le cas où je serois autorisé à lui laisser une copie de la dépêche que j'allois lui lire. Bien que celle-ci ne m'en ordonnoit qu'une lecture, cependant j'aurois cru le but manqué, en n'accédant pas au désir du principal Secrétaire d'État, surtout qu'il paroit que c'est une nouvelle méthode établie depuis peu—je lui observai donc que l'on ne m'avoit pas chargé d'en laisser une copie, mais que je prenois sur moi de le faire confidentiellement. Après avoir fait la lecture de ce document que Mr Canning écouta avec une grande attention, il me dit que sur le Continent on partoit d'un principe entièrement faux—que les Puissances croyoient pouvoir s'ériger en tribunal pour exercer leur influence sur toutes les affaires quelconques ; que cette erreur existoit depuis le Congrès de Vienne—que les transactions qui en avoient été la conséquence avoient eu pour but de détruire la trop grande prépondérance qu'une Puissance avoit exercé sur les autres, et que les affaires qui devoient former l'objet d'un concert des Cabinets Alliés, avoient été specifiées par ces mêmes transactions—qu'il n'avoit jamais été question d'aller au delà—que l'histoire des derniers tems étoit marquée par trois époques—celle de Naples, de Verone et la présente—que dans la première l'Angleterre s'étoit séparée de l'Alliance, que cette séparation avoit été marquée par la réponse que le Cabinet Anglois avoit du faire à la circulaire de Laybach—qu'à Verone—l'Angleterre avoit protesté contre ce qui s'y étoit fait, et avoit pris une attitude de neutralité entre la France et l'Espagne, que la guerre avoit heureusement été de si courte durée, que cette neutralité n'avoit pas été compromise—mais que la troisième époque arrivoit à une question entièrement maritime et de commerce, et par conséquent du domaine d'Angleterre, que l'influence des Puissances cessoit là où se trouvoient les bornes du Continent—qu'il croyoit qu'Elles se fésoient illusion sur les intentions de la France relativement à la question des Colonies, qu'il étoit sûr, qu'elle l'envisageoit différemment—qu'il y avoit la même nuance entre les Puissances et la France, qu'entre celle-ci et l'Angleterre.—Mr Canning revint

sur tout ce qu'il m'avoit déjà dit antérieurement ainsi qu'à Mr de
Lieven sur cette affaire—disant qu'une autre marche de l'Angleterre eût rapproché les nouveaux Gouvernemens de l'Amerique
Espagnole, des Etats Unis du Nord qui n'attendoient que cette
circonstance pour étendre leur influence et leur prépondérance sur
tout ce vaste continent—que la position degagée et libre où l'Angleterre se trouvoit avoit seule pu arrêter ce mal, qui eût été incalcul-
able en ce qu'il y eût consacré le principe démocratique et séparé
d'une manière bien plus positive entre les Colonies et la mère
patrie—que c'étoit pour cette raison qu'il désiroit tant que le
Brésil pût s'arranger avec le Portugal afin de voir une forte
Monarchie s'élever dans le nouveau monde qui puisse servir
d'exemple et de base pour les autres Etats—que c'étoit peut-être un
des principaux motifs qui avoit retardé la reconnoissance de l'indépendance de Colombie ou du Buenos Ayres—qu'on oublioit sur le
Continent que le Gouvernement Anglois même étoit une conséquence d'une révolution, qu'on avoit passé ici par toutes ces phases,
qu'on étoit habitué à de pareils changemens et ne les envisageoit
pas sous le même point de vue que chez nous ; que nous fésions un
acte très honorable et de grande générosité en déclarant que nous
ne reconnoîtrions jamais l'indépendance de ces Colonies à moins
que la métropole ne le fît,—que la position, l'organisation, l'intérêt
de ce pays-ci et l'esprit de ses habitans ne lui permettoient pas de
faire la même chose—que l'histoire offroit plus d'un exemple de
pays qui s'étoient détachés de la mère patrie et que l'on avoit
reconnu avant celle-ci, comme les Pays-Bas, dont l'Espagne n'avoit
reconnu l'indépendance que 70 ans après, qu'elle pourroit en
mettre autant pour reconnoître la partie de ses Colonies qu'il
seroit hors de son pouvoir de reconquérir, que si l'Angleterre
vouloit suivre cet exemple, ces nouveaux états Américains se diri-
geroient vers la Puissance qui leur offriroit l'avantage de les reconnoître, et que cette puissance seroit l'Amerique Septentrionale, qui
retireroit tous les bénéfices de cette mesure. Que le gouvernement Anglois avoit eu plus d'égards pour l'Espagne que celle-
ci et la France n'en avoient eu pour l'Angleterre lorsqu'elles se
lignèrent pour aider la révolte de ses Colonies de l'Amérique du
Nord—que la France avoit été la première à reconnaître leur
indépendance et à former une alliance avec elles—tandis que
l'on avoit prévenu de ce côté-ci, sur ce que l'on seroit obligé de
faire, afin que l'Espagne eût l'avantage de le faire elle-même—
qu'il avoit eu soin dans sa réponse au discours de Sir James Mackintosh dernièrement (le 15 Juin) de distinguer avec précision le
sens de la phrase *reconnaissance de l'indépendance* qui devoit être
considerée sous un double point de vue, savoir : 1º, quand une
Colonie se déclaroit indépendante et que la Métropole la recon-
noîssoit comme telle, alors l'autorité de celle-ci sur la première
cessoit, et 2º, quand une Colonie annonçoit à un autre état son
indépendance, et que celui-ci la reconnoissoit ce n'étoit ni plus

ni moins que l'énoncé d'une opinion, ou d'un fait qui n'affectoit en rien la situation relative de la mère patrie avec cette Colonie— et qui n'impliquoit aucune obligation d'Alliance ou de co-opération quelconque.

Le Principal Secrétaire d'Etat ne répondant pas directement à la question posée d'une manière si claire dans la dépêche de Votre Altesse—je pris la liberté d'attirer son attention sur cette partie essentielle de la dépêche—il éluda d'entrer en explication à cet égard, et me dit qu'il me verroit encore la semaine prochaine.—Je me permis néanmoins d'observer à Mr Canning que je voyois qu'il soupçonnoit la France de diverger avec nous sur cette question et que ce n'étoit pas le cas ; qu'elle avoit également déclaré ne pas vouloir préjuger les droits de Sa Majesté Catholique en reconnoissant avant elle l'indépendance de ses Colonies—qu'elle étoit donc parfaitement d'accord avec nous sur le principe, et que si comme puissance maritime et commerçante elle avoit peut-être quelques ménagemens à prendre rélativement à l'intérêt de son commerce, cela n'avoit rien à faire avec le fond de la question, qu'elle envisageoit comme nous—que nous étions les premiers à réconnoitre les différentes positions selon les différentes conformations des Gouvernemens, que l'intérêt particulier de l'Angleterre pouvoit très bien marcher à côté de l'intérêt politique d'une nature générale et commune à toutes les Puissances, que personne ne contestoit à l'Angleterre le droit de mettre à couvert cet intérêt particulier, qu'au contraire on seroit bien aisé de lui voir exercer sa prépondérance maritime dans un but salutaire—que si j'avois bien compris sa réponse à Sir James Mackintosh—j'y avois vu que le Gouvernement Anglois mettoit une grande importance à ce que celui d'Espagne fît le premier pas envers ses Colonies—que s'il le jugeoit ainsi, il falloit laisser à celui-ci non seulement les moyens de le faire, mais encore les lui fournir ; que l'Angleterre au lieu d'aider l'Espagne par des Conseils et des bons offices—se plaçoit entr'Elle et ses Colonies d'une manière à ce qu'Elle ne puisse les atteindre. Ici il m'interrompit pour me dire, que bien que les Puissances n'en soyent pas informées il pouvoit m'assurer qu'on avoit donné plus d'un conseil et fait l'offre de services qu'Elle avoit rejetés, qu'entr'autres on lui avoit conseillé de se faire payer l'abandon de son droit de souveraineté sur les provinces, qu'il semble le moins probable de recupérer,—comme la Colombie et Buenos-Ayres—qu'elle auroit pu obtenir pour cela une bonne somme d'argent qui eût servi à rétablir ses finances et à arranger ses affaires intérieures—mais qu'il sembloit qu'elle ne vouloit entendre rien, qui n'eût pour objet la suprématie générale sur la totalité de ses anciennes possessions, et qu'il craignoit que cet aveuglement sur l'état réel des choses, ne lui fît perdre le tout, et que certainement l'Angleterre ne pouvoit se soumettre à cet aveuglement—que les Puissances qui avoient si généreusement promis de ne pas dévancer Sa Majesté Catholique dans la reconnoissance de quelques-uns de ces états, verroient avec le temps si elles y trouveroient leur compte, qu'en attendant tous les avantages de commerce qu'elles pourroient partager également avec tout le monde, passeroient en des mains d'où il seroit difficile de les retirer lorsque le temps et l'habitude les y auroient placés.

Je lui dis que je doutois que l'Espagne fût aussi peu éclairée sur ses véritables intérêts qu'il le prétendoit, que je savois indirectement qu'elle étoit occupée d'un plan pour la pacification de ses Colonies, et qu'en supposant que ce plan fut présenté aux Puissances, et par conséquent aussi au Gouvernement Anglois, je lui demandai s'il se réfuseroit à le prendre en considération, et à donner au Cabinet de Madrid des avis qui fussent dans son intérêt—il m'assura que, si dans l'intervalle qui s'écouleroit jusqu'au moment où l'on croiroit devoir prendre une décision ici, l'Espagne présentait un pareil plan, on se prêteroit volontiers à l'examiner, mais non de concert avec les Puissances, que celles-ci devoient cependant exercer leur influence sur l'Espagne pour l'engager à rédiger un plan qui fût raisonnable et practicable.

Voilà tout ce que j'ai pu obtenir de Mr Canning pour le moment, et quand l'on considèrè avec quelle persévérance il avoit évité de répondre à toute insinuation ou demande quelconque faite dans cette vue, l'on doit regarder comme une grande concession de sa part la promesse de ne pas se refuser à être utile à l'Espagne si Elle fait un appel aux bons offices du Gouvernement Britannique d'une manière qui puisse lui convenir pour la forme et pour le fond.

Veuillez agréer, Mon Prince, l'hommage de mon très-profond respect.

NEUMANN.

APPENDIX II

CANNING ON THE DOCTRINE OF GUARANTEE

(a) *Canning to Sir Wm. À Court,* 18*th September* 1823;
received 30*th September, No.* 54

[This classic despatch points out the danger of guaranteeing the internal institutions of a country. There are several others on the same lines in the despatches to Portugal, but none are so brilliantly expressed.]

" The British Government will not, in any case, undertake any guaranty (*sic*) whatever, either of territory or internal Institutions.[1]

" The scrupulousness with which England is in the habit of fulfilling her obligations makes it the more necessary for her not to contract them lightly. A guaranty is one of the most onerous obligations which one State can contract towards another. A defensive Alliance binds the Government contracting it to come to the aid of its Ally, in case of an unprovoked attack upon his Dominions : and to make in his behalf, every reasonable and practicable exertion,—practicable in extent, and reasonable in duration. But it does not bind the assisting Government to the alternative of either a successful result, or an indefinite prolongation of the War. A guaranty (*sic*), strictly construed, knows no limits either of time, or of degree. It would be, unless distinctly restricted in that respect, claimable in a War commenced by the Power to whom the guaranty (*sic*) is given, as well as in a War of unjust aggression against that Power ; and the integrity of the territory of that Power must be maintained, at whatever cost the effort to maintain it is prolonged : nay, though the guaranteed Power itself should contribute almost nothing to the maintaining it. If . . . the engagement is to be restricted in these particulars, it would constitute an unilateral defensive Alliance, but it would cease to be a guarantee. Objectionable as a territorial guaranty is shown to be, the objections to a guaranty of internal institutions are infinitely stronger. It is difficult to say whether these objections

[1] This is printed in Stap., *Pol. Life,* i. 427–30, but with some mistakes. The version here given is from the original despatch, *F.O. Spain,* 185/91. Canning to À Court, Sept. 18/23, No. 54, received Sept. 30. The spelling of the word guarantee is varied at different times in the original.

539

apply with greater force to the party giving, or to that which receives, such a guaranty (*sic*).

" The very principle on which the British Government so earnestly deprecated the War against Spain, was, that of the right of any Nation to change or to modify its internal Institutions.

" Is that War to end in His Majesty's consenting to assume to Himself the province of defending, against all Challengers, from within, as well as from without, the Institutions, whatever they might be, which the War may leave standing in Spain ?

" Is His Majesty to guaranty (*sic*) the Constitution of 1812, indifference to which, to say the least . . ., is the single point upon which anything like an Agreement of opinion has been found to exist in Spain ? or is He to guaranty (*sic*) the antient despotism, the restoration of which, with all its accompaniments, appears to be the object of by far the largest party in the Country ? or is it to be in behalf of some new system, struck out at a heat, at the winding up of affairs at Cadiz, that the faith of Great Britain is to be pledged, and that Her blood and treasure are to be forthcoming ? or is it only to the undoubted right of the Spanish Nation to reform its own Government, that the sanction of His Majesty's guarantee is to be added ? If such a guarantee were anything more than the mere affirmance of an abstract proposition, against whom would it have practically to operate ? clearly against the Spaniards themselves : and in the endless struggles which might be expected from the then distracted state of parties in that Country, against every party by turns ?

" Could anything be more unbecoming than the assumption of such a right by a foreign Power ? Could anything be more intolerable to the Country with respect to which it was assumed?

" It is hardly necessary to add that while His Majesty must decline accepting such a right for Himself, he could not acknowledge it in any other Power.

" The exercise of such a right must necessarily lead to an intermeddling with the affairs of the guaranteed State, such as to place it, in fact, at the mercy of the Power who gives the guarantee.

" Russia, in former times, guaranteed the Constitution of Poland.

" The result is known—and it was inevitable. The natural and necessary course of things must, in such a case, overbear even the most sincere and studied abstinence from interposition on the part of the guaranteeing Power.

" There can be no doubt that His Majesty's Allies will feel how little such an arrangement would be compatible with the Engagements by which they stand bound to each other : to maintain the State of territorial possession established at the Peace, and the rights of independent Nations."

(b) *Maritime Guarantees*, 1824–6

Canning offered two maritime guarantees, of which neither were accepted; but the scope and limitation of them are interesting. On the 2nd April 1824 (*F.O. Spain*, 185/95. Canning to À Court, 2nd April 1824) Canning offered " a formal engagement on the Part of Great Britain to employ, when called upon, her maritime Power to defend that Colony for Spain against any external aggression; unwilling as this Country is generally, and upon principle, to undertake any engagement in the nature of a guarantee, His Majesty's Government would consider this as a case in which they might be justified in departing, in a certain degree, from their accustomed cautious policy. They would not hesitate to contract such an engagement; so soon as Spain shall, on her side, have adopted the suggestions of my other despatch," *i.e.* to accept our good offices to recognise the independence of the Spanish Colonies.

Canning subsequently pointed out to France (*F.O. France*, 146/71 : to Granville, 21st January 1825, No. 8) that this guarantee was " simple and gratuitous . . . it stipulates for no compensation, requires no condition (beyond that of the previous acceptance . . . of our good offices), and, above all, that, far from hinting at the introduction of a British garrison into the Havannah (a point on which, I understand, the jealousy of Prince de Polignac to be particularly excited), it expressly negatives that notion, by specifying maritime protection."

In the dispute between Brazil and Buenos Aires, Canning offered to guarantee the navigation of the Rio de la Plata, if both sides desired it. This was an even more limited guarantee than that offered over Cuba. But it was purely maritime, and only offered in case both Buenos Aires and Brazil agreed. As they did not, Canning refused to do anything in the matter.

(c) *Interpretation of Territorial Guarantee to Portugal,*
12th January 1825

F.O. Austria, 120/68. Canning to H. Chamberlain [British Consul-General at Brazil], 12th January 1825, enclosed to Sir H. Wellesley.

" The context and spirit [of our Ancient Treaties with Portugal] undoubtedly gives to Portugal a claim upon us for general protection, if not for a specific guarantee. Such guarantee, indeed, is argued by the Marquis de Palmella to extend even to the *Colonial* Possessions of the Crown of Portugal. We do not admit that extension [we must act according to the general spirit of the agreement].

" If Brazil were acknowledged as independent without the concurrence of the Mother Country, and if after such Concurrence

Brazil were to make war upon Portugal ?   Whatever may be the construction of our Treaties as applicable to the unforeseen case of a contest between two parts of the Portuguese Monarchy, these Treaties unquestionably bind us to defend Portugal against any *foreign* Power, and Brazil would have been made a foreign Power, in respect to Portugal, by our Act."

(d) *Guarantees to Greece*

This was mainly territorial, and refused by Canning for the whole Ottoman Empire.   When confined to Greece, he showed some disposition to concede it, if all five Great Powers agreed.   When Austria and Prussia refused, England refused also (*v. supra*, pp. 400–1).

It may be contended here, therefore, that Canning wavered with respect to his fixed determination not to grant territorial guarantees, other than those already existing.   This is unquestionably true, but the point seems to be that he was prepared to modify this rule if all the Great Powers agreed to give the guarantee, and if it was confined to Greece.   What he was not prepared to do was to guarantee Greece alone territorially against future Russian or Turkish aggression.

APPENDIX III

CANNING AND SPANISH AMERICA

(a) *Canning's Notes on a Despatch from Monsieur de Chateaubriand to the Prince de Polignac, 26th January* 1824, enclosed in *F.O. France,* 146/62. Canning to Sir C. Stuart, 13th February 1824, No. 12.

[These notes were circulated to Paris, Petersburg, Berlin, and Vienna, in reply to Chateaubriand's despatch of 26th January 1824 (printed in Stap., *Corr.,* i. 139-44). They were not to be read *in toto,* but to form a basis for conversation and explanation. They were thus never published.]

Note I

Monsieur de Chateaubriand sets out with instituting a comparison between the conduct of France last year towards Spain, and that which we have reserved to ourselves, the free discretion to adopt towards Spanish America.

The two cases appear to be not only not alike, but to have no features of resemblance. A question as to the justice or injustice of a direct, hostile, armed invasion of a neighbouring State, on the plea of danger to be apprehended, either from its positive institutions or from the unsettled character of its Government, has nothing surely in common with the simple question of fact : at what period a Colony or Dependency, which has declared its separation from the Parent State, may properly be acknowledged by other Powers as having established its independent political existence ?

[*N.B.*—A third paragraph omitted here owing to Wellington's comment, *W.N.D.,* ii. 211.]

Note II

Monsieur de Chateaubriand says that Spain asks for ' Arbitrators ' and not for ' Advisers.' Monsieur de Chateaubriand contends that, in giving our advice to Spain singly, we do not comply with her request ; while, by consenting to go into a Conference with the other Allies of Spain, we should fulfil it to the letter.

543

The obvious difference between advice and arbitration consists, not in the number of Counsellors or Judges, but in this : that an adviser gives counsel to the party who requires the counsel, alone ; whereas an arbitrator hears both the party requiring it, and the party with respect to whom it is required. Now as to 'Arbitration' in *this* sense, that is, as to the hearing of the Colonies as well as of the Mother-Country, we do not understand it to be proposed by Spain, nor is it anywhere suggested by Monsieur de Chateaubriand.

We have advised Spain to make a proposition to the American Provinces, founded on the only basis on which we think any proposition likely to be successful, or advantageous, to Spain ; but what Spain asks is the 'aid of her Allies' to maintain *Her Legitimate Sovereignty* over the American Provinces. *It is no fault of ours that the time for this object is gone by* ; [1] but, believing it to be gone by irrecoverably, it would not be friendly in us, but deceitful and dishonest, to encourage His Catholic Majesty in an attempt which appears to us utterly hopeless.

Note III

Monsieur de Chateaubriand supposes the use of the words 'Sovereignty' and 'Rebellion' by Spain, to have shocked the feelings of the British Government ; and he argues upon those words as if they were used by Spain in reference to the same part of the question. But the word 'Rebellion' is applied, in the Spanish Circular, not only to Spanish America, but to Spain itself. It was certainly a surprise to the British Government (and they presume that it must have been a surprise no less to the French Government) to learn, that, not from the period of what Monsieur de Chateaubriand calls *la déchéance* of His Catholic Majesty at Seville, but that for three years before that time, during the whole of which period His Majesty [*i.e.* of England], and during the greater part of which His Most Christian Majesty [*i.e.* of France], had Ambassadors at Madrid ; and up to the very conclusion of which period His Most Christian Majesty professed the most pacific relations with Spain, that country was in a state to be qualified as a state of 'Rebellion.'

But we do not claim any right to discuss the relative situation of His Catholic Majesty [of Spain] and His Subjects, so long as that situation is matter merely of internal dispute. Our concern is not with this or that Party or Faction in Spain ; but with *Spain*, whether purely monarchical, or constitutional ; just as (to cite a much more striking instance) our concern was with *France*, when we made peace with the Consulate in 1802 ; and just as the concern

---

[1] Wellington, *W.N.D.*, ii. 212, wanted to add to this passage, 'if it ever existed.' Canning did not adopt this. The italics are my own.

of every other Power in Europe was with France, when they contracted or maintained pacifick relations with that Country, under all the varying phases which the French Revolution assumed, in returning, as Monsieur de Chateaubriand describes it, " from the Convention to Legitimacy, through Robespierre and the Directorate, and Bonaparte."

Note IV

With "these recollections fresh on his mind, it is not a little singular that Monsieur de Chateaubriand should exclaim against the acknowledgment of a state of things in any country not sanctioned by the Will of the Sovereign, as a thing hitherto unheard of ; and should pronounce all new governments to be ' incurably vicious,' which are not preceded by a formal abdication of the legitimate Sovereignty."

Had the August House of Bourbon abdicated Its Rights, before the successive recognitions of each successive order of things in France, by all the Powers of Europe without exception—by England, it must be confessed among them, but not till every other Power had set Her the example ?

Note V

But we are far from denying the truth of Monsieur de Chateaubriand's argument, that the unrenounced Sovereignty of Spain might, *in its mere ' passive ' existence*, be inconvenient to the new States of America, even after the acknowledgment of their Independence by other Powers.

So strongly do we feel the truth of this argument, that our advice to Spain, and our offer of Intervention with the American Provinces, are grounded upon it.

[The italicised passage was added as a result of Wellington's comment, *W.N.D.*, ii. 212.]

Note VI

But did not England herself " talk of Sovereignty and Rebellion," says Monsieur de Chateaubriand, " till the day on which she signed the Treaty that raised her own American Colonies into a Nation ? "

She did so—but She signed that Treaty as soon as She was convinced that the practical means of maintaining Her Sovereignty were exhausted—and assuredly what England did, and what She lost in that Contest, must assign to Her Counsels, on the present occasion, a weight which can hardly belong to those of any other Power. Her experience may naturally and usefully operate, both as an example and as a warning.

Note VII

But if Spain should refuse to waive Her Rights of Sovereignty, and if we should, nevertheless, acknowledge the independence of the American States, " are we prepared" (Monsieur de Chateaubriand enquires) "to declare War against Spain ? "

Why should we ? When France, in 1778, announced to this Country that she had signed a treaty of amity and alliance with the United States of America, she accompanied that intelligence with the Assurances of a desire to remain at peace with Great Britain.

War, it is true, followed—because this last act of France was not one of simple recognition—it was the consequence and consummation of a series of foregone acts of little less than direct hostility, by assistance more or less openly furnished to our Enemies—acts of ' generosity ' as Monsieur de Chateaubriand characterises them ; but not the less directly aimed against the vital interests of Great Britain. War followed upon these acts ; but we have given no such cause of offence to Spain. We have preserved, throughout her contest with her Colonies, a strict and impartial neutrality ; or, if in anything partial, we have leant decidedly to Spain, prohibiting any supply of the munitions of war to her Adversary, while we left open that supply to the Mother Country ; and passing a new law for the express purpose of preventing the subjects of Great Britain from flocking to the standard of the Insurgents.

Besides, in 1778, the War in British America was in its full vigour. It was almost impossible, therefore, to form an alliance with one State without hostility to the other.

In Spanish America any remains of contest now are to be found only in one of the five Provinces—Peru—and in the Castle of St John d'Ulloa [in Mexico].

Lastly, it is now about fourteen years since some of the South American Provinces first declared their separation from Spain. In 1778, the Declaration of Independence by British America was not two years old.

There are, therefore, no such causes of War on the part of Spain against England, as there were on that of England against France in 1778 ; and the profession of the desire of France, at that period, to remain at Peace with England, shows, at least, in the opinion of France herself, there was no inevitable necessity for a Declaration of War on the part of the Power recognising American Independence.

[Wellington, *W.N.D.*, ii. 213, objected to the italicised passage, but Canning retained it.]

Note VIII

But the Independence of the Colonies, although acknowledged, Monsieur de Chateaubriand contends, will never be secure if Spain shall withhold her recognition. The force of this argument has already been admitted to a certain degree—but that admission has its limits.

We do not complain that Monsieur de Chateaubriand exacts from Great Britain even an excess of honourable forbearance. But the evils of delay, not to the interests of Great Britain only, but of the World, cannot be left wholly out of contemplation. If we are to wait till Spain shall think fit to abdicate her passive Sovereignty, who shall guaranty the extent of that delay? The Low Countries threw off their Allegiance to Spain in 1576—they were independent *de facto*, and were acknowledged by England in 1577, and by France, as well as England, in 1596. The recognition of their independence by Spain, however, was not obtained till the Treaty of Münster, in the year 1648. Is it now intended to be proposed, that the like passive resistance on the part of Spain, in regard to Spanish America, shall be respected for the like period of half a century?

What is to be, during such an interval, the situation of so large a portion of the habitable Globe, proscribed from all legitimate rank among Nations?

Note IX

But the different States of America, says Monsieur de Chateaubriand, are in different degrees of forwardness, both as respects their separation from Spain and as regards their own internal settlement. And there are, not one, but five or six States to be acknowledged.

It follows that they may be acknowledged, if necessary, at five or six successive periods ; and that we may, if we think fit, measure our advances to acknowledgment according to their respective advance towards a fitness to be acknowledged.

There is not one of them that is not superior in point of extent, and not far inferior in population, to many of the States of Europe ; and there is not one in which the succession of changes in the form of government has been more rapid during the last fourteen years, than it was in France during the period (of about equal length) referred to by Monsieur de Chateaubriand, that of the transit from the Convention to the Empire. It must be remembered too, that, as in respect of the internal state of any country, recognition is not alliance, so, in respect to the internal state of such country, recognition is not guarantee.

We have, however, taken means to inform ourselves of the progress of each State towards a settled and stable form of Government.

The French Government has done the same. It has lately had Emissaries in Mexico, who may have reported to it on the Affairs of that great Province ; and the State of Buenos Ayres (*sic*) has at least not retrograded since 1819, when France thought it ripe for the offer of a Bourbon Prince to consolidate its institutions.

What may be the form of Government best suited to the Provinces, when independent, it is not for us to decide ; still less to make any particular form of Government a condition of our acknowledgment of that Independence.

Whatever our wishes may be, such is not the mode of accomplishing them.

Note X

Nor can we agree with Monsieur de Chateaubriand in thinking that an European Congress would have a greater influence *in this respect* than Great Britain alone.

On the contrary, the opinion of a Nation in possession of a free Constitution is surely, *in this respect*, more likely to be listened to with complacency than that of a Congress of Powers, the greater part of whom might be suspected, however unjustly, of wishing to impose upon the new States a model more strictly Monarchical. Nor must it be forgotten that the ' moral influence ' of the European Alliance (on which Monsieur de Chateaubriand is disposed so greatly to rely) has, in the instances in which it has been successful, been backed by practical interference.

The ' moral influence ' of Laybach was enforced by Austrian Arms in Piedmont and in Naples. The ' moral influence ' of Verona was aided by a successful invasion of Spain.

We doubt not that, in the present instance, the abjuration of force is sincere. But is it possible to flatter ourselves that implicit faith will be placed at once by the American Provinces in the sincerity of that abjuration ? or that, even when events shall prove it to be sincere, the abstinence from force will be attributed merely to unwillingness to employ it ?

In the long interval which (Monsieur de Chateaubriand admits) must elapse before the designs of a Congress of Five Powers could be fully matured and developed, what would be *our* situation if we suffered our determination as to the *not* employing force to remain doubtful ? What would be the situation of the *Alliance* if by us *alone* that determination were declared ?

Such are the principal arguments suggested in Monsieur de Chateaubriand's Despatch. Upon the whole, there is nothing in these amicable suggestions that leads us to repent of the answer which we have given to the Spanish Government.

To that answer, itself, we refer for the positive grounds on which our decision has been founded, and for a justification of the disinterestedness of that decision to Spain, to the Alliance, to the Old World, and the New.

(b) *Canning's Interpretation of the Polignac Memorandum* [1]

[The suppressed passages of the Polignac Memo were printed for the first time by me in *Cambridge History of English Foreign Policy*, ii. 633–7.]

F.O. Mexico, 204/4, No. 11, 9th September 1825. Canning to H. G. Ward.

" In reply to your No. 7 of 3rd June. As to the intentions of this Country with respect to any future possible contest between the New States of Continental America and the Allies of Spain in Europe.

" It did not occur to me that His Majesty's intentions in this respect could be liable to any misconstruction.

" The declaration made by me in the Conference with the Prince de Polignac in October 1823 was calculated to produce the effect (which in fact it did produce) of warning other Powers against intermeddling in the Contest between Spain and the American Provinces which had declared their independence—not by holding out to these Provinces any promise of co-operation on behalf of this Country, but by intimating that, in the event of any other Powers taking an active part in the contest, His Majesty reserved to himself the discretion of considering what course the interests of His People might call upon His Majesty to adopt, in a War which would then assume a general, instead of a civil, character.

" In consequence of this declaration, the Countries of Spanish America have been able to arrive unmolested at that point at which it has appeared to the British Cabinet that their character of independent Governments is fully established. As such His Majesty has acknowledged them ; and it is certainly from no want of effort on the part of His Majesty that His Majesty's acknowledgment has not been accompanied by that of the Mother Country.

" It never was intended by the British Government that this declaration should be held out to the American Provinces, or understood by them, as a Treaty of defensive Alliance, and yet such would be the character of an Engagement which pledged this Country generally and indefinitely to defend the New States of America against all attacks from Europe.

" That any such attack should be made is highly improbable : it is perhaps scarcely less improbable, that, in the event of an extension of the War, now unhappily existing between Spain and her late Colonies, to other Powers, England could long avoid being drawn into its vortex.

" But while every consideration, alike of interest and of humanity, will induce the British Government to continue to employ every effort to avert a calamity so grievous to Mankind as such a

---

[1] [Canning here points out that the situation of Mexico, recognised as independent in 1825, is different from that of 1823 under the Polignac pledge.]

War would be, it must not be conceived that this Country either has contracted, or is disposed to contract, any engagement, express or implied, such as would make its taking part in any War, which its efforts may not be successful in preventing, a matter of positive obligation."

F.O. Mexico, 204/4, No. 14, 14th October.   Canning to H. G. Ward.

" You went a little too far.   You represent yourself to have stated that, ' in the event of direct Hostilities being contemplated, then, indeed, H.M.'s Govt. was PLEDGED to take a *part in the Contest*.'

" That in the event of such Hostilities, Great Britain could not long avoid being involved in the Contest, may be true ; but that She is positively, and for all time to come, pledged to take part in any Contest which may arise between any Power of Europe and *independent* Mexico is a Proposition which you are to be very careful neither to advance yourself, nor to admit if advanced by the Mexican Government.

" The British Government has given no such pledge to Mexico, and it is not the policy of the British Government to fetter by such pledges its Decision upon future contingencies, and with respect to cases hypothetically proposed."

(c) *The Third Cabinet Memo on Recognition, December* 1824

[This Memo is in the Vansittart papers, unsigned and undated, but is written *after* the 10th December 1824.   Stap., *Corr.*, i. 212, shows evidence that Canning is returning Liverpool a paper " in heads of which there is one more than Hydra had."   The Memo here given has eight heads only, and unless subsequently altered, cannot be the one thus indicated, which seems to be a Memo of Liverpool's, *i.e.* the second Memo.   This was therefore, the third. On 14th December Canning writes, ' I am recasting mine,' and this would seem to indicate that the Memo here quoted is, in fact, by Canning.   The use of ' I ' throughout, with regard to diplomatic questions, seems inappropriate to anyone except the Foreign Secretary, and certain indications (*e.g.* the reference to Guatemala) suggest Canning.   At anyrate, this, the third, Memo on recognition is of fundamental importance.]

1. "The answer of M. de Damas and M. Villèle to Lord Granville is very unsatisfactory and embarassing (*sic*) with a view to our Parliamentary and Diplomatic proceedings, and it is difficult, after what has already taken place, to pass it by without serious notice.   Yet I am inclined to consider it as an honest and candid proceeding ; and as indicating much less of hostile intention than might have been enveloped in very civil and courtly language. M. de Villèle fairly stated the situation of Spain and the embarassments (*sic*) of France ; and I believe his description to be a true

one, and that the French Government would willingly renounce the advantages to be derived from the entrant it now possesses to be extricated from the difficulties in which it has been involved by its interference in Spanish affairs.[1]

I am, therefore, most anxious to take any course consistent with our honor which may render it possible to avoid any angry notice of the French answer. I think L[or]d Bathurst's suggestion of an appeal to the Allied Powers worthy of consideration, though it is certainly open to objection. I have no doubt the Allied Powers would support and justify the proceeding of France; but I think it likely they would explain and limit the occupation of Spain in a way which might relieve us from part of our difficulties. It would at all events gain time, which may be of importance in a question like this, which is one affecting honor at least as much as of substantial interest. Other measures may be suggested which, without leading to a hostile collision, would avoid the appearance of acquiescence in a long occupation of the Spanish fortresses. I do not believe that any progress has yet been made in the incorporation of the power of Spain (such as it is) with that of France : and I think it not at all improbable that in no long time we may see either very angry discussions arise between the two gov[ernmen]ts, or such a state of contest in Spain as may occupy a great part of the French power and resources.

2. The great practical question for us seems to be how, in the event of an actual incorporation of the resources of Spain with those of France, such an accession to the power of France can best be counteracted. I have no hesitation in saying that this must be by a separation of the resources of Spanish America from those of Spain : and it is (at least in this point of view) a fortunate circumstance that this state of things has already taken place; and that we are in a situation to avail ourselves of it without any imputation of bad faith; or even any cause of just resentment on the part either of France or Spain. We have only to pursue the course in which, deliberately, and with full notice to all parties concerned, we have for some years been engaged, and which (so far as I recollect) has never been made the subject of a distinct complaint. The least which can be said of the actual

---

[1] "It may be necessary here to state what I believe to have been the objects of the French Gov[ernmen]t in the invasion of Spain : (1) to terrify the Revolutionists of France by crushing those of Spain; (2) to recover the credit of the French arms and to attach the army to the Royal Family; (3) to gain the honor of freeing a Bourbon King from thraldom and thereby to re-establish something like the influence possessed by France over Spain during the Family Compact. In the first two objects the French Gov[ernmen]t has been successful, and if it could have obtained the third it would have been better pleased to withdraw the army wholly than to retain the Spanish fortresses at all the risk it may lead to, and the expense it must occasion. For the 30,000 men left in Spain will cost France at least £1,000,000 a year—a sum equal to the income of the indemnity proposed to the Emigrants."

situation of Spain is that she is incapable of making any effectual effort, without foreign assistance, for the recovery of those Colonies which have wholly thrown off their dependance (*sic*) on her, though she may be able to afford some aid to the Royalists in these provinces in which they still maintain the contest. With regard to the former, therefore, we are quite at liberty (consistently with all our former proceedings and independently of any considerations arising out of the French occupation of Spain) to take such a course as may appear most conducive to our own interests and policy. We have in fact not only established a great commercial intercourse with those Colonies, but we have taken several steps towards forming political relations with them, by the appointment of Consuls—of Commissions of Inquiry, and more recently by the measures taken towards entering into a commercial treaty with Buenos Ayres (*sic*) [23rd July 1824]. These very measures render it, however, more difficult longer to defer some similar proceeding with regard to the much more important States of *Mexico* and *Colombia*. With respect to Colombia, it may indeed be said that the same objection, which in the opinion of several members of the Gov[ernmen]t principally opposed the recognition of that State, continues to exist : and that, while the chief of the Columbian Gov[ernmen]t [Bolivar], at the head of its principal army, is carrying on a precarious warfare in a distant country [Peru], the very existence of the independant [*sic*] Gov[ernmen]t might be endangered by his meeting with any great reverse. Though I believe that such a reverse would rather produce some internal convulsion and change in the system of Colombia than do anything to reestablish the influence of Spain there, yet I think that, having waited so long for the crisis of the contest in Peru, it may be advisable to wait a little longer for its decision.

3. With respect to Mexico the case is different. Since our last consideration of the question an event has happened which adds materially to the firmness of that Gov[ernmen]t,[1] and though our official intimation from them is but meagre, I think circumstances of public notoriety, or known from other quarters, sufficiently establish the fact of the complete separation of New Spain from the Mother Country. I am aware that the possession of Fort Juan d'Ulloa gives the Spaniards the control over the Port of Vera Cruz, and a nominal possession in the Mexican territory. I cannot, however, consider the possession of this insulated point, which is only maintained from its inaccessible situation, as materially affecting the question of the independence of the country.

If, then, we are of opinion that the independence of Mexico is substantially established, there are two reasons which powerfully weigh with me in favour of an immediate step towards opening a friendly connection with its Gov[ernmen]t.

[1] The attempt of Iturbide to recover his empire, its failure, and his execution.

4. The first is the magnitude of British interests which are involved in our intercourse with that country. M. de Villèle's observation that by the effect of British Capital and Industry we were effectually appropriating to ourselves the resources of the vast regions of Sp[anish] Am[erica] is peculiarly applicable to Mexico. The Capitals [*sic*] remitted *there* are in great part vested in concerns of a less transient and temporary nature than mere commercial speculations. They are sunk in mining and territorial concerns, which are extending every day to a vast amount, and which cannot be reached, nor indeed rendered lucrative, but at a considerable distance of time. It is impossible but that questions must arise out of these concerns in which the intervention of our Gov[ernmen]t will be required, or that it can be given with propriety and effect but through the medium of diplomatic relations.

5. The other and perhaps still more powerful motive is my apprehension of the ambition and ascendancy of the U[nited] S[tates] of Am[erica]. It is obviously the policy of that Gov[ernmen]t to connect itself with all the Powers of America in a general Trans-Atlantic league, of which it would have the sole direction. I need not say how inconvenient such an ascendancy may be in time of peace, and how formidable in case of war.

6. I believe we now have the opportunity (but it may not last long) of opposing a powerful barrier to the influence of the U[nited] S[tates] by an amicable connection with Mexico, which from its position must be either subservient to or jealous of the U[nited] S[tates]. In point of population and resources it is at least equal to all the rest of the Spanish Colonies ; and may naturally expect to take the lead in its connections with the powers of Europe. I by no means think it at present necessary to go beyond the mere relations of amity and commercial intercourse ; but if we hesitate much longer, and especially if our commercial treaty with Buenos Ayres should not take effect, all the new States will be led to conclude that we reject their friendship upon principle, as of a dangerous and revolutionary character, and will be driven to throw themselves under the protection of the U[nited] S[tates] as the only means of security.

7. The new State of Guatimala [*sic*] is in some respects similarly circumstanced with Mexico ; and of importance from the Ports it possesses both on the Atlantic and Pacific : but I have not yet sufficient information respecting its internal state to induce us to proceed in recognising it at present. It appears also that considerable and important portions of the territory it claims are likewise claimed by Colombia ; and these portions seem to comprise the British settlements in Honduras, Campeachy, and the Mosquito Shore.

8. It affords an additional reason for taking this opportunity of opening a political intercourse with Mexico, if we have an opportunity in doing so of again offering our mediation between that

country and Spain. I do not, indeed, expect any good effect from such an offer ; nor are we in any degree bound to make it : but it may give our recognition of Mexico a less offensive character towards Spain.

9. I would not connect the proceeding with the French occupation of Spain ; as it might appear that by taking an equivalent, we afforded a tacit sanction to that occupation; but represent it as a further advance in measures in progress, and in which we had already sufficiently announced our intention to proceed."

[*Note*.—This Memo is unsigned and undated, and in *B.M.* Add. MSS. 31237, ff. 258–65.]

APPENDIX IV

BOLIVAR'S OVERTURES TO CANNING (1825-6)

[In the text, Chapters VI and VII, reference is made to the views of Bolivar generally. Here the special nature of his relation to England is shown, together with some indication of his preference for monarchy in South America. Some of the following despatches have been quoted by Villanueva, but none of them *in toto* or in English. That of Maling is given here, therefore, *in extenso*. It will be seen that Bolivar made definite overtures to England for an alliance and a guarantee. Canning never replied to them, but he sent a letter to Bolivar on the opening of the Congress of Panama. It was not delivered, as Bolivar was still in Peru, and in consequence was returned to London. I have been unable to find a copy of it.

The tendencies of Bolivar towards monarchy have been alluded to by many Spanish-American writers and are fully given here; but the proposal to renounce power himself, and to accept an English candidate for the throne, is less well known.]

(a) *Bolivar's Interview with Captain Maling* (18th and 20th March 1825)

F.O. Peru, 61/6. Captain Maling to Lord Melville

Cambridge—Chorillos, 18/20 *March* 1825.

(Private and Secret.)

MY LORD,

I am just returned from an interview with General Bolivar who sent for me ostensibly to communicate some intelligence which he had received by express from Columbia, it must however be of so old a date to Your Lordship, from the much quicker communication with the Eastern Coast of America, that I need only name to you that it had reference to Mons. Chasseriau's instructions as given in the *Morning Chronicle* of the 1st September 1824, and to the information contained in the Paper, of which I have the honor to enclose a copy and translation. Colombia I am told is taking every precaution against such a surprise, but if there ever was any serious intention on the part of France to land a force at Venezuela, I am inclined to think it will not now be carried into effect. That the French have only been waiting a favourable moment to give their assistance to the Spanish party, I have long been of opinion, and if Your Lordship has any grounds for believing that Admiral Jurien was prepared to land a force in South America, Your Lordship will perhaps agree that it was most probably intended that force should only act overtly after the great victory the Spaniards had fully calculated upon gaining previous to the battle of Ayacucho, when the hand of Providence seems to have given to the weaker party, one of the most extraordinary and most brilliant victories recorded in history, and inferior to none in point of importance to the New World. Had the Spaniards succeeded as they expected they should, and *butchered to a man* the whole of the Independent Army, then Rodil was commanded to leave only 50 old men in the Castles, and to harrass and protract the flight of Bolivar with all the troops he could collect together. And in that event it is by no means improbable that the French would have succeeded against Columbia, whilst Rosamel was lying at Valparaiso ready to co-operate with the *Asia* in the reduction of Chile, where the French have been indefatigable in their intrigues, and where they had managed to create considerable disaffection to the Government.

Thus they would have accomplished one of the Articles of their instructions which directs the blow shall be struck at the same moment throughout South America, and by this by no means illconcerted plan of co-operation, I am of opinion South America or the greatest part of it would have passed into the hands of France, as proposals were again sent to that country not long ago, proposing to place a French prince upon the Throne; I have no doubt the standard of France would now have been flying at Callao had it not been for the extraordinary success, which turned the whole aspect of affairs in favor of the Independent cause. But I must now bring under Your Lordship's notice the conversation which I had with the Dictator of Peru, and which seemed in fact to be his principal object in sending for me. Having conversed with me upon his Despatches from Colombia, and said he in some degree believed the account, for they were actually arming in Colombia from a conviction of its truth, he added, " But what can France or Spain expect to gain; they can never obtain a permanent footing in our Country. France has declared she will not tolerate popular Governments; that revolutions have distracted Europe for the last 30 years, and that America can never see Peace so long as she gives way to the popular cry of equality. And in truth I am of the opinion of France, for although no man is a greater advocate for the rights and liberties of mankind, which I have proved by devoting my fortune and the best years of my life to their attainment, still I must confess, this country is not in a state to be governed by the *people*, which one must allow after all is generally better in thought than in practice. No country is more free than England, under a well-regulated Monarchy ; England is the envy of all Countries in the world, and the pattern all would wish to follow in forming a new Constitution and Government.

"Of all Countries South America is perhaps the least fitted for Republican Governments. What does its population consist of but of Indians and Negros who are more ignorant than the vile race of Spaniards we are just emancipated from. A country represented and governed by such people must go to ruin.

"*We must look to England for relief*, we have no other resource. And you have not only my leave but my request that you will communicate our conversation and bring the matter under the consideration of H.B.M.'s Government in any manner which may seem best to you either officially or otherwise. You may say I never have been an enemy to Monarchies upon general principles ; on the contrary, I think it essential to the respectability and well-being of new nations, and if any proposal ever comes from the British Cabinet for the establishment of a regular Government, that is, of a Monarchy or Monarchies in the New World, they will find in me a steady and firm promoter of their wishes, perfectly ready to uphold the Sovereign England may propose to place and support upon the Throne.

" I know it has been said of me, *I* wish to be a king, but it is *not*[1] so ; I would not accept the Crown for myself, for when I see this Country made happy under a good and firm Government, I shall again retire into private life ; I repeat to you, if I can be of service in forwarding the wishes and views of the British Cabinet in bringing about this desireable object they may depend upon my service. I owe it to England, and I would infinitely sooner be indebted to England for its always generous and liberal assistance than to any other Country. France or Spain would treat with me no doubt, were I to make similar proposals to them, but never will I submit to any interference with America on the part of those odious and treacherous nations.

" The title of King would perhaps not be popular at first in South America and therefore it might be as well to meet the prejudice by assuming that of ' Inca ' which the Indians are so much attached to. This enslaved and miserable Country has hitherto only heard the name of King coupled with its miseries and Spanish Cruelties, and a change of Vice-King has invariably proved a change of one rapacious oppression for another. Democracy has its charms for the people, and in theory it appears plausible to have a free Government which shall exclude all hereditary distinctions, but England is again our example ; how infinitely more respectable your nation is, governed by its King, Lords, and Commons, than that which prides itself upon an equality which holds out little temptation to

[1] [Doubtful.]

exertion for the benefit of the State, indeed I question much whether the present state of things will continue very long in the United States. Indeed I wish you to be well assured I am not an enemy either to Kings or to an Aristocratical Government provided they be under the necessary restraints which your Constitution imposes upon the three degrees. If we are to have a new Government let it be modelled on yours, and I am ready to give my support to any Sovereign England may give us."

Thus I have endeavoured to give you, My Lord, the substance and as nearly as I could the words which were used by His Excellency, to which I merely replied, " I concluded a new Consul or Minister might soon be expected from England, that I had no authority to enter into any political discussion or arrangement with him, and that all I could do was to make it my duty to write to you privately an account of what had passed and I had no doubt Your Lordship would, if it appeared requisite, bring his wishes under the consideration of His Majesty's Ministers upon this private communication, in a sufficiently authentic form to expect they would be replied to in due time."

His Excellency was satisfied with my intention of writing to Your Lordship and more by my expedition, observing that the French were so busy in their intrigues, that unless advantage was taken of this favorable moment, when they might say they had no enemy in their Country, more difficulty might attend the measure. I have now only to add to this unavoidably long letter the brief account of what is passing here.

The Castles of Callao still hold out, they are closely besieged by land and sea, but the Batteries are not yet completed against them. Rodil keeps up the spirits of his men by assuring them the *Guerrero* (84) and two frigates may be hourly looked for, that they are bringing supplies of every description, and 2000 picked Troops. We have not however any reason to believe him to have received news of the *Guerrero* having passed Cape Horn. It is not improbable he has no news whatever of the *Guerrero*, but is trusting to the promises of General Serigo, a Spaniard of distinguished military talents, who went home a passenger in the *Aurora*. When he left this in June last, he went home confident in the success of the Spanish cause, from the immense exertions then making in Upper Peru. And I now mention to Your Lordship, I have since discovered he had a twofold object in going home, which I believe he managed to conceal from Captain Prescott under an assurance he was only going to Europe to be married. General Serigo took home with him an exact account of the Spanish forces in Peru, of their resources, and of their hopes ; he also took with him a plan of the year's campaign as it was intended to be carried on, and he took these for the information of the French Government, to whom he was in the first instance to apply, and to urge the necessity of their sending a French Prince and a French Army to deliver Peru. If General Serigo be traced, I think Your Lordship will find his first object in Europe was with the French Government.

When Serigo took leave of Rodil he promised faithfully to return within the year, and had the representations sent home by him been attended to immediately, Affairs in America would probably have been the reverse of what they are. The delay of the *Aurora* on her passage was a truly fortunate event for the Peruvians.

The only force now in Upper Peru is Obaneta's. His riches and great popularity enable him still to maintain himself there, and it is difficult, from the contradictory reports that reach us, to say whether his Army is really dwindled to nothing, as some assert, or he be not gaining recruits from the fugitive Spaniards of Ayacucho. Obaneta's endeavours to embark and send off his immense property induces me to believe he cannot maintain himself long.

The Dictator having discovered some weeks ago that Captain de Moges, who was sent off by Adml. Rosamel to reside at Lima, had been intriguing, sent him off at two hours' notice. This was a strong measure, and I was anxious to know how it would be borne by the French Admiral.

He arrived here on Thursday and on Friday had his interview with the Libertado, expecting to see him, in order that he might explain away a circumstance at which he felt highly indignant. Bolivar appointed the hour, and I am told both parties got very earnest and warm. Most of the conversation passed in the presence of several. Rosamel tried to take up the business with a high hand ; he first insisted upon an explanation with regard to his Captain being sent off, which he considered as an insult to France. Bolivar told him he had done no more to Captain de Moges than France had done by the South American Agents who had landed on her territory and who not only were sent away, but had their papers seized. When France retracted and apologised, Peru would also submit. The Admiral protested his instructions were most positive and unequivocal, to observe a most strictly neutral part, but that the Libertador had not only insulted his country by turning out a gentleman who held no public situation there, but also by certain paragraphs in his journals ; alluding to one, which I enclose, in which the French are spoken of as the " *invincibles* of Egypt, St Domingo, and Waterloo." Bolivar allowed he was aware of the whole point of the paragraph, and that he admitted it might not be very palatable to his (Admiral Rosamel's) Countrymen, but, he added, "that style of writing began with France ; I have in the next room a collection of French papers, each containing *personal* insults to me. I have not descended to that yet, but you must not talk to me of giving you satisfaction for anything you may read in my papers till France, who was the first to offer insult, has apologised to me."

In short, after sparring in this way for 3 hours, the Admiral, finding he could make nothing of him, in some degree cooled, and they parted friends. I visited the Admiral the next morning, but he seemed mortified and full of spleen against Bolivar and his cause.

I think Your Lordship may calculate with certainty, that unless a large force arrives here from Spain, strong enough to drive off two heavy frigates and half a dozen corvettes, the Castles of Callao will not hold out beyond the beginning or middle of May. The *Blonde* [1] proceeded on her voyage (perfectly healthy) on the 17th inst., and I expect the *Briton* hourly here from Valparaiso. I should mention to Your Lordship that General Bolivar made his communication to me confidentially and that it is totally unknown to every one here, for I should add that although Bolivar is himself extremely popular, as popular as it is possible a Columbian should be in Peru, still there is such a jealousy, if not hatred, between the Peruvians and Columbians that there can be no real cordiality between the two people, until time and intercourse may lessen the prejudice, but I mention this with a view of explaining to Your Lordship why I feel justified in saying that notwithstanding the late successes of the Columbians in favor of Peru, the Country can scarcely be called in a quiet state, from the contending interests of party, which now they have no external enemy to fear will be getting more troublesome every day, and open a fine field to those who are employed by France and Spain to sow dissensions, and keep up an opposition to any plan for a settled Government, which either Bolivar or any one else might propose.

In conclusion, I have only to assure Your Lordship that I have placed no further faith in the news from Columbia than may be necessary to thwart any surprise which might be intended on this side, it merely keeps me alive to what is passing without my deviating from the line of conduct I am commanded to pursue as a Neutral. And having thus intruded upon Your Lordship's patience where I thought it my duty to do so, I have only to apologise for any part of my letter which may not be so intelligible as I could wish to make it at the distance I am from you.—I have, &c.

(*Signed*) THOS. MALING.

[*Endorsed*].—Copy of a letter from Capt. Maling to Lord Melville, dated Chorillis 18/20 March 1825. Recd. 25th July.]

(b) *Bolivar's Conversations in* 1826 *on the Congress of Panama*

[These are of less importance than that with Maling in 1825 and can, therefore, be summarised with illustrative extracts. They are all despatches by the British Consul-General, Ricketts,

[1] Lord Byron's ship. [In pencil.]

in Peru. They certainly do not suggest that Bolivar thought that the Congress of Panama had been a failure.]

F.O. Peru, 61/7. Ricketts to Canning, 18th February 1826, secret.

Bolivar expressed his great sense of the obligation, never to be forgotten, of this country [Colombia or Peru?] for the high and liberal policy towards it which you [Canning] had so firmly, ably, and irresistibly maintained.

" So long as she [England] did not form the ' Bridge ' to this country, he [Bolivar] had nothing to fear from others. England was the Ally he most sought and should most court. . . . There might be jealousies among each other (*sic*) and could be none with us [England]." He [Bolivar] " did not uphold a Republican form of government as superior to any other." Brazil had an Empire, there was a Federation in the States of the Rio Plata (Buenos Aires). He did not care much about the Federal System. He had ' his own notions ' for Colombia, and ' other forms again ' for Upper and Lower Peru. The Congress of Panama should produce closer political relations between Spanish America, Great Britain, and the United States. He was anxious for Great Britain to be represented there. If the League (of Spanish-American States) was achieved, he personally would retire to France or to Italy.

F.O. Peru, 61/8. 1st June. Ricketts to Canning.

Bolivar said he had ' every friendly disposition ' and ' no hostile feeling against Brazil.' He was ' decided in taking no part with Buenos Aires ' in the war against Brazil, and turned to England to negotiate an armistice.

14th July. Ricketts to Canning, secret, received 11th December 1826.

Bolivar pleased at the appointment of a representative of England at Panama. He looked to her for ' guarantee and alliance.' " England must necessarily take in her hands the needle of this balance." There was in South America ' anxiety to be guided by the counsels of Great Britain '. . . . " The several States required to be upheld by the power and influence of Great Britain, without which no security could be expected, no consistency preserved, and no secret compact maintained."

5th September 1826. Ricketts to Canning (summarised).

Bolivar stated himself as pleased with the results of the Panama Congress and its transfer to Tacucayba.

He hopes to apply the Bolivian (*i.e.* monarchical) system to Colombia. He did not like the proposed Mexican-Colombian attack on Cuba. As regards the Spanish-American States obtaining recognition of their independence by Spain, he thought the money-compensation idea now quite impossible. He hoped that Great Britain would mediate in the matter. Ricketts adds that Bolivar may possibly become head of the three States, Peru, Bolivia, and Colombia.

APPENDIX V

GEORGE IV., METTERNICH, AND HANOVERIAN DIPLOMACY (1825–7)

[The following despatches throw light on some of the most obscure transactions in Hanoverian Court history and diplomacy. The diplomacy of the first three Georges was made clear in *Great Britain and Hanover*, by A. W. Ward [1899]. That of George IV. after 1822 has always been obscure. It was, however, plainly at variance with that of his Minister between 1823–4. On 11th March 1825 (Stap., *Corr.*, i. 258) Canning writes to Granville as to " some incredibly ill-advised expressions in a letter from too high a quarter to Prince Metternich himself." The text of this I have not found in *V.S.A.*, though there is an allusion to it. The first step in recantation was taken by George in a letter of 10th May 1825, which he directed Münster to write to Metternich (v. *supra*, p. 250). On the 13th October 1825 Canning wrote to Granville (Stap., *Corr.*, i. 298), " I have still another reason as part and proof of that new footing : the King has of late directed Münster to communicate to me all the Hanoverian correspondence. *Comprenez-vous ?* " The further sign of this surrender is the despatch of 8th November, here reproduced as (*a*). Canning sent off the text to Granville on 13th November (Stap., *Corr.*, i. 322). " You are not to show it, nor copy it, and are to return it to me by the return of the messenger. When you consider who and what the writer is, what are his necessary prejudices, and of what sort his former connections, and of what character the transactions in which he has for so many years been engaged, you will see that such an *exposé* precisely at such a moment is the most unequivocal proof that it was possible to receive of a most important conversion [the King]. You will make allowance, as I do, for certain expressions, especially at the beginning, with regard to language used in relation to Spain),[1] which are probably employed in reference to former declarations of opinion at the time when the event to which they relate [invasion of Spain 1823] occurred. But with these and such like qualifications, the way in which every topic is treated is as nearly as possible what I myself would have

[1] *Vide infra*, p. 564 n.

prescribed, and certainly is not what I should have myself have ventured to expect from this quarter this time twelve months."

But we shall see how this exposition of Münster to Metternich on 8th November 1825 (a) developed, during 1826-7, into a regular set quarrel, v. (b).]

(a) *H. de W. MSS.*, 360/3. *Count Münster, London, to Count Grote (Hanoverian Envoy), Paris, 8th November* 1825. Translated.

" As the policy of the British Government with respect to the revolutions in various countries is regarded in different lights, I think it my duty to state to Your Excellency the manner in which it views of the more important political events of the present moment. Generally speaking, great injustice is done to this Cabinet if it is represented as entertaining a predilection for what is (*sic*) called the liberal ideas of this age. It is known here, as well as at other courts, that every Government, however perfect, is exposed to the attacks of the revolutionists, that manifest errors in those Governments facilitate those efforts, and that the wisest measures to counteract the mixed attempts of (*sic*) overturning existing institutions are not wholly efficacious. What, therefore, could England gain by fostering so dangerous a principle ? England, on the contrary, is sincerely desirous to (*sic*) overcome this principle, and it is only the manner in which this end is to be attained that causes differences of opinion, and such difference must naturally arise in England the moment that other courts lay it down, as an axiom, that they are called upon unconditionally to interfere in every quarrel between governments and their subjects, to lift their swords on behalf of the former, without considering that the quarrel *may have arisen from abuses above the measure of indurance* (sic) *which may reasonably be required of human nature.*

" Your Excellency, perhaps, remembers that during the negotia-tions at Vienna, for completing the laws of the Confederation, we endeavoured to establish the principle of interference on the part of members of the Confederation, in differences between the German Governments and their States, upon a basis calculated to prevent that error. Now, in similar occurrences, upon the great Theatre of the World, where the interest to maintain existing things by the force of arms, regardless of the question whether what exists does so justly or not, becomes manifest or becomes probable, a Cabinet like that of Great Britain, which is obliged to render an account of its conduct to Parliament, cannot possibly follow in the steps of other Nations —a party assuming the right of interference *admits that the opposed party has the same right* in similar circumstances. To act upon this principle in England were Treason against the Constitution. For instance, in the Spanish Revolution, objectionable as it was, and great as was the right of France to put an end to it for the sake of her own security, England could not pursue the same line of conduct as her Allies, England, for the purpose of liberating Spain from foreign domination, had made enormous sacrifices ; King Ferdinand, by errors of the first magnitude, *had almost compelled his subjects to revolt.* Thus circumstanced, was King Ferdinand to be simply restored to a throne which his own measures, more than rebellious subjects, had overturned ? Would it not have been proper to have established something more durable ? This error England could not commit. I have no doubt that, in other quarters likewise, it is regretted that King Ferdinand should have frustrated the attempt of the Allies to introduce a better order of things in Spain by dismissing a Minister [1] agreeable to them and who shared their equitable views, and throwing himself into the arms of a Priest cast (*sic*) of which 45 Bishops out of 50 voted for the establishment of the Inquisition.

" These circumstances ought to serve as an apology for the political conduct of England with respect to Spain, though some of the sentiments entered in the course of these transactions are not perhaps to be approved.[2] Her conduct relative to the Spanish Colonies is founded upon similar grounds. They have paid too little attention upon the Continent to what Spain, the Mother Country, has herself effected in South America during the two Revolutions ; to the fact that she herself had losened (*sic*) the tie of subjection and granted an equality of civil rights. Could it be required, or was it to be expected, that *these extensive Countries, so long oppressed, should patiently return to their former slavish* condition, or could any hopes be entertained that *a feeble and miserable Government* would find the means of *reducing those* Colonies to its sway ? Could this be effected by mediation, whilst Spain at home was incapable of enjoying such tranquillity ? *How long was England to suffer this state of uncertainty* which hovers over the fate of the New World ? Commerce had intervowen (*sic*) enormous capitals with the industry of that portion of the Globe : how were these to be protected ? how were the numerous trans- actions arising from this intercourse to be adjusted while South Americans were to be regarded in the light of rebels ?

" In the case of Brazil, England *has furnished proofs of its desire to preserve the Portuguese Monarchy.* Though much has been said about the division of this Monarchy, the Brazils could be pre- served to the House of Braganza only by the steps taken by Don Pedro, and at first with the express approbation of the King, his father," [*i.e.* by Pedro declaring himself Emperor.]

[This affair concluded by the Treaty (29th August 1825) between Portugal and Brazil.]

" The affairs of Greece still threaten Europe with fresh dis-

---

[1] Zea de Bermudez.
[2] A reference to Canning's speeches of 14th and 30th Apr. 1823.

turbances. The mediation of the Allied Continental Powers, as Your Excellency knows, has led to no result. *This was to be expected*, since no coercive measures were to be employed. The Greeks were not satisfied with a mere *garantie verbale*, and better treatment on the part of their cruel oppressors, who in return required unconditional subjection. England could be no party in the mediation at Constantinople, *as she foresaw the way in which it would terminate*, and clearly perceived that the object of the Cabinets was more to prevent Russia from taking up arms, and *procuring the Porte time to suppress the revolt of the Greeks by the sword*, than to settle the existing differences upon an equitable basis. England, however, without recognising the independence of the Greeks, granted them the rights of a belligerent power, *in order to confine the war within the bounds fixed by civilisation.*

" This has been regarded by the Turks, and other Powers who desire that the Turks should be considered as rebels and not entitled to the rights of neutrality, in an unfavourable light. Thus circumstanced, the Greeks, convinced that their reverses in the last campaign were owing in some measure to their internal divisions, formed the resolution of placing themselves under English protection. That this idea did not originate in this country is evident from Mr Canning's answer to the Greek deputies and the royal proclamation respecting the strict neutrality to be observed, and which was not issued till after the interview had taken place. Mr Canning explicitly stated to the deputies that Great Britain was bound by European treaties, and by treaties with the Porte ; that the former prevented the increase of one State at the expense of another—and that upon the treaties with the Porte, which the latter faithfully observed, depended the trade with the Levant ; and that the Greeks probably benefited more by the neutrality of England than by a declaration in their favor, as such a declaration might lead to a war in which their interests would be put in the background." [1]

MÜNSTER.

Dorso. London, 8th November 1825.

[Copy of a letter from Count Münster to Count Grote.

Similar despatches were written to Hanoverian Envoys at Vienna and Petersburg.]

Count Ruisby Philipp (Hanoverian *chargé d'affaires* at Paris) acknowledged this on 21st November 1825 : " I must confess that the twofold character of our gracious Monarch has often excited in me doubt and perplexity, when drawing up my reports, as to

---

[1] The italics represent passages underlined in pencil, apparently by Canning himself. He cannot have liked the allusion to his speeches of Apr. 1823. But this was obviously rendered necessary by former correspondence which has perished. George IV. held to the principle that he defended the actions, but was not obliged to defend the speeches of his minister. He assented to the former, but not to the latter.

the nature of many terms I have employed. But your Excellency's most important despatch of the 8th of this month has rendered my task perfectly easy."

(b) *Despatches Illustrating the Münster-Metternich Quarrel* (1826–7)

(i) *Count Münster, London, to Cte. de Merveldt (Hanoverian Envoy), Vienna, 14th November 1826.*[1]

Les dépêches que Vous avez adressées au Roi me sont exactement parvenues jusqu'à celle du 18 Octobre inclusivement. Je n'ai pas tardé à les soumettre à Sa Majesté qui les a lues avec tout l'intérêt que réclament les circonstances compliquées qui agitent les régions orientales et occidentales de l'Europe. Le Prince de Metternich parait donc encore mécontent de la conduite de la Grande Bretagne. Je n'ai pas hésité à lire au Roi la communication que Son Altesse Vous avait faite le 25 Septembre et dont Elle avait eu l'intention de m'entretenir, si j'avais pu me présenter au Johannisberg.

Vous connoissez, Monsieur le Comte, la correspondance que j'eus avec le Prince sur le même sujet lors de Son dernier séjour à Paris. Mon opinion n'a pas changé depuis. Je ne puis que rendre hommage à la justesse des raisonnemens qui guident le Cabinet Britannique dans les affaires du moment ; mais je n'en regrette pas moins sincèrement une divergence dans les opinions des deux Cabinets qui pour le bonheur de l'Europe ne devraient jamais agir que de concert.

Le Prince de Metternich en impute la faute au Ministre qui dirige dans ce moment les rapports politiques de la Grande Bretagne. J'avais espéré que Son opinion sur lui aurait changé par les efforts que celui-ci a faits, pour montrer en toutes occasion aux Cours alliées dans leur véritable jour les vues et les motifs qui dirigent la politique du Cabinet de Londres.

1. and 2. *Si les raisonnements sur lesquels ils sont basés ne sauraient être réfutés*, on ne peut lui supposer des vues cachées, lorsqu'il pretend travailler à rétablir un repos durable dans l'orient. Certes notre Roi n'est pas homme à se laisser tromper par des paroles, et rien ne Lui ferait consentir à des instructions par lesquelles un Ministre voudrait circonvenir les principes connus qui guident sa politique.

3. *On peut vouloir le même but et différer grandement sur les moyens d'y parvenir.* Le système politique de la Grande Bretagne est moins sujet à varier d'après les opinions personelles des Ministres qui se succèdent que ce n'est le cas ailleurs. Les intérèts de l'Empire sont publiquement discutés et (4) *la Constitution Britannique prescrit des bornes qu'on ne saurait outrepasser arbitrairement.*

5. *Je crois ne pas me tromper en observant qu'il s'est opéré un*

V.S.A., England, *Varia*, 1821, enclosed by Metternich to Esterházy, Italics my own. The *examen* by Metternich which follows (ii) was written end of November or early December 1826.

*changement dans la manière de voir du Prince de Metternich depuis
les dernières années.* Ce changement, s'il dure, me parait de nature
à devoir augmenter de jour en jour la divergence dans la marche
politique des Cabinets de Londres et de Vienne, que nous regrettons
sincèrement, car quelque soit le Ministre qui se trouvera au timon
des affaires de l'Angleterre, il lui serait impossible de suivre la marche
que le Prince de Metternich paraît s'être tracée depuis l'époque dont
je parle. Le maintien du système monarchique a de tout temps
été, et avec raison, un but principal de la politique de l'Autriche.
Ce but a dû mettre le Prince en opposition directe avec ceux qui
veulent le renverser. 6. *Mais faut-il, pour le soutenir, devenir
absolutiste, devenir le défenseur des abus de ce système, et l'ennemi des
garanties contre le pouvoir arbitraire?* Ce n'était pas là la foi
politique du Prince de Metternich après le rétablissement de l'ordre
en Europe. 7. *Relisez ses déclarations faites au Congrès de Vienne
à l'égard de l'acte fédéral de l'Allemagne et comparez-les à la marche
tenue par la Cour directorial à la Diète.* Quel est l'abus contre
lequel une plainte ait pu prévaloir, et y a-t-il encore quelqu'un en
Allemagne qui puisse espérer que le droits confirmés par l'acte
fédéral et garantis par toutes les Puissances de l'Europe seraient
soutenus et garantis par la Diète fédérale, lorsque le Prince le plus
insignifiant trouverait à propos de les violer? Il est inutile de
Vous citer des examples. Ils Vous sont suffisamment connus.

Quelle serait la suite de l'opinion que cette marche des affaires
a excité contre ma constitution dont devait dépendre la stabilité
de l'organisation politique de l'Allemagne, si jamais l'ordre actuel
serait ménacé d'un bouleversement? Certes, dans la pluspart des
Etats de l'Allemagne on ne compterait plus sur le soutien de la
Nation, auquel on est principalement redevable des succès obtenus
contre la France. Et à quoi a-t-on sacrifié cet immense avantage
de l'opinion publique? Etendons cette même observation aux
vicissitudes que le reste de l'Europe a subies depuis le même époque.

8. *Nous voyons le Cabinet de Vienne prendre une part active dans
les troubles qui ont éclatés dans d'autres pays.* Je ne voudrais pas lui en
faire une reproche, car je ne prétends pas, que toute autre Puissance
devrait suivre en cas pareil le système de la Grande Bretagne. Comme
celle-ci n'oserait jamais admettre une ingérence étrangère chez elle,
elle ne doit pas s'en arroger à là étranger. Les intérêts des Etats
continentaux peuvent leur prescrire une autre marche, parceque
les troubles excités dans un pays voisin peuvent facilement se
répondre au delà de ses frontières. Mais dans un tel cas d'urgence,
il ne devrait pas seulement être question de réprimer les troubles,
mais plustot de remonter à leur source, afin de prévenir leur
retour. Une Cour étrangère ne saurait avoir le droit de punir les
auteurs des troubles, bien que sa sûreté peut exiger de les calmer.
Elle devrait donc, pour ses propres intérêts, s'efforcer d'agir contre
la cause du mal, non contre les troubles qui n'en sont ordinairement
que les symtômes ou les suites.

9. *Le Prince de Metternich, de son côté, ne paraît soutenir que l'absolutisme.* La politique que *l'Autriche suit à* Madrid et à Constantinople, ainsi qu'à Paris, lui en donne l'apparence.

Vous savez tout ce qu'on a tenté pour faire modifier les constitutions données à leur pays par plusieurs des membres du Corps germanique au sud de l'Allemagne. Ce qui arrive aujourd'hui en Portugal, prouve encore ce que je viens d'avancer. Le Souverain légitime de Portugal renonce conditionellement à cette Couronne, en faveur de Sa fille, et de Son frère, en lui octroyant une constitution.

La grande majorité de la Nation Portugaise se montre satisfaite de cet acte, et la pluspart des principales Cours de l'Europe croient devoir la reconnaître comme émanant de la volonté Souverain. Il n'y a que l'Espagne qui employait jusqu'ici tous les moyens pour y mettre obstacle. Ses mesures devenaient même tellement hostiles, qu'elle refusait à recevoir le Ministre de Portugal comme tel à Sa Cour, et de rendre les armes des deserteurs portugais, auxquels elle avait accordé asyle en Espagne. Ce n'est qu'après que la Grande Bretagne lui fit sentir, qu'elle se verrait obligée à défendre le Portugal, si l'Espagne causerait une rupture, et que le Ministre Britannique quitterait Madrid, que le Roi d'Espagne enfin céda.

Mais le repos du Portugal n'en reste pas moins ménacé. La Reine qui a si souvent conspiré, a tâché de gagner les soldats qui étaient de garde à Son palais, et l'Infant D. Miguel sert de mot de ralliement aux ennemis de la Régence.

D'après les dépêches du 13 Octobre, il a été proclamé Roi absolu, par le Marquis de Chaves, près de Villa-réal. Cette tentative a échoué, mais une plus sérieuse s'est opérée en Algarve, où des troupes se sont declarées en faveur de l'Infant. Le Gouverneur de la province, Comte Alva, a été arrêté un moment. Il a fallu envoyer des troupes pour combattre les revoltés, et la Régente s'est vue obligée à réclamer la protection des troupes de marine des vaisseaux anglais dans le Tage, pour la sûreté de la famille Royale. Or, cette guerre civile n'est elle pas en partie provoquée par la conduite de *l'Infant D. Miguel, qui à son tour est dirigé par le Cabinet d'Autriche ?* [1]

Ce Prince ne saurait avoir aucun droit au Trône, tant qu'existe Son frère l'Empereur et Sa descendance mâle, qu'en vertu de l'acte auquel Il a si longtemps refusé Son assentiment. Pour Le soustraire au danger qui pourrait en resulter pour Lui, on Lui a cependant fait prêter secrètement et conditionellement le serment ; et au lieu de Le faire partir pour le Brésil, où l'Empereur l'a invité à venir, le Prince de Metternich vient d'y expédier le Baron Neumann, pour négocier des modifications à la Constitution qui déplait à Vienne.

Cette manière de faire prêter le serment à Dom Miguel, ne saurait

---

[1] Referred to in Metternich's despatch, heading No. 11, p. 574.

guères convenir à l'Empereur du Brésil, et moins encore au repos du Portugal, qui reste compromis, tant que la parti de la Reine et de l'infant et de l'Espagne pourra se prévaloir de Son nom pour fomenter des troubles. Ce n'est aussi qu'avant le départ des dernières dépêches de Sir H. Wellesley que le Prince de Metternich a mis cet Ambassadeur au fait de cette prestation de serment ; délai qu'on a tâché d'expliquer, en alleguant qu'il fallait attendre la dispense du Pape pour le mariage projeté entre Dom Miguel et Sa nièce.

Comment expliquer la politique de l'Autriche dans ce conflit entre l'Empereur D. Pedro et Son Frère ? L'acte du premier est une émanation de Sa puissance Souveraine applaudi par la majorité des Portugais. Cet acte peut être mal avisé ; mais il est capable d'être modifié et corrigé par l'autorité légitime. De l'autre côté, nous voyons un Prince qui n'est connu en Europe que par ses principes anti-libéraux. Peut-on espérer, que revêtu d'une autorité absolue, il sera moins redoubtable pour le Portugal, qu'une Régence limitée par une Constitution, sujette à être corrigée facilement ?

Faut-il une autre preuve qu'on protège l'absolutisme, lorsqu'on se déclare même contre l'autorité royale, là où on les croit en opposition ? Et que penser des prétendus efforts pour le maintien de la paix, lorsqu'on donne lieu, pour ainsi dire, à l'éclat d'une guerre dans la Peninsule ?

J'en reviens à la question orientale, qui fournit principalement matière de doléance contre l'Angleterre. L'Autriche se plaint, que l'Ambassadeur d'Angleterre ne communique plus avec l'Internonce d'Autriche. Ici on observe, au contraire, que ce Ministre n'a jamais accueilli les vues de l'Angleterre. Ce n'est pas là la ligne sur laquelle devrait se trouver les Agens de deux Cours amies. Mais elle est encore la suite de la divergence des vues sur le chemin à choisir pour rétablir le repos dans l'Orient.

La décision de la Porte sur l'Ultimatum russe ne saurait mettre un terme aux inquiétudes que sa position inspire. Elle vient d'accepter les conditions qu'on lui dicte ; mais elle tardera à les accomplir. En attendant la lutte contre les Grecs insurgés tiendra le dénouement de la question en suspens. La communication officielle du Protocôle de St Petersbourg du 4 Avril, qui a été faite de concert par la Grande Bretagne et la Russie, aux Cours alliées à la fin d'Août, Vous prouvera qu'on jugeait trop légèrement à Vienne cet arrangement. Les Cours alliées n'avaient-Elles pas déclaré Elles-mêmes, à l'ouverture des Conférences de St Petersbourg sur le sujet de la Grèce, que l'intérêt de Leur Peuple et de l'Europe entière exigeait, qu'on mît fin à une lutte qui laisse l'Europe dans un état d'inquiètude ?

Cependant ces Conférences n'ont eu aucun résultat satisfaisant. On voit continuer une lutte qui excite tant de passions, et qui, par les cruautés qui l'ont provoquée, et dont le spectacle révoltant se répète sans cesse, réunit les vœux des Peuples pour le succès des opprimées.

Ce que l'Angleterre a prédit en leur accordant le caractère de belligérantes ce qu'Elle a désiré éviter par ce moyen, est arrivé. Le commerce maritime de la Méditerranée souffre par une nuée de Pirates grecs et les malheurs de la Grèce se sont accrus. Il faudra voir maintenant à quel point la Cour de Vienne voudra concourir avec l'Angleterre et la Russie pour faire entendre raison à la Porte.

À quoi a mené un système qui a isolé l'Autriche, que l'opinion publique place à la tête de l'absolutisme ? On en voit les suites en Russie ainsi qu'en France. Il en a dû résulter que le Cabinet anglais s'éloigne d'un Ministre qui parait se montrer hostile aux garanties d'une liberté civile raisoñable et modérée ; car c'est un pareil système constitutionnel qu'on regarde ici comme le plus sûr soutien des trônes tout comme on croit que l'arbitraire absolu doit finir par les renverser en provoquant les révolutions. C'est entre ces deux systèmes que s'est établi aujourd'hui la lutte et non entre la Monarchie et les Revolutions.

10. *Il est inutile que je m'étende sur les rapports dans lesquels le Prince de Metternich se trouve avec les principales Cours de l'Allemagne, ou sur le degré de confiance dont il jouit parmi la nation allemande.* Vous êtes à même, Monsieur le Comte, d'en juger sur les lieux, et Vous déplorerez avec moi, qu'une Cour qui réellement mérite la plus grande confiance et un Ministre aussi habile et tellement fait pour être aimé, comme l'est incontestablement le Prince de Metternich, a cédé à un désir trop vif de se mettre à la tête du parti qui voudrait soutenir le système monarchique à en outrepasser les bonnes. Peut-il servir sa cause en tâchant d'établir l'opinion, comme si le Cabinet Britannique se trouvait placé au premier rang du parti liberal ? La faveur dont jouit ce Cabinet pourrait par là annoblir une' mauvaise cause, et l'éloigner de la bonne.

Le contenu de cette dépêche pourra peut-être servir à expliquer dans une conversation avec le Prince de Metternich ce qui me paraît la cause du manque de concert dont il se plaint. Je les ai détaillées parcequ'il m'a fait l'honneur de me communiquer ses plaintes, et parceque je crois me rendre digne de sa confiance en ne pas cachant mes véritables sentimens dont il ne revoque pas en doute (: je m'en flatte du moins :) la pureté quant à ma profession de foi politique qui lui est dès longtemps connue et qui n'a jamais varié.

J'ai l'honneur d'être etc., etc.

(ii) *Examen d'une dépêche du Comte de Münster à l'Envoyé d'Hannovre à Vienne, en date de Londres du 14 Novembre 1826* [1]

Le Comte de Münster, Ministre dirigeant de L. M. le Roi d'Hannovre résidant à Londres, a addressé le 14 Novembre une dépêche

[1] *England, Varia,* 21, end of November or early December 1826. Metternich to Esterházy. The italics are Metternich's.

ostensible à l'Envoyé de sa Cour à Vienne ; comme cette pièce nous a paru contenir plus d'une assertion hazardie, on a vu qu'elle meritoit la peine de la˙soumettre à un examen rigoureuse. A cet effet on citera souvent le texte de la dépêche, qu'on fera suivre des remarques applicables.

1. *Si les raisonnements* (: de Mr Canning :) *ne sauroient être refutés.* Cette supposition dont on deduit la conclusion que l'on ne peut lui supposer des vues cachées est tout au moins hazardie. Comment établir la proposition, que tels ou tels *raisonnements* d'un Ministre ne sauroient être refutés. Il faudroit au moins specifier le cas, s'il s'agissoit, par ex[emple] du raisonnement par lequel Mr Canning a voulu justifier par sa dépêche au chargé d'affaires britannique à Berlin le protocolle du 4 d'Avril et la conduite de la Grande-Bretagne dans la question de l'intervention, il a éprouvé une refutation, qui ne laisseroit pas de replique aux plus ardents amis de Mr Canning.

2. *Notre Roi ne consentiroit pas à signer des instructions par lesquelles on voudroit circonvenir les principes connus.* Du moment où il s'agit des principes *connus* de Mr Canning, il est certain que les instructions qu'il soumettra à S. M. B. ne seront pas de nature à circonvenir aux ci. C'est parceque les principes *connus* de Mr Canning et ceux des Ministres qui défendent le sistème conservateur diffèrent entre eux que le Comte de Münster ne doit point être surpris de ce que les instructions du ministre anglois pour l'Ambassadeur britannique doivent être différentes de celles que le Prince Metternich fait passer à l'Internonce autrichien.

3. *On peut vouloir le même but et differer sur les moyens d'y parvenir.* Voilà une vérité incontestable ; mais il reste à prouver que le ministre anglois actuel veuille arriver *au même but* que le ministre autrichien, et il est permis d'en douter.

4. Il en est du même du passage ou il est dit pag. 3 que la Constitution britannique prescrit des bornes aux ministres qu'ils ne sauroient passer *arbitrairement.* Cela est vrai dans le sens le plus restreint de cette parole, mais non dans le sens plus étendu. On présente du Portugal le Casus fœderis pour fournir des secours à la régence par l'Angleterre *existoit ou non.* Il auroit peu être plus facile de prouver la négation qu'il n'a été à Mr Canning par toute la subtilité de sa dialectique de prouver qu'il existoit. N'est-ce pas s'abandonner à une détermination arbitraire que de justifier et de faire dependre un parti aussi décisif d'une argumentation casuiste ?

5. *Je crois ne pas me tromper en observant qu'il s'est opéré un changement dans la manière de voir du Prince de Metternich depuis les dernières années.* Ce passage se lie à celui qui se trouve rapporté plus bas sous No. 7. Nous sommes d'avis que peu de Cabinets ont suivi sous le rapport des principes une marche plus regulière que le Cabinet de Vienne ; de même le Prince Metternich n'a-t-il jamais songé à ce que dans toutes les differentes questions le

Cabinet à Londres suive la même marche que le Cabinet autrichien ? Il n'ignore pas que sous plus d'un rapport il doit y avoir une difference dans la marche de l'un et de l'autre, mais si *le maintien du sistême monarchique* ainsi que l'assure le Comte de Münster *est avec raison* le but de la politique de l'Autriche, ce seroit l'endroit ou il pourroit associer à cette même tendance le ministre britannique et l'on pourroit induire de ce que le ministre hannovrien ne hazarde pas même dans ce passage à affirmer que le but de Mr Canning est également de conserver et non de bouleverser ou qu'il est plus avancé dans la confidence des vues de ce ministre qu'il n'ose l'avouer ou qu'il n'a point eu la sagacité de les penetrer.

6. Le Comte Münster va plus loin dans sa rédaction, il qualifie, le Prince Metternich *d'Absolutiste,* d'être le défenseur *des abus* de ce sistême et *ennemi des garanties contre le pouvoir arbitraire :* toute la page 4 renferme une diatribe contre le Chancelier de Cour et d'Etat, qui autorise que l'on demande au Comte Münster de fournir les preuves des propositions hazardies qu'il avance.

7. Quand il dit, *relisez les déclarations* (: du Prince de Metternich :) *faites au congrès de Vienne à l'égard de l'acte federal de l'Allemagne,* nous avouens n'en connoitre aucune qui soit en opposition *avec la marche tenue par la Cour directoriale à la diète.* D'avoir signé l'article 13 de l'acte de fédération germanique n'est point, arborer la banniere des fabricants de constitution ni en général ni en application particulière à l'Allemagne. Il faudroit pour qui tout ce paragraphe puisse se justifier, fournir avant tout des preuves, quels *sont les abus du sistême monarchique que le Prince Metternich a defendu ?*—qu'ils sont *les abus dont il a été porte plainte à la dicté* et contre les quels aucune plainte n'ait pu prevaloir ?—Il est dit à la fin de ce passage *qu'il est inutile de citer des exemples, ceux-ci était suffisament connus.* C'est précisement le contraire et c'est le cas de demander qu'on en cite : enfin, il faut que le Comte de Münster ignore la valeur du terme Absolutiste et Absolutisme repetés plusieurs fois dans sa dépêche, pour l'employer sans croire blesser par là et les égards dus au ministère autrichien et sans chocquer même aussi la consideration qu'il doit personnellement au Prince de Metternich.

8. *Nous voyons le Cabinet de Vienne prendre une part active dans les troubles qui ont éclaté dans d'autres pays.* Quand on écrit une pièce dogmatique, on devroit ne pas se meprendre sur les regles les plus simples de la langue dont on fait usage. Qui croiroit que la phrase *le Cabinet de Vienne prend une part active aux troubles qui ont éclatés dans d'autres pays* doit signifier, *le Cabinet reprime les troubles,* et cependant le passage qui suit *je ne voudrois point lui en faire un reproche* indique que le Comte Münster a dit ici le contraire de ce qu'il vouloit dire. Il consent et admet que le Cabinet autrichien agit dans ces circonstances selon son véritable intérêt parceque dit-il pag. 6 *les troubles excités dans un autre pays peuvent facilement se répandre au dela des frontières ;* mais ajout-

il *une cour etrangère ne sauroit avoir le droit de punir les auteurs des troubles et devroit s'efforcer d'agir contre la cause du mal.*

Il est evident, que tout ce passage se rapporte à l'intervention autrichienne dans la révolution de Naples de l'année 1820 et de celle du Piemont en 1821 aux operations des congrès de Troppau et de Laibach.

Le Comte de Münster paroit avoir en partie confondu et en parti oublié les transactions de cette époque.

La Cour de Vienne n'a agi que sur les réclamations des Souverains dans les états des quels des mouvements revolutionnaires avoient éclatés. Lors de l'occupation du Piemont par un corps d'armée d'observation, la Cour de Vienne proposa à l'Empereur de Russie de s'en charger. Quels sont les auteurs des troubles napolitains qui ont été punis par l'Autriche ? Elle a detenu sur la requisition du Roi de Naples quelques uns des principaux coupables, d'autres ont eu pour lieu de residence les états autrichiens; ce n'est pas là une punition infligie par l'Autriche. Quant au second point : savoir d'agir contre la cause du mal l'Autriche a fait ce qu'elle a peu ; c'est à ses conseils en partie qu'on doit les sages dispositions organiques emanées du Roi de Naples de Laibach au mois de 1821.

Nous verrons si l'influence angloise en Portugal engagera le gouvernement constitutionel à des mesures aussi propres à concilier les esprits que l'etoient celles qui furent adoptées alors par l'impulsion du Cabinet de Vienne.

9. La dépêche répète que le Prince de Metternich ne paroit vouloir soutenir que l'Absolutisme et après avoir ajouté *que la politique* de l'Autriche à Madrid, à Constantinople et à Paris le prouve, elle articule la question, que l'on sait et que cette puissance a fait pour modifier les constitutions données par plusieurs membres du corps germanique au midi de l'Allemagne? (Voyez fin de page Cet commencement de page 7.)

Cette accusation est encore d'une si insigne fausseté que l'on a de la peine à la combiner avec les notions et les souvenirs des transactions que le Comte de Münster devroit avoir et aux quelles le Cabinet hannovrien n'est pas resté étranger. Le Comte Münster a assisté lui même aux conferences qui eurent lieu à Vienne pendent l'hiver de 1819–1820 et concurrent à l'acte supplementaire de l'acte de la fédération germanique. Il a aidé à rediger les articles 54, 55, 56, 57, 58, 59, 60, and 61 de ce traité conclu sous les auspices et la presidence du Cabinet autrichien.

On abandonne au jugement de chaque lecteur impartial l'esprit et la tendence de ces articles qui attestent le desir de voir gouverner les royaumes et les principautés qui composent la confédération germanique non pas d'un regime constitutionel, mais de leur donner ou laisser des états qui prennent part au pouvoir legislatif.

Si la memoire du Comte Münster le sert avec exactitude il se rappellera à qui l'on dût la redaction de l'art. 59 qui ne cherche que dans des reglements disciplinaires le rémède contre les abus signales des lors par des gouvernements qui s'étoient donnés ce que l'on appelle une constitution. Plus tard quand ces mêmes gouvernements manifestèrent leurs embarras non seulement au Cabinet autrichien, mais encore à d'autres Cours de la confédération, le Cabinet de Vienne notamment, limita ses conseils aux mêmes moyens, savoir les reglements bien ordonnés, et ce sont là des démarches que le ministre hannovrien qualifie d'une action, qui tend à modifier les constitutions de membres du corps germanique du midi de l'Allemagne.

10. Le passage allegué est en rapport avec celui de la fin de pag : 13 et le commencement de pag. 14, où le ministre hannovrien interpelle l'Envoyé de cette cour pour le rendre juge *du dégré de confiance dont joint le Prince Metternich parmi la nation allemande et à déplacer qu'il se soit mis à la tête d'un parté qui veut depasser les bornes du sistême monarchique.* Il est inutile d'observer que le terme *de dégré de confiance* est employé en sens ironique, et ce la nous remarquerons que nous pensons être un juge aussi competent qu'un autre sur l'opinion des Allemands à l'égard de la politique de l'Autriche et du chef de son Cabinet. Il existe en Allemagne comme ailleurs dans le reste de l'Europe un parti qui peut se qualifier de *conservateur* et un autre au quel on est convenu de donner l'attribution de *liberal* ou de *révolutionaire*, sans ajouter ici quelques autres termes moins menagés, et qui sont devenus sygnonimes.

Le premier parti considère l'Autriche comme son appuy naturel, comme la puissance qui depuis la restauration de l'Europe a constamment employé ses moyens pour maintenir l'ordre établi, combattre les mauvaises doctrines et leurs effets, soutenir le foible contre l'oppresseur et persuader tous ceux qui auroient été disposés, sous quelque forme et sous quelque pretexte que cela fut, à abuser de leur pouvoir que l'Autriche tentera de reprimer cet abus.

Le second est le parti libéral dont la tendence se trouve en opposition manifeste avec des semblables principes, si le Comte de Münster entend parler de celui-ci, quand il dit que le Prince Metternich a perdu la confiance en Allemagne, on peut en convenir avec lui et doit ajouter que le ministère autrichien n'a jamais été jalouse de la mériter.

11. La partie politique que le ministre hannovrien discute avec le plus d'étendue et s'il est permis de le dire, avec le plus d'amertume, est celle qui se refère à la question portugaise ainsi que celle de la lutte entre la Porte et ses sujets Grecs insurgés ; accordons un instant d'attention aux reproches qu'il fait en ces deux points à la conduite du ministère autrichien.—Tout l'article relatif au Portugal pag. 7, 8, 9, 10, 11 fourmille d'assertions hazardiées et de fausses inductions.

Le ministre hannovrien affirme le 14 Novembre que la grande majorité de la nation portugaise se montre satisfaite de la constitution *octroyée* et six semaines après ses adherents auroient été obligés s'enfuir ou au Brésil ou en Angleterre si un corps d'armée angloise ne les soutenait contre la majorité de la nation portugaise.

Plus loin pag. 8 il est dit *que la guerre civile en Portugal est provoquée par la conduite de l'Infant D. Miguel dirigé à son tour par l'Autriche.*

Si on admet que l'Autriche dirige la conduite de l'Infant D. Miguel c'est donc à ses conseils qu'il faut attribuer et le serment qu'a prêté ce Prince et à ce que à l'heure qu'il est on ne le voit pas à la tête des royalistes en Portugal ?

Mais ajoute-t-on *le serment a été prêté secrètement et conditionnellement et on expédie M. Neumann à Rio Janeiro pour negotier des modifications à la Constitution qui déplait à Vienne.*

Le serment n'a pas été prêté secrètement, il a été prêté le 4 d'Octobre ; les fiançailles qui auraient lieu le furent à l'époque où il convenoit de parler des deux actes que l'Empereur Don Pedro avoit demandés être réunis ; si le ministère autrichien a tardé quelques jours à en donner connoissance officielle à l'Ambassadeur d'Angleterre on seroit tenté de demander sur quoi le ministère britannique fonde la prétention d'une confidence aussi precipitée et quelles sont les temoignages qu'il a donné dans les derniers tems en réciprocité au ministère autrichien de cet abandon de confiance qu'il exige ?

Le serment est tout aussi peu conditionel ; il a été prêté dans les termes prescrits dans les mains de l'Empereur du Brésil et non en celles de la régente. Cette reserve qui a mis à couverts les droits de D. Miguel à la régence n'a rien de commun avec la constitution et n'est nullement conditionelle relativement à celle-ci.

Quant aux modifications de la nouvelle constitution portugaise que M. Neumann doit négotier au Brésil, on est d'autant plus surpris de voir relever avec désapprobation au Comte Münster cette mission en ajoutant que la constitution déplait à Vienne, que M. Canning lui-même, dont *les raisonnements ne sauroient être refutés,* a exprimé dans son trop fameux discours du 12 Décembre que cette constitution n'avoit pas son entière approbation.

Plus loin pag. 10 le Comte de Münster convient lui même que cet acte peut-être malavisé qu'il est capable d'être modifié et corrigé par l'Autorité légitime, tandis qu'il faisoit pag. 9 quasi un reproche au Prince de Metternich d'avoir expedié à cet effet M. Neuman à Rio Janeiro.

12. On a-t-on pris enfin pag. 10 *que le Cabinet autrichien ne soit déclaré contre l'Autorité royale et qu'il donne lieu pour aussi dire à l'éclat d'une guerre civile ?* Enfin comment ose-t-on avancer pag. 13 que le Prince Metternich se montre *hostile* contre les garanties d'une liberté civile raisonnable et *moderée ?* Ce sont des graves accusations et si le Prince Metternich n'a pas demandé ou qu'on prouve cette assertion, ou qu'on la retracte, il a fait certes preuve de beaucoup de modération.

13. Venons à la manière dont le ministre hannovrien traite pag. 11 la question orientale. Il dit l'Autriche *se plaint de ce que l'Ambassadeur d'Angleterre à Constantinople ne communique plus avec l'Internonce autrichien,* plus bas à la fin de pag. 14 il repète que le Prince Metternich lui a fait l'honneur de lui communiquer ses *plaintes.* On doute que le Chancelier autrichien se soit jamais *plaint* de la conduite de M. Strattford Canning envers l'Internonce autrichien. Cela seroit au dessous de la dignité du Cabinet autrichien; autre chose est faire des observations sur la conduite politique d'un ministre, autre chose *s'en plaindre,* et d'après le sistême que la Grande-Brétagne a adopté à l'égard de la question orientale depuis sa declaration de neutralité en 1825 et la conduite tenue envers la Porte dans cette lutte entr'elle et ses sujets revoltés on savoit trop à quoi on avoit encore à s'attendre pour s'étonner ou se *plaindre* de la conduite du représentant de la Grande-Brétagne à Constantinople.

Le Comte Münster dit pag. 11 que l'on *s'étonne* que l'Internonce n'ait pas *accueilli* les vues de l'Angleterre.

L'Angleterre a persisté longtems à ne coopérer d'aucune manière à la pacification entre la Porte et ses sujets chrétiens revoltés. Cette isolation des 4 autre puissances alliées ne pouvoit certainement être accueilli par l'Internonce. Après la signature du Protocolle du 4 Avril elle juge à propos de s'en mêler en menaçant la Porte de l'emploi de mesures coercitives en cas de refus de l'intervention, principe que le Cabinet autrichien a constamment combattu et voilà que le ministère britannique prétend être étonné de voir ses vues non accueillies par le ministre autrichien à Constantinople?—En verité, il n'y-a pas là lieu à l'étonnement.

Plus bas le Comte Münster dit, que l'acceptation par la Porte de l'Ultimatum russe ne sauroit mettre un terme aux *inquiétudes* que *sa position* inspire et ajoute qu'elle tardera à les accomplir.— On retrouve dans cette dernière prédiction celles dont le Journal des Débats n'a cessé d'entretenir les lecteurs.

Quant à l'inquiètude que la position de la Porte inspire, on avoue ne pas entendre le sens de cette phrase, quand c'est le Comte Münster qui la prononce. Il ne paroit pas disposé à éprouver de la sollicitude par la position critique où est placée la Porte; et il n'abusera pas assez de notre bonne foi pour feindre que la Porte puisse inspirer de l'inquiétude à ses voisins?

On lit pag : 12 *qu'on a jugé à Vienne trop legèrement l'arrangement du 4 d'Avril.* On l'y a jugé d'après le texte de sa redaction dont l'obscurité et le manque de précision étoient palpables. Si les Cabinets anglois et russes jugent à propos d'y ajouter des nouveaux developpements, l'affaire pourra prendre alors un autre aspect. Ceux qui nous sont connus aujourd'hui 31 Janvier ne paroissent guères plus conséquents et plus logiques que n'étoit cette première redaction du 4 d'Avril.

14. La dépêche en question dit pag : 12. Ce que *l'Angleterre a*

prédit en lui accordant (: savoir aux Grecs :) *le caractère de belli-gérants et ce qu'elle a desiré éviter par ce moyen est arrivé.* Nous prenons acte de cet aveu du ministre hannovrien qui pour le coup ne paroit guères apologétique pour la déclaration du mois de Novembre 1824 par laquelle l'Angleterre reconnut au gouverne-ment grec provisoire les droits de Puissance belligérante.

Le Comte Münster demande pag : 13 comment la cour de Vienne voudra concourir avec l'Angleterre et la Russie *pour faire entendre raison à la Porte.* Il est à noter pour l'intelligence des termes que les Philohellenes comprennent par la phrase " faire entendre raison à la Porte," contraindre celle-ci à reconnoitre l'indépendance de ses sujets revoltés. C'est ainsi sans doute que la France à la paix de Versailles fit entendre raison à l'Angleterre quand celle-ci fut obligée de réconnoitre l'indépendance des états unis d'Amérique. Le Cabinet autrichien attache à ces termes une autre acceptation, sa reponse du 22 Décembre à l'office britannique en donne la mesure ; le Comte Münster y reconnoitra qu'il offre de concourir à chaque moyen pour parvenir à terminer les Calamités actuelles de la Grèce sauf à ceux qu'elle juge être contraires aux principes *du droit.*

Nous terminons ici l'analise d'une pièce, à laquelle nous n'avons donné tant d'étendue que parcequ'elle est émanie de la plume d'un ministre dont la sagacité a depuis bien des années tout autant merité l'approbation genérale que la loyauté de ses principes, et s'il s'agit de déplorer des erreurs, c'est l'égarement dans lequel les sophismes de Mr Canning ont fait tomber l'esprit du Comte Münster qu'il sera permis de déplorer.

(iii) *Count Münster to Count de Merveldt,* 9th February 1827
(communicated to Esterházy) [1]

" He [Metternich] drags the Emperor [Francis II.] into the contest and forgets that his attacks upon the policy of England affect my King. Mr Canning's speech is that minister's own work, he must answer for it ; but measures of the Cabinet, sanctioned by the King, the King himself defends when attacked from abroad. Of the political sins of Prince Metternich which I have mentioned, and which he denies, those committed in Spain I thought it my duty not to let pass unnoticed. Prince Metternich takes shelter behind his ostensible despatches ; King Ferdinand did the same. This prince had given orders to disarm the Portuguese deserters, but at the same time allowed them to be organised and encouraged for an attack upon Portugal. Count Villa Real's complaints against the Austrian Minister and the Marquis de Moustier prove

[1] *H. de W.,* 360/5. This is a sequel to the very angry dispute between Münster and Metternich at the end of 1826. *V.S.A.,* Metternich to Ester-házy, Nov. 3, Dec. 26/26, in Weisungen nach England. Metternich refused to continue the discussion, so Münster took this way of express-ing his views.

that although the public declarations breathed nothing but pure monarchical principles, they secretly promoted the attempt to overturn the new constitution by means of the Portuguese rebels before the English, who had declared that they would not interfere in the internal affairs of Portugal, could undertake any serious measures. I claim some merit in not admitting the contrast between the unchangeable policy of Austria and that of England; Prince Metternich knows the saying, *che in questo mondo mutabile e legrero e spesso il variar parsieu*. When he accuses England of fickleness, he certainly forgets his residence at Paris, Napoleon's marriage with the archduchess, his alliance against Russia, and the correspondence communicated by Baron Fain.   Münster.

" *P.S.*—Prince Esterházy tells me that he is going to transmit my answer to Prince Metternich, and he begs me to bear in mind how highly Prince Metternich values my confidence, though he cannot subscribe to my opinions. Let our friend Hardenberg see this correspondence. They seem to have taken it into their heads to send England to Coventry so long as Canning remains at the head of the Foreign Office. What a pretty sort of continental system that would lead to ! "

APPENDIX VI

THE CORRECTED AND ORIGINAL VERSIONS OF CANNING'S SPEECH ON PORTUGAL OF 12TH DECEMBER 1826

[The study and comparison of these two versions is of the highest importance, as the numerous corrections inserted have, many of them, great significance.]

Speeches of Canning

Therry [1836], vol. vi. pp. 89–92.

Star, 13th December 1826

[The *Star* was in close touch with the entourage of Canning, and the report represents a correct momentary impression of the Speech.]

It will be for Spain, upon *knowledge* [1] of the step now taken by His Majesty, to consider in what way she will meet *it. The* earnest hope and wish of His Majesty's Government is, that she may meet it in such a manner as to avert *any ill consequences to herself,* from the measure into which we have been driven by the unjust attack upon Portugal.

a communication

the call.   My

to avert the consequences of the Message before us.

Sir, I set out with saying that there were reasons which *entirely satisfied my judgment* that nothing short of a point of national faith or national honour *would justify* at the present moment, any voluntary approximation to the possibility *of war.* Let me be understood, however, distinctly, as not meaning to say that I dread war in a good cause (and in no other may

induced me to think

I will not say would justify, but would make desirable of a dangerous war.

[1] Where any serious divergences occur, the beginning only is in italics, and the other version will be found in the right-hand column.

it be the lot of this country ever to engage !) from a distrust of the strength of the country to commence it, or of her resources to maintain it. I dread it, indeed—but upon far other grounds : *I dread it from an apprehension* of the tremendous consequences which might arise from any hostilities in which we might now be engaged. Some years ago, in the discussion of the negociations respecting the French war against Spain, I took the liberty of adverting to this topic. I then stated that the position of this country in the present state of the world was one of neutrality, not only between contending nations, but between *conflicting* principles ; and that it was by neutrality alone that we could maintain that balance, the preservation of which I believed to be essential to *the welfare of mankind*. I then said that I feared that the next war which should be kindled in Europe, would be a war not so much of armies, as of opinions. *Not four years have elapsed, and behold my apprehension realised !* It is, to be sure, within narrow limits that this war of opinion is at present confined : but it *is* a war of opinion that Spain (whether as Government or as nation) is now waging against Portugal ; it is a war which has commenced in hatred of the new institutions of Portugal. How long is it reasonable to expect that Portugal will abstain from retaliation ? *If into that war* this country shall be compelled to enter, we shall

I dread it from a consciousness of the tremendous power Great Britain possesses of pushing hostilities in which we may be engaged, to consequences which I shudder to contemplate (*Hear, hear, hear.*)

contending

peace and safety of the world.

Four years' experience . . . has confirmed rather than altered my opinion.

I fear that the next war to be kindled in Europe, if it spread beyond the narrow limits enter into it with a sincere and anxious desire to mitigate rather than exasperate—and to mingle only in the conflict of arms, not in the more fatal conflict of opinions. But I much fear that this country (however earnestly she may endeavour to avoid it) could not, in such case, avoid seeing ranked under her banners all the restless and dissatisfied of any nation with which she might come in conflict. It is the contemplation of this new *power* in any future war which excites my most anxious apprehension. It is one thing to have a giant's strength, but it would be another to use it like a giant. The consciousness of such strength is, undoubtedly, a source of confidence and security ; but in the situation in which this country stands, our business is not to seek opportunities of displaying it, but to content ourselves with letting the professors of violent and exaggerated doctrines on both sides feel that it is not their interest to *convert an umpire into an adversary.* The situation of England, amidst the struggle of political opinions which agitates more or less sensibly different countries of the world, may be compared to that of the Ruler of the Winds, as described by the poet :

of Spain and Portugal, will be a war of most tremendous character—a war not merely of conflicting armies, but of conflicting opinions. (*Cheering.*)

I know that if into that war this country enters (and if she do engage, I trust it will be with a most sincere desire to mitigate rather than exasperate, and to contend with arms, rather than with the more fatal artillery of popular excitation), she will see under her banners, arrayed for the contest all the discontented and restless spirits of the age, all those who—whether justly or unjustly—are dissatisfied with the present state of their own countries. The consciousness of such a situation excites all my fears, for it shows there exists a power to be wielded by Great Britain, more tremendous than was perhaps ever yet brought into action in the history of mankind. (*Hear.*)   But, though it may be " excellent to have a giant's power it may be tyrannous to use it like a giant."   The knowledge that we possess this strength is our security ; and our business is not to seek, etc. . . .

" their umpire into their competitors." (*Hear.*)

The situation of this country may be compared to that of the Ruler of the Winds.

" Celsâ sedet Aeolus arce,
Sceptra tenens ; mollitque
    animos et temperat iras ;
Ni faciat, maria ac terras
        coelumque profundum
Quippe ferant rapidi secum,
    verrantque per auras."

The consequence of letting loose the passions at present chained and confined, would be to produce a scene of desolation which no man can contemplate without horror ; and I should not sleep easy on my couch, if I were conscious that I had contributed to precipitate it by a single moment.

This, then, is the reason—a reason very different from fear—the reverse of a consciousness of disability—why I dread the recurrence of hostilities in any part of Europe ; why I would bear much, and would forbear long ; why I would (as I have said) put up with almost any thing that did not touch national faith and national honour, rather than let slip the furies of war, the leash of which we hold in our hands—not knowing whom they may reach, or how far their ravages may be carried. Such is the love of peace which the British Government acknowledges ; and such the necessity for peace which the circumstances of the world inculcate. I will push these topics no farther.

I return, in conclusion, to the object of the Address. Let us fly to the aid of Portugal, by whomsoever attacked ; because it is our duty to do so ; and let us cease our interference where that duty ends. We go to Portugal, not to rule, not to dictate, not to prescribe constitutions—but to defend and to preserve the independence of an ally. We go to plant the standard of England on the well-known heights of Lisbon. Where that standard is planted, foreign dominion shall not come.[1]

REPLY ; *Speeches*, vol. vi. pp. 108–112

Besides, Sir, I confess I think that the effects of the French occupation of Spain have been infinitely exaggerated.

I do not blame those exaggerations ; because I am aware that they are to be attributed to the recollections of some of the best times of our history ; that they are the echoes of sentiments which, in the days of William and of Anne, animated the debates and dictated the votes of the British Parliament. No peace was in those days thought safe for this country while the crown of Spain continued on the head of a Bourbon. But were not the apprehensions of those days greatly overstated ? Has the power of Spain swallowed up the power of maritime England ? Or does England still remain, after the lapse of more than a century, during which the Crown of Spain has been worn by a Bourbon, niched in a nook of that same Spain—Gibraltar ; an occupation which was contemporaneous with the apprehensions that I have described, and which has happily survived them ?

Again, Sir, is the Spain of the present day the Spain of which the statesmen of the times of William and Anne were so much afraid ? Is it indeed the nation whose puissance was expected to

---

[1] There are a number of small differences in these last three paragraphs, which do not seem worth recording.

shake England from her sphere ?   No, Sir, it was quite another
Spain—it was the Spain within the limits of whose Empire the sun
never set—it was Spain ' *with the Indies* ' that excited the jealousies
and alarmed the imaginations of our ancestors.

But then, Sir, the balance of power !   The entry of the French
army into Spain disturbed that balance, and we ought to have
gone to war to restore it !   I have already said that, when the
French army entered Spain we might, if we chose, have resisted
or resented that measure by war.

But were there no other means than war for restoring the
balance of power ?   Is the balance of power a fixed and unalterable standard ?   Or is it not a standard perpetually varying, as
civilisation advances, and as new nations spring up and take their
place among established political communities ?   The balance of
power a century and a half ago was to be adjusted between France
and Spain, the Netherlands, Austria, and England.   Some years
afterwards, Russia assumed her high station in European politics.
Some years after that again, Prussia became not only a substantive,
but a preponderating monarchy.   Thus, while the balance of power
continued in principle the same, the means of adjusting it became
more varied and enlarged.   They became enlarged, in proportion
to the increased number of considerable states—in proportion, I
may say, to the number of weights which might be shifted into the
one or the other scale.   To look to the policy of Europe, in the
times of William and Anne, for the purpose of regulating the
balance of power in Europe at the present day, is to disregard the
progress of events, and to confuse dates and facts which throw a
reciprocal light upon each other.

Star, 13th December

It would be disingenuous, indeed, not to admit that the
entry of the French army into
Spain was, in a certain sense, a
disparagement—an affront to
the pride—a blow to the feelings
of England : and it can hardly
be supposed that the Government did not sympathise, on
that occasion, with the feelings
of the people.   But I deny that,
questionable or censurable as
the act might be, it was one
which necessarily called for our
direct and hostile opposition.
Was nothing, then, to be done ?
Was there no other mode of
resistance than by a direct

It was not Spain they (our
ancestors *temp*. Queen Anne)
feared ;   India [The Indies ?]
was the cause of their apprehension ; and I admit that if, when
France made that attack, Spain
had still been placed in possession of the same resources,
there might have been ground
for a more decisive interference.
I will admit, for argument's
sake, that the occupation of
Spain by France was a disparagement to the character of this
country ; I will admit even that

attack upon France—or by a war to be undertaken on the soil of Spain? What if the possession of Spain might be rendered harmless in rival hands —harmless as regarded us— and valueless to the possessors? Might not compensation for disparagement be obtained, and the policy of our ancestors vindicated, by means better adapted to the present time? If France occupied Spain, was it necessary, in order to avoid the consequences of that occupation, that we should blockade Cadiz? No. I looked another way. I sought materials of compensation in another hemisphere. Contemplating Spain, such as our ancestors had known her, I resolved that if France had Spain, it should not be Spain '*with the Indies.*' I CALLED THE NEW WORLD INTO EXISTENCE, TO REDRESS THE BALANCE OF THE OLD.

it was a blow to the policy which ought to be maintained in the regulation of the balance of power. What, then, was to be done? There were two means to be adopted in our resistance to it, one of them was to attack the French troops which entered Spain ; the other was to render the Conquest harmless as far as regarded us, and valueless, or something worse, actually injurious, to the possessor. I say, then, that if we have been for the present dispossessed of anything in our situation as forming part of the balance of power, we are fully compensated. Was it necessary to blockade Cadiz, I say, to restore the situation of England? No. I look at the possessions of Spain on the other side of the Atlantic; I LOOK AT THE INDIES AND I CALL IN THE NEW WORLD TO REDRESS THE BALANCE OF THE OLD. (*Great cheering.*)

It is thus, Sir, that I answer the accusation brought against His Majesty's Government, of having allowed the French army to usurp and to retain the occupation of Spain. That occupation, I am quite confident, is an unpaid and unredeemed burden to France. It is a burden of which, I verily believe, France would be glad to rid herself. But they know little of the feelings of the French Government, and of the spirit of the French nation, who do not know that, worthless or burdensome as that occupation may be, the way to rivet her in it would be, by angry or intemperate representations, to make the continuance of that occupation a point of honour.

I believe, Sir, there is no other subject upon which I need enter into defence or explanation. The support which the Address has received, from all parties in the House, has been such as would make it both unseemly and ungrateful in me to trespass unnecessarily upon their patience. In conclusion, Sir, I shall only once more declare that the object of the Address which I propose to you is not war—its object is to take the last chance of peace. If you do not go forth on this occasion to the aid of Portugal, Portugal will be trampled down, to your irretrievable disgrace—and then will come war in the train of national degradation.   If, under circumstances like these, you wait till Spain has matured her secret machinations into open hostility, you will in a little while have the sort of war required by the pacificators—and who shall say where that war will end ? [1]

[1] These last two paragraphs have some minute discrepancies which do not seem worth recording.

APPENDIX VII

THE ANGLO-RUSSIAN PROTOCOL OF 4TH APRIL 1826

(a) *Text of Protocol* (4th April 1826)

S.M. Britannique ayant été invitée par les Grecs, à interposer ses bons offices afin de les réconcilier avec la Porte Ottomane, ayant conséquemment offert sa médiation à cette Puissance et désirant se concerter à cet égard avec S.M. l'Empereur de toutes les Russies ;

d'un autre coté, S.M. Impériale étant également animée du désir de faire cesser, par un arrangement conforme aux voeux de la religion, de la justice et de l'humanité, la lutte dont la Grèce et l'Archipel sont aujourd'hui le théâtre ;

les soussignés sont convenus :

§ 1. Que l'arrangement à proposer à la Porte, si elle accepte la médiation qui lui a été offerte, placerait les Grecs dans les relations suivantes envers l'Empire Ottoman :

Les Grecs relèveraient de cet Empire et lui payeraient un tribut annuel, dont le montant serait fixé une fois pour toutes, d'un commun accord ;

Ils seraient gouvernés par des autorités qu'ils choisiraient et nommeraient eux-mêmes, mais à la nomination des quelles la Porte aurait une certaine part ;

Dans ce mode d'existence ils jouiraient d'une entière liberté de conscience et de commerce et gèreraient exclusivement eux-mêmes leur administration intérieure ;

Pour opérer une séparation entière entre les individus des deux nations et pour prévenir des collisions, suite nécessaire d'une lutte aussi longue, les Grecs feraient l'acquisition des propriétés Turques qui pourraient être situées ou sur le continent ou dans les îles de la Grèce.

§ 2. Que si le principe d'une médiation à interposer entre la Turquie et la Grèce avait été admis à la suite des démarches déjà faites dans cette vue par l'Ambassadeur de S.M. Britannique à Constantinople, la Russie ferait dans tous les cas servir son influence au succès de la dite médiation.

Le mode d'après lequel elle s'associerait aux négociations ultérieures que cette médiation amènerait avec la Porte Ottomane, et l'époque où elle y prendrait part, seraient déterminés ultérieurement d'un commun accord, entre le Cabinet, de St Pétersbourg et celui de Londres.

§ 3. Que dans le cas où la médiation offerte par S.M. Britannique à la Porte Ottomane, n'aurait pas été acceptée par cette Puissance, et quelque soit d'ailleurs l'état des relations de S.M. Impériale avec le Gouvernement Turc, la Russie et la Grande Bretagne regarderont toujours les termes de l'arrangement mentionné au § 1 du présent Protocole, comme la base de la réconciliation à effectuer par leur entremise, soit en commun soit séparément, entre la Porte et les Grecs, et ils saisiront toutes les occasions favourables de faire valoir leur influence auprès des deux Parties, afin d'opérer cette même réconciliation sur la dite base.

§ 4. Que la Russie et la Grande Bretagne se réservent d'adopter par la suite, les mesures nécessaires pour déterminer les détails de l'arrangement en question, ainsi que les limites du territoire et les noms des îles de l'Archipel, auxquelles il sera applicable et qu'il sera proposé à la Porte de comprendre sous la dénomination de Grèce.

§ 5. Que de plus dans ce même arrangement S.M. Impériale et S.M. Britannique ne chercheront, ni l'une ni l'autre, aucune augmentation de territoire, aucune influence exclusive, aucun avantage de commerce pour leurs sujets, que ceux de toute autre nation ne puissent également obtenir.

§ 6. Que S.M. Impériale et S.M. Britannique, désirant que Leurs Alliés puissent participer aux arrangemens définitifs dont le présent Protocole renferme une première esquisse, porteront le dit Protocole, confidentiellement à la connaissance des Cours de Vienne, de Paris et de Berlin, et leur proposeront de garantir, de concert avec la Russie, la transaction finale qui réconciliera la Turquie et la Grèce, cette transaction ne pouvant être garantie par S.M. Britannique.

NESSELRODE.
LIEVEN.
WELLINGTON.

Fait à St Pétersbourg,
le 23 mars (4 avril) 1826.

(b) *The Comments of Lebzeltern*

V.S.A., Russland, Bd. 9 (1826). Lebzeltern an Metternich.
Trés secret

St Pétersbourg, le $\dfrac{\text{7 Avril}}{\text{26 Mars}}$ 1826.

Enfin, mon Prince, le grand mystère est dévoilé ; le Duc de Wellington est hier à 4 heures du matin parti ; avant-hier il a diné chez l'Empereur, ensuite il a vu le Comte de Nesselrode ; Sa Majesté a été plus tard Elle-même congé de lui, de sorte que le Duc la veille de son départ a été invisible pour tout autre. Sa Majesté l'a comblé d'attentions, lui a donné le régiment de Smolensk, lui a fait de superbes cadeaux en vases de malaquite, de Porphyre, etc.

Je dis le jour même au Comte de Nesselrode chez qui j'avais dîné, qu'il avait signé la veille quelqu'acte avec le Duc et que, si je ne me trompais fort, lui Comte de Nesselrode avait réussi à faire revenir l'Empereur sur Ses opinions au sujet de l'affaire grecque et à rattacher celle ci à la marche actuelle de la Russie, en s'entendant avec l'Angleterre sur cette question.

En effet hier il me recut et avant de me faire sa communication, il me demanda, où j'avais puisé mes conjectures de veille. Dans le langage de l'Empereur, lui répondis-je, dans le vôtre tout opposé au sien, dans les terreurs dont je Vous ai vu frappé, dans les joies qui y ont bientôt succédé, dans la marche du Duc de Wellington qui sans cela serait inexplicable à mes yeux, dans l'embarras que trahissait sa physionnomie envers moi, enfin dans vos mystères mêmes envers vos Alliés et dans vos contradictions manifestes envers leurs Ministres. Il voulut me contester le dernier point, mais l'évidence était de mon côté.

Eh bien, reprit il, si nous étions convenus avec l'Angleterre de bases, qui seraient tout à fait dans le sens et les principes de Votre Cour . . . si en suivant vos conseils, qui portaient que sans la participation de l'Angleterre, l'œuvre de la pacification était très difficile, nous l'avions écoutée . . . et si les intérêts de l'Alliance se trouvaient ménagés, que diriez-Vous ?

Je lui répondis qu'une chose pouvait être bonne dans son essence, mais devenir mauvaise par les moyens adoptés pour y parvenir ; que je le voyais en ce moment dans la joie d'un triomphe, mais que son préambule me disait assez, qu'il ressentait un grand embarras à annoncer aux Cours, qu'elles se trouvaient exclues de cet arrangement quelqu'il soit ; qu'au reste je ne pouvais rien prononcer avant d'avoir lu la pièce.

Il me la donna, en me prévenant qu'il avait obtenu non sans peine du Duc de Wellington de m'en faire la communication confidentielle, ainsi qu'à Mr de la Ferronnays, pour l'information préalable de nos Cours ; mais que la communication officielle ne pouvait leur en être faite avant que l'on n'apprît ici l'accueil que recevrait à Londres cette transaction ; que même alors, l'intérêt de sa réussite exigeait qu'elle demeurât secrète ; et qu'à plus forte raison le Cabinet de Vienne était prié de garder la plus grande réserve sur cette communication anticipée.

Je lus ce Protocole et je lui dis, que le voyant révêtu de trois signatures, je pouvais me dispenser de toute observation . . . mais, avez Vous quelque chose à objecter sur le fond de la pièce ? . . . elle ne contient, lui ai-je répondu, sûrement pas davantage, mais plustôt moins que ce depuis trois ans j'ai été autorisé à signer moi-même ; mais où est l'artiçle de l'emploi des moyens coercitifs dont vous faisiez dépendre le salut de la Russie . . . si la Porte refuse, que ferez Vous avec l'Angleterre pour la forcer et pour éviter à la

Russie un aussi sanglant affront ou bien pour le punir ? Je ne vois ici qu'une chose ; après avoir éprouvé pendant cinq ans l'extrême déférence des Cours alliées pour toutes vos idées, après avoir risqué de Vous brouiller avec elles parcequ'elles ne pouvaient dans leur conscience reconnaitre la justice d'un moyen qui était injuste, ni convenir de ce moyen parcequ'il était à la fois inadmissible et dangereux, après une opiniâtreté invincible de votre part, l'Angleterre se présente ; dès lors vous vous séparez inopinément de vos Alliés dans une question, que Vous avez caractérisée ces jours ci encore comme européenne, pour Vous arranger avec elle à huit clos, sur les mêmes bases convenues avec nous, mais en renonçant aux prétentions sur lesquelles Vous aviez tant insisté.

Le Comte de Nesselrode me dit (1) que c'était la conséquence de ce que la Russie n'avait pu s'entendre avec ses Alliés et de ce qu'ils avaient rejeté ses propositions ; (2) que c'était une suite de nos conseils de travailler à ramener les opinions en Angleterre quant à l'affaire de la Grèce ; (3) que c'était le résultat de la rupture de toute négociation avec les Alliés depuis l'automne passé et que cette rupture ayant eu lieu, ils ne pouvaient se plaindre de ce que la Russie n'eut pas repoussé les propositions de l'Angleterre, pour parvenir au même but que nous voulions atteindre.

Je lui répondis, qu'avant tout je l'assurais qu'il n'était point digne de la position des Alliés de se plaindre, et je récusais cette expression ; que de même il était digne de lui de ne point s'écarter des vérités historiques ; à sa place je ne rechercherais point à employer des excuses, parcequ'en général elles dénoncent par elles mêmes l'existence de quelque tort. Que cela posé, je me permettrais de lui répondre . . . ad Primum, que la Russie avait toujours trouvé ses Alliés prête à s'entendre sur tout, sauf sur *l'impossible* sur une seule chose inadmissible ; que la preuve en était, que ce Cabinet n'avait pas même abordé vis à vis de celui de Londres la question des moyens coercitifs, parcequ'elle portait en elle-même sa propre condamnation . . . ad Secundum, qu'en effet nous avions toujours reconnu l'avantage de ramener l'Angleterre dans l'Alliance et la *difficulté d'une* réussite sans elle, bien plus ne sachant point si elle ne se prononcerait pas contre nous ; que notre travail, d'ailleurs approuvé ici, avait tendu ou bien à obtenir sa co-opération morale dans nos démarches, ou bien la définition de l'attitude qu'elle prendrait, disposés que nous étions à marcher sans elle, dès que nous aurions appris le parti auquel elle s'arrêterait ; or, je demandais, si *de bonne foi* le Cabinet russe avait cru suivre nos conseils, en s'arrangeant isolément avec l'Angleterre sans en dire le mot à ses Alliés. *Ad Tertium,* que je niais qu'il y eut en *rupture* de négociations ; que je n'avais aperçu d'une part que dépit et bouderie, et de l'autre le même empressement à continuer des explications sans humeur, sans manifester aucun ressentiment et dans le désir de parvenir au but proposé, comme dans la confiance que ce nuage passerait avec le calme de la reflexion et l'examen de la vérité. Enfin, il me paraissait plus analogue à la circonstance et à son propre rôle, que le Comte de Nesselrode se retranchât sur un changement de systême à la suite d'un changement de Règne plustôt que de tomber dans la répétion de récriminations, que je connaissais toutes dont je n'admettais point la justice et sur la valeur desquelles j'interrogerois avant tout sa propre conscience.

Le Comte de Nesselrode me contesta faiblement mes réponses et me dit, que je devais relever dans ce Protocole d'abord qu'on s'y était tenu aux choses mêmes dont nous étions convenus, ensuite combien l'Empereur avait veillé aux intérêts de l'Alliance . . . que si la Russie avait repoussé les propositions du Cabinet Anglais, il n'aurait pas moins continué à agir seul dans l'affaire de la pacification, ce qui aurait pu tourner en désavantages et compromissions pour tous . . . qu'il croyait avoir rendu en cela un service à l'Alliance, en ramenant l'Angleterre dans une question où les Puissances devraient en dernière analyse intervenir . . . et que nous communiquer préalablement ce travail ou le négocier de concert avec nous, eut répondu à ses vœux ; mais que nous n'ignorions pas que l'Angleterre s'était irrevocablement opposée à toute marche collective.

Je répliquai, que je voyais difficilement de quelle manière il avait cru rendu un service à l'Alliance tandis qu'à mes yeux il n'en avait rendu qu'à Mr Canning, qui montrerait avec orgueil la Russie, cette Puissance prépondérante dans l'Alliance, détachée de cette Alliance par ses soins, marchant seule avec lui comme *adhérante* à son plan et agissant dans un sens opposé à ses déclarations précédentes. Cette idée déplut singulièrement au Comte de Nesselrode et il la combattit avec vigueur. Je lui répondis, que dans tous les cas ce n'était point la Russie qui avait ramené l'Angleterre, mais bien cette Puissance qui avait fait sortir la Russie de ses anciennes voies et de l'Alliance. La preuve en était clairement démontrée à mes yeux par le désaveu même, donné par Mr Canning au Vicomte de Strangford. Il ne l'a désavoué aussi durement que parceque cet Ambassadeur moyennant le projet qu'il avait présenté au Cabinet russe, avait risqué de faire entrer l'Angleterre dans le systême de l'Alliance en l'associant à la marche des Puissances. Agir seul est ce que Mr Canning voulait, et c'est ce qu'il a obtenu par votre assentiment à marcher *après lui* en auxiliaire.

Une chose encore m'est particulièrement sensible dans cette affaire, lui ai-je dit, et c'est le rôle que Vous y faites jouer à Votre jeune Empereur dès le début de sa carrière. Pendant qu'Il répète à tous ceux qui L'approchent, *qu'Il ne se reconnait pas le droit d'intervenir dans l'affaire de la pacification et qu'Il y renonce ;* Il signe un engagement basé sur cette *intervention* plus encore sur *une médiation* qui supposait des conditions n'existant pas. . . .
Le Comte de Nesselrode m'interrompit et chercha à démontrer,

que l'Empereur avait dit, qu'Il ne se reconnaissait pas le droit de faire la guerre pour la cause des Grecs . . . Brisons sur cet objet, répliquai-je, il est pénible à toucher ; Vous savez bien dans quels détails l'Empereur est entré pour développer son opinion et l'Europe connait ses paroles aussi bien que Vous ; or, s'étant montré jusqu'ici aussi digne de confiance, je suis d'autant plus affligé de l'impression morale que recevront tous ceux qui en connaissant ses déclarations précédentes, liront votre Protocole. . . . Le Comte de Nesselrode se tût.

Et c'est Vous cher Comte, qui L'avez entrainé, et pourquoi ? parceque Vous avez cru atteindre d'un coup le but de votre travail de trois ans en dépit de tout ce qu'on Vous a dit d'amical et déraisonnable à ce sujet. Ce moyen coercitif qui nous a si longtems divisés, Vous l'employez indirectement et c'est l'Angleterre qui y applaudit. Vous ne l'appliquez pas ostensiblement à la question des Grecs, le Cabinet Britannique n'aurait osé le promettre ; mais en enflant autant que possible l'importance de Vos griefs directs, de ces mêmes griefs que Vous aviez naguères jugés peu de chose et en menacant la Porte de guerre, Vous êtes entrés au prémier acte de Votre système de coercition, et en traitant par le voie de l'Angleterre l'affaire grecque, votre système devient par le fait applicable à cette affaire. Vous avez tout obtenu du Duc et Vous êtes dans un moment d'exaltation, qui ne Vous permet pas d'entrevoir toutes les conséquences possibles de cette marche. Le Comte de Nesselrode ne contesta aucune de ces observations et convint par ses gestes de leur justesse.

Je continuai : je ne dirai pas que Vous ne deviez être satisfait (1) d'avoir enfin tiré cette question du cercle vicieux, où Vous la retenez ; (2) de l'extrème condescendance du Duc ; mais ne craignez-Vous pas que Mr Canning ne désapprouve ce Plénipotentiaire pour sa facilité à Vous tout accorder sur la question directe, ce qui Vous place dans la position d'exercer votre moyen coercitif dans le moment, où il serait de fait applicable dans ses effets à la négociation pour la Grèce ? Je ne crois pas qu'il se soit exprimé dans ce sens, mais plustôt dans celui que l'Empereur renonçait *à faire la guerre* pour la question ou la cause des Grecs ; au reste je n'ai point vu ce qu'il a écrit. . . . Ce n'aurait été qu'un jeu de mots, ai-je répliqué. Vous voilà donc entre les mains du Cabinet de Londres et celui ci a obtenu les coudées franches de votre part dans sa négociation en Orient, en Vous les abandonnant de son côté dans la question directe et en consentant à une invasion armée de votre part du territoire ottoman, dès que vous la colorez par des motifs puisés dans la non exécution des Traités. . . . Le Comte de Nesselrode me répondit, que le contraire de ma prémiere assertion se trouvait dans le texte du Protocole, puisque le Cabinet de Londres se trouvait lié par des bases fixes et entièrement conformes à celles, que les Alliés auraient eux mêmes adoptées dans leur plan de pacification. Mr le Comte de Nesselrode me fit valoir le

Chapitre où il était stipulé, qu'aucune des parties intervenantes ne s'adjugerait d'avantage d'aucun genre, qui ne fut commun aux autres Alliés.

Je dis à ce Ministre que la pièce etant signée et le parti de la Russie pris, je lui avais fait les observations qui précédent confidentiellement et *extra-office* . . . que je pouvais l'assurer, qu'il n'était point dans les principes ici [en] usage de ma Cour de s'arrêter à des considérations personnelles ou d'être susceptibles de petites jalousies ; qu'Elle planait trop haut pour cela et que sa maxime avait toujours été, *que le bien se fasse, n'importe par qui* ; mais que sous des rapports d'intérêt général, de tranquillité européenne et de maintien de l'Alliance, la nouvelle marche adoptée ici me semblait gravement compremettante. En effet d'un coté la guerre pouvait éclater d'un moment à l'autre et quels immenses dangers ne sauraient pas liés à un dénouement pareil ? et d'un autre côté Vous sortez de l'Alliance déja si affaiblie pour Vous réunir à son principal adversaire, à celui à qui Vous n'avez cessé Vous-même de reprocher une marche double, contradictoire et équivoque ; plus même, Vous Vous associez à ses principes, car employer le mot de *médiation* entraine avec soi la reconnaissance implicite *des droits des parties bélligérantes*, et cela lorsque Vous m'avez dit Vous-même que Vous n'aviez point de confiance dans les démarches de Mr Stratford Canning, ni dans ses succès.

Mr le Comte de Nesselrode voulut rejeter la faute du présent sur la conduite de l'Alliance depuis quatre ans envers la Russie ; mais je lui répondis constamment que cette conduite n'avait tenu qu'à l'insistance mise à l'admission d'un principe injuste et qui se trouvait aujourd'hui condamné par la nature même de l'engagement qu'on venait de prendre avec l'Angleterre, qui emportait avec soi la renonciation complète à l'emploi des moyens coercitifs contre la Puissance légitime en faveur de l'insurrection.

Comme cet entretien etait purement confidentiel, suivi sur le ton de l'amitié de part et d'autre, et que j'avais pris sur ma responsabilité de promettre que votre Altesse n'en ferait aucun usage, comme enfin je vis le Comte de Nesselrode souvent remué par mes observations ; je continuai :

Vous m'avez dit plusieurs fois, que j'avais pénétré vos pensées et répété les paroles que vous auriez prononcées ; eh bien, permettez-moi, pure et honnête comme je vous connais et attaché à la système de l'Alliance comme je vous ai toujours remontré, de vous dire quelle est votre position au moment ou je vous parle. . . . Vous êtes partagé par des sensations de contentement et de régrêt. Vous êtes à l'aise en vous trouvant placé dans un attitude plus libre et suivant une marche determinée ; vous êtes flatté par l'éspoir de faire jouer à la Russie le rôle auquel vous aviez visé, par l'espoir de satisfaire ainsi à ce que vous avez appelé *la dignité et les opinions nationales*, enfin par la circonstance de n'avoir plus à redouter l'opposition de l'Angleterre ni de la trouver sur votre chemin et contre vous ; mais au fond vous sentez des remords envers les Alliés et Vous êtes régrêt des formes mises à cet arrangement, vous craignez l'impression sur l'ésprit des Puissances, vos amies et vous craignez plus encore que ce premier pas à fait ne vous jette plus loin que vous ne le voudriez Vous-même. Le Comte de Nesselrode me dit, que je lisais trop bien dans sa pensée, pour qu'il eût rien à ajouter à ce que je venais de prononcer ; que les formes suivies lui laissaient en éffet des régrêts et qu'il n'avait pas tenu à lui qu'elles ne fussent différentes ; qu'il ésperait néanmoins être jugé avec bienveillance par les Alliés, s'ils meditaient avec ce sentiment les conditions du Protocole.

Je priai le Comte de Nesselrode de me permettre de marquer au crayon au moins les principaux passages de cette pièce ; il n'y consentit pas. Ce n'est donc, mon Prince, que par un éffort de mémoire, que j'ai tracé l'extrait ci-joint et à l'exception de deux paragraphes, je ne crois pas m'être éloigné de sa substance.

Ce Ministre me pria de ne rien dire de tout ce qui précède à Mr le Vicomte de Strangford ; je le promis. L'attitude où Mr Canning a placé cet Ambassadeur merite une mention particulière.

Je n'ajoute point d'observations à ce réspectueux rapport, mon Prince. Elles seraient superflues.

Mr le Comte de la Ferronnays se trouve avoir fait à peu près les mêmes observations que moi au Comte de Nesselrode. Ce Ministre lui a fait promettre de n'écrire à aucun de ses Collègues sur les évènemens qui viennent de se passer.

Deux chances se présentent encore devant nous au milieu de ce conflit d'inconvéniens : . . si la Porte sacrifiant son amour propre, se met en règle avec la Russie, ainsi que Votre Altesse le lui a éternellement conseillé, cette dernière Puissance malgré ses nouveaux engagemens, se trouvera en déhors de la question grêcque ; car, si la Porte répousse la médiation du Cabinet Britannique, celui ci se permettra difficilement de l'Empire à la Porte moyennant des voies coércitives et cette affaire restera dès lors dans le caractère d'une négociation, à laquelle chaque Puissance pourra prendre la part qui lui conviendra. . . . L'autre chance serait celle où Mr Stratford Canning rencontrât des facilités à Constantinople, et près des Grecs une opposition, augmentée par la tournure qu'auraient pris les différends entre la Russie et le Gouvernement Ottoman, car les Anglais ne sauraient employer la force contre les Grecs. Néanmoins il resterait un point à eclaircir, sur lequel les dernières paroles de l'Empereur (sub Nr. 173, C.) portent mon attention. Le Cabinet Britannique croit qu'il pouvoit traiter Ibrahim Pacha ainsi que le Pacha d'Egypte, comme il a traité le Dey d'Alger, sans pour cela se brouiller, avec la Porte ? L'Empereur ne peut avoir répété cette assertion, que parcequ'Il l'a tenue du Duc ; en la supposant vraie, à quoi conduirait elle ? au pouvoir qu'aurait l'Angleterre de forcer le Pacha d'Egypte à cesser de prêter des secours à la Porte contre les Grecs : mais dès lors ceux ci deviendraient indépendans et le Duc déclare, que l'Angleterre ne veut pas plus que la Russie de l'indépendance de la Grèce ; et au moins ne seraient ils plus disposés à accepter sa médiation.

Veuillez agréer, mon Prince, l'hommage de mon respect.

LEBZELTERN.

P.S.—J'étais surpris que le Comte de Nesselrode n'eut point mis d'opposition au départ de mon Courrier et à ce que Votre Altesse recut des communications préalables de mon côté. Il m'écrit le billet conçu en ces termes : " Ne pourriez-Vous pas, cher Comte, différer le départ de Votre Courrier jusqu'au Dimanche ou Lundi ; il arriverait alors à Vienne à peu près en même tems que le mien, qui sera porteur d'une dépêche explicative de tout ce qui s'est passé, laquelle Dépêche ne pourra être soumise à l'Empereur que demain soir et à Vous-même que dans la matinée du Dimanche. Je Vous promets que mon Courrier ne partira pas avant le Vôtre et comme cette fois c'est un Prince qui fera le Courrier, le Vôtre le devancera dans tous les cas de beaucoup. Tout à Vous N——."

Je lui ai répondu : " Je désire trop, cher Comte que Vous puissiez expliquer à Vienne tout ce qui s'est passé ici, d'une manière plus éclairé et plus satisfaisante que je ne saurais le faire, pour ne point adhérer à vos vœux en retardant l'expédition de mon Courrier jusquà Dimanche. Tout à Vous Lebz——."

LEBZELTERN.

APPENDIX VIII

THE MAKING OF THE TRIPLE ALLIANCE (1827)

(a) *The Damas Projet Compared with the Granville and Pozzo di Borgo Projet* (19th January 1827)

[It is not often that we can trace the different stages in the making of a Treaty, and it is most instructive to do so. In (*a*) we have the original French version (left-hand column), and the Pozzo-Granville amended version (right-hand column).

On p. 599 the Canning-Lieven version (right-hand column) represents the results of the revision of the two versions given below. The left-hand column of (*b*) gives the text of the Treaty as actually signed. It will be found most valuable to compare the gradual evolution of the Treaty from the embryonic stage to the final version. Comments, where given, are in square brackets.]

Damas' Projet

Les Puissances Alliées, s'étant depuis longtems, pénétrées de la necessité de mettre un terme à la Guerre qui a éclaté en Orient et aux maux qui en résultent pour leur propres sujets : plusieurs d'entr'elles ayant reçu, d'ailleurs, soit directement, soit indirectement, de la part des Grecs, l'invitation de s'interposer en leur faveur, près la Porte Ottomane, elles ont jugé que le moment etait arrivé d'unir, par un traité formel, leurs efforts, pour amener une pacification que réclament le bien de la religion

Pozzo-Granville Projet
[Both in *F.O. France*, 146/85. Granville to Canning, 19th January 1827.]

La nécessité de mettre un terme à la guerre qui depuis six ans désole la Morée, les Isles (*sic*) de l'Archipel, et une partie de la Grèce, et qui occasionne, à la Chrétienneté en général, et aux Sujets des Puissances Contractantes en particulier, des Maux très graves et insupportables et les Cours de Russie et d'Angleterre, ayant dans un esprit de Paix et de Concorde, et à l'invitation même d'une des Parties Belligérantes, avisé aux moyens de terminer de la manière la plus equitable cette lutte sanglante, et consigné

Damas' Projet

et de l'humanité de même que l'intérêt du repos de l'Europe.

Dans cette vue, et à cet effet, elles ont nommé leurs Plenipotentiaires pour discuter, arrêter et signer le dit traité.

S.M., etc.

[Granville's comment, 19th January 1827. " We thought it necessary that the Preamble should contain a reference to the Protocol, and should state the grounds on which it was proposed to convert its provisions into the more formal act of a Treaty."

Damas did not object.]

Pozzo-Granville Projet

dans un Protocole, en date du 4 avril de l'année 1826, le mode, et les principes d'un arrangement désirable entre la Porte Ottomane et cette portion de ses sujets qui sont en armes contre elles, et ce Protocole ayant été communiqué aux les Cours de France, de Vienne, et de Berlin, dont chacune en particulier a fait connoître son opinion à ce sujet, leur Majestés l'Empereur de Toutes les Russies, le Roi de France et le Roi des Royaumes Unis de la Grande Bretagne, persuadés que la Conversion des Principes consignés dans le Protocole — susmentionné en un Traité formel donnerait à cet acte la solennité et la force propres à lui assurer le résultat qui en est le but principal, et voulant procéder à la confection du dit Traité, ont nommé, etc.

Damas' Projet

I. Les Puissances contractantes[1] *offriront* simultanément à la Porte Ottomane, leur médiation dans la vue de réconcilier avec elle les Sujets des Provinces de la Grèce.

Cette offre de médiation sera faite à cette Puissance immédiamment après la ratification du présent traité, au moyen d'une déclaration collective des Plénipotentiaires des Cours Alliées à Constantinople.

II. Il est convenu, que si la Porte Ottomane accepte la médiation qui lui aura été offerte,

Pozzo-Granville Projet

I.

continueront à offrir

[and last sentence, ' cette offre,' etc., therefore omitted. *Cp.* Pozzo to Lieven, 22nd January, *F.O. Russia*, 65/168.]

[Damas was asked if France would sign the Treaty without waiting for the consent of Vienna and Berlin. He answered he must ask for instructions.]

II.

[*Cp.* Art. 1 of Protocol.]

---

[1] Where the Drafts are the same the right-hand column is left blank. Alterations are italicised in the left-hand column, and the other version inserted in the right. Comments are in square brackets.

Damas' Projet

l'arrangement qui lui sera proposé reposera sur les bases
suivantes : Les Grecs payeront
à l'Empire Ottomane un tribut
annuel, dont le montant sera
fixé, une fois, pour toutes,
d'un commun accord.

Ils seront gouvernés par des
autorités qu'ils choisiront et
nommeront eux-mêmes, mais
à la nomination des quelles la
Porte aura une certaine part.

Dans ce mode d'existence ils
jouiront d'une entière liberté de
conscience et de commerce et
géreront exclusivement, eux-
mêmes leur administration intérieure.

Pour opérer une séparation
entière entre les individus des
deux nations et pour prévenir
des collisions, suite nécessaire
d'une lutte aussi longue, les
Grecs feront l'acquisition des
propriétés Turques qui pourront
être situées ou sur le Continent
ou dans les îles de la Grèce.

III. Les mesures nécessaires
pour déterminer les détails de
l'arrangement cité dans l'article
Deux, ainsi que les limites du
territoire et les noms des îles
de l'Archipel aux quelles il sera
applicable et qu'il sera proposé
à la Porte Ottomane de comprendre sous la dénomination de
Grèce, seront préparées et dis-
cutées, de concert avec la dite
Puissance, et dans des conférences établies à Constantinople
entre les Plénipotentiaires des
Cours Alliées.

IV. Si l'arrangement pro-
posé à la Porte Ottomane est
accepté et converti en une transaction finale qui réconcilierait
les Grecs avec elle, et si une

Pozzo-Granville Projet

III.
[*Cp*. Art. 2 of Protocol.]

IV.
[*Cp*. Art. 6 of Protocol.]

Damas' Projet

garantie est jugée nécessaire, cette transaction sera placée sous celle des Hautes Parties Contractantes. Cette garantie sera exercée collectivement et par l'intermédiaire de leurs Plenipotentiaires à Constantinople.

V. Dans le cas où la Porte se refuserait à l'offre de médiation qui, en vertu de l'article Premier *doit lui être faite au nom des* Puissances [qui] lui declareront formellement, que si, dans un délai, dont ou conviendra, elle ne se décide point à l'accepter, elles-mêmes sont résolus à établir, avec les Grecs, des rélations commercialles à leur envoyer, à cet effet, et à en recevoir, des agens publics, en attendant qu'elles reconnaissent la forme de leur Gouvernement et entretiennent avec lui, des rapports politiques. Cette déclaration sera faite, également, et dans une forme collective par les Plenipotentiaires de l'Alliance près le Divan.

VI. Il est bien entendu que soit dans l'arrangement à proposer à la Porte Ottomane en faveur des Grecs soit dans les relations à établir avec ceux-ci en cas de refus de la dite Puissance d'admettre la médiation, les Hautes Cours contractantes ne rechercheront aucune augmentation de territoire aucune influence exclusive, aucun avantage de commerce, pour leur sujets que ceux de tout autre nation ne puissent également obtenir.

[Nothing in Damas corresponds to No. VII. in Pozzo-Granville version.]

Pozzo-Granville Projet

V.

This italicised passage omitted. les for des.

[No. 24, 19th January, Granville observes :
" The sending of agents . . . is more clearly pronounced than in the Protocol."]
Cp. Art. 1 of Protocol.

VI.
[*Cp.* Art. 5 of Protocol.]

[*Cp.* Art. 6 of Protocol.
This article added by **Pozzo** and **Granville**.]

VII. Le présent Traité sera communiqué aux Cours de Vienne et de Berlin, avec

Damas' Projet

Pozzo-Granville Projet

l'invitation de devenir Partie Contractante, ou d'y prendre part de la manière dont elles jugerait le plus convenable.

VII. Le présent Traité sera ratifié et les ratifications en seront échangées, dans le délai de deux mois, ou plûtot, si faire se peut.
En foi de quoi, etc.

[Same but numbered VIII. in Pozzo and Granville.]

(b) *Text of Treaty* (6th July) *and the Canning-Lieven Version of 22nd May*

Canning-Lieven Version, 22nd May

Text of Treaty as Signed, 6th July

F.O. France, 146/89. Dudley to Granville, *Projet de Traité à conclure entre la Russie, l'Angleterre et la France, dans le but de la pacification du Levant.*

S.M. l'Empereur de toutes les Russies, S.M. le Roi de France et de Navarre, et S.M. le Roi du Royaume Uni de la Grande Bretagne et d'Irlande, pénétrées de la nécessité de mettre un terme à la lutte sanglante qui en livrant les provinces Grecques et les îles de l'Archipel à tous les désordres de l'anarchie, apporte chaque jour de nouvelles entraves au commerce des Etats Européens, et donne lieu à des pirateries, qui, non seulement exposent les sujets des hautes Parties contractantes à des pertes considérables, mais exigent en outre des mesures onéreuses de surveillance et de répression.
S.M. le Roi de France et de Navarre, et S.M. le Roi du Royaume Uni de la Grande Bretagne et d'Irlande, ayant d'ailleurs reçu de la part des

Sa Majésté Le Roi du Royaume Uni de la Grande Bretagne et d'Irlande ayant été invitée par les Grecs à interposer ses bons offices, afin de les réconcilier avec la Porte Ottomane, ayant accepté cette demande—et désirant s'unir à Ses Alliés pour y donner suite :
Et Sa Majesté L'Empereur de toutes les Russies, ainsi que Sa Majesté Le Roi de France et de Navarre, ayant reconnu avec Sa Majesté Britannique combien il étoit à désirer de terminer une lutte dont les inconvéniens se font ressentir de plus en plus chaque jour—puisqu'elle met des entraves au commerce, qu'elle donne occasion à des pirateries qui commandent des mesures de répression onéreuses à toutes les nations, et qu'elle expose les Sujets des trois Puissances à

Text of Treaty as Signed,
6th July

Grecs l'invitation pressante d'interposer leur médiation auprès de la Porte Ottomane, et, étant, ainsi que S.M. l'Empereur de toutes les Russies, animées du désir d'arrêter l'effusion du sang, et de prévenir les maux de tout genre que peut entrainer la prolongation d'un tel état de choses ;

Ont résolu de combiner leurs efforts, et d'en régler l'action, par un Traité formel, dans le but de rétablir la paix entre les parties contendantes, au moyen d'un arrangement réclamé, autant par un sentiment d'humanité, que par l'intérêt du repos de l'Europe.

A ces fins, elles ont nommé leurs plénipotentiaires pour discuter, arrêter et signer le dit Traité, savoir :

S.M. l'Empereur de toutes les Russies :

le sieur Christophe, prince de Lieven, Général d'Infanterie des armées de S.M. Impériale, son aide-de-camp général, chevalier des ordres de Russie, de ceux de l'Aigle noire et de l'Aigle rouge de Prusse, etc., son Ambassadeur extraordinaire et plénipotentiaire près S.M. Britannique ;

S.M. le Roi de France et de Navarre :

le sieur, prince Jules, comte de Polignac, Pair de France, chevalier des ordres de S.M. très Chrétienne, maréchal de camp de ses armées, etc., et son Ambassadeur à Londres ; et

S.M. le Roi du Royaume Uni de la Grande Bretagne et de l'Irlande :

Canning-Lieven Version,
22nd May

des pertes et à des maux devenus intolérables :

De plus, les Hautes Parties Contractantes étant animées du désir de faire un effort pour arrêter l'effusion du sang et de prevenir les maux de la guerre dans une des plus belles parties de l'Europe, et en outre de celui de préserver la Porte Ottomane des dangers que doit inévitablement entrainer pour Elle-même, la prolongation d'un tel état de choses.

Leur Majestés sont convenus de combiner, par un Traité formel, leurs efforts pour amener une pacification entre les parties belligérantes, au moyen d'un arrangement conformé aux vœux de la réligion, de la justice, et de l'humanité.

Dans cette vue, et à cet effet, Elles ont Nommé Leur Plenipotentiaires, etc.

Text of Treaty as Signed, 6th July	Canning-Lieven Version, 22nd May
le sieur Jean Guillaume, vicomte Dudley, Pair du Royaume Uni de la Grande Bretagne et de l'Irlande, conseiller de S.M. Britannique en son Conseil privé, et son principal Sécrétaire d'Etat, ayant le Département des Affaires Etrangères, etc., etc.	
Lesquels, après s'être communiqué leurs pleinspouvoirs, trouvés en bonne et dûe forme, sont convenus des articles suivans :	

Article I

Les Puissances contractantes *offriront* à la Porte Ottomane leur médiation, dans la vue d'amener une réconciliation entre elle et les Grecs.	offriront simultanément [Canning insisted on Lieven accepting ' les Grecs ' for ' les sujets.']
Cette offre de médiation sera faite à cette Puissance immédiatement après la ratification *du Traité*, au moyen d'une déclaration *collective*, signée par les plénipotentiaires des Cours alliées à Constantinople, et il sera fait en même temps aux deux parties contendantes la demande d'un armistice, immédiat entre elles, comme condition préliminaire indispensable à l'ouverture de toute négociation.	du présent Traité, simultanée, et il sera fait en même tems la demande, adressée également aux deux parties belligérantes, d'un armistice immédiat entre Elles, comme condition indispensable à l'ouverture de toute négociation.

Article II

L'arrangement à proposer à la Porte Ottomane reposera sur les bases suivantes :	
Les Grecs relèveront du Sultan, comme d'un seigneur suzerain, et *en conséquence* de cette suzeraineté, ils payeront à l'Empire Ottoman une redevance annuelle, dont le montant	en vertu

Text of Treaty as Signed, 6th July	*Canning-Lieven Version, 22nd May*

sera fixé, une fois pour toutes, d'un commun accord.

Ils seront gouvernés par des autorités qu'ils choisiront et nommeront eux-mêmes, mais à la nomination desquelles la Porte *aura une part déterminée.*

Pour opérer une séparation entière entre les individus des deux nations, et pour prévenir des collisions, suite *inévitable* d'une lutte aussi longue, les Grecs entreront en possession des propriétés Turques, situées ou sur le continent ou dans les îles de la Grèce, *à la charge d'indemniser les anciens propriétaires, soit moyennant une somme annuelle à joindre à la redevance qu'ils payeront à la Porte, soit à l'aide de quelqu' autre transaction de la même nature.*

aura une certaine part.
[Inserted after this sentence.]
 " Ils jouiront d'une entière liberté de conscience et de com-[nécessaire]
merce, et gèreront exclusivement eux-mêmes l'administration de leurs propres affaires."

[The passage italicised first added in the Canning-Lieven version. *Cp.* last par. Art. II of Damas' Projet.]

Article III

Les détails de cet arrangement, ainsi que les limites du territoire sur le continent, et la désignation des îles de l'Archipel, auxquelles il sera applicable, seront déterminés dans une négociation à établir ultérieurement entre les hautes Puissances et les deux parties *contendantes.*

en litige.

Article IV

Les Puissances contractantes s'engagent à poursuivre l'œuvre salutaire de la pacification de la Grèce sur les bases posées dans les articles précedens, et à munir, sans le moindre délai, leurs représentans à Constantinople de toutes les instructions que réclame l'exécution du Traité qu'elles signent.

Text of Treaty as Signed, *6th July*	*Canning-Lieven Version,* *22nd May*

Article V

Les Puissances contractantes ne chercheront dans ces arrangemens aucune augmentation de territoire, aucune influence exclusive, aucun avantage de commerce pour leurs sujets, que ceux de toute autre nation ne puissent également obtenir.

Article VI

Les arrangemens de réconciliation et de paix, qui seront définitivement convenus entre les parties *contendantes*, seront garantis par celles des Puissances *signataires* qui jugeront utile ou possible de contracter cette obligation. *L'action et les effets de cette garantie deviendront l'objet de stipulations ultérieures entre les hautes Puissances.*

en litige,

contractantes

[This last sentence omitted in Canning-Lieven version.]

Article VII

Le présent Traité sera ratifié, et les ratifications en seront échangées dans le terme de deux mois, ou plutôt, si faire se peut.

En foi de quoi, etc.

Fait à Londres, le 24 juin (6 juillet) 1827.

(L.S.) Lieven.
(L.S.) Le prince de
Polignac.
(L.S.) Dudley.

Article additionnel et secret

Dans le cas où la Porte Ottomane *n'accepterait pas, dans le terme d'un mois, la médiation* qui lui sera proposée, les hautes Parties contractantes conviennent des mesures suivantes :

rejetterait (added in pencil, n'accepterait pas dans le terme d'un mois) la proposition,

[The shortening to a month was suggested by Pozzo, the

Text of Treaty as Signed, *6th July*	*Canning-Lieven Version,* *22nd May*

(1) Il sera déclaré à la Porte, par leurs représentans à Constantinople, que les inconvéniens et les maux *signalés* dans le Traité patent comme inséparables de l'état de choses qui *subsiste* dans l'Orient depuis six ans et dont la cessation, par les moyens à la disposition de la Sublime Porte Ottomane, paraît encore êloignée, imposent aux hautes Parties contractantes la nécessité de prendre des mesures immédiates pour se rapprocher des Grecs.

subsequent shortening to a fortnight by Canning.]

désignés

existe

Il est entendu que ce rapprochement s'opérera en établissant avec les Grecs des relations commerciales, en leur envoyant à cet effet, et recevant d'eux des agens consulaires, en tant qu'il existera chez eux des autorités capables de maintenir de telles relations.

(2) Si dans ce même terme d'un mois [1] la Porte *n'acceptait pas* l'armistice proposé dans l'article I du Traité patent [ou, si les Grecs, se refusaient à son exécution], les hautes Puissances contractantes *déclareront* à celle des deux parties contendantes qui voudroit continuer les hostilités, ou, à toutes deux, s'il devenait nécessaire, que les dites hautes Puissances vont s'efforcer, par tous les moyens, que les circonstances suggéreront à leur prudence, d'obtenir les effets immédiats de l'armistice dont elles désirent l'exécution, en prévenant, autant qu'il sera en leur pouvoir, toute collision entre les Parties con-

(right column, aligned:)

Numbered (3). [For 2 *v*. below.]
Se repose (crossed out and added in pencil, "dans le même terme d'un mois n'accepte pas"). [ou . . . exécution] omitted.

il lui sera déclaré par les Représentans des Hautes Puissances Contractantes qu'elles vont réunir leurs Escadres, dans le but d'empêcher tout secours d'hommes, d'armes, de vaisseaux, et de munitions, Egyptiens ou Turcs, d'arriver par mer en Grèce ou dans l'Archipel : et, dans ce cas, la réunion de ces Escadres aura lieu immédiatement, et les Hautes Parties Contractantes traiteront dès lors les Grecs en amis, sans prendre

[1] Ultimately shortened to a fortnight by Canning ; agreed to by Polignac, July 20.

Text of Treaty as Signed,
6th July

Canning-Lieven Version,
22nd May

tendantes, et en effet, aussitôt après la susdite déclaration, les hautes Puissances employeront conjointement tous leurs moyens pour en accomplir l'objet, sans toutefois prendre part aux hostilités entre les deux parties contendantes.

part toute fois aux hostilités entre les deux parties belligérantes.

En conséquence, les hautes Puissances contractantes, immédiatement après la signature du présent article additionnel et secret, transmettront des instructions éventuelles, conformés aux dispositions énoncées ci-dessus aux amiraux commandant leurs escadres respectives dans les Mers du Levant.

[Last paragraph " En conséquence . . . du Levant " omitted.]

(2) Si au bout d'un mois, la Porte n'accepte pas la médiation des Hautes Parties Contractantes, elles rappelleront simultanément de Constantinople leur Représentans accrédités auprès de la Porte (added in margin, 'L'adoption ou le rejet de cette clause est au choix de la France'). [Granville reported rejection by France on 30th May 1827, and it was therefore omitted in the Treaty.]

(3) *Enfin, si, contre toute attente,* ces mesures ne suffisent point encore pour faire adopter les propositions des hautes Parties contractantes par la Porte Ottomane, ou si, de l'autre coté, les Grecs renoncent *aux conditions stipulées* en leur faveur dans le Traité de ce jour, les hautes Puissances contractantes n'en continueront pas moins à poursuivre *l'œuvre de la pacification,* sur des bases dont elles sont convenues entre elles, et en conséquences, elles autorisent dès à present leurs représentans à Londres à discuter et arrêter les moyens ultérieurs dont l'emploi pourrait devenir nécessaire.

(4) Si, la Porte Ottomane ayant accepté la proposition d'un armistice, les Grecs rejettoient cette proposition, ou, après l'avoir acceptée, agissoient en contravention de l'Armistice, les Escadres réunis des Hautes Puissances Contractantes veilleront à son maintien, sans prendre part toutefois aux hostilités entre les deux Parties belligérantes.

(5) Enfin, si, contre toute [same as par. 3 of secret article of Treaty]. Except 'les Grecs renoncent à la base sur laquelle le Protocol a été fondé'; and 'le but' for 'l'œuvre.' [Rest to . . . entre elles omitted.]

Le présent article additionnel et secret aura la même force et valeur que s'il était inséré mot à mot au Traité de ce jour: *il sera ratifié,* et les ratifications en seront échangées en

il sera compris dans la Ratification du dit Traité [from

Text of Treaty as Signed, *6th July*	*Canning-Lieven Version,* *22nd May*
même tems que celles du dit Traité.	" les ratifications . . . Traité " omitted].

En foi de quoi, etc.

Fait à Londres, le 24 juin (6 juillet) 1827.[1]

(L.S.) LIEVEN.
(L.S.) LE PRINCE DE
      POLIGNAC.
(L.S.) DUDLEY.

[1] Text from Martens. *Traités conclus par la Russie*, xi. 355–62. Except that the order of precedence is naturally different, and that there is a different use of capitals, the text is the same as that in *F.O. France*, 94/93 and 94, and in *F.O. Russia*, 93/45/29. The latter is the original text. Martens terms the agreement incorrectly a convention; it was a treaty. As regards *ratification*, the French took place on July 11, and the Russian was exchanged with the British on Aug. 8.

APPENDIX IX

METTERNICH'S EPITAPH ON CANNING
(12TH AUGUST 1831)

Metternich (Vienna, 12th August 1831) to Esterházy (London)[1]

Metternich begins by taking exception to Lord Palmerston's views on Italy.

" The Ministry of Mr Canning marked an era in the history of England and of Europe. We must regard the short duration of that Ministry as equivalent to a league for drawing us from the correct and practical old order of things towards that policy of fantasy which in a few years brought France to the year 1789, which has only made the Triple Alliance assent to the occupation of the Morea by French forces, which has caused the Emperor Nicholas to lose an army, the loss of which to-day puts his power within an ace of ruin (*deux doigts de sa perte*), which has given a stimulus (*essor*) to liberalism on the Continent threatening to engulph all thrones and all institutions, which finally has led England to radical reform and to political impotence.[2]

" These facts being established, it is certain that the existing English administration, that singular amalgam of pure Whigs, Radicals, and Canningites, is better than that of the defunct patron of this last party. It is he who gave to evil the frightful stimulus (*essor*) that we have seen it take. But evil is always inseparable from some remedies; and the Cabinet of England to-day begins to fix its eyes on some remedies. It is so far true that open evil is better than evil which wears a veil."

[1] *V.S.A.*, Weisungen nach England, 1831. I owe this quotation to the kindness of my friend, Professor Lingelbach. It will be noted that Metternich means the Premiership, not the Foreign Ministry, of Canning.

[2] The French drove the Turks from the Morea in 1828; the Emperor Nicholas suffered heavy losses during 1828–9 ; the French Monarchy fell in July 1830.

GENERAL INDEX

INDEX TO BOOKS AND AUTHORITIES

(The contemporary newspapers will be found listed in the previous index.

N.B.—The references are generally to footnotes.)

631